Philosophical Aesthetics
An Introduction

Edited by Oswald Hanfling

 **Blackwell**
Publishing

 The Open
University

Blackwell Publishing in Association with the Open University

© 1992 by The Open University 1992

THE OPEN UNIVERSITY
Walton Hall, Milton Keynes, MK7 6AA, UK

BLACKWELL PUBLISHING
350 Main Street, Malden, MA 02148-5020, USA
108 Cowley Road, Oxford OX4 1JF, UK
550 Swanston Street, Carlton, Victoria 3053, Australia

First published 1992
Reprinted 1992, 1994, 1995, 1997, 1998, 1999, 2000, 2002, 2004, 2005

Library of Congress Cataloging in Publication Data

Philosophical aesthetics: an introduction/edited by Oswald Hanfling
    p.   cm.
Includes bibliographical references and index.
    ISBN 0–631–18034–6 (hbk) — ISBN 0–631–18035–4 (pbk)
    1. Aesthetics. I. Hanfling, Oswald
BH39.P472   1992
111'.85—dc20   91–27476
                                                     CIP

A catalogue record for this title is available from the British Library.

The book forms part of an Open University course *Philosophy of the Arts* (AA301). For further information about this and other Open University Courses, please write to the Central Enquiry Service, The Open University, PO Box 71, Milton Keynes, MK7 6AG, UK

Set in 11 on 13 pt Times
by Text Processing Services, The Open University

The publisher's policy is to use permanent paper from mills that operate a sustainable forestry policy, and which has been manufactured from pulp processed using acid-free and elementary chlorine-free practices. Furthermore, the publisher ensures that the text paper and cover board used have met acceptable environmental accreditation standards.

For further information on
Blackwell Publishing, visit our website:
www.blackwellpublishing.com

Contents

Acknowledgements

Grateful acknowledgement is made to the following sources for permission to reproduce material in this text:

Auden, W.H. (1968) 'Musée des Beaux Arts' in *Collected Shorter Poems, 1927–1957*, Faber & Faber Ltd and *Collected Poems* edited by E. Mendelson, © 1940 and renewed 1968 by W.H. Auden, reprinted by permission of Random House, Inc.; Lévi-Strauss, C. (1970) *The Raw and the Cooked*, Jonathan Cape Ltd, Harper & Row Inc.; Gardner, H. (1972) 'A Structural Analysis of the French Intellectual Tradition' in *The Quest for Mind*, Coventure Ltd, reproduced by kind permission of Sigo Press; Larkin, P. (1964) 'Love Songs in Age' in *The Whitsun Weddings*, Faber & Faber Ltd; Segal, D.M. 'The Connections between the Semantics and Formal Structure of a Text' in *Mythology*, edited by P. Maranad, first appeared as 'O svjazi semantiki teksta s ego formal' noj strukture' in *Poetica II,* Varsovie (1966), pp. 15–44.

Introduction

This volume has been compiled and written for the Open University's course 'Philosophy of the Arts', and is intended to provide introductions to the main areas of interest in the subject. The essays may be read separately, and no special knowledge of the arts or of philosophy has been assumed.

A question that might occur to anyone who reflects on the arts is how such a thing should be possible at all. From the point of view of usefulness, or of survival in the natural world, the arts might seem an inexplicable and irrational activity, and perhaps would seem so to a rational observer from another planet. Here is something that sets human beings apart from the animal world; and here also is a fit subject for that sense of wonder of which Aristotle spoke, as a motive for philosophical enquiry.

The activity of art is much older than philosophical reflection about the arts, and artistic objects and activities can be found in almost every society, including those in which there is no explicit concept of art. But, since the beginnings of Western philosophy, the arts have been an important object of philosophical investigation. Both Plato and Aristotle were impressed by the importance of the arts, and their discussions remain as starting-points for the philosophy of the arts today.

Among other well-known philosophers who wrote about the arts were Aquinas, Hume, Kant, Schopenhauer and Marx, as well as twentieth-century writers such as Collingwood and Wittgenstein. The views of all these are discussed in this volume, as well those of writers of more recent date.

The volume begins with three essays under the collective title 'What is Art?' It is not unusual, in discussions of a given concept, to begin by defining, or trying to define, the concept. But the quest for definition should not be regarded as a mere preliminary, something to get out of the way before the main discussion begins. On the contrary, 'The Problem of Definition', to quote the title of the first essay, is a difficult and central problem in the philosophy of the arts. The concept has had a long and complicated history; and because of the importance of art in our lives, there has been much argument about what qualities an object or performance must have in order to qualify as art: whether, for example, it must serve a useful purpose in order to do so, and what that purpose might be. The definition of art has often been connected with questions of value, and according to some writers, the questions 'What is art?' and 'What is good art?' are inseparable.

The main 'theories' of what art is are introduced in Essay One, in the quest for a definition, along with the question of how art and value are related. In this way the main topics of the subsequent essays are foreshadowed in this first one. The main theories, as discussed in Essays Four to Six, are: (i) art is whatever provides 'aesthetic experience'; (ii) art is a vehicle for the expressions or communication of feeling; and (iii) works of art are 'imitations of nature' or 'representations of reality'. (These theories can be regarded as providing definitions of art, but, as will become clear, this does not exhaust their interest.) The later essays in the volume deal mainly with evaluative aspects of art. They include 'Art, Society and Morality', 'The Evaluation of Art', 'Criticism and Interpretation', and two final essays in which recent Continental and Marxist theories are discussed.

This is the shape of the book in broad outline. Let me now introduce the essays in more detail. The first, written by myself and entitled 'The Problem of Definition', begins with a brief historical survey of the concept , to give some sense of the complexity of its development, and the controversial way in which it acquired its present form. Next I discuss and criticize a definition proposed by the art historian W. Tatarkiewicz, which has the virtue of containing all of the 'standard theories' of art, including those just mentioned, in a complex formula devised by this writer. After this I introduce a question which has become prominent, both in aesthetics and elsewhere, since the appearance of Wittgenstein's *Philosophical Investigations* in 1951: whether the quest for such definitions is not altogether misguided. Some writers have argued that there is not, and could not be, a definition of art, and that this approach to the concept can only lead to distortions of it. In contrast to this, there is the more recent 'institutional theory', put forward by George Dickie. According to this, the traditional approaches and theories are indeed incapable of yielding a definition, but another sort of definition is proposed: roughly, that 'work of art' means whatever has been put forward as such by a suitable person or institution. This has been, and continues to be, an influential theory, not only in philosophical discussion, but in the art world itself. A notable feature of it is that, unlike more traditional approaches, it places no qualitative constraints on what is to be counted as art, leaving open the possibility of the most innovative creations to be admitted as works of art.

In the final section, 'But is it art?', I try, contrary to this view, to do justice to the bewilderment experienced by many ordinary observers when confronted by putative works of art which have been produced in accordance with this and similarly accommodating views of art.

The question 'What is art?' can be understood in ways other than the quest for definition. It may be about the intrinsic qualities of art, such as beauty; and these are the topic of the second essay, 'Aesthetic Qualities'. The question here is not so much about defining art in terms of such qualities, but to examine the qualities themselves. The most prominent example is that of beauty; for, whatever surprises the continuing history of art may have in store for us, it is likely that the traditional association of art with beauty will remain. The nature of beauty is discussed in this essay, including the 'classic' view, that beauty is an objective property, consisting in the balance and proportion of parts, and describable, according to some thinkers, in mathematical terms. Opposed to this are 'subjectivist' views, according to which beauty is, or is to be identified by, a feeling experienced by the viewer or listener.

After this I turn to a quality that has been prominent in discussions of art since the work of 'formalist' critics such as Fry and Bell in the early years of the twentieth century. In expounding the new non-representational art of certain painters to a reluctant public, these writers treated *form* as the fundamental quality of art. How far this idea can be applied to works of art in general, and what exactly is meant by 'form', is discussed in this essay.

This is followed by a review of the more recent work of Frank Sibley on 'aesthetic concepts'. Sibley draws attention to the fact that the vocabulary actually used in discussing works of art is far wider than the traditional 'beauty', 'form', etc. It includes such terms as 'delicate', 'sombre', 'dynamic', 'garish', 'a telling contrast', 'sets up a tension', and many others. The main questions here are (i) in what sense, if any, these qualities are objects of perception; and (ii) what the logical relations are between them and the 'supporting' non-aesthetic qualities, such as 'pale colours', 'curving lines', 'has a great number of characters', 'deals with life in a manufacturing town', and so on. Can the former be deduced from the latter, so that, for example, the presence of certain colours will *entail* that a picture is garish?

A final section is devoted to the puzzling phenomenon of 'expressive qualities', such as 'sad' and 'plaintive', as applied to music. If a piece of music is described in these terms, are we to think it is because the composer had these feelings when writing it? The difficulties of this view are discussed in this section, but a much fuller treatment of 'expression theories' is provided in Essay Five.

In Essay Three, 'The Ontology of Art', the question 'What is art?' is taken in another sense again. This time the focus is on the mode of existence (ontology) of works of art. In this context, as in many others throughout the book, it is important to notice distinctions between the arts, as opposed to the assumption (which crystallized only in the eighteenth century), that the different arts can all be subsumed under the general heading of 'art' or 'fine art'. The distinction that is important for ontology is that between 'unique' arts, such as painting, in which the works are particular physical objects, and arts such as poetry and music, where this is not so. Beethoven's First Symphony cannot be identified with a particular object or performance. In what sense does the work 'exist'? Philosophers have found it helpful to speak of such existence in terms of 'type' and 'token', and these terms are discussed in the essay.

Such ontological questions may seem at first rather technical, but it soon appears that, in the arts especially, they are connected with important matters such as the authentic performance of works of music and drama. What we have, in the case of such works, are the scores or texts. But these are necessarily 'incomplete', leaving room for a great variety of possible interpretations, all of which might be claimed as authentic according to various criteria. If, for example, we want to give authentic performance of a piece by Chopin, should we construct and use a piano such as those existing in his time? What if we think that the composer himself would have preferred the superior instruments of today? Again, can we, people of the twentieth century, *experience* a work of music or drama in the same way as people of another age? If not, what is the point of 'authentic performance'?

The final section is about authenticity in another sense, which arises when we are confronted with (a) reproductions or (b) imitations of original works. In this discussion I consider some famous cases of forgery, and the contention of some thinkers, that in such cases it is irrational for us to attach a lower value to reproductions or limitations than to original works. They argue that what matters, or should matter, are only the intrinsic qualities of the work before us, such as its beauty or form, and that these, and the work itself, can be appreciated without any knowledge of the circumstances of its creation. This issue, connected with what is known as 'the intentional fallacy', is further discussed in

Essay Nine. Such issues have acquired a new importance in recent times, when techniques of reproduction and imitation, perhaps with the aid of computers, are becoming more and more advanced. (There is also the possibility of 'original' works of music, and perhaps poetry, by means of computers.)

Essay Four, on 'Aesthetic Experience', introduces us to one of the major 'theories' of what the arts are essentially about. (As in other cases, it would be more accurate to speak of a 'type' or 'group' of theories, but the simplification may be allowed for these introductory remarks.) The approach of aesthetic experience might seem more plausible than any other. What, after all, are the arts for? Why do we spend money on them, and take time and trouble to experience them? To these questions two main answers may be given, one social and the other personal. The arts, it may be said, contribute, or are capable of contributing, to the welfare of society, and should be promoted for that reason, in so far as they conform to it; and this approach is discussed in Essays Seven and Eleven. But few would claim that social benefit is the main reason or justification for artistic activity. The personal answer, on the other hand, will be in terms of an individual's experience – the pleasure, delight, thrills, or whatever, that we experience when we listen to music, read a poem or contemplate a painting. It is clear that such experiences, however described, are, as Diané Collinson points out, 'prized very highly'. For many people they are among the greatest pleasures of life, and much has been written and said about their importance. According to one writer, quoted by Collinson, aesthetic experience is 'uniquely marked out' and 'extraordinary in its delight'. Such remarks will not, however, take us very far towards understanding *how* this kind of experience is uniquely marked out, or how it could serve to provide a theory of the arts in general.

The trouble is that when we think about the experiences in question, we find them to be extremely various. This is so for two reasons, the first of which is personal: one person's reaction to a given work of art will be different from that of another: even if both are positive, they may describe their experiences – what they get out of the work – in very different ways. (This may even be true of the same individual at different times.) The second reason is connected with the great variety of what we call 'works of art'. (Here we are reminded of the point made in Essay One, that the arts have been unified under one concept only in recent times.) Is it really plausible to think that there is a particular kind of experience, to be called 'aesthetic', that is common to all the different kinds of art? Even within a given genre, say the novel, we may be more impressed by the variety of the works, and the corresponding readers' reactions, than by anything they have in common. 'No single account' of aesthetic experience, writes Collinson, 'seems able... to yield a characteristic or group of characteristics that can serve as the basis of a definition of the experience'.

Nevertheless a number of writers have tried to provide such characterizations, and their attempts are reviewed in this essay. A major contributor to this literature was Schopenhauer, who described the kind of absorption that we often experience in the contemplation of art, as well as of other aesthetic objects, such as a landscape. 'We *lose* ourselves entirely in this object... we forget our individuality, our will... ' In Schopenhauer's philosophy, as Collinson explains, the will was of central importance; and our 'contemplative' stance towards aesthetic objects was to be characterized by a suspension of will.

The word 'contemplation' is prominent in this part of the essay, but in later sections it is the negative term 'disinterested' that plays a central role. 'To be disinterested', as Collinson explains, 'describes the absence of the kind of interest that relates to one's own advantage or disadvantage... It is to be concerned with the object itself, not with how it relates to oneself'. She devotes a section to Kant's aesthetics, in which this concept plays an important role. According to Kant, writes Collinson, 'it is by a feeling of delight that we come to judge that something is beautiful'. But this delight has to be distinguished from two other 'interested' kinds of delight, the first being a 'merely sensory agreeableness, such as a liking for strawberries', and the second 'a delight in something that is recognized as morally good'. 'Disinterested', as I said, is a negative concept, and as such avoids the difficulties of positive characterizations of aesthetic experience. But there is more to Kant's account than the negative point, as readers of this essay will find.

In the following section there is a discussion of the formalist Clive Bell (who is also considered in Essay Two, 'Aesthetic Qualities'). The case of Bell provides an illustration of the difficulty of trying to arrange the views of writers on aesthetics in a neat classification, such as that adopted in the structure of this volume. Bell is commonly, and reasonably, classified as a formalist. But he can also be regarded as belonging to the aesthetic experience camp, in view of his appeal to 'a peculiar... aesthetic emotion' by means of which the essential quality of works of art, 'some quality common and peculiar' to them all, was to be identified. (This quality turns out to be what he called 'significant form'.) Finally, Bell might also be classified under 'expression theories', as discussed in Essay Five, since he held that what makes form significant is that it 'conveys an emotion felt by its creator'.

Another account of the 'disinterested' kind is that of Edward Bullough, with his notion of 'psychical distance'. Here it is appropriate, as Collinson writes, to make a distinction 'between an aesthetic *attitude* and an aesthetic *experience*: the aesthetic attitude being a certain kind of stance or approach required as a necessary condition of aesthetic experience'. On this view, what is fundamental is our manner of viewing the object, rather than the resulting experience. What is necessary, according to Bullough, is that, in a certain sense, we 'distance' ourselves from it. In a famous illustration he describes a fog at sea, which might well be regarded as terrifying by passengers on a ship; inviting us, by means of an eloquent description (quoted in the essay), to see that the same people might be able to view the same fog as an object of great aesthetic enjoyment. This they could do by distancing themselves from the practical implications of the object.

A more recent exponent of aesthetic experience and aesthetic attitude theories has been Monroe Beardsley. In this essay we are introduced to his attempt to provide a positive characterization of aesthetic experience, in the form of 'five criteria', and his modifications of these in response to criticisms by George Dickie. Dickie has been a strong critic of this whole approach, describing the aesthetic attitude as a 'myth'. I have already mentioned Dickie as one of the chief advocates of the 'institutional theory', discussed in Essay One; and his opposition to such writers as Bullough and Beardsley is not unconnected with this; nor is the fact that Beardsley has been a strong critic of the institutional theory. The point is that according to the Bullough or Beardsley approach, it must be possible to characterize art in terms of an appropriate experience or attitude, however difficult it may be to define these accurately. The point of the institutional theory, by contrast, is that allowance must be made for anything whatever to count as a work of art, provided only that it has been put forward as such by a suitable member of the art world. This presupposes nothing about the intrinsic qualities of the work, or about the experiences or attitudes of those who view or hear it.

The accounts just considered may be described as consumer-oriented: according to them, art is to be viewed from the perspective of a person viewing or hearing the work. In Essay Five we are introduced to theories in which the central role is played by the person creating the work, and art is to be defined or characterized by reference to the creator's feelings rather than those of the consumer. This is not to say that the latter are always left out of account. Tolstoy's theory, which is the first to be discussed, is one of *transmission*, and like some others in this group, he regarded art as comparable to language. 'By words a man transmits his thoughts to others, by art he transmits his feelings'. The feelings, according to Tolstoy, must be of a certain kind: they must be (a) feelings that the artist himself has 'lived through', and (b) such as to promote 'the brotherhood of man'; and the work itself must be understandable by simple people, so as to enable it to achieve this end.

The latter requirements take the theory beyond the scope of mere expression or transmission theories, into the realm of issues about the social and moral roles of art, such as those discussed in Essays Seven and Eleven. (In this respect Tolstoy was an important precursor of Marxist views about the arts.) But they also raise questions, of a general kind, about the nature of definitions of art and indeed definitions in general. Robert Wilkinson writes that when Tolstoy's book was published, it 'evoked both dismay and protest'. The reason for this lay in the drastic consequences of the author's definition. For, as Tolstoy himself pointed out, a large proportion of Western art, including many works regarded as masterpieces, would fail to qualify as art, being either not accessible to simple people, or containing feelings at variance with the 'brotherhood of man'. Tolstoy himself did not baulk at these consequences, and indeed named and discussed many of the rejected works at length.

Tolstoy's definition, we may say, has teeth. It is not one that conforms to Wittgenstein's dictum: 'Philosophy leaves everything as it is'. Such definitions may be more interesting and challenging than those which merely record ordinary usage, but an objector may not be willing to accept them. So far from agreeing to exclude the non-qualifying works from the description 'art', the objector may cite them as *counter-examples* to the definition, arguing that any definition which would exclude them must be mistaken.

In Essay One there is a discussion of 'persuasive definitions', and the view of one writer that what appeared to be a mere definition of existing usage was in truth one that had 'work to do'; its work was to 'teach people a new way of looking at pictures'. Perhaps Tolstoy's definition can be understood in a similar way.

The question of definition arises again in the case of Collingwood, who stated explicitly that his intention was to define art in a way that 'harmonizes with common usage'. Now, according to Collingwood, works of art are 'expressions of emotion'. But is this in accordance with common usage? Perhaps many people would accept this statement as a definition, or partial definition, of art. But would their actual usage of the term be in accordance with it? What exactly does the statement mean, and what does it entail? Collingwood's account of the matter is rightly regarded as a classic of its kind. But, as Wilkinson shows, when the implications are followed through, the results may strike us as strange, and far removed from ordinary ideas and common usage. (One is reminded of Bertrand Russell's remark that philosophers often begin by saying something so obvious as not to be worth saying, and end with something so paradoxical that no one will believe it.)

Collingwood's account differs in interesting ways from that of Tolstoy and other expression theorists. According to Collingwood, the artist's emotion is of a very special kind; it is not a feeling to which one can give a ready name, such as 'sentiment of human brotherhood'. Instead there is, as Wilkinson puts it, 'a burden of inchoate emotion the nature of which is unclear'. Artists are motivated to rid themselves of this burden by making the emotion 'articulate to' themselves, which they can do by creating a work of art suitable to it. These may be plausible ideas, but their implausible consequences are brought out by Wilkinson. They include the claim that works of art exist essentially in the mind, and that, in Collingwood's words, 'every utterance and every gesture that each one of us makes is a work of art'.

A constant source of interest, but also of possible confusion, in the philosophy of the arts, are the differences between the arts. A statement or definition that seems plausible for some of the arts may not seem so when we turn to others. In the case of literature, drama and representational painting, a good deal of explaining can be done by reference to the events narrated, objects described or depicted, etc. These play an important role, at least, in accounting for our interest in the relevant works. But this is not so in the case of music, which, with a few exceptions, is non-conceptual and non-representational. Hence the expression theory has been especially prominent in the case of music.

But is music non-representational? Is this how it differs from language? Some theorists have claimed that music is a kind of language – a 'language of the emotions'. Such a view is expounded in Deryck Cooke's *The Language of Music*, in which he presents, in great detail, a systematic correlation between emotions and musical patterns. Another account, in which music is compared with language, is that of Suzanne Langer. Drawing on ideas and terminology from Wittgenstein's *Tractatus*, she spoke of musical patterns as sharing 'formal properties' with human feelings of motion and rest, etc. 'Music', she wrote, 'articulates forms which language cannot set forth'. These theories are critically discussed in the essay, but a general difficulty about them all concerns the question of value. What, we may ask, would be the point of producing musical sounds, and other artistic works, if their only function was to express or symbolize somebody's feelings? Even if the alleged correspondence between music and feelings were proved, this would leave unexplained the value that we place on music, and the delight we experience in our encounters with works of art in general.

Such questions are readily answered if we appeal to intrinsic qualities of art, such as beauty, as opposed to facts about the artist's feelings or other facts extrinsic to the work. Theories based on facts of the latter kind are described by Wilkinson as 'heteronomist', because they rely on something *other* than the work; and they are contrasted with Edward Hanslick's ideas in *The Beautiful in Music*. Hanslick rejected all theories of the 'language of the emotions' type, insisting that the value of music is to be found in its 'purely musical' features. He maintained that insofar as a piece of music is representational, this diminishes its beauty. We are not to think of music, as we think of language, in terms of meaning: music 'pleases for its own sake, like an arabesque, a column or some spontaneous product of nature – a leaf or flower'.

Hanslick is presented, in the context of this essay, as an opponent of the expression theory, but his 'autonomist' stance can be seen in a wider context. In his emphasis on intrinsic properties he shares the purist conception of art maintained by Clive Bell; and his rejection of representationalism in music may be compared with Bell's denigration of representationalism in painting, and his insistence that aesthetic appreciation is of formal properties alone. Such autonomist or purist views are opposed, not only to the expression theory, but to any other views allowing a knowledge of the artist, or the circumstances in which a work was produced, to be relevant to its appreciation. This issue is connected with the problem of imitations and forgeries (Essay Three) and is discussed again, in connection with interpretation, in Essay Nine.

Of the various theories and ideas that have been held about art, one stands out for its antiquity, and its prevalence throughout the history of art. This is the idea for which the Greek *mimesis* (roughly: imitation, copy, representation) is often used. According to mimetic views, our interest in works of art, and the value we ascribe to them, are due to their ability to represent or imitate reality. Such a view was expressed by Aristotle when he wrote that 'the poet is an imitator, just like a painter or any other image-maker' (*Poetics*, 1460b).[1] The idea that art is essentially mimetic was taken for granted by the Greeks and by many later writers up to the present day. It is also often expressed in ordinary talk about the arts. Thus a portrait may be praised as 'an excellent likeness' or criticized for being 'not a bit like him'; while the presentation of offensive material in television drama is sometimes defended on the ground that 'that's how life really is'.

In a survey of mimetic views of the arts, it is natural to begin with the writings of the ancient Greeks; and in the opening pages of Essay Six we are introduced to Plato's largely hostile views about the arts. The mimetic view, as I have said, was taken for granted, and Plato's criticisms were based on this assumption.

Now in critical discussions of theories of art, such as those of Essays Four to Six, two main kinds of questions may be distinguished. The first, connected with Essay One, is about definition. Here the question will be whether the theory under discussion can be made to yield a necessary and sufficient condition of art; and a critic would try to produce counter-examples that do not conform to the proposed definition. (An obvious difficulty for mimetic definitions is the existence of non-representational arts such as music.) But a second kind of question is about making sense of the relevant description of art, even if this is applied only to some kinds of art and not as an overall definition. I have already mentioned one difficulty that arises here, which is about the *point* of producing works of art, supposing they conformed to that description. Thus we may ask what the point would be of producing imitations of reality, or of paying artists to express their feelings, if this is what art, or some art, is really about. Some of Aristotle's views on this are discussed in Essay Six. According to him, writes Rosalind Hursthouse, 'we enjoy accurate representations of things because we enjoy learning'. The question whether, or in what sense, we *learn* from works of arts, and whether this could be their main function, is discussed at length in this essay.

The statement I have just quoted may be used to draw attention to two main aspects of the mimetic view. The first is that the arts serve to 'represent things', and the second that they are beneficial by providing knowledge. This division is reflected in the structure of the essay. The first aspect, representation, is discussed with reference to painting; the second, knowledge, with reference to literature.

It would be generally agreed that paintings are, or may be, representational. (Here we must set aside non-representational painting, which may be classified, in this respect, with most music and most architecture.) But how do paintings represent? An answer that suggests itself is that the artist 'copies what he sees', thereby producing a likeness of the reality. This view has been criticized by Ernst Gombrich as involving 'the myth of the innocent eye'. The trouble is that 'what the artist sees' depends on the cultural and conceptual equipment that he brings with him to the scene, and a similar point may be made about the viewer. After expounding these and other difficulties about the 'resemblance' view, Hursthouse presents us with a choice. If the way in which a picture represents its object is not that of resemblance, then it must be one of 'convention'. The conventionalist view of Nelson Goodman is expounded in the next section. Goodman has claimed that 'almost any picture may represent almost anything'; and that 'pictorial representation' is analogous to 'verbal description', the former being no more dependent on resemblance with the object than the latter. (This view of representational art invites comparison with views about non-representational arts such as music, as discussed in Essay Five, including the idea that music is a language or symbolic system.)

The final sections of Essay Six are concerned with the question of truth and knowledge; and this time literature, and particularly the novel, is the main topic of discussion. An extreme view, expressed by Arnold Isenberg, is that aesthetic experience has nothing to do with truth; and this is criticized by reference to examples taken from R. K. Elliott, in which the appreciation of certain poems depends essentially on the reader's knowledge of relevant facts.

But if it is accepted that truth has an important role in the appreciation of literature, this does not entail that, as Aristotle thought, the latter can *teach* us anything; for the truths in question may be ones we already know, and can then *recognize* in what we read. In any case, why should we expect a work of fiction, a product of the writer's imagination, to impart knowledge? What, for example, can we expect to learn from a novel by Dostoevsky? According to Ilham Dilman, we can learn many things: 'the way pride, humiliation [etc.]... can turn into a force for evil'; how someone 'under the guise of innocent motherly concern' can try to manipulate her son's thoughts; 'how a bad conscience and passivity can drive a man to a violent act'; and so on.

Here it may be useful to distinguish between 'learning how' (how certain motives can produce such and such results), and 'learning that' (that such and such events occur or occurred, etc.). What the novel teaches us is not the obvious fact that, for example, pride can be a force for evil; but *how* this can happen in a given set of circumstances. What we gain may be a deeper understanding, rather than a knowledge of facts previously unknown.

Essay Seven, 'Art, Society and Morality', again takes its departure from Plato's criticism of the arts, and this time the emphasis is on their social and moral role. The arts, according to Plato, belong to a class of 'luxuries', existing over and above the 'healthy' society – the ideal state – that he aimed to describe in *The Republic*; and he saw no need for a class of 'professional imitators' in such a society. Such imitators were liable to be harmful because their motivation was of the wrong kind: to entertain rather than to instruct. A poet, for example, might present gods and heroes in a shameful or ridiculous light for the sake of better entertainment, and thereby set a bad example to the young. Another of Plato's criticisms is that the poet may act out, say, a doctor's or a general's role without having a proper knowledge of these activities.

These and other arguments of Plato may strike a modern reader as crude, and based on an excessively narrow conception of art. But, as Tom Sorell points out, they are readily applicable to some, at least, of today's art. Thus a modern novelist, or TV scriptwriter of 'drama-documentaries', may be motivated by a desire to capture an audience, rather than by a scrupulous pursuit of accuracy and truth, or by thoughts about the moral effects of a work.

Nevertheless, as Sorell shows, there are weaknesses in Plato's argument. He seems not to allow for the difference between our responses to a representation or imitation which we recognize as such, and the feelings that would be provoked in us by the real thing. Moreover, his arguments are applicable only to certain kinds of art, leaving aside the many artistic creations and activities which have no particular bearing on morals.

Plato's criticism of the arts is connected with his views about knowledge, and moral knowledge in particular. He held that true knowledge is to be had by communion with eternal, immutable entities, the 'Forms', and that the knowledge (so called) that we gain through our senses is only of secondary validity. The best example of this is our knowledge of mathematical truths, which might be described as 'eternal', in contrast to empirical facts, knowledge of which may be gained from particular experiences of the physical world. But Plato had a similar view about moral knowledge, ascribing the same eternal, non-empirical status to moral truths as to those of mathematics. But, as Sorell argues, it is wrong to deny that we can gain instruction in moral matters by empirical means. Experience, both of life and of literature, may not teach us moral truths, but it can enrich and deepen our understanding of moral situations, our sympathy for people different from ourselves, and so on.

Another thinker who has appeared before in these essays is Tolstoy. In Essay Five he featured mainly as a protagonist of the expression theory; this time the emphasis is on his ideas about the moral and social functions of art. Tolstoy's insistence on moral function is comparable with that of Plato; but he had a different idea about what that function should be. According to Tolstoy the function of true art is to 'unite people', to promote 'the brotherhood of man'. This led him to stipulate, first, that art must have a wholesome content and, secondly, that it must be accessible to everyone. Sorell poses two questions for this conception of art. The first is whether a work of art may not be 'essentially part of a local tradition', and none the worse for that; the second, whether it is right to evaluate works of art according to 'the fulfilment of a *non-aesthetic* purpose'. In connection with the first question he is able to point out that even the stories of the bible – regarded by Tolstoy as paradigms of good art – would be understood in different ways by people of different cultures and languages.

On the second question, concerning a 'non-aesthetic purpose' of art, Sorell points out that 'aesthetic and political purposes [may] pull in opposite directions', with negative consequences for the quality of art. A similar difficulty arises for Marxist views of art, as discussed in Essay Eleven.

A notable opponent of instrumentalist views of art was Oscar Wilde; but according to Wilde, the instrumentalist fallacy arises in connection with *mimesis* – 'the aim of being true to nature or true to life'. Sorell quotes an eloquent passage in which Wilde denounces those who think that good art results from the mere imitation of reality. Wilde's rejection of mimesis might be compared with Hanslick's rejection of 'meanings' in the case of music, as discussed in Essay Five, and his insistence that music 'pleases for its own sake'. These are all ways in which the intrinsic and peculiar qualities of art, and aesthetic experience, are defended against the imposition of extrinsic purposes or values, whatever they might be.

Instrumentalist views such as those of Plato and Tolstoy may be regarded as inadequate and perhaps philistine. But, however much we may wish, contrary to them, to stress the intrinsic values of art, questions about the effects of art on society cannot be set aside. In recent times especially, there has been much concern about the capacity of works of art to give offence and cause harm. According to one authority, quoted in the essay, 'pornography is basically rapists' television'. Another problem concerns the offence given to religious people by certain portrayals, in works of art, of figures such as Jesus and Muhammad. In the essay such problems are addressed largely via the 'Williams Report' on obscenity and censorship. Sorell brings out the difficulties of defining such concepts as harm and offence, and of balancing the admittedly pornographic content of a given work against its admitted artistic virtues. It may be easy enough to legislate against extreme cases that are devoid of any artistic content; but this would leave much of the problem untouched. Nowadays controversial works are often defended in the interest of 'free expression'; but Sorell raises some sceptical questions about the importance of this value.

So far, the discussion has been mainly about the effects of art on society and morality. But other questions arise about the role of social forces in the evaluation of art. According to the sociologist Janet Wolff, there is a problem about accepted evaluations of art because they are based to a large extent on the judgement of a small class of 'establishment' people, who are clearly unrepresentative of the population at large. This criticism is questioned by Sorell, as is the argument of Roger Taylor, who blames élitist attitudes towards art, and 'high' art, for their deleterious effects on 'low' art and popular culture. According to Taylor, the latter is constantly 'in danger of being appropriated by bourgeois culture', which 'can suck the life out of what were previously vital activities'. One of his examples is jazz which, originally part of the life of an underprivileged class, was later taken up by the bourgeoisie so as to become part of their artistic culture.

The moral and social effects of art, important as they may be, cannot be sufficient for the evaluation of works of art. But how, by what other criteria, are they to be evaluated? The main 'theories' of art, discussed in earlier essays, will not take us far towards answering these questions. Mimesis, if it means a mere copying or imitation of things, leads to the absurd result that a *trompe-l'oeil* painting which is so lifelike as to be mistaken for the real thing, should be valued more highly than paintings in which this is not the aim. According to expression theories, the highest praise would go to works that are most effective in expressing their author's feelings. Finally, the approach of aesthetic experience, being consumer-orientated, seems more relevant to the value that we place on art; but it tells us little about which, or whose, experiences are to be valued.

But what actually happens when we discuss the quality of a work of art? Such discussions proceed largely by pointing out features *of the work* – aesthetic qualities such as those discussed in Essay Two. A work is praised because it is graceful or witty, or denigrated for being garish or sentimental. But what is the status and validity of such judgements? Are they, as some would maintain, 'merely subjective'? This is the main topic of Essay Eight.

The subjectivist view is at odds with the fact that there is such a thing as aesthetic *reasoning*, with reasons being exchanged in support of particular judgements. But what kind of reasoning is here involved? Colin Lyas discusses the question with reference to the traditional dichotomy of deductive and inductive reasoning. Aesthetic reasoning, he points out, is not deductive: we do not, in a deductive sense, 'prove' that a given work is witty or garish. Is there a role for inductive reasoning? One might argue that because this painting is by Rembrandt, it is likely to be good; and this would be good inductive reasoning. But, as Lyas points out, it would not give us what we want, which is to *see for ourselves* that the work is good, and to see for ourselves the aesthetic qualities that make it so.

Another example of inductive reasoning is that of the Golden Section. There is, as Lyas explains, a certain proportion between two distances on a line or other object, which has been found by experience to be more pleasing than other proportions. Here we seem to have an objective, measurable aesthetic datum, which would give inductive grounds for thinking that any work containing it is likely to be good. This idea, which is criticized in the essay, invites comparison with Aristotle's statement that 'the chief forms of beauty are order and symmetry and definiteness, which the mathematical sciences demonstrate in special degree' (Essay Two, p.41).

Lyas, following Sibley, argues that aesthetic reasons are of a special kind, conforming neither to deductive nor to inductive models; but that this does not make them subjective. Comparing aesthetic statements with statements of colour ('this light is green'), he shows what reasons there are for regarding aesthetic statements, as well as those of colour, as objective; but he concludes by questioning the 'simple dichotomy' of objective and subjective.

The evaluation of a work of art presupposes that we understand it in some sense; and this in turn may mean that we have *interpreted* it correctly. The question of correct interpretation has been hotly debated by writers on the arts, especially in connection with literary texts; and it is the main topic of Essay Nine. To understand such a text we must know the language in which it is written; but is this sufficient for understanding it? It is well known that a given text, say a poem or part of a poem, may lend itself to different interpretations; and a good deal of critical discussion is devoted, not to evaluating the work, but to determining how it is to be understood. But should the question be 'What does *it* mean?' or 'What did the author mean?' According to the view of Beardsley and Wimsatt in their famous paper 'The Intentional Fallacy', an author's intention is irrelevant in determining the meaning of his text.

The meanings of words, as Lyas reminds us, are not fixed by individuals; they belong to the words themselves, and knowledge of them is shared by those who speak the language. Hence, it seems, 'if we are in doubt, we need to consult dictionaries and not authors'. This view is not, however, accepted by Lyas.

There is more to knowing the meaning of what someone has written or said than a mere knowledge of the words. We need also to know something of the context in which they are written or said. This might tell us, for example, that the words were meant ironically and not in their normal sense. Lyas takes up a famous example, first introduced by Beardsley, in which the concluding line of one of A. E. Housman's poems was taken to be ironic. When this was put to the author, he assured his correspondent that his meaning had not been ironic. But was *his* meaning the meaning that mattered? Is it the one that matters for us, who read the poem today? According to Beardsley, the line may still be ironic, regardless of the author's intention; the latter being a fact about him, and not about the poem. But this claim is criticized by Lyas.

There is more to the 'intentional fallacy' issue than just intention. The arguments of Beardsley and Wimsatt take in all kinds of 'extraneous' material – anything that is not to be found in the work itself. They are part of that purist strand of thought to which Bell gave expression when he wrote that 'to appreciate a work of art, we need bring with us nothing from life, no knowledge of its ideas and affairs... nothing but a sense of form and colour and a knowledge of three-dimensional space' (quoted in Essays Two and Four); and also part of the argument for a distinctive 'aesthetic experience', as postulated by Bell, Beardsley and others.

One of the difficulties of this position is brought out by Lyas, using a satirical example from Swift. To appreciate the point of the piece we must have, 'not only a knowledge of intention, but also of the artist's historical and other circumstances'. Without this, the piece might amount, for us, to no more than a work of pure imagination.

In this debate there are, it seems to me, two extreme positions: one is that extraneous knowledge is never relevant to aesthetic appreciation; the other, that it always is. I doubt if either position is plausible.

There is a tendency among philosophers in English-speaking countries to equate 'philosophy' with what is sometimes called 'the English-speaking tradition'. But other ways of doing philosophy are to be found in France and Germany, for example; and this is true, not least, for philosophy of the arts. In recent times, 'Continental' approaches to the subject have enjoyed a considerable vogue in English-speaking countries, especially in literary studies. In Essay Ten we are introduced to theories, such as 'structuralism', which stem largely from the work of the Swiss linguist Saussure. Structuralism is the view that the essential meaning of a work it to be found in its 'deep structure' – one that it may share with others of its kind. According to the Russian formalist G. Propp, there may be basic elements which are available for 'transformation' by different authors and in different cultures. This is especially noticeable in folk-tales, where what is essentially the same story appears in many different guises. Similarly, in the case of a literary genre, such as murder mysteries, there may be stock formal elements which are available for combination in different ways, without undermining the fundamental 'structure' that all these works have in common. The French anthropologist Lévi-Strauss used this approach to analyse primitive myths, claiming that the same structural elements could be discerned in a number of them, in spite of their apparent diversity; and he showed how the relevant 'transformations' could be displayed formally in a diagram with, as Sim says, 'quasi-mathematical precision'.

In this approach there is much emphasis on the systematic wholeness of a text. Its components 'have no value except within the system in question, and are interdependent'. Hence, value was to be regarded as 'relative to a system', much as the value of a knight or pawn is relative to the game of chess; but 'there is no such thing as *intrinsic* value', which might be ascribed to the work (system) as a whole. Contrary to more traditional views, the task of the critic was not evaluation, but structural analysis. According to Lévi-Strauss, such analysis is to be recommended because of its power, as he put it, to 'reduce messages of a most disheartening complexity' to a simple perspicuous pattern.

The value of this reduction of complexity is questioned by Sim. Structualism has also been criticized from within the French tradition by Jacques Derrida. According to him, it is an illusion to regard the elements or words of a text as having stable, determinate meanings. The meanings shift and change in an eternal play of mental associations, leading to the construction of puns and other word-play. Derrida himself engages in such word-play in his use of the words '*différence*' and '*différance*'. These words are indistinguishable in speech, but whereas the first means 'difference', Derrida uses the second to mean 'deferral'. 'The constant possibility of shifting' writes Sim, 'illustrates Derrida's point that meaning is never determinate and stable'. The choice between *different* meanings is, so to speak, constantly being *deferred*.

For Derrida, as Sim explains, the opposition to structuralism – 'the tyranny of forms' – is associated with 'the authoritarianism of Western thought' and 'Western metaphysics'. But, as Sim points out, the traditional kind of criticism is not *necessarily* authoritarian', even if the qualified critics may be described as 'authorities'. As regards the question of meaning, he accuses Derrida and his followers of presenting the issue 'in a polarized form'. The truth is that while meaning is not always stable, it is not always unstable either. Moreover, if it were always unstable, must not the meaning of Derrida's text itself be regarded as indeterminate?

A feature of all the main theories discussed in Essay Ten is that they are hostile to, or at least silent on, the question of evaluation, unlike more traditional approaches. Thus, if we accept that works of art are to be analysed according to their 'deep structure' or, on the other hand, that there are no stable meanings to be found in them, this gives us no guidance on the evaluation of particular works. The Marxist approach, discussed in Essay Eleven, is quite the opposite. In it the concern with value is dominant, and the value in question is social and political. It is an approach of the same type as that of Plato and Tolstoy, discussed in Essay Seven. Tolstoy's requirement, that art must be (a) 'realistic' and (b) accessible to the mass of ordinary people reappears in the writings of Marxists quoted in this essay, who hold that art is to be judged and justified for its didactic benefits. The theory of art as a method of 'social engineering' was expounded and practised in Stalin's Russia. Its function was to be 'the ideological remoulding and education of the toiling people', as Stalin's cultural commissar put it.

However, as Sim points out, this is only one side of Marxist aesthetics; for many different views have been put forward by writers belonging to this tradition. A particularly interesting difference, expounded in the essay, is that between realism and anti-realism. A paradox of 'socialist realism' is its tendency to lead to an art that is conservative and static; for if the appreciation of art is to be easily accessible to the majority of people, then the advantage will be with 'straightforward', rather than with innovative, adventurous art. Such art may also be conservative in the sense of being in accordance with traditions existing in pre-revolutionary times. This would make it objectionable according to the Marxist 'reflection theory', whereby the art of a given society reflects the nature of that society. From this theory it would follow that the art of a capitalist society, including traditional realistic styles, would be suitable for a capitalist and not a socialist state.

Other Marxist thinkers, however, have opposed realism, maintaining that, in various ways, non-traditional (revolutionary) art is more likely to promote the cause of improvement and education, perhaps by being more likely to 'make people think'. A notable example, discussed in the essay, is Bertolt Brecht, who recommended and practised an '"alienation effect", whereby the audience is actively prevented from treating the drama on the stage as reality, or identifying with the dramatic characters'.

Such issues are usually discussed in relation to literature and the visual arts. Are they also applicable to music? The term 'realism' is not readily applicable to music, but the issue of traditionalism versus modernism in music has been discussed, among others, by Adorno. Defending such composers as Schoenberg, Adorno objected to the traditional 'tonal combinations'. 'It is not simply that these sounds are antiquated and untimely, but that they are false.' The function of today's music was to 'express the tensions' of modern life, and composers should abstain from the 'reworking of older styles'. (Here again we have the assumption, criticized at length in Essay Five, that music serves as a medium of expression, perhaps a kind of language.) Yet, as Sim points out, those who follow Adorno in his opposition to traditional forms are 'exposing themselves to charges of élitism (one of the cardinal sins of Marxist politics)'.

Oswald Hanfling, September 1991

Note

[1] I am grateful to Dr C. Osborne for this translation. In the Penguin edition, page 69, the relevant passage begins 'Like the painter or any other artist...' This may be puzzling to readers who are aware that in Aristotle's vocabulary the same word, usually translated 'artist', is used to cover craftsmen such as carpenters and shoemakers, as well as flautists and sculptors (see Essay One, p.5). Aristotle would not, however, have wanted to speak of carpenters and shoemakers as 'imitators'.

PART ONE WHAT IS ART?

1   The problem of definition

Oswald Hanfling

Introduction

Questions of the form 'What is X?' have been prominent in philosophy since the time of Socrates. What is knowledge? What is truth? What is virtue? What is time? What is beauty? What is art? Such questions have baffled thinkers through the ages, and a vast amount has been written on each of them. There has been an assumption that it should be possible to *define* the words in question, and that we do not really know what we are talking about if we cannot define our words. 'Either', wrote Clive Bell in his book *Art* (1915), we mean by 'works of art' a class of objects having some 'quality common and peculiar to all members of this class', or else 'we gibber' when we use the expression 'works of art'. His aim, he said, was to discover 'the essential quality... that distinguishes works of art from all other classes of objects' (Bell, 1915, p.7).

Nowadays it is no longer assumed so widely that definitions of this kind must or should be available. According to Wittgenstein, this assumption rests on a false conception of language, the truth being that language can, and for the most part does, function perfectly well without such definitions, and this does not undermine our ability to know what we are talking about when we use the words in question. Even so, it may be useful to pursue the quest for a definition, for this may throw light on the concept in question. It may be illuminating to investigate the conditions that have been or might be put forward by way of definition, to understand what they contribute towards the meaning of the word, and why they fall short of capturing it entirely.

These remarks are applicable to the question 'What is art?' no less than to others of this kind. Even if no answer will be forthcoming, the quest for a definition may still be worthwhile. Moreover, this will be a convenient way of introducing the main 'theories' of art that have been put forward – about what art is, what makes it important and valuable, what makes the difference between good and bad art, and so on.

The attempt to define art has a certain urgency which makes it different from attempts to define knowledge, truth, etc. It is sometimes said that philosophical questions are 'merely verbal', as if this were to diminish their interest or importance. Against this it may be argued (though I shall not do so here) that 'merely verbal' questions of this kind may be among the most important questions we can ask, having to do with fundamental concerns of human life. In the case of art, however, it can be shown directly that the question 'What is art?' is not 'merely verbal' in any trivial sense. The great novelist Tolstoy, who used the question *What is Art?* for the title of his book on art, began by drawing attention to the vast expenditure of human resources devoted to the production and performance of art of all kinds, for those who could afford it. What, he asked, was it all for? What benefits were to be gained from all this expenditure and industry? In reply he offered a definition of art which would make it subservient to moral concerns. True art, he maintained, would serve a good purpose, and he set out to explain what this was and how it could be achieved. (As with some other definitions of art, Tolstoy's answer gives us not only a definition but also a criterion of quality: the answer to 'What is art?' is at the same time an answer to 'What is good art?')

Nowadays we are less prepared to lay down criteria for good art in terms of moral benefit, for we may hold that art has its own special kind or kinds of value. But the point about the expenditure of human effort and wealth is as valid today as in Tolstoy's time. And if we do not insist on moral criteria, we do at least want the expenditure to be on something that is valuable in some sense – a sense that is appropriate to art if not to morality. But this means that the expenditure must be on *art*, and not on some substitute pretending to be art. In this way the 'verbal' question about art can become an important question of public policy. But the question also arises at a personal level. If I, an ordinary consumer of art, have gone to some trouble to visit an art gallery, theatre or concert hall, I may complain that my time and money have been wasted, that what has been presented to me is not merely not good art (which may be a matter of taste), but that it is not to be recognized as art at all, since it does not conform to what is normally understood by this word. Here we see that the question 'What is art?' is of immediate practical concern, unlike some of the other questions of definition.

In investigating a given concept, it is sometimes illuminating to consider its history, for this may throw light on the ideas that have gone into the concept – or, as the case may be, how we come to have such a concept at all. Concepts such as those of art, knowledge and truth do not spring up at random; they are reflections of human needs and interests, of the situation in which we find ourselves and our perception of the world in which we live. There is, however, a difference in this respect, between the concept of art and some others that have been of interest to philosophers. The difference is not one of different histories, but of having a history at all. P.F. Strawson has spoken of a 'central core of human thinking which has no history', of 'categories and concepts which, in their most fundamental character, change not at all' (Strawson, 1959, p.10). It can be argued that concepts like those of knowledge, truth and time belong to this class; they are part of the fabric of human life and language as such, and are not subject to variation in different times and places. (This is not to deny the obvious fact that *what* people know, regard as true, etc., varies in different times and places; the point is about the existence of the *concepts* of knowledge, truth, time, and so on.) If this is so, then those who aim to find a correct definition of knowledge, say, are at least shooting at a fixed target. But this is not so in the case of art. Even the most cursory examination of the history of this concept will show that it has been subject to much change; and the very existence of the concept cannot be taken for granted, but depends on the state of a given culture at a particular time. There is no reason to suppose, for example, that the pre-industrial societies studied by anthropologists must have such a concept, must make use of words and statements which would be translated into our 'art'.

The art historian Tatarkiewicz writes that our modern concept of art is 'a confluence of concepts' – an inheritance consisting of a number of ideas and strands of thought, dating back to ancient times.[1] Now this may also be said about many other concepts that have developed in the course of time, but what further distinguishes the concept of art is that the ideas that have gone into it are sometimes in conflict with one another, reflecting opposing views not only about what art is but about what it ought to be; what is important about it and which of the activities in question are to be valued most.

Controversy has been a characteristic feature of the concept of art. But it may be said that today it is in a state of crisis unlike any that existed before. Almost daily we are confronted with new kinds of objects or performances which challenge our notions of what art is or ought to be. Such traditional qualities as beauty, aesthetic experience and 'the imitation of nature' have come under challenge, and even the minimal requirement that a work of art should be a *work* – an object made by human hands – has been flouted. But as these qualities have fallen away, one other quality, that of innovation, has taken on a new importance.

'The essence of art', according to the painter Dubuffet, 'is novelty. Likewise should views on art be novel. The only system favourable to art is permanent revolution' (quoted in Tatarkiewicz, p.264).

If the only requirement on art is that of novelty, then we must not be surprised to find an ever wider range of objects and performances being put forward as art, until, it would seem, anything whatever might be describable as art. We have already witnessed such 'works' as *Invisible Sculpture*, consisting of a hole that was dug in New York's Central Park and then filled up again; while in the field of music we have been given John Cage's work entitled *433"*, which consists of four minutes and thirty-three seconds of silence. Moreover, the difficulty of distinguishing art from what is not art is proving difficult in practice as well as theory, as when we read in a newspaper report that 'a three-ton sculpture made from 90ft of steel girders, intended for a municipal park in Eindhoven, Holland, was taken to a workshop for painting, mistaken for scrap, cut up and sold to a steel mill'; while in another incident a certain artist was banned from a gallery 'for eating fellow artist's Robert Gober's latest "creation" – a bag of doughnuts on a pedestal'.

These problems are characteristic of our time, and we might look with envy towards other times when the nature and role of works of art was more clearly identified. But, as I said, controversy about art is not peculiar to our time, and it may be said that the seeds of the present crisis have always been there within the concept, though it has taken certain other ingredients of modern life to bring them to fruition.

Historical background

The story of the concept of art is a complicated and fascinating one, and much scholarly research has been devoted to it. My aim, however, will be only to draw attention to certain aspects of the story, so as to bring out the unstable and controversial nature of the concept, thus preparing the ground for a discussion of what is meant by 'art' today. The concept of art with which we are familiar has not always been in existence and cannot be regarded as part of the permanent furniture of human thought. This point can be made by reference to other periods and other cultures than our own, but it is usual to make the comparison first of all with the views expressed by ancient Greek writers, because of their importance as originators of Western thought.

A familiar difficulty in discussing ancient Greek views about virtue, art and other matters is that of translation. For example, it is often pointed out that the word *eudaimonia*, which is important in Aristotle's ethics, has no exact counterpart in modern languages. The nearest concept we have is *happiness*, and that is how the word is usually translated. But other notions, such as those of flourishing and prospering, are also invoked to explain the ancient concept. The issue is important, because, when confronted with some striking claim about 'happiness' in Aristotle's writings, we need to consider whether he was indeed speaking of happiness as we understand the term. If what he says about it strikes us as unusual or implausible, then we may regard this as evidence that he cannot have meant happiness in our sense of the term.

Similarly, when we read ancient Greek discussions about 'art', we must take them to be about a concept to which the translation 'art' approximates more or less. The Greek word in question is *techné* (from which the modern word 'technique' and similar words are derived). But the Greek word covered a variety of activities other than those we would classify as art. There is a passage in Aristotle in which he makes a point about 'a flautist or a sculptor or any artist', and in the next sentence mentions 'joiners and shoemakers' as further examples of artists (Aristotle (a), 1097b, p.75). Aristotle was not *claiming* that the latter are artists; he was merely following an accepted usage which his readers, unlike ourselves, would regard as straightforward. (In the Penguin edition the translator gives 'art, craft, skill' as corresponding to the Greek *techné* (p.370).)

The wider use of 'art' is also present in modern English, for we do speak of the art of joinery, of shoemaking and so on. But when the words 'art' or 'the arts' are used by themselves, we do not mean to include joinery or shoemaking; and similarly when we speak of 'works of art'. In this respect the ancient concept was wider than ours.

This difference was connected with different views about the function of an artist, and about what constituted *good* art. Thus, to take the same passage again, Aristotle could put it to his reader, without qualification, that the 'goodness and proficiency' of an artist lay in the performance of his 'specific function'. Now it is true, for us no less than for Aristotle, that the goodness of a shoemaker lies in the making of shoes, the goodness of a sculptor in producing works of sculpture and so on. But we may wish to qualify this by saying that the function of the artist – the 'creative artist' – is not circumscribed like that of the shoemaker or carpenter. For whereas there are fairly definite constraints on what counts, say, as a good pair of shoes, this is not so in the case of a work of art. A good pair of shoes, we might say, is a more predictable product than a good work of art.

A related difference between ancient and modern ideas lies in the role of *reason* in the production of art. According to Aristotle, art is 'essentially a reasoned productive state', one that is 'truly reasoned' (Aristotle (a), 1140a, p.208). Such a view may sound strange to us (unless we remember what was included under the term 'art'), for we think of art as involving feeling and inspiration, and not merely as an exercise of reason. Here, we might wish to say, lies an essential difference between the artist, as we use the term, and the joiner or the shoemaker.

Ancient ideas of beauty – or rather, of what we translate as 'beauty' – also differed from ours in being more connected with rational pursuits. 'The chief forms of beauty', wrote Aristotle, 'are order and symmetry and definiteness, which the mathematical sciences demonstrate in a special degree' (Aristotle (c), 1078b). Such a view of beauty implies that the perception of it is reserved for the rational faculties of the mind, which are supposed to distinguish human beings from the rest of the animals. Hence, according to Aristotle, animals are 'insensible' to the pleasures of 'harmony and beauty'. Such views were still being expressed two thousand years later. Thus Shaftesbury, in the seventeenth century, maintained that whereas animals are 'incapable of knowing or enjoying beauty', man enjoys it 'by the help of what is noblest, his mind and reason' (Shaftesbury, 1964 edn, p.259). There is little room in these accounts of beauty for such qualities as creativity, innovation and personal expression which have become prominent in modern times and are important ingredients of our concepts of art and beauty.

In the case of poetry, however, these remarks must be qualified by certain views which are to be found in Plato's writings. According to Aristotle, the poet was to be regarded 'like the painter or other maker of likenesses'; all of them, he held, were aiming to 'represent things... either as they were or are, or as they are said or thought to be or to have been, or as they ought to be' (Aristotle (b), 1460b, p.1483). (His book, known as the *Poetics*, was in effect a kind of instruction manual for the achievement of this aim.) But a very different conception of poetry is expressed in some of Plato's writings. 'All good epic poets', he wrote,

> recite all that splendid poetry not by virtue of a skill (*techné*), but in a state of inspiration and possession... So too it is not when they are in control of their senses that the lyric poets compose those fine lyric poems... A poet... cannot compose before he gets inspiration and loses control of his senses and his reason has deserted him... They utter these words of theirs not by virtue of a skill (*techné*), but by a divine

power... It is not they who say such supremely valuable things as they do, who have not reason in them, but... it is the god himself who speaks...

(Plato (a), 533E–534E; the passage is quoted by Tatarkiewicz, p.99)[2]

Yet we can also find, elsewhere in Plato's writings, an 'Aristotelian' conception of the poet as a mere 'artist'. In a passage in which he gave a ranking of human occupations, Plato put the poet only in sixth place, along with 'some other imitative artist' (Plato (b), 248E; Tatarkiewicz, p.99). A similar vacillation existed in the case of music. Both music and poetry, according to Tatarkiewicz, 'were comprehended as acoustic productions and both were supposed to have a "manic" character, i.e. to be a source of rapture' (p.51). But the status of music changed when it became known that its harmonies were governed by mathematical laws, which would, it was thought, make it amenable to the same kind of treatment as other arts.

It seems ironic that the quality of being inspired, which for us is an important ingredient of art, should be thought to disqualify poetry from being an art. But we must remember that 'art' in the ancient sense corresponded with our concept only to some extent. One of the differences, as can be seen from Plato's ranking in the *Phaedrus*, is that what came under 'art' did not enjoy the same prestige as art today. When, on the other hand, the poet (or musician) was regarded as inspired by the gods, then his prestige was high (*cf.* Plato (b), 245A, 248D).

So there existed a different grouping of activities as between art and non-art, and this is relevant to the question of definition today. Nowadays we may take it for granted that there is a group of activities, 'the arts', which come naturally together as activities of the same general kind; and on this basis we proceed to ask what it is that they all have in common, which makes them different from other activities. The truth is, however, that 'The Modern System of the Arts', as P.O. Kristeller has called it, only emerged, after a good deal of argument, in the eighteenth century.

It is usually held that the decisive and most influential statement of the 'modern system' was that of Charles Batteux, who, in his treatise *Les beaux arts réduits à un même principe* ('the fine arts reduced to a single principle') of 1746, separated the 'fine arts' from the 'mechanical arts', and listed the former as consisting of music, poetry, painting, sculpture and the dance (P.O. Kristeller, 'The Modern System of the Arts' (1951 and 1952), reprinted in Weitz, 1970, pp. 139–40). Batteux tried to show that the principle common to the fine arts was the 'imitation of beautiful nature' (*ibid.* p.140). But his main influence lay, not in the particular principle that he put forward, but in his clear separation of the fine arts – the arts, as we might say – from other activities, according to some principle or definition. What distinguished the 'modern system' was not that it replaced some previously existing system, but the very idea of treating the arts in a systematic way. 'Classical antiquity', according to Kristeller, 'left no systems or elaborate concepts of an aesthetic nature, but merely a number of scattered notions and suggestions that exercised a lasting influence down to modern times' (*ibid.* pp. 117–8). It was only then that a systematization of the arts was attempted.

Is the 'modern system', with its separation of the 'fine arts', an improvement on previous ideas? The poet Goethe, writing in 1772, thought it was something that might appeal to a 'fashionable dilettante', but was not to be taken seriously. He spoke of the 'bad reasoning' and 'theoretical trickery' which led people to suppose that 'certain activities and pleasures of mankind... could be classified under the rubric of arts, or fine arts' (quoted by Kristeller, *ibid.* pp. 157–8).[3] Kristeller himself, after reviewing the history of the 'modern system', comments that it 'begins to show signs of disintegration' (*ibid.* p.163). He pointed out how the status of various arts has vacillated at different times, depending on 'the particular cultural and social conditions' of the time (*ibid.* p.162). Thus 'gardening has lost its standing as a fine art since the eighteenth century', while the cinema 'is a good example of how new techniques' may lead to forms of art for which there was no place in earlier systems of the arts. Again, such forms as 'stained glass and mosaic, fresco painting and book illumination, vase painting and tapestry, bas relief and pottery have all been "major" arts and in a way they no longer are now' (*ibid.*).

It seems clear, however, that there is more to the modern system than these remarks would suggest. For that idea did, after all, take root, and in spite of many disagreements about what should be included within the arts, and why, there is a more or less clear continuity between what we mean by art and the 'modern system' that emerged in the eighteenth century. It is appropriate to say 'emerged', because this system was not invented out of the blue by Batteux. His formulation was something for which the world was ready, and it was felt that it, or something of the sort, reflected a valid and important classification. This feeling remained and survived in spite of subsequent developments and controversies, and today the term 'art' (or 'fine art') is still used for various purposes, practical and otherwise, and it would be difficult to do without it. It is not surprising, then, that the question of definition continues to be regarded as important.

Again, turning to the conceptual situations that existed before the 'modern system', it might be claimed, with a kind of conceptual hindsight, that modern ways of classifying arts are applicable to the activities of other times (such as the ancient Greek), even though these classifications did not exist then – perhaps even that our classifications are superior to theirs, that we now see things in a clearer light than was possible before. And this again would bestow importance on the quest for a definition.

The problem of definition today

The ingredients that make up the modern concept of art have been inherited from earlier times, and some of them were present in the ancient concepts, as discussed above. Beauty, inspiration, skill and craftsmanship, the imitation or representation of nature – these are still important to the concept of art that we have inherited. But in the course of time these ingredients underwent changes, and new ones made their appearance or became more prominent. Inspiration is nowadays understood in a less literal sense than in ancient times (when it was attributed to the gods). Innovation and invention became rivals to older ideas according to which the artist was a craftsman, following traditional techniques to make a satisfactory product. Beauty came to be regarded as a distinct quality, not to be identified with order and symmetry, but having more to do with feeling than with the rational faculties. And in one way or another, the role of feelings became prominent in ideas about art and beauty. In recent times it has been held, by such writers as Roman Ingarden and Monroe Beardsley, that the essential quality of art is a certain 'aesthetic experience' which is produced by the contemplation of works of art, and various attempts have been made to explain what this consists in. Others, such as Edward Bullough and Jerome Stolnitz, have invoked a special 'aesthetic attitude' which would explain what the experience of art, and art itself, are all about. Others again, notably R.G. Collingwood, have regarded art as being essentially an expression of the artist's feeling, while according to Tolstoy the purpose of art is to transmit certain feelings to the audience.

Batteux, as I said, had made a sharp separation between the fine and mechanical arts; and a similar separation has been made between 'pure' and 'useful' arts. According to these views an object produced by a mechanical method (such as a photograph) could not count as art, and neither could an object designed for a useful purpose (such as a vase or an office block). But these restrictions have been challenged in recent times. Another kind of restriction that has moved in and out of the concept of art is that of intellectual content or moral seriousness. In the nineteenth century, remarks Tatarkiewicz, some people found it difficult to accord the title of 'art' to light operas, and similar reservations have been felt about 'high art' versus 'low art', the latter including folk art, jazz and so on.

The restrictions mentioned in the last paragraph have not proved very durable. Nowadays the exclusion of useful works from the category of art would seem arbitrary, and few would be prepared to defend it. And the requirement of high intellectual content, though certainly relevant for the interpretation and evaluation of a work of art, would not be regarded as a necessary condition of art. But other ideas about art have proved more durable. Such qualities as beauty, form, expression and representation might be regarded as essential to art and it may be thought that the concept can be *defined* in terms of one, or perhaps more than one, of these qualities.

But can such a definition be produced? It is usual to approach questions of definition in terms of necessary and sufficient conditions, and this has been so in the case of art. Suppose that quality X is put forward as a definitive condition of art. Then we can test the definition in two ways. First, we can ask whether there are examples of art which do *not* have quality X. (If so, X is not a necessary condition of art.) Secondly, we can ask whether some things have quality X, but are not art. (If so, X is not a sufficient condition of art.) In other words: if the definition is to succeed, then anything that is art must have quality X (X is a necessary condition); and anything that has quality X must be art (X is a sufficient condition).

Consider beauty, for example. Most people would agree that art and beauty are connected. But is beauty a sufficient condition of art? No; for many natural objects, scenery, etc. are beautiful without being works of art. Is beauty a necessary condition of art? (Must a work of art be beautiful?) Again, the answer seems to be 'no', but this point is more contentious and I shall not pursue it here. (The role of beauty in art is discussed in Essay Two.) But the negative answer to the first question is enough to show that art cannot be defined by reference to beauty alone.

As another example, consider Aristotle's claim that 'like the painter or other maker of likenesses', the poet aims at the representation of life (Aristotle (b), *ibid.*, see p.6 above). Can the representation of life be regarded as a necessary condition of art? Not unless music and other 'non-representative' arts (including abstract painting, for example) can somehow be accommodated.

Next let us take a definition in terms of feeling. According to Tolstoy,

> art is a human activity consisting in this, that one man consciously by means of certain external signs, hands on to others feelings he has lived through, and that others are infected by these feelings and also experience them.
>
> (Tolstoy, 1930, p.123)

This definition raises a number of difficulties, including that of identifying 'these feelings' in a given case. But leaving such difficulties aside, let us consider whether Tolstoy's formula provides a necessary condition of art. Cannot something be art without satisfying his formula? The answer seems to be 'yes', for someone may create a work of art, say a beautiful vase, without any intention of passing on 'feelings he has lived through'.

A more sophisticated kind of definition was attempted by Tatarkiewicz. He drew together the threads of his historical survey and summarized six main types of conditions that had been regarded as definitive of art. They were: the production of beauty, the representation or reproduction of reality, the creation of forms, expression on the part of the artist, the production of aesthetic experience, and the production of shock – the last being 'a characteristic product of our own times' (Tatarkiewicz, 1980, pp. 28–32). Some of these, he observed, could not stand as necessary conditions of art, while others could not stand as sufficient conditions. The 'creation of forms', for example, may be acceptable as a necessary condition, but cannot be regarded as a sufficient one, since many human artefacts, other than works of art, satisfy this condition. (To say that something has a form is not, after all, to say very much.) These and similar difficulties, he pointed out, have affected all of the conditions in his list. (The condition about producing shock, which is 'characteristic of our time', would obviously not do as a necessary condition, for it would exclude the art of other times.)

It appears that while all of these conditions are connected with our concept of art, and are relevant in determining whether something is a work of art, none is decisive or capable of yielding a definition of art. According to Tatarkiewicz, however, it is possible to combine them all into a formula that is articulated in such a way as to yield a satisfactory definition. He first stated that the conditions in question may be classified as being concerned either with the artist's intention or 'with the *effect* of art on the recipient' (*ibid.* p.38). A '*definition of art*', he went on, 'must take into account both its intention and its effect', and it must take in all of the six main features of art that he had identified. He thought that this could be achieved by a disjunctive formula, i.e. one containing several alternatives, as follows:

> A work of art is either a reproduction of things, or a construction of forms, or an expression of experiences such that it is capable of evoking delight or emotion or shock.
>
> (Ibid.)

The first three items (following 'either... ') take into account the artist's intention, while the last three ('such that... ') represent the effect on the recipient. None of the six, however, is given as a necessary condition of art by itself; it is only when they are joined in a disjunction that, according to this author, a necessary and sufficient condition results.

This definition, claimed Tatarkiewicz, was 'immune from attack on the part of those who are against defining art at all (especially Kennick)' (*ibid.* p.39). W.E. Kennick, in a well-known article first published in 1958 (to be discussed shortly), had argued that art could not be defined because it had no single function, but Tatarkiewicz's formula was designed to accommodate this point, since a number of different functions were included.

Even so, is the definition satisfactory? It may be asked why beauty, so long a major component of the concept of art, does not appear in it. Tatarkiewicz explained that he wanted to stay clear of 'evaluative terms', and he thought this could be done by subsuming beauty under 'evoking delight'. But, leaving this point aside, we may agree that a disjunctive definition, giving several alternatives, is more likely to succeed than the simple kind of definition, such as those considered before, in which only one condition is given. For it may be that although something can be an instance of X (in this case, art) without satisfying one particular condition, it cannot be an instance of X without satisfying at least one of a stated *set* of conditions. In this sense a disjunctive definition is less demanding than a single-condition one, and more likely to accommodate all the instances.

But does the present definition succeed in doing this? May not something be a work of art and yet be neither a reproduction of things, nor a construction of forms, nor an expression of experiences? Consider again the example of a vase, which was used earlier as a counter-example to a definition of art in terms of expression. This example might also fail to satisfy the condition about being a reproduction of things.

But what about the second condition, concerning the construction of forms? This does seem to be satisfied by the vase. However, as mentioned earlier, there is a difficulty about the vagueness of 'form'. If this word is taken in its widest sense, then 'construction of forms' can stand as a necessary condition by itself, and there is no need to bring in the other alternatives; for everything that exists has some form. But in that case the condition would contribute nothing to the definition of art, for it would not pick out anything that is distinctive of this concept. If, on the other hand, the word 'form' is given a narrower sense, then we may find that some works of art will *not* be constructions of form in that sense – as well as failing to satisfy the other two alternatives. But however this may be, no such definition of form is attempted in Tatarkiewicz's formula, so that this condition about form contributes virtually nothing to the overall definition. (The role of form in art is further discussed in Essays Two and Four.)

Turning to the second part of the definition ('capable of evoking delight or emotion or shock'), we may find a similar difficulty with the scope of these words. To bring these out, let us consider the definition from the point of view of *sufficient* conditions. In other words, if an object satisfies the definition, does it follow that it is a work of art? If I evoke shock by expressing my experiences in foul language, then I will have satisfied the definition; but it would hardly follow that I have produced a work of art. Similarly, if a tourist 'reproduces things' by taking snapshots of scenery, or if fond parents takes photographs of their children, these may well be capable of producing delight, emotion or even shock; but it would not follow that they were works of art. Here again what seems to be needed is to give a more specific sense to these three words, but it seems unlikely that this could be done without excluding recognized works of art. In any case, no such attempt is made by Tatarkiewicz.

Another difficulty is that the definition does not seem to allow for art of poor quality, which fails to evoke the appropriate response. It may be said that the works displayed in a local exhibition of amateur paintings, for example, are works of art, even if they fail to evoke the appropriate response – whatever this is taken to be. Here again the definition fails to provide a necessary condition: it is not necessary that a work should actually be capable (good enough) of evoking a suitable response.

It may be thought that this fault can be remedied by inserting the phrase 'intended to be' before 'capable'. But in that case the condition would be too demanding in another sense. For many of the objects we recognize as works of art were not (or may not have been, for all we know) produced with any such intention. Religious art, for example, may have been produced with the intention of glorifying God, or for magical purposes (Plates 1 and 3); a Chinese vase (Plate 2), now regarded as a valuable work of art, may have been made for practical purposes and without any thought of evoking an aesthetic response; and so on.

A more promising solution might be to introduce another disjunction: '… capable *or* intended to be capable…'. This would assume that art of poor quality must at least be intended to evoke a suitable response, if it is to count as art; while art that was not so intended (like the examples just mentioned) would satisfy the definition by actually being capable, etc. (What would then be excluded are works that are neither good enough to evoke the response, nor made with that intention.)

I have given examples of the difficulties that may arise in trying to find a satisfactory definition of art. These do not, of course, show that no such definition will ever be forthcoming. Moreover, the separate conditions of beauty, representation, expression and so on, in various senses and combinations, have all been discussed much more fully than I have attempted; and some of the relevant literature will be surveyed in later Essays.

Another approach, however, has been to suggest that the very idea of looking for a definition of art is misguided. This approach was inspired by the appearance of the 'later' philosophy of Wittgenstein from 1953 onwards. Wittgenstein did not address the problem of defining art, but he presented a wide-ranging philosophy of language, with implications for the idea of definition in general. He argued against the assumption that, in general, our uses of words must be definable in terms of necessary and sufficient conditions, and claimed that a word may do its work perfectly well even if no such definition can be given.

In a passage which has become famous he used the word 'game' as an example. This word, he pointed out, is associated with a number of conditions such as amusement, winning and losing, skill and so on; but we should not assume that there must be a set of necessary and sufficient conditions governing the use of the word, that without these it would not be able to function. He challenged his reader to produce a set of conditions that games, and only games, have in common.

> Consider… the proceedings that we call 'games'. I mean board-games, card-games, ball-games, Olympic games, and so on. What is common to them all? – Don't say: 'There *must* be something common or they would not be called "games" – but *look and see* whether there is anything common to all… Look for example at board-games, with

their multifarious relationships. Now pass to card-games; here you find many correspondences with the first group, but many common features drop out, and others appear. When we pass next to ball-games, much that is common is retained, but much is lost. – Are they all 'amusing'? Compare chess with noughts and crosses. Or is there always winning and losing, or competition between players? Think of patience. In ball games there is winning and losing; but when a child throws his ball at the wall and catches it again, this feature has disappeared. Look at the parts played by skill and luck; and at the difference between skill in chess and skill in tennis. Think now of games like ring-a-ring-a-roses...

(Wittgenstein, 1953, I, 66–7)

What we find here, he concluded, is not a set of features that is 'common to them all', but 'a complicated network of similarities overlapping and criss-crossing', which he proposed to characterize as 'family resemblances'. In viewing the members of a family we may find that some are similar in build or in the way they walk, while others may share certain facial features, such as an upturned nose or a certain shape of the mouth, and so on. On the basis of such similarities we may be able to recognize them as belonging to the same family; but there is no need to suppose that there must be some feature or set of features that all the members, and only they, have in common – that without this we could not recognize them as belonging to the same family. Similarly, according to Wittgenstein, there is no need to suppose that if we are to recognize certain activities as games, then there must be something that they, and only they, have in common – in other words, a set of necessary and sufficient conditions for this concept.

Wittgenstein's claim may also be understood in an historical, developmental sense. We have seen something of how the concept of art has developed, with various features waxing and waning in the course of its history. Now Wittgenstein did not use this concept in his discussion, but another of his examples was the concept of a number. If we think of numbers such as nought, negative numbers, irrational numbers and so on, we become aware that our concept of a number is the result of development in the course of its history. 'Why', asked Wittgenstein, 'do we call something a "number"?' Perhaps, he replied, because it is related in suitable ways to what has 'hitherto been called number'. He introduced another of his analogies.

We extend our concept of number as in spinning a thread we twist fibre on fibre. And the strength of the thread does not reside in the fact that

> some one fibre runs through its whole length, but in the overlapping of many fibres.
>
> *(Ibid.* I, 67)

As I have said, Wittgenstein was making a general point about language (and did not use 'art' as one of his examples). But it was soon noticed that the point would be relevant to a number of contentious concepts, including art, science, religion, democracy and many others. In an article first published in 1956, Morris Weitz quoted Wittgenstein on games and family resemblances and applied this idea, not only to the concept of art, but also to 'its sub-concepts' – literature, music, painting and so on.

> Consider questions like... 'Is Virginia Woolf's *To the Lighthouse* a novel?'... On the traditional view, these are construed as factual problems to be answered yes or no in accordance with the presence or absence of defining properties. But... what is at stake is no factual analysis concerning necessary and sufficient properties but a decision as to whether the work under examination is similar in certain respects to other works, already called 'novels', and consequently warrants the extension of the concept to cover the new case.
>
> (Weitz, 1956; reprinted in Margolis, 1987, p.148)

There is a difference, however, between the concept of art and concepts such as that of a game; for it may be argued that the former is more volatile and, therefore, even more resistant to definition than the latter. The boundaries of the concept of a game, even if not reducible to a definition, are generally agreed in practice; and if there is disagreement about borderline cases this is not likely to be profound or troublesome. (It may be possible simply to agree that these are borderline cases and leave it at that.) But this is not so in the case of art. Here we have a concept that is inherently contentious, and disputes about what should or should not count as art have often been troublesome and even heated, especially in modern times. No one, for example, would want to claim that anything whatever might qualify as a game, but the view that anything whatever might qualify as art has had a considerable following, resulting in the appearance of various controversial works whose status as art, while strongly defended by some, is indignantly denied by others. Hence the issue about definition is more urgent, and has a more practical bearing, in the case of art than in the case of most other concepts. The concept of a game, for example, is largely allowed to take its own course, adapting itself to such new instances or new circumstances as may arise in the course of its history. But in the case of art – or, to take another example, democracy – there is active intervention, especially from those with vested interests. They may want to 'shape' the concept to their interests, persuading us to see such and such instances as being, or not being, instances of that concept.

One group of people with an interest in subverting any existing definition of art are the creative artists themselves, who may wish to exercise their creativeness by going beyond the generally accepted notions. According to Weitz, 'the very expansive, adventurous character of art, its ever-present changes and novel creations, make it logically impossible to ensure any set of defining properties' (*ibid.* p.149). It is, no doubt, possible for a creative artist to be adventurous and innovative without calling into question the existing notions of what art is. But sometimes these motives do take the form of challenging and upsetting the existing notions – so that if a definition of art *were* accepted, it might be the artist's aim to break it down. Thus the first painters of abstract art may have wanted to challenge the idea of art (or visual art, at least) as 'the imitation of nature'; and writers such as Virginia Woolf and James Joyce may have wanted to challenge accepted ideas about conditions that must be satisfied if something is to qualify as a novel. And in recent times we have seen a spate of works whose main point seems to be philosophical, demonstrating in a practical way that there are no limits to the concept of art. The idea, for example, that works of art are *made* as such is challenged by the exhibiting of 'ready-mades' – ordinary objects that may be found in shops or on building sites – as works of art.

The quest for a definition of art was also rejected by W.E. Kennick in his article 'Does Traditional Aesthetics rest on a Mistake?'. Kennick argued that a person's competence in using a word, such as 'art' and others, does not depend on an ability to define the word, nor on the existence of a definition. We are able to distinguish works of art from other objects, he claimed, simply 'because we know English' (Kennick, 1958, p.321), and this does not imply knowledge of a definition, or even the existence of one.

> If anyone is able to use the word 'art' correctly, in all sorts of contexts and on the right sort of occasions, he knows 'what art is', and no formula in the world can make him wiser.
>
> (*Ibid.* p.321)

He asked the reader to 'imagine a large warehouse, filled with all sorts of things' including paintings and other works of art, as well as all sorts of miscellaneous objects.

Now we instruct someone to enter the warehouse and bring out all the works of art it contains. He will be able to do this with reasonable success, despite the fact that, as even the aesthetician must admit, he possesses no satisfactory definition of Art in terms of some common denominator, because no such definition has yet been found.

(Ibid. pp. 321–2)

However, another difference between the concept of art and others (including 'game') is that the former is and has been influenced by an establishment of experts, whose ideas and judgements are more authoritative than those of ordinary speakers of English. This affects Kennick's claim about an ordinary person's ability to select works of art from a warehouse full of miscellaneous objects. Such a claim would be true enough in the case of games, for someone with a normal knowledge of English would indeed be sufficiently well equipped to distinguish games from other activities (though even here, mere visual inspection would not be enough); and there is no establishment of experts to whom one would or should appeal for instruction in the matter. But this is not so in the case of art. The recent history of art is rich in examples of works which, because they did not conform to commonly held notions of art (of poetry, music, drama, painting, sculpture, etc.), seemed to the public not to be art at all, and which nevertheless were later accepted as art – perhaps even great art – because of the fact that certain experts recognized them as such and persisted in expounding them to a reluctant public.

Kennick's example of the person sent to the warehouse would work well enough if the works stored there conformed to existing notions and paradigms, such as would be known to a normal speaker of the language (with, let us say, a reasonable degree of interest in art); but it would not work if some of the works were innovative or revolutionary. If, for example, one had been sent to the warehouse when non-representational paintings first made their appearance, then one would probably have been at a loss on finding some of these among the stored items. And in that case it might have been appropriate to take advice from an expert. Kennick may have been right in saying that 'no formula in the world can make him wiser', but it could still be the case that an expert's understanding, going beyond a mere knowledge of the English word 'art', would make him wiser. 'At the cutting edge of art history', wrote one of Kennick's critics,

most of us do not know an artwork when we see one; we have to be told by someone – an 'expert' – who is going on something more than the accepted usage of the expression.

(Matthews, 1979, p.46)

However, if Kennick was wrong in his reliance on an ordinary person's knowledge of English, his (and Weitz's) rejection of the quest for definition may still be valid, for it cannot be assumed that the experts are deducing their verdicts from a set of necessary and sufficient conditions.

According to Kennick, those who have put forward definitions of art have sometimes been mistaken about their true purport. He referred to Clive Bell's statement in his book *Art*, published in 1914, that 'Art is Significant Form'. This statement, he commented, 'does not help us to understand what art is at all' (Kennick, p.324). Yet the statement, made at a time when a new kind of painting (abstract and non-representational), in which formal properties had a new importance, first appeared on the artistic scene, 'has a *point*' (*ibid.*). What Bell had discovered, said Kennick, was not the true definition of art – not 'the essence of Art... although he thought that this is what he found, *but a new way of looking at pictures*... [Bell's] slogan... has work to do'; its work was to 'teach people a new way of looking at pictures' (*ibid.* p.325).

Kennick's position may be compared with C.L. Stevenson's work on 'persuasive definitions' in his article under that title, which first appeared in 1938. One of Stevenson's examples was the claim, made by certain critics in the nineteenth century, that Alexander Pope was not really a poet, because his verse lacked certain qualities. According to Stevenson, this was a case of 'persuasive definition'. It was not as if these critics could appeal to an established definition to show that Pope's work failed to meet its conditions; what they were, in effect, doing was to advocate a 'narrow sense of "poet" ', and this 'had the function of stressing, in the reader's attention, certain features common to most poetry, but lacking in Pope's' (Stevenson, 1938). What was at issue, again, was not the *true* sense of 'poet', such as might be given by a 'true definition', but the advantage of attending to, or emphasizing, certain features of the art in question.

The result of accepting the persuasive definition in Stevenson's example would be to exclude certain works from the category of poetry; while the result of accepting Bell's definition would be to admit, or to value more highly than before, certain works of painting.

The Institutional Theory

In spite of difficulties and objections, the quest for a definition of art has continued. But some thinkers have turned away from the traditional qualities, feelings and experiences associated with art, in quest of a different type of definition.

In the passage quoted above, in which Wittgenstein challenged the reader to 'look and see whether [games] have anything in common', he mentioned some of the more obvious features of games and quickly dismissed them by pointing out that they were not present in all instances of games. But some critics replied that perhaps something more than a mere 'look and see' was required, for there might be some less obvious feature that games, and only games, had in common – something that would require philosophical insight for its discovery and exposition. (See, for example, Haig Khatchadourian 'Common Names and "Family Resemblances"', in Pitcher, 1966.) The same approach has been used in the case of art, with the suggestion that there might be a 'non-exhibited property' that works of art, and only works of art, have in common (Mandelbaum, 1965); and George Dickie has claimed to have identified such a property. What makes something a work of art, according to Dickie, is not some special quality that can be observed within the work, but a certain status that has been conferred on it by what he called (following Arthur Danto) 'the artworld'. Danto had claimed that 'to see something as art requires something the eye cannot descry – an artworld' (Danto, 1964).

What is meant by 'the artworld'? Its 'core personnel' explained Dickie, 'is a loosely organized, but nevertheless related, set of persons including artists (understood to refer to painters, writers, composers), producers, museum directors, museum-goers, theatre-goers, reporters for newspapers, critics... art historians, art theorists, philosophers of art, and others' (Dickie, 1974, pp. 35–6). Moreover, 'every person who sees himself as a member of the artworld is thereby a member' (*ibid.* p.36). He admitted that this concept was rather vague, but claimed that, nevertheless, 'the artworld carries on its business at the level of customary practice', and that this practice 'defines a social institution' (*ibid.* p.35).

Now a 'central feature' of this institution was 'the *presenting* of particular works of art' (*ibid.* p.31); and it was this presenting, or 'conferring of status', that made an object a work of art. Here was the property that all works of art had in common, and in terms of which the concept was to be defined.

A work of art in the classificatory sense is (1) an artefact (2) a set of the aspects of which has had conferred upon it the status of candidate for appreciation by some person or persons acting on behalf of a certain social institution (the artworld).

(*Ibid.* p.34)

The main idea of this definition is expressed in the clause about conferring, but I shall first comment briefly on a number of other points.

First, a general point about the scope of Dickie's argument. As we saw above, he intended 'artists' to 'refer to painters, writers, composers'; and the definition of art that I have just quoted is meant to cover all the arts, and not just art in the narrow sense of painting and sculpture – as in 'art gallery' and 'art school'. But his discussion, and those of others of similar views, are conducted largely in terms of art in the narrow sense. In these discussions it is sometimes assumed that the points made about 'art' have their counterparts in the other arts, though, for the sake of convenience, these need not always be stated explicitly. This point should be borne in mind in reading the discussion that follows.

Next, a point of detail. The phrase 'a set of aspects' in the quoted definition is there to allow for the exclusion of irrelevant aspects, such as 'the colour of the back of the painting' (*ibid.* p.40), which would not be part of what is intended in the conferring of status.

The word 'classificatory' serves to indicate that Dickie is not interested in questions of value; his question is 'What is art?' and not 'What is good art?'. It is sometimes held that the word 'art' has an honorific connotation, so that to describe something as art is to praise it. But according to Dickie, the word can be used in a neutral sense, without any commitment to value, and this is the sense he intends. (I shall return to this issue.)

Condition (1), about being an artefact, is surprising, given the general motivation of Dickie's and Danto's arguments, which was to accommodate the modern avant-garde examples of art. The traditional qualities of art, such as were used in earlier definitions, can be seen as restrictions on what may count as art, and all of them were flouted by artists of the avant-garde. Why, then, should the institutional definition stipulate that the object must be an artefact? If, as Dickie himself asked, 'Duchamp can convert such artefacts as a urinal... into works of art, why can't natural objects such as driftwood also become works of art...?' (*ibid.* p.44).[4] His reply (consistent with his main position) was that such objects would indeed be works of art, if they were offered as candidates for appreciation (e.g. by being shown in an exhibition) (*ibid.*); but in that case, he claimed, the object would also be transformed into an artefact, for 'artefactuality is conferred on the object rather than worked on it' (*ibid.* p.45). But whatever may be said for this claim, it is clear that the gist of Dickie's definition lies in the second clause, about the conferring of status. It is this that is supposed to make an object – be it a piece of driftwood, or one of Duchamp's 'ready-mades', or a more traditional specimen of art – into a work of art.

A similar treatment is given by Dickie to the question of works of art produced by a chimpanzee. Here again, whether they 'are art depends on what is done with them' and not on their intrinsic qualities or agency of production (*ibid.* p.45). On show in a museum of natural history, they are not art; but if

> they had been exhibited a few miles away at the Chicago Art Institute they would have been works of art... One institutional setting is congenial to conferring the status of art and the other is not.
>
> (*Ibid.* p.46)

It is, indeed, in dealing with works of art that are physically indistinguishable from other objects that the Institutional Theory can be best appreciated; for in these cases there is, *ex hypothesi*, no intrinsic difference between the object that is a work of art and another that is not. Why is it, asked Danto, that 'Warhol's Brillo boxes *were* works of art while their commonplace counterparts, in the backrooms of supermarkets... were not?' (Danto, 1981, p.vi). Andy Warhol's *Brillo Box*, exhibited in 1964, was in fact a plywood replica of the commercial cartons, but, as Danto pointed out, being made of plywood is not what makes the difference. The difference, the crucial difference between being a work of art and not being one, must be found elsewhere; and the Institutional Theory tells us where it is to be found.[5]

The Institutional Theory, remarked Dickie, is rather like claiming that ' a work of art is an object of which someone has said "I christen this object a work of art"' (Dickie, p.49). But can an object be made what it is by a mere statement to this effect? We normally think that facts are independent of statements, and that things are what they are independently of what anyone may say. 'Wishing will make it so' is a pleasant fantasy, but a fantasy none the less; is it not the same with saying?

Dickie's approach is comparable with J. L. Austin's work in the philosophy of language. Austin had drawn attention to a remarkable, though common enough, type of language, which he called 'performative' (Austin, 1961 and 1962). He pointed out that in making such statements as 'I promise...', 'I apologize...' and 'I congratulate you', we create, and do not merely state, the facts in question. The promising is done, the fact is brought into being, by the very act of saying 'I promise... ' – by *performing* this act. When such a speech-act is performed, it makes no sense to ask whether the statement is *true* or not, for it is made true by the very act of saying it; and similarly with 'I apologize', 'I congratulate you' and a number of other examples. This is not to deny, of course, that a promise may be broken or may be insincere at the time of utterance. The point is that, whether sincere or otherwise, a person who says these words *has made* a promise, and is held responsible if he fails to keep it.

However, a suitable situation is required for the performance of these acts. One can apologize only if there is something suitable to apologize for, and if the person concerned is available to receive the apology. Promising to do *X* usually presupposes that *X* is something desired by the other person, and so on. Now in the case of some performative statements, the required setting is an institutional one. American dollar notes bear the inscription 'This note is legal tender for all debts, public and private'. This statement, again, is not being used to record an independent fact; it is the statement, made in a suitable setting, that *makes* these notes legal tender. In this case, however, it is essential that the statement be made by or on behalf of a suitable institution (the United States Treasury). Made by an unauthorized person, such a statement would have no force, except perhaps as a joke.

Another example is that of christening. 'I name this child Jane' (or again, 'I name this ship Queen Elizabeth'), uttered in suitable surroundings by an authorized person, brings it about that the child is named Jane (or the ship Queen Elizabeth). But without such surroundings and authority, these are futile utterances. The same is true of the use of 'declare', in such contexts as 'I declare the meeting open' and 'This forest is declared to be a Special Conservation Area'. These declarations are 'performative', but the performance can take place only in a suitable institutional setting.

The Institutional Theory fits in well with these developments in the philosophy of language, as Dickie's reference to christening indicates. It includes both the institutional setting – the relevant institution being the artworld – and the performative act; for the action of, for example, displaying a painting in an art gallery is tantamount to a declaration that it is a work of art.

Dickie's description of the artworld as a 'customary practice' (quoted above, p.20) also invites comparison with money in another way. Consider a paper currency other than the American dollar, which does not carry a declaration, but which is and has been used for all the normal purposes for which money is used. Suppose, furthermore, that this money is not backed by any formal institution, but that it evolved informally out of an earlier system of barter. Now imagine someone questioning whether this is really money. After all, he might point out, it is only pieces of paper; and while it is true that it is *used* as money, does it follow that it really is money? To this one may reply that what makes it money *is* its use (or 'customary practice'). If everyone uses it as money, then there can be no question whether it is really money. Moreover, it would be correct to speak of this as an *institution*, albeit an informal one, not defined or regulated by legislation (and in this way comparable with the artworld, as Dickie sees it).[6]

Similarly, Timothy Binkley has commented as follows on the question whether some of today's controversial works are really works of art.

> I don't know what to say except that they are made (created, realized or whatever) by people considered artists, they are treated by critics as art, they are talked about in books and journals having to do with art, they are exhibited in or otherwise connected with art galleries, and so on.
>
> (Binkley, 'Deciding about Art', in Aagaard-Morgenstern, p.95)

What more could be required to show that something is a work of art?

There is something magical about the way in which, according to these views, an ordinary object may be transformed into a work of art; it is, to quote the apt title of Danto's book, a 'Transfiguration of the Commonplace' (Danto, 1981). Left to lie on a scrap-heap, an object such as one of Duchamp's 'ready-mades' is nothing more than a piece of scrap. But once a certain treatment has been given to it, it is transformed into a work of art, something to be examined and appreciated as such by the public. It is, and yet it is not, the very same object that was lying on the scrap-heap.

Objections to the Institutional Theory

In criticisms of traditional definitions of art the point is sometimes made that they are motivated by a desire to deal with or advocate a particular kind or aspect of art, which may become important at a particular time, rather than to give an accurate description of the whole concept as it exists in our language. We saw above (p.19) how this point was made by Kennick about Bell's definition of art as 'significant form'. It was no accident that this and other 'formalist' theories arose at a time when a new kind of painting, not conforming to accepted criteria but strong in formal qualities, came into prominence. The new definition of art, if acceptable, would accommodate these works, as well as promoting a correct appreciation of art in general, which would now be seen as consisting essentially in the creation of forms of an aesthetically satisfying kind. To take another example, Tolstoy's definition of art as the transmission of feelings from author to recipient may have had more to do with his desire to advocate a particular kind of art (involving good and socially valuable feelings) than to do justice to the existing concept; and this again can probably be attributed to social circumstances of the time.

The Institutional Theory too made its appearance in response to a problem that arose at a particular time: namely, what to do about 'ready-mades' and other offerings which seem to flout all the accepted ideas. The theory would be able to accommodate these works, in contrast to previous ideas which would exclude them from the domain of art. And in doing so it would pin-point the essential difference between art and non-art, a difference that could emerge clearly only in the light of the modern developments. But is the theory acceptable? How well can it deal with art in general?

Let us consider whether it is satisfactory in giving a *necessary* condition of art. The clause about conferring the status of candidate for appreciation will probably suggest a work that is exhibited in an art gallery, performed in a concert hall, or published in print. But may there not be a work of art that has had no such treatment? Suppose someone paints a picture, composes a piece of music, or writes a poem, and these are never exhibited or published. Would it follow that they are not works of art? Do they become works of art only when they are offered for appreciation? This implausible conclusion seems to be entailed by Dickie's theory. It appears, however, that the condition about conferring the status of candidate for appreciation is not what it may have seemed. Dickie concedes that 'Many works of art are seen only by one person – the one who creates them – but they are still art.' He claims that in such cases, 'The status in question... is usually conferred by a single person, the artist who creates the artifact' (Dickie, p.38). But these statements are hard to understand. In what sense does such a person act on behalf of an artworld, and in what sense does he *confer* the status in question? And why, in any case, should we accept that an artefact cannot be a work of art without such conferral? With some of the modern works, the idea of conferral is obviously important. In the case of Duchamp's *Fountain*, for example, it makes all the difference whether the object is left in its normal position as a urinal, or exhibited for appreciation in a gallery. We might agree that it becomes an artwork if, and only if, this is done. But this is not so in the case of more straightforward works, which we can recognize as art without any conferral of status as required by the theory.

The same problem may arise about a whole class of artefacts as opposed to particular items. Consider religious art such as Russian icons, or useful artefacts such as vases, or folk-art of various kinds (e.g. dancing), in modern as well as tribal societies. These kinds of art may have been produced or performed without any thought of candidacy for appreciation. There may have been no such thing as an artworld, and the very concept of art may have been non-existent. Are we to say that these things became art only if and when that status was conferred on them by an artworld? We commonly speak of recognizing, seeing, claiming, that such items *are* works of art, as opposed to merely conferring that status on them by a performative act. Thus, if the pre-historic cave-paintings at Altamira are works of art (see Plate 1), then, it may be said, they were works of art *before* their recognition by the artworld and not as a result of this. Hence the conferring of status is not a necessary condition of art.

The example of the Lascaux paintings was used by Danto in his discussion of 'ready-made' art. Such art, he pointed out, only makes sense at a certain time in the history and theory of art. 'It is the theory that takes it up into the world of art, and keeps it from collapsing into the real object which it is'. To see such things as art,

> one must have mastered a good deal of artistic theory as well as a considerable amount of the recent history of New York painting. It could not have been art fifty years ago. But then there could not have been, everything being equal, flight insurance in the Middle Ages or Etruscan typewriter erasers. The world has to be ready for certain things, the artworld no less than the real one. It is the role of artistic theories, these days as always, to make the artworld, and art, possible.

> (in Margolis, *op. cit.*, p.164)

It would, he concludes, 'never have occurred to the painters of Lascaux that they were producing *art* on those walls'.

This may be so, but does it follow that they were *not* producing art on those walls? If it is indeed 'the role of artistic theories... to make... art possible', then this is the conclusion we must draw, following Danto (assuming that artistic theories were not current among the cave-dwellers). But in this respect Danto's comparison with flight insurance in the Middle Ages is misleading. For while it would be nonsense to suppose that some medieval activity might come to be recognized as flight insurance, it is not nonsense to say that pre-historic paintings came to be recognized as works of art. And 'recognized' in this case would mean that we recognize them for what they are: they *are* works of art, and do not acquire this character only by being recognized.

Another example, used by Kennick in his arguments against definition, was that of funeral art in ancient Egypt, made for the purpose of
being buried in the grave in order to provide magical benefits for the
deceased (Plate 3). He used this to support his conclusion that 'the
attempt to define Art in terms of what we do with certain objects is as
doomed as any other' (Margolis, *op. cit.*, p.330; quoted by Dickie, pp.
27–8). Here was an example of art, even though what was done with it
was entirely different from the appreciation of art in today's artworld, as
envisaged by Dickie. In reply, Dickie suggested that the Egyptians may,
after all, have put the works there 'for the dead to appreciate' (Dickie,
p.28). But even if this were so, it would still be questionable whether this
is a necessary condition of their being works of art.

Another point made by Dickie was that the Egyptians may have had
a different concept of art from ours; and he wanted only 'to be able to
specify the necessary and sufficient conditions for the concept of art
which we have (we present-day Americans, we present-day Westerners
…)'. But this does not remove the difficulty which *is* about the present
concept. If the Egyptian items were works of art without having fulfilled
Dickie's condition, then it would make no difference if their concepts
were different from ours: they would have been works of art, as we
understand this term, without fulfilling Dickie's condition.

It may be thought that the way out of these difficulties is to make the
condition about conferral hypothetical rather than actual. In other
words, the object would be a work of art, not only if the status of
candidate *was* conferred on it by someone acting on behalf of the
artworld, but also if this status *would be* conferred by such a person,
were that person to find out about it. This would accommodate the
Lascaux paintings, for it was always true that they *would be* regarded as
candidates for appreciation when suitable conditions came into being.
Accordingly, they were always works of art and did not become so only
when that status was conferred on them. Again, take some of Schubert's
masterpieces which, undervalued or neglected at the time, were destroyed or mislaid. Though they were not actually offered for appreciation, we might say that they qualify as art because they *would* have been
so offered, if a suitable representative of the artworld had known about
them. Some of these works were, indeed, discovered and published
many years later.

But this hypothetical version of the theory would still not allow for
the existence of art which, unlike Schubert's masterpieces, is not and
would not be exhibited, for the simple reason that it is not good enough.
Such works might well be described as art, in the 'classificatory sense',

because of their intrinsic character and circumstances of production, regardless of any prospect of being put forward as candidates for appreciation. Thus it appears that the Institutional Theory, accommodating as it is towards the controversial works of recent times, is unduly restrictive when it comes to art that is recognizable as such according to traditional ideas.

Another recent account, resembling the Institutional Theory, is that of Timothy Binkley. Like advocates of the Institutional Theory, Binkley claims that 'properties are fundamentally irrelevant to art status... To be an artwork is not to share, by identity or consanguinity [i.e. family resemblance], properties which delineate "art"' (in Aagaard-Morgenstern, 1976, p.97). But neither, according to Binkley, is it necessary that the object should have the relevant status conferred by someone acting on behalf of the artworld; what matters is only the artist's intention. As with the Institutional Theory, what makes an object a work of art is not anything in the object itself; but this time it is the intention of the artist that makes all the difference. Binkley described how, when visiting an exhibition of 'conceptual' art, he came across 'a small brown spiral notebook'.[7] Was the notebook a work of art – part of the exhibition? (*ibid*. p.90). Then he noticed that it bore the inscription 'Not part of the exhibition'. His first reaction was to disregard the notebook as not worthy of attention. But then he wondered whether the book, *with* that inscription, might not after all be one of the artworks on exhibition. Might not this be one more way in which the ingenious artist had gone against accepted conventions and thereby produced something highly original?

Binkley concluded that the fundamental criterion of 'art status' must be the author's intention. 'The reason it is hard to say whether the notebook is a work of art is that it is unclear what the intentions of its author(s) were regarding art status, making it difficult for us to "read" the piece' (*ibid*. p.98). In order to do that we must know the author's intention; but nothing more would be required.

In another article Binkley spoke of the artist's role in 'indexing' the object in question. 'The concept of "work of art"', he wrote,

> does not isolate a class of peculiar aesthetic [objects]. The concept marks an indexical function in the artworld. To be a piece of art, an item need only be indexed as an artwork by an artist. Simply recategorizing an unsuspecting entity will suffice.
>
> (Binkley, 'Piece: Contra Aesthetics', in Margolis, p.83)

As with the Institutional Theory, what makes an object a work of art is not anything in the object itself; but this time it is the intention of the artist that makes all the difference. Binkley's approach avoids the requirement of the Institutional Theory (that the status of art must be conferred by an artworld), but it still imposes a condition – that of being 'indexed as an artwork by the artist' – which would exclude many examples of what is generally recognized as art. Among these are the cave paintings of Lascaux and the beautiful antique Chinese vases exhibited in museums today (see Plate 2). These things were not indexed as artworks by an artist, but this would not count against their being recognized as such today.

So much for the question whether the Institutional Theory, and the alternative just considered, are acceptable as statements of necessary conditions of art. Let us now consider the theory from the point of view of *sufficient* conditions: if an object satisfies the institutional definition, does it follow that it is a work of art? This question is one that has troubled many visitors to galleries of modern art (and similarly with other arts, such as music and poetry). Confronted with a work such as *Brillo Box*, or some other work or performance lacking – or flouting – all the traditional qualities of art, ordinary observers may well question whether they are art at all. Having gone to considerable trouble and expense to come to the gallery in the hope of experiencing and enjoying some new art, they find objects that they cannot even recognize as art and may complain of having been cheated. Now if the meaning of 'art' were as described in the theories we have considered, then to deny that these are works of art would be self-contradictory. A person who made the denial would be like someone who admits that a duly authorized person christened the child Jane and yet denies that the child's name is Jane. This position would be unintelligible. But is this so with the person who denies that the objects on show are really art? Must this person accept that they are art, just because they are exhibited in a gallery belonging to the artworld?

In this respect the comparison with such performances as christening may be misleading, and it may be that the Institutional Theory should rather be compared with certain other speech-acts which are performative only to some extent. Consider a game, such as tennis, in which the umpire is empowered to declare the ball 'out' and assume that, according to the rules of the game (when played in championship conditions, say), a ball is out if and only if the umpire says so. We might say that the umpire's saying so makes it the case that the ball is out. Now in the case of christening, promising and so on there is, as we saw, no question of truth beyond the performance: given the statement 'I name this child Jane', made in appropriate circumstances, we cannot ask whether the statement is *true*, or whether it is true that the child now has this name. But this is not so in the case of the umpire's 'out'. Here it is possible to ask whether he spoke truly, for besides the institutional fact (brought into being by his declaration) there is also a non-institutional fact, concerning the actual position of the ball when he spoke, which is independent of his declaration. Similarly, it may be that even if the artworld's declaration of an object to be a work of art has a certain institutional and performative force, this does not exclude the possibility of asking – like our disappointed visitors to the gallery – whether it is really art.

Another difficulty for the Institutional Theory lies in the meaning of 'appreciation', in the condition about an object having 'conferred upon it the status of candidate for appreciation'. Would any kind of appreciation be relevant? It might be said that what is meant is appreciation of an appropriate kind, i.e. *aesthetic* appreciation. But this would make the definition circular: it would be like saying that something is a work of art if it is to be appreciated in the way appropriate for a work of art. It seems that we need to identify a kind of appreciation that is specific to art and to build this into the definition. But this would destroy the openness of the definition, which would then exclude works of art not amenable to that kind of appreciation, whatever it might be. If the appreciation in question were identified by reference to accepted paradigms of art, then it might not be suitable for innovatory works, such as the new theory was designed to accommodate. Hence it is not surprising that Dickie was at pains to explain that he did not mean by appreciation a 'special kind of aesthetic consciousness, attitude or perception', such as had been invoked by those (such as Bullough, Stolnitz and Beardsley) who try to define art in such terms; and in his article 'The Myth of the Aesthetic Attitude', *American Philosophical Quarterly*, 1964) he criticized such views at length.

In his book *Art and the Aesthetic* Dickie explained that what he meant by appreciation was 'something like "in experiencing the qualities of a thing one finds them worthy or valuable"' (*op. cit.,* pp. 40–1). But this is not specific enough, for an object may be offered for appreciation, in this sense, without being offered, or regarded, as a work of art. 'A brief biography of the artist mounted on the gallery wall beside his works', writes Binkley (*op. cit.,* p.101), would satisfy Dickie's definition; for it would be placed there in the hope of being valuable to visitors to the gallery. Yet it would not, on that account, qualify as a work of art. A similar criticism was made by Beardsley, who had tried to formulate a 'distinction between *aesthetic* appreciation and other forms or types' of appreciation (Beardsley, 1982, p.311). Dickie, he said, 'aims to bypass' this distinction; but he could not see how, according to Dickie's notion of 'appreciation', one could 'rule out the idea that, say, in seeing and responding to ("experiencing") the changing colours of a traffic light I find them valuable as signs for regulating traffic' (*ibid.*). But such value would not be thought to entail that they are works of art.

So far I have dealt with criticism of the Institutional definition, in terms first of necessary, and then of sufficient conditions. But it may be asked whether the formula in question can be regarded as a definition at all. A definition of art should supply an answer to someone who asks whether a particular object is art; and this requirement would be fulfilled by the traditional definitions. Now in one sense it would also be fulfilled by the Institutional formula (leaving aside the question of its truth). Thus if I am wondering whether *Brillo Box* is really art, then this formula will provide the answer, by reference to the status that has been conferred. But what if I happen to be the person who must decide whether to confer the status? On what basis am I to make the decision? Should I conclude that the work is *not* art, because the relevant status has not, or not yet, been conferred? On this account nothing would ever become a work of art!

The Institutional definition of art says nothing about the traditional qualities of art, such as might be used as *reasons* for calling something a work of art. But those who decide, on behalf of the artworld, to put a work forward for appreciation, do not, of course, do it merely by drawing lots. Such decisions are often made after a lot of discussion, in which recognized qualities of art are invoked. How could we make sense of their decisions otherwise? 'How can we possibly believe', writes Richard Wollheim, that the 'representative of the artworld' is putting an object

> forward for appreciation, unless we can also attribute to him some idea of what it is about the artifact that we should appreciate, and further, believe that it is because of this that he is drawing our attention to it?... When Ruskin accused Whistler of flinging a pot of paint in the public's face, he was in effect saying that Whistler could not be putting his paintings forward as candidates for appreciation: he must be engaged in some other cause: and why Ruskin said this was that he could not see what it was in Whistler's paintings that Whistler could possibly be asking us to appreciate.
>
> (Wollheim, 1980, p.165)

Someone who puts an object forward for appreciation must be prepared to answer the question 'Why?' – to tell us why it should be regarded as being worthy of this treatment; and the answer must be in terms of reasons that we can at least recognize as such. Without this the action of putting an object forward for appreciation would be unintelligible.

'But is it Art?'

I have argued that the Institutional definition is not satisfactory as a sufficient condition of art, since it makes sense for someone to deny that, or question whether, an object is a work of art in spite of the fact that it has been put forward for appreciation. Even so, it is sometimes assumed that the recent controversial works, if recognized as art by those in authority, must be art for that reason; so that any definition or theory which fails to accommodate them must be deficient. 'Since any definition of art must compass the Brillo boxes' writes Danto, 'it is plain that no such definition can be based upon an examination of artworks' (Danto, 1981, p.vii). It cannot be so based, he argues, because mere examination will not reveal any difference between the 'ready-made' artwork and the same object lying, untransfigured, on a supermarket shelf. But may we not challenge Danto's starting-point? Who is to say that such works are really art? Such a challenge has been posed by B.R. Tilghman in his book *But is it Art?*. 'Danto', he writes, 'assumes unquestioningly' that such objects are works of art; but 'this assumption is one that wants arguing for' (Tilghman, 1984, p.98).

Now one way of arguing for it is by reference to the judgement of those who put these works forward for appreciation by exhibiting or publishing them. As I pointed out earlier (p.18), it is part of our concept of art that there is a place in it for expert judgement, such as may override the ordinary person's opinions. Is it not futile, in the long run, for such a person to oppose the verdict of the experts? There may still be a point in saying (though not in the sense of the Institutional Theory) that art is whatever is declared to be art by suitable representatives of the artworld. The point would be, not that an object *becomes* a work of art by being declared one, but that the experts' declaration is more likely to be correct.

There have been cases in the history of art, in which an initially hostile public opinion was changed through the efforts of artists and promoters of art, so that what was originally avant-garde, and viewed with suspicion or disdain by the public, became in due course part of the acknowledged corpus of art. The works of the French Impressionists, now among the most admired art treasures, were scorned and derided on their first appearance. An art critic of *Le Figaro* reported that

> An exhibition – supposed to be an exhibition of paintings – has just been opened at the Durand-Ruel Gallery... It really is frightful seeing such an aberration of human vanity and lunacy. Do tell Monsieur Pissarro that trees aren't really purple and the sky isn't really the colour of butter; tell him the things he paints don't really exist anywhere and no intelligent person can be expected to accept such rubbish... Try and make Monsieur Degas see reason... Try and explain to Monsieur Renoir...
>
> (Albert Wolf, *Le Figaro*, 3 April 1876; quoted in Kulka, 1988, pp. 22–3)

Tolstoy, who insisted that art should be 'comprehensible to normal people' (*op. cit.*, p.156), poured scorn on the modern literature, painting and music of his time, including such works as Ibsen's *The Master Builder*. He quoted at length from 'the diary of an amateur of art' (it was in fact his daughter), who had visited the French exhibitions and described her bewilderment. But nowadays we have learned to smile at such reactions, acknowledging that the judgement of a contemporary 'amateur of art' may be subject to correction by those who know better.

It can be argued, however, that the art which bewildered art-lovers of earlier times was not as radical a departure from existing norms as that which bewilders us today. Tilghman has illustrated this by reference to arguments which were put forward in defence of another avant-garde movement of the past, that of 'post-impressionism'.

> In an article in *The Nation* Fry defended the post-impressionists in the following way. He admitted that although 'they were in revolt against the photographic vision of the nineteenth-century...', nevertheless they are the most traditional of recent artists... Now, Fry tells us, don't look at Cézanne as you look at the nineteenth-century academics; see him, instead, as doing the kind of thing that Giotto was doing.
>
> (*Op. cit.*, pp. 74–5)

By going back to a much earlier period, Roger Fry was able to draw attention to certain 'values of form, design, and expression' which were present both in the work of the old master and in the new art of his time. In this way he could persuade the public that this was really art, and art that was worthy of attention, in spite of appearances to the contrary.

But this kind of argument is not applicable to some of today's innovatory art, where the whole point and motivation is to go against accepted values. Indeed, if some present-day critic, corresponding to Fry, undertook to defend such a work by comparing it with the art of some old master, his defence would be self-defeating, for it would undermine the very feature (the rejection of accepted values) which was supposed to give the work its interest and justification.

On the other hand, it may be doubted whether the comparison with Giotto would have been decisive in getting the public to appreciate the aesthetic qualities of the new work. For if these qualities are in the work, then they are so regardless of the comparison with Giotto. Someone who enjoys the work today may do so without any knowledge of the comparison, and with altogether very little knowledge of the art of past ages. It was, indeed, another defender of the new art, Clive Bell, who declared that, 'to appreciate a work of art we need bring with us nothing but a sense of form and colour and a knowledge of three-dimensional space' (*Bell*, p.27). This is an extreme position, but if one disagrees with it, one may still hold that what is at issue between those who condone and those who reject the avant-garde art of today, is the absence of aesthetic qualities within the work, and not the connection with acknowledged works of the past. Thus Binkley, a defender of the new art, takes his stand on the issue about aesthetic qualities: 'being aesthetic', he claims, 'is neither a necessary nor a sufficient condition for being art' (Margolis, p.85).

But is the recent avant-garde art devoid of aesthetic qualities such as might be appreciated by an observer? According to Tilghman, this is so. What, he asks, 'would one be missing if one took *Brillo Box* merely as – a Brillo box? It is not that one would be lacking in appreciation for there is no aesthetic character to appreciate. Nor would one be lacking any normal reaction to something of abiding human significance' (Tilghman, p.118). Yet if we consider a work such as *Brillo Box* or Duchamp's *Fountain*, we may say that these objects are not devoid of aesthetic qualities – qualities of form, colour, texture, etc. which might be appreciated as such. They were, after all, probably designed by an industrial artist with aesthetic qualities in mind. This shows that having aesthetic value and being designed by an artist are not sufficient conditions for being a work of art, since these products are not regarded as such without some act of 'transfiguration'; and it may be thought that what makes all the difference is, after all, the institutional 'christening' postulated by Dickie.

There are other ways, however, of explaining what makes these items art (or of defending their claim to be art). It is sometimes said, of accepted and admired works of art, that their value lies in getting us to see the real world in a new way. In the case of visual arts this may mean that we come to see beauty and other aesthetic qualities in quite ordinary objects, which would otherwise not be thought worthy of attention. Van Gogh, for example, taught us, by means of his pictures, how to see such objects as an ordinary chair or an old pair of boots in a new, aesthetic way (see Colour Plate 1); and it may be claimed that similar benefits can be obtained from the exhibition of ready-mades and similar objects.

> In pop art a great proportion of the creative activity... consists in making the aesthetic judgement: 'This object is worthy of detached sustained contemplation. This is beautiful – out of all context of its place and use in ordinary life – stop and look.'
>
> (Fröhlich, 1966, p.19)

The comparison with Van Gogh must not, however, be taken too far, for in the latter case the artist did more than simply put the objects before us. He 'transfigured' their appearance by means of his artistic skill and insight. The same may be said of a great writer who depicts some sequence of ordinary life in a novel. Here again we are led to see ordinary things in a new way, but this is not done just by presenting them as they are – as might be done, say, by playing back a simple video recording of ordinary life.

When we turn to literature and music the idea of ready-mades is anyway less easy to implement than in the case of works like *Fountain*. An interesting literary example, however, is the poem 'Tiermarkt/Ankauf' by the German poet Erich Fried. The poem consists of an advertisement which appeared in 1970 in a Berlin newspaper, in which the chief of police offered to purchase dogs having such qualities as 'ruthless sharpness', 'a pronounced pursuing instinct', 'undisturbed by shooting' etc. (Fried, 1987). This poem is not quite a ready-made, for the lines of the original have been broken into short fragments which are printed in the form of blank verse, with surprising success. In this case the work has aesthetic qualities, of the kind appropriate to that kind of verse, which were not present in the advertisement as printed.

However, a different kind of justification has been put forward by Danto for such works as *Fountain* and *Brillo Box*. Rejecting the Institutional Theory (Danto, 1981, p.viii), Danto maintains that when something is called a work of art, this description of it has to be '*earned*, and the question is what entitles something to this honour' (*ibid*. p.31). Now one might think the answer in the case of *Fountain* would be by reference to its visible qualities – its 'gleaming surfaces and deep reflections', to quote Danto. But this is not Danto's answer. Such qualities, he argues, are irrelevant to the status of this object as a work of art, since they do not distinguish *Fountain* from its ordinary urinal counterparts. The relevant qualities, which are crucial in turning such objects into works of art, are, according to Danto, of a very different kind. 'The work itself has properties that urinals themselves lack: it is daring, impudent, irreverent, witty and clever' (*ibid.* pp. 93–4). These are the qualities that entitle it to be designated a work of art.

Now these are certainly recognizable and indeed important qualities in terms of which we appreciate established works of art of various kinds. But is Danto right to ascribe them to such a work as *Fountain*? We may agree that the work had these qualities when it was first exhibited, but it is not clear that we should speak of it as having them *now*, so many years, and so many other outrageous offerings, later. (Perhaps we would say that by now the joke has worn off.) But Danto himself emphasized the dependence of art on historical context. An 'aesthetic object', he wrote, 'is not some eternally fixed Platonic entity, a joy forever beyond time, space and history… The aesthetic qualities of a work are a function of their own historical identity' (*ibid.* p.111). Presented at a given moment in history, and in a particular cultural context, an object is a work of art, with suitable aesthetic qualities; presented at another time and in another context, it is nothing of the sort.

An important question in the philosophy of the arts has been to what extent a knowledge of historical context, and also of the artist's intentions, are relevant to the appreciation of a work of art. (This is discussed at length in Essay Five.) Most people would agree (avoiding extreme positions such as that of Bell discussed above) that the appreciation of a work may at least be enhanced by a knowledge of context, though this would vary greatly with different types and specimens of art. In some cases it might make a lot of difference (as when we learn, for example, that the author of 'Ode to a Nightingale' was himself near to death), while in others it would be unimportant or irrelevant. Now the new 'daring' kind of art, as expounded by Danto, is characterized by its heavy dependence on contextual knowledge. So much so, that a critic might complain that whereas in established works of art appreciation is *enhanced* by such knowledge, there is in the new kind of art nothing there to be enhanced, but only, so to speak, the enhancement without the substance. Hence the qualities of daring, wit, etc. that Danto ascribes to *Fountain* can be appreciated without even seeing the work. And indeed thousands of people interested in the arts have read about this and other works of a similar kind, and have appreciated those qualities without any need to inspect the works themselves – or, to take the musical example mentioned on page 4 above, actually to 'listen' to John Cage's *4'33"*.

There is a kind of originality that wears off and another kind that does not. This may be illustrated by a passage in Thomas Love Peacock's *Headlong Hall*.

MR GALE   I distinguish the picturesque and the beautiful, and I add to them, in the laying out of grounds, a third and distinct character, which I call *unexpectedness*.

MR MILESTONE   Pray, sir, by what name do you distinguish this character, when a person walks about the grounds for a second time?

Here it looks as if the laugh is on Mr Gale. But this is not really so. For the truth is that one may experience a view as unexpected, surprising, etc. even though one has seen it many times. ('Every time I turn the corner, it strikes me afresh', etc.) Similarly there are qualities of unexpectedness, surprise, originality, in works of music and literature whose impact we experience again and again. Such qualities are intrinsic to the work, unlike originality in the merely historical sense of having done or said something that no one had thought of before. The latter kind of originality, which is prominent in works like *Fountain*, is not something to be experienced again and again, each time we contemplate the work.

The importance of such works in theoretical discussions about art is indeed out of proportion to their function as *art*. While it is true that they are strong in certain qualities (those mentioned by Danto) they have these only in an ephemeral way. And there are no other ways in which we can enjoy them or be inspired by them. No one would pretend that such art is, to quote Tilghman again, 'about depth and mystery, the conflicts within the human soul and a view of life and human relationships' (Tilghman, p.117). Art, concludes Tilghman, 'is important in our lives and cannot be a matter of indifference and... any theory permitting it to be otherwise has to be mistaken' (*ibid.* p.116).

But here again we must be careful not to regard what is true of some art as a necessary condition of all art. It is true and important to our concept of art that the themes mentioned by Tilghman appear in many works of art – especially, perhaps, in great works of art. But there is also much other art, of well-established status, where this is not so. A work of art, whether visual, literary or musical, may be beautiful or moving without dealing with any such themes. In the case of non-representational art, especially music, it is in any case difficult to read such thoughts into a work. (The description of certain music as 'profound' is discussed in Essay Two.)

Once again we get into difficulties if we try to impose a necessary condition on art. It does not follow, however, that in the case of art 'anything goes', or that we must humbly accept whatever is put out for us by the artworld. We are entitled, on the basis of our knowledge of the concept, to put forward reasons, appealing to established qualities of art, for or against the recognition of an object as art – or, as the case may be, art that is worthy of public display.

In appealing to such reasons, would one be committed to a definition of art? Would one have to maintain that an object is a work of art if, and only if, it satisfies conditions X, Y, and Z? No; reasons may be given without commitment to such a definition. A similar point may be made about Wittgenstein's discussion of the word 'game'. In that discussion he mentioned some typical features of games, such as amusement, skill, and winning and losing, and denied that any one or combination of these could be treated as necessary and sufficient for the concept. But this would not mean that one cannot justify one's description of a particular activity as a game by reference to one of more of these typical features. It was, after all, no accident that Wittgenstein mentioned these features, and not all sorts of others having nothing to do with our idea of games. One might say that these features are *part of the concept*, without thereby implying that they are necessary conditions, satisfied by every instance of a game.

It is also useful to think of the matter in terms of Wittgenstein's further discussion. How, he asked, 'should we explain to someone what a game is', since we cannot give him a definition? His reply was: 'I imagine that we should describe *games* to him, and we might add: "This *and similar things* are called 'games'"' (Wittgenstein, 1953, I, 69). Now we may assume that the games we would choose for this purpose would be paradigms such as chess or football, and not out of the way examples whose status might be disputed. In this way the meaning of the word is tied to certain paradigms, such as would occur to us for the purpose of explaining its meaning.

These remarks are also applicable to the concept of art. In this case too there are paradigms – works to which one would refer if one had to explain what art is, and the meaning of the word is tied to these. In addition, there are (as in the case of games) various other examples which conform to the paradigms to a greater or lesser extent. The status of some of these will be questionable and precarious, because they lack too many of the features that are typical of the concept and are too far removed from the paradigms which would be cited as typical examples of the art. In the case of the latter one could not without absurdity deny that such a work is really art; but in the case of the 'way out' examples, this is certainly possible, and indeed desirable. This kind of art may perform a useful service in challenging accepted notions of art; but it is also useful – and important – to challenge its credentials as art; and this can be done by someone with a normal understanding of the concept, and is not the prerogative of experts alone.

On the other hand, we must not lose sight of the fact that our concept of art cannot be regarded as part of the permanent furniture of human thought. It may be that sooner or later, and perhaps due to the innovatory pressures of today's art and the institutional forces behind it, the conceptual geography will have changed to such an extent that the word 'art' will no longer mean what it means now. Such a change would not, of course, be 'merely verbal'. It would include fundamental changes in the practice and appreciation of art, which in turn would entail a different conception of human culture and civilization.

Bibliography

Aagaard-Morgenstern, L. (ed.) (1976) *Culture and Art*, Nijborg.
Aristotle (a) (1976 edn) *Ethics*, Barnes, J. (ed.) 2nd edn, Penguin Books.
Aristotle (b) (1941 edn) *Poetics*, in *The Basic Works of Aristotle*, McKeon, R. (ed.), Random House.
Aristotle (c) (1941 edn) *Metaphysics*, in *The Basic Works of Aristotle*, McKeon, R. (ed.), Random House.
Austin, J.L. (1961) *Philosophical Papers*, Oxford University Press.
Austin, J.L. (1962) *How to do Things with Words*, Oxford University Press.
Beardsley, M. (1982) *The Aesthetic Point of View*, Cornell University Press.
Bell, C. (1915) *Art*, 2nd edn, Chatto and Windus.
Danto, A.C. (1964) 'The Artworld', *Journal of Philosophy*.
Danto, A.C. (1981) *The Transfiguration of the Commonplace*, Harvard University Press.
Dickie, G. (1974) *Art and the Aesthetic*, Cornell University Press.
Fried, E. (1987) *100 Gedichte ohne Vaterland*, Wagenbach.
Fröhlich, F. (1966) 'Paradoxes of Abstract Expressionism and Pop Art', *British Journal of Aesthetics*.
Kennick, W.E. (1958) 'Does Traditional Aesthetics rest on a Mistake?', *Mind*.
Kulka, T. (1988) '?', *British Journal of Aesthetics*.
Mandelbaum, M. (1965) 'Family Resemblances and Generalizations concerning the Arts', *American Philosophical Quarterly*.
Margolis, J. (ed.) (1987) *Philosophy Looks at the Arts*, Temple.
Matthews, J.R. (1979) 'Traditional Aesthetics Defended', *Journal of Aesthetics and Art Criticism*.
Nash, R. (1987) 'The Demonology of Verse', *Philosophical Investigations*.
Pitcher, G. (ed.) (1966) *Wittgenstein*, Macmillan.
Plato (a) (1987 edn) *Ion*, Penguin Books.
Plato (b) (1952 edn) *Phaedrus*, Hackforth, R. (trans.), Cambridge University Press.

Shaftesbury, Lord, 'Characteristics of Men, Manners, Opinions, Times' in Hofstadter, A. (ed.) (1964) *Philosophies of Art and Beauty*, Chicago University Press.
Stevenson, C.L. (1938) 'Persuasive Definitions', *Mind*, 47; reprinted in Stevenson, C.L. (1963) *Facts and Values*, Yale University Press.
Strawson, P.F. (1959) *Individuals*, Methuen.
Tatarkiewicz, W. (1980) *A History of Six Ideas*, Nijhoff.
Tilghman, B.R. (1984) *But is it Art?*, Blackwell.
Tolstoy, L. (1930) *What is Art?*, Oxford University Press.
Weitz, M. (1956) 'The Role of Theory in Aesthetics', *Journal of Aesthetics and Art Criticism*; reprinted in Margolis (1987).
Weitz, M. (ed.) (1970) *Problems of Aesthetics*, Macmillan.
Wittgenstein, L. (1953) *Philosophical Investigations*, Blackwell.
Wittgenstein, L. (1960) *The Blue and Brown Books*, Blackwell.
Wollheim, R. (1980) *Art and its Objects*, 2nd edn, Cambridge University Press.

Notes

[1] W. Tatarkiewicz (1980) *A History of Six Ideas*. As the title of his book implies, Tatarkiewicz identifies six main ingredients of our concept of art.

[2] A similar view, concerning the special place of poetry, was still being expressed by Goethe in the nineteenth century: 'The arts and sciences are achieved through thought, but not so poetry, since it is a thing of inspiration; one should not call it either art or science but genius'. (*'Man sollte sie weder Kunst noch Wissenschaft nennen, sondern Genius'*) (Quoted by Tatarkiewicz, p.117. See also Nash, 1987, for discussion of this view in Plato and at later times.)

[3] Goethe's remarks are comparable with Wittgenstein's criticisms, two centuries later, of what he called 'the craving for generality' – the desire to subsume a range of diverse things under a single principle – which he diagnosed as one of the main pitfalls of human thought.

[4] In 1917 Marcel Duchamp submitted a work entitled *Fountain* to an exhibition of the New York Society of Independent Artists. It consisted of an ordinary porcelain urinal. Duchamp was responsible for a variety of 'ready-mades' and other innovative conceptions in the course of his career.

[5] In spite of similarities between Dickie's and Danto's positions, the latter does not accept Dickie's solution, as we shall see later.

[6] There is more than a surface resemblance between these remarks about money and Wittgenstein's dictum that 'the use of a word *in practice* is its meaning' (Wittgenstein, 1960, p.69). Wittgenstein was concerned to show that there is nothing behind the *use* of a word, in virtue of which it has meaning.

[7] Conceptual art has been defined as 'art in which the artist's intent is to convey a concept rather than create an art object'.

Aesthetic Qualities

Oswald Hanfling

1 Beauty and Proportion

What qualities are characteristic of art? Beauty is probably the first that comes to mind. What is beauty? The first thing that may strike us here is the enormous variety of beautiful things. Is it likely that they all share some common element or elements in virtue of which they are all beautiful? The difficulty of finding 'what they have in common' is likely to be as great in the case of beauty as in the case of art itself.

There is an ancient view, and one that has persisted through the ages, that beauty consists essentially of such properties as symmetry and proportion. 'The chief forms of beauty', wrote Aristotle, 'are order and symmetry and definiteness, which the mathematical sciences demonstrate in special degree' (Aristotle (a), 1078b). St Augustine, writing in the fifth century AD, declared that 'beautiful things please by proportion... with pairs of equivalent members responding to each other' (Augustine, p.191).

In the seventeenth century the Earl of Shaftesbury declared that 'all beauty is truth. True features make the beauty of a face; and true proportions the beauty of architecture; as true measures that of harmony and music' (Shaftesbury, p.241). These 'true proportions', he claimed, have 'natural beauty, which the eye finds as soon as the object is presented to it', so that even an infant is 'pleased with the first view' of such regular objects as spheres, cubes, etc.; and similarly with the beauty of 'fair and shapely' actions (*ibid.* pp. 254–5).

Is beauty perceived by animals? We have no hesitation in ascribing to animals the perception of sounds, colours, smells and various objects such as food, other animals, and so on; but it is doubtful whether we would ever ascribe the perception of beauty or ugliness to an animal. Why is this so? According to the thinkers discussed in Essay One, the perception of beauty is reserved for beings endowed with the higher, rational faculties of the mind, as implied by Aristotle's reference to 'the mathematical sciences'. These, he held, 'demonstrate in a special degree' the 'order and symmetry and definiteness' which were the main characteristics of beauty (Aristotle (a), 1078b). Animals, according to Aristotle, are 'insensible' to the pleasures of 'harmony or beauty'; and this is so, not because their senses are not acute enough, but because they lack the appropriate rational faculties. Animals, to quote Shaftesbury again, are 'incapable of knowing or enjoying beauty', whereas man enjoys it 'by the help of what is noblest, his mind and reason' (*op. cit.* p.259).

In the eighteenth century Rousseau resorted to the 'regularity' conception of beauty when comparing the feelings of primitive man with those of his civilized descendants. According to Rousseau, the emergence of man from the savage state was a great misfortune and the source of most of the evils of human existence. But there was at least one compensation. The finer feelings of sexual love, he held, were not available to the savage, since 'his mind cannot form abstract ideas of proportion and regularity', such as are required for the perception of female beauty; here was one respect, at least, in which civilized man had the advantage over his savage ancestors (Rousseau, p.70).

The nature of beauty is of interest to practising artists and not only to people who merely think or philosophize about the concept. In this way the quest for a definition of beauty may turn into a quest for a recipe for *producing* objects of beauty. Having established what beauty is, the creative artist would know what to do, or at least aim at, if the creation of beautiful things is what is desired. One practising artist who approached the subject in this spirit was the painter William Hogarth, whose *Analysis of Beauty* appeared in 1753. In this work the reader is directed to the author's own illustrations, showing how his theory of beauty is to be put into practice.

Hogarth found the traditional 'regularity' view deficient. 'If the uniformity of figures, parts, or lines were truly the chief cause of beauty, the more exactly uniform their appearances were kept, the more pleasure the eye would receive' (Hogarth, p.18). But, he pointed out, this is not so. We are not satisfied with perfect regularity, but need something in the way of variety. And this, he said, is in fact supplied by practising artists, whose 'constant rule in composition in painting [is] to avoid regularity' (*ibid.* p.19).

He sought to show, with the help of illustrations, how different kinds of line would be more or less beautiful according to their potential for variety. Least satisfactory were perfectly straight lines, which 'vary only in length, and therefore are least ornamental' (*ibid.* p.38). Next came 'curved lines', and after that 'straight and curved lines joined'. These were followed by 'the line of beauty', consisting of a 'waving line' with 'two curves contrasted'; and finally, in supreme place, came the 'line of grace', which provided the greatest amount of variety. This line was to be represented by 'a fine wire, properly twisted round the elegant and varied figure of a cone' (*ibid.* p.39). (See Figure 1.)

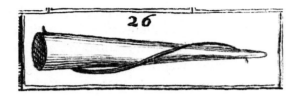

Fig. 1 Illustration from Hogarth's Analysis of Beauty.

It will be seen that, for all his critical remarks about regularity, Hogarth's line is nevertheless connected with regularity. The cone is obviously a regular figure and appears as such in classical geometry; and there is regularity even in the way the artist has chosen to twist his 'fine wire' in the illustration. It may be said, therefore, that Hogarth's recipe for beauty is a refinement of the regularity view, rather than a rejection of it.

A rejection is to be found in *A Philosophical Enquiry into the Origin of Our Ideas of the Sublime and the Beautiful* by Edmund Burke, first published in 1757. Flowers, remarked Burke, are objects of beauty; but is this due to their regularity?

> What proportion do we discover between the stalks and the leaves of flowers, or between the leaves and the pistils? How does the slender stalk of the rose agree with the bulky head under which it bends? but the rose is a beautiful flower; and can we undertake to say that it does not owe a great deal of its beauty even to that disproportion?
>
> (Burke, p.94)

He concluded with a definition of beauty which contained no fewer than seven conditions. A beautiful object, he said, had to be 'comparatively small' and 'smooth', and to have certain kinds of variety, delicacy and coloration, which he spelled out in detail (*ibid.* p.117).

The first of these conditions is perhaps the most surprising. In support of it, Burke maintained that we hardly ever describe large objects as beautiful; and in support of the condition about delicacy, he claimed that 'it is not the oak, the ash, or the elm, or any of the robust trees of the forest, which we consider as beautiful' (*ibid.* p.116).[1]

Such implausible claims about what we say or think usually betray some ulterior motive on the part of the writer. Burke rejected these objects from the domain of the beautiful because he wanted to make room for another aesthetic quality which came into prominence at that time, and which challenged the place of beauty as the only or most important aesthetic quality. This was 'the sublime', a quality that was to be contrasted with beauty in several ways.[2] 'Sublime objects are vast in their dimensions, beautiful ones comparatively small'; 'beauty should be smooth and polished', sublime objects 'rugged and negligent' as well as 'dark and gloomy'; beautiful things must be 'light and delicate', sublime things 'solid and even massive' (*ibid.* p.124). The sublime is 'fitted... to excite the ideas of pain, and danger, that is to say, whatever is in any sort terrible... or operates in a manner analogous to terror' (*ibid.* p.39). Burke, Kant and others tried to explain how these ideas of pain, danger, etc., could affect us in such a way as to produce a satisfying aesthetic experience.

The development of 'the sublime' and other concepts in the aesthetic thought of the Eighteenth Century is a topic for art historians and will not be pursued here. What we must note, first, is the dethronement of beauty from its pre-eminent position in aesthetics. The assumption that beauty is a necessary condition of art – or rather, of good, successful art – could now be challenged, and various other qualities put forward by which to judge and appreciate a work of art. Secondly, without going into the details of Burke's analysis of beauty, and others that were put forward, it seems that once the regularity view of beauty is given up, no obvious alternative suggests itself. There was, and perhaps still is, a self-evident quality about the connection of beauty with regularity, and this is not so with other connections or definitions that might be suggested. The regularity view could survive virtually unquestioned until quite recent times; but once it is surrendered, there is no obvious successor. It now becomes plausible to suppose that beauty exists in an infinite variety of forms and cannot be captured by any overall definition or recipe.

2 Beauty and feeling

The analyses of beauty considered so far have been in terms of objective qualities, such as size, proportion, smoothness and lightness. But it may be thought that the place to look for an analysis of beauty is within ourselves rather than in the objects. This was the view of one of the most important philosophers of the time, David Hume (1711–76). Hume pointed out that there must be more to the perception of beauty than the perception of particular objective qualities.

> A man may know exactly all the circles and ellipses of the Copernican system, and all the irregular spirals of the Ptolemaic, without perceiv-

ing that the former is more beautiful than the latter.

(Hume (a), p.124)

It is clear from Hume's examples (circles, etc.) that the regularity view was still prevalent when he wrote. However, his main concern was to question the objectivity of beauty, rather than to take issue about any particular set of objective qualities.

> Euclid has fully explained every quality of the circle, but has not, in any proposition, said a word of its beauty. The reason is evident. Beauty is not a quality of the circle. It lies not in any part of the line... It is only the effect which that figure produces upon a mind, whose particular fabric or structure renders it susceptible of such sentiments. In vain would you look for it in the circle.[3]

(Ibid. p.125)

Euclid's business was to describe the qualities of the circle. Why then did he say nothing about that quality which we call its beauty? Because, according to Hume, there is no such quality. Beauty, he holds, is something that exists in the mind of the observer; it cannot properly be ascribed to objects outside the mind. We do of course ascribe beauty to such objects in ordinary language, but according to Hume this is a confusion which is due to the close association between the perception of the object and the feelings it arouses in us. 'The mind', he writes,

> is not content with merely surveying its objects, as they stand in themselves: it also feels a sentiment of delight or uneasiness... consequent to the survey; and this sentiment determines it to affix the epithet beautiful or deformed [to the objects that it surveys].[4]

(Ibid. p.124)

Hume's account of beauty may be described as 'subjectivist', for according to it beauty is, or is dependent on, a subjective occurrence: a feeling or 'sentiment' within the observer. This view gains support from the widespread disagreement that exists concerning the beauty of particular objects. In the case of objective qualities, such as would be described by Euclid, any disagreement that occurs can be resolved by examining the object. Thus if one person thinks the object is circular while another takes it to be elliptical, this can be resolved by examining or, if necessary, measuring the object. Again, if there is a disagreement about colours, this can be settled by examining the object more carefully, in a better light, etc. (though some disagreement may remain in borderline cases). But this is not so in the case of beauty. In this case, the object may be displayed to both parties in a good light, its measurements and proportions may be agreed, and so on; and yet one person may describe it as beautiful while the other does not.

> One person may even perceive deformity, where another is sensible of beauty... To seek the real beauty, or real deformity, is as fruitless an inquiry, as to pretend to ascertain the real sweet or real bitter. According to the disposition of the organs, the same object may be both sweet and bitter [i.e. what is sweet to one person may be bitter to another.]
>
> (Hume (b), p.6)

Similarly, if beauty is or depends on a feeling within the observer, then it too will vary 'according to the disposition of the organs' of the person concerned.

Hume's account of beauty may also be compared with the effect that a drug may have on our feelings. If we ascribe, say, the quality of pain-killing to a particular drug, then it is understood that this quality exists only in relation to the effect of that drug on those who take it; and it may well be that it has this quality in relation to some people but not in relation to others. And the same would be true of beauty, if the description of an object as beautiful depended on a feeling or sentiment 'consequent to the survey' of the object in question.

That there is a *connection* between beauty and feeling can hardly be disputed. We speak of the love of beauty, and of getting pleasure from beautiful things. Listening to a piece of beautiful music or poetry, we may experience feelings of considerable intensity. But according to Hume beauty and feeling are not merely connected; his view was that beauty is itself feeling. This view has the consequence that beauty cannot exist in the absence of a suitable observer, with, as Hume put it, 'an intelligent mind, susceptible to those finer sensations'.

> Till such a spectator appear, there is nothing but a figure of such particular dimensions and proportions: from his sentiments alone arise its elegance and beauty. [In Hume's English the word 'sentiment' was closer to 'sensation' than it is today.]
>
> (Hume (c), p.292)

A similar view was expressed by the American philosopher Santayana in *The Sense of Beauty*, first published in 1896. According to Santayana, there is 'a curious but well-known psychological phenomenon' whereby we take 'an element of sensation' to be 'the quality of a thing'. Hence, 'if we say that other men should see the beauties we see, it is because we think those beauties *are in the object*, like its colour, proportion, or size'. But this notion, he said,

> is radically absurd and contradictory. Beauty… cannot be conceived as an independent existence… It exists in perception, and cannot exist otherwise. A beauty not perceived is a pleasure not felt, and a contradiction.
>
> (Santayana, pp. 28–9)

Just as it would be 'absurd and contradictory' to suppose that pleasure can exist independently of anyone feeling pleased, so it is with beauty, given that beauty is a sensation – a 'felt pleasure' – and not 'the quality of a thing'.

These remarks by Hume and Santayana remind us of the saying that 'beauty is in the eye of the beholder', which expresses the view that beauty is a subjective quality, depending, as Hume put it, on a 'disposition of the organs' of the person concerned, in the same way as the qualities of sweet and bitter. There is a further element, however, in the views expressed by Hume and Santayana. According to them, beauty is not merely a subjective quality, but one that consists in a feeling or sensation. Thus Santayana, having said that beauty does not exist independently but only 'in perception', goes on to indicate that beauty is a pleasure that we feel and that it is 'an element of sensation'; and Hume speaks similarly of feelings and sensations. The claim that beauty is a feeling seems to be a necessary ingredient of the subjectivist view, for it is hard to conceive what beauty would consist in if it were neither an objective quality nor a feeling. (The idea that it is something 'in the eye of the beholder' cannot be taken literally.)

Now the idea that beauty is a feeling may seem plausible because of the undoubted connection between beauty and feeling. It is true that the perception of beauty makes us feel good, that ugliness is depressing and so on. But to speak of beauty itself as a feeling is to go much further, and further away from our normal use of this word. Asked how I feel when in the presence of beautiful or ugly things or surroundings, I might reply 'happy', 'thrilled', 'delighted', 'sad', 'disappointed', 'disgusted', etc.; but it would make no sense to reply that I feel beautiful or ugly.

Again, if beauty were a feeling, then, to quote Santayana again, it would be 'absurd and contradictory' to suppose that it might exist independently of being perceived; and a similar view was quoted from Hume. But there is nothing absurd or contradictory in making this supposition. In a book about the development of our planet in past ages, we may read that long ago, before the appearance of any 'intelligent minds' on earth, such and such a region, now an arid desert, was full of beautiful plants. This would strike us as an interesting and by no means unintelligible statement. Similarly, we might talk, perhaps in a discussion about conservation, about the beauty of wild places existing today, which no one has ever visited. One might indeed be arguing that they should be preserved in spite of this. Now on the Hume-Santayana view such statements and discussions must be nonsensical. They would be like talking about a world in which there is pleasure, but no beings capable of feeling pleasure. Such talk would indeed be 'absurd and contradictory'. But this is not so in the case of beauty.

3   Causal theories of beauty

There is another way, however, of defining beauty by reference to feeling. Beauty, it may be said, is a quality of objects and not itself a feeling; but this quality is identified by the feelings it causes in us. In some passages Hume seems to have maintained this view. 'Beauty', he wrote,

> is such an order and construction of parts, as... is fitted to give a pleasure and satisfaction to the soul... beauty is nothing but a form, which produces pleasure, as deformity is a structure of parts, which conveys pain; and... the power of producing pain and pleasure make in this manner the essence of beauty and deformity.
>
> (Hume (d), p.299)

This view does not entail that beauty cannot exist in the absence of suitable spectators, for an object might be 'fitted to give pleasure', even though it is not actually doing so (because no spectators are present).

A causal treatment of beauty is also to be found in Burke's *Enquiry*. 'By beauty I mean, that quality or those qualities in bodies by which they cause love, or some passion similar to it' (Burke, p.91). As we saw on p.43, he went on to state what these qualities were, but that statement must be regarded as subservient to the definition just quoted, for its correctness must depend on whether the qualities mentioned do indeed 'cause love, or some passion similar to it'. If not, then the list would have to be amended.

More recently a causal view has been maintained by Herbert Read, among others. In *The Meaning of Art*, published in 1931, he remarks that there are 'pleasing forms' which 'satisfy our sense of beauty', and he regards this as a matter of cause and effect.

> Certain arrangements in the proportion of the shape and surface and mass of things result in a pleasurable sensation, whilst the lack of such arrangement leads to indifference or even to positive discomfort and revulsion.
>
> (Read, p.18)

The causal approach to aesthetics was rejected by Wittgenstein in his *Lectures on Aesthetics* of 1938.[5] In this discussion, as in the quotation from Read, the word 'discomfort' is used, but Wittgenstein used it by way of contrast with what he called 'discontent'. It was, he held, the latter which was more characteristic of discourse about the arts. By 'discomfort' he meant, like Read, sensations resulting from suitable causes, whose occurrence would be a matter of trial and experiment. 'Discontent', on the other hand, was not a sensation but an attitude; and in expressing discontent with an aesthetic object one was criticizing the object as being 'not right', and not commenting on its power to cause sensations. To make his point he sometimes drew attention to aesthetic situations of a modest, everyday kind. One might, he said, express 'discontent' with the shape of a door, or approval of a suit which is of 'the right length' (Wittgenstein, 1966, p.5). The expression of discontent, he said, is not 'an expression of discomfort *plus* knowing the cause'; it is not 'as if there were two things going on in my soul – discomfort and knowing the cause' (*ibid.* pp. 13, 14).

Now on the view taken by Hume, Burke and Read, the description of a thing as beautiful or ugly does amount to a double statement of this kind. In describing a thing as beautiful, one would be saying both that one felt a pleasurable sensation and that this was caused by certain qualities in the object. But according to Wittgenstein aesthetic descriptions are descriptions of the objects themselves and not of their causal powers with regard to sensations.[6]

Wittgenstein was not denying the importance of feelings when seeing or hearing works of art. Moreover, 'you could play a minuet once and get a lot out of it, and play the same minuet another time and getting nothing out of it' (*ibid.* p.29); and this suggests that hearing the music and responding to it are two separate occurrences, related by way of cause and effect. On this view, our interest in a work of art, and our evaluation of it, would depend on its efficacy in producing certain feelings. There was, Wittgenstein says, 'a tendency to talk about "the effect of a work of art" – feelings, images, etc.', so that if one were asked why one was listening to that minuet, one might be inclined answer 'To get this and that effect'. But, he asked, 'doesn't the minuet itself matter? – hearing *this*: would another have done as well?' (*ibid.* p.29).

If the model of cause and effect were correct, then the answer to this question should be 'yes'. In that case, the point of listening to a minuet would be to get a certain feeling, and then any other piece that produced the same feeling would do just as well. The same would be true of a picture or poem, so that 'if you gave a person the effects and removed the picture, it would be all right' (*ibid*. p.29n.). But if this were so, would not 'a syringe which produces these effects on you do just as well as the picture' or the minuet? According to the causal account, the answer should again be 'yes'. On this view, we might suppose that the shelves of record shops, instead of containing recordings of pieces by Beethoven, Mozart, etc., were furnished with a supply of suitable syringes and drugs, classified under composers' names, and equally effective in producing the desired feelings, but at a lower cost.

In some cases, such as that of the door being too low, it is in any case implausible to think that the aesthetic response must always involve feelings. But even where an aesthetic response does involve feelings, it is still wrong, according to Wittgenstein, to regard the production of feelings as accounting for our interest in aesthetic objects, or as being what we mean when we ascribe aesthetic qualities to them.

4   The normative force of judgements of beauty

As we saw at the start of the previous section, a supposed advantage of subjectivist accounts of beauty was that they would accommodate the widespread disagreement that exists in judgements of beauty. According to these accounts, the disagreements would be no more surprising than the fact that what tastes sweet to one person tastes bitter to another, or the fact that what gives a headache to one person does not do so to another. Hume, having described beauty as a 'sentiment' (i.e. sensation), commented that 'all sentiment is right, because sentiment has a reference to nothing beyond itself' (Hume (b), p.6); and he quoted the saying 'it is fruitless to dispute concerning tastes'. One might say that it makes *no sense* to describe a sensation as either right or wrong. If I get a certain sensation when climbing a high ladder and you do not, we cannot say that one of us must be right and the other wrong.

The fact is, however, that we do 'dispute concerning tastes', and we sometimes claim that others are wrong, or deficient in taste, if their descriptions differ from ours. How could this be so, on Hume's account? In his essay 'Of the Standard of Taste' he tried to explain how there could be such a standard, and what it means to describe some people's taste as superior to that of others. In spite of the subjectivity of sensation, it can also be observed that people's sensations correspond to a large extent; and here lay the key to the problem, as Hume saw it.

> The rules of art are founded... on the observation of the common sentiments of human nature... Their foundation is the same with that of all the practical sciences, experience; nor are they any thing but general observations, concerning what has been universally found to please in all countries and in all ages.
>
> (Hume (b), pp. 8, 7)

On this view, to describe an object as beautiful would be to make a general claim about its ability to please, and in this matter some people might be less skilled, or less well informed, than others.

> Though the principles of taste be universal, and nearly, if not entirely, the same in all men; yet few are qualified to give judgment on any work of art, or establish their own sentiment as the standard of beauty.
>
> (*Ibid.* p.17)

According to Hume, 'the rules of art' are, like laws of nature, to be discovered by scientific observation. Just as scientific observation may lead us to discover a regular connection between, say, a type of diet and a type of disease, so scientific observation can lead us to discover correlations between types of aesthetic objects and 'the common sentiments of human nature'.

In the first of the passages just quoted, Hume seems to think that such discoveries can be made of 'what has been universally found to please in all countries and all ages', and this phrase may strike us immediately as excessive. But let us take his claim to be about rules or laws of a general rather than of a universal kind. (This would not undermine their scientific status, for many scientific laws are about probabilities and do not aspire to universality.) On this view, the description of an object as beautiful would be a claim about its ability to please, let us say, most people most of the time. But is this how the word 'beauty' is used? Someone who described an object as beautiful would not thereby be committed to any such generalization.

In this matter, as in others, there is a disagreement between Hume and Kant, whose *Critique of Judgement* appeared in 1790. What distinguishes attributions of beauty, according to Kant, is their normative force, involving claims about what people *ought* to feel rather than general judgements about what they would feel or have felt. He first contrasted this normative force with expressions of mere personal preference, as when we describe something as 'agreeable'. When some-one 'says the Canary-wine is agreeable', he wrote, this means no more than 'agreeable *to me*'; and in this case 'the axiom holds good: *Every one has his own taste*' (Kant (a), pp. 51–2). But to describe a thing as 'beautiful' involves a larger and normative claim: larger because it involves other people, and normative because it says that they *ought* to describe it likewise, even if they do not. If the thing

> merely pleases *him*, he must not call it *beautiful*. Many things may be charming and agreeable to him – no one cares about that; but when he calls something beautiful, he demands the same delight from others... Thus he says: the *thing* is beautiful; and he does not merely count on the agreement of others... because he found them agreeing with him on several occasions in the past, but he *demands* their agreement. He blames them if they judge differently, and denies that they have taste, while still demanding that they ought to have it; and to this extent one cannot say: everyone has his own taste.
>
> (Kant (b), pp. 19–20, my translation. See also Kant (a), p.52)

Kant's view, like that of Hume, is that ascriptions of beauty involve other people; but whereas for Hume they are 'general observations', based on past experience of what has been 'found to please', Kant regards them as normative rather than experiential; it is not that the speaker 'counts on the agreement of others' on the basis of past experience, but that 'he *demands* their agreement' and accuses them being at fault if they think otherwise.

The normative account of beauty was vehemently rejected by Santayana (though he did not mention Kant by name). 'It is unmeaning', he declared, 'to say that what is beautiful to one man *ought* to be beautiful to another' (Santayana, p.27). Whether it is so will depend 'upon similarity of origin, nature, and circumstance among men'. If these are the same, 'then the same thing will certainly be beautiful to both', but otherwise it will not. In that case, 'the form which to one will be entrancing' will not be so to another, and he may see no more than 'a shapeless aggregate of things, in what to another is a perfect whole' (*ibid.* p.27). But beyond these facts of nature we cannot go: 'it is absurd to say that what is invisible to a given being *ought* to seem beautiful to him'.

Santayana seems not to recognize that there is such a thing as *teaching* someone to see a perfect whole, or some other pattern of aesthetic significance, where previously he saw only a shapeless aggregate; and similarly with other aesthetic qualities in the various arts. A perceptive critic may make the invisible visible to us. This is not to say that having seen the aesthetic significance of a work we are bound to agree about its beauty. Whether we do so may indeed depend on our nature and circumstances, as mentioned by Santayana. However, what is at issue is not the existence of such disagreement, but the normative force of what is said when one describes something as beautiful. According to Kant, as we have seen, such descriptions are not merely reports of personal liking, nor are they (as Hume would have it) statements about the power of an object to please all or most people. What one is saying, according to Kant, is that others *ought* to see this beauty, and that they are deficient in taste if they do not. It is this kind of normative claim that Santayana rejects as 'unmeaning'.

In this matter ordinary usage seems to be on Kant's side. It is perhaps an exaggeration to say that we would accuse a person of lacking taste merely on the basis of one object, as Kant seems to think (though this may depend on the object in question); but we may well do so if the disagreement is sufficiently extensive. This is especially noticeable in the case of negative judgements. Someone who ascribes beauty to objects that we regard as garish, sentimental or hideous, would be accused of being deficient in taste.

5 The decline of beauty

How important is beauty in the conception, practice and appreciation of art? That beauty is not a *sufficient* condition for art has always been clear from the recognition of beauty in nature. Here we find many objects of beauty, but they would not be described as art. There are also many artefacts, for example bridges and windmills, which might be described as beautiful without thereby being regarded as works of art. We may also speak of the beauty of moral qualities and actions, as Shaftesbury and others have done, but again, we would not normally regard these as works of art.

In modern English the word 'beautiful' is used very widely, so that almost any kind of object may be called beautiful by way of praise. At one time it was usual, as Clive Bell reminds us in his *Art* (1915, 2nd edn), to speak of 'beautiful huntin'' and 'beautiful shootin'' (Bell, 1915, p.14). (This was one of his reasons for rejecting beauty as the distinguishing feature of art.) Collingwood, in his *Principles of Art* (1938), drew attention to such expressions as 'a beautiful demonstration' in mathematics, 'a beautiful stroke' in billiards and 'a beautiful claret' (Collingwood, p.39). Even 'a beautiful day', he pointed out, may mean merely 'one which gives us the kind of weather we need for some purpose or other' (*ibid.*). He also claimed that 'if we go back to the Greek, we find that there is no connection at all between beauty and art' (p.37). 'To call a thing beautiful in Greek', he said, 'is simply to call it admirable or excellent or desirable'.

> A poem or painting may certainly receive the epithet, but only by the same kind of right as a boot or any other simple artifact. The sandals of Hermes, for example, are regularly called beautiful by Homer, not because they are conceived as elegantly designed or decorated, but because they are conceived as jolly good sandals which enable him to fly as well as walk.[7]
>
> (*Ibid.* p.38)

These examples show that beauty cannot be regarded as a sufficient condition of art. Can it be regarded as a necessary condition? Must a work of art have beauty? This is clearly not so if we allow for the existence of art of poor quality, where, perhaps, the artist intended to create a beautiful work but produced only an inferior one. So let us put the question differently: must a work of art be either beautiful, or intended to be so? If we understand 'beautiful' in the very broad (one might say diluted) sense to which Bell and Collingwood drew attention, then the answer may seem to be 'yes'. If the word means no more than 'good', and if we assume that artists normally try to produce work that is good, then the answer will be 'yes'. (Some qualification would have to be made about those who, for some reason, do not intend this.) However, 'beautiful' is also used in a narrower, more specific sense, to mean not just good, but good in a particular way. This is borne out by Kant's distinction between 'beautiful' and 'agreeable', and also by the distinction made by Burke, Kant and others, between 'beautiful' and 'sublime'. In this sense of the word, it would seem that beauty is *not* a necessary condition of art. According to Burke, for example, beauty and sublimity would be *alternative* qualities to which an artist might aspire, and a good work of art might be sublime without being beautiful.

Nowadays the word 'sublime' no longer has its former importance, and also its meaning has changed to some extent. But qualities of that kind are still recognized in our conception and appreciation of art. A work of fiction may be praised for being thrilling and exciting – because, to quote Burke again, it 'excites the ideas of pain and danger... or operates in a manner analogous to terror'. Why these evocations of pain and terror should be found satisfying is a question on which various theories have been advanced. (Some of these are discussed in Essay

Four.) But there is no doubt of the importance of these qualities in works of art, including some of the greatest art.

Now it might be said, returning to a broad use of the word 'beautiful', that such works could *also* be described as beautiful, by way of overall praise. But this may not seem an appropriate way of describing them. As John Passmore has put it, 'we wouldn't feel quite comfortable if we called the etchings of Goya or the engravings of Hogarth beautiful' (Passmore, p.50). The subject-matter and mood of such works would make the description of them as beautiful inappropriate, if not absolutely wrong.

According to Read, there is the tendency 'to force this one word "beauty" into the service of all [the] ideals expressed in art' (Read, pp. 22–3). But, he maintained,

> if we are honest with ourselves, we are bound to feel guilty sooner or later of verbal distortion. A Greek Aphrodite, a Byzantine Madonna and a savage idol from the Ivory Coast cannot one and all belong to this... concept... The last one, at least, we must confess to be unbeautiful, or ugly.
>
> (*Ibid.*)

In describing the piece from the Ivory Coast as 'unbeautiful', Read was not, of course, saying that it would be inferior to the examples of European art; his point was that such an object might possess aesthetic qualities *other* than beauty, which would qualify it as a work of art, no less than the other two. His choice of all three examples was meant to draw attention to the diversity of art. 'All these objects' he concluded, 'may be legitimately described as works or art'; but there was no need to stretch the word 'beauty' so as to accommodate them all.

If beauty is not a necessary condition of art, it may still be an important ingredient of art, and the discussion of art. But this too has been disputed. According to Passmore, 'artists seem to get along quite well without it; it is the café-haunters, the metaphysicians, and the calendar-makers who talk of beauty' (Passmore, p.50); while Wittgenstein claimed that in actual discussions about art the word 'beauty' 'plays hardly any role at all'.

> You say: 'Look at this transition', or... 'The passage here is incoherent'. Or... 'His use of images is precise'. The words you use are more akin to 'right' and 'correct'... than to 'beautiful'...
>
> (Wittgenstein, 1966, p.3)

These remarks have been criticized by Mary Mothersill in her *Beauty Restored* (1984). She concedes that 'the term "beautiful" doesn't figure prominently in the talk of "someone who knows what he's talking about"', but claims that 'when a point about a poem or a musical performance is made, the concept of beauty is in the background' (Mothersill, p.257). She also maintains that beauty is

> like knowledge or action, a 'standing' concept, that it is taken for granted in critical discussion of the arts, and that it is indispensable. One mark of a concept's being indispensable is that, given the instruction, 'Get along without it', one is at a loss as to how to proceed.
>
> (Mothersill, p.247)

Now it might be accepted that the concept of beauty is indispensable in this sense. But it would not follow that it is involved in all discussions of the arts, or even that it is the most important ingredient. It might be indispensable in some discussions but not in others. The comparison of the concept of beauty with those of knowledge and action may also be questioned. It can be argued that knowledge and action are indispensable to any human language (and in that sense, any human society). But is the same true of the concept of beauty? Could there not be a society, with a human language, in which there is no such concept? (This is not a question about whether beautiful things are in fact made in that society, for such things may be made even if there is no concept of beauty – just as works of art may have been made by prehistoric people even if they had no concept of art.)

As we have seen, a number of difficulties await those who try to define beauty, and hence art in terms of beauty. Does this mean that there is no connection between art and beauty, or that the connection is unimportant? No: people who visit galleries, read poetry and so on, do, after all, look for beauty, and may be disappointed if they don't find it, or enough of it. Even if this is not always so, if beauty is not a necessary condition of art, the connection may still be important. Again, while it may be true that no satisfactory definition of beauty can be produced, and that people disagree about what things are beautiful, it does not follow that the word is meaningless or that there are no limits to the disagreement. If I am told that a certain object is beautiful, then I shall have a reason for going to see it and will have certain expectations about it.

6 The rise of formalism

As we have seen, one reason for challenging the pre-eminent place of beauty in art was the recognition of other qualities such as the sublime. Another quality, which became prominent in more recent times, was that of form. This has been regarded by some as an alternative to beauty, and by others as being what beauty consists in.

The latter view is comparable with ancient ideas about proportion and symmetry. But the modern formalism was based on personal feelings rather than on any particular type of formal qualities. The appropriate forms were those which, to quote Read again, 'result in a pleasurable sensation'. This, and not any objective definition, was the criterion of good form. According to Clive Bell, a leading proponent of the new formalism, 'the starting-point for all systems of aesthetics must be the personal experience of a peculiar emotion'; and 'the objects that provoke this emotion we call works of art' (Bell, 1915, p.6). The emotion in question is produced, according to Bell, by the perception of a certain kind of form, which he called 'significant form'; but this form was itself defined in terms of the relevant emotion. 'When I speak of significant form, I mean a combination of lines and colours that moves me aesthetically'(*ibid*. p.12).

In this respect the new formalism was more akin to the subjectivism of Hume than to older views which were based on objective qualities of form. And as in the case of Hume's subjectivism, questions arise about the status of aesthetic judgement and aesthetic value – about what Hume called 'the standard of taste'. If the criterion of quality were merely 'what moves me aesthetically', then judgements of quality would be purely personal, as when – to take Kant's example again – one person finds Canary wine agreeable while another does not.

The main concern of the formalists, however, was about the importance of form, in both theory and practice. They insisted on the distinctness and overriding importance of formal qualities and they applied this principle in their critical practice.

The new formalism was connected with a distinction between intrinsic and extrinsic qualities. To illustrate the distinction, let us take a painting of a beautiful landscape. In this case we may speak of the beauty of the landscape as extrinsic to the painting, contrasting this with the intrinsic beauty (or other aesthetic qualities) of the painting. It is, indeed, not uncommon to praise a painting for its intrinsic beauty, when the object depicted is not itself particularly beautiful. This contrast can also be made in the case of literary art. The words of a poem, such as *The Ancient Mariner*, refer to events that are distinct from the poem and are in that sense extrinsic to it. (They might have taken place without the poem.) But the poem also has intrinsic qualities of form and beauty – its rhythms, choice of words and so on, which belong to the poem and not to anything outside.

The distinction between intrinsic and extrinsic may also be made in connection with certain thoughts and feelings that a work may produce in us. To take an example from architecture, we may find that a Gothic building has a religious or historic atmosphere, and this is part of our experience when we contemplate the building. But it may be argued that these properties of the building are extrinsic in comparison with such intrinsic properties as form and beauty. The latter can be appreciated without any thought or even knowledge of religious or historical associations, while, on the other hand, the religious or historical associations that the building conjures up may be had without the building.

Which of the two kinds of qualities is more important, intrinsic or extrinsic? Which is essential to art? It may seem as if the answer must be: intrinsic. Here, it may be said, lies the distinctive contribution that art makes to our lives. If what we want is to enjoy a beautiful landscape, then the best thing to do is to visit such a landscape, and the enjoyment of a painting of it would be only derivative and secondary. There must be something else, distinct from the beauty of the landscape, for the sake of which we want to see the painting; and this must be its essential quality. Again, if we want to reflect on certain thoughts, or hear about certain events, then we can have them told in ordinary language, and there is no need for a work of art to be created. There must be something special to the work of art, for the sake of which we value it.

A similar point may be made about 'functional' theories of art, whereby the value of art lies in serving some useful purpose. According to an ancient Greek theory, the different musical 'modes' (known as Dorian, Phrygian, Lydian and so on), were commended for their efficacy in producing certain qualities of character, such as courage and fidelity. This view was disparaged by Eduard Hanslick (1825–1904) in his book *The Beautiful in Music* (1854).

> If the function of the Phrygian mode were merely to animate the troops with courage in the face of the enemy, or a Dorian mode to ensure the fidelity of a wife whose husband was far away, then the loss of Greek music is a melancholy thing for generals and husbands, but aestheticians and composers need not regret it.
>
> (quoted by Wind, p.136)

To get at the essential qualities of a work of art, it may be helpful to consider an object similar to it, which shares the essential qualities but not the inessential ones. A striking application of this point was made by Heinrich Wölfflin (1864–1945), who claimed that 'the essence of the Gothic style is as evident in a pointed shoe as in a cathedral' (quoted by Wind, p.21). (Presumably he was thinking of the Gothic arch, in particular.) The essence of that style was to be found in certain formal properties, and these are better appreciated, on this view, away from any religious or historical associations.

In the case of pictorial art, the issue of intrinsic versus extrinsic came to a head at the turn of the century, with the emergence of non-representative painting. The matter was now put to the test by the subtraction, so to speak, of the (allegedly) inessential component, leaving only the intrinsic qualities behind. Critics such as Roger Fry and Clive Bell, who could appreciate and expound the merit of the new works, argued that the essence of aesthetic value lay in formal properties as opposed to any representative function. Moreover, the lessons they had learned from non-representative painting were now to be applied to painting in general, including works produced long ago. According to Fry, 'we are liable to have our aesthetic reactions interfered with' if we look at such a painting as Raphael's *Transfiguration* with its 'dramatic overtones and implications' in mind. It is only by becoming 'absorbed in [its] purely formal relations... by the pure contemplation of the spatial relations of plastic volumes', that we can isolate that 'aesthetic quality' of the work which is 'the one constant quality of all works of art' (Fry, pp. 197–8).

A similar approach was taken by Bell in his book *Art*. According to Bell, the 'irrelevant representative or descriptive element' may detract from both the creation and the proper appreciation of art. It can be 'a sign of weakness in an artist', who may, if he is 'too feeble to create forms... try to eke out' his talents by 'suggesting the emotions of life' by means of representative content (Bell, 1915, p.28). He thought that Frith's *Paddington Station*, with its wealth of human detail, was feeble in this sense; it was 'an interesting and amusing document' but 'not a work of art' (*ibid.* p.18).

A corresponding weakness was that of spectators with 'defective sensibility', who, unable to appreciate formal properties, 'read into the forms of the work those facts and ideas for which they are capable of feeling emotion', coming 'straight home to the world of human interests'. Such people, Bell said, are like 'deaf men at a concert' (*ibid.* p.29).

He claimed that:

> To appreciate a work of art we need bring with us nothing from life, no knowledge of its ideas and affairs, no familiarity with its emotions... We need bring with us nothing but a sense of form and colour and a knowledge of three-dimensional space.
>
> *(Ibid.* pp. 25, 27)

This is strong medicine, which some will be less able, and less willing, to take than others. In many cases it will be difficult, in a psychological sense, to set aside our knowledge of human interests and emotions when contemplating a given work, and it may be that the effort needed to do so would interfere with our enjoyment of the work. On the other hand, it is true that too much attention to the representative and other extrinsic qualities of a work may distort and impoverish our appreciation of it. Such a work may be valued for its efficacy in calling up ideas and emotions, which might be of a personal, religious or political kind, even though it lacks artistic merit. (It might, for example, be regarded as shallow or sentimental by people of aesthetic sensibility.) And in this sense the advice given by Bell and Fry may lead us to a more perceptive appreciation.

However, in some respects it is not possible to separate formal from representative properties, as Anne Sheppard has pointed out. She invites us to consider a 'carefully balanced' painting, *The Battle of San Romano* by Uccello, in which *movement* is an essential ingredient of balance (Sheppard, p.46). Prominent in the picture are two mounted soldiers whose horses are rearing towards one another. But to see this we need to bring with us something more than the bare 'sense of form and colour and... three-dimensional space' of which Bell speaks. We need to see the lines and colours as animals in motion, and motion directed towards one another. Similarly, 'the slanting lines on the left of the picture which represent the pikes of the victorious army as it advances are not slanting some to the right and some to the left just to make a pretty pattern' (*ibid.* p.46); they serve to convey the movement of an army. This movement is part of the formal composition, the balance, of the picture; but we cannot recognize it unless we bring with us some knowledge of the objects and practices in question.

The new formalism was expounded mainly in the context of visual art. How would it work in the case of other arts? Music may be regarded, from the formalist point of view, as the purest art form, since musical works do not, generally speaking, have any outside reference. A work such as Beethoven's First Symphony is not 'about' anything, as *The*

Ancient Mariner is, nor is it 'of' anything, as Raphael's picture of the Transfiguration is.[8] Some musical works, it is true, contain imitations of natural sounds (Beethoven's *Pastoral Symphony* is an obvious example), and there is also such a thing as musical 'quotation', in which a piece of music contains material from another piece. But these are special cases.

In the case of literary art, however, there is a problem with meaning: should the meanings of words be regarded as extrinsic to a work of literary art – a poem, let us say? It may seem so, for these meanings exist independently of the poem, and it may be thought that the essential qualities of the work are its purely 'musical' ones – the sounds of individual words, and the rhyme, metre, etc. that result from their combination in formal patterns. This view seems to have been taken by Fry. On one occasion, reported by his friend Bell, he composed a 'poem' which sounded similar to Milton's ode 'On the morning of Christ's Nativity', but which consisted of 'deliberate gibberish – a collection of sounds so far as possible without meaning'. He claimed that this composition possessed 'all, or almost all, the merits of the original' (Bell, 1956, p.76). These merits would of course have been the 'purely aesthetic' ones, consisting of formal properties untainted by any outside reference. Another way of illustrating and, so to speak, experiencing Fry's point would be by listening to a poem in a foreign language of which one had no knowledge. A less clear-cut example, but one that may be more familiar, is that of Edward Lear's nonsense poems. These do contain some elements of English but consist largely of nonsense words. It is sometimes said that these poems have a special beauty just because the words are 'pure sounds', untainted by meaning.

But in the case of poetry there is a difficulty similar to that which arose in connection with painting, as illustrated with the example from Uccello. The difficulty is that of separating intrinsic from extrinsic qualities. As we have seen, the meanings of words are to be treated as extrinsic, not relevant to the purely aesthetic (formal) merits of the poem. Yet some formal properties are essentially connected with meaning. Thus, to take an example from Milton, consider the interruption of rhythm which occurs in Sonnet XVI, (on his blindness), in the lines

> And that one talent which is death to hide
> Lodged with me useless, though my soul more bent
> To serve therewith my Maker...

Reading these lines aloud, we notice that the word 'useless' has to be read in such a way as to disrupt the steady rhythm of the verse; and in this way the negative sense of this important word is stressed. But this is a point about a relationship *between* form and meaning, which would be lost if one were to exclude meaning.

Again, in discussing a drama or a novel, we may want to talk about the balance between plot and sub-plot, and this would make no sense if we were to set aside the meanings of the words. Such a discussion might also have to take in the emotional content of the plots, etc. These considerations were supposed to be prohibited by the strict formalist approach, and yet they may be essential for a discussion of formal properties.

Does it follow that the distinction between formal and other properties is untenable? No; it only follows that the distinction is not as clear-cut, not as easy to apply, as some advocates of formalism seem to have thought. It is still true that if one were asked to mention the formal properties of a work, one would give one kind of answer; and asked to mention other properties, a different kind of answer. And the same is true of 'intrinsic' and 'extrinsic', as was shown by the examples given at the beginning of this section (pp.57–9). The fact that a distinction is not always clear-cut does not entail that it is invalid or unimportant.

A more fundamental accusation that may be made against formalism is, to quote Wittgenstein, 'the craving for generality' – a desire to subsume a large and varied range of things under a single principle. Arnold Isenberg has characterized the formalist argument as follows:

> You deduct from an admittedly great altarpiece or historical painting those factors which you think have been proved by experience either to be not necessary or not sufficient conditions of value in art; and since you believe that the principles which govern aesthetic effect must be the same everywhere, you identify these principles with the mystic remainder... Your reader is persuaded by this proof to imagine that he does not see what he sees and does not like what he likes but is being affected in an uncanny manner by hidden relationships, the same in Giotto, Titian, Picasso, and Mondrian. The method, in short, is *subtraction*.
>
> (Isenberg, p.31)

It is, however, mere prejudice to suppose that aesthetic satisfaction must be attributable to a single kind of quality; and while it is true that formal qualities are important – sometimes most important – in the creation and appreciation of a work of art, this does not entail that it must be so in all cases. A rambling, episodic novel may be described correctly as formless, but admired none the less for its other qualities – its beauty or originality of language, insight into human nature, and so on. And a painting, similarly, may be admired for these and other qualities, rather than for any formal merits it may possess.

7 Aesthetic and non-aesthetic qualities

So far this discussion of aesthetic qualties has included beauty, form and the sublime. But our aesthetic vocabulary is much richer than this, encompassing, according to Frank Sibley, 'an almost endless variety'. We say, for example,

> that a poem is tightly-knit or deeply moving; that a picture lacks balance, or has a certain serenity or repose... that the characters in a novel never really come to life, or that a certain episode strikes a false note.

> (Sibley, 1959, p.421)

We use such terms as 'integrated', 'sombre', 'dynamic', 'powerful', 'vivid', 'delicate', 'trite', 'sentimental' and 'tragic', 'graceful', 'delicate', 'handsome' and 'garish'; as well as 'a telling contrast', 'sets up a tension', 'conveys a sense of' and 'holds it together'. These and other examples were listed by Sibley as 'aesthetic concepts' (Sibley, 1959, pp. 421–2). He contrasted them with descriptions of art which he called 'non-aesthetic', as when we say that 'a novel has a great number of characters and deals with life in a manufacturing town; that a painting uses pale colours... and has kneeling figures in the foreground; that the theme of a fugue is inverted at such a point' (*ibid*. p.421). The two kinds of language are to be characterized by what was needed in order to perceive the relevant qualities. Qualities of the non-aesthetic kind, he said, can be 'pointed out to anyone with normal eyesight, ears and intelligence', whereas those of the aesthetic kind 'require the exercise of taste, perceptiveness or sensitivity, of aesthetic discrimination or appreciation' (*ibid*. p.421).

In speaking of the 'perception' of aesthetic qualities Sibley did not mean only visual and aural qualities, such as are to be found in the visual arts and in music. As is clear from the examples quoted above, he also meant those which are perceived in the sense in which one can perceive (or 'see') that 'the characters in a novel never really come to life, or that a certain episode strikes a false note'. What would not be included, however, are qualities of an historical or circumstantial kind, such as the originality, daring, cleverness, etc., which were ascribed to works like *Fountain* and *Brillo Box*, as discussed in Essay One (pp.21–5). These qualities could only be appreciated by someone with a knowledge of the historical circumstances and could not be perceived in the works by themselves. (Such qualities may also of course be ascribed to more traditional works.)

Sibley's argument deals with two main topics: the perception of aesthetic qualities, and the relation between aesthetic and non-aesthetic. Unlike those who regard aesthetics as being mainly about the production of feelings, he held that 'broadly speaking, aesthetics deals with a kind of perception... People have to *see* the grace or unity of a work, *hear* the plaintiveness or frenzy in the music, *notice* the gaudiness of a colour scheme' (Sibley, 1965, p.137). Now in order to see and hear these aesthetic qualities, we must be 'in possession of good eyesight, hearing and so on', just as we must in order to perceive non-aesthetic qualities. But the possession of these faculties is not enough in the case of aesthetic perception, for 'people normally endowed with senses and understanding may nevertheless fail to discern' the relevant qualities. What they need, in addition, is to exercise taste, sensitivity, etc. In this matter critics have a role to play. 'A major occupation of critics is the task of bringing people to see things for what, aesthetically, they are' (*ibid.* p.141).

There are, however, relations of dependence between aesthetic and non-aesthetic qualities. 'Any aesthetic character a thing has depends upon the character of [its] non-aesthetic qualities... and changes in its aesthetic character result from changes in its non-aesthetic qualities' (*ibid.* p.138). Hence it is that

> often when we apply aesthetic terms, we explain why by referring to features which do *not* depend for their recognition upon an exercise of taste: 'delicate because of its pastel shades and curving lines', or 'it lacks balance because one group of figures is so far off to the left and is so brightly illuminated'.
>
> (Sibley, 1959, p.424)

The dependence of aesthetic on non-aesthetic is not, however, one that can be stated in the form of sufficient conditions. 'There are no sufficient conditions, no non-aesthetic features such that the presence of some set of them will beyond question justify or warrant the application of an aesthetic term' (*ibid.* p.424). We cannot, for example, 'make *any* general statement of the form "If the vase is pale pink, somewhat curving, lightly mottled, and so forth, it will be delicate"' (*ibid.* p.426). Although these features might be mentioned in support of the statement that the vase is delicate, they would not amount to a proof of it; and neither could they serve as a set of sufficient conditions for the delicacy of vases in general. Such generality, according to Sibley, can be found only on the negative side. Thus it may be said that a thing could *not* be garish 'if all its colours are pale pastels, or flamboyant if all its lines are straight' (*ibid.*). But these statements have no positive counterparts. We cannot say, for example, that if a thing has bold colours then it must be garish, or that if it has such and such curving lines, then it must be flamboyant.

In using aesthetic terms, Sibley said, 'we learn from samples and examples' and not from rules. He describes 'a man who failed to realize the nature' of aesthetic concepts, or who, 'knowing he lacked sensitivity in aesthetic matters [and] did not want to reveal this lack... provided himself with some rules and generalizations', on the basis of which 'he might frequently say the right things'. Such a person, he said, 'could have no great confidence or certainty; a slight change in an object... might ruin his calculations' (*ibid.* p.432).

It is not clear whether Sibley had any real people in mind. But it is not unusual to find people who, though well versed in talking and theorizing about art, are suspected to be lacking in sensitivity when it comes to aesthetic perception. Such people may persuade us (and themselves, perhaps) that such and such merits or demerits are present in a given work, by inference from suitable non-aesthetic qualities. But a more sensitive observer may find, on inspection, that the relevant qualities are not really there.

So far is the relationship of non-aesthetic to aesthetic from being one of sufficient conditions, that, as Sibley points out, a given non-aesthetic description may serve to support two different aesthetic descriptions, one favourable and the other unfavourable. A work may be described as graceful or delicate, because of its 'pale colour, slimness, lightness, lack of angularity'; but the same reasons might be given for describing it as 'flaccid', 'washed out', 'lanky' or 'insipid' (*ibid.* p.428).

> Thus an object which is described very fully, but exclusively in terms of [non-aesthetic] qualities characteristic of delicacy, may turn out on inspection to be not delicate at all, but anaemic or insipid.
>
> (*Ibid.*)

Similarly, 'many of the features typically associated with 'joyous', 'fiery', 'robust' or 'dynamic', are the same as those associated with 'garish', 'strident', 'turbulent', 'gaudy', or 'chaotic'. And again, 'one poem has strength and power because of the regularity of its metre and rhyme; another is monotonous and lacks drive and strength because of its regular metre and rhyme' (*ibid.* p.429).

Sibley distinguished two senses of 'reason', which I shall refer to as 'inferential' and 'explanatory'. A reason in the inferential sense is 'roughly, a true statement or fact such that, on the basis of knowing *it*, it would be reasonable, right or plausible to infer, suppose or judge' that something is the case (Sibley, 1965, p.146). Suppose, to take a non-aesthetic example, I said that the Eiffel Tower is the tallest building in Paris. Asked why I said this, I might refer to the fact someone told me, or that I read it in a book. These would be facts from which I can reasonably infer that it is so. But another kind of question would be: why is it so? What is wanted this time is an *explanation* of its being so, and this might require knowledge, which I may or may not have, about the facts behind the building of the Tower, and other circumstances. Reasons in the inferential sense are essentially reasons that the speaker knows; they are used by the speaker to defend or justify what was said, to show that the belief is reasonable. But this is not true of reasons in the explanatory sense. Such reasons might be put forward by way of hypothesis or speculation, but one is not obliged to do so, or to have any knowledge of them at all.

Now in the case of aesthetic and non-aesthetic qualities the relation-ship, according to Sibley, is explanatory and not inferential. The non-aesthetic quality or qualities may serve to *explain* the presence of a perceived aesthetic quality, but we cannot *infer* that the latter must be present from the fact that the former are. And as with other cases of explanation, someone who perceives an aesthetic quality may or may not know an explanation for its presence, in terms of non-aesthetic qualities. Thus 'a person might notice that something is graceful... without yet knowing or being able to specify exactly the reason why' (Sibley, (b), p.146). According to Sibley, the discovery of such reasons is 'one of the central activities of critics: *explanation*' (*ibid*. p.140). This explanation may be interesting in itself, but it may also bring it about that 'our appreciation is deepened and enriched and becomes more intelligent in being articulate' (*ibid*.).

The inferential kind of reason, on the other hand, is not appropriate for aesthetic statements. 'It is absurd to ask', says Sibley, that such a statement '(involving, as it does, perception) be based upon reasons' in the inferential sense (*ibid*. pp. 146–7). 'The reason the music is sad at a certain point may truly be that just there it slows and drops into a minor key. The reason a man's face looks funny may be that he screws up his eyes in an odd way'. But these non-aesthetic facts

> would be very poor reasons for believing or inferring that the music
> must be, or even probably is, sad, or that the face looks funny. The

music might instead be solemn or peaceful, sentimental, or even characterless; the face might look angry or pained or demonic.

(Sibley, 1965, p.148)

The two aspects of Sibley's argument, concerning the perceptual nature of aesthetic qualities, and the manner of their dependence on non-aesthetic qualities, are connected. It is because we have to '*see* the grace or unity of a work', etc. (as quoted on page 64), that the existence of such qualities is not to be established by inference. Notwithstanding the dependence of aesthetic on non-aesthetic, the gracefulness of a vase or the sadness of a piece of music cannot be *inferred* from their non-aesthetic qualities, but must be perceived directly.

This is not to say that the critic's role must be confined to explanation. For besides the two kinds of reasons (only one of which, the explanatory, is appropriate for aesthetics), there are ways of 'helping people to see and judge for themselves that things have those [aesthetic] qualities' (Sibley, 1965, p.141). This may indeed be done by pointing out non-aesthetic features that we had not noticed – though 'sometimes, although these *were* seen, the resultant aesthetic quality was still missed' (*ibid*. p.141). But in any case, the critic's role is to get us to see the aesthetic quality for ourselves, and this is not to be achieved by inferring its presence from that of non-aesthetic qualities, or by any other inference.

Sibley's insistence on the *perception* of aesthetic qualities may be contrasted with the theories discussed in earlier sections, whereby the presence of such qualities, or our knowledge of them, would depend on feelings. It may seem plausible to regard beauty in this way, because it is readily associated with feelings such as love and delight. But the situation is different when we turn to such qualities as 'vivid', 'delicate', 'dynamic', 'trite' and so on, for there is little temptation to think that these qualities are to be identified by corresponding feelings, one for each quality. It is, however, largely in terms of such qualities that aesthetic discourse is conducted. Moreover, the description of a thing as beautiful is itself often supported by reference to qualities of this kind.

8 'Expressive' qualities

On the other hand, there is a type of aesthetic quality where the connection with feelings seems especially strong and direct. A piece of music may be described as sad or cheerful. Is this because it expresses the composer's feelings? Is it due to feelings produced in the audience? Again, what if someone speaks of 'a plaintive melody'? This example was introduced by Wittgenstein who went on to ask: 'Does he hear the complaint?' (my translation; see Wittgenstein, 1953, p.209). One's first impulse may be to answer 'yes'. What else can it mean to describe a melody as plaintive? But if this answer is given, then further questions arise. Who is doing the complaining? What is the complaint about? Again the answers may seem straightforward. The complaint, it may be said, is made by the composer or performer of the music. And while we may not know what the complaint is about, we can easily imagine a suitable object.

> Perhaps the plaintive numbers flow
> For old, unhappy, far-off things,
> And battles long ago:
> Or is it some more humble lay,
> Familiar matter of today?
> Some natural sorrow, loss or pain,
> That has been, and may be again?
>
> (Wordsworth, 'The Solitary Reaper')

Such qualities as 'sad' and 'plaintive', when ascribed to music, are known as 'expressive', and this reflects a widespread view that music, but also art in general, serves to express an artist's feelings (the 'expression theory'). But this view (as can be seen in Essay Five) is open to serious objections; and the description of such qualities as 'expressive' may be misleading, if it implies that the expression theory is correct.

This implication was challenged by J.O. Urmson in his paper 'Representation in Music' (1973). Urmson did not deny that 'some composers have from time to time expressed their sadness in their music', but he questioned whether this is what is *meant* in describing a piece of music as sad. This cannot be so, he argued, for he could himself easily 'write a short piece of music that would be recognizably sad without thereby expressing sadness or anything else' (Urmson, 1973, p.141).

Another suggestion has been that there is a resemblance between sad music and the appearance or behaviour of sad people. But is there such a resemblance? Or are we inclined to 'read' this into the music even if it is not there? Peter Kivy has drawn attention to the way in which we 'tend to "animate" what we perceive'.

> Tie a piece of cloth around the handle of a wooden spoon and a child will accept it as a doll; more to the point, *you* will see it as a human figure... Put three lines in a circle,

and you will inevitably see it as a face. Why? Not simply because it resembles the features of a human countenance. After all, it also resembles many other things.

(Kivy, 1990, p.57)

In a later chapter, however, he regarded resemblance as the key to an explanation in the case of music. We hear a given piece of music as 'expressive of sadness', he wrote, 'because we hear it as a musical resemblance of the gesture and carriage appropriate to the expression of our sadness' (*ibid.* p.53). But will not the music too 'resemble many other things' – and resemble them more than human expressions of sadness? Kivy used a passage from J.S. Bach as an example. 'Don't we hear the melodic line droop', he suggested, 'in the oboe solo of the first Brandenburg?' (*ibid.* p.55). But what if we do? Does this drooping *resemble* that of a human being? (And do people normally express sadness by drooping?)

How can the drooping attitude of a human body be said to resemble a sequence of notes? It may be replied that in both cases there is a movement from higher to lower. However, the description of notes as high and low is just as puzzling as the description of music as sad or plaintive. We describe a building as high because of its spatial relation to the ground; but no such relation exists in the case of a sound. In some languages, I understand, high and low, as applied to notes, are reversed; and this seems no less reasonable than our usage. But in that case, would Kivy's melodic line be soaring rather than drooping? And what if pitch were not described in terms of elevation at all, but, let us suppose, in terms of sharp and blunt? (The existing use of 'sharp' in music raises similar questions.)

On the other hand, the *differences* between sad music and normal expressions of sadness are evident. Normally we express sadness either in words, in which case we may say what we are sad about and why, or by means of gestures or non-verbal sounds (though in this case too we can be asked what we are sad about). But may not a piece of music at least resemble an expression of sadness of the non-verbal kind? Kivy, referring to a certain passage in Bach's *St Matthew Passion*, claims that 'the music quite literally sounds like a cry'. But, as Urmson, has pointed out, 'sad music does not much resemble the sounds that people make to express their sadness, which are typically disagreeable and even raucous' (Urmson, p.141). Again, 'sad music is pleasant to listen to', and listening to it may make us happy (*ibid*. p.142), but this is not so with normal expressions of sadness.

The example given by Kivy is, in any case, rather special. There are not so many passages of music in which it would be plausible to find a resemblance with a human cry or any other non-musical sound. Kivy's example may perhaps remind us of those passages in Beethoven's Pastoral Symphony where we hear imitations of the cuckoo and other birds. But such examples, as well as being fairly rare, comprise only a small part of the music in which they occur. And what we are concerned with is the description of a whole work or section of a work as sad or plaintive – or pastoral, perhaps. What would be needed to support the resemblance theory is an example in which the music is wholly or largely composed of sounds resembling human expressions of sadness, etc. (or in the case of a pastoral work, of imitations of birds and other countryside noises). And then it would need to be shown that the example is typical – that the same kind and quantity of resemblance can be found in all other music described as sad, and so on.

Another point to be noticed about Kivy's example is that it contains words as well as music. Now words may of course be, and in this case are, expressive of various feelings; and when we hear such music it is difficult to separate the emotional content of the music from that of the words. Therefore it would be better, in discussing the resemblance theory, to use examples of music that are not settings of words – whose emotional content is not mingled with that of words. (The way in which words and music suit one another in settings of words to music is itself a fascinating topic which I shall not pursue.)

But why, if not because of resemblance, do we describe music as sad, plaintive, etc.? Is it because it makes us feel sad? It is true that music evokes feelings in us, but can it make us feel sad? Listening to music, sad or otherwise, is something that gives us pleasure; but feeling sad does not normally give us pleasure. Again, if I say I feel sad, I should be able to say what I feel sad about, but what would this be in the case of music? (If the music were awful, this might be a suitable reason for sadness, but it would not, or not necessarily, be a case of sad music.) Finally, this attempt to deal with sad music would not be applicable to plaintive music, for there is no such feeling as 'plaintive'.

Another suggestion is that sad music is suitable for expressing sadness that we already feel; it is the kind of music that would be chosen for sad occasions. But such occasions may be far from our thoughts when we enjoy a piece of music of this kind. Yet, as Sibley put it, we '*hear* the plaintiveness or frenzy in the music', and likewise we hear that it is sad or 'solemn or peaceful, sentimental, or even characterless' (quoted p.67), as we see or hear other aesthetic qualities.

Another example, discussed by Kivy in another work, is the description of certain music as *profound*. In the case of literature, this word can be explained by reference to the subjects treated. We would expect such a work to be about important human concerns, and to deal with them in certain ways (which are explored by Kivy). But what can it mean to describe, say, the late quartets of Beethoven as profound? Are they 'about' human concerns? Do they contain questions, statements and discussions about the human condition? The claim that music is, indeed, a kind of language, is explored in Essay Five. But unless this can be maintained, the description of music as profound remains puzzling. (In this case, after various attempts at explanation, Kivy confessed that he had 'failed to find any rational justification' for this use of 'profound' (Kivy, 1990).)

When the subject is further opened out, it appears that these puzzling uses of language are not peculiar to aesthetics. This point has been brought out well by Isenberg. 'Every area of experience', he wrote, 'borrows from nearly every other'. The word 'light' is used in contrast to 'dark', but also in contrast to 'heavy'; but what do these meanings have in common? Again, we may describe a person as 'light-hearted', but how can a heart be light? Hence 'it seems rather silly to ask how music can be *light-hearted*, as if you already knew how a heart can be light' (Isenberg, p.9). Another example, given by Urmson, is the word 'dull': 'the weather, a conversation, a person, a colour, a knife-blade and a pain may all be called dull', yet 'they could scarcely all share exactly the same feature' (Urmson, p.140). (The word 'exactly' may be misleading here, for it seems to imply that there is some feature that is *nearly* the same in all these instances, in virtue of which they are called dull. But this is not so: the problem would be the same with 'nearly' as with 'exactly'.)

These uses of language, both inside and outside aesthetics, are sometimes called 'metaphorical'. But they are not metaphors in the same way that 'sifting the evidence' or 'the head of the company' are. In these cases we can explain how the metaphor works, by drawing attention to the relevant analogies. We also have the option of saying the same thing non-metaphorically. But this is not so in the other cases. 'If "dull pain" is metaphorical, what is the literal equivalent?' (*ibid*. p.140).

Thus it appears that the problem of 'expressive' qualities is part of a much larger issue in the philosophy of language: whether, or to what extent, our uses of words are explicable. To say this is not, of course, to solve the problem; but it may serve to put it in a truer perspective.[9]

Bibliography

Aristotle (a) (1941 edn) *Metaphysics*, in *The Basic Works of Aristotle*, McKeon, R. (ed.), Random House.

Aristotle (b) (1976 edn) *Ethics*, Barnes, J. (ed.), Penguin Books.

Augustine, 'De Musica' in Hofstadter, A. (ed.) (1964) *Philosophies of Art and Beauty*, Chicago University Press.

Bell, C. (1915) *Art*, 2nd edn, Chatto and Windus.

Bell, C. (1956) *Old Friends*, Chatto.

Burke, E. (1958 edn) *A Philosophical Enquiry into the Origin of Our Ideas of the Sublime and the Beautiful*, Routledge and Kegan Paul.

Collingwood, R.G. (1938) *The Principles of Art*, Oxford University Press.

Fry, R. (1926) *Vision and Design*, Chatto.

Hogarth, W. (1969 edn) *Analysis of Beauty*, Scolar Press.

Hume, D. (a) 'The Sceptic' in Lenz, J.W. (ed.) (1965) *Essays*, Bobbs-Merrill.

Hume, D. (b) 'Of the Standard of Taste' in Lenz, *op. cit.*

Hume, D. (c) (1975 edn) *Enquiries concerning Human Understanding and concerning The Principles of Morals*, Selby-Bigge, L.A. (ed.), Oxford University Press.

Hume, D. (d) (1978 edn) *A Treatise of Human Nature*, Selby-Bigge, L.A. (ed.), Oxford University Press.

Isenberg, A. (1973) *Aesthetics and the Theory of Criticism*, Chicago University Press.

Kant, I. (a) (1952 edn) *Critique of Judgement*, Meredith, J.C. (trans.), Oxford University Press.

Kant, I. (b) (1924 edn) *Kritik der Urteilskraft*, Felix Meiner.

Kivy, P. (1980) *The Corded Shell*, Princeton University Press.

Kivy, P. (1990) *Music Alone: Philosophical Reflections on the purely Musical Experience*, Cornell University Press.

Mothersill, M. (1984) *Beauty Restored*, Oxford University Press.

Passmore, J. 'The Dreariness of Aesthetics' in Elton, W. (ed.) (1954) *Aesthetics and Language*, Blackwell.

Read, H. (1972 edn) *The Meaning of Art*, Faber.

Rousseau, J.-J. (1973 edn) *Discourse on Inequality*, Cole, G.D.H. (ed.), Dent.

Santayana, G. (1955 edn) *The Sense of Beauty*, Dover.

Shaftesbury, Lord 'Characteristics of Men, Manners, Opinions, Times' in Hofstadter, A. (ed.) (1964) *Philosophies of Art and Beauty*, Chicago.

Sheppard, A. (1987) *Aesthetics*, Oxford University Press.

Sibley, F. (1959) 'Aesthetic Concepts', *Philosophical Review*.

Sibley, F. (1965) 'Aesthetic and Nonaesthetic' *Philosophical Review*.

Urmson, J.O. 'Representation in Music' in Vesey, G. (ed.) (1973) *Philosophy and the Arts*, Macmillan.

Wind, E. (1963) *Art and Anarchy*, Faber.

Wittgenstein, L. (1953) *Philosophical Investigations*, Blackwell.

Wittgenstein, L. (1966) *Lectures and Conversations*, Barrett, C. (ed.), Blackwell.

Notes

[1] Aristotle too held that size is relevant to beauty, but for different reasons. 'Beauty is a matter of size and order, and therefore impossible either... in a very minute creature, since our perception becomes indistinct as it approaches instantaneity; or... in a creature of vast size... as in that case, instead of the object being seen all at once, the unity and wholeness of it is lost to the beholder' (*Poetics*, 1450b; in McKeon, R. (ed.) (1941) *The Basic Works of Aristotle*, Random House).

[2] Burke was influenced by a work attributed to a writer of the first century AD known as Longinus and which was usually translated under the title *The Sublime*. The first such translation into English appeared in 1698 and interest in the concept developed after that.

[3] A similar discussion may be found in Hume (c), pp. 291–1.

[4] Hume's use of 'deformed', rather than 'ugly', as the opposite of beauty again reminds us of the traditional connection of beauty with regularity, proportion, etc.

[5] I have written 'aesthetics' rather than 'beauty', because Wittgenstein's discussion was not in terms of beauty. As we shall see later, he denied that beauty is an important concept in our appreciation of art. However, his criticism of what I have called 'the causal approach to aesthetics' would also apply to beauty.

[6] Wittgenstein's example of the shape of a door is reminiscent of his work as architect on the house built for his sister in Vienna in the 1920s, when his obsession for getting things right, even in matters of detail, was noted. 'The strongest proof of Ludwig's unshakable attitude with regard to dimensions is perhaps the fact that he caused the ceiling of a large room to be raised by three centimetres... after the building of the house had been completed.' In another passage his sister spoke of the immense trouble that had been taken over getting the doors right: 'but what resulted was really worth the upheaval and effort that it had cost, and as I write I am overcome by a great longing to see those noble doors again, in which, even if the rest of the house fell into ruin, one could recognize the spirit of its creator' (Wittgenstein, H., 'Familienerinnerungen', in Nedo, M. (ed.) (1983) *Wittgenstein*, Suhrkamp, pp. 208, 218, my translation).

[7] A recent edition of Aristotle gives 'fine, admirable, noble', as well as 'beautiful', as possible translations of the Greek *kalos* (Aristotle (b), p.368).

[8] The view that music is, contrary to what I have said, a kind of language, is examined in Essay Five.

[9] For a fuller treatment of issues discussed in this section, see Hanfling, O. 'I heard a plaintive melody' in Phillips Griffiths, A. (ed.) (1991) *The Wittgenstein Centenary Essays*, Cambridge University Press.

The Ontology of Art

Oswald Hanfling

Introduction

The question 'What is art?' can be understood in several ways. In Essay One it was taken to be about defining the concept in terms of necessary and sufficient conditions. Essay Two was about certain qualities, such as beauty and form, which are or have been regarded as characteristic of art, even if not put forward as a definition of it. In the present essay we shall be concerned with questions of ontology: 'How, and in what sense, do works of art exist?'

Ontology is 'the study of being in the abstract', and it has long been at the centre of philosophical enquiry. What is being? What is existence? What kinds of entities may be said to exist? Do facts, for example, exist as well as things? Are there negative facts (e.g. the print on this page is not red) as well as positive ones (e.g. this print is black)? Again, do universals (such as redness) exist as well as particulars (such as red objects)? And is it correct to say that all existence is really physical?

These are large topics, extending beyond the scope of this essay and the philosophy of the arts. Nevertheless, as we shall see, some of them are connected with the arts, and the arts give rise to peculiar problems of ontology. These are connected with important questions about the appreciation and value of works of art: questions about the uniqueness of a work, the authenticity of a performance, and so on.

Are works of art physical objects? This would be the view of materialists, who hold that all existence is physical or material. Are they particulars? This would be the view of thinkers such as John Locke, who, in the seventeenth century, declared that 'all things that exist are only particulars', and that '*general* and *universal* belong not to the real existence of things' (*An Essay Concerning Human Understanding*, III,3,6 and 11).

Like so much of Locke's writing, this may seem no more than common sense; for it seems hard to conceive how and where universals could have their existence, as distinct from the existence of particulars. Nevertheless the existence of universals was accepted in ancient Greek philosophy and to a large extent throughout the Middle Ages; and it was reaffirmed in the twentieth century by Bertrand Russell.

The existence of universals has been debated through the ages, but here we need only consider whether, if universals exist, works of art should be counted among them, or regarded as particulars. The view that they should be regarded as particular physical objects may seem straightforwardly correct if we have certain kinds of art in mind. A statue, for example, is obviously a particular, physical thing. Yet even this example may give rise to problems. In the Tate Gallery in London there is a sculpture by Rodin, called *The Kiss*. But this, we are told in the catalogue, is only one version of the work. For Rodin 'used a studio system for the production of his marbles. They were carved by professional marble sculptors under his supervision with finishing touches by the master.' Now if we spoke of Rodin's *The Kiss*, would we be referring to one physical object (the one before us, perhaps), or to all the versions that were made? Which is the work of art in this case? In what sense does such a work of art exist?

Thus problems of ontology may arise even in the case of sculpture, where we seem to be dealing with objects that are both particular and physical in a straightforward way. Such problems are all the more evident, however, when we turn to such arts as music and literature. When we listen to a work of music, what we hear and enjoy is a particular performance. But can we identify the work with a performance? When we read a literary work, say a novel, we read a particular volume. But can we identify the work with a particular volume? Such views would have absurd consequences, as Richard Wollheim has pointed out.

> It would follow that if I lost my copy of *Ulysses*, *Ulysses* would become a lost work. Again, it would follow that if the critics disliked tonight's performance of *Rosenkavalier*, then they dislike *Rosenkavalier*.
>
> (Wollheim, p.5)

One might reply that what is wrong here is that the wrong objects have been mentioned. The objects that matter, it might be said, are not the copy on my table or tonight's performance, but the manuscripts originally produced by the authors; these are the objects that the works of art really consist in. But this would still leave us with problems. 'The critic, for instance, who admires *Ulysses* does not necessarily admire the manuscript' (*ibid*. 6–7); and again, 'it would be possible for the manuscript to be lost and *Ulysses* to survive' (*ibid*. 7). This has indeed happened with very many works of literature.

1 Are works of art in the mind?

If these works are not to be identified with a physical entity, are they mental entities? This view has been maintained by Benedetto Croce (1866–1952) and R.G. Collingwood (1889–1943).[1] It is perhaps most plausible when considered from the point of view of creation. 'When a man makes up a tune…', wrote Collingwood, 'The actual making of the tune is something that goes on in his head, and nowhere else.' (Collingwood, 1938, p.134).

He compared the creation of a work of art with that of a bridge. In this case too the real 'creation' was the plan in the engineer's mind, and this must not be confused with the *plans*, 'that is, the pieces of paper with these notes and sketches on them'. These, said Collingwood, 'only serve to tell people (including [the engineer], for memory is fallible) what the plan is' (*ibid.* p.132). In the case of the bridge, however, 'there is a further stage. The plan may be "executed" or carried out; that is to say, the bridge may be built' (*ibid.*); and then the bridge itself would be that physical object and not an imaginary thing, the plan in the engineer's head (nor, of course, the pieces of paper containing the notes and sketches). But the case of art is different. In this case too a 'plan may be executed' (e.g. a musical composition may be performed in accordance with the score), but the status of this performance would not correspond to that of the bridge.

> The noises made by the performers, and heard by the audience, are not the music at all; they are only the means by which the audience, if they listen intelligently… can reconstruct for themselves the imaginary tune that existed in the composer's head.
>
> (*Ibid.* p.139)

The bridge itself is that particular physical object, built in accordance with the plans (and the plan). But the work of art itself is not a particular performance; it exists, or existed, 'in the composer's head'.

In speaking thus of 'the composer's head' Collingwood seems to imply that the question is one of existence in one place as opposed to another, rather as one might wonder whether an object is on the table or in the cupboard, whether a performance took place in a concert hall or in the open air, etc. But 'the composer's head' cannot be meant in a straightforward spatial sense; it is not as if, were we to open the composer's head, we would find the tune existing there. The sense of 'in the head' that is meant here is sometimes conveyed by the expression 'in the mind', which does not have the spatial, physical connotations of 'in the head'; and Collingwood's position could be expressed in terms of 'the mind' rather 'the head'. Therefore I shall, in what follows, sometimes use 'mind' rather than 'head' in discussing this and similar views.

Collingwood's claims about the existence of a work of art were expressed mainly in terms of music, though he went on to defend the same position with regard to other arts. 'The painted picture', he wrote, 'is not the work of art in the proper sense of that phrase', the latter being 'something existing solely in the artist's head' (*ibid.* p.305). But how plausible is Collingwood's position in the case of music? It is clearly possible for someone to compose a piece of music 'in his head' without ever committing it to paper or making it public in any sense (the same is true of a poem). This is especially so if the piece is fairly brief and simple; indeed, most of us could probably do this without difficulty (leaving aside any question of quality). Again, there is the spectacular case of Mozart, who was apparently able to compose extensive and complex works entirely in his head, writing them down afterwards in a mechanical fashion, rather like the print-out of a computer. He spoke of these mental compositions as 'finished', and was sometimes engaged in another composition while carrying on with the notation of the 'finished' work.

We may agree that in these cases the work existed, prior to the notation, 'solely in the artist's head'. But is this still so after the notation? And are all cases of composition like those just described, that is, having an initial mental existence? In dealing with the second question we must notice the kind of composing that is done, say, at the piano and not in the head. In this case the composer may try out various combinations of melody and harmony on the instrument *without* any prior mental composition. (Similarly, a painter may try out combinations of colour and brushwork on the canvas without a prior mental composition.) Here the work comes into being, bit by bit, in the course of an overt activity, and cannot be said to have a prior existence in the mind. Nor does it have to exist in the mind afterwards, for the artist may proceed from one overt act to another, progressively writing down preferences in a manuscript, playing them over from time to time, and so on.

We must also consider the kind of music that is performed impromptu or by way of improvization. In these cases the music comes into being in the act of performance, and has no separate existence either in the mind or on paper. A defender of the mental theory would have to claim either that this is inconceivable or that what is produced is not art.

However, let us consider a work that *has* existed first in the composer's mind. Does it continue to exist there, and only there, even after it has been written down or performed? The mental ontology was rejected by Roman Ingarden. 'The musical work', he wrote, 'does not form any part of mental existence, and, in particular, no part of the conscious experiences of its creator; after all, it continues to exist even when the composer is dead' (Ingarden, 1986, p.2). Now there are cases in which a work would *not* exist after the composer is dead. If he composed it only in his head and never wrote it down or performed it, then the work would die with the composer. But this is not so with works that *have* been written down or recorded in some way. It would be indeed be absurd to deny the existence of all the great works of past ages, on the ground that their composers are dead. (We describe such composers as 'immortal', because their works live on, but this does not mean that they live on in the minds of those composers.)

Another 'mental' view, rejected by Ingarden for similar reasons, was that the work exists in the minds of the listeners. The work, he pointed out, 'continues to exist after these experiences have ceased' (*ibid*.). He also rejected the idea that a work exists in the form of particular performances. If this were so, then 'there would be no way of distinguishing the performance of a musical work from the work itself' (*ibid*. p.5). Yet this is something we often do, for example in judging that one performance of a work 'was faithful while the other departed from the original in many ways' (*ibid*. p.6).

Having rejected the identification of the work with any particular mental or physical entity, Ingarden posed the question; 'how can a thing exist if it is not mental (pertaining to consciousness) or physical and can exist even when no one takes any conscious interest in it?' (*ibid*. pp. 2–3). It might be thought that if a thing exists neither as a mental nor as a physical entity, then it must indeed be non-existent.

It seems clear that a work of art may exist without having any physical existence. To take an example from literature, if all the copies of Milton's sonnet 'To the Nightingale' were lost or destroyed, it would not follow that the poem was lost. (Indeed, it might not have been written down in the first place, as is the case with the poetry of pre-literate societies.) Nor would the existence of the poem depend on its being recited at the time of existence. (It would not go in and out of existence depending on whether someone, somewhere, was reciting it.) In such a case the poem must exist at least in people's memories; it must be the case that someone *can* recite or perform the work if the occasion arises. A work which existed neither in any physical form nor in anyone's memory would indeed be non-existent. (This is so with the many 'lost works' of antiquity, for example.) But does a work that someone can recite from memory exist in that person's mind? Not if this means that the person must be conscious of it or 'takes a conscious interest in it'. In that sense the work may be far from the person's mind. All that is required is an ability; the ability to recite or perform the work when the occasion arises.

In that case, would the work be identified with that ability? Would the memory be what the work consists in? No, for if we say that the work exists in someone's memory, this would not mean that the work and the memory are one and the same. As with other memories, what is remembered must be something distinct from the memory. To say that someone remembers a song, for example, is to imply that the song has or had a separate existence from that person's memory of it now.

2 Types and tokens

How then is the work itself to be conceived? When Richard Wollheim considered the matter, he resorted to an ontological idea that had been introduced by Charles Peirce (1839–1914). Works such as the novel *Ulysses* and the opera *Der Rosenkavalier* were to be characterized, he said, as 'types', and the copies or performances of them as 'tokens'. Thus '*Ulysses* and *Der Rosenkavalier* are types, my copy of *Ulysses* and tonight's performance of *Rosenkavalier* are tokens of those types' (Wollheim, 1980, p.75).

The terminology of type and token is widely used by philosophers nowadays, and is recognized as the expression of an important ontological insight. It is important, however, to treat the words 'type' and 'token' as technical terms, setting aside their ordinary meanings and connotations. What is meant by them is best explained by examples. An example given by Wollheim was 'the Red Flag', where this is taken to mean 'not this or that piece of material, kept in a chest or taken out and flown at a masthead, but the flag of revolution, raised for the first time in 1830 and that which many would willingly follow to their death' (*ibid.*). In this case the tokens are 'this or that piece of material': entities which might be kept in a chest, for example. They are 'tokens', in the same sense as 'my copy of *Ulysses*' and 'tonight's performance of *Rosenkavalier*'. The 'type', on the other hand, is what is meant when we speak of 'the Red Flag'. What is meant by this is not any particular piece of material, nor any collection of such pieces. The type, in this sense, has a peculiar ontological status, and cannot be reduced to any collection of pieces or other items. Nevertheless, certain pieces of material stand in a particular logical relation to the type 'the Red Flag', which is expressed by saying that they are tokens of that type. And the same relation obtains, according to Wollheim, in the case of a novel or an opera.

Among other examples of types mentioned by Wollheim are 'the Minuet', 'the Boeing 707' and 'the Penny Black' (*ibid.* p.78). The Minuet is a type whose tokens are particular minuets composed by various composers; tokens of the Boeing 707 are particular aircraft located at airports or in the air; and tokens of the Penny Black are the Penny Black stamps to be found in the albums of collectors and so on. Another interesting example is that of words. The word 'red', for instance, is a type, of which the particular occurrences of the word in sound or print are tokens. And when we speak of the word 'red' it is usually the type that is meant and not any particular occurrence.

The logic of types, and different kinds of types, is far more complicated than I have described so far, and it has given rise to a considerable amount of literature, some of it rather technical. These complications will not be pursued here, but it is worth drawing attention to interrelations of types (or as we might say, types within types), such as exist in the case of the Minuet. The minuets composed by Bach, Mozart and others are tokens of this type, but these compositions are (as we have seen) themselves types when considered in relation to particular performances of them. Similarly, the type *Rosenkavalier* becomes a token when considered in relation to 'the Opera', and so on. Conversely, we find that performances may themselves be regarded as types and not tokens. For example, if we speak of 'Ashkenazy's performance' of Beethoven's opus 109, we may mean, not a particular occurrence, but a type of which particular occurrences are the tokens.[2] And further relations of type and token are to be found when we turn to recordings of performances. Whether something is a type or a token may depend on the point of view from which it is considered.

The description of works of art in terms of type and token enables us to locate these entities in a wider logical framework, one that is to be found in many areas of language. Indeed, the type/token ontology pervades our conception of the world and our language. This ontology may come as a surprise to someone who assumes (following the tradition of Cartesian dualism) that all existence must be either mental or physical, or who accepts Locke's dictum that 'all things that exist are only particulars'. Contrary to these views, a type cannot be regarded as a particular, nor can it be classified within the traditional mental/physical dichotomy.

Locke's assertion, as we saw earlier, was coupled with a denial of the existence of 'universals'. (The type/token ontology had not yet been recognized.) Now in my discussion I have spoken of tokens as particulars (particular performances, etc.). But it is important not to confuse the type/token ontology with that of universals and particulars (such as redness versus particular red things). The difference is brought out by Wollheim by reference to a 'transmission' of properties, which occurs in the case of type and token, but not in the case of universal and particular. In the case of the latter,

> no property that an instance of a certain universal has necessarily, i.e. that it has in virtue of being an instance of that universal, can be transmitted to the universal... [Thus] redness cannot be red or coloured, which its instances are necessarily... In the case of types, on the other hand, all and only those properties that a token of a certain type has necessarily, i.e. that it has in virtue of being a token of that type, will be transmitted to the type... [Thus] the Union Jack is coloured and rectangular, properties which all its tokens have necessarily.

> (Wollheim, 1980, p.77)

It should be noted that the point is about properties that a token has 'necessarily, i.e.... in virtue of being a token of that type'. It would not apply to properties that the tokens merely happen to have, but which are not 'necessary' in that sense. Thus, 'even if all its tokens happened to be made of linen, this would not mean that the Union Jack itself was made of linen' (ibid.).[3]

Similarly, to take an example from the arts, let us take it that a token (a performance) of opus 109 will necessarily have three movements if it is to count as a token of that work; then it will follow that having three movements is a property of the work (the type) itself. But this will not be so with non-necessary properties of the tokens, such as being played with feeling, or in front of an audience.

3 'The work of music and the problem of its identity'

As we have seen, 'being rectangular' and 'having three movements' may be regarded as necessary properties of tokens of the relevant types; but these tokens would also have many other, non-necessary properties, that would not prevent them from being tokens of the relevant types. Thus tokens of the Red Flag might be made of linen or of terylene, but this would not affect their belonging to that type. Similarly, a performance of opus 109 would be a token of that type, regardless of whether it were played by Ashkenazy or Brendel, played in a concert hall, tent or drawing room, etc. And considerable differences of performance are compatible with their all being tokens of the same type. Thus a given work may be played at different speeds, with different dynamics and so on, without calling into question the status of all these performances as tokens of the work in question. (There are limits, of course, and the question whether a given performance, or adaptation, can still count as a token of a particular work may be a matter of dispute.)

These variations were of particular interest to Roman Ingarden, in a book whose title I have used to head this section (Ingarden, 1986). Ingarden did not use the terminology of type and token, but he made a comparable distinction in terms of 'schema' and 'profile'. A musical work, he said, 'is first a schema designated by the score', and the different performances are so many profiles of the schema. This terminology may be more suitable than that of token and type for bringing out certain aspects of music and its performance.[4] The word 'schema' conveys the idea of an *instruction*, to be followed by those who perform the work. And in using the metaphor of a profile, Ingarden draws attention to the variety of performances of a given work, corresponding, perhaps, to the variety of profiles of a particular face. (This is not, of course, the sense of 'profile' in which a face has only two profiles, right and left.)

Ingarden was especially interested in what he called 'the problem of identity' of a work of music. Given 'the possibility of its realization many ways' (*ibid.* p.150), which, if any, would represent the true identity of the work? Which, if any, would be 'the most faithful' realization of it? The schema, he pointed out, does not fully determine how the work is to be performed. Musical notation

> fixes certain sounds, their duration and co-presence or sequence, their approximately determined absolute and relative pitch, their intensity and their colouring. Sometimes we find in the score such instructions as *legato* or *staccato* or a slur sign to indicate that a number of notes are to be played as a unit. Finally, we often find in the score such verbal instructions as 'gaily', 'seriously', 'with feeling' and so on...
>
> (*Ibid.* pp. 138–9)

In some respects the notation determines the performance absolutely ('fixes certain sounds'), and leaves no room for interpretation. The performer must not, for example, play a sequence of notes which contravenes that given in the notation. But in other respects (*legato*, 'gaily', etc.) there is clearly room for interpretation; and indeed these directions may be altogether lacking from the composer's notation, leaving it to the performers (or perhaps to an editor) to use their judgement.

Thus there is a discrepancy between schema and performance. The schema is necessarily indeterminate; it cannot fully determine how the work is to sound. But there can be no such indeterminacy in a performance. The schema leaves open various possibilities; in the performance these are closed. In the schema we have 'a variety of imprecisions and blurrings... which in specific performances are necessarily removed and replaced with sharp, univocal determinations', which depend on 'the talent and artistic sensibility of the performer' (*ibid.* p.139). We are, in a sense, cut off from the composer's creation, the musical work; for 'it is impossible to perform the schema on its own'. We cannot 'hear the work in this schematic shape, and we cannot even imagine it in this way' (*ibid.* p.141).

It may be thought that this discrepancy could be remedied by making the schema more determinate. In certain phases of musical history schemas have indeed tended to become more determinate, with more, and increasingly precise, directions being given. The invention of the metronome enabled Beethoven, for example, to give a more precise indication of tempo than had been possible before. But to what extent must such instructions be obeyed? There are obviously limits to what is a tolerable interpretation. The composer Stravinsky spoke of 'the notorious liberty, especially widespread today, which prevents the public from obtaining a correct idea of the author's intention' (Stravinsky, 1975, p.101). He referred to Beethoven's Eighth Symphony, 'which bears the composer's own precise metronomic directions'. But, he protested,

> are they heeded? There are as many different renderings as there are conductors! 'Have you heard *my* Fifth, *my* Eighth' – that is a phrase that has become quite usual in the mouths of these gentlemen, and their mentality could not be better exemplified.
>
> (*Ibid.* p.151)

Perhaps some of these conductors are to be criticized for departing too much from the composer's instructions; but we would hardly expect them to obey those instructions absolutely. If they are not obeyed, or not obeyed entirely, is the performance no longer a performance of that work? This would depend on the degree of the divergence, but few would insist on absolute fidelity to the score as a condition of the performance being a performance of the work in question.

Again, even if a metronome indication is obeyed, this still leaves room for a variety of interpretations. For such indications are not to be followed mechanically, giving exactly equal values to each unit. The more subtle variations of tempo could still take place within the overall prescription, and they may make all the difference, aesthetically, between one performance and another.

It would be impossible to make the schema completely determinate without destroying its character as a schema. Such completeness would require nothing less than a full realization in sound, which would have to be recorded on disc or tape. But if this were done, it would no longer be a schema, for the idea of a schema is correlative with those of interpretation and performance. And in the supposed case there would only be the mechanical repetition of a single performance. The ontology of such music would be different from that of Western classical music of the kind discussed so far. Examples of it are to be found in modern popular music, some of which exists only in the form of a recording.

But what if, in addition to a schema, there existed a performance of the work by the composer on disc or tape? Stravinsky, concerned about future performances of his works, went to some trouble to provide such recordings as guidance for future performances. He describes how he became interested in the Pleyel 'mechanical piano' (pianola) for this purpose, and later, following the development of the gramophone, signed a contract with a major gramophone company, whereby he was to 'record [his] work both as a pianist and conductor, year by year' (*ibid.* pp. 101, 150).

> Here, far better than with the piano rolls, I was able to express all my intentions with real exactitude. Consequently these records... have the importance of documents which can serve as guides to all executants of my music.
>
> (*Ibid.* p.150)

'Unfortunately', he complained, 'very few conductors avail themselves of them'. 'Is it not amazing', he continued,

> that in our times, when a sure means which is accessible to all has been found of learning exactly how the author demands his work to be executed, there should still be those who will not take any notice of such means, but persist in inserting concoctions of their own vintage?
>
> (*Ibid.*)

But how much weight should be placed on composers' performances of their own work? If, wrote Ingarden,

> we were able to hear Chopin himself play, we would have no guarantee that he performed his own works well or that he interpreted them in the

only possible manner, even assuming that, technically speaking, he was equal to the task.

(Ingarden, 1986, p.145)

Again, we cannot assume that Chopin played his compositions only once; 'in fact, he must have played them many times, not in the same way in every instance and not in every instance in the best way' (*ibid.* p.148).

Stravinsky's renderings of Stravinsky obviously have a special authority, but are they beyond criticism? Some critics have regarded them as perverse. Again, many people who hear recordings of T.S. Eliot reading his own works are dissatisfied with the performance, and consider that they would be better read by somebody else.

It might be thought that the true identity of a work can be captured by means of an 'ideal' performance, such as would be 'the most perfect musical product that we can possibly imagine arising out of the schema' (*ibid.* p.142). But, as Ingarden pointed out, such a product could never be identified. For one thing, there are different styles of playing at different periods, so that what would be perceived as an excellent performance at one time might not be so perceived at another. But even if we confine ourselves to one period (say the present), we cannot maintain that of several possible interpretations of a work, one must be 'the most perfect', for it may be that several of them are recognized to be excellent, each in its own way.

Another problem is that of determining a composer's intentions. Stravinsky thought he could 'express all [his] intentions with real exactitude' by means of his recordings. But how far can such intentions reach? Could the intentions of a past composer, such as Chopin, reach out to the sound of his music today? 'Chopin', wrote Ingarden,

> could not have foreseen how his works performed on today's instruments would sound. He naturally 'heard' them within those qualities of sound colouring [which were] possible in the prevailing state of piano manufacture.

(*Ibid.* p.140)

Perhaps, had he been able to hear the instruments of today, he would have preferred their sounds to those available in his time, in terms of which he conceived and created his music. Suppose, then, that Chopin could be brought back from the dead and given an opportunity to hear the pianos of today; would this enable him to decide the matter? No; to do that he would need to hear their sound as we do, hearing it as the sound that is *normal* for piano music.

In any case, we cannot assume that composers have fully determinate conceptions of their works, even with regard to performances in their own time. This is especially so in the case of highly complex works.

> [E]ven the composer himself does not know the profile in all its qualifications; at best he imagines it more or less precisely and at times he may merely be guessing at it. With regard to symphonic works it is probably always... difficult to imagine the complex profile of an orchestral work in all its detail and full tonal colouring.
>
> (*Ibid.* p.149)

Not infrequently it happens that the creator of a work, be it music or drama, is surprised and delighted by what can be done with it – the realizations of which it is capable – in the hands of a gifted performer or director. There are also cases in which composers or writers will alter their scripts in the light of such experience. They may do so on grounds of aesthetic quality (this version is more beautiful, more dramatic, etc.), but they may also feel that the new version is a better expression of what they 'wanted to say' than what they had themselves written; rather as another person may help me to find the right words for what I want to say in the course of a conversation.

Thus, in one way and another, the work reaches out beyond its creator's knowledge and competence. 'His creation extends beyond his artistic intentions...' (*ibid.* p.150). Ingarden's 'problem of identity' cannot be solved by any of the approaches we have considered (following his discussion). If we ask which is the true work, which realization comes closest to the work itself, there is no straightforward answer.

4 Recreating the past

Problems about the ontology of art are not problems only for philosophers. They are connected with practical questions about how the works concerned should be performed. Nowadays there is a vigorous debate about whether performances should be 'authentic' – faithful to what the composer or writer wrote down or intended. We have already seen some of the difficulties of applying this principle, and others will be discussed in this section. But it may be asked, first of all, why authenticity should be regarded as desirable. Is it so on aesthetic grounds? Is it a matter of morality?

It may be a matter of morality if the case is one of deception. If the audience is led to believe that they are hearing what Bach or Shakespeare wrote, when in fact the score or text has been substantially altered by a performer or producer, then this may be a case of deception which deserves moral censure. But what if the audience is aware of the alteration? What if they don't care very much whether the performance is in accordance with the text or not? It may still be felt that to tamper with the original work would be an injustice to its creator and therefore wrong. This is especially so if the result is, or is thought to be, inferior to the original. In such a case we may say that the performance is unfair to the creator, that it is doing an injustice. (The same may be said of an inferior performance as distinct from an altered version.) But what if the performance is not judged to be inferior to the original? Perhaps the creator would resent it nevertheless. But would this matter if the creator were long dead – or for that matter, recently dead?

These are difficult questions, which I shall not pursue. What is clear is that opinions about them may well differ, and that present views about authenticity are only of recent origin. In the nineteenth century, for example, it was regarded as acceptable to 'improve' the works of Shakespeare by deleting or altering various passages which were found offensive, but such tampering would hardly be tolerated nowadays. This is not to say that nowadays the works are always performed in their entirety and without any alteration whatever. In the case of an unusually long work, for example, some cuts may be made for practical reasons. But in general we are more cautious than our forebears in making such cuts or other alterations, if this endangers the ideal of authentic performance.

Again, in the case of music, it was not unusual in the past to detach movements from Beethoven's works, for example, and play them in juxtaposition with other works. At the first performance of Beethoven's Violin Concerto, the soloist performed a novelty piece between movements, holding the violin upside down. Nowadays such practices would hardly be tolerated. Even Beethoven himself sometimes detached movements from his works, juxtaposing them with other pieces, so we cannot be sure to what extent such practices were contrary to his wishes.

Can the preference for authenticity be supported on aesthetic grounds? In 1989 it was reported that the original manuscript of Mendelssohn's Violin Concerto had been discovered in a library, and that the version with which music-lovers had been familiar over the years contained unauthorized alterations by an unknown hand. In certain passages there was a considerable difference between the two versions which could easily be heard when they were played one after the other. As often happens in such cases, the person who claimed to have discovered the original manuscript also insisted on the superiority of what the composer himself had written; and if this were so, we would have good aesthetic reasons for reverting to the authentic version. Yet we cannot assume that authenticity and superior quality will always coincide. And if an altered version is judged by qualified people to be superior, then it may not be easy to decide which version ought to be performed in the future. Those who say that it should be the improved version may claim to have 'aesthetics' on their side, arguing that works of art should be valued for their aesthetic qualities and not for 'extraneous' facts concerning authorship, etc. (This issue is discussed in section 6 below.)

Let us assume, however, that authenticity is a desirable ideal. To what extent can it be attained? One requirement, obviously, is to refrain from altering or 'improving' authors' manuscripts without their permission (though a certain amount of editorial emendation may be acceptable where the author is thought to have made a slip). Another aim, in the case of music, would be to try to recover the sounds that a composer might have had in mind. As we saw in section 3, with the example of Chopin, this would depend on the instruments that were available, or commonly used, at that time. And what is often meant by 'authentic performance' nowadays is the use of instruments – 'period instruments' – which are the same, or as similar as possible, to those in use at the time of the composition. A prominent example is the reintroduction of the harpsichord, by such pioneers as Wanda Landowska, for playing music that was written before the invention, or widespread use, of the piano. For a long time it was considered that the earlier keyboard instruments had been superseded by the piano, and to play old music on the new instrument was considered entirely proper and normal. But nowadays many people prefer to hear Bach's harpsichord music played on that instrument. This may be for purely aesthetic reasons – because they prefer the sound; but it may also be for reasons of authenticity – because they want to hear something as close as possible to the original work.

But is authentic performance a coherent ideal? Some of its difficulties have been discussed in an article by James O. Young.[5] He first draws attention to difficulties that may arise through lack of knowledge, as in the case of Mozart's clarinet concerto.

> As is well known, the piece was written for Anton Stadler. What is less well known is that he did not play a clarinet at all but a basset clarinet. Precisely what sort of instrument Stadler would have played is unknown and, in all probability, will remain unknown. Moreover, the original manuscript of Mozart's concerto does not survive.
>
> (Young, 1988, p.229)

According to Young, the earliest existing score of the work is that of a printed edition, published ten years after the composer's death, in which 'the basset clarinet part is rewritten so as to be playable on a clarinet' (*ibid.*). No doubt such examples could, if we go back to still earlier times, be multiplied indefinitely.

However, the problem is not merely one of ignorance, as can be seen if we try to formulate the ideal of authenticity. It may be thought that a performance will be authentic if it 'reproduces music as it was heard at the time of its composition' (*ibid.*). But, as Young points out, this might lead to results which no one, not even an advocate of authentic performance, would desire, for 'music must often have sounded perfectly atrocious at the time of its composition' (*ibid.* p.230). It is known that, in some cases at least, the instruments used were in bad repair, the performers less competent than what we take for granted today, and so on.

> Handel's Chandos Anthems were first played by the Duke of Chandos' domestic staff. One of the players was recommended because 'He shaves very well & hath an excellent hand on the violin & all necessary languages'. [But] however good his hand may have been on the violin, it is unlikely that he played as well as a modern professional.
>
> (*Ibid.* pp. 230–1)

The professional standards that we take for granted today have developed in fairly recent times, and there is reason to think that, on the whole, past performances were inferior and indeed faulty. But it would be perverse to advocate authentic performance, if this meant (or included) a return to lower standards.

To avoid the difficulty we might appeal to the composer's intention, declaring a performance to be authentic if it 'sounds the way its composer intended it to sound' (*ibid.* p.231). But, as I pointed out on page 86 above, we cannot assume that the composer of a work will be the best judge of performances of it. According to Young, 'many musicians, including those interested in authentic performance, disregard Frescobaldi's instructions simply because they believe that following them does not result in very successful interpretations' (*ibid.* p.232). Moreover, as pointed out before, we cannot be sure that a composer (such as Chopin) would have preferred the 'authentic' sound – that produced on original instruments – to that of a modern piano, for example. In this case we could hardly say that the modern sound was what the composer *intended*, and yet there might be grounds for thinking that it is what the composer would have preferred, had it been available at the time.

A third formula, considered by Young to avoid these difficulties, is that a performance is authentic if it 'makes a piece sound as it would have sounded at the time of its composition, had conditions been ideal' (*ibid.*). But this still leaves another kind of difficulty. A musical performance, we may say, is an action on the part of the performers, but it can also be regarded as a *transaction* between them and their audience. How a piece of music 'would have sounded', and how it sounds today, is not merely a function of how it is played; it also depends on the audience's receptivity. It is not just a question of how it sounds in the physical sense (of pitch, timbre, etc.), but of how it sounds *to* someone. And how a piece sounds to a given audience will depend on their musical experience and on the cultural world in which they live.

> Mediaeval listeners hearing (under ideal conditions) a composition which contained a third would hear the interval as dissonant. Modern listeners hearing the same mediaeval composition will hear the thirds as consonant.
>
> (*Ibid.* p.233)

Again (to take an example not used by Young), when we read today that in the Fifteenth Century thirds were denounced as 'lascivious' and therefore not fit for religious music, we may be amused or astonished. But we may be sure that behind this apparently ludicrous statement there was a difference of aural perception. The sound may have been the same as that which we hear today, and yet what the listeners heard was not the same as what we hear today.

We do not have to go back to the Middle Ages to make this point about works of the past, for, as Young argues, after we have been exposed to the sounds of twentieth-century music, 'almost nothing sounds dissonant any longer. It is even difficult for us to hear the dissonances of the eighteenth and nineteenth centuries' (*ibid.*). In such cases we may be astonished when we read about the hostile reception which a 'dissonant' work received at its first performance.

It would, no doubt, be an exaggeration to say that we cannot hear the dissonances of eighteenth and nineteenth-century music at all, for, however accustomed to dissonance we may have become in hearing later works, we may still recognize or experience a dissonance, or a 'surprising' change of key, occurring in the context of an older work. It is indeed one of the qualities of great works of art that they can continue to shock or surprise us even after we have experienced them many times, and after having been exposed to more extreme surprises in more recent works. The point remains, however, that our experience of the older dissonances and other features of a work must be affected, at least, by our wider experience; and this prevents us from experiencing the work in the same way as a contemporary audience.

Our experience of art is also affected by the wider cultural and historical context, as Young points out. Audiences in the eighteenth century 'would have heard many passages for oboe and flute in Bach or Handel' as recalling 'the rustic bagpipe and shepherd flute', given that these instruments, and the activities associated with them, were familiar at the time; but we cannot hear the music in that way today (*ibid.*). Similarly, certain operas by the seventeenth-century composer Lully may be experienced by us as 'affected and sycophantic', but, given the assumptions and moral attitudes of their world, 'the courtiers at Versailles heard them quite differently' (*ibid.*).

A more recent example (not used by Young) is that of Gilbert and Sullivan. Their operettas are full of topical jokes and allusions whose meaning would have been obvious to most members of their audience. But for us many of them are obscure or pointless. It may be thought that this difficulty can be overcome if we take the trouble to learn about the relevant facts and personalities. (In this way the example differs from that of dissonance in music.) But if we take this trouble, the jokes may still seem quaint or stilted, because for us the context is no longer a living one. Thus what was at the time pungent and actual is now meaningless or lifeless. Again, after exposure to the humour of our own time, our 'ear' for humour is different from that of our forebears. (In this respect the example is similar to that of dissonance in music.)

What can be done in such cases about authentic performance? It can be argued that what is needed to recreate the original work is not repetition of the same words (and music), but the introduction of topical, present-day material which will recapture the spirit – as opposed to the letter – of the original. (This would be analogous to playing the works of Chopin on a modern piano rather than on one resembling the instruments of his time, claiming that this is more faithful to the spirit of the music.) Thus an allusion to a political scandal of that time might be replaced by what is judged to be its modern counterpart, and so on. Such alterations have indeed been made in productions of Gilbert and Sullivan since the expiry of the original copyright, under which they were forbidden. It is true that they have not usually been defended in the name of authenticity, but someone who appeals to the spirit as opposed to the actual text of the work might do so in the name of authenticity. However, this approach would open the door to all kinds of alterations, depending on the judgement and taste of those in charge. The identity of the work might be thrown further into doubt, and the underlying idea of authenticity diluted beyond recognition. (There is a difference between this example and that of the modern piano, for in the case of the latter we may assume that the same notes, at least, are being played.)

Similar difficulties arise if we turn, say, to the works of Shakespeare. We may consult a glossary to translate some of Shakespeare's vocabulary into modern English, but this will not convey the authentic 'flavour' of the words: the resonance and associations that they would have had for a contemporary audience. Thus, if, to quote Anne Sheppard, we are bored by the 'punning and verbal sparring' that takes place in some of the plays, we can try to 'put ourselves in the position of the original audience', finding out 'all sorts of things about them – not only what they liked in literature, music and art, but their social background, their ways of thinking, their attitudes to religion, sex and politics...' (Sheppard, 1988, p.96). Such efforts may help us to understand the plays better; understanding not merely what the words mean, but also why they were written in the ways they were. But this will still fall short of *experiencing* the works as a contemporary audience would have done. Thus, having found out all the relevant information about an exchange of 'punning and verbal sparring', we may find it just as tedious as before. As twentieth-century people, shaped by the experiences, beliefs and tastes of our time, we cannot interact with the works of Shakespeare in the same way as the audiences for whom they were written.

These differences must affect the ways in which the plays are performed, and we may be sure that today's productions differ significantly from those of Shakespeare's time. This is not just because of the general point that a given 'schema' always leaves room for a variety of realizations, but because of the differences in audience receptivity. Even if there had been (contrary to Ingarden's arguments) a single, absolutely correct realization at the time (perhaps one of those sanctioned by the dramatist himself), this would not be accessible for an audience of today. Given the difference of receptivity, they could not be affected by the performance in the same way as audiences of the time.

How does this affect the ontological status of a Shakespeare play? The ontology of a play is less dependent on performance than is the case with music. For it is, after all, possible to treat the play merely as a piece of writing, something we can read for ourselves without any thought of performance. On the other hand, we cannot disregard the aspect of performance. This is an essential part of the work, and in this respect 'the problem of its identity' arises no less than in the case of music. If we ask which is the true *Hamlet* – the work itself – then we are brought back to the problem of authentic performance, as before.

We have now considered purely musical works (such as those of Chopin), works containing words as well as music (opera), and works containing only words (drama). All of these are 'performing' arts, involving the special ontology of schema and performance. But the problem of authentic experience also arises in the case of non-performing arts, such as poetry and the novel. To a modern reader the heroines in Trollope's novels may appear quaint and lacking in character; but presumably this would not have been so for contemporary readers, for whom the novels were written. Their aesthetic experience is one that we may be able to understand, but it is not one that we can easily share. Again, should we read the *Canterbury Tales* in Chaucer's fourteenth-century English or in a modern translation? The original, authentic work is that which was written by Chaucer. But, again, the authentic *experience* is beyond our reach, given that we cannot experience the language of that time as our own, living language. And in some respects the modern translation, if skilfully done, may give us a better feeling of the original than we would get from reading the original text. However, in these cases the problem is one of experience and not ontology. The identity of the work is not in question; the work itself is that which was written by the author and the multiplicity of realizations (performances) does not arise.

I have drawn attention to a number of difficulties about the concept of authentic performance. If these cannot be removed, does it follow that the concept is incoherent, and that the pursuit of authenticity is altogether illusory? No. For while it may be agreed that authenticity is an ideal that cannot be fully realized, it may still be thought preferable, or interesting, to hear a work performed on the instruments of the time. We would indeed be under an illusion if we thought that this would give us just the same experience as that of contemporary listeners; but there remains a sense in which we are hearing the same as they did. If we hear the piece played, say, on a harpsichord rather than a piano, then the physical sounds, at least, are like those, or more like those, heard by contemporary audiences, than the sounds produced by a modern piano would be. And to wish to hear the work performed on the old type of instrument is perfectly reasonable, even if we are under no illusions about the limitations of this kind of authenticity.

5   The Ontology of Painting and Sculpture

So far the discussion has been largely about arts which are multiple in certain ways. In the case of music and drama there is the multiplicity of performances, and in the case of a text, such as the novel *Ulysses*, there is the multiplicity of copies, none of which can be identified as the work itself. (The two kinds of multiplicity were discussed together under the heading of type and token.) But there are other kinds of art where the ontological situation is different, and where a work of art may be identified with a single physical object. Such are the arts of painting, sculpture and architecture. Michelangelo's statue of David is a single physical object, and so is Leonardo's painting, the *Mona Lisa*.

The ontological status of works of art is connected with the kind of value we place on them. Great music and literature are valued no less than great works of graphic or plastic art; but they are not valued in the same way. A sonata is not an object to be carefully locked away or insured against theft or damage, but the value of paintings and sculptures is expressed in these ways. This is because of the uniqueness of their existence, as opposed to the multiple existence of other arts.

But is this an essential feature of the graphic and plastic arts? Consider the difference between paintings and engravings. When Leonardo painted the *Mona Lisa* he created a unique physical object, and this was, and is, the work of art. But what about the engravings which he and others produced of various subjects? In this case too unique physical objects were created: the original plates from which prints were taken. But in this case the work of art exists – or also exists – in the form of those prints. (In one sense, indeed, the latter would be more authentic than the plate, for they would be 'the right way round' as regards left and right, whereas the plate must reverse them.) And a similar multiplicity may exist in the case of sculpture created in the form of a mould. In these cases the ontological situation is akin to that of a text. It is not quite the same, for whereas I can own the novel *Ulysses* in the form of a cheap paperback, I cannot have a Leonardo engraving (print) without paying a lot of money. This is because, whereas a novel can be reprinted *ad infinitum*, there is a limit to the number of prints that can be taken, or were taken, from the engraver's plate. (There are various possibilities. The artist may stipulate the number of prints to be taken, the plate may be destroyed or may have deteriorated, and so on.)

Thus we find, within the category of graphic and plastic arts, works that exist in multiple ways, as well as works that exist in the form of unique objects. But how secure is this status of uniqueness? A painting can easily be copied, and in the case of the *Mona Lisa* innumerable copies have been made and will probably go on being made. In this case, however, we make a clear distinction between the copies and the original. It is the painting itself, the original work executed by the master

95

himself, that we value so highly, and the value of a copy, however well done, is negligible by comparison.

But is this distinction always so clear-cut? What if the master himself had made a copy? Should we still treat the original, the one he did first, as far superior in value? What if the second work, the copy, were of better quality? Again, what if we found out (or, as the case might be, judged) that the second work was not so much a copy of the first as another attempt at the same subject? 'Rubens, Rembrandt and Raphael', writes Crispin Sartwell, 'were among many artists who churned out copies of their own works, of mixed quality, on demand' (Sartwell, 1988). He lists and illustrates no fewer than twenty-one different senses in which a work might be described as spurious.

From these and other examples we see that the distinction between original and non-original is not as straightforward as may have been thought, and this affects the idea of uniqueness as applied to paintings. Nevertheless there are many works in existence (including the *Mona Lisa*) whose uniqueness is unquestioned and unaffected by complications of the kind just considered. In such a case we may know that the artist himself painted the very work that we see before us, and never painted anything else that might be described as a copy. Here the work of art as a unique object is clearly exemplified, and the distinction between this and non-unique forms of art is sharp and clear.

But how permanent is this situation? What if the technique of reproduction were developed to such an extent that we could not tell the difference between an original and a reproduction? There are, for all we know, no limits to what technological progress might achieve in this direction. As P.F. Strawson has pointed out, it is

> a merely contingent fact that we are, for all practical purposes, quite unable to make reproductions of pictures and statues which are completely indistinguishable, by direct sensory inspection, from the originals.
>
> (Strawson, 1974, pp. 183–4)

According to Strawson it is a mistake to distinguish between art that consists of types and tokens, and art consisting of 'particulars' (unique objects). 'All works of art', he claims, 'are equally types and not particulars' (*ibid.* p.184). Were it not for the 'practical limitations' of reproduction, the originals of paintings and works of sculpture, like the original manuscripts of poems, would not as such have any but sentimental value, and, perhaps, some technical-historical interest as well.

We should be able to speak of the same painting being seen by different people in different places at one time, in just the way in which we now speak of the same sonata being heard by different people in different places at one time (*ibid.*).

It may be questioned, however, whether the ontology of paintings and works of sculpture can be assimilated quite so readily to that of music or poetry. We may admit that the reproduction of the former might one day be perfected in the way described by Strawson, but as long as this is not so, we cannot properly say that 'all are equally types'. Moreover, our contemplation and appreciation of such works is bound up with the knowledge that, as things are, they are unique and not multipliable in the manner of types. Standing before the *Mona Lisa*, we are aware that this, and this alone, is the object that was formed by the master's hand. This knowledge, together with the content and aesthetic qualities of the work, makes up the whole experience that we get from such a work. In an age of perfect reproductions such experiences would perhaps no longer exist, and our concept and experience of art would differ accordingly. But that age has not yet arrived.[6]

6 The Problem of Forgeries

As we have seen, the ontology of graphic and plastic arts is complicated, and the conception of such works as consisting of unique particulars must be qualified in view of various possibilities of multiple production and reproduction. Another possibility affecting the uniqueness of works of art is that of imitation. It is possible to produce works in the style of a great painter as opposed to reproductions of them, and this would be another way of undermining their unique status. In this case 'unique' means something rather different from the uniqueness of a physical object. This can best be shown by reference to acknowledged type/token arts, such as music and literature. Beethoven's compositions may be described as unique, but not in the same sense as the *Mona Lisa*. The compositions do not exist in the form of unique physical objects, but they are unique in the sense in which Beethoven's style is unique. And this uniqueness would be undermined by the existence of other compositions in the same style.

This kind of uniqueness also exists in the case of 'particular' works of art, such as paintings. The paintings too, apart from being unique objects in the physical sense, may have unique qualities, corresponding to those of the musical work. So a painting is (or may be) unique in two ways, and its uniqueness may be undermined in two ways: by reproduction, or by paintings done in a similar style. In the case of music only the latter is possible; one might write music in the style of Beethoven, but one cannot make reproductions of his works. (One can, of course, make reproductions of his manuscripts, but these are not to be identified with his works.)

Both kinds of uniqueness, and both kinds of undermining of uniqueness, affect our conception and evaluation of art. If perfect or near-perfect reproductions of paintings became commonplace, this would affect the importance we attach to seeing the original works; and if the practice of producing high-quality works in the style of the great artists became commonplace (whether in painting or in music), this might affect the value we attach to works produced by the masters themselves. Thus, in one way or the other, we might come to think that as much value should be attached to a 'Leonardo' – either a reproduction or a picture in the style of the master – as to a Leonardo, such as the original *Mona Lisa* hanging in the Louvre.

On the whole, we feel uneasy about works done in the style of great artists, and the terms 'imitation' and 'pastiche' are sometimes used in a derogatory sense in this connection. But is this rational? What does it matter, one might ask, whether the work before me is a type or a particular, a unique original or a reproduction, a Leonardo or a 'Leonardo' – if, as I can see, it is a thing of beauty? According to some writers, it matters little. They maintain that such distinctions are irrelevant if we are considering the work of art as such, and from a purely aesthetic point of view.

The issue was brought into focus by the notorious van Meegeren affair in 1947. Han van Meegeren, a Dutch artist who was active in the thirties, became interested in the techniques and materials used by old masters such as the seventeenth-century painter Vermeer. After much study and practice he was able to produce a number of pictures in the style of Vermeer, though of subjects different from those the master himself had painted. He was able to pass off these works as genuine Vermeers, and supplied them to the art market through an ingenious system of middlemen. In due course the paintings made a public appearance, were hailed by leading experts as masterpieces of the great Vermeer, and exhibited as such in public galleries. Van Meegeren became a rich man on the proceeds of his sales, but after some years the fraud was exposed and a trial of the forger took place in 1947.[7]

This exposure of the 'Vermeers' completely changed the attitude of the public towards these works, reducing their value to a fraction of what it had been before. But was this change of attitude justified?

The first thing that may occur to us here is the dishonesty of what the forger did. We have good reason to object if someone becomes rich by fraudulent means. (On the other hand, it appears that van Meegeren's success in making fools of the experts made him a popular figure with the Dutch public of the time.) But why should the dishonest circumstances of the production of the work make a difference to our enjoyment of it? Suppose we found out that Vermeer himself cheated his customers when fulfilling their commissions: would this reduce the value that we place on his works? In this case we might think less of the man, but our admiration of his works would continue unchanged.

Another objection to forgery, especially on the scale of the van Meegeren case, is that it may distort our knowledge of art history. The number of known works by Vermeer is rather small, with certain subjects predominating. The discovery of several additional works, unknown hitherto, might have a considerable effect on our understanding of this artist's work and personality, and the context in which he worked. Some of the pictures produced by van Meegeren, though in the style of Vermeer, were of subjects rather different from those that the master himself had painted. These large-scale, important-looking works must have had a considerable effect on contemporary ideas about Vermeer.

This point, however, is applicable only to some cases and only to a limited extent. We might suppose, contrary to what actually happened, that the forgeries were not of a kind that could make much difference to our understanding of the artist (they might have been works of similar subjects, etc.). Or we might suppose that the forgery was done openly and without any dishonest intention.

Finally, even if a dishonest and misleading act were committed, it would no longer be misleading after the exposure. Why then should we not go on exhibiting the forger's works, clearly labelled 'van Meegeren', and enjoy them for their beauty and other aesthetic qualities? And if these are equal to those of the Vermeer (as appeared to be the case), why should we not value them as highly?

But can we be sure that they are equal to the old master's works? And, going back to the question of reproductions, can we be sure that a reproduction which looks perfect is really so? Strawson envisaged that there might be reproductions 'which are completely indistinguishable, by direct sensory inspection, from the originals'. But is direct sensory inspection good enough? It may be thought that something more scientific is needed; and indeed scientific tests may be conclusive in establishing, say, that a given painting was done within the last twenty years, or that it cannot have been painted by such and such an artist. (In this respect, no doubt, we have advanced beyond the tests available at the time of van Meegeren.)

Such tests, however, would not be relevant to the *aesthetic* qualities of the work, such as its beauty and other aesthetic qualities, of the kind identified by Sibley (see my discussion in Essay Two). In this case it is sensory inspection that is relevant, for it is by means of our senses – by using our eyes – and not by scientific tests, that we find out whether a work is beautiful, well balanced, graceful, etc. And if this is what we are interested in, and is that for which we value the works in question, then sensory inspection is the criterion that should be applied.

Yet this criterion is not as straightforward as it may seem, for, as Nelson Goodman has pointed out, 'we must ask who is assumed to be doing the looking' (Goodman, 1968, pp. 99–123; Margolis, 1987, p.262). It might be that 'at least one person… can see no difference', but clearly this would not be enough to show either that two works are indistinguishable or that they are equally good; for, as Sibley remarked, the perception of aesthetic qualities calls for a certain kind of sensitivity which is more developed in some people than in others.

Suppose then that a sufficient number of suitably qualified people agreed about the merits of a given reproduction. Would not this be a sufficient criterion for settling the matter? According to Goodman, no such consensus could ever settle the matter. There may be a case in which 'nobody, not even the most skilled expert can ever tell the pictures apart by merely looking at them', but this would still not suffice to settle the matter. For 'no one can ever ascertain by merely looking at the pictures that no one ever has been or will be able to tell them apart by merely looking at them' ((Margolis, 1987, p.262). Hence we can never be sure that they are indistinguishable.

It might be objected that this requirement, stretching indefinitely into the future (and the past), is excessive and indeed far-fetched. Is it not enough, for present purposes, if a sufficient number of qualified people cannot tell the pictures apart? In that case, would we not set aside speculations about differences that might be perceived, one day, by experts of the future? But according to Goodman this would be a mistake. For my knowledge that the picture on the left is an original and that on the right a copy is 'evidence that there may be a difference between them that I can learn to perceive' ((*ibid*. p.264) even though I cannot perceive it now. And this evidence, according to Goodman, must make 'an aesthetic difference between them for me now'.

It might be thought that if the difference between the original and the copy is not easily perceptible to a reasonably competent viewer of art, then it cannot make much difference to one's aesthetic enjoyment. But, as Goodman points out, in the area of aesthetics 'minute perceptual differences can bear enormous weight'.

> Extremely subtle changes can alter the whole design, feeling, or expression of a painting. Indeed, the slightest perceptual differences sometimes matter the most aesthetically; gross physical damage to a fresco may be less consequential than a slight but smug retouching.
>
> (*Ibid.* p.266)

The experience of 'learning to perceive', perhaps under the guidance of a teacher, is one with which most viewers of art are familiar. And I may have reason, in a given case, to believe that there are qualities that I might learn to perceive even though I cannot perceive them now. There is, one might say, more to the visual qualities of a painting than meets the eye.

So far the argument has been about reproductions or copies. But the same kind of argument is applicable to imitations, such as those by van Meegeren. If, as far as I can tell, the paintings by van Meegeren are as good as those by Vermeer, and even if I am joined in this opinion by 'the most skilled expert', I ought not to conclude that they really are as good, or even nearly as good, as those of the old master. The fact that a painting was done by an artist whose works have 'stood the test of time', makes it reasonable for me to believe that it is worth special attention, and this is not true of the imitation. There is reason to think that I may learn to see special merits in the former, even if I cannot see them now; and, conversely, there is reason to think that the work done by the imitator will, in the course of time, reveal shortcomings which may be invisible to me now. This seems to have been so in the case of van Meegeren, for few people nowadays would claim that the aesthetic merits of his works are comparable with those of great painters such as Vermeer.

But do these considerations dispose of the problem? Do they fully explain, and justify, our preference for original works? The fact that a work was painted by a great artist is a good reason for believing that it will turn out be superior to any imitation or reproduction, even if we cannot see this now. But may we not also have good evidence for believing that an imitation or reproduction is of high merit, comparable, perhaps, to that of an original?

When van Meegeren was brought to trial, the spuriousness of most of the 'Vermeers' had been established. But one or two of them, notably one entitled *The Supper at Emmaus*, were (or were thought to be) so good that the defendant found himself in the position of *claiming*, rather than confessing, that this was indeed his work. So great was the disbelief of the court that *The Supper* was, so to speak, a *genuine* forgery, that the forger asked for permission to prove his skill by turning out another 'Vermeer' under the court's supervision; and this request was granted. The work produced by van Meegeren under these conditions was inferior to his best, but still good enough to convince the court of his ability as a forger. Nevertheless some of the leading experts of the time continued to believe in the authenticity of *The Supper* (as a work by Vermeer), and to extol the outstanding merits of this work. The distinguished expert J. Decoen described his 'moment of greatest anguish' when he feared that, in accordance with an ancient Dutch law, the court was about to order the destruction of this work, along with others whose spuriousness was not disputed. Insisting on the preservation of this and another work, Decoen believed that he had thereby 'rescued two capital works of the Dutch school of the seventeenth century' (quoted in Dutton, 1983, p.61). Subsequent laboratory tests showed that Decoen was wrong and that these pictures were no more authentic than the others.

These facts were recounted by Alfred Lessing in support of his argument that the value which we place on authenticity 'leads to absurd or improbable conclusions' (in Dutton, p.59). 'What does it matter', asked Lessing, 'that Decoen is wrong?'

> What, after all, makes these paintings 'capital works'? Surely it is their purely aesthetic qualities... [Why then] should Decoen not be justified in his actions, since he has preserved a painting which is aesthetically important for the only reason that a painting can be aesthetically important – namely, its beauty?
>
> (*Ibid.* pp. 61–2)

'The plain fact', he concluded, 'is that aesthetically it makes no difference whether a work is authentic or a forgery', and the experts, 'instead of being embarrassed at having praised a forgery', should 'take pride in having praised a work of beauty' (*ibid.* p.62).

Now we have already seen that, to establish that something is a 'capital work', the verdict of contemporary experts, even if unanimous, is not enough. For we cannot be sure that this verdict will not be reversed in the future, and this is especially so in the case of an imitation. Nevertheless the praise of contemporary experts, together with our own perception perhaps, must give us *some* reason to believe that a given work is really of high merit. This, after all, is all we have to go on in the case of contemporary artists who are *not* forgers or imitators, but whose work has not yet had a chance to stand the test of time. It would be absurd to withhold our admiration and valuation of these merely on the ground that our judgements may be reversed at a later time.

In the case of van Meegeren, as it happens, judgements were reversed quite soon, and nowadays his works are not rated very highly in terms of 'purely aesthetic qualities'. (This is also true of those which he painted under his own name.) But this need not have been so, for we can imagine a forger or imitator whose works stand the test of time over a long period. It may even come about that his works are judged to be better than those of the old masters whose imitations they are. We cannot assume that in every case first is best. Again, we may suppose that such imitations became commonplace and that many of them were judged, over a long period of time, to be of equal merit, in purely aesthetic terms, to the corresponding original works. In this case we would have good reason to believe that an imitation may really be as good as an original, even if we agree with Goodman's reservations.

Yet our attitude to imitations is not consistent with these remarks. The knowledge, or discovery, that a work is an imitation is usually enough to reduce its value to a fraction of what it would otherwise have been. (This is also the case when it is discovered, say, that a work which was thought to be by Rembrandt was really by one of his followers or associates.) But is this attitude rational?

If we think of the matter from a purely financial point of view, we may be struck first of all by the extraordinarily high prices at which original works by the great artists are bought and sold nowadays. Such prices are fuelled partly by financial speculations, national interests and other extraneous factors, and they may well be regarded as irrational or even absurd. But whatever may be said to this effect, the prices are, to some extent at least, reflections of the 'real' value of these works – the value that is ascribed to them by ordinary art-lovers who are not engaged in dealing or speculating. But is it, from their point of view, rational to make such a big distinction between the value of an original and that of an imitation?

According to Lessing, as we have seen, it is not. The greatness of a work of art, he argues, must not be confused with the greatness of an artist. Of course van Meegeren could not become as great an artist as Vermeer merely by painting pictures in the style of the latter, however good they might be in themselves. For the latter was 'not a great artist only because he could paint beautiful pictures', but also because of the originality of his work, 'the fact that he painted pictures in a certain manner at a certain time in the history and development of art' (*ibid.* 73–4). But these historical facts should not be allowed to affect our evaluation of the pictures.

Originality, according to Lessing, is 'but the means to an end', the end being 'the production of aesthetically valuable or beautiful works of art'. The experience of such works, he says, is 'wholly autonomous', and anything not 'perceivable in the work of art itself' is 'wholly irrelevant to the pure aesthetic appreciation...' (*ibid.* 75–6).

Lessing's position invites comparison with a passage written some fifty years earlier by Clive Bell.

> Great art remains stable and unobscure because the feelings that it evokes are independent of time and place, because its kingdom is not of this world... What does it matter whether [such works] were created in Paris the day before yesterday or in Babylon fifty centuries ago?
>
> (Bell, 1914, p.37)

In Essay Two I discussed how Bell and other formalists tried to insulate the purely aesthetic qualities of works of art (which they took to be qualities of form) from 'extrinsic' features such as meaning and connection with human affairs. This, as we saw, was a difficult position to maintain, for it appeared that 'pure form' could not be isolated in the required way from other aspects of a work. But this difficulty would not affect the exclusion of facts about the creation of a work, as advocated by Lessing, and by Bell in the passage just quoted.

But is it right to exclude such qualities as achievement and originality from the domain of aesthetic qualities and aesthetic appreciation? This question arose in connection with the problem of definition, the subject of Essay One. As I said there, some recent innovative works of art, lacking in aesthetic qualities of the intrinsic kind, have been defended on grounds of originality alone. According to Arthur Danto, this is enough to admit them, at least, to the category of art, contrary to those who deny that they are art at all. Such works, he says, may be 'daring', 'impudent' or 'clever' in virtue of their relation to the artistic context of the time. Hence 'the aesthetic qualities of a work are a function of their own historical identity' (Essay One, p.36). Here we have a conception of aesthetic qualities that is very different from that of Lessing. Not only are qualities of a historically dependent kind to be included as aesthetic qualities, but, according to Danto, they make all the difference in the recognition of certain objects as works of art.

The expression 'aesthetic qualities' may certainly be used to cover qualities of the historical kind as well as those, such as beauty, which are apparent from the mere inspection of a work, independently of any historical knowledge. It has been claimed, however, that the two kinds of qualities are not separable. According to Gregory Currie, 'the aesthetic judgements we make are *essentially* bound up' with knowledge about the artist's achievement (Currie, 1989, p.41). But it is not clear why judgements of beauty and many other aesthetic qualities should not be made without such knowledge – which is indeed what happens if we approach a work without any knowledge of that kind. (We also ascribe aesthetic qualities to natural objects where the question of artistic achievement does not arise.) If subsequently we acquire knowledge about the origin and other circumstances of the work, this may enhance our enjoyment of it, but it would not affect the apparent (intrinsic) qualities of the work. The work would not, for example, become more – or as the case might be, less – beautiful through that knowledge.

Moreover, the apparent qualities are in a sense more fundamental than the others, for, as Lessing put it, originality is 'but the means to an end', the end being 'the production of aesthetically valuable or beautiful works of art' (quoted above, p.103). The point is that a work is of aesthetic value only if it has qualities of the apparent kind. Knowledge that a work was the first of its kind, was produced only after much struggle, etc., cannot by itself give us aesthetic pleasure, if the work lacks intrinsic merit. Such knowledge may *enhance* aesthetic pleasure, but it cannot provide it independently. By contrast, the apparent qualities of a work may be enjoyed independently of the non-apparent ones.

This is not to deny, of course, that achievement and originality are important qualities – whether we call them 'aesthetic' or not. But to what extent can they explain our preference for original or authentic works as opposed to imitations or copies? Is our preference for Vermeer over van Meegeren to be explained by the greater achievement of the former? The achievement of van Meegeren was considerable – one might well describe it as staggering. Must we say that the achievement of Vermeer was greater? This will depend on what qualities we have in mind. In terms of the qualities exhibited by van Meegeren – painstaking study and experiment, skill and ingenuity in developing a particular style and technique – the achievements of Vermeer were probably smaller.

Do we, or should we, value a work of art according to the difficulty of its production? Denis Dutton, commenting on Schubert's setting of one of Goethe's poems, sees it 'as a way of overcoming various problems' posed by the text. 'It is surely more than merely a pretty piece of music sprung from the mind of someone on an autumn afternoon in 1815' (Dutton, 1983, p.177). But what if it *had* sprung from the composer's mind with little effort on his part? Mozart, it appears, found that much of his music came to him with little effort. But this would not be a good reason for valuing it less highly than the music of others. And if, as Coleridge tells us, the poem *Kubla Khan* came to him while he was asleep and only needed to be written down next morning, this would not count against its being a masterpiece.

Perhaps, however, the relevant kind of achievement is that involving innovation rather than difficulty. Creative artists such as Beethoven and James Joyce are celebrated for their innovative boldness, breaking away from established ways of writing and opening up new possibilities of aesthetic enrichment. But is this a reason for valuing their *works* more highly? There have been other great artists, creators of great works of art, who are not noted for breaking new ground. They were content to work within an existing tradition, producing their works in accordance with established rules and practices. Yet this would not prevent them from being masterpieces of the highest order. On the other hand, a highly innovative work may fall short of this quality, perhaps just because of its pioneering character.

Moreover, the importance of innovation is relative to the temporal distance from which we contemplate a work. Its impact on us is greatest if the work has only just appeared, but it diminishes as we go back in time. Sometimes we find it hard to appreciate the innovative character of a work now familiar to us, and we may be surprised when we read about its impact on contemporary audiences. In many cases we do not know, and perhaps do not care very much, whether the work of art that we are enjoying was breaking new ground or not. And finally, we must remember that for most of the history of art, other than Western art in fairly modern times, innovation and originality were neither prized nor attempted, and yet much great art was produced without these qualities.

Now Lessing, as we have seen, regarded it as 'a plain fact' that the authenticity of a work is irrelevant to its aesthetic value. But if the fact is so plain, how is it that so many people fail to see it, and allow their aesthetic appreciation to be affected by such non-apparent qualities as authenticity? This problem was considered by Arthur Koestler, whose views were similar to those of Lessing, but who took a more diagnostic approach. Among his many interesting examples was that of a friend who had been given a drawing by Picasso, which she took to be a reproduction. On learning that it was an original, she transferred it from its place in the staircase to a more honourable position in the drawing-room. But since it was a line-drawing in black ink on white paper, it would have been quite impossible for her to tell the difference. (Here is an example where Goodman's argument is less effective than in the case of paintings.) On being questioned about her reason for the transfer, 'she answered... that of course the thing had not changed, but that she *saw* it differently since she knew it was done by Picasso himself' (Koestler, 1969, p.407.) Koestler then asked her 'what considerations determined her attitude to pictures in general', to which she replied that they were 'considerations of aesthetic quality – composition, colour', etc.

Koestler had no difficulty in showing that this reply was in conflict with her treatment of the Picasso drawing, but, he conceded,

> there is something of her confusion in all of us... We are unable to see a work of art isolated from the context of its origin or its history... In our minds the question of period, authorship and authenticity, *though in itself extraneous to aesthetic value*, is so intimately mixed up with it, that we find it well-nigh impossible to unscramble them.
>
> (*Ibid.* p.408)

Now one might have thought that this diagnosis, if correct, would be sufficient to deal with the problem. On this view it is just a psychological fact that our experience of works of art cannot be detached from what we know about their non-apparent qualities – even if we agree that the latter are, in a sense, 'extraneous'. According to Koestler, however, there was an underlying motive for the 'confusion'. It was, he claimed, due to snobbery. His friend, he said, would not have been a snob if in her reply she had admitted that the original would be indistinguishable from a reproduction, and that she had made the transfer 'for reasons which have nothing to with beauty'; but as it was, she stood convicted of snobbery.

It is true that snobbery may be involved in the acquisition and display of original works of art, as well as other rare and expensive objects. But if Koestler's friend confused aesthetic with other values, it does not follow that she was a snob. Her logic may have been weak, but that is not a moral failing, as snobbery is. Again, the 'confusion' which, as Koestler says, 'is there in all of us', need not be a *logical* confusion. If, as Koestler and Lessing maintain, there is a pure 'aesthetic value' which is logically distinct from questions of period, authorship and so on, it does not follow that this can or ought to be experienced in isolation from what one knows about period, authorship and so on. Perhaps this is what Koestler's friend was getting at in her first reply (before walking into the logical trap he had set for her), when she said that 'she *saw* it differently since she knew it was done by Picasso himself' (*ibid.* p.407). It was not that she could now discern qualities of composition, colour, etc. which would be there in the original but not in a reproduction, but that her perception of these qualities, and her experience of the work as a whole, were affected by her new knowledge.

This point was in effect conceded by Koestler in another passage, in which he asks us to imagine that an old painting in a second-hand dealer's shop were suddenly discovered to bear the signature of some great artist of the past. Such a discovery, he said, 'has nothing to do with beauty, aesthetics' and so on, 'and yet, God help us, the sheep and the mill and brook *do* suddenly look different and more attractive...' (*ibid.* p.408). But in experiencing this change one would not, or not necessarily, be guilty either of snobbery or of logical confusion.

Another aspect of the matter, to which Koestler drew attention, is the value we place on antique or historic objects having no great aesthetic pretensions, such as Galileo's telescope or a shirt worn by Nelson (*ibid.* p.409). In such cases it matters to us whether the object we are contemplating is authentic – the very same object that the great man held or wore – or merely a reproduction. Again, this is not a matter of market value, but of the way we experience the object as we contemplate it in the museum. But this also applies to our contemplation of paintings in a museum of art. Here too our experience is affected by the knowledge that this is the very object that Vermeer or Picasso had before them and on which they worked out their creative ideas. We may also be affected by the sheer antiquity of a work, or by knowledge about its original function, for example, in a religious context. (It is interesting that whereas in Britain 'gallery' is used as distinct from 'museum', corresponding to the distinction between aesthetic and historical or antiquarian interest, in other countries the word 'museum', or its counterpart in other languages, is used throughout.)

As we have seen, our experience of art is affected in certain ways by facts of ontology. In the case of unique arts such as painting our consciousness of the unique identity of a work is an important element in our experience of it, and this is not so in the case of multiple arts, such as music. In this case there may also be a unique object – the manuscript that was written by the composer's hand. But the thrill that we might get from being in the presence of this object is quite separate from our experience of the music, for this requires a performance.

This feature of the aesthetic experience of unique arts remains important as long as the 'perfect' reproduction of paintings is not possible, or is not in fact practised to any large extent. We cannot assume, however, that this will always be so. Perhaps the day will come when such reproductions will be possible and widely practised and when their quality will have stood the test of time to a sufficient extent to overcome the doubts engendered by Goodman's argument. Works such as the *Mona Lisa*, as well as masterpieces of the future, would be hanging in people's houses, and if one went to see the original in the

Louvre it would be only for antiquarian interest. The expression 'Mona Lisa' might come to mean a type and not the original object on which Leonardo laid his hands; and the ontological status of such works would be more like that of works which are intended as types from the beginning – such as engravings or, let us say, cartoons whose tokens appear in newspapers. (There would still be a difference between works of the future, which would have this status from the beginning, and those of the past, which would have it conferred on them, so to speak, retrospectively.)

Similarly, the day may come when the practice of imitation (as distinct from reproduction) becomes widespread and acceptable, with many practitioners, perhaps aided by computers, turning out pictures in the style of Vermeer, Leonardo and others, of such high quality that no one can tell the difference. Perhaps such works will be referred to as 'vermeers' and 'leonardos', and these words will no more call those personages to mind than when we use the word 'watt' without any consciousness of the person James Watt. Such developments (unlike the case of reproduction) are also conceivable in the case of music, so that, for example, the term 'a Beethoven sonata' will come to mean a sonata in the style of Beethoven, and people would not care very much whether it was composed by the master himself or by a modern imitator; and similarly with works of literature. They might indeed be grateful for the enlargement of the relevant class of works – just as one may regret, as things are, that Beethoven wrote only such and such a number of sonatas, that Brahms composed only four symphonies, and that only a small number of plays were written by Chekhov.

The idea of enlarging these classes of works by producing imitations of them, and by undermining the distinction between originals and imitations to a point where it no longer seems of importance, would probably be unacceptable to most people today and may indeed horrify us. Yet in some of the other arts such ideas and practices have been accepted to a considerable extent. Reproduction furniture, made in modern workshops in imitation of old styles, is widely used and appreciated; and while it does not command the same monetary value as genuine antiques, it is not regarded with the same distaste as would be aroused by the 'reproduction' of music or literature, as envisaged above. And in the case of architecture the reproduction of old styles is and has been widely practised. In these cases, however, the reproductions are usually conceived in terms of period (Regency, etc.) rather than in terms of individual artists' names (though there are exceptions).

Whether the arts of music and literature, as practised and

appreciated in our culture, will ever move in this direction, is a matter for speculation. But the mere possibility of this cannot serve to show that our present attitudes to art, and the ontology of art, are irrational or reprehensible. As things stand, the distinction between unique and multiple arts is real enough, and it is natural and proper that the uniqueness of a work should affect our aesthetic experience.

Bibliography

Bell, C. (1915) *Art*, 2nd edn, Chatto and Windus.
Collingwood, R. G. (1938) *The Principles of Art*, Oxford University Press.
Currie, G. (1989) *An Ontology of Art*, Macmillan.
Dutton, D. (ed.) (1983) *The Forger's Art: Forgery and the Philosophy of Art*, University of California Press.
Goodman, N. (1968) *Languages of Art*, Oxford University Press.
Ingarden, R. (1986) *The Work of Music and the Problem of its Identity*, Macmillan.
Koestler, A. (1969) *The Act of Creation*, Pan Books.
Margolis, J. (ed.) (1987) *Philosophy Looks at the Arts*, Temple.
Sartwell, C. (1988) 'Aesthetics of the Spurious', *British Journal of Aesthetics*.
Sharpe, R.A. (1979) 'Type, Token, Interpretation and Performance', *Mind*.
Sheppard, A. (1988) *Aesthetics*, Oxford University Press.
Stravinsky, I. (1975) *An Autobiography*, Calder and Boyars.
Strawson, P.F. (1974) *Freedom and Resentment and Other Essays*, Methuen.
Wollheim, R. (1980) *Art and its Objects*, 2nd edn, Cambridge University Press.
Young, J.O. (1988) 'The Concept of Authentic Performance', *British Journal of Aesthetics*.

Notes

[1] Collingwood's position will be further discussed in Essay Five.

[2] It has been argued that 'a work of music is not a type whose tokens are performances. Rather performances are tokens of an interpretation of that piece of music...' (See Sharpe, 1979.)

[3] An exception to this criterion of 'transmission' seems to be the property of *being located in space*. This is essential to being a token of the Red Flag, but it cannot be ascribed to the type.

[4] The difference is not merely one of terminology. Ingarden was interested in certain problems about music and did not explore the same ontological issues as those who have written about types and tokens.

[5] Young, 1988. For criticism of Young, see R.A. Sharpe, 'Authenticity Again', *British Journal of Aesthetics* [forthcoming].

[6] A more recent advocate of the view that 'all works of art are equally types' is Gregory Currie in *An Ontology of Art* (1989). His reasons, however, are very different from those of Strawson. According to Currie 'no work of art is a physical object... A work of art is rather an *action type*' (*ibid*. p.7). Like Strawson, he claims that 'all kinds of works are multiple; capable, in principle, of having multiple instances' (*ibid*. p.8); but this is because, according to him, a work of art is essentially an *action*, and actions are to be regarded as types. Thus the action of painting *Guernica* is a type of which Picasso's act is a token; but there might have been other tokens of the same type, i.e. not copies of an original work, but all of them equally original performances (*ibid*. p.9).

[7] The story of the affair is told by Hope B. Werness, in Dutton, 1983.

PART TWO ART AND FEELING

Aesthetic Experience

Diané Collinson

Introduction

Is there a way of experiencing works of art that is *the* appropriate way? If there is such a way of experiencing works of art, how is it to be described and what are its major characteristics? How does it differ from other kinds of experience and what is its significance in human life?

A traditional response to these questions has been to say that there is an appropriate way of experiencing works of art, one that is distinguishable from other kinds of experiences, and that may be described as aesthetic experience. But the difficulties of justifying and substantiating that response are legion. Descriptions of aesthetic experience are so various and make such diverse claims that it is difficult to find any clear defining characteristic of it or any single feature that is shared by all its descriptions. It has been described as an experience that imparts knowledge, as one that does not impart knowledge, as will-less, as disinterested, as active, as passive, as cathartic, as contemplative. It has been declared to be on the one hand not essentially unlike other sorts of experiences and on the other to be a type of experience that is uniquely different from others. Some theorists have maintained that it is an experience that occurs only as the consequence of adopting a certain attitude, the aesthetic attitude, others that aesthetic experience proper is evoked only by works of art. Still others have argued that it is possible to experience almost anything aesthetically.

This essay investigates some of the philosophical issues arising from those diverging accounts of aesthetic experience. It examines a range of descriptions of aesthetic experience, the concept of an aesthetic attitude, and the debate between those who uphold such concepts and those who regard them as untenable. Its broad conclusion is that there is a tenable concept of aesthetic experience, that it is importantly connected with, although not exclusive to, experience of the arts and that it is a valuable element in human life.

1 Historical considerations

There is an important historical dimension to the enquiry into aesthetic experience. In dealing with it and with related concepts such as those of art and beauty we shall not be dealing with fixed concepts. Art, for example, has been variously defined in terms of imitation, expression, illusion, play, truth, imagination, and so on. Then, the assumption that anything that is a work of art is also beautiful has undergone careful critical scrutiny and revision. And the whole notion that there is a particular kind of sensibility and experience that can be characterized and distinguished as 'aesthetic' has been challenged. As a preliminary, therefore, we need to grasp the complexity of that tricky word: 'aesthetic'.

Investigating the roots and applications of a word can often be a dull and pointless thing to do, but this is not the case with 'aesthetic'. Knowing its roots tells us what kind of sensibility aesthetic sensibility is generally taken to be. Knowing its original application and something of how that application has changed helps us to understand the scope of its present use. For the Greeks at the time of Aristotle (384–322 BC) the word was 'aesthesis'. It referred to both sensation and perception and meant, in general, 'perception by means of the senses'. At that time it had no special application to the perception of works of art and beauty; it described every kind of perception based on the senses and it marked out one side of a division that was important in Greek thought, namely, the division between the sensory perception of things and the intellectual apprehension of them. It was not until the eighteenth century that it began to be used more specifically in connection with art and beauty. In 1735, Alexander Gottlieb Baumgarten introduced the term 'aesthetics' to name his 'science of perception'. Baumgarten's study was not confined to the perception of art and beauty but in due course, as others adopted his terminology and became influenced by his ideas, 'aesthetics' and 'the aesthetic' came to be used predominantly in discussions of art and beauty, though not always with the exact meanings given to them by Baumgarten.[1]

Such variations in meaning need not trouble us greatly. The benefit of knowing something of the origins and applications of 'aesthetic' is that we are thereby reminded that much aesthetic experience is grounded or has its beginnings in sense experience. It is, for example, through seeing its forms, lines, colours, spaces and textures that we come to aesthetic experience of a painting, experiencing, as we see those elements of it, its liveliness or calm, harshness, boldness or serenity, lyricism or wit, joyousness or foreboding. This does not mean that aesthetic experience can be straightforwardly characterized as essentially sensuous. Literary works of art, for example, are not sensuously perceived except in that we see or hear the words that are the means to experiencing them. Perhaps all that can be ventured, as a minimal starting point, is the claim that aesthetic experience is to do with having perceptions. Frank Sibley, in a paper discussing the differences between the aesthetic and the non-aesthetic has pointed out that:

> aesthetics deals with a kind of perception. People have to *see* the grace or unity of a work, *hear* the plaintiveness or frenzy in the music, *notice* the gaudiness of a colour scheme, *feel* the power of a novel, its mood or its uncertainty of tone... the crucial thing is to see, hear, feel.
>
> (Sibley, 1965, p.137)

There are two things to note here. The first is that although aesthetic experience may begin with the senses it does not end with them. If we reflect on what is involved in 'sense perception' or 'sensory experience' we realize we are not referring simply to physical stimuli and responses. In trying to give an account of perceiving a painting we might well begin with a fairly straightforward report of the physiological mechanisms of sight, describing the impact of light rays on the retina, the functions of lenses, processes of refraction and similar events. We would probably continue with talk of seeing colours, shapes, dark and light areas, roughness and smoothness; then depth, space, distance; eventually of perceiving objects, forms, impressions of movement or stillness, scenes, events, figures, and also moods, emotions and meanings. In so describing the perception of a picture we have moved – somehow – from physical processes to meanings and from the sensuous to the mental. It is clear that perception is a complex philosophical topic and that its complexity is presupposed in any detailed account of aesthetic experience.

The second thing to note is that aesthetic perception is perception of certain *aspects* of what is perceived. The Sibley quotation refers to grace, unity, plaintiveness, frenzy, gaudiness, power, mood and tone, and this suggests that there may be a range of qualities that could be grouped together as aesthetic qualities, thereby establishing a distinctive character for aesthetic experience.

In what has been said so far, there have been certain assumptions of close but undefined connections between three important concepts: art, beauty and the aesthetic. Baumgarten's coining of 'aesthetics' to describe his particular area of enquiry brought out and reinforced any such connections that already existed between the three, but it also gave rise to confusions about the exact nature of the connections. One kind of confusion is dispelled by realizing that the kind of experience described as aesthetic experience need not be confined to works of art. We can be moved in much the same way by natural phenomena, things and beings, by vistas, sunsets, seas, sounds, creatures, and the human face and form. The concept of the aesthetic is therefore not coextensive with the concept of art: the aesthetic can embrace more than works of art, whilst not all dealings with art are aesthetic dealings (think, for example, of the dealings with art which are not aesthetic dealings and which take place at Sotheby's and Christie's).

Further understanding is achieved by realizing that aesthetic experience, although traditionally linked with beauty, need not be confined to experience of the beautiful, for we can say that things which are ugly, dull, repulsive or indifferent are also candidates for aesthetic perception. The aesthetic, therefore, need not be defined either in terms of art or in terms of beauty, even though it may be closely connected with both. In recent years the differentiation of these three has been urged by those who have maintained that there is nothing essentially aesthetic nor essentially beautiful about art; that art is concerned with changing outlooks, shocking people and introducing radically new ideas (for a discussion of these matters, see Binkley (1977)). What we can derive from all this is that aesthetic experience, in spite of its close relationship with beauty and with art, need not be of art nor of the beautiful, and that art need not be aesthetic and need not be beautiful.

A related matter, needing only brief mention here, concerns a confusion that exists between aesthetics and the philosophy of art. The experience of art and beauty had of course been written about and discussed long before Baumgarten used the term 'aesthetics' to bring the study of them together under that head. But art, beauty and the aesthetic, although they may be taken to overlap to some extent or to be importantly connected, are not co-extensive. Because of this it is possible to delineate two separable but overlapping areas of enquiry: the philosophy of art, the main focus of which is on the nature of art and its creation, and aesthetics, the main focus of which is on the perception of aesthetic qualities.[2] The notion of beauty seems to provide an overlap between these two. But the distinctions just described are not ones to which we need adhere with rigour in what follows and, indeed, are often ignored by writers on aesthetics and the philosophy of art. Their importance in the present context is this: they may cause difficulties if we are not aware that they are sometimes made.

2 The nature of aesthetic experience

One point of agreement concerning aesthetic experience is that it is an experience to be prized very highly. The following remarks reveal the kind of value that has been placed on it.

> I think it [the aesthetic experience] a type of experience uniquely marked out, extraordinary in its delight, and often in its difficulty and pain, but above all an experience that is not always nor readily to be had, that it involves the concentration, the mental undistractedness, even the bodily euphoria and lightness that we too often cannot muster at all.
>
> (Findlay, 1967, p.4)

> Our whole considering and admiring or condemnatory mind is captured, our imagination taken possession of, by the words we read or hear; they work in our mind as our own; as words we utter with a whole mind behind them, enforcing a shift of conception and value through a wide area of our own mental habits. We are not only with it, we are in what we read as we are in our own sincere utterances.
>
> (Meager, 1964, p.215)

> The attention is no longer directed to the motives of willing, but comprehends things free from their relation to the will. Thus it considers things without interest, without subjectivity, purely objectively; it is entirely given up to them... Then all at once the peace, always sought but always escaping us on that first path of willing, comes to us of its own accord, and all is well with us... aesthetic pleasure... is delight from pure knowledge and its ways.
>
> (Schopenhauer, 1969 edn, vol. I, p.196)

The general import to be taken from those remarks is that aesthetic experience at its highest and best is arresting, intense and utterly engrossing; that when fully achieved it seizes one's whole mind or imagination and conveys whatever it does convey so vividly that the result is delight and knowledge. I cannot of course now present a particular work of art in such a way as to guarantee that it will evoke a response of the quality and richness suggested by those remarks. But consider, as something that I believe invites such an experience, a short poem by Philip Larkin:

Love Songs in Age

She kept her songs, they took so little space,
   The covers pleased her:
One bleached from lying in a sunny place,
One marked in circles by a vase of water,

One mended, when a tidy fit had seized her,
   And coloured, by her daughter –
So they had waited, till in widowhood
She found them, looking for something else, and stood

Relearning how each frank submissive chord
   Had ushered in
Word after sprawling hyphenated word,
And the unfailing sense of being young
Spread out like a spring-woken tree, wherein
   That hidden freshness sung,
That certainty of time laid up in store
As when she played them first. But, even more,

The glare of that much-mentioned brilliance, love,
   Broke out, to show
Its bright incipience sailing above,
Still promising to solve, and satisfy,
And set unchangeably in order. So
   To pile them back, to cry,
Was hard, without lamely admitting how
It had not done so then, and could not now.

(Larkin, 1988, p.113)

Perhaps that poem, 'Love Songs in Age', does not yield for everyone an experience of the intensity implied in the three descriptions given above. Yet it can, I suggest, generate an experience that exemplifies at least some of the characteristics mentioned in the descriptions. Certainly, in reading the poem's first verse, my imagination at once becomes possessed by images of the marked and faded songs and of the incident of their rediscovery. As soon as I have read the whole poem and grasped something of the denser meanings of the other two verses I find I want to return to the beginning, to dwell again on the images there and then to explore, with much greater care this time, the more complex thought of the second and third verses. I find I am able to do this with an easy concentration. I am engrossed, moving back and forth within the world of the poem, from any one phrase to any other, letting each show its own significance as well as its relationship to its context. When I read the poem through again completely it seems to me that I inhabit its world. I experience both the thoughts and feelings of the woman and the poet's comprehension of them. I seem to have exemplified some of the words of the second quotation: 'We are in what we read as we are in our own utterances'. When I reflect on the experience of the poem I find that in reading it I am able to conceive of and feel a sadness that is at once overwhelming and yet unmomentous. At the same time, one aspect of the complex experience derived from this poem is a profound pleasure. I turn away from it with reluctance and cannot quite break from it. In reverie I brood over its images and phrases, feeling again its particular sadness. It is difficult to understand why acquaintance with such sadness should please me so much; why I should want to continue dwelling on and in it.

No single account of a particular aesthetic experience, such as the one just given, seems able to yield a characteristic or group of characteristics that can serve as the basis of a definition of the experience. It seems to have a variety and complexity that defy attempts to state its essential conditions. It can be intense or gentle, sustained or fleeting, immediate or cumulative, or combinations of any of these. And this variety is increased and made more complex by the different media in which works of art come to us. For example, the whole of a painting can be present to one's gaze whereas music and dramas unfold through a period of time; novels and poems are realized wholly in the imagination; and a large or lengthy work will have a different impact from one that can be encompassed immediately or quickly. A further source of variety is the fact that people often respond differently to the same work and that an individual may respond to a particular work differently at various times. We sometimes experience something almost in the manner of a revelation: the work seizes us and we are taken effortlessly into its world. But when, at a later date, we return to the work to renew the experience, it eludes us and all we can say is that we did once experience the work thus. Conversely, aesthetic understanding can sometimes develop unawares, especially in the case of a work such as Milton's *Paradise Lost*, over which most of us have at first to labour as a task rather than read with ease. But one's engrossment in the details of its language and context can suddenly become augmented into an overwhelming realization of the poem's magnificence. In a somewhat similar way, it is possible for aesthetic perception to occur in retrospect; as, for instance, when one visits a picture gallery intending to absorb a particular *genre* or major work but then may derive very little, it seems, from the visit. Yet subsequently, perhaps days or weeks later, the paintings come to mind, compelling the kind of imaginative participation that had not come about before.

3   Contemplation theory

Although aesthetic experience varies widely, there have been many attempts to identify a characteristic or characteristics common to all its manifestations. Probably the most widely-affirmed of these attempts are those that maintain that aesthetic experience is essentially contemplative. If we think of 'contemplation theory' as a broad heading, then a range of accounts, all of which depend on the notion of being a spectator or beholder, may be subsumed under that heading. There is no need to elaborate the general conception of contemplation as it relates to the arts for it is an integral part of our traditional approach to them. Traditionally, audiences at plays, concerts and other performances are seated in reasonable comfort, often in darkness and in such a way as to allow and encourage attentive contemplation; one becomes absorbed or 'lost' in a book, dwells on a lyric poem, stands gazing at a painting, a sculpture, the façade of a building, and so on. All these attitudes presuppose contemplation, in some sense of that word. But contemplation, in a general or rather loose sense, cannot of course be *the* distinguishing feature of aesthetic experience, for contemplation is also characteristic of much religious experience and is regarded as at least an element in such matters as solving mathematical and other problems, the resolution of moral dilemmas and the conceiving of next year's vegetable garden. It is therefore the question whether there is a particular kind of contemplation, a kind held to be the distinguishing mark of aesthetic experience, that must be the central concern here.

One strand of contemplation theory can be traced back to Aristotle. Aristotle's main discussion of artistic matters is contained in his writings known now as the *Poetics* or *On the Art of Poetry*. The work is largely an analysis of the structure and composition of tragic drama and it offers no sustained or systematic account of the experience of art and beauty. But from Aristotle's remarks on how tragic drama should be constructed and on how it should impact on the spectator, and from further remarks occurring in other of his works, a good deal may be gleaned. In the *Poetics* he maintains that the spectator experiences, or should experience, pleasure in witnessing tragic drama and that there is a pleasure that is 'proper to it'; proper in that the well-made tragedy engenders in the spectator both the experience and the resolution of the emotions of pity and fear. In the *Eudemian Ethics* he points out that looking and listening, however rapt one may become, are never regarded as intemperate in the way that appetites such as eating and drinking may be, even though looking and listening, like eating and drinking, begin with the senses. He says,

> If a man sees a beautiful statue, or horse, or human being, or hears singing... only with the wish to see the beautiful and to hear the

singers, he would not be thought profligate any more than those who were charmed by the sirens.

(Aristotle, Eudemian Ethics, 1230b)

What Aristotle is trying to bring out in that last remark is the contemplative character of the proper perception of dramatic tragedy and of beauty in general. He distinguishes between our responses to the sight of luxurious food and goods or a voluptuous human figure, which often stimulate intemperate appetites and desires, and the experiencing of a pleasure that is generated simply in the perception and contemplation of something, and that is quite different from the pleasure of satisfying an appetite. He also points out that we do not condemn rapt, contemplative attention as profligate in the way in which we condemn strong appetites and desires: the stillness, or *stasis*, of aesthetic pleasure is not the object of moral disapproval in the way that the movement to procure what one desires might be.

What is the exact nature of the contemplation that is characterized by stillness or *stasis*? An Aristotelian reply to this question has to be derived from those brief and somewhat enigmatic remarks about pity and fear, already mentioned, that have been the subject of extensive discussion and interpretation in classical, literary and philosophical writing.

> A tragedy, then, is the imitation of an action that is serious and also, as having magnitude, complete in itself... with incidents arousing pity and fear, wherewith to accomplish its catharsis of such emotions.

(Aristotle, Poetics, 1449b)

The word 'catharsis' has attracted many interpretations, and perhaps too much has been made of it, for there does seem to be a fairly straightforward understanding of what Aristotle says, one that is consonant with his whole analysis of tragic drama and the effects it should seek. Throughout his account his insistence is on the structure and plot of a tragedy being so organized that the whole representation evokes pity and fear in the beholder and in such a way that it imparts its proper pleasure.

This proper pleasure is connected, for Aristotle, with knowledge and also with the human propensity to enjoy representations and imitations. He says:

> it is... natural for all to delight in works of imitation... we delight to view the most realistic representations of [objects] in art... to be

learning something is the greatest of pleasures... [T]he reason of the delight in seeing the picture is that one is at the same time learning – gathering the meaning of things...

(*Ibid.* 1448b)

The pleasure from well-wrought tragedy, for Aristotle, is the pleasure of seeing and knowing what is represented in it. Pity and fear are engendered in us as spectators of the tragedy but when those emotions are contained by the structure of the well-wrought tragedy, instead of provoking us to movement and action as they normally do in daily life, they are able to be experienced contemplatively; for the sake of knowing what they are like rather than as spurs to action. We are purged of them, it seems, in being able to experience and know them fully. They yield their proper pleasure: the pleasure, according to Aristotle, of an untrammelled knowledge of their natures. For him, a drama that invites a non-aesthetic or non-contemplative regard is not properly tragedy. We are able to experience its proper pleasure if the drama is constructed so that it is like an organism in that each part is essential to the whole, is harmoniously related to all the other parts, and the whole is complete.

If the structural conditions specified by Aristotle are satisfied then any intrusion of the spectator into the drama is resisted or held at bay; yet at the same time, and indeed *because* of that resistance to personal intrusion, the spectator is able to engage totally with the work. If we now ask how this can be, why the integrity and internal relatedness of a well-wrought drama resist practical intrusion and yet invite involvement of another kind, the answer must, I think, be along the following lines. First, something that reveals itself as complete and whole in itself is recognized as something upon which, in a certain sense, one cannot and would not want to intrude. There is nothing to be *done* in respect of such an entity; all one may properly do is admire or contemplate its meaning and entirety. But, second, the very properties that render it in one sense unapproachable also render such an entity peculiarly apt for profoundly attentive contemplation, for its excellence and clarity, its richness and wholeness, arrest and maintain spectators' attention so commandingly that they are taken into its world, though not as intruders or as additional elements in it.

The Aristotelian thread of contemplation theory became incorporated into Western culture and Christian doctrine in the thirteenth century through the scholarship of Thomas Aquinas. Aquinas's exposition and development of Aristotelianism established it as the dominant and profoundly influential element in both religious and secular scholarship, and when he came to write about the experience of art and beauty he developed the kind of distinction Aristotle had made between the *stasis* induced by beauty perceived as beauty and the desiring movement towards the possession of something. Thus Aquinas maintained that beauty and goodness in a thing, although fundamentally identical, are logically different,

> for goodness properly relates to the appetite (goodness being what all things *desire*); and therefore it has the aspect of an end (the appetite being a kind of movement towards a thing). On the other hand, beauty relates to the cognitive faculty; for beautiful things are those which please when seen.
>
> (Aquinas, *Summa Theologica*, Pt I, Q5, A5)

That passage shows Aquinas following Aristotle not only in characterizing aesthetic perception as contemplative but also in regarding it as cognitive. The kind of logical distinction he makes between responding to good or desirable things by movement towards them and to beauty by an entranced contemplation has prevailed in much aesthetic theory. It is expressed in a most lively and interesting way in some of the work of the twentieth-century writer, James Joyce. In Joyce's *Portrait of the Artist as a Young Man* there is a conversation in which Stephen Dedalus discusses the experience of art and beauty with a fellow-student, Lynch. Both young men are steeped in a Jesuit education derived from the doctrines of Aristotle and Thomas Aquinas. The starting-point of their talk is Aristotle's famous remark, already cited, that tragedy is 'a representation of an action that is worth serious attention... by means of pity and fear bringing about the purgation of such emotions'. Stephen complains that Aristotle did not define pity and fear and he offers his own definitions of them:

> Pity is the feeling which arrests the mind in the presence of whatsoever is grave and constant in human sufferings and unites it with the human sufferer. Terror* is the feeling which arrests the mind in the presence of whatsoever is grave and constant in human sufferings and unites it with the secret cause.
>
> (Joyce, 1972 edn, p.212)

[* 'Terror' is used by James Joyce where the Bywater translation uses 'fear'.]

The important word there is 'arrests'. Stephen reminds us that Aristotle had said that 'not every kind of pleasure should be demanded of tragedy, but only that which is proper to it'. He argues that it is the arresting of the mind that ensures the proper pleasure of experiencing a well-wrought tragedy, and he says,

The tragic emotion, in fact, is a face looking two ways, towards terror and towards pity, both of which are phases of it. You see I use the word *arrest*. I mean that the tragic emotion is static. Or rather the dramatic emotion is. The feelings excited by improper art are kinetic, desire or loathing. Desire urges us to possess, to go to something; loathing urges us to abandon, to go from something. The arts which excite them, pornographical or didactic, are therefore improper arts. The aesthetic emotion (to use the general term) is therefore static. The mind is arrested and raised above desire and loathing.

(*Ibid.* p.213)

Lynch tries to puncture Stephen's high seriousness. Wanting to maintain that great art *can* incite a person to movement or action, he reminds Stephen that he, Lynch, one day wrote his name in pencil on the backside of the Venus of Praxiteles in the Museum. 'Was that not desire?' he asks. But Stephen is undismayed. He is not, he says, trying to deny that 'we are all animals', but Lynch's act was no more than a physical response, 'a purely reflex action of the nervous system' and, as such, something quite different from the proper response to art; for beauty expressed by the artist, he maintains,

awakens, or ought to awaken, or induces, or ought to induce, an aesthetic *stasis* (stillness), an ideal pity or an ideal terror, a *stasis* called forth, prolonged and at last dissolved by what I call the rhythm of beauty.

(*Ibid.* pp. 213–14)

Stephen reinforces his argument with more references to Aquinas. (Elsewhere he describes his theory as 'applied Aquinas'.) He reminds Lynch that Aquinas said that beautiful things are those which please when seen. Stephen says that the Latin word used by Aquinas for 'seen', '*visa*', is a vague word but nevertheless 'clear enough to keep away good and evil which excite desire and loathing. It means certainly a *stasis* and not a *kinesis* [movement]'. He invokes three words that are used by Aquinas to describe something that is beautiful. These are integrity (*integritas*), harmony (*consonantia*) and clarity (*claritas*). They relate closely to Aristotle's requirements for a well-wrought drama but Stephen uses them to expound the way in which we *experience* beauty. He asks Lynch to look at a basket that a butcher's boy has slung inverted over his head.

In order to see that basket... your mind first of all separates the basket from the rest of the visible universe which is not the basket. The first phase of apprehension is a bounding line drawn about the object to be apprehended. An aesthetic image is presented to us in space or in time... But temporal or spatial, the aesthetic image is first luminously apprehended as selfbounded and selfcontained upon the immeasurable background of space or time which is not it. You apprehend it as *one* thing. You see it as one whole. You apprehend its wholeness. That is *integritas*.

(*Ibid.* pp. 218, 219)

Stephen is equally explicit about *consonantia*, or harmony:

Then... you pass from point to point, led by its formal lines; you apprehend it as balanced part against part within its limits; you feel the rhythm of its structure... the synthesis of immediate perception is followed by the analysis of apprehension. Having first felt that it is *one* thing you now feel that it is a *thing*. You apprehend it as complex, multiple, divisible, separable, made up of its parts, the result of its parts and their sum, harmonious. That is *consonantia*.

(*Ibid.* p.219)

Claritas is more difficult for Stephen to explain. It describes not simply the illumination of mind one experiences in the perception of beauty but also the clarity and glory of what is perceived. Stephen is well aware that the word has a significance deriving from its theological use by Aquinas. When discussing the Holy Trinity, Aquinas speaks of the Son as 'the *art* of the omnipotent God' and as exemplifying Beauty and its three conditions, *integritas, consonantia* and *claritas* (Aquinas, Part 1, Q.39, Art. 8). The Son, he says, is the Image of God but is also a separate being. We therefore have to think of a work of art or a beautiful object as analogous with 'the art of the omnipotent God', that is, as created and as existing separately and having its own meaning. And just as, in Aquinas's theology, it would be a mistake to suppose that the Son is simply an instrument or means to the Father rather than a distinct being, so, for Stephen, would it be a mistake to suppose that something beautiful is simply a means to some further glory rather than a glorious being in itself. *Claritas*, as an element in aesthetic perception, implies a recognition of the separate existence and self-contained meaning of a beautiful object. From this Stephen argues that what is made clear and knowable in *claritas* is the beautiful object's *quidditas*, that is, quiddity or 'whatness'.

When you have apprehended that basket as one thing and have then analysed it according to its form and apprehended it as a thing, you

make the only synthesis which is logically and aesthetically permissible. You see that it is that thing which it is and no other thing. The
radiance of which he [Aquinas] speaks is the scholastic *quidditas*, the
whatness of a thing. This supreme quality is felt by the artist when the
aesthetic image is first conceived in his imagination.

(Joyce, 1972 edn, p.219)

Quidditas is not an easy concept to grasp fully. It has been variously
described as the essence, the being, the nature, the definition, or the form
of something. Aquinas described it in the following way:

> It is what the Philosopher [Aristotle] frequently calls 'the what a thing
> is to be', that is, that through which something is a certain kind of
> being. It is called 'form', moreover, inasmuch as 'form' signifies the
> certitude of anything... It is also called by the name 'nature', when
> nature is said of anything that can be grasped intellectually in some
> way.

(Aquinas, 1965 edn, pp. 34, 35)

Stephen seems to be working towards the idea that the experience of
beauty is the experience of a clarity that enables us to recognize a thing's
essential being or form. *Claritas* describes both our apprehension of an
object and a quality of the object. Stephen speaks of the experience as of
a revelation

> the instant wherein that supreme quality of beauty, the clear radiance of
> the aesthetic image, is apprehended luminously by the mind which has
> been arrested by its wholeness and fascinated by its harmony is the
> luminous silent stasis of aesthetic pleasure...

(Joyce, 1972 edn, pp. 219, 220)

In another novel, *Stephen Hero*, James Joyce describes the experience as
an epiphany, 'a sudden spiritual manifestation... the most delicate and
evanescent of moments' (Joyce, 1956 edn, p.216). Epiphanies, he says,
should be recorded by writers with extreme care. One such careful
recording is to be found towards the end of Jean-Paul Sartre's novel,
Nausea, (Sartre, 1956 edn, p.248) and has the merit not only of being an
exact account of what Joyce calls an 'epiphany' but also of bringing out
what it means to recognize *quidditas*. In the novel, the main character,
Roquentin, has lost everything that once made life meaningful for him.
In despair he plans to leave the town, and goes for the last time to his
usual café to hear his favourite jazz record, 'Some of These Days'. As
the record plays Roquentin suddenly recognizes that the tune has a life
of its own that is inviolable; that the tune *itself* is not something that

could be destroyed by smashing records or tearing up music. In fact, the tune is not an existing *thing*, an object at all: it has *being* rather than mere physical existence (*cf.* Essay Three, pp.82–7). He says:

> *It* does not *exist*. It is even irritating in its non-existence; if I were to get up, if I were to snatch that record from the turntable which is holding it and if I were to break it in two, I wouldn't reach *it*. It is beyond – always beyond something, beyond a voice, beyond a violin note. Through layers and layers of experience, it unveils *itself*, slim and firm, and when you try to seize it you meet nothing but existents, you run up against existence devoid of meaning. It is behind them: I can't even hear it, I hear sounds, vibrations in the air which unveil it... it has nothing superfluous: it is all the rest which is superfluous in relation to it. It *is*.
>
> (*Ibid.*)

4 Will-lessness

In the passage from the *Eudemian Ethics* (1230b), Aristotle wrote of people who were 'charmed by the Sirens', those sea creatures whose songs were of such beauty that sailors became transfixed and will-less so that their ships ran on to rocks. This same notion of loss of will as an important characteristic of aesthetic experience is found in the philosophy of Arthur Schopenhauer (1788–1860).

Schopenhauer's views on art and the experience of it are dependent on the structure of his philosophy as a whole and although the details of that structure are complex they derive from a single thought. It is the thought that the world as we understand it in everyday life, with its apparent orderliness, variety, its comprehensibility and manipulability, is fundamentally nothing but one immense, blind driving force which Schopenhauer calls *will*. It is important to understand that, for Schopenauer, there are not two separate things, the world *and* will, but that the world *is* will and will *is* the world. However, we may think of the world under two aspects. Under one aspect it may be conceived of as blind, irrational will; under another, the same force is experienced as the world of our everyday understanding, a world in space and time, operating under causal laws and explicable to the human mind. Schopenhauer writes of the world as a whole as 'the objectification of the will'; it is will made manifest. And just as we are to think of the world as a whole as the objectification of will as a whole, so we are to think of any individual human body as the objectification of a particular, individual, human will. Everything one does or is, all human lives and all the multifarious creatures and things comprised by the world, are particular objectifications of the universal and perpetual struggle of the will as a whole. The world conceived of as under natural laws and as containing beings capable of autonomy and choice is the world as we represent it to ourselves in virtue of the capacities of mind possessed by human beings; but the world as will, as a blind force without lucidity or reason, is how it also is. If we understand this, Schopenhauer says, we understand the truth of the human situation.

His view of things has sombre implications. It offers a picture of human life as an inescapable struggle in which all things and all beings are pitted against each other as each is driven to persist in its own willing. It means that the sense we make of the world when we conceive of it as being in space and time, and as operating under causal laws, and of ourselves as creatures capable of reason and choice, is undermined by the recognition that the mainspring of all this is a blind power that has no intelligence or purpose. For what we think of as knowledge of the world is, Schopenhauer maintains, subordinate to the irrational power of will. Our minds, using the capacities they have, simply organize the meaningless chaos that is the world as will. But ultimately it is will that is dominant and any knowledge that we have serves the will. The will simply *wants*, blindly, but knowledge knows the way to meet the want. The will is 'the strong blind man carrying the sighted lame man on his shoulders' (Schopenhauer, 1969 edn, vol. II, p.209).

Schopenhauer offers the possibility of salvation from our subjection to will. He points out that even though we recognize that this is how things are there is often also a feeling that 'behind our existence lies something else, that becomes accessible to us only by our shaking off the world'. This something else is revealed when what he calls 'a denial of the will' takes place. One cannot deliberately rid oneself of will, so its denial cannot be brought about by choice; but it occurs as the result either of great suffering or of aesthetic contemplation. It involves a perception of things that is entirely different from the everyday perception of them as in space and time, and as under causal laws, and it yields a knowledge that is quite different from the knowledge acquired by means of that everyday framework of understanding. Schopenhauer says that when denial of the will occurs:

> we no longer consider the where, the when, the why and the whither in things, but simply and solely the *what*... we... devote the whole power of our mind to perception, sink ourselves completely therein, and let our whole consciousness be filled by the calm contemplation of the natural object actually present, whether it be a landscape, a tree, a rock, a crag, a building, or anything else. We *lose* ourselves entirely in this

object... we forget our individuality, our will, and continue to exist only as pure subject, as pure mirror of the object, so that it is as though the object alone existed without anyone to perceive it, and thus we are no longer able to separate the perceiver from the perception, but the two have become one, since the entire consciousness is filled and occupied by a single image of perception.

(Ibid. vol. I, pp. 178, 179)

The structure and ramifications of Schopenhauer's thought are quite different from Aristotle's or Thomas Aquinas's. Yet their accounts of the will-less nature of aesthetic perception are strikingly similar in many ways. All three refer in some way to a profoundly attentive contemplation, to the exclusion of everything save the object of that attention, to the vivid presence of what is perceived, to loss of will or desire, to the compelling nature of the experience and to the delight and knowledge attendant upon it. Schopenhauer's claim that the knowledge acquired in aesthetic contemplation is of a special kind is intrinsic to the general structure of his philosophy. He maintains that when something 'suddenly raises us out of the endless stream of willing' (*ibid.* p.196) the knowledge that is then available is not of a particular object but of 'the Idea of its species'. Ordinarily it is as individual willing subjects that we perceive things but in aesthetic contemplation, when the individual will is denied, what is perceived is not a particular object but the Idea of the object.

We have to think of the Ideas much as Plato did, that is, as non-material, as more real than physical things, and as perfect and unchanging. In Schopenhauer's scheme of things Ideas occupy a place between the will as a whole, which is unknowable, and all the particular physical phenomena of the world, the particular trees, tables, creatures, mountains, statues, buildings and so on, that are known to us in daily life. In his philosophy, as in Plato's, the Idea consists of all that is essential in the perceived object and nothing that is inessential. In knowing the Idea of something, what is known is the fundamental structure that makes it the *kind* of thing that it is rather than the particular variations that make it an individual instance of that kind. Thus Schopenhauer says:

> To the brook which rolls downwards over the stones, the eddies, waves, and foam-forms exhibited by it are indifferent and inessential; but that it follows gravity, and behaves as an inelastic, perfectly mobile, formless, and transparent fluid, this is its essential nature, this, *if known through perception*, is the Idea... only the *essential*... constitutes the *Idea*.

(Ibid. p.182)

Schopenhauer maintains that it is possible to become the knower of an Idea only through a loss of one's individuality, by becoming a will-less 'pure subject of knowing'. Just as the particular, contingent variations of an object must fall away to reveal its Idea, so does the individual will of the perceiver give way to a pure knower. Schopenhauer writes of the perceiver as 'pure subject of knowledge, free from individuality and from servitude to the will'. The individual, he says, can know only particular things; the person who, in perceiving, becomes the pure subject of knowing knows only Ideas. We have to think of ourselves as somehow outside space and time, as free from our ordinary ways of apprehending things and free as well from any kind of wanting or practical relationship to what we perceive. If, for instance, it is a tree I am able to contemplate in this way, then the whole of my consciousness is filled by its image and there is a fusion of myself as pure knowing subject with the known object, the tree: 'the subject, by passing entirely into the perceived object, has also become that object itself, since the entire consciousness is nothing more than its most distinct image' (ibid. p.180). As an individual who wills and apprehends the world in the ordinary way, one knows the things in the world as objects that relate to one's individual will. At such times the tree is for the provision of shade, or for firewood, or is an obstruction to the sunlight, a danger in high winds, or a pleasant environmental amenity. But if it is as a 'pure knower' that I perceive the tree then what is known is not just a particular object but an aspect of will as a whole. The perceived tree, Schopenhauer says, is plucked from the stream of the world's course and becomes 'a representative of the whole, an equivalent of the many in space and time'. In knowing it as Idea one comes as close as it is possible to get to knowing the will as a whole.

If the denial of the will necessary for aesthetic contemplation cannot be brought about by an act of will then how exactly does Schopenhauer see it occurring? Philosophically speaking, it requires that will, which is normally dominant, gives way to knowledge. Physiologically, a strong stimulation of perceptual activity demanding one's full attention (the kind of 'arrest' described by Stephen Dedalus) is required, so that consciousness of one's self, or will, is wholly ousted by consciousness of something else: 'one is conscious no longer of oneself, but only of the perceived objects' (ibid. vol. II, p.369). Schopenhauer points out that alcohol and opium are not conducive to the kind of acute perception that is required. Instead we need to be well rested and calm so that we can the more easily lose awareness of the self and entertain the consciousness of other things. He says: 'For we apprehend the world purely objectively, only when we no longer know that we belong to it; and all things appear the more beautiful, the more we are conscious merely of them, and the less we are conscious of ourselves' (*ibid.* p.368). The denial of will is a denial or loss of one's individuality and an achievement of pure perceptual contemplation.

It follows from Schopenhauer's views that it is possible for anything to be regarded purely objectively since everything is to some extent or at some level a manifestation of an Idea. It is, nevertheless, works of art that most readily and most easily effect the nullification of will that is required to bring us to the purely objective viewpoint. Works of art, he says, can do this because they emphasize the essential and eliminate the inessential. When something is 'picturesque' or 'poetical' it becomes set apart and is less accessible to the will. The perceiver is then more easily able to contemplate without will. In a sense, the perceiver becomes identified with the thing perceived, and being without will and 'without burden and hardship' (*ibid.* p.371), finds the experience pleasurable. 'Everything', Schopenhauer remarks, 'is beautiful only so long as it does not concern us' (*ibid.* p.374).

Schopenhauer says that we have to assume that the ability to apprehend Ideas, to lose one's individuality, is present to some extent in almost everyone. Anyone lacking the ability, he maintains, must be incapable of aesthetic pleasure. The person of genius possesses this ability to the highest degree and can retain the state of contemplation long enough to be able to 'repeat what is thus known in a voluntary and intentional work, such repetition being the work of art' (*ibid.* vol. I, p.195). The genius has 'separated out' the Idea and 'lets us peer into the world through his eyes' (*ibid.*). The ability to perceive so well is the inborn gift of the genius, and the ability to embody this perception in an artefact that enables us to see what the genius saw is, Schopenhauer says, an acquired technique. Whether the gifted perceiver knows Ideas through nature or through art makes no essential difference to the character of the experience. The person naturally disposed to this kind of apprehension may find it occurring in any circumstances or environment.

Although we need to understand something of the metaphysical framework of Schopenhauer's thought, we do not need to accept that framework in order to acknowledge what is of value in his account. We can separate much of his characterization of aesthetic experience from the metaphysics on which he grounds it. We can, for example, accept the existence of a sense of a restless striving in human life without embracing the belief that the world is ultimately pure will. We can entertain the thought that in aesthetic perception we perceive things in a certain way and acquire knowledge without accepting that what we perceive and know are Platonic Ideas. In particular, we can explore, by means of Schopenhauer's eloquent accounts of the enriching and liberating nature of aesthetic experience, the full character of this kind of human experience. At the same time, even as we savour his insights, we begin to recognize that his metaphysical framework places certain restraints and emphases on his account of aesthetic perception.

For example, we intuitively understand a work of art as a created, new object that is valued not because it points us to something beyond or other than itself but because it is meaningful in virtue of its own particularity. This is the kind of logical status Aquinas ascribes to a beautiful object when he speaks of Beauty as separate and distinct, in the way that the Son is separate and distinct from the Father; and it is part of what Sartre's character, Roquentin, recognizes in the song he hears in the cafe when he realizes that it has a being and meaning of its own that are inviolable. Yet Schopenhauer seems to take a quite different stand. For him it is knowledge of Ideas that is of supreme importance and the particular work of art is simply a means to that more important vision. At one point he says: 'the purpose of all the arts is merely the expression and presentation of the Ideas' (*ibid.* p.252). A question that therefore needs to be asked is whether his metaphysical scheme accords too little importance, or the wrong kind of importance, to the particular aesthetic object or work of art.

A full answer to that question would occupy many pages. But this much may briefly be said in defence of Schopenhauer's account. In spite of his emphasis on Ideas he does regard the particular object or work as *necessary* for the perception of the Idea it instantiates. Without matter, Ideas could not become apparent to us, could not be aesthetically perceived. So the work of art, or object, cannot be seen as something that is dispensable once we get through and beyond it, so to speak, to the Idea; for the object or work *is* the Idea made perceivable. It is not merely an instrument that clears the way towards the Idea. It is its ineliminable embodiment.

The apparent fusion or union of Idea and object raises two further problems. The first is that of how exactly an Idea, which is essentially abstract and general, can be exemplified in a particular material object. Once again, any comprehensive treatment of this difficulty would take up a great deal of space, for it is one which permeates much traditional philosophy and which has not been satisfactorily resolved. All that can be said briefly is that Schopenhauer, like other metaphysicians, is trying to give an account of an underlying coherent and systematic structure of reality that will be recognized as the ground and justification of our everyday experience and beliefs. We do often describe aesthetic experience as furnishing us with insights into a deeper and more universal reality, and the notion of a plurality of eternal Ideas, capable of some sort of instantiation in particular things, is a possible explanation of such experiences and a possible account of what reality fundamentally is like. But it is a deficiency in any such account if it cannot make clear the relationships between any of its categories or parts, and Schopenhauer's account is deficient in that he is not, in the end, able to say *how* Ideas can be instantiated in particular things. His metaphysical structure, therefore, does not manage to provide the kind of grounds or justification that are needed to support his account of aesthetic experience and of reality in general.

The second, related, difficulty concerning Ideas is about how the maker and the percipient of an object or work are able to recognize that they are apprehending an Idea. For if, as Schopenhauer insists, we cannot know Ideas independently of their embodiments in particular things, then we have no means of checking a particular perception – putatively of an Idea – against a standard that would confirm or disconfirm the perception. Once again, the metaphysical structure Schopenhauer has erected produces problems that cannot be satisfactorily resolved.

In spite of these and other difficulties, the notion of Ideas is a fruitful one in the context of aesthetic experience. Schopenhauer contrasts Idea with concept, describing the former as resembling a living organism that has 'generative force, which brings forth that which was not previously put into it'. In contrast, concepts, although useful in daily affairs, are 'eternally barren and unproductive in art' (*ibid.* p.235). The artistic genius, Schopenhauer says, perceives and feels the Idea as something original and generative, apprehending it as something sensuous and richly productive. Here Schopenhauer is using his conception of the Idea to elucidate important characteristics of works of art and of the production and experience of them, and also to distinguish the domain of art as essentially involving perception, feeling and imagination from the domain of reason, reflection and conceptualization. He says that every work of art offers an incomplete and temporary answer to the question, 'What is life?' Each work is 'a fleeting image, not a permanent, universal knowledge' and it is so because 'all the arts speak only the naive and childlike language of *perception*' (*ibid.* vol. II, p.406). Perception gives what is particular; it supplies fragmentary examples rather than rules. It is left to philosophy, he says, to provide the concept, a permanent and comprehensive answer to the question 'What is life?' At the same time he regards philosophy and the arts as fundamentally related in that both seek to answer that question, albeit by different means: art by percepts, philosophy by concepts.

5 Contemplation again

Before going any further with particular accounts of aesthetic experience we should look more closely at the notion of contemplation. So far the term has been used in a general sense to mean something such as 'perceiving', 'dwelling on', 'regarding' or 'attending to'. It contrasts with 'acting upon', 'wanting', 'desiring' or 'bringing about something', and it suggests stillness rather than movement. From this it is sometimes assumed that contemplation is a wholly static and passive state and cannot be an activity. The bodily stillness characteristic of many of our contemplative moments or moods lends some weight to these assumptions.

The assumptions need to be questioned. It is arguable that contemplation does not necessarily require stillness, that movement is sometimes essential to it, and that stillness does not imply passivity. The proper contemplation of a large building such as a cathedral requires one to walk about it, not only in order to take in its different parts and aspects but also to obtain a sense of its spaces and masses, and the diffusion and gradations of light among them. One needs to move round a sculpture, seeing it close to and from a distance, looking at it from different angles; this is an essential element of the attentive contemplation that a three-dimensional object merits. Similarly, one may move about before a painting, shifting one's point of vision, or may place the painting in different lights or at different heights for the sake of contemplating it fully.

Even when bodily stillness does seem to be the appropriate concomitant of contemplation there is no reason to assume that the contemplation is passive. Contemplating is something one does rather than something that happens to one. 'Attending to', 'dwelling upon', 'regarding' and 'looking at' are activities often involving great concentration and intensity. The inward feeling of contemplation can be one of abounding vitality and movement: one seems to be transported into the world of the work and then explores that world. And when this dynamic quality of contemplation is acknowledged, when it is recognized that its inward side is not the equivalent of what may outwardly show itself as a fixed gaze or glassy stare, then it is possible to allow that it is not essentially static or passive. The Aristotelian *stasis* described by Stephen Dedalus is a sustained focusing of attention rather than an inert recipience. In the case of a painting the activity of contemplation consists of a visual exploration, a recognition of shapes and representations and an understanding of their relationships and meanings. The case of listening to a piece of music is analogous. For although it may seem that here is an instance of much greater passivity in that one is simply led through, or follows through, a temporal sequence of sounds, that is by no means the full story. Knowledge and memory have to be employed actively in order to recognize and connect the heard themes, rhythms and harmonies, and to produce the expectations of their recurrences, developments and resolutions. In dwelling on a poem, as the remarks on Larkin's 'Love Songs in Age' may have suggested, one gradually investigates images and thoughts, moving imaginatively among the poem's phrases and meanings and searching them in ways that deepen and extend percipience.

In spite of the above considerations it would be entirely wrong to try to maintain that there is nothing of passivity in aesthetic contemplation. It has both passive and active aspects and C.S. Lewis was surely right when he observed that 'The first demand any work of art makes on us is surrender' (Lewis, 1961, p.19). But contemplation maintains a dialogue with what is perceived. It includes that will-less receiving in which a person is entranced, as if experiencing a revelation, as well as a searching attentiveness. It includes thinking *about* something by imagining it as well as apprehending it directly: I may contemplate the vista that lies before me or the images evoked in the reading of a lyric poem, but recalling them and dwelling on them afterwards are also contemplations of them. But perhaps the contemplation that is most typical of an aesthetic situation is one marked not by the empty passivity that may seem to be implied by a complete absence of will, but more by a *willingness* to dwell on something, to be contained and move within the evocations of *this* work, its forms, qualities and moods. Even Schopenhauer's will-less perception is not that of a wax-like *tabula rasa* receiving impressions; the striving will is absent but knowledge is not. He writes:

> everyone who reads the poem or contemplates the work or art must of course contribute from his own resources... [everyone] has to stand before a picture as before a prince, waiting to see whether it will speak and what it will say to him. What we grasp of the work depends on what capacity and culture allow.
>
> (Schopenhauer, 1969 edn, vol. II, p.407)

6 Disinterestedness

A feature of aesthetic contemplation as considered so far is that it seems to require both an involvement with and a detachment from the perceived object. What we understand from the accounts derived from Aristotle, Aquinas and James Joyce is that the completeness and harmony of the well-wrought work of art sets it apart so distinctly that it resists one type of involvement, that in which one might intervene to act upon or within the work in some way, while at the same time creating the conditions for another type, an imaginative participation in the work's character and meaning. Schopenhauer's view is comparable in that it includes not only a detachment but also an involvement that is a near-mystical union with what is known.

The kind of impersonal detachment characteristic of aesthetic contemplation is generally known as 'disinterestedness'. It has probably been the single most important concept in the last three centuries of aesthetic theory, has been expounded in a variety of ways and has been given different emphases by different writers. To be disinterested concerning something is not the same as being uninterested in it. 'Disinterestedness' can describe the absence of the kind of interest that relates to one's own advantage or disadvantage; or it can describe an impartial and unbiassed attitude in which one has no personal axe to grind in a matter. It requires us to consider something on its own merits and not in relation to what might accrue from it for ourselves: to be concerned with the object itself rather than with how it relates to oneself. Or it can refer to a concern solely with the look or appearance of something and an absence of any interest in the actual existence of what appears.

The notion of disinterest as an important characteristic of aesthetic consciousness was given explicit and detailed exposition by Immanuel Kant (1724–1804) in his *Critique of Judgement* (Kant, 1973 edn). Kant, like Schopenhauer, whom he preceded and influenced, produced a comprehensive and architectonic philosophy, replete with its own elaborate terminology. In his philosophy as a whole Kant systematically investigated three modes of human consciousness: knowledge, desire and feeling. For each of these topics he wrote a critique. His *Critique of Pure Reason* examines knowledge, and his *Critique of Practical Reason* morality. The third *Critique*, the *Critique of Judgement*, examines our consciousness of beauty, approaching the matter by means of what Kant calls 'the judgement of taste', that is, the kind of judgement we make when we feel and pronounce that something is beautiful.

Kant starts from the fact that we do make judgements such as 'This is beautiful' and he investigates their character, logical status and presuppositions. His fundamental question is: 'How are judgements of taste *possible*?' In asking this what he wants to find out is whether such judgements are well-grounded: that is, whether we are justified in affirming the kind of thing we do affirm in them. If they do turn out to be justified then Kant regards them as 'possible' in the sense that the justification *entitles* us to make such judgements.

Kant presents four Moments, or aspects, of the judgement of taste. He first points out that the judgement that something is beautiful arises from 'being conscious of this representation with an accompanying sensation of delight' (*ibid.* p.43). Simply, one feels delight in the apprehension of a perceived appearance and thereby judges it to be beautiful, as for example, when one delights in a view or landscape and exclaims at its beauty. The judgement, according to Kant, is not cognitive, that is, it does not lay claim to any knowledge. It is based entirely on feeling, which he describes as 'a quite separate faculty of discriminating and estimating'. Moreover this feeling of delight is a response to the *representation* or perceived appearance, not to some feature that depends on the actual existence of what is represented. If it did depend on the object's existence then our feeling of pleasure, Kant maintains, would not be disinterested. He says: 'everything turns on the meaning which I can give to this representation, and not on any factor which makes me dependent on the real existence of the object. Everyone must allow that a judgement on the beautiful which is tinged with the slightest interest, is very partial and not a pure judgement of taste. One must not be in the least prepossessed in favour of the real existence of the thing, but must preserve complete indifference in this respect, in order to play the part of judge in matters of taste' (*ibid.*).

To refine and emphasize the point that the judgement that something is beautiful arises from a disinterested pleasure, Kant carefully distinguishes it from two other kinds of delight: delight in what is agreeable and delight in what is good. He claims that both delight in what is agreeable and delight in what is good involve a desire of some sort towards an object and therefore an interest in it. What is agreeable, he maintains, makes a direct appeal to the senses and so arouses an inclination to possess the agreeable object or to possess something like it. Our pleasure is therefore related in some way to its real existence and so is not disinterested pleasure. We have a comparable interest in the real existence of the good in that we desire the good thing or action to exist. In contrast 'the judgement of taste is simply *contemplative*, i.e. it is a judgement which is indifferent to the existence of an object, and only decides how its character stands with the feeling of pleasure and displeasure' (*ibid.* p.48). Kant does not mean by this that someone who judges that, for instance, a particular oriental rug is beautiful is wholly indifferent to the real existence of the rug but simply that *in judging its beauty* one's attention is directed to its visual qualities or appearance rather than to the existence of what makes such perceptions possible. The judgement of taste may well be succeeded by an interest in the real existence of the rug and by a desire to possess it but that interest and that desire are not elements in the judgement of taste, the pleasure of which accrues in the contemplation of beauty and is unaffected by the reality or unreality of what it contemplates. All the time, in these carefully made distinctions, Kant is working to provide a precise characterization of the kind of experience that results in a judgement of taste. He says:

> Of all these three kinds of delight [in the beautiful, in the agreeable, in the good], that of taste for the beautiful may be said to be the one and only disinterested and free delight; for with it, no interest, whether of sense or reason, extorts approval... For FAVOUR [that is, the pleasurable liking that does not depend on either a desire or a moral requirement] is the only free liking.
>
> (*Ibid.* p.49)

He regards both the judgement of agreeableness and that of beauty as aesthetic judgements, for both are based on feeling, but maintains that only the judgement of beauty is a judgement of *taste*. Taste is a person's capacity to judge things by means of a contemplative delight in their beauty; it is the capacity for disinterested aesthetic experience.

In the second Moment Kant identifies another distinguishing characteristic of the judgement of taste, one that arises from the fact that the feeling of delight from which the judgement of taste springs is subjective while the form of the judgement, 'This is beautiful', is objective. It is objective in that it seems to impute beauty to the object: we do not express the judgement subjectively by saying 'I like it'; instead, Kant says, we 'speak of the beautiful as if beauty were a quality of the object' (*ibid.* p.51). He points out that in the case of a judgement that something is agreeable we can allow that there can be a difference of opinion: 'a person does not take it amiss if, when he says that Canary-wine is agreeable, another corrects the expression and reminds him that he ought to say: It is agreeable to me' (*ibid.*). But Kant has to explain why the judgement of beauty is not like that; why it is grounded in feeling yet at the same time is stated in terms that imply some sort of objectivity and that invite the agreement of others.

Kant's justification of these characteristics of aesthetic judgement is a complex one and I will do no more than outline it here. What he wants to show is that it is possible for aesthetic judgement to be subjective in that it is grounded in feeling, but also objective in that it may legitimately demand the agreement of others. The justification involves reference to a view Kant has already expounded in the *Critique of Pure Reason*, where he argues that we have to assume that humankind in general possesses faculties of Imagination and Understanding, since it is these faculties that make knowledge and communication possible. Imagination and Understanding, he maintains, interact: Imagination unites the sense perceptions that are the raw material of experience and Understanding supplies concepts and higher level classifications for the resulting syntheses, thereby rendering them objective and shareable, and so able to count as objects of knowledge.

We may ignore the details of Kant's account of knowledge here, because we know already that he does not think that the judgement of taste involves knowledge. What we have to hold fast to is the notion of the interaction of Imagination and Understanding. For, whereas in the production of knowledge our mental activity is ruled by *definite concepts* and commonly possessed mental structures that furnish conditions for objectivity, in the pure judgement of taste, Kant holds, the Imagination and Understanding engage in an *indefinite*, although harmonious, interaction that is not dependent on a concept. Thus we do not judge that, for example, a rose is beautiful by reference to a definite concept of beauty, but by reference to our feelings concerning it. Accordingly, Kant describes the judgement of taste as a free one: it is free not only from the constraints of desires and morality but also from constraints that would be imposed on it by a definite concept of beauty. In this kind of free activity the Imagination, he writes, 'induces much thought, yet without the possibility of any definite thought whatever, i.e., a concept, being adequate to it, and which language, consequently, can never get quite on level terms with or render completely intelligible' (Kant, 1973 edn, p.176.)

Although the Imagination's activity in the judgement of taste cannot be bounded by a concept, the Understanding does exert an influence on it by requiring that its explorations, although free, are not chaotic or incoherent. The interaction of the two faculties must have a formal structure of the sort it has in the generation of knowledge. Thus Imagination enlivens Understanding by stimulating it to a wealth of indefinite thought, while Understanding regulates the Imagination's activity. But although there is this similarity to the kind of interaction that generates knowledge, the result is not knowledge because the judgement of taste depends on feeling rather than concepts. Its free delight is the feeling and percipience of beauty. At the same time, Kant has argued that all rational beings possess formally similar faculties and mental structures and may therefore be supposed capable of such feeling and percipience. From this he is able to conclude that we are justified in claiming the possibility of a shared delight and universal agreement in the judgement of taste. He has a neat way of encapsulating all this. He says, 'The beautiful is that which, apart from a concept, pleases universally' (*ibid.* p.60).

Why does Kant not regard the judgement of taste as a cognitive one? It is because it does not conform to the standards he has laid down for knowledge in the first *Critique*, the *Critique of Pure Reason*. But his account does allow for the judgement's having what might be described as the *feeling* of knowledge: that vivid sense of a profound understanding or awareness that is characteristic of much aesthetic experience.

In the third Moment Kant turns to considering the beauty that is judged in the judgement of taste. He describes the beautiful object or representation as possessing 'the form of finality' or, in a phrase that has become well-known, as having 'purposiveness without purpose' (*ibid.* pp.62–3). By this he means that we apprehend the beautiful object *as if* it were something designed for a purpose. It is not that we think of it as actually having a particular purpose that it might be possible to discover, but that it has the *form* of purposiveness. The point Kant is making here is perhaps best understood by reference to beauties of nature. The forms and patterns of flowers and crystals and of certain natural formations of stones and rocks seem to have the purposiveness he describes, appearing to possess meaning and significance in virtue of their shapes and patterns and the arrangement of their elements, and yet to have no definite or particular meanings.

It is precisely this unfettered form of purposiveness or finality in a representation that quickens the interaction of Imagination and Understanding in a free and pleasurable way. The activity of these two faculties corresponds to the unfettered purposiveness in the perceived form, for they interact in a way that is both lawlike and free, just as the representation that quickens their activity is at once both free (in that it fulfils no particular end or purpose) and lawlike (in that it has the *appearance* of having been designed for a specific purpose). In the free but lawlike interaction, of Imagination and Understanding evoked by the representation, one experiences the delight that is the judgement of taste.

The fourth Moment of Kant's analysis of the judgement of taste takes up and develops something he raised in the second Moment, namely, the claim that the judgement 'This is beautiful' implies that 'everyone *ought* to give the object in question his approval' (*ibid.* p.82) and also describe it as beautiful. What he is pointing out, once again, is that the judgement seems to imply that it is *possible* for us to agree in such judgements and that, ideally, we *ought* to agree in them. But the only basis or justification for assuming all that is by presupposing a 'common sense': an ability in everyone to experience pleasure 'from the free play of our powers of cognition' (*ibid.* p.83), that is, of Imagination and Understanding. Of course, very often and for a variety of reasons we are unable to exercise this ability to the full and so we disagree in our judgements of taste; but the *possibility* of agreement is given a foundation if we presuppose such an ability. It is an 'ideal norm' which, if or when realized, is an example of how judgements of taste would concur under ideal conditions.

It may be useful, before going any further, to summarize the main points of Kant's account of aesthetic experience. We need to remember that he approaches the matter by analyzing the kind of judgement we make when we experience beauty and that his chief claim is that it is by a feeling of delight that we come to judge that something is beautiful. This delight has to be distinguished from the delight that is merely a sensory agreeableness, such as a liking for strawberries, and from a delight in something that is recognized as morally good. Both these latter kinds of delight are 'interested' in that the person who finds strawberries agreeable wants there to be actual strawberries to eat, and the person who is rational cannot, according to Kant, do other than desire the real existence of anything that is morally good. Delight in beauty is free delight, not only because it is disinterested but also because one's activity of mind in respect of it is not circumscribed by a definite concept that imposes limits on one's reflections. This does not mean that apprehension of the beautiful is chaotic; for Imagination and Understanding interact in a way that is *formally* similar to the way in which they interact when they work by means of concepts to produce knowledge. They interact as harmoniously *as if* they are still concept-governed, albeit with a much greater scope to their activities than when they are determined by particular concepts.

According to Kant, beauty in a representation is its formal properties, its appearance of being designed, but for no specific purpose. This purposiveness without purpose generates and corresponds to the harmonious, lawlike but unconfined interaction of the cognitive faculties. When we experience beauty we are recognizing and responding to formal qualities.

Kant's account of genius further illuminates the character of the experience of beauty, for he sees the activity of mind of the producer of works of art as similar in many ways to the activity of mind of the perceiver of beauty. He describes genius as 'the innate mental aptitude (*ingenium*) *through which* nature gives the rule to art' (*ibid.* p.168). It is a talent for producing that for which no definite rule is given. Genius itself 'gives the rule to art'. The genius is someone who has a natural ability to produce works without the constraint of definite concepts, although this does not mean that works of genius are not law-like. The essential property of genius is originality and this originality consists in following the law of one's own nature in producing a work of art. Of course, this does not mean that anything one does out of one's own nature is an act of genius, for one might merely produce original nonsense. Kant therefore maintains that a work of genius must be *exemplary* in that it must furnish a model, not for imitating, but for following. It would be pointless to try to be a genius by imitating the work of a genius. Imitation can never furnish us with such a work because the copy it produces is the result of investigation and working to rules and so is the result of an activity that is logically distinct from acting in accordance with the ruling of one's own original nature. One can only seek to follow the example of the way in which a genius works.

The intelligibility that the work of genius must possess if it is not to be judged merely as original nonsense depends on the vital and generative activity that takes place between the Imagination and the Understanding. Kant speaks of the Imagination as a productive faculty that is a powerful agent for creating 'a second nature out of the material supplied to it by actual nature'. This rich profusion of thought and ideas, if it is to be apprehended, must satisfy the demands of Understanding. It may not be a merely fanciful association of ideas but must follow 'principles which have a higher seat in reason (and which are every whit as natural to us as those followed by the Understanding in laying hold of empirical nature' (*ibid.* p.176). Kant maintains that when the creative artist borrows material from nature and develops it into 'what surpasses nature', his imagination produces 'aesthetic ideas' that endeavour to embody 'rational ideas'. These 'rational ideas' have no instantiations in the natural world. They are large, composite notions such as peace, justice, brutality, purgatory and so on. But they may achieve the appearance of reality through being represented aesthetically in particular, sensuous, complex images. Kant writes:

> Such representations of the imagination may be termed *ideas*. This is partly because they at least strain after something lying out beyond the confines of experience, and so seek to approximate to a presentation of

rational concepts (i.e. intellectual ideas), thus giving to these concepts the semblance of an objective reality. But, on the other hand, there is this most important reason, that no concept can be wholly adequate to them... The poet essays the task of interpreting to sense the rational ideas of invisible beings, the kingdom of the blessed, hell, eternity, creation, etc. Or, again, as to things of which examples occur in experience, e.g. death, envy, and all vices, as also love, fame, and the like, transgressing the limits of experience he attempts with the aid of an imagination which emulates the display of reason in its attainment of a maximum, to body them forth to sense with a completeness of which nature affords no parallel; and it is in fact precisely in the poetic art that the faculty of aesthetic ideas can show itself to full advantage. This faculty, however, regarded solely on its own account, is properly no more than a talent (of the imagination).

(Ibid. pp. 176, 177)

A simple example can perhaps illustrate all this. If we consider the rational idea of peace and, using Kant's terminology, attach to it the image of a dove, then we have a wealth of attributes to dwell on: whiteness, purity, the freedom of flight, soft-voicedness and pastoral quiet; and all these images expand and enrich one's intellectual conception of peace. As well as the logical, intellectual understanding of peace we have an aesthetic idea of it that expands it almost limitlessly. The Imagination 'spreads its flight' over a vast, related, but indefinite and unformulable area. In Kant's philosophical system, once thought has developed beyond concepts that can be instantiated in objects of sense and moves into the realm of ideas, what it dwells on cannot count as knowledge. Yet such thought has the *form* of knowledge, for it deploys Imagination and Understanding in a way that is formally similar to the way in which they are deployed in the acquisition of knowledge. Concepts such as eternity, hell, and the kingdom of the blessed are, in Kant's terminology, ideas or concepts of reason. This means that they may be rationally conceived but not *known* in sense experience; and they may be explored and enriched by means of aesthetic ideas.

One great value of Kant's account of the judgement of taste is that it sharpens and organizes our intuitive understanding of what aesthetic experience is like, identifying and analyzing its elements with great precision. Another major value of his account is its placing of the judgement of taste within a larger conception of human capacities and activities. By delineating the wider relationships in which aesthetic sensibility stands to cognition and desire, to reason, sense, Imagination and Understanding, it provides us with an account that is at once exact and comprehensive. We are able to recognize both the particular character of what he calls the faculty of taste and its connections with other faculties. Thus the judgement of taste, or aesthetic judgement, is identified as arising from feeling. It is a feeling of pleasure that is distinguishable from pleasurable feelings concerning the agreeable or the good in that it is disinterested; it is disinterested in that it is concerned with the representation or appearance rather than with the real existence of what is perceived. The pleasure that arises from the mutual quickening of rational and imaginative faculties is subjective and the judgement arising from it is not made by reference to any definite concept of beauty, but at the same time invites the agreement of others.

All of that is consistent with many of our more informal descriptions of aesthetic experience. Kant also encompasses in his account two other characteristics that often feature in our informal descriptions. These are, first, the sense of the illimitability of the aesthetic experience and, second, our intimations of some sort of connection between the beautiful and the morally good. The illimitability, the unbounded proliferation of harmoniously related images and thoughts, has its source and justification for Kant in the imagination's freedom from the restraint of definite concepts. The sense of a connection between the beautiful and the morally good is a more complex matter, requiring a fuller grasp than can be given here of the place of reason in Kant's moral philosophy, so I shall do no more than indicate the kind of connection Kant expounds. He maintains that full reflection on something that is beautiful cannot fail to lead to reflection also on the morally good. This is because, in his view, a beautiful representation, natural or made, is a rendering of moral ideas in terms of sense: the beautiful is the symbol of the morally good. Kant is not wanting to suggest here that experiences of beauty are to be sought in order to come to what is morally good, but that if we do attend appropriately to beauty we shall have, at the very least, some intimations of its necessary connections with the morally good. Nor, in speaking of beauty as the symbol of the morally good, is he saying that, for example, a painting of a morally good person such as Socrates symbolizes moral good by depicting a virtuous person. His meaning is more profound than that. It is the *formal* properties of the work, of any beautiful work, be it a depiction of a saint or of a carcass in a slaughterhouse, that for him symbolize the morally good; and there is a formal resemblance, too, between the way in which we judge beauty and the way in which we ascertain what is morally good, for both involve a freedom that is nevertheless lawlike, and both have, in Kant's view, an ultimate grounding in the faculty of reason.

Kant's account of the disinterestedness of aesthetic pleasure has been criticized for ambiguity. His formulations, it has been said, 'are not clear enough and unequivocal and the explications provided by him do not coincide' (Mitias, 1986, p.142). This line of criticism has been developed by pointing out that the Kantian notion of disinterested pleasure seems to have at least three basic meanings: first, it can refer to a satisfaction that is independent of whether the object exists or not; second, to a satisfaction that is independent of any desire to possess the object; and third, to a satisfaction that is devoid of personal interest. But it is difficult to see why these three features of aesthetic disinterest should be seen as constituting *ambiguity*. Why should they not be understood as three different aspects of aesthetic disinterestedness? One's pleasure in the look or sound of something is distinguishable from any interest one may or may not take in its actual existence, from any desire to possess it and from any personal involvement with it. It is surely distinctions such as these that Kant sought to make in order to sharpen understanding of the nature of aesthetic sensibility. His analysis certainly is not immune to criticism, but it does seem to be a mistake to regard its complexity as ambiguity.

A general criticism of Kant's account, and one that has greater cogency delivered from a twentieth-century perspective than from an eighteenth-century one, derives from the fact that it works largely within that trilogy of concepts, art, beauty and the aesthetic, that have so often been loosely defined or understood in terms of each other. For Kant, the judgement of taste is a judgement arising from the feeling of pleasure in the *beautiful*, and because of the close connections between art and beauty it is then very easy to assume that the account of what it is to experience beauty is also the account of what it is to experience a work of art. But this identity should not be assumed, and we need to think about the worth of Kant's account of aesthetic experience separately from the question of its worth as an account of the experience of art, just as we may think of the aesthetic as dealing with concepts other than beauty. Another limitation of Kant's account is that he does not discuss what is involved in judging something *not* to be beautiful. We have to infer that an appropriately disinterested contemplation of something lacking the form of purposiveness yields no pleasure and that the object is thereby judged *not* to be beautiful.

There is much more to Kant's *Critique of Judgement* than it has been possible to outline in the preceding pages. It explores the nature of art, genius and the sublime, as well as the logical characteristics of aesthetic judgement, and many other things besides. Here the main emphasis has been placed on the notion of disinterest, not only because of its importance in Kant's own account of aesthetic experience but because of the influence it has exerted on so many subsequent developments in aesthetics and the philosophy of art. From the complexity of Kant's analysis of the judgement of taste has developed the view that to experience something aesthetically is to experience the perceived properties of the object and to do so for the sake of that perception rather than for the sake of any other relation in which one may stand to the object.

7 Form and 'Significant Form'

Several of the views discussed so far have emphasized the importance of form in aesthetic experience. The concept of form is not a simple one. Even the most rudimentary reflection on it quickly encounters complexities of meaning and reveals that thinkers use the term in different ways or with different emphases. For Aristotle form is the balanced structure that relates the elements of a whole. For Aquinas, it is something similar: 'a due proportion', a harmony, wholeness and clarity the perception of which constitutes a revelation of essential being. For Schopenhauer, as for Plato, form is the metaphysical structure of reality that is perceivable and also knowable only under certain conditions. With Kant, only form, in the sense of design, can be beautiful. For him, colour is a non-formal property and cannot be an element of beauty because its appeal is only a sensory one. He allows that a colour may be agreeable and its agreeableness may attract us to the beautiful form, but any pleasure taken in it is distinct from the pleasure taken in the beautiful. Non-formal properties, on Kant's account, are therefore not objects of the judgement of taste. He writes:

> In painting, sculpture, and in fact all the formative arts, in architecture and horticulture, so far as fine arts, the *design* is what is essential. Here it is not what gratifies in sensation but merely what pleases by its form, that is the fundamental prerequisite for taste. The colours which give brilliance to the sketch are part of the charm. They may no doubt, in their own way, enliven the object for sensation, but make it really worth looking at and beautiful they cannot.
>
> (Kant, 1973 edn, p.67)

An influential theory of the aesthetic enjoyment of form was presented in a book written by Clive Bell (Bell, 1915). Bell's theory applies predominantly to the visual arts and was written at a time when the work of Impressionist and Post-Impressionist painters was a source of perplexity to many people who could see no merit of any kind in the new styles of painting and who had been accustomed to judging paintings more by reference to their content and subject matter rather than to their formal aspects. Bell launches into his exposition by stating:

> The starting point for all systems of aesthetics must be the personal experience of a peculiar emotion. The objects that provoke this emotion we call works of art. All sensitive people agree that there is a peculiar emotion provoked by works of art... This emotion is called the aesthetic emotion; and if we can discover some quality common and peculiar to all the objects that provoke it, we shall have solved what I take to be the central problem of aesthetics.
>
> *(Ibid.* pp. 21, 22)

Bell goes on to ask what quality is shared by all objects that provoke our aesthetic emotions. He replies:

> Only one answer seems possible – significant form... lines and colours combined in a particular way, certain forms and relations of forms, stir our aesthetic emotions. These relations and combinations of lines and colours, these aesthetically moving form, I call 'Significant Form'; and 'Significant Form' is the only quality common to all works of visual art.
>
> *(Ibid.* p.23)

When Bell speaks of 'all works of art' he is using the term 'work of art' in an evaluative sense to mean '*good* work of art'. Significant form is the essential characteristic of a good work of art. Unlike Kant, Bell does not exclude colour as an element in significant form. He regards the distinction between form and colour as an unreal one, remarking that

> You cannot conceive a colourless line or a colourless space; neither can you conceive a formless relation of colours... when I speak of significant form, I mean a combination of lines and colours (counting white and black and colours) that moves me aesthetically.
>
> *(Ibid.* p.26)

Nor does Bell place much importance on aesthetic experience of nature. He concedes that

> some people may, occasionally, see in nature what we see in art, and feel for her an aesthetic emotion; but I am satisfied that, as a rule, most people feel a very different kind of emotion for birds and flowers and the wings of butterflies from that which they feel for pictures, pots, temples and statues.
>
> *(Ibid.* pp. 26–7)

Beautiful insects, creatures and natural objects, he maintains, do not exhibit significant form and so do not move us aesthetically. What makes form significant is that it 'conveys an emotion felt by its creator', whereas beauty conveys no such emotion. But Bell's main concern in all this is to draw attention to an important difference in the ways in which we may experience visual works of art. It is the difference between works that may excite interest and admiration, that may 'move us in a hundred different ways, but... do not move us aesthetically' and works that do move us aesthetically (*ibid.* p.30). Among the interesting but non-aesthetic works he includes 'portraits of psychological and historical value, topographical works, pictures that tell stories and suggest situations, illustrations of all sorts' (*ibid.* pp. 29–30). He singles out Frith's popular *Paddington Station*, a painting full of incidents, characters and social detail. He remarks on the fascination of all it depicts but declares that it is not a work of art, even though it contains 'several pretty passages of colour'. Then he says:

> In it line and colour are used to recount anecdotes, suggest ideas, and indicate the manners and customs of an age: they are not used to provoke *aesthetic* emotion. Forms and the relations of forms were for Frith not *objects* of emotion, but means of *suggesting* emotion and conveying ideas [my emphasis].
>
> (*Ibid.* pp. 30–1)

What Bell is insisting on here is that the aesthetic emotion is a response to form itself, not to the human circumstances or characters or events that form may be used to depict. But he does not want to say that realistic representation must necessarily be bad; it may well be significant, but its aesthetic value, in his view, lies in its formal aspects. Sumerian sculpture, pre-dynastic Egyptian art, archaic Greek, and early Chinese and Japanese works are cited as sharing three characteristics: absence of representation, absence of technical swagger, sublimely impressive form.

Bell's conclusion is that 'to appreciate a work of art we need bring with us nothing from life, no knowledge of its ideas and affairs, no familiarity with its emotions... For a moment we are shut off from human interests; our anticipations and memories are arrested; we are lifted above the stream of life' (*ibid.* p.36). These words are vividly reminiscent of Schopenhauer's remark that art 'plucks the object of its contemplation from the stream of the world's course and holds it isolated before us' (Schopenhauer, 1969 edn, vol. I, p.185). Bell maintains that significant form, the one essential characteristic of art that induces true aesthetic emotion, is unaffected by cultural and historical change. He writes: 'great art remains stable and unobscure because the feelings that it awakens are independent of time and place, because its kingdom is not of this world'. Yet he does not believe that the *same* unchanging forms are universally and perpetually reappearing in art, for 'the forms of art are inexhaustible; but all lead by the same road of aesthetic emotion to the same world of aesthetic ecstasy' (Bell, 1915, pp. 45–6).

The claim that we need bring nothing with us from life in order to appreciate art is worth pondering. Bell elaborates it by saying that 'we need bring nothing with us but a sense of form and colour and a knowledge of three-dimensional space' (*ibid.* p.37). But can he be right in regarding the representational aspect of a painting as in no way relevant to an aesthetic perception of it? When we dwell on a painting such as Picasso's *Woman Weeping* (Colour Plate 2) it is not simply that its lines, colours and shapes are satisfyingly related in a formal complexity but that in being so related they perfectly and movingly exhibit *grief*. It is the mutually enriching union of form and content in the work that seems to be the source of its *aesthetic* excellence. But on Bell's account, a purely aesthetic contemplation of *Woman Weeping* would not even begin to engage with – if that is psychologically possible – the depiction of tears and a woman's face; for him, the aesthetic emotions experienced by the percipient should be evoked by the work's formal elements and not by anything represented or embodied in or by those forms. Bell might well reply to the point that it is the indissolubility of form and content that is aesthetically potent, that those who hold such a view in fact lack the capacity to respond to significant form in the required way.

Bell's separation of content from form and his near-exclusive linking of the aesthetic emotion to art bring about a bifurcation between on the one hand, art and the aesthetic, and on the other, what he calls 'life'. For him, in experiencing the visual arts aesthetically we turn away from everyday living and enter another world, 'a world with an intense and peculiar significance of its own... that... is unrelated to the significance of life' (*ibid.*). In this other world the emotions of life, Bell says, 'have no place... it is a world with emotions of its own'. This seems to run counter to the intuition that aesthetic perception and appreciation of painting, and of the arts in general, can be of profound significance in everyday life, and in part II of his book Bell acknowledges and endorses this intuition. He declares:

though art owed nothing to life, life might well owe something to art…
Art does affect the lives of men; it moves to ecstasy, thus giving colour
and moment to what might otherwise be a rather grey and trivial affair.

(*Ibid.* p.77)

He concedes, too, that art is affected by life, 'for to create art there must
be men with hands and a sense of form and colour and three-dimensional
space and the power to feel and the passion to create'. And he provides a
more exact account of how the objects and scenes of daily life, depicted
in so many paintings, feature in the aesthetic perception of significant
form. He writes:

Artists are often concerned with things, but never with the labels on
things. These useful labels are invented by practical people for practical purposes… A practical person goes into a room where there are
chairs, tables, sofas, a hearth-rug and a mantelpiece… if he wants to set
himself down or set down a cup he will know all he needs to know for
this purpose. The label tells him just those facts that serve practical
ends; of the thing in itself that lurks behind the label nothing is said.
Artists, *qua* artists, are not concerned with labels… They are concerned with things only as means to a particular kind of emotion which
is the same as saying they are concerned only with things perceived as
things in themselves; for it is only when things are *perceived* as ends
that they *become* means to this emotion… when we do succeed in
regarding the parts of a landscape as things in themselves – as pure
forms, that is to say – the landscape becomes, *ipso facto*, a means to a
peculiar, aesthetic state of mind… because they *perceive* things as
ends, things become for them [the artists] 'means' to 'ecstasy'.

(*Ibid.* pp. 79, 80)

Bell's words there cannot but remind us that in his emphasis on the
importance of form in aesthetic experience he is in the mainstream of
philosophical thinking on the topic. Like others before him he holds that
to perceive the forms of things is to experience the deeper reality of the
world. When he turns, in the third chapter of *Art*, to what he calls 'the
metaphysical hypothesis', his question is: Why do certain arrangements
and combinations of forms move us so strangely? Part of his answer we
know already from remarks already quoted. We are moved aesthetically
by forms that express the emotions of those who create works of art; the
artist, more than the ordinary spectator, finds material beauty expressive
and is able to see things 'as ends in themselves' rather than as means to
something other than themselves. And when something is seen stripped
of all its associations and all its significance as means, the formal

significance that is revealed is, Bell says, 'the significance of Reality'. The artist's emotion is an emotion felt for reality and the work of art is an expression of that *emotion*: 'Not what he saw but only what he felt will necessarily condition his design' (*ibid*. p.79). We have to suppose, Bell writes, that when we consider anything as an end in itself,

> we become aware of that in it which is of greater moment than any qualities it may have acquired from keeping company with human beings. Instead of recognising its accidental and conditioned importance, we become aware of its essential reality, of the God in everything, of the universal in the particular, of the all-pervading rhythm.
>
> (*Ibid*. p.72)

Few have denied the attractiveness, boldness and vitality of Bell's view but numerous charges have been laid against it. One charge often made is that of vicious circularity. Bell first states that art evokes aesthetic emotion; he then says that aesthetic emotion is evoked by significant form. But significant form, we are then told, consists of such lines and colours as evoke aesthetic emotion: aesthetic emotion and significant form have been defined in terms of each other instead of independently of each other. What is needed to break this circle is a description of aesthetic emotion that distinguishes it from other emotions without reference to significant form.

Another complaint is that Bell's theory is highly subjective. He says that 'the starting point of all systems of aesthetics must be the personal experience of a peculiar emotion' and he maintains that an aptitude or gift of aesthetic appreciation is rare and requires constant cultivation and practice: 'Only those for whom art is a constant source of passionate emotion can possess the data from which profitable theories may be deduced' (*ibid*. pp. 21 and 19). All this means that it is difficult to disagree effectively with his theory, since any criticism of it can be dismissed or, at the very least, undermined by the response that it must be emanating from someone lacking in the sensitivity required to respond to significant form. At the same time Bell seems to believe, in a somewhat Kantian mode, that it is part of what it is to be a human being to possess some capacity to respond to significant form. But he makes no sustained attempt to say how agreement in aesthetic judgement might be possible.

Another criticism levelled against the theory of significant form relates to its fundamental simplicity. Bell assumes that aesthetic experience can be characterized by reference to a single essential quality: significant form. Such a view, as we have already seen, can be challenged. To be fair to Bell, we have to remember that he does not put forward his theory as one that he would want to assert for all the arts. His concern is with the visual arts only. But even there the theory seems to be over-simple in its claim that 'to appreciate a work of art we need bring with us nothing from life, no knowledge of its ideas and affairs, no familiarity with its emotions'. What Bell wants to exclude are those irrelevant, associative, extraneous connections that 'life-experience' can lead us to make and that can so disastrously obscure the intrinsic character of the object that is before us. What he did not seem to recognize was that his own superb appreciative capability did not so much exclude representational elements as deploy or assimilate them with complete appropriateness in the service of his aesthetic delight in formal properties. Nor does he fully consider the point already made that form and content are often fused together, as in Picasso's *Woman Weeping*, or when, for example, the depiction of a tempest is given by means of rough and forceful brush strokes.

Such criticisms of Bell's theory do not mean that the notion of significant form is without value. For anyone struggling to find a way to a certain kind of enjoyment of paintings the doctrine surely was and is a supremely illuminating one. The fact that it stands in need of refinement and correction is as much a merit as a failing since it thereby evokes an immediate critical interest and debate.

Bell separates art and significant form from beauty. He does not define art in terms of the beautiful; beautiful form is not the same as significant form and it is significant form that is, for him, the essential quality of works of art. It is the aesthetic rather than the beautiful that Bell connects with art. He regards aesthetic experience as experience of art, except in the case of the artist who, he says, is capable of experiencing the aesthetic emotion in respect of many things.

8   Experience and 'an experience'

All the talk of aesthetic experience as something distinct and different from other kinds of experience presupposes an understanding of what is meant by 'experience'. But the presupposition merits investigation. The term 'experience' can be used in a very broad sense to cover almost every aspect of conscious living and also in a quite narrow sense to refer to a particular and perhaps very brief incident or episode. These different applications are discussed and related to aesthetic experience by John Dewey in his book *Art as Experience* (Dewey, 1934).

Dewey is firmly opposed to theories such as Bell's that banish works of art and our experience of them to a separate realm so that their origins and associations with the human conditions that brought them into being are ignored and the experience of them is severed from its connections with everyday experience. He sees art and the experience of it as within the mainstream of human life yet as having characteristics of their own. He points out that 'life goes on in an environment' (*ibid.* p.13), that we continually interact with our surroundings, seeking enrichment and stability and a harmony with them. In all this, he says, there is a rhythm of loss and recovery of union but when we come to terms with our environment in a non-illusory way happiness and delight can occur. Dewey writes of 'a fulfilment that reaches to the depths of our being – one that is an adjustment of our whole being with the conditions of existence' (*ibid.* p.17). This, he says, is the source of aesthetic meaning, and the artist 'cares in a peculiar way for the phase of experience in which union is achieved' (*ibid.* p.15).

Dewey distinguishes between experience which occurs continuously and *an* experience. Experience in general is often inchoate: 'Things are experienced but not in such a way that they are composed into *an* experience' (*ibid.* p.35). In contrast, *an* experience is both integrated with and demarcated from the rest of experience. *An* experience might be a meal in Paris, a quarrel, a storm: 'in an experience, flow is from something to something' (*ibid.* p.36). There are pauses and fluctuations but no real gaps in an experience. Correlatively, in a work of art, different acts, episodes, occurrences, fuse into a unity, 'just as in a genial conversation there is a continuous interchange and blending, and yet each speaker not only retains his own character but manifests it more clearly than is his wont' (*ibid.* pp. 36–7). Within the unity of an experience much may be going on, Dewey says, but the *quality* of the experience unifies it so that we can identify it as *that* meal, *that* summer evening, *that* quarrel, and so on. He sees the difference between aesthetic experience and intellectual experience as being a difference in their materials. The material of the fine arts consists of qualities, that of intellectual experience of signs or symbols 'having no intrinsic quality of their own' (*ibid.* p.38). The signs or symbols of intellectual experience stand for or refer in some way to other things, whereas qualities may be appreciated for what they are. The difference between these two, qualities and signs, is, he says, enormous; but an experience of thinking can have an aesthetic quality in virtue of its structure, and aesthetic experience thinks by means of the thought embodied in the aesthetic object. Thus an experience of thought and an aesthetic experience each contain something of the other; it is only their different emphases that earn them different names. What Dewey wants to urge here is that there is no *fundamental* difference between experiences of all kinds and that most of our experience is non-aesthetic. By and large experience is either 'a loose succession of events' or a strictly mechanical connection of things, so that when the aesthetic appears with its vividness, coherence and vitality, it is often accorded a special status. But in fact any experience that is *an* experience rather than a formless continuity is so in virtue of possessing aesthetic qualities that unify it. Dewey remarks that 'the enemies of the aesthetic are neither the practical nor the intellectual. They are the humdrum...' (*ibid.* p.40).

There is an insistence on movement, development, change and culmination in Dewey's account of aesthetic experience. The movement towards a closure of an experience is, he says, 'the opposite of arrest, of *stasis*' (*ibid.* p.41). This looks at first sight very much like a view that is in exact opposition to that of all those who speak of the poised entrancement of aesthetic contemplation. Yet on examination it does not really show up as a contradiction. The users of the term 'stasis' do not maintain that the perceiver's whole activity is necessarily halted and frozen. It is more as if the actual passage of time is irrelevant and that the stasis occurring in the percipient refers to the steady focusing of the shaft of attention that is directed upon an object. Within that shaft of attention occurs everything that Dewey includes in an experience: an undergoing or receiving that may be difficult or painful, a searching absorption that may be charged with suspense and emotions of all kinds, an extension of understanding and an enrichment of meanings. Dewey believes that aesthetic perception involves activities comparable with those of the creative artist. He contrasts perception with recognition. Bare recognition of something or someone merely attaches a tag or label, imposes a role name: 'we recognize a man on the street in order to greet or to avoid him, not so as to see him for the sake of seeing what is there' (*ibid.* p.52). But when we perceive something aesthetically we do not see it as a pointer to something else, as a signpost that may lead to an experience, for the perception itself is the aesthetic experience. An object, Dewey says, 'is peculiarly and dominantly aesthetic, yielding the enjoyment characteristic of aesthetic perception, when the factors that determine anything which can be called *an* experience are lifted high above the threshold of perception and are made manifest for their own sake' (*ibid.* p.57).

Dewey's insistence on the cohesion of the aesthetic experience with experience in general contrasts sharply with certain elements of Bell's theory of significant form. Nevertheless Dewey approves Bell's emphasis on the importance of formal relationships and his rejection of painting as simply representational. What he cannot accept is the tenet that 'we need bring with us nothing from life' in order to appreciate a painting's aesthetic qualities; nor can he agree with the view that what a painting represents is entirely lacking in aesthetic import.[3] His own claim is that the painter is able to organize a scene, say of a bridge, buildings, a figure, to present a *new* object that is an expression of an emotion having a unique meaning. This new object, the painting, is not 'expressive' either of the scene alone or the emotion alone but only of the unique meaning brought about by their fusion. This means that Dewey cannot accept the implications in the theory of significant form that lines and colours have meanings simply in their relations to each other, for then, he argues, 'the meanings of lines and colours would completely replace all meanings that attach to this and any other experience of natural scene' (*ibid.* p.98). This would make the meaning of an aesthetic object different from the meanings of experiences of other things. The work of art would express something that belonged only to art instead of to every part of life and this would be contrary to Dewey's whole conception of aesthetic experience as not fundamentally different from other kinds of experience. He argues that it is impossible for an artist to approach a scene with no interests, attitudes and background of values drawn from prior experience and insists that a scene must be observed with meanings and values brought from experience *before* it is reconstructed in terms of the relations of lines and colours. He says:

> No matter how ardently the artist might desire it, he cannot divest himself, in his new perception, of meanings funded from his past intercourse with his surroundings, nor can he free himself from the influence they exert upon the substance and manner of his present being. If he could and did there would be nothing left in the way of an object for him to see.

(Ibid. p.89)

Imagination is important in Dewey's account. His analysis of it in chapter 12 of *Art as Experience* reinforces his claims concerning the dependence of aesthetic meaning on experience in general. He argues that all conscious experience has some imaginative quality and that it is only through imagination that meaning is donated. What he is maintaining can be exemplified by reference once again to Picasso's *Woman Weeping*. When we see this painting we comprehend it within a context of meanings and values derived from former experiences of the tears, the pain and wretchedness of grief, because we are able to *imagine* all those in relation to the work. Thus Dewey says: 'the conscious adjustment of the new and the old *is* imagination' (*ibid.* p.272). When the meanings aroused by something in the present fail to find an embodiment in that present they form the matter of reverie and dreams; emotions adhere to them and they seem fanciful and unreal. But in works of art these imaginings, or meanings, do become embodied in a material and it is this fact that constitutes what Dewey calls 'the peculiarity of all experience that is definitely aesthetic' (*ibid.* p.273). The work of art operates imaginatively rather than as a physical existent. It enlarges immediate experience by expressing imaginatively evoked meanings.

Although he affirms that imagination plays a vital part in aesthetic experience and the work of art, Dewey wants to reject theories that regard both of them merely as forms of illusion or make-believe. He regards reverie and dream-like states as significantly contributive to aesthetic states, especially to the creation of works of art, since they supply conditions for the emergence of deeply-stored meanings, but he does not see them as constituting the whole story. Descriptions in terms of reverie and dream omit the elements of control and purpose that transform the reverie from something subjective to something objective, intelligible and communicable. Dewey maintains that the kind of controlling purpose that is required relates only to the *matter* of the work. The imaginative element of a work that is to be a painting has to be conceived in terms of colour and shapes; of one that is to be a dance, in terms of movement, rhythms and deployment of space. The whole purpose is to produce an *object* in which the subjective reverie is embodied and which is attended to for what it is. In connection with this last point Dewey writes:

> the one who experiences the work of art loses himself in irrelevant reverie unless his images and emotions are also tied to the object, and are tied to it in the sense of being fused with the matter of the *object*. It is not enough that they should be occasioned by the object: in order to be an experience of the object they must be saturated with its qualities... the qualities of the object and the emotions it arouses have no separate existence. Works of art often start an experience going that is enjoyable in itself, and this experience is sometimes worth having, not merely an indulgence in irrelevant sentimentality. But such an experience is not an enjoyed perception of the object because it is provoked by it.
>
> (*Ibid.* p.276)

The issues addressed in those remarks are important ones. They concern the relationship between the work of art and its percipient. Dewey is pointing out that if we are to apprehend the work for what it is then *its* qualities and meanings must inform our experience of it. It must not be used merely as a trigger to revive personal and idiosyncratic memories or associations that render it, in the words of José Ortega y Gasset, 'only the cause and alcohol... of pleasure'. Instead, the elements of the work, however strange they may seem, must be allowed to shape and define one's sensibility. Thus Adrian Stokes, reflecting in a similar vein, wrote: 'The work of art should be to some extent a strait-jacket in regard to the eventual images that it is most likely to induce' (Stokes, 1966, p.247). The relationship has also been likened to that which is appropriate between persons. On that analogy we do not see a work of art as a means to some further end but as an end in itself. We do not impose preconceptions on it but let it reveal itself. We give it time, attending to it, and we allow that it has a plurality of meanings that are not immediately perceptible. If we find we like it we wish to repeat and deepen our experience of it. We wish to look again and to extend and refine intuitions through more careful enquiry, just as, if we like and love another person, we wish them to flourish, to continue being just as they are, and to enter into our lives. We see the work as another subject, a being in its own right. A painting, a novel, a poem, is like a world within the larger world, constituted as its own domain by its integrated internal order and unity. It is as if it has taken something of the larger world into itself and composed it there in such a way that when we contemplate it we are not, as it were, sent back into the larger world where meaning would become attenuated or diffused or interrupted, but find more and more of the world contained within the meaning of the work itself. One's imagination is not dispersed randomly by such a work. That is why, at best, we can be entranced by a painting, held to it by a shaft of attention that excludes everything else and that finds illimitable meaning in it. If we think of the painting as having taken something of the world into itself, we can understand why a contemplative exploration of the work can extend and deepen our experience of the forms and the life of the world. This is as true of paintings predominantly concerned with shapes, lines, colour and light as it is of those that tell some kind of human story, since any or all of those elements have been derived in some way from perceptions of the world and have then been embodied in the painting.

Dewey's constant concern in his philosophy is to avoid setting up a rigid system that disguises the real nature of experience. He wants to give a comprehensive account of aesthetic experience, presenting its several strands in such a way that they are never distorted by having the structure of a pre-conceived theory imposed on them. But his pursuit of those aims has sometimes provoked charges of a lack of clarity in his account. An example of this occurs in his remarks on the cognitivity of aesthetic experience. He does not want to say that aesthetic experience yields knowledge in any of the senses in which other philosophers such as Plato, Aristotle and Schopenhauer maintain it does. Instead, he writes of knowledge being *transformed* in aesthetic experience so that it becomes 'something more than knowledge because it is merged with non-intellectual elements to form an experience worth while as an experience' (Dewey, 1958, p.290). In speaking of 'experience worthwhile as an experience' Dewey is no doubt reaffirming his view that aesthetic experience is valued as an end rather than as a means. But it is difficult to know how exactly to understand the notion of knowledge being 'transformed' into 'something more than knowledge'. Yet the words serve to remind us of the special character of aesthetic experience and the high value placed on it by those who enjoy it. Dewey writes:

> The trouble I find with the representative and cognitive theories, is that they, like the play and illusion theories, isolate one strand in the total experience, a strand, moreover, that is what it is because of the entire pattern to which it contributes and in which it is absorbed. They take it to be the whole.
>
> (*Ibid.*)

But although he is ostensibly rejecting those traditional theories of aesthetic experience the general affinity of much of his account with some of the views of Plato, Aristotle, Aquinas, Kant, Schopenhauer and Bell is obvious, even when, as in the following passage, he is endeavouring to bring out the essence of his own conclusions.

> A work of art elicits and accentuates this quality of being a whole and of belonging to the larger, all-inclusive, whole which is the universe in which we live. This fact, I think, is the explanation of that feeling of exquisite intelligibility and clarity we have in the presence of an object that is experienced with aesthetic intensity. It explains also the religious feeling that accompanies intense aesthetic perception. We are, as it were, introduced into a world beyond this world which is nevertheless the deeper reality of the world in which we live in our ordinary experiences.
>
> (*Ibid.* p.195)

9 'Psychical distance'

A major question arising from the accounts discussed so far is whether aesthetic experience is to be thought of as depending on certain qualities or features of objects (where 'objects' includes not only particular things but scenes, events, persons, creatures and so on) or on a special attitude towards or way of perceiving things; or on some sort of conjunction of the two. Bell's theory of significant form is an example of the view that it is certain qualities of an object that furnish logically necessary conditions of aesthetic experience. Schopenhauer's theory is an example of the view that a certain attitude – in the case of his theory, an attitude of will-lessness – is its logically necessary condition. As already noted, those two theories of aesthetic experience, in common with others such as Aristotle's and Kant's, seem to require both a detachment and an involvement: a detachment from the practical or utilitarian aspects of the object and, as a result, a contemplative involvement with its essential being.

Reflection on those two features of detachment and involvement suggests that a distinction may be drawn between an aesthetic *attitude* and an aesthetic *experience*; the aesthetic attitude being a certain kind of stance or approach required as a necessary condition of aesthetic experience. On this view, the will-lessness described by Schopenhauer is the attitude of detachment that is necessary to bring about aesthetic experience. From this we may be tempted to think of the experience as a whole as a temporal, psychological process in which one is first rid of one's individual will and then, in consequence and if all goes well, enjoys an aesthetic experience of some sort. But this can lead to misunderstanding and error. For to think of Schopenhauer's account only as a description of a psychological process is to obscure the philosophical point for which he argues, namely, that denial of the individual will is the *logically* necessary condition for the impersonal knowledge of Idea that, for him, characterizes aesthetic experience. Will-lessness is a logically necessary condition of aesthetic experience because it would be logically absurd to attribute impersonal knowledge to a knowing subject who is personal and individual. Loss of will, or self, is therefore the logically necessary condition of Schopenhauerian aesthetic experience.

This does not mean that we have to think of the complete aesthetic experience as a process that conforms to a fixed pattern or rigid procedure. For example, in enjoying the Canteloube setting of the Auvergne folk song, 'Passo pel Prat' (Canteloube, 1983 recording, no 4) one does not first undergo an identifiable period of 'will-lessness' that precedes an actual aesthetic delight in its rapturous sounds. It is more as if, to use Schopenhauer's terminology, one's will is dissolved or snatched away in the entrancement of hearing the first phrases of the music. The logical conditions are effected, so to speak, in an instant rather than as part of an identifiable process. Conversely, there are times when, however propitious circumstances may seem to be for aesthetic experience, the immediate result is disappointing. A museum room lined with twelfth and thirteenth-century paintings may well have little effect when first viewed. But it is possible that days later one's mind may become overwhelmingly possessed by the images, forms and colours that had seemed to make so negligible an impact when they were actually seen.

A theory of the aesthetic attitude that attempted to encompass the variety of aesthetic experience and at the same time to define it exactly was expounded by Edward Bullough in a set of lectures he gave in the University of Cambridge in 1907 (Bullough, 1977 edn). The lectures were the first of their kind to be given there. They generated a widespread interest and ever since have exerted an influence on the philosophy of aesthetic experience. Bullough's account depends on what he calls 'psychical distance', a concept which he explains by reference to the experience of a fog at sea. He points out that a fog at sea can be strange and very frightening, 'all the more terrifying because of its very silence and gentleness'. Everyone present is anxious, nervous and strained. He writes:

> Nevertheless, a fog at sea can be a source of intense relish and enjoyment. Abstract from the experience of the sea fog, for the moment, its danger and practical unpleasantness... direct the attention to the features 'objectively' constituting the phenomenon – the veil surrounding you with an opaqueness as of transparent milk, blurring the outline of things... observe the carrying power of the air... note the curious creamy smoothness of the water... and the experience may acquire, in its uncanny mingling of repose and terror, a flavour of such concentrated poignancy and delight as to contrast sharply with the blind and distempered anxiety of its other aspects. This contrast, often emerging with startling suddenness, is like a momentary switching on of some new current, or the passing ray of a brighter light, illuminating the outlook upon perhaps the most ordinary and familiar objects – an impression which we experience sometimes in instants of direst extremity, when our practical interest snaps like a wire from sheer over-tension, and we watch the consummation of some impending catastrophe with the marvelling unconcern of a mere spectator.

> (Bullough, p.94)

Bullough attributes this switch in outlook to the phenomenon he calls 'Distance'. The Distance is between the self and its affections or, what he regards as much the same thing, between the self and the sources of those affections. In the case of the fog at sea Distance is produced by perceiving the phenomenon without being affected by the personal terror it can occasion. When 'distanced', even if we see the fog as something that causes terror we see the terror as in the fog rather than in ourselves: the distanced view of things is not our normal view of them. Distance works such that it cuts out the practical side of things, and allows the elaboration of what is thereby revealed.

It seems to be implicit in Bullough's account that 'distancing' is both a phenomenon one may consciously try to produce in order to achieve an aesthetic experience and also one that may just occur without conscious effort. He regards Distance as an aesthetic principle that enables us to distinguish agreeable pleasures which, he says, are non-distanced, from aesthetically valuable experiences that are impossible without the insertion of Distance. He rejects characterizations of art and our consciousness of it as objective, subjective, realistic, idealistic, sensual, spiritual, individualistic, typical, and so on. The conflicts between such descriptions, he says, can only be reconciled by the more fundamental conception of Distance. The notion of Distance, he maintains, provides a criterion of beauty and a distinguishing feature of the 'artistic temperament' as well as being one of the essential characteristics of aesthetic consciousness. It is what makes *aesthetic* contemplation possible.

Bullough wants to maintain that the relationship in which one stands to the aesthetically perceived object is a personal one, albeit of a peculiar character. Its peculiarity is that its personal character has been filtered: 'cleared of the practical, concrete nature of its appeal, without... losing its original constitution' (*ibid.* p.97). He cites our attitude to drama as an example. Enactments in the theatre often appeal to us in the way that people and events in daily life appeal, except that in the theatre we do not respond, as we might in daily life, by involving ourselves practically or physically in what is taking place before us. This non-participation is often explained by pointing out that we know the drama is 'unreal' and consequently do not intervene in it. But Bullough wants to turn this explanation on its head. It is not, he says, that knowing the unreal nature of the drama creates the Distance that prevents our intervention in it, but that 'Distance, by changing our relation to the characters, renders them seemingly fictitious' (*ibid.* p.98). His proof of this is that 'the same filtration of our sentiments' and the same 'unreality' of *actual* men and things occur, when at times, by a sudden change of inward perspective, we are overcome by the feeling that 'all the world's a stage' (*ibid.*).

Bullough also detects a paradox which he calls 'the antinomy of Distance'. He asks us to agree with him that a work of art makes its strongest appeal when we have sympathies and experience that let us apprehend it fully: when we have what he calls a *concordance* with the work. A man who is deeply jealous in his relationship with his wife might well experience a profound concordance in witnessing a performance of *Othello*. This ought to qualify him to appreciate the play fully; but, Bullough observes,

> He will probably do anything but appreciate the play. In reality, the concordance will merely render him acutely conscious of his own jealousy; by a sudden reversal of perspective he will no longer see Othello apparently betrayed by Desdemona, but himself in an analogous situation with his own wife.
>
> (*Ibid.* p.99)

He concludes that the concordance required for aesthetic perception should be as complete as is compatible with maintaining Distance; there must be '*the utmost decrease of Distance without its disappearance*' (*ibid.* p.100).

Bullough maintains that Distance may be variable in that there may be degrees of it that vary according both to the nature of the object and with the individual's capacity. The individual's capacity may also vary from occasion to occasion. For example, I may be unable to appreciate the collection of Byzantine icons I went to see today. Tomorrow, if I go again, it may be different; I may achieve a suitable Distance. This variability of Distance, Bullough argues, allows for variability in aesthetic experience in a way in which concepts such as 'objectivity' and 'detachment' do not. More importantly, he points out, it permits the notion of a particular kind of personal involvement as the hallmark of experiences that are aesthetic experiences. It recognizes, too, that Distance can depend on both the perceiver and the perceived object. 'Under-distancing', when it occurs, is usually a failing in the subject, as in the example of the jealous husband attending a performance of *Othello*. But it can also be occasioned by a failing in the object, by, for example, the kind of repulsive naturalism characteristic nowadays of some television soap operas. Excess of Distance, according to Bullough, is more often the result of some feature or features of the work of art, or can be brought about by the temporal gap that the passing of several centuries produces. Thus it may be that I find the icons difficult to approach or engage with because I can find no concordance of feeling with their somewhat cloistral solemnity and privacy; time has made their style and mood an alien antiquity for me until I, or they, effect some change in my sensibilities.

A criticism of the theory of psychical distance and of aesthetic attitude theory in general was presented by George Dickie in papers and a book written between 1961 and 1971. Dickie's claim is that the notion of an aesthetic attitude is a myth, once useful but now harmful to aesthetic theory. He is critical of Bullough's terminology: of the use of the word 'distance' to name a phenomenon and of the word 'distancing' to describe an action. For everything that is thereby referred to can, he maintains, be accounted for by using the concept of 'attention'. He asks: 'Do we, in order to appreciate some object, commit a special act of distancing? Or, if in a given case it is not a question of doing something, are we ever induced into a state of being distanced when faced with a work of art or a natural object?' (Dickie, 1971, p.50). His answer is that neither of these seems to occur because what we are actually doing is simply *attending* to an object. 'What', he enquires, 'is the point of introducing new technical terms and speaking as if these terms refer to special kinds of acts and states of consciousness?' (*ibid.* p.57). He says that if the distance-theorist asks: 'But are you not usually oblivious to noises and sights other than those of the play or to the marks on the wall around the painting?', his answer is: 'Yes, of course that is how it is; but it simply means that "one's attention is focused" and not that any special action has been performed or that any special psychological state has been induced' (Dickie, 1964, p.57). Dickie recognizes that aesthetic apprehension cannot be characterized merely by saying that one attended to a play, for the attention might be to the stagecraft manifested in it or to its likelihood of being a financial success; and so he suggests that the kind of attention required is attention *to the action of the play* and that this is a better description of what is going on than saying, as Bullough would say, that one puts the play (or any work of art) out of gear with one's practical interests.

What errors does Dickie believe will result from Distance theory? He objects to the use of the single notion of Distance to characterize aesthetic experience, to the proliferation of special terms, and to the rigid demarcations and categorizations that tend to result from such theorizing. The resulting framework, he maintains, just does not accommodate actual experience. More specifically, the upholders of Distance theory see it as having far-reaching implications, not only in taking

Distance to be a necessary condition of aesthetic experience but also in its being a yardstick for evaluating works of art. This is brought out in an article by Sheila Dawson (Dawson, 1961). Dawson, an advocate of Distance theory, refers to a part of *Peter Pan* in which Peter turns to the members of the audience and asks them to clap their hands in order to save the life of the fairy, Tinkerbell. She claims that this produces a 'horrible loss of distance' for most children: the magic has gone because distance has been abolished (*ibid.* p.168). This suggests to Dickie that 'loss of distance' might be used as a measure of the failure of something to be a work of art, and to rebut the idea he points out that *King Lear* and *A Taste of Honey* are plays in which an actor addresses the audience but which are not thereby disvalued. His own view of what is going on is that the author of *Peter Pan* is giving the children 'a momentary chance to become actors in the play' and that the children do not suffer loss of distance because they never were in a state of being distanced. Contrary to Dawson, Dickie maintains that 'Peter Pan's request for applause is a dramatic high point to which children respond enthusiastically' (Dickie, 1964, p.57).

We do not have to agree with Dickie's claims here. It is open to us to argue that the children who happily participate in *Peter Pan* by clapping their hands when requested, do so not because they are never distanced and accordingly suffered no loss of distance, but because they *are* distanced and remain so throughout the time in which they participate in the play. It may be that they have the imagination or sophistication to participate in that way *and* maintain distance. This does not contradict Bullough's own exposition of his theory of psychical distance, for he nowhere states that audience participation is incompatible with being distanced.

Dickie concedes that Bullough's theory has some plausibility when it has to do with 'threatening natural objects'. What he is thinking of here is the way in which strange or startling phenomena such as fog at sea or the freakish variations in wind, cloud and light that sometimes precede a violent storm, can bring about a sudden dramatic shift in one's perception of a scene or landscape. But he doubts the efficacy of the theory as it relates to works of art. It is not, he insists, that the jealous husband at the performance of *Othello* has lost or failed to achieve distance but simply that, because it reminds him of his own jealousy, he finds it difficult to attend to the action of the play. To a supposed defender of distance theory who wants to argue that a member of the audience who mounted the stage in order to save the heroine is someone suffering from loss of psychical distance, Dickie replies that 'a better explanation would be that he has lost his mind and is no longer mindful of the rules and conventions which govern theatre situations' (Dickie, 1971, p.50). He points out that there are similar kinds of conventions for each established art form and that being distanced certainly cannot be characteristic of our approach to all the arts because some arts, especially dancing and singing, will sometimes draw in the spectator to become a participant in the work. He observes that there are 'intermediate cases: hissing the villain and cheering the hero in the old-fashioned melodrama situation, applauding during an act because of an especially well-performed piece of acting, and so on'. He concludes that:

> It is not that we are detached or distanced from a work of art, we are barred from the work of art by the rules of the art game. It is not that picture frames, raised stages, and the like are devices which help cause a peculiar kind of psychological phenomena, as Bullough thought. These devices serve (along with other purposes) merely as a signal (if any is needed) that certain rules are to be obeyed. It would be better to speak of the aesthetic barrier than of psychical distance.
>
> (Dickie, 1962, p.299)

Dickie's criticisms have considerable cogency. They are certainly efficacious in casting doubt on the idea of a special kind of psychological mechanism that comes into play in order to generate aesthetic experience. And here it should be noted that his remarks are part of a broader attack he has made on what may be described as *psychologism* in aesthetics. This psychologism is the tendency to think of the aesthetic attitude wholly in terms of a subjective process occurring in individuals instead of seeing it as a concept that is a part of a philosophical account of what it *means* for an attitude or an experience to be *aesthetic*. Dickie wants to undermine the view that there is a special and somewhat mysterious mechanism in need of close, introspective examination, an examination which, if successful, would resolve problems about the nature of the aesthetic. He does not want a subjective process such as 'distancing' to be seen as the necessary and sufficient condition of aesthetic experience. For if 'distancing' an object becomes the guarantee of aesthetic experience of it, the notion of a specifically aesthetic object falls into abeyance and aesthetic qualities then depend on the psychological capacities of individuals. Against such subjectivism Dickie wishes to maintain that the close attention we pay to a work of art depends on objective features of the work – its wholeness, clarity and completeness – rather than on the performance of a special act by the perceiver.

Although his criticisms reveal inadequacies in Bullough's account of the aesthetic attitude and in subjectivist accounts in general, Dickie does not succeed in convincing us that the notion of Distance is one that should be abandoned. This is partly because Bullough's description of the 'feel' of those experiences we tend to call 'aesthetic' is extremely apt: we easily recognize what he is talking about and are able to acknowledge the considerable metaphorical and explanatory force of the notion of Distance even if we reject it as a complete and definitive account of the nature of aesthetic perception. And it is in just this respect, that is, as an adequate description, that Dickie's own account is unconvincing. The notion of attending to something, although it admits of greater and lesser degrees of attention, does not carry within it the rich phenomenological possibilities that are traditionally associated with aesthetic perception. Unlike the concept of contemplation, it suggests little or nothing of the selfless absorption, the engagement of heart and mind, commonly regarded as characteristic of the aesthetic point of view. It is more redolent of blinkered concentration than of a complex and variable experience of perception. It fails also to exhibit the character of an approach, captured in Keats's notion of Negative Capability, in which one is 'capable of being in uncertainties, mysteries, doubts, without any irritable reaching after fact and reason' (Keats, 1954 edn, p.179). In short, although Dickie succeeds in giving warning of a barren kind of psychologism that can result from Distance theory he does not thereby succeed in discrediting the whole account. Bullough's views are consonant with the mainstream of intuitive understanding of the character of the aesthetic domain and they embody issues that are still importantly alive in the philosophy of the arts.

An interesting question arising from discussions of the aesthetic attitude concerns the nature of our emotional involvement with works of art. Bullough, as we have seen, argues that Distance renders characters fictitious, so that we are not tempted to treat them as real beings, while Dickie maintains that observing theatrical conventions achieves the same result. But this awareness of the 'unreality' of works of art has evoked puzzlement. For how is it that we can be profoundly moved by depictions and representations which we know not to be real?

A suggestion that is somewhat different from both Bullough's and Dickie's views is that we engage in 'a willing suspension of disbelief' concerning characters and events in books, plays, paintings, and so on: we temporarily believe in their real existence and so are able to be moved by them as we would be in reality. But this is not a satisfactory analysis of what takes place. For one thing, if we did sometimes believe that fictional characters were real we would surely, on occasion, find ourselves intervening in the action of plays in the manner suggested by Bullough and we would react to paintings, statues, novels and poems in what would turn out to be entirely inappropriate ways. For another thing, we would be in a false relationship with these works, since to see them as real rather than as representations would deprive them of their true status as created entities. A work of art is *art*. It employs, as Kant pointed out, material that is borrowed from nature but that is 'worked up by us into something else – namely, what surpasses nature' (Kant, 1973 edn, p.176). If we suspend our belief that art is what it is then our engagement with art is not rational. It is therefore much more feasible to argue that we need to retain unimpaired the belief in the artifice of what we perceive, along with all our other beliefs concerning life, actions, and emotions, if we are to respond to such creations in a rational and intelligible way. It is clear that we are able to understand and feel deeply for characters in a book without knowing whether they are real or fictional, but the capacity to feel for them does not depend on either truly or falsely believing in their actual existence but on understanding the world of the book through its relation to the whole world of our beliefs. I do not have to believe in the actual existence of Romeo and Juliet in order to understand and feel the tragic nature of their deaths, because the meaning and import of what goes on *within* the drama is not affected by its being fictional or unreal.

This is not a topic that can be fully examined here but one further observation is worth noting. If it is puzzling or remarkable that we are able to feel anguish or any other strong emotion in experiencing something we know is not real then it is surely equally puzzling and remarkable that we can feel anguish at, for example, the envisaged or imagined loss of a person we love at a time when that person is safely with us. Indeed, this latter anguish should be seen as somewhat more remarkable and puzzling than the former, since it can occur without the prompting of a depiction or representation. But in fact we do not find such imaginings problematic except, perhaps, when they are pathological; and then it is the pathology rather than the ability to imagine that requires explanation. We do usually accept that most human beings possess, in varying degrees, the ability to imagine not only circumstances, events and situations which are not factual but also the responses and emotions they invite, just as we accept that they possess abilities to think, reason, remember, conjecture and dream.

10   A well-considered view

In the latter half of the twentieth century the American philosopher,

Monroe C. Beardsley, has made a sustained attempt to develop a satisfactory account of aesthetic experience. Beardsley avoids charges of subjectivism because he takes aesthetic experience to be largely of aesthetic objects and, he says, 'the object controls the experience' (Beardsley, 1958, p.527). His aim has been to provide criteria of aesthetic experience rather than a definition couched strictly in terms of necessary and sufficient conditions, and he offers five such criteria. In his paper 'Aesthetic Experience' he uses the term 'artkind instance' to refer to the entities that characteristically occasion aesthetic experience but he holds that the experience is also 'obtainable in some degree from other objects or situations (especially natural objects) that are often grouped with artkind instances in respect to an interest we take in them' (Beardsley, 1982, p.285).

Beardsley's five criteria of the aesthetic character of experience are: object directedness, felt freedom, detached effect, active discovery and wholeness. 'Object directedness' refers to the willingness to be guided in one's perceptual activity by certain properties of an object or a perceptual field. This includes not only an absorption in, say, the painting before us but also in its symbolism; or in the case of a novel, in its plot or in some aspect of its characterization. He sees this criterion of object directedness as a necessary condition of aesthetic experience.

'Felt freedom' is the release from considerations that are extraneous to the intrinsic meaning of what is present to one in aesthetic experience. Beardsley writes of 'that lift of the spirit, sudden dropping away of thoughts and feelings that were problematic... a sense of... having one's real way, even though not having actually chosen it or won it' (ibid. p.290). If I have understood aright, this felt freedom is the feeling of engaging in an untrammelled perception and understanding of something. It is a freedom from the dross that can so often intervene between oneself and the object of attention, and it generates a sense of being more aware of and more vitally at ease within the abundance of life. Beardsley perceives certain dangers of escapism in this feature of aesthetic experience and he does not want it to count as a necessary condition of the aesthetic. He points out that it may be absent in some of our encounters, especially 'with artkind instances that are intricate and puzzling and hard to make out, that offer resistances and obstacles to understanding or perception' (ibid.).

Beardsley observes out that his criterion of 'detached effect' somewhat resembles the notions of 'psychical distance', 'disinterestedness' and 'will-less contemplation' but he does not want it to carry the same philosophical implications as those notions. The major point he wishes to make by means of it is that our feelings about a depicted event or act or situation are significantly different from our feelings about their real life instantiations. He rates detachment as an 'important and extremely common feature of art experience' (*ibid*. p.291) but not as a necessary condition of it; for, he observes, an experience of an artkind instance that lacked such detachment might well qualify as aesthetic on other grounds. What is so difficult, he observes, is 'to capture in words the exact ways in which the practical or technological aspect of an object can and cannot enter into the experience of it if that experience is to have this third feature of detached effect' (*ibid*.). This is surely a central problem in any attempt to elucidate the nature of aesthetic experience.

Beardsley regards his fourth criterion, 'active discovery', as a central component in aesthetic experience. It refers to the cognitive element in the experience, to the exploratory quest that may range from a powerful exertion of intellectual capacities on a complex object to a calm perception of quite minimal formal relationships. Beardsley's account of this criterion is not entirely clear. Having said that he regards it as 'one of the central components' in aesthetic experience he then goes on to say that by itself and in its minimal manifestations it does not make an experience aesthetic. He does not say that he counts it as a necessary condition but remarks that 'there must always be *something* there to be apprehended, and there is always something going on that can be called, in a broad sense, understanding' (*ibid*. p.293).

When he first propounded 'wholeness' or unity as a criterion of aesthetic experience Beardsley developed the idea in terms of both a *complete* unity and a *coherent* unity. His claim was that the perceived unity of a work of art causes feelings, emotions and expectations in the perceiver, that these various affects are unified among themselves and that together with the objective elements of the work they constitute a unified experience. This account was subjected to criticism from George Dickie. Dickie maintained that although it is entirely possible to say of an artwork that it is unified, coherent and complete, it is not possible to say the same of our experience of it: we cannot intelligibly speak of 'aesthetic experience' mainly because

we cannot capture, or take hold, in our mind, of the reality to which the expression refers; and we cannot capture this reality because it lacks a structure, a specific identity, which we can conceive or in some way describe-because it lacks, in other words, a unity, i.e., coherence and completeness.

(Dickie, 1974, pp. 188–92)

Dickie's conclusion was that the unity, etc., that we certainly ascribe to the artwork has been wrongly ascribed by Beardsley to the *experience* of it. He pointed out that a unity of feelings is not possible in respect of some works of art because some works of art, such as ' a certain kind of abstract painting which has a good but simple design and which can be taken in, as it were, at a glance', do not affect our feelings. Further, he argues that not all works of art, especially works such as *Hamlet* that produce a great welter and variety of feelings, generate an effective unity in the perceiver (*ibid.* p.192).

In his response to these criticisms Beardsley modified his view. He relinquished his claim concerning the completeness of aesthetic experience because he wants to say that even if one listens to the middle of a string quartet for a minute or two, 'something aesthetic has happened to you – without completeness or consummation' (Beardsley, 1982, p.287). Aestheticness therefore does not depend on a unity of the experience in what he calls 'the dimension of completeness'. He concentrates accordingly on what he describes as unity in the dimension of coherence. He counters Dickie's objection that some works of art do not generate affects in us by saying that whatever elements such works *do* include 'may still more or less cohere' (*ibid.* p.294). More fundamentally, he challenges Dickie's view that there are experiences with aesthetic character that are without feelings, arguing that a scanning glance may indeed be without affect but that if it is, then it will also lack scope for the inclusion of other aesthetic elements. He meets Dickie's claim that a succession of a variety of emotions is not a coherent unity by pointing out that such a succession is made coherent in that the emotions are 'all muted by a degree of detachment through the fictionality of their objects, and this helps to keep them from flying off in different directions'; that the emotions can be felt to follow naturally upon one another; that considered as responses to the plot the emotions form certain patterns, rhythms and so on; and that underlying all the different emotions in a work such as *Hamlet* are pervasive feelings concerning the development of the tragedy. The feelings, Beardsley maintains, 'give the experience of the play much of the unity that it has' (*ibid.* p.295).

These modifications to the criterion of unity are well conceived. Much has been made, from time to time, of the importance of unity as a mark of aesthetic experience but it is difficult to see how it can be regarded as an essential characteristic of it, especially if it includes experience of phenomena other than works of art. We actually 'notice the world in small bits': we notice a fragment of bird song, glimpse the shining river from a moving train, momentarily register a single, pure colour, or encounter a word or phrase that seems to leap from the page into one's imagination (I think of 'October is marigold').[4] If such experiences have a unity it is more in virtue of their separateness or distinctness from more humdrum perceptions than in an internal coherence.

What are the merits of Beardsley's account of aesthetic experience? Certainly, by emphasizing criteria rather than necessary and sufficient conditions, he manages to loosen up the concept considerably, making it applicable to a very wide range of experiences. This is surely an important requirement in an account of something that has such a great variety of manifestations and that relates to such differing phenomena. At the same time, Beardsley manages not to loosen the concept beyond the bounds of useful applicability. As he points out, 'the proposed account of aesthetic character does enable us to admit numerous clear-cut cases of artkind instances to the class of things capable of providing experiences of this character... and it shows us how to rule out other phenomena that either have some pretensions to provide aesthetic criteria or may be expected or mistakenly believed to do so' (*ibid.* p.298). He offers two examples of the application of his criteria. The first is an account of the experience of some 'colour-field optical paintings' which a critic describes as largely unpleasant in that the painter has attempted to 'dazzle, blind, overwhelm' in a spectacular way. On Beardsley's criteria as listed on page 166 such an experience is not an aesthetic one. The second example is also of an experience that fails his criteria. It is the same critic's description of some objects at an exhibition as containing 'a sustained, sinister threat of imminent de-struction'. These threatening objects are

> a pile of rough hewn bricks stacked up on a glass plate that leans out towards the viewer, a low glass bench that, if sat upon, could splinter into painful pieces, a doorway stretched tight with rubber strips that pinch and press when you try to go through them and two sets of blinding hot lights set up on door jambs so as to cause great discomfort when you pass them.

> (Beardsley, 1982, p.297)

Only the sweep of a conveyor belt and the poised weight of the bricks have any aesthetic import. The other objects, although physically threatening, remarks the critic, 'never challenge us on an aesthetic level'. Beardsley points out that this is a proper critical discrimination. It distinguishes works that expand aesthetic experience from those that 'abandon it in favour of something else, something quite different' (*ibid.* p.297).

Beardsley's analysis should not be seen just as a well-considered defence of the claim that there is a kind of experience that is distinctively aesthetic. It certainly *is* such a defence and it does serve to mark the culmination of an important aspect of the debate; but it is more than that because Beardsley does not pretend to put every difficulty to rest. He is always aware of the formulation of fresh perspectives on art and the aesthetic, and this openness both to old problems and new ideas means that his analysis provides a basis for the discussion of developing issues. And that is how I shall use it in the last section of this essay; that is, as the starting ground from which to comment further on one or two of the persisting themes and developing issues in accounts of aesthetic experience.

11   Recurring and developing themes

Something that quickly becomes clear from the examination of a range of accounts of aesthetic experience is that the experience has no single defining feature. At the same time it is obvious that most accounts of it focus on groups of features or characteristics that are broadly similar; for example, concepts such as stasis, will-lessness, detachment, distance and disinterestedness have a good deal in common, even though they have differing emphases and differing significances within the philosophical systems or theories to which they respectively belong.

It seems to be the case, too, that the more one explores the topic of aesthetic experience the greater reluctance there is to commit oneself to any one account of it. No single theory seems able to do it justice, partly because the concept is a complex one that refers to a broad variety of phenomena and experiences, partly because it is a concept with a history that is linked to cultural history and to the history of philosophy. We cannot do other than regard earlier accounts of aesthetic experience from the point of view to which new works of art and new arts have brought us and in doing so we often find the earlier accounts, or parts of them, inadequate or irrelevant to the present-day concerns. There is always a growing edge to the study of aesthetic concepts and so it has been remarked that 'The writings of aestheticians very quickly come to appear dated' (Proudfoot, 1988, p.835). Nevertheless, certain themes endure and continue to emerge in one form or another, demanding clarification or reappraisal in the light of new ideas in the arts and of changing sensibilities.

One recurrent theme is that of the pleasure or delight of aesthetic experience. In many discussions of it there is an assumption sometimes implicit, sometimes explicit, that a positive aesthetic experience is always enjoyable. Numerous writers refer to pleasure, delight, enjoyment, rapture or satisfaction as characteristic of it. For present purposes I shall use the word 'delight' to encompass all these feelings, even though it is possible to discriminate in interesting ways between them.

When delight is ascribed to aesthetic experience that ascription cannot mean that one experiences delight as the *direct* response to all the works of art or phenomena that one is capable of experiencing aesthetically; for particular, immediate experiences may range from those of pure terror or grief, dread or melancholy, to those of rapture, rejoicing, amusement or mirth. Of course, there are works of art that are delightful in that they represent something delightful, express delight and engender delight in the perceiver. That kind of multiple delight attends the reading of a single line such as Laurie Lee's 'The hedges choke with roses fat as cream' (Lee, 1955). But something quite different from delight is imparted by, for instance, the last, anguished words of Dr Faustus as he waits to be taken by the devil to eternal damnation: 'O soul be changed into little water drops,/And fall into the ocean ne'er to be found' (Marlowe, 1976 edn, p.338). Nor do we respond with delight to the menace and deformity typical of so many of the figures in the paintings of Francis Bacon. Yet I am as glad to have seen a Bacon painting and a performance of Marlowe's *Doctor Faustus* as I am to have read Laurie Lee's poem, even though I find despair and suffering in the first two and am enchanted by the last. And it is perhaps the fact of this ultimate gladness that lets us see more exactly the nature of what has been loosely described as 'aesthetic delight'. It is probably better understood as an aspect of Beardsley's notion of 'felt freedom', so that it is taken not as a description of the character of every appropriate direct response to works of art but of an ultimate aesthetic approval that is experienced as a delight in a new clarity, a broadening or deepening or enrichment of sensibilities. A newspaper advertisement for the 1989 production of William Nicholson's play *Shadowlands*[5] cited plaudits acclaiming it as 'unbearably moving' and 'a joy to the end'. Those plaudits may seem somewhat contradictory at first sight but there is no real discrepancy between them if they are understood in the light of the foregoing remarks. The asserted joy is a joy in having been so deeply moved and enlightened in a way that is proper to a well-wrought drama. Nor, comparably, is there difficulty in explaining why we can be pleased and grateful to have seen a profoundly moving performance of a tragedy such as *King Lear* or *Othello*; for it is not that we are gladdened by Lear's suffering, by the wrong done to Desdemona or by Othello's blind passion, but that we have been admitted to an understanding of meanings and realities that are of great importance in human life. There is a sense of knowing something with vivid clarity and certainty. Rebecca West has written of this delight as 'a blazing jewel' and an 'intense exaltation', stimulated by a work of art 'which through its analysis of some experience enormously important to humanity... creates a proportionately powerful excitary complex'. This feeling, she maintains, is the result of perceiving the transformation of an experience which, left in its crude state, would make us feel that life is too difficult. Transformed, it becomes a joyful triumph: 'It is the feeling of realized potency, of might perpetuating itself'. This is not her own might that she feels; it is a sense that she has been helped to go on living, and also an intimation of something more. She writes: 'And that I should feel this transcendent joy simply because I have been helped to go on living suggests that I know something I have not yet told my mind, that within me, I hold some assurance regarding the value of life, which makes my fate different from what it appears' (West, 1979 edn, pp. 379–80).

Another recurrent theme, noted near the beginning of this essay, is that of the relationship between art and the aesthetic. There it was pointed out that aesthetic experience is not the equivalent of experience of art or experience of beauty even though, traditionally, it has been closely connected with both. Monroe Beardsley is among those who maintain that there is a very close connection between art and the aesthetic. He holds that a work of art is something that is produced with the intention of meeting an aesthetic interest and that when aesthetic experience is obtained from other than art objects or situations then they are ones 'that are often grouped with artkind instances in respect to an interest we take in them' (Beardsley, 1982, p.285). Thus he allows that aesthetic experience occurs outside as well as inside the realm of art and so is not specific to art. At the same time he is reluctant to accept the view that it is not an essential aim of art to generate aesthetic values and aesthetic experience. Once again it is important to recognize that cultural developments influence the scope of what can be said on this topic. Bohdan Dziemidok has pointed out that 'Contemporary artistic practice proves that it is possible to create... works of art which completely (or almost completely) lack aesthetic values of any kind. Not always, however, has it been thus, and not always will it have to be thus. Art is a cultural phenomenon and the cultural context has its final say in art's determination' (Dziemidok, 1988, p.15).

What is perhaps most significant in that remark of Dziemidok's is its qualifying parenthesis 'or almost completely'. It reveals a doubt as to whether it makes conceptual sense to describe a proffered work as a work of art if it is entirely lacking in aesthetic qualities. That is a large question which I shall not examine here. But let us suppose for a moment that the concept of the aesthetic is detachable from, even though it may often be significantly connected with, the concept of art. Then it may seem, as T.J. Diffey has pointed out, that there is 'no other place for it to go or context for it to occupy, so that it is left dangling in mid-air, as it were' (Diffey, 1986, p.5). But such a detachment might turn out to be instructive. Freed from any essential relationship with art, the concept of the aesthetic, although apparently homeless, might show its character more plainly so that on the occasions when it did have a connection with art the nature of that relationship would be better understood. By distinguishing the idea of experience of art from that of aesthetic experience we would be able to speak of experience of art as sometimes including an aesthetic element, sometimes as not doing so. We would perhaps be encouraged to acknowledge that a pure and *sustained* aesthetic experience is somewhat rare: that the occasions when we are held aesthetically entranced are few compared with those when our regard shifts rapidly between aesthetic, practical, economic, historical and other considerations. The experience of art in its broadest sense might be seen to include, in addition to aesthetic elements, much of the social and cultural razzle-dazzle of theatre-going, concerts, exhibitions and events as well as awareness of the techniques and media of the arts, of stagecraft, direction, production, criticism and the *modus operandi* of artists and performers of every kind, while aesthetic experience might be seen as obtainable from a postcard reproduction. That would not be to narrow or diminish the idea of aesthetic experience. Taking seriously its detachability from experience of art could foster more careful enquiry into the view that aesthetic experience is latent in many of our explorations of and dealings with the world; that it is an element in conscious activity in general and is manifested in many small domestic deeds and perceptions. It seems to be undeniable that 'In various ways, human beings seem to be endlessly and hopelessly caught up in an urge to render the world around them an aesthetically pleasing one' (Zuñiga, 1989, p.43).

In his paper already quoted, Diffey suggests that 'aesthetic' can mean something which comprises neither art nor beauty. In saying that, he is not denying that art and beauty are especially apt to generate aesthetic experience. What he proposes is that the nature of aesthetic experience might be more fully understood if we 'widen our sensitivity to the possibilities within the notion of the aesthetic' (Diffey, 1986, p.10). He cites a passage from Dostoevsky's *A Friend of the Family* in which the story's narrator describes the pleasure and admiration evoked by a certain beautiful child whom people felt was 'born to be happy'. Then the narrator observes: 'Perhaps my aesthetic sense, my sense of the artistic, was for the first time excited; it took shape for the first time, awakened by beauty, and that was the source from which my love arose'. Diffey points out that although this example may seem not to support his case for looking beyond the artistic and the beautiful for the meaning of aesthetic, 'it does encourage us when exploring the aesthetic to look for connections and relationships between art and beauty' (*ibid*.). It is true that it offers that encouragement. But it surely does also support the case for looking beyond art and beauty for the meaning of the aesthetic. For it speaks of an *awakening* and of that awakening as the source from which *love* arose. The implications there are that a new vision, or perception, and a deeper, or finer, feeling are involved in aesthetic experience.

Diffey considers another passage of literature from John Cowper Powys:

> It was not only a blow to her love, to her pride, to her happiness. It was a blow to something deeper than these, to that innate respect for life as a thing of quite definite aesthetic values, which made up the very illusion of her soul.
>
> (*Ibid*. p.11)

What Diffey seizes upon here is the question why aesthetic perception, construed as perception for its own sake, is deemed good and valuable. The problem, he says, 'is to explain why such experience should matter or is important to human beings'. His own suggestion is that the term 'aesthetic' is a term that 'extends thought, stretches the mind, and leads us into new and uncharted territory' and that our language 'is leading us by means of as yet such inadequately understood expressions as aesthetic experience to new possibilities of experience of which philosophy has not yet become self-conscious, is not yet cognizant'. For those reasons he believes that further systematic clarification of the notion of aesthetic experience is worthwhile (*ibid*. p.11).

There is another aspect of aesthetic experience which, like those aspects referred to by Diffey, merits closer examination because it, too, could reveal more about what it is we value so highly in aesthetic experience. It is the aspect which concerns what we ordinarily call the self. We should enquire more carefully into descriptions of what happens to the self in aesthetic experience. We speak of 'losing ourselves' in a book, a film, and so on, or of being 'taken out of' ourselves or 'transported'. This has to be distinguished from mere escapism, described by Schopenhauer as 'the common way' in which imagination is used 'to build castles in the air, congenial to selfishness and to one's own whim, which for the moment delude and delight' (Schopenhauer, 1969 edn, vol. I, p.187). In Schopenhauer's terminology such dreaming is wilful fantasy that wants the world to be a certain way and refuses to dwell on it as it actually is.

But what does happen to the self in aesthetic experience? And what is the value of the experience? We may begin to answer by saying that what happens is that we lose and regain the self. The self is lost in that it becomes absorbed in what it contemplates and explores. When it is regained, what has been experienced has become a part of it. By means of the senses, imagination and reason, one has encompassed phenomena and ideas that have widened and deepened consciousness in such a way that something of the life of the world, or the *possibilities* of the world, have become part of the personal realm of one's own life. The loss of the self is of course connected with the detachment characteristic of aesthetic experience and variously described as disinterestedness, will-less contemplation, psychical distance, stasis. Its regaining is connected with accounts of felt freedom, delight, knowledge, clarity, a sense of acquaintance with reality or truth. It is well described by Gadamer who writes that

> To the ecstatic self-forgetfulness of the spectator there corresponds his continuity with himself. Precisely that in which he loses himself as a spectator requires his own continuity... the absolute moment in which a spectator stands is at once self-forgetfulness and reconciliation with self. That which detaches him from everything also gives him back the whole of his being.

(Gadamer, 1986, pp.113–14)

It is, perhaps, the experience of music that exemplifies this most vividly. In listening to Canteloube's setting of 'Baïlèro' (Canteloube, 1983 recording, no 3) one can seem to inhabit and become inhabited by the song's sound. It takes up its life in the hearer and the hearer lives within and through its flow and vitality. In hearing it thus, we do not weave stories in it, even though we know it is a song that is meant to be redolent of skies and hills, space, air and radiant light. The sound itself is the whole 'story'. It is quite ungraspable; but there is no desire to grasp it for all that is wanted is that it shall be present to the hearer as it is. It is as if one is engaged, with the utmost accord, understanding and enlightenment, with a living presence.

Considerations of matters such as these may yield a fuller under-standing of aesthetic experience. In reflecting on them we quickly come to see that they are in many ways developments and reconstructions – representations or re-inventions, perhaps – of ideas contained in earlier accounts of aesthetic experience. Kant, for example, and as already noted, wrote of a felt freedom as an element in the experience of beauty, and Schopenhauer made much of the transformation of the self as the condition of aesthetic experience. It is true that we nowadays reject the metaphysical systems within which these thinkers organized their analyses; in particular we reject their positings of some kind of transcen-dental or metaphysical Reality as the ground of aesthetic experience. Yet it does not seem that Diffey, in writing of 'aesthetic' as a term which 'extends thought, stretches the mind, and leads us into new and uncharted territory' is describing something that is experientially dif-ferent from what was described by means of the older metaphysical ter-minology. This is not in any way to denigrate Diffey's insights and the particular focus of attention to the aesthetic that he proposes. Rather, it shows that there are features of aesthetic experience that endure, that cannot easily be left out of accounts of it, and that invite further exploration.

We should not slip into the error of thinking that when Diffey speaks of 'aesthetic' as a term that 'extends thought, stretches the mind, etc.' that he is thereby offering a definition of aesthetic experience. Aesthetic experience may well yield such expansions of mental life but the suggestion is not that it is its essential end or purpose to do so. What must not be lost sight of here is that the analysis of aesthetic experience is the analysis of an experience that is in itself an end rather than a means to some further end. In aesthetic experience the means *is* the end. Aesthet-ically speaking, I do not attend a performance of *King Lear* or contem-plate Picasso's *Guernica* (Plate 4) or engage with any other work of art or phenomena in order to learn something more about the world, but to live in and with the world in a particular way: aesthetically; that is, as an imaginatively participating perceiver. It is this way of inhabiting life and the world that is valued, as is so often said, for its own sake. Exactly what it means to value such an experience for its own sake is something else that merits discussion.

Bibliography

Aquinas (many editions) *Summa Theologica*.
Aquinas (1965 edn) 'On Being and Essence' in Goodwin, R.P. (trans.) *Selected Writings of Thomas Aquinas*, Bobbs-Merrill.

Aristotle (many edns) *Poetics*. Quotations are from the Ingram Bywater translation; references are to the Bekker numbering.

Aristotle (many editions) *Eudemian Ethics*.

Beardsley, M.C. (1958) *Aesthetics: Problems in the Philosophy of Criticism*, Harcourt Brace.

Beardsley, M.C. (1982) 'Aesthetic Experience' in Wreen, M.J. and Callen, D.M. (eds) *The Aesthetic Point of View: Selected Essays of Monroe C. Beardsley*, Cornell University Press.

Bell, C. (1915) *Art*, Chatto and Windus, and Grey Arrow, 1961 edn (to which page references are made).

Binkley, T. (1977) 'Piece Contra Aesthetics' in *Journal of Aesthetics and Art Criticism*, vol. 35, pp. 265–77.

Bullough, E. (1977 edn) *Aesthetics*, Greenwood Press.

Canteloube de Malaret, M.-J. (1983 recording) in *Songs of the Auvergne*, Series 1–3, Decca Record Company, Third Series, sung by Kiri Te Kanawa.

Dawson, S. '"Distancing" as an Aesthetic Principle', *Australian Journal of Philosophy*, vol. 39, 1961, pp. 155–174.

Dewey, J. (1958) *Art as Experience*, Capricorn Books.

Dickie, G. (1962) 'Is Psychology Relevant to Aesthetics?', *Philosophical Review*, vol. 71, pp. 297–300.

Dickie, G. (1964) 'The Myth of the Aesthetic Attitude', *American Philosophical Quarterly*, vol. 1, no 1, January, pp. 56–7.

Dickie, G. (1971) *Aesthetics: An Introduction*, Pegasus Press.

Dickie, G. (1973) 'Psychical Distance: In a Fog at Sea', *British Journal of Aesthetics*, vol. 13, no 1, Winter, pp. 17–29.

Dickie, G. (1974) *Art and the Aesthetic: An Institutional Analysis*, Ithaca.

Diffey, T.J. (1986) 'The Idea of Aesthetic Experience' in Mitias, M.H. (ed.) (1986) *Possibility of the Aesthetic Experience*, Nijhoff Publishers.

Dziemidok, B. (1988) 'Controversy About the Aesthetic Nature of Art', *British Journal of Aesthetics*, vol. 28, no 1, Winter.

Findlay, J.N. (1967) 'The Perspicuous and the Poignant', *British Journal of Aesthetics*, vol. 7, no 1, January.

Gadamer, H.G. (1986) *Truth and Method*, Barden G. and Cumming J. (trans.), Crossroad.

Joyce, J. (1956) *Stephen Hero*, Jonathan Cape.

Joyce, J. (1972 edn) *Portrait of the Artist as a Young Man* in Levin, H. (ed.) *The Essential James Joyce*, Penguin Books.

Kant, I. (1973 edn) *Critique of Judgement*, Meredith, J.C. (trans.), Oxford University Press.

Keats, J. (1954 edn) Letter, 21 December 1817 in Walsh, J.H. (ed.) *Selected Letters and Poems of John Keats*, Hart-Davies, Granada Publishing.

Larkin, P. (1988 edn) 'Love Songs in Age' in Thwaite, A, (ed.) *Collected Poems*, The Marvell Press and Faber and Faber.

Lee, L. (1955) 'Home from Abroad' in *My Many-Coated Man*, Deutsch.

Lewis, C.S. (1961) *An Experiment in Criticism*, Cambridge University Press.

Marlowe, C. (1976 edn) 'The Tragical History of Dr Faustus' in Steane, J.B. (ed.) *The Complete Plays*, Penguin Books.

Meager, R. (1964) 'The Sublime and the Obscene', *British Journal of Aesthetics*, vol. 4, no 3, July, pp. 214–27.

Mitias, M.H. (ed.) (1986) *Possibility of the Aesthetic Experience*, Nijhoff Publishers.

Proudfoot, M. (1988) 'Aesthetics' in Parkinson, G.H.R. (ed.) *An Encyclopaedia of Philosophy*, Routledge.

Sartre, J.-P. (1956 edn) *Nausea*, Baldick, R. (trans.), Penguin Books.

Schopenhauer, A. (1969 edn) *The World as Will and Representation*, Payne, E.F.J. (trans.), Dover Publications.

Sibley, F. (1965) 'Aesthetic and Non-aesthetic', *Philosophical Review*, 74, pp. 135–59.

Stokes, A. (1966) 'The Image in Form', *British Journal of Aesthetics*, July, vol. 6, no 3.

West, R. (1979 edn) 'The Strange Necessity' in *The Essential Rebecca West*, Penguin Books.

Zuñiga, J. (1989) 'An Everyday Aesthetic Impulse: Dewey Revisited', *British Journal of Aesthetics*, vol. 29, no 1, Winter, p.43.

Notes

[1] The term 'aesthetica' was first used by Baumgarten in 1735 in his *Meditationes Philosophicae de Nonnullus ad Poema Pertinentitous*. He used it to refer both to sensuous knowledge and the science of the beautiful, and maintained that the aesthetic knowledge resulting from these two complemented and was as reliable as intellectual knowledge.

[2] There is a discussion of the relationship of aesthetics to the philosophy of art in Edwards, P. (ed.) (1967) *Encyclopedia of Philosophy*, Macmillan vol. I, pp. 35–40.

[3] Dewey discusses this view at some length in *Art and Experience*, pp. 86–9 but in relation to a remark made by Roger Fry (a close friend and supporter of Bell) to the effect that the subject matter of a work of art is always irrelevant.

[4] This is the opening phrase of Ted Hughes' poem, 'October Dawn', in Alvarez, A. (ed.) (1962) *The New Poetry*, Penguin Books, p.149.

[5] *Shadowlands* is about C.S. Lewis's marriage to Joy Davidman and their deep relationship until the time of her death from cancer in 1959. Joy was already seriously ill when they married in 1957.

Art, Emotion and Expression

Robert Wilkinson

Introduction

Works of art are logically problematic for a number of reasons, and one of these is that we are apparently ready to ascribe to them qualities normally predicated of persons or other living organisms as well as those predicable of inanimate objects. Thus it is said of successful works of art that they have 'organic form' or that they have a 'life' of their own; or that bad works of art are 'dead' or 'lifeless'. Closely related to this is an equal readiness to regard them as essentially expressive of or embodying or communicating emotions (which are primarily properties of persons), and this line of thought has occurred nowhere more frequently than in Europe since the Romantic movement. It has often been assumed that all significant art in some way takes its rise in an emotional crisis of the artist, who seeks then to create a work of art such that those who come into contact with it are made to feel the artist's original emotion and are in some way thereby enriched. Again, and more formally, it has been held that art can be defined in terms of emotional expression; or that expression is the mental process distinctive of the artist properly so called. Again, the notion either of expression or of a very close link between art and emotion has been called on repeatedly in attempts to explain one of the most elusive of all the problems of the philosophy of art, the nature and aesthetic value of music. In this essay, some of the classic theories which use the concept of expression are examined, both those which seek to use it to define the concept of art and those in which it is used more specifically in the context of musical aesthetics. Then, in section 3, 'Expression and the Aesthetic Transaction' below, I examine each stage in the process of aesthetic communication (the artist, the work of art, the person experiencing the work of art) to see whether this process is illuminated by the concept of expression, and conversely how this concept is illuminated by it. Again, as is inevitable and proper in discussing this subject, a number of points will emerge as we go along about the nature of emotion, and the role of art in our emotional lives. A number of related but distinct topics will occur and recur, in different combinations, as we proceed. Is expressing emotion what artists do when they create works of art? How do they manage (if they do) to embody emotion in a work of art? What do we feel when we encounter the work? What is it to be in a mood or feel an emotion? What do we mean when we describe works of art in terms specifying expressive properties? What are these properties like? By the time we arrive at the end of the essay, I hope that the outline of a coherent view on these subjects will have begun to emerge.

I will begin with two theories which have in common the thesis that art is definable as the expression of emotion, of which the first is from Tolstoy. Before turning to this view, however, I would like to stress a point about terminology, which follows from some remarks I made above. In what follows, I will speak repeatedly of the 'expressive properties' of works of art. By this term I will mean only: 'whatever features it is that works of art possess which incline us to describe them in terms drawn from the description of human moods and emotions'. This usage of the term does not presuppose the truth or falsity of any of the theories to be discussed. The link (if any) between the expressive properties of works of art and the emotions of either the artist or the audience is one of the issues to be investigated. My use of the term 'expressive properties' is intended to be neutral on this matter.

1 Expression as a Defining Property of Art

Tolstoy's theory in What is Art? *(1898)*

Tolstoy approaches the question of the nature of art initially from a concern over what various individuals are made to suffer or at least put up with in its name: large sums of money are spent on it which could be put to other uses; people are treated cruelly in its service and sacrifices are enforced for its sake, and so on. Any human institution which induces behaviour of this sort needs a justification, and the start of a justification must be, in Tolstoy's view, a definition of the institution in question (Tolstoy, 1969, chapters 1 and 2). Tolstoy lists a number of the definitions of art he finds in standard works from roughly the mid-eighteenth century to his own time and finds them all confused (*ibid.* chap. 3). He therefore sets out to construct his own definition of art, and this task he begins by asking the question: what purpose does art serve in the life of humanity? Looking at the matter in this way, Tolstoy contends, 'we cannot fail to observe that art is one of the means of intercourse between man and man' (*ibid.* p.120). By words a man transmits his thoughts to others; by art he transmits his feelings. Art (like language) is a means to a goal Tolstoy valued very highly: that of union among humankind. Art produces a sense of spiritual union: 'In this freeing of our personality from its separation and isolation, in this uniting of it with others, lies the chief characteristic and the great attractive force of art' (*ibid.* p.228). Art brings about union by means of the transmission of feeling. Hence Tolstoy defines art as follows:

> Art is a human activity consisting in this, that one man consciously by means of certain external signs, hands on to others feelings he has lived through, and that others are infected by these feelings and also experience them.
>
> (*Ibid.* p.123)

That is, an object is a work of art if and only if:

(a) it causes its audience to experience feelings;

(b) it is deliberately intended to do so by its maker; and

(c) its maker has him/herself lived through the feelings thus aroused.[1]

Tolstoy supplements this definition with his second major claim, for not only does he limit the class of works of art to those which are expressive in the manner just defined, but he also wishes to stipulate which emotions are worthy of being communicated by works of art. In order to rank emotions in an evaluative way, Tolstoy needs a principle, and the principle he uses is drawn from the religious beliefs he held at the time of writing *What is Art?*. Tolstoy was at this stage of his life a fervent Christian of an ascetic cast. He denounced the pleasures of the flesh, and advocated as the goal of all action the bringing about of the brotherhood of man, which he regarded as 'true Christianity' (*ibid.* p.151). Valuable emotions, then, are those which bring about or exemplify the brotherhood of man, and it is these emotions which art should seek to transmit.[2]

It becomes rapidly clear that in Tolstoy's view very little of the accepted canon of European art in any form satisfies this test for the transmission of valuable emotions because of the way in which the test is interpreted. Society he regards as being divisible into the rich and the poor, and any art worthy of the name, in Tolstoy's view, will serve to break down the pernicious apartness of classes and persons which this division brings with it. From this it is a short step to Tolstoy's contention that 'true' art is such as to be immediately understandable by children and untutored souls, and so to everyone (*ibid.* p.177), and to his further assumption that any art which can do this is of a fairly simple and straightforward kind. Since (as Tolstoy goes on) most Western art since the Renaissance has been made to titillate the idle and bored rich, very little of it (in his view) is really art at all. In this period, religious belief amongst members of the upper classes all but evaporated, and to divert them from facing the spiritual vacuum left by its absence, the rich have commissioned from artists works ever more involved, affected, obscure and impoverished in respect of subject matter. Indeed, the entire canon of Western art (Tolstoy contends) transmits only three feelings, 'pride, sexual desire, and weariness of the world', and none of these is of any value (*ibid.* p.152). He reserves particular scorn for the French poetry of his time, that of Baudelaire, Verlaine and above all Mallarmé, who made special virtues in poetry of obliquity, allusiveness and difficulty (*ibid.* p.158). Tolstoy quotes a few lines from Mallarmé to make clear what he means:

> [In poetry] I think there should be nothing but allusions… To name an object is to take away three-fourths of the enjoyment of the poem, which consists in the happiness of guessing little by little: to suggest it, that is the dream.
>
> (*Ibid.*)

Very little music or painting fares any better: he rejects as unintelligible by the many all Symbolist, Impressionist and Neo-impressionist painters; and also the music of Liszt, Wagner, Berlioz, Brahms and Richard Strauss (*ibid.* pp. 170ff.). He also condemns nearly all his own works, including *War and Peace*, for the same reasons (*ibid.* p.246, n.1).

What remains standing as 'art' after this onslaught? Tolstoy gives a few examples of what he considers to be 'Christian' art: the works of Schiller, Victor Hugo and Dickens; *Uncle Tom's Cabin* and *Adam Bede*; the paintings of Millet; perhaps a dozen fragments (not whole works) from the combined *oeuvre* of Haydn, Mozart, Schubert, Beethoven and Chopin (*ibid.* pp. 242ff.). Special praise is reserved for what he considers the best (because universally intelligible and affecting) art: the Book of Genesis; the parables in the Gospels; folk legends; fairy tales and folk-songs (*ibid.* p.177); these last are greatly to be preferred to Beethoven's piano sonata op. 101, which in Tolstoy's view is characterized by 'obscure, almost unhealthy, excitement' (*ibid.* p.222).

When *What is Art?* was published it evoked both dismay and protest, both in Russia and abroad,[3] not surprisingly, since here was a writer of undoubted genius apparently condemning most art out of hand in an almost fanatical manner. The difficulties to be discussed here, however, are not those connected either with Tolstoy's ethics or with the critical verdicts he considers to follow from an application of his moral views. Tolstoy employs a number of assumptions and arguments of philosophical interest, and these illuminate the complexities of the concept of expression.

The first point to consider (which arises in connection with many variants of expression theory, not only Tolstoy's) is the assertion that expression is a necessary condition for art. Tolstoy's claim concerning the definition of art can be put in this way: x is a work of art if and only if x is expressive of feeling. (Let us leave aside for the moment the requirement that it must express a feeling its creator has felt.) The claim that only expressive objects count as works of art is difficult to sustain: there are many examples of minor pieces of music from the mid-eighteenth century, for instance, which are well-formed, elegant and pleasing but not in any significant way expressive, and yet these are undoubtedly works of art; and the same is true for many poems and paintings and so on. Works can enter the class of works of art by possessing a set of aesthetic virtues which do not include expressive qualities. A defender of Tolstoy would reply, perhaps, that these works are on his view desiccated and effete and not works of art at all. The response to this is that this only follows if Tolstoy's definition is accepted as a recommendation as to how to use the concept 'art': his definition is certainly not a record of how it *is* used, as the objection shows. Whether it is worth considering as a recommendation will depend to a large extent on whether Tolstoy's theory involves other difficulties: if it does, any recommendations as to conceptual revision will be to that extent less attractive.

One such difficulty is Tolstoy's conflation of moral criteria with aesthetic ones for the purpose of the evaluation of works of art. If further confirmation (i.e. beyond the text of *What is Art?*) is needed for Tolstoy's adherence to this view, it can be found in an entry in his diary for 17 November 1896:

> The aesthetic is merely one expression of the ethical... If feelings are fine and noble, art will be fine and noble too, and vice versa.
>
> (cited in Troyat, 1990, p.735)

(This subordination of the aesthetic to the moral is by no means unique to Tolstoy, it having been held by certain Utilitarians earlier in the nineteenth century and certain Soviet Marxist theorists in the twentieth, to give only two examples.) A critical consequence of this view is that the subject-matter of a work of art largely or wholly determines its aesthetic merit or demerit. That is, for anyone holding the Tolstoyan premise, it follows that the presence of whatever subject-matter is ideologically approved of guarantees success in a work of art, and its absence or contradiction guarantees indifference or failure, and this is very remote from the way in which works of art are generally assessed. Generally speaking, a large part of the assessment of aesthetic value depends on how the subject is handled, which is in effect to say whether or not the work has aesthetic virtues or vices or both. For example, Tolstoy wants to bring about the brotherhood of man, and one way of doing this is to promote the feeling of kindness between people. Therefore, good works of art, it follows in his view, will show the value of kindness: whether this subject is treated in an artistically satisfying way is irrelevant, for example, it is unimportant whether the characters are credible, or the style pleasing to read and so on. These features, which are aesthetic virtues, are on this view of no account in determining the value of the work of art as a work of art.

But to pay attention to these features is not to downgrade the importance of the subject matter. (These matters are discussed further in Essays Six and Seven.) There is a distinction to be drawn, as the critic A.C. Bradley pointed out, between two views:

(a) that the subject-matter of a work of art *guarantees* nothing with regard to its aesthetic value; and

(b) that the subject-matter of a work of art *counts for* nothing, i.e. that no subject-matter is more promising than any other.[4]

Proposition (a) does not entail proposition (b). Nor does the denial of Tolstoy's view (which is to accept as true proposition (a) above) entail that one's assessment of the truth or falsity of the content of a work of art (if it has a content which can be either true or false: generally speaking, buildings and pieces non-vocal music do not have a subject-matter of this kind) has no role to play either in the impact the work makes or in one's final estimate of its value.

Tolstoy's view concerning the relation of moral and aesthetic virtues leads to a third very serious difficulty (though, again, it is by no means unique to his own presentation of the expression theory). Since he regards the subject-matter of art as all-important and the handling of it as having little importance, it follows that for him the art object itself, the vehicle of expression, is of negligible value. The goal of art is to convey feeling type x, and if two art objects, A and B both do this equally well, then it will be a matter of indifference which I encounter or, indeed, if one of them is lost. But this is at variance with the way in which works of art are thought of. They are usually regarded as being in an important way individual or unique – once again, more like persons or higher animals than like mere objects – and the loss of any is the loss of something irreplaceable. What is crucial is the *way* in which each work is expressive: if this were not so, they would be substitutable the one for the other without loss, but they are not. To give only one example: there are a number of pieces of music dating from roughly the turn of the century which are 'farewells to life', for example the Ninth Symphony of Bruckner or the Tenth of Mahler. If Tolstoy is right, it is unimportant if one of these works is lost, but to say this is to see at once that it is false. The reason for the falsehood lies in the fact that in each case the poignancy is embodied in a unique fashion, and the uniqueness is constituted by the special combination of aesthetic properties employed in each case. Any theory of aesthetic expression must acknowledge that the vehicle of expression – the particular work of art itself – makes an ineliminable contribution to the expression.[5]

Beyond these general difficulties raised by the expression theory, there are two which are more closely allied to Tolstoy's particular version of it. First, as we have seen, Tolstoy urges that all good art is universally intelligible, and uses this test to dismiss most of the accepted canon of Western art. It might be argued against him, he notes, that a great deal of classical poetry, painting and music, which would have been unintelligible to the masses when it was produced is now widely understood and well-loved. Tolstoy's reply to this is that 'this only shows that the crowd, especially the half-spoilt town crowd, can easily (its taste having been perverted) be accustomed to any sort of art' (Tolstoy, 1930, p.147). By using an argument of this kind, Tolstoy is in effect refusing to allow anything to count as evidence against his initial assertion that good art is universally intelligible, since he is prepared to assert that the wide appreciation of any art he does not like is to be regarded as a perversion of taste. Nothing can falsify a theory couched in this way, and any theory which both (a) claims to tell us about the way things are in the world but (b) cannot be disconfirmed in any way by evidence about the world is logically suspect.

Secondly, Tolstoy's view entails some unacceptable consequences concerning the creative processes of artists. He insists that in any art worthy of the name, the artist must have lived through the feelings she or he wishes to express and that, having felt them, the artist seeks for a way of communicating these feelings to others. On both these points, Tolstoy's views (in this text) are somewhat over-simple. To anticipate briefly some points taken up later on in this essay, it is usually the case that the initial idea or inspiration for a work comes to the artist inchoate and unbidden, rather than being a clear-sighted, deliberate seeking after a form in which to embody an experience already fully thought through and conceptualized. Generally, the full embodiment of the inspiration in the work of art goes hand in hand with the understanding on the part of the artist of what the full implications of the initial idea might be. Nor is there any such simple correlation between what has been lived through and what is artistically convincing as Tolstoy suggests: many writers report, for instance, that characters they have created seem to take a direction of their own, and undergo experiences the artist can only imagine, but are none the less convincing as a result.

Since it involves difficulties such as these, Tolstoy's version of the expression theory is unacceptable; but it is not to be dismissed (as some have dismissed it) as the petulant, almost fanatical, outburst of an old man with pretensions to sainthood. The issues Tolstoy raises are important and profound: we do make and enforce sacrifices in the name of art, and it is not always obvious with what justification we do so; nor is it odd or cranky to suggest that the reason is located somewhere in a relation between art and our emotional constitution. This is a theme which will be taken up again in later sections of this essay.

As we have seen, one of the difficulties with Tolstoy's view is that it does violence to the complexity of the creative process of the artist; the same cannot be said of the second of the classic theories of expression to be considered here, that developed by R.G. Collingwood in his book *The Principles of Art* (1938).[6]

Collingwood's theory in The Principles of Art

Collingwood sets out with the same objective as Tolstoy, i.e. to answer the question: what is art? His avowed method is to derive the answer by examining common talk and convictions about art, and unveiling the normally unarticulated (but none the less present) general assumptions which underlie our everyday usage of the term 'art'. As he puts it, his aim is 'to clarify and systematize ideas we already possess... there is no point in using words according to a private rule of our own, we must use them in a way which fits on to common usage' (Collingwood, 1938, p.1).[7] Thus it is to be borne in mind, as each stage of Collingwood's argument unfolds and definitions are offered of terms such as 'art', 'expression' and 'imagination', that in his view '...no one can define a term in common use until he has satisfied himself that his personal usage of it harmonizes with common usage' (*ibid.* p.2). This is an important point to which further reference is made in what follows.

The first stage of the argument is to clear the ground by contrasting what Collingwood calls 'art proper' with other activities with which (he contends) it is generally confused. Of these, the most important is what he terms 'craft', which is characterized by six properties:

(1) Craft involves a distinction between means and end, each easily and independently identifiable.

(2) Craft involves a distinction between planning and execution.

(3) In planning, the end is prior to the means whilst in execution the reverse is the case. (E.g. if a carpenter plans to make a table, the end or goal – making the table – is prior to the devising of the means of the making, i.e. which wood, which tools, etc. Conversely, in the making itself, the means – the wood and tools – exist before the goal – the table.)

(4) There is always a distinction to be drawn between raw material and finished product.

(5) There is a distinction between form and matter: matter is identical in raw material and finished product; the form is changed by the exercise of the craft.

(6) There is a hierarchical relation between various crafts, one supplying what another needs (e.g. the timber merchant supplies pit props to the miner; the miner coal to the blacksmith, etc.) (*ibid.* pp. 15–17).

Collingwood denies that any of these six properties can be predicated of 'art proper', and one consequence of this is that he rules out at once the view that art can be defined as representation. This is because he equates representing something with imitating it, i.e. producing something that looks like it; and it follows from his definitions that representation is a craft, since it involves manipulating raw materials in the service of a goal ('making something that looks like *x*') known before the execution of the work begins.

A little reflection will show that certain common assumptions about art are also ruled out by the above analysis of craft and the denial of its applicability to art. He is committed to denying that an artist can distinguish between the goal (or end) and the means used to achieve it; or that the execution of the plan of a work of art can be distinguished from the plan itself; or that there is any meaningful distinction to be drawn between the materials of a work of art and the finished work composed of them. These assertions prepare the way for a definition of 'art proper' in terms of two concepts: expression and imagination. In Collingwood's view, the term 'work of art' does not refer to a public, physical object (or class of such) of any kind; rather, it refers to a mental object, a state of mind of the artist. These special mental objects can be defined as imaginative expressions of emotion. To appreciate fully what this means, it is necessary to grasp what Collingwood has to say about the nature of expression and the activity of the imagination.

Before the creation of a work of art, Collingwood contends, the artist feels oppressed by a burden of inchoate emotion the nature of which is unclear. In Collingwood's sense of the term, expression is a mental process the goal of which is to allow artists to articulate the nature of their emotion to themselves. The aim of this process is not the communication of the emotion to anyone else (e.g. an audience): this may occur, but it is incidental to the expression (*ibid.* pp. 109–11). Collingwood stresses that expressing an emotion is different from simply describing it. To say, for instance, 'I am in love,' or 'I feel angry' is not in Collingwood's sense to express an emotion, but simply to classify it. What expression does is to exhibit the special features of *this* instance of *my* feeling. Expressions are unique: 'Expressing [an emotion]... has something to do with becoming conscious of it; therefore, if being fully conscious of it means being conscious of all its peculiarities, fully expressing it means expressing all its peculiarities' (*ibid.* p.113). Put another way, expression individuates emotions. Again, expressing an emotion is to be contrasted with betraying it. To shake while feeling fear, for example, is not to express fear, since we can betray emotions without being fully aware ourselves of what it is we are feeling: 'The characteristic mark of expression is lucidity or intelligibility' (*ibid.* p.122), and mere betrayals of emotion do not share these properties of expression.

From this definition of expression certain corollaries follow, first concerning the division of the emotions expressed by art into the comic, the tragic, and so forth. Since *ex hypothesi* no artist knows the nature of what is to be expressed before the expression has taken place, no artist can set out to write, e.g. a comedy or a tragedy: such a distinction can only be made *ex post facto* (*ibid.* pp. 115–6). Secondly, the distinction between artists and non-artists is abolished, where the former are regarded as possessors of a special mental endowment called genius. A spectator who understands the feeling an artist has expressed, is to that extent also an artist, for on this view, to understand an expression is to recreate and re-experience it oneself (*ibid.* p.117).

Expression, then, is the rendering individual and intelligible to oneself of a burden of previously inchoate emotion. The faculty of the mind which carries out this activity, in Collingwood's theory, is the imagination, the central function of which is creative thought. The imagination makes the expression, but it is a type of making which (to use Collingwood's term) is non-technical. By this he means that the creative activity of the imagination is not like the use of a technique or skill (which, as we have seen, Collingwood takes to be an identifying property of craft) (*ibid.* p.128). Again, this creative activity cannot be the giving of a new form to an already existing bit of material of some kind, since this again is a feature of craft (*ibid.* p.133). Granted these stipulations as to what imaginative creation is not, Collingwood has to adopt the position that the real work of art is the expressive state of mind of the artist: he must locate the work of art in the realm of the mental in order to be consistent with his definition of craft. Hence: 'A work of art may be completely created when it has been created as a thing whose only place is in the artist's mind' (*ibid.* p.128). What we commonly refer to as the work of art (physical objects or performances) are in Collingwood's view to be regarded as merely externalizations of the work of art proper. These externalizations are designed to be such that, if properly executed and sensitively studied, we the spectators will be able to reconstruct for ourselves the same state of mind that was initially created by the artist. The work of art will then exist as *our* state of mind (*ibid.* pp. 134–5). Yet these externalizations are incidental: no work of art need be externalized at all. On this view, a mute (and inglorious) Milton is still a great artist, though no one will ever know it.

From this theory of imaginative expression, certain further consequences follow, of which we may pick out four. First, in Collingwood's sense of 'expression', there is no distinction to be drawn between an emotion and the expression of that emotion: the expression is *constitutive* of the emotion (*ibid.* p.244). From this in turn it follows not only that there cannot be an unexpressed emotion (*ibid.* p.238), but also that 'there is no way of expressing the same feeling in two different media' (*ibid.* p.245). Secondly, any activity which counts as an expression of an emotion is a work of art. Hence Collingwood writes: 'Every utterance and every gesture that each one of us makes is a work of art' (*ibid.* p.285). Thirdly, since (in Collingwood's view) all language expresses emotion, and since poetry and philosophy are both linguistic, there is no distinction to be drawn between them (*ibid.* pp. 297–8). Fourthly and finally, there is a state of mind on the part of someone contemplating a work of art which counts as the correct response to that work of art. The correct response is the reconstruction in the mind of the spectator of 'a total imaginative experience identical' (*ibid.* p.309) with that of the artist who created the initial state of mind which we are enabled to share as a result of the encounter with its physical externalization.

These consequences, taken together with a number of points raised earlier, indicate the first type of difficulty raised by Collingwood's views. It will be recalled that he claims to be systematizing common beliefs and convictions about art, but it is difficult to sustain this claim in the light of the positions set out in the preceding paragraph. For example, he contends that no artist can set out to produce a work with a particular emotional content yet this is at variance with how talk about the creation of art proceeds. If Collingwood were right in this respect, it is difficult to see how any artist could sensibly be commissioned to produce a work of a given type (as they regularly are), for example, a setting of the requiem mass, or a wedding poem or anthem, and so on, since what the artist produced might bear no relation to the mood of the commission at all. Again, he asserts that there is a correct response to a work of art, i.e. the one which duplicates that of the artist in creating it. Yet this again is not how such matters are usually viewed. Our response to works of art changes as we change with age and experience. What seems the last word in excitement and sophistication at twenty can appear twenty years later a jejune expression of hopes credible only on the basis of kindly inexperience, and who is to say which of these views is 'correct'? And on what grounds? (This is not to say, of course, that aesthetic responses cannot be roughly ordered in terms of, for example, sensitiveness or perceptiveness, at whatever age they are made, though the criteria we use to make such discriminations are themselves very subtle. The point is that ordinarily we do not regard aesthetic responses like problems in mathematics, to which more readily statable standards of correctness do apply.) The situation embedded in ordinary usage, which Collingwood claims to be summing up, is rather that there is a range of non-eccentric responses to a work of art, just as there is a range of defensible judgements which can be made. (From this it does not follow that such judgements are 'subjective' in any important sense, any more than this follows for the enormous range of non-aesthetic situations which can be defensibly interpreted in a number of ways, within the constraints of rationality.)

A further consequence of Collingwood's 'correct response' view is that with respect to music, drama and dance there must be such a thing as an ideal performance, approachable by others but ultimately admitting of no peer. Once again, this is difficult to square with the ordinary usage Collingwood is supposed to be summing up. Ordinarily, one accepts that, for example, two performers may interpret a musical score in quite different ways, but produce performances which are equally valid, and the same is true of plays. Scores and scripts, in their different ways, are not exhaustive specifications for performance; some aspects of the performance (and sometimes a good many) are left to the judgement of the performer. Collingwood draws attention to this last point himself (*ibid*. pp. 320–1), but does not note the implication of his views with respect to ideal performance.

Again, Collingwood says that every gesture and utterance we make is a work of art, and this is remote from common usage. Croce's version of this theory entails the same consequence, and as George Santayana once remarked in criticism of this latter version, any theory of aesthetics which entails 'that a perfect Neapolitan sigh is aesthetically equal to *The Iliad*' has very little to do with real life (Santayana, (a), p.54). To be fair, Collingwood is not committed to holding the sigh equal in aesthetic value to *The Iliad*; but he is committed to regarding both as works of art.

Now Collingwood lays great stress on the point that his theory is to contain nothing mysterious, nothing not contained in or implied by ordinary usage; yet, as we have seen, his view entails consequences which are not those of common usage. Since these consequences *are* entailed by his theory, it follows that one or more of his principal premises must be false. The problem seems to me to lie in his notion of what it is to express an emotion, combined with his view that works of art are mental objects.

Two facts about expression in art clearly and properly impressed Collingwood deeply: first that to construct expressive aesthetic objects requires imaginative power (such construction is neither spontaneous nor easy), and secondly, that where a work of art is successfully expressive, no other work of art can stand in for it – successful works of art are unique in respect of the way in which they embody expressive properties. Collingwood's view on this point is at the other end of the spectrum from that of Tolstoy who, as we have seen, regards works of art simply as a means to an end, paying no heed to their uniqueness. The difficulties arise when Collingwood combines the premise that expressions in art are unique with the further premise that works of art are mental objects. This latter position he wants to take up for a number of reasons, chiefly in order to be able to distinguish sharply between 'art proper' (imaginative and expressive) and craft (mere skill without imagination). In taking this view, he is responding to an idea which has been common coin for some time, i.e. that there is more to art than mere technical skill.

From his definition of expression, it follows that there cannot be an unexpressed emotion; and from the view that works of art are mental objects, it follows that there need be no physical externalization of the work and so that communication between the artist and anyone else is incidental to expression. Let us consider these points in order. There cannot be an unexpressed emotion, because by definition to be aware that one has an emotion is to that extent to individuate it and so to the same extent to express it. Combined with the premise that works of art are mental (and therefore private) objects, this commits Collingwood to a view of expression remote from the common usage from which he began. In common usage, the expression of an emotion is something which is in principle public: it is the aspect of the experience which manifests itself in a typical piece of behaviour. In common usage, the expression of emotion is something which, if it is to be inhibited, must be inhibited deliberately, and sometimes at great cost. Put another way, the point is that for Collingwood, 'express' means essentially 'to articulate uniquely' and involves no necessary reference to a public manifestation; but that in common usage, whatever else 'express' means, it does involve a necessary reference to such a manifestation.

Perhaps it will be replied that Collingwood is speaking of expression in an aesthetic context, and that that is significantly different from the non-aesthetic one; but here he faces a further problem over the role of the public, physical work of art which he calls the externalization and which he regards as in principle eliminable from the artistic enterprise. He has to try to deal with a serious difficulty (of which he is aware) which arises from the way in which artists work. The difficulty is that many artists report that they articulate their experience ('express' it, in Collingwood's sense) through working with the materials of their chosen medium. Collingwood puts the objection into the mouth of a painter, who sums up the reports made by a number of artists:

> One paints a thing in order to see it... You see something in your subject, of course, before you begin to paint it... but only a person with experience of painting, and of painting well, can realize how little that is, compared with what you come to see in it as your painting progresses... a good painter – any good painter will tell you the same – paints things because until he has painted them he doesn't know what they are like.
>
> (*Ibid.* pp. 303–4)

Thus, as Collingwood himself notes, the position is that,

> There is no question of 'externalizing' an inward experience which is complete in itself and by itself. There are two experiences, an inward and imaginative one called seeing and an outward and bodily one called painting, which in the painter's life are inseparable, and form one single indivisible experience, an experience which may be described as painting imaginatively.
>
> (*Ibid.* pp. 304–5)

Now this admission can be made verbally consistent with Collingwood's theory. He goes on to point out that he has not conceded that the painting (the physical object) *is* the work of art (which is the artist's imaginative expression); but what he does concede is that the production of the physical object 'is somehow necessarily connected with the aesthetic activity, that is, with the creation of the imaginative experience which is the work of art' (*ibid.* p.305). However, such a concession cannot be accommodated in Collingwood's theory: if the work of manipulation of the artistic medium is 'necessarily connected' with the realization of the inner state, then the externalization is essential to the process of creating the work of art, even if it is not identical with the latter. Once this is allowed, Collingwood can no longer maintain the sharp distinction he wants between artistry and craftsmanship.

There is a further difficulty related to externalizations which, whilst not a formal consequence of his theory, is important. Collingwood's theory is such as to encourage neglect of an important aspect of works of art, namely the role played by the materials of the work in question. It is obvious that, in varying degrees, the materials of a work of art play a significant role in its impact. This is most clearly so in sculpture and architecture, where the materials have a limiting effect on the form: metal statues of human beings can stand on their own ankles; stone ones cannot, hence the need for certain accessories or poses in stone. Concrete and steel buildings can be made in different shapes from those in brick and stone, because of the different strengths of the materials involved. In other arts the effects are subtler (like that of different kinds of pigment in paint, or timbres in music) but none the less they are equally important, since tiny changes of colour or sound can produce quite considerable aesthetic differences.[8] A theory like Collingwood's which identifies the work of art proper with a mental state, and regards externalizations as incidental, would not lead one to think carefully about this unjustly neglected aspect of aesthetics.

Finally, Collingwood's theory cannot sustain the objection to which Tolstoy's is also liable in that Collingwood's view also asserts that the expression of feeling is a necessary condition for any work to count as a work of art, and this is not so. Many objects are accepted as works of art which are not in any meaningful sense of the word expressive. If Collingwood counters that this is to mistake externalizations for works of art proper, the reply is that his notion of work of art proper is utterly remote from the common usage he claims to elucidate, and involves him in the difficulties noticed above.

To sum up, we have seen that Collingwood is sensitive to some important features of expression in art: that expressive objects are unique, and not easy to make; and that there is more to art than technical skill. However, the way in which he tries to do justice to these points in his theory, chiefly by means of his location of the work of art in the realm of the mental, leads him to conclusions remote from the common usage he claims to sum up. Again, certain facts about the way in which artists work lead him into inconsistency over the role of the physical objects which externalize the work of art.

If the last objection advanced above holds, it follows that all theories, like those of Tolstoy or Collingwood, which try to link expression to the *definition* of art, are unacceptable. From that, however, it does not follow either that there is nothing to be learned from considering these views (I hope I have shown that a good deal about expression and other matters does come up in such a consideration), or that the notion of expression is not important in an understanding of art. It has often been held that the expression of emotion, or a special relation between art and emotion provides the key to one of the most elusive of all the questions in aesthetics, the source of the power of music. To this issue we turn next.

2   Three Theories of Music

The power of music to stir the emotions has been acknowledged in both East and West for over two thousand years, even to the extent of being regarded as dangerous by those interested in safeguarding the state.[9] Yet it has proved extraordinarily difficult to give an account of how music can affect us in this way, and it is not hard to see why this should be so. The earliest and most enduring of Western theories of art identified art with the imitation of nature; but music will not fit happily within this definition. It cannot represent visual forms or colours; nor can it describe the world in conceptual terms, as language does; and its ability to imitate naturally occurring sounds plays only a tiny part in its impact, and composers rarely have recourse to it. Yet this non-mimetic, non-conceptual medium of organized sound has consistently provided aesthetic experiences of all levels of value, from the mildly diverting to aesthetic encounters which touch the centre of the personality and move us to a degree which is never excelled. What kind of art can this be?

The theories of musical aesthetics, which attempt to answer this question, fall into two broad classes:

(a) *heteronomist theories* which try to explain the aesthetic value of music in terms of its relations to something outside the music, and this 'something' is usually emotion; and

(b) *autonomist theories* which maintain that the aesthetic value of music depends on nothing outside itself, but solely on features intrinsic to the music.

In this section, we will look at three theories, two heteronomist and one (more or less) autonomist, all of which contribute to building up a clearer picture of what is involved in aesthetic expression and the relation of art and emotion. We begin with the heteronomist views, each of which links music with emotion, though in different ways. The first view is that of the musicologist Deryck Cooke.

Music as the language of the emotions

Cooke's views are of interest for many reasons, not the least of which is that they summarize and systematize in a learned and scholarly way ideas which many lovers of music implicitly accept as an account of the musical transaction (i.e. of what composers are doing, how they do it, and what listeners experience as a result). Cooke argues that music has a content, that it expresses feelings, and that an objective basis for understanding it may be found, (Cooke, 1959, pp. xi–xii) 'since music is, properly speaking, a language of the emotions, akin to speech' (*ibid.* p.33). The book as a whole is an attempt to assemble evidence to justify this assimilation of music to verbal language in certain respects. He admits (as he must) that, unlike verbal language, music does not embody concepts (*ibid.* pp. 25–6), but he does consider that it contains elements, like words, of constant signification which can be endlessly recombined to make new utterances understandable by any user of the language.[10]

The basic signifiers, the 'words', so to speak, of the language of music are the notes and intervals of the European diatonic scale, major, minor and chromatic (Cooke deliberately leaves out non-European systems, a point to be returned to below). These notes and intervals, and certain phrases derived from them, have (Cooke argues) 'inherent emotional characters' (*ibid.* p.xii). This is to say in effect that the notes, etc. of these scales have a meaning and this meaning is to be conceived of as a constant emotional significance. His method of argument to support this central contention is to assemble examples of European music from 1400 to 1900, and to isolate those common elements in the music that have closely comparable or identical expressive characters.

Some examples will make this clearer. It is obvious, in Cooke's view, that there is a general connection between music composed in major keys and pleasant emotion (e.g. joy, confidence, love, serenity, triumph) and between that composed in minor keys and unpleasant emotions (e.g. sorrow, fear, hatred, disquiet, despair) (*ibid.* pp. 50–1). Why should this be? A property which the intervals of both major and minor third have in common is fixedness, i.e. they do not need to resolve into another note, so long as they retain their basic character as part of a triad. Within the context of the triad, each has a constant significance: the major third is satisfied, contented and joyful, whilst the minor third is 'the supremely stern, straightforwardly and dignifiedly tragic note, firmly "looking on the dark side of things"' (*ibid.* p.64). The intervals of major and minor sixth likewise have respectively an inherently joyful or sad significance, but with the important difference that each needs to resolve into another note, and so express joy or sorrow in a state of flux, rather than as a settled condition (*ibid.* pp. 64–9). The intervals of seventh and second, major and minor, have less direct and emphatic similarities to the major and minor third, but nevertheless, Cooke argues, they have clearly discernible significance which emphasize joy and sorrow respectively (*ibid.* pp. 72–9). Cooke extends his account to cover all the intervals of the major and minor scales.

Musical phrases constructed from these notes and intervals have analogous expressive properties. Cooke gives examples of such phrases as the following:

(a) Ascending 1–(2)–3–(4)–5 (major): this phrase has always been used to express an outgoing, active, assertive emotion of joy (*cf.* the opening of the last movement of Beethoven's Fifth Symphony).

(b) Ascending 5–1–(2)–3 (major): as for (a), but with more exuberance, triumph or aspiration.

(c) Ascending 1–(2)–3–(4)–5 (minor): this phrase expresses pain; an assertion of sorrow, a complaint, a protest against misfortune.

(d) Ascending 5–1–(2)–3 (minor): this phrase expresses pure tragedy – and so on (Cooke, 1959, pp. 115ff.).

Cooke gives detailed examples to support seventeen basic phrases of this kind.

Thus baldly stated, it might seem that Cooke is implying a view of musical composition and reception of a crudely mechanical kind: I want to write a sad piece, so I consult my dictionary of intervals and phrases, select suitably sad ones, and begin writing; but Cooke was far too sensitive and knowledgeable to believe anything like this (*ibid.* pp. 168ff.). Throughout the book, he is at pains to stress that these basic significances can be modified in countless ways by other features of music, a fact which gives this language an unparalleled subtlety. These other musical features he divides into two classes which he calls (a) *vitalizing* agents and (b) *characterizing* agents. The vitalizing agents are volume, time and pitch. Generally speaking, volume determines musical emphasis (the louder, the more emphatic) (*ibid.* pp. 95–6). Time in music has two aspects: tempo and rhythm. The tempo of the music determines the speed at which it is played: the faster the tempo, the greater the animation. The rhythm determines which notes are accented or stressed (*ibid.* pp. 97–101). The root of the effect of pitch change is to be found in the naturally felt analogy between increasing the frequency of a sound and the idea that it is going up, and between diminishing its frequency and the idea that it is going down. Cooke in turn correlates this with a distinction between what he terms 'outgoing' and 'incoming' emotions: some forms of joy, for example, are exuberant and can be called 'outgoing' while, by contrast, grief in many instances causes a person to look inward and so can be described as 'incoming' (*ibid.* p.102ff.).

The characterizing agents are tone-colour (or timbre) and texture. Tone-colour Cooke regards as the chief means of dramatic characterization in music: the timbre of different instruments gives them different personalities, so to speak, which greatly affect the significance of what is played on them (imagine the same notes played on a piano, a harpsichord, a flute, a violin, a distorted electric guitar) (*ibid.* p.112). The texture of a piece of music is determined partly by the instrumental forces for which it is scored (from solo to full orchestra) and partly by the way these forces are used. What Cooke calls a 'thick' texture is often exemplified by Wagner or Richard Strauss; a 'spare' texture by Stravinsky or Satie or Hindemith (*ibid.*).

The language of music, then, in Cooke's theory, is made up of notes and intervals, and phrases derived from them, which have an inherent emotional significance, but these significances or meanings can be modified with infinite subtlety by the other features of music: volume, time, pitch, timbre and texture. Far from being a simple language to use, its endless permutations require the full capacity of genius if their potential is to be fully explored.

The first thought provoked by Cooke's views is this: how is he to account for the differences of opinion which listeners have over the emotional character of various pieces of music? Such disagreements do occur and are not confined to non-professionals: the pages written by cognoscenti are filled with often rancorous argument over what a given piece expresses. If music is a language by virtue of having notes of inherent significance, why are such disputes so routine? Cooke is aware of this objection to his theory, and replied as follows:

> Could it not be that some listeners are incapable of understanding the feeling of the music properly?... The fact is that people can only react to the emotions expressed in a work of art according to their own capacity to feel those emotions.
>
> (*Ibid.* p.21)

But this line of reply is suspect for at least two reasons. First, in order to make it work, Cooke must say what he means by 'understanding the feeling of the music properly' in a manner which does not involve him in logical circularity, and it is not easy to see how he can do this. It is difficult to envisage a test of 'proper understanding' which does not consist in accepting Cooke's views on musical significances, but this is to beg the question. The second sentence quoted above does not help to make matters any clearer. Cooke is apparently advocating the following principle: For any emotion E, I can 'react' to an aesthetic expression of E if and only if I can feel E; but this is false. I can react to an aesthetic expression of cruelty without either feeling cruel or ever having felt it.

Even if these problems could be circumvented by suitable changes to definitions, there remain further difficulties in Cooke's views of a more serious kind. The first concerns his central assertion that the notes of the major, minor and chromatic diatonic scales have an emotional significance or character which can be described as 'inherent'. Writing almost a hundred years before Cooke, the great critic Hanslick, whose own view we will come to presently, noted the following point:

> many of the most celebrated airs from *The Messiah*, including those most of all admired as being especially suggestive of piety, were taken from secular duets (mostly erotic) composed in the years 1711–1712, when Handel set to music certain madrigals by Mauro Ortensio for the Electoral Princess Caroline of Hanover.
>
> (Hanslick, 1957, p.35)

The piece generally known as 'For unto us a Child is born' is unaltered both in key and melody from one of these secular duets where it accompanies the words of a lover's complaint.[11] What has happened to any 'inherent emotional significance' the notes and phrases of the melody must have in Cooke's theory? He could reply that they have been 'extensively modified' by the other elements of the work, notably the words; but this is to equate 'modification' with 'obliteration'. To take an example from popular music, there are countless rock guitar solos based on fast twelve-bar sequences which include many minor thirds and minor sevenths, often played against a background of major chords and thereby (if Cooke is right) potentially producing violent semitonal discords expressive of intense disquiet; but the effect (if they are well played) is usually exciting, with an expressive character of a positive kind. The point is that if the 'inherent emotional characters' of the notes can be in effect obliterated (not just changed) by other features of the musical context, it is difficult to see what justification there is for the use of a term like 'inherent': if it is used properly, it must mark an invariable concomitance (if x is inherently y, then whenever x occurs, y occurs); but this is not true of some of the musical intervals on which Cooke relies.

The notion of inherence is involved in a further difficulty connected with Cooke's theory. To appreciate this problem, it is necessary to focus on a point mentioned in passing above: right from the start, Cooke restricts the scope of his theory to music in the European classical tradition from 1400 to 1900. He explicitly excludes recent atonal music, and all indigenous music from Africa, India, China and Japan: music from these parts of the world he refers to, significantly, as 'utterly alien' (Cooke, 1959, p.55). He is quite open on the point that: 'if music is an international language within a given continent, it is certainly not an inter-continental language' (*ibid.* p.xii). It is not difficult to see why he restricts his theory as he does, since some of the technical features of music from other continents would add considerable complications to his theory. For example, Cooke's view is only applicable to musical systems which operate with readily identifiable individual notes of definite pitch, and this notion is of little use in connection with certain Indian *ragas*, in which some 'notes' are played with a vibrato so wide and so slow that the Western idea of a note of a certain pitch is inapplicable to them. Again, in some circumstances notes are raised by sub-semitonal intervals not included in Cooke's theory. Again, much Chinese music is based on a pentatonic scale, which does not allow the construction of many of the 'phrases' of Cooke's musical vocabulary. One general point which emerges is that Cooke's theory, were it acceptable at all, would work only as an account of one period in the history of the music of one continent

(Europe), and would leave unexplained the undoubted expressive power of music from different traditions.

This of itself is not a reason for disputing that music might usefully be assimilated to language, since natural languages are not intercontinental either, but the restriction of the account to one cultural tradition is in tension with Cooke's hints as to how the terms of his vocabulary gain their significance. Cooke considers that the language of music (as he defines it) is more than a collection of formulae whose significance has come about merely by their habitual association with certain types of emotional expression (*ibid.* p.24). He considers that the correspondences between certain tone patterns on the one hand and certain emotional reactions on the part of listeners on the other are 'inherent, as are, for example those between certain faces we pull and certain emotions we intend them to express – delight, scorn or disgust' (*ibid.* p.25). Now emotional reactions of this kind are not the property of one cultural tradition only, and to attempt to locate the roots of musical significance in psychological reactions which are supra-cultural is inconsistent with Cooke's declared view that his theory does not work for non-European musical traditions. It is an indication of a tension which underlies Cooke's entire theory: on the one hand, he wishes to assimilate music to verbal languages, which have a vocabulary but in which nearly all words signify by convention; and on the other, he wants to locate the basis of musical meaning not in convention but in 'inherent significance', and if that were true, music would to that extent be quite unlike verbal language.

Cooke's theory has lead him to a confused position on a profound issue in the theory of the aesthetic response, an issue which is not restricted to the aesthetics of music but which surfaces with particular acuteness in the discussion of non-mimetic, non-conceptual art forms. The issue is to identify whether there are any elements of any art which derive their aesthetic impact or significance from perceptual responses so deeply embedded in the human psyche that we can regard them as (so to speak) built-in and automatic – 'tropism' is the psychological term generally used to refer to a response of this kind. If there are any such, they will form an important strand in the explanation of how aesthetic objects affect us as they do. Cooke does not address this issue in any detail and, as has been indicated, his remarks are not entirely consistent or clear. He does not advance a theory of human nature or perception, both of which are necessary if this problem is to be faced squarely. What these generalizations mean will become clearer if we digress from music briefly to glance at some ideas put forward by the Purist painter Amédée Ozenfant (1886–1966).

Ozenfant sought a theoretical basis for Purism, the style of painting he hoped would supersede Cubism, and hoped to ground this style in a theory of universal human responses. In his writings on this issue, he maintains very clearly that human nature includes such responses or tropisms and contends that art should be 'based on' such invariant features of human beings (Ozenfant, 1952, pp. xiii–xv). Colours and forms (insofar as these can be meaningfully separated), he contends, stimulate responses of this kind. The colour red always excites and the colour green always pacifies (*ibid.* p.251); again, some colours are painful to contemplate simultaneously or when mixed, for example, blue and red, and the mixture reddish-violet (*ibid.* pp. 252–3). And, no amount of conventional usage could 'make the curve express what the straight line expresses' (*ibid.* p.250). He is quite specific about where he thinks the roots of visual significance are to be found. 'The language of the visual arts is made up of categorical forms, which are only signs, as it were, inadvertently' (*ibid.* p.249). (A 'categorical form' is one which induces a tropism.) Interestingly, though he does not develop the point, he thinks music very similar to painting in this respect: 'Compare the effect of high or low notes on our state of being. All the affective value of music resides in the opportune utilisation of diverse auditory tropisms' (*ibid.* pp. 251–2). Painting and music derive their aesthetic impact from universal features of perceptual experience; not so literature, in Ozenfant's view, because literature uses language. Language embodies the forms imposed on experience by conceptual thought, and there is no set of concepts (he thinks) which is universal: 'Words are symbols whose sense depends entirely upon the conventions specific to each language. As a result, you have writing's extreme difficulty in being universal' (*ibid.* p.308). It would take us rather too far afield to attempt to assess Ozenfant's remarks here – it is, for instance, very doubtful that the theory of tropisms would take us as far in understanding the aesthetic impact of painting as Ozenfant thinks: he certainly belittles the role of learned responses to style.

In the present context, the point to stress is that, whatever the truth of his assertions, the theoretical framework within which they are exhibited does at least have the merit of discriminating clearly between different sources of significance (tropism and/or convention) and embodies a view on the nature of perception. This necessary apparatus is absent from Cooke, whose theory is the more imprecise as a result.

These reflections suggest a general point about the attempt to assimilate music to verbal language, namely that such an attempt is profitless unless it is approached with a considerable theoretical framework already in place: there must be at least a theory of meaning or significance (absent from Cooke). It is difficult to proceed far in this assimilation without a reasoned view on the points exhibited in the structure of Ozenfant's theory.

Finally, there is a more basic objection to Cooke's entire strategy. Even supposing that Cooke has succeeded in his attempt to establish a series of invariant correlations between notes and intervals on the one hand, and emotional significances on the other, it would not follow from this that music could properly be called a language. Most of the functions of natural languages are not considered by Cooke. Even if music were correlated with emotion, could I ask a question in music? Could I give an order? Make a request? Could I pray? Make up a fiction? (For a fuller list, *cf.* Wittgenstein, 1953, pp. 11–12, §23.) If Cooke has succeeded in his argument, all I could do in music would be to make sounds with predictable expressive properties, but that does not make music a language in any significant sense.

If the foregoing considerations are satisfactory, it follows that Cooke's attempt to explain the impact of music by a partial assimilation to language is not satisfactory; and an acceptable view, if it could be worked out, would have to deploy a great deal more by way of theoretical apparatus than is fielded by Cooke. However, Cooke's view is only one of those which attempt to locate the aesthetic significance of music in a relation between it and the emotions. The American philosopher Susanne Langer retains this premise but denies that music is a language (and so avoids all the difficulties over significance which beset Cooke). Music for Langer is a special sort of symbol.

Music as a symbol of emotion

Susanne Langer's theory of music is part of her general theory of art, which in its turn is consequent upon her philosophy of mind. The central concept in these divisions of her philosophy is that of a symbol. Thus Langer takes as her starting point an assumption which has been widely subscribed to in the philosophy of mind since Kant, namely that the structure or articulation of experience is the result of the processing by the mind of data furnished by the senses and by introspection. Before the imposition of a structure by the mind, experience is (to use William James's phrase) a 'buzzing, blooming confusion'. The fundamental operation of the mind on this array of data Langer calls abstraction, and abstraction is defined as 'the perception of form' (Langer, 1964 edn, p.59). A symbol is any device by means of which we give a form to the data of experience: the primary function of all symbols is not to communicate experience, but to give it form.

There are two major, distinct types of symbol in Langer's philosophy: discursive and presentational, and the primary example of a discursive symbolism is verbal language. The features she takes to be distinctive of language are modelled on the views of the early Wittgenstein, as set out in his *Tractatus Logico-Philosophicus*.[12] For present purposes, the most important of these features as they appear in Langer's philosophy are: (a) every language has a vocabulary and a syntax, i.e. elements of fixed meaning, and rules for their meaningful combination; (b) it is possible to construct a dictionary of a language, since words can be found equivalent in meaning to one another; (c) languages, being based on conventions, can be translated (Langer, (a), p.94).

Langer contends that there is a limit to what can be formulated by means of a linguistic (i.e. discursive) symbolism. Discursive symbols can properly formulate only what can be set out in the sequential manner such symbol systems (in her view) necessitate. Any facet of experience which does not lend itself to sequential ordering cannot be spoken of: it is ineffable. In particular, discursive symbols are of little use when it comes to the articulation of our emotional life:

> Everybody knows that language is a very poor medium for expressing our emotional nature. It merely names certain vaguely and crudely conceived states, but fails miscrably in any attempt to convey the ever-moving patterns, the ambivalences and intricacies of inner experience, the interplay of feelings with thoughts and impressions, memories and echoes of memories, transient fantasy, or its mere runic traces, all turned into nameless, emotional stuff.
>
> (*Ibid.* pp. 100–1)

In order to lend form to this emotional life, and so to render it conceivable and comprehensible, a different type of symbol is needed, and this Langer calls a 'presentational' symbol.

Presentational symbols do not employ a vocabulary or a syntax, and do not impose the sequential ordering of experience required by discursive symbols. A presentational symbol is a complex formulation produced by the process of abstraction (i.e. the imposition of form on experience by the mind) such that its constituent elements 'are understood only through the meaning of the whole, through their relations within the total structure. Their very functioning as symbols depends on the fact that they are involved in a simultaneous, integral presentation' (*ibid.* p.97). What presentational symbols have in common with what they symbolize is logical form (a concept again derived ultimately from Wittgenstein's *Tractatus*), and it is in virtue of having a common logical form that a presentational symbol can symbolize what it symbolizes. In

Langer's usage, 'logical form' means 'structure, articulation, a whole resulting from the relation of mutually dependent factors' (Langer, (b), p.15). Two lampshades of different sizes and colours, but of the same shape, have, in Langer's usage, the same logical form; so do a person's two hands (*ibid.*).

Langer claims that works of art are presentational symbols. What a work of art does is to present for our contemplation an aspect of experience which cannot be captured by discursive (i.e. verbal) means, and renders it perceivable by means of a presentational symbol: 'Artistic form is congruent with the dynamic forms of our direct sensuous, mental, and emotional life' (*ibid.* p.25; *cf.* Langer, 1953, chap.3 *passim*). Or again, a work of art 'articulates what is verbally ineffable – the logic of consciousness itself' (Langer, (b), p.26). Presentational symbols (and so works of art) do not have meaning in the linguistic sense; but they have a type of significance, which Langer calls 'import'. A work of art, she writes, 'carries with it something that people have sometimes called a quality... sometimes an emotional content, or the emotional tone of the work, or simply its life' (*ibid.* p.129) and it is this which constitutes its import.

Music is an art; pieces of music are works of art, and therefore, in Langer's view, are presentational symbols.

Thus she dismisses the view (held by Cooke, for example) that music is a language: it fails to satisfy her distinguishing criteria for language, since it does not possess elements of fixed connotation (Langer, (a), p.228). Nor is it to be regarded in any simple way as a form of self-expression on the part of the composer who feels an emotion and then in some obscure fashion conceives a musical theme with the same emotional character (*ibid.* pp. 215–6). Music is neither 'the cause [nor] the cure of feelings, but their logical expression' (*ibid.* p.218). Music is a presentational symbol by means of which we articulate or render con-ceivable to ourselves the life of the emotions (*ibid.* p.222). It follows from Langer's theory of symbolism that music and what it symbolizes (the life of the emotions) must share a common logical form:

> there are certain aspects of the so-called 'inner life' – physical or mental – which have formal properties similar to those of music – patterns of motion and rest, of tension and release, of agreement and disagreement, preparation, fulfilment, excitation, sudden change, etc.
>
> (*Ibid.* p.228)

What has prevented recognition of this fact is that the forms shared by music and emotion have no verbal equivalents, and so cannot be spoken of in the discursive medium of language: 'music articulates forms which language cannot set forth' (*ibid.* p.233). Moreover,

> Because the forms of human feeling are much more congruent with musical forms than with the forms of language, music can *reveal* the nature of feelings with a detail and truth that language cannot approach.

> (*Ibid.* p.235)

This assertion, however, requires an important qualification. It can be objected that, if music is so perfectly congruent with the patterns of felt life as Langer contends, why is it that certain pieces of music seem to bear diverse emotional interpretations equally well? Langer is aware of this difficulty and has a reply. Music does indeed share the logical form (or morphology, as she sometimes says) of feeling, but *only* its logical form. If two feelings have the same pattern (e.g. a gradual rise to a climax, or a sharp rise with a gradual decay), music will not be able to do more than articulate the pattern: it will not be able to individuate feelings which are different in nature but have the same logical form. The symbolism provided by music is therefore incomplete: she chooses to acknowledge this by declaring that music is an 'unconsummated' symbol:

> *what music can actually reflect is only the morphology of feeling*; and it is quite plausible that some sad and some happy conditions may have a very similar morphology... *Music at its highest, though clearly a symbolic form, is an unconsummated symbol...* tor the *assignment* of one rather than another possible meaning to each form is never explicitly made.

> (*Ibid.* pp. 238, 240)

To summarize, Langer contends that music is a symbol which shares the logical form of the inner life of the emotions and renders it conceivable by us. Music is a presentational symbol and not a language; and it differs from other presentational symbols in being unconsummated, i.e. it is incomplete, since it can symbolize only one aspect of felt life – its logical form or morphology or pattern – and it cannot individuate feelings which are similar or identical in respect of their logical form but differ in emotional tone.[13]

It will be clear that Langer's account of music avoids the most serious problems faced by Cooke: it is not necessary for her to try to set up a vocabulary of music, since she denies that it has one, and all the difficulties over 'inherent significances' do not appear in her theory. Again, if her view is true, it will not be subject to restrictions of style or culture: the patterns or logical forms of felt life, whether they are different in different cultures or not, will be symbolized in the music which the given culture produces. Moreover, the theory makes explicit allowance for the varied responses pieces of music seem readily to evoke, and yet preserves the intuitively satisfying link between music and emotion. Langer's view does, however, involve some difficulties peculiar to itself, of which I will mention four.

In the first place, the application of her general theory of symbolism to the act of artistic creation makes the latter process even harder to understand than it already is. It follows from her theory that a work of art gives form to a previously inconceivable element of experience, yet it is one of the well-established data in the psychology of creativity, and one which Langer herself acknowledges (Langer, 1953, pp. 121–2), that artists often have a sense of what it is they wish to do whilst a work is in process of creation, and try various alternatives to see which is most coherent with this governing intuition of the work (*cf.* pp. 188ff. of this essay for more on the process of creation in art). If Langer is taken strictly at her word, then the creation of works of art becomes all but inexplicable, since, *ex hypothesi*, artists cannot know what they are making until they have finished.[14]

Secondly, her assertion that all works of art are presentational symbols has some odd consequences for works of literary art. Works of literature use the medium of discursive symbolism, language, which, we are told, is a notoriously poor instrument for the articulation of the forms of emotion. It follows from her theory that works of literature are works of art only insofar as they are presentational symbols, and that any aesthetic value they have can reside only in the articulation of ineffable elements of experience in the formal properties of these works; yet to deny that any insight into emotion can be derived from the discursive symbolism (i.e. language) in literary works is absurd. It would be odd to be committed to the view that neither Stendhal nor Proust nor Musil nor Henry James, for example, are able to give any form to their understanding of the emotional life.

This point is linked to a third difficulty, mentioned also in one of its forms by Malcolm Budd (Budd, 1985), which is this: Langer bases her theory of the value of music on the assertion that the forms of the emotional life cannot be articulated in discursive symbolism in an adequate way, but there is no reason to accept that this is true. The examples Langer gives of 'logical forms' said to characterize feelings – of acceleration and deceleration, crescendo and diminuendo and so on (*cf.* the quotations from the psychologist Köhler, Langer, (a), p.226) – are all perfectly statable in words and indeed routinely reflected by stylistic devices in literary works, most obviously by change of rhythm.

Finally, the concession that music is an unconsummated or incomplete symbol is a dangerous one. Langer admits that music symbolizes only the form of an emotion, not its emotional content, and therefore if there are any two emotions with the same form, music will be unable to express them individually. Once it is presupposed, however, that there is a form of feeling isolable from content, the link between music and emotion is in danger of being broken. As Budd has pointed out, Langer's examples of logical forms (slow rise to a climax, and so on) are not peculiar to emotion, but occur in non-emotional natural phenomena (Budd, 1985, pp. 114–5), and if this is the case, it follows that *all* that music can provide is a symbol in sound of certain logical forms. Langer asserts that there is a special link between music and emotion, and that the value of music resides in its power to articulate emotion to us; but once it is admitted that (a) emotions have logical forms isolable from their contents and (b) that these logical forms are not peculiar to emotion, then there is no logical justification for the assertion that music is a symbol specifically of emotion. A further argument would need to be given to show why we link the logical forms in music with emotion in particular, rather than any of the other phenomena which share these logical forms; but this central thesis is not argued for, it is merely assumed. This objection to Langer raises a point of great importance in the philosophical understanding of aesthetic expression, and that is that the way in which the concept of emotion is analysed is central to the adequacy of theories which link the aesthetic value of art with emotion. This point will be taken up again in the following sections.

These objections show that Langer's attempt to explain the relation between music and emotion is unsuccessful, as, in a different way, is Cooke's attempt to establish a language of emotion. Both views presuppose that the aesthetic value of music is to be explained by reference to something outside the music, i.e. emotion. The next view I will consider denies this, yet, I hope to show, brings to our attention very clearly some fundamental aspects of the concept of aesthetic expression.

Hanslick: 'The essence of music is sound and motion'

The two theories of music we have considered so far are examples of heteronomist theories, that is, theories which seek to locate the source of the aesthetic value of music in the relation between music and an extra-musical feature of the world. I will now consider a theory of music which is much more nearly, if not unqualifiedly, autonomist – that is, one that does not look beyond music for the source of its aesthetic value – put forward by the Viennese critic Eduard Hanslick (1825–1904) in his short classic *The Beautiful in Music* (1854). By 'the beautiful', Hanslick means, 'the aesthetically valuable'; that is, he is using 'beauty' as a portmanteau term for all the aesthetic virtues: he is not addressing the question of how one particular aesthetic virtue (beauty) is manifested in music.

The heteronomist theories of Cooke and Langer are both fairly recent, but this style of view is anything but new in Western thought. Hanslick cites twenty-two examples of the 'music is a language of the emotions' type, from the eighteenth and early nineteenth centuries (Hanslick, 1957, pp. 16–19). This whole approach Hanslick regards as profoundly in error. He argues that music is incapable of representing any definite emotion, and that the locus of aesthetic value in music is to be found in what he terms its 'purely musical' features. He does not deny that music is linked to the emotions in certain ways, but argues that the links are not as they are generally taken to be. What are his arguments?

His first major argument is that 'Definite feelings and emotions are unsusceptible of being embodied in music' (*ibid.* p.21), because a definite emotion involves not only an affective state of a person, but also a definite thought:

> The feeling of hope is inseparable from the conception of a happier state which is to come, and which we compare with the actual state. The feeling of sadness involves the notion of a past state of happiness. These are perfectly definite ideas or conceptions, and in default of them – the apparatus of thought, as it were – no feeling can be called 'hope' or 'sadness', for through them alone can a feeling assume a definite character. On excluding these conceptions from conscious-ness, nothing remains but a vague sense of motion which at best could not rise above a general feeling of satisfaction or discomfort... A determinate feeling (a passion, an emotion) as such never exists without a definable meaning which can, of course, only be communi-cated through the medium of definite ideas.
>
> (*Ibid.* pp. 21–22)

In other words, to feel an emotion which can be classified (as love or hatred or fear or anger or awe, and so on) always involves not only an affective state but also a belief or set of beliefs concerning the object of the emotion. Love is never just love but love of someone; awe is awe in the face of someone or something; anger is about something and directed at someone, and so on. Now music, since it is neither conceptual nor mimetic, can never represent a definite thought; therefore music can never in principle represent a definite emotion. Hanslick assumes that a definite emotion is a complex, having as one of its constituents what is sometimes called a propositional content, and asserts that in no way can the propositional content be conveyed by music.

I said above that Hanslick's theory is not unqualifiedly autonomist, and the reason for the qualification is the next step in his argument. Even if music is a non-conceptual, non-mimetic medium, Hanslick considers that there is one class of ideas it can express very well. These are the ideas 'associated with audible changes of strength, motion, and ratio: the ideas of intensity waxing and diminishing; of motion hastening and lingering; of ingeniously complex and simple progression, etc.' (*ibid.* p.23). These ideas can be represented in music because sound can be changed in directly analogous ways. It is in virtue of this that music, in Hanslick's view, can represent what he calls the 'dynamic properties' of emotions, even if it can never represent their propositional content:

> It may reproduce the motion accompanying psychical action, according to its momentum: speed, slowness, strength, weakness, increasing and decreasing intensity. But motion is only one of the concomitants of feeling, not the feeling itself.
>
> (*Ibid.* p.24)

This is a very stringent restriction, as he goes on to make clear. Music cannot, for instance, represent the affective condition which is a component of an emotion, even apart from its propositional content. It cannot represent love, 'but only the element of motion; and this may occur in any other feeling just as well as in love, and in no case is it the distinctive feature' (*ibid.*). Beyond this very limited capacity of the medium to represent the dynamic aspects of emotion, the power of music to represent emotion rests only on what Hanslick calls symbolism. What he has in mind is similar to the view of Ozenfant (referred to above in the discussion of Cooke), which it prefigures strikingly, though it is not developed at any length. Certain sounds, Hanslick contends, like certain colours, strike human beings in invariant, non-conventional ways, producing responses in us which are effectively tropisms:

> Sounds, like colours, are originally associated in our minds with certain symbolical meanings which produce their effects indepen-

dently of and antecedently to any design of art. Every colour has a character of its own; it is not a mere cipher into which the artist blows the breath of life, but a force. Between it and certain states of mind, Nature herself has established a sympathetic connection... In like manner, the first elements of music, such as the various keys, chords, and timbres, have severally a character of their own.

(Ibid. p.25)

He is careful to point out at once, however, that music cannot be composed out of these basic elements as a house can of bricks, simply by putting them together in the right order. Once the musical elements are combined, they produce unpredictable results. As he puts it, 'Aesthetically speaking, such primordially distinctive traits are nonexistent when viewed in the light of those wider laws to which they are subordinate' *(ibid.* p.26). Hanslick was well aware that works of art cannot be produced merely by following rules.

He concludes the first major phase of his argument (i.e. against the thesis that the value of music lies in its power to represent emotion) with a supplementary claim. Whilst accepting what he has said so far, some might argue in reply (he thinks) that, even if music cannot at present represent feelings, such representation is the goal toward which it should strive. Against this assertion, Hanslick contends that 'The beautiful in music would not depend on the accurate representation of feelings even if such a representation were possible' *(ibid.* pp. 38–9). His argument for this supplementary claim is that musical value diminishes in direct proportion as the music aims to become specific in its attempted depictions of non-musical situations. The type of music which (Hanslick assumes) aims at such highly specific depiction is recitative, where the music is entirely at the service of the words: take away the words, and the music which remains is of next to no aesthetic interest. The same is true for other types of music.

The beautiful tends to disappear in proportion as the expression of some specific feeling is aimed at; for the former can expand only if untrammelled by alien factors, whereas the latter relegates music to a subservient place.

(Ibid. p.40)

Hanslick is here relying on a principle which is important and which he makes fully explicit only later on, and that is that the demands of the evolution of a musical theme and those of the development of a non-musical situation or a conceptual idea are unlike and independent.

Music is unlike language in a very important way:

> The fundamental difference [between language and music] consists in this: while sound in speech is but a sign, that is, a means for the purpose of expressing something which is quite distinct from its medium, sound in music is the end, that is, the ultimate and absolute object in view.
>
> *(Ibid.* p.67)

This autonomist notion lies behind his remarks concerning the deep tensions which are in his view inherent in art forms which employ both words and music, notably opera: 'The principles in which music and drama are grounded, if pushed to their logical consequences, are mutually destructive; but they point in so similar a direction that they appear almost parallel' *(ibid.* p.41).

Having established to his satisfaction that the aesthetic value of music does not lie in any supposed capacity to represent emotion, Hanslick then offers a positive account of the nature of this aesthetic value. In his view, the aesthetic value of music resides purely in aesthetic properties of the music itself, not in anything outside itself that it is supposed to represent or express. As he puts it, the source of the beautiful in music,

> *is specifically musical.* By this we mean that the beautiful is not contingent upon nor in need of any subject introduced from without, but that it consists wholly of sounds artistically combined. The ingenious co-ordination of intrinsically pleasing sounds, their consonance and contrast, their flight and reapproach, their increasing and diminishing strength – this it is which, in free and unimpeded forms, presents itself to our mental vision.
>
> *(Ibid.* p.47)

It is just a fact about human beings that we are so constituted that these musical sounds delight us aesthetically:

> [our imagination, which is so constituted as to be affected by auditory impressions] delights in the sounding forms and musical structures and, conscious of their sensuous nature, lives in the immediate and free contemplation of the beautiful.
>
> *(Ibid.* p.49)

Musical sounds, as has been noted, do not express anything extra-musical. The subject of music is only successions of sound which have no reference beyond themselves (*ibid*. p.119): if anything could be said to be the subject of music, it can only be musical ideas:

> Now, a musical idea reproduced in its entirety is not only an object of intrinsic beauty but also an end in itself, and not a means for representing feelings and thoughts.
> The essence of music is sound and motion.
>
> (*Ibid.* p.48)

Put in another way, Hanslick's positive thesis concerning the aesthetic value of music is this: musical sounds just strike us as aesthetically interesting (though Hanslick would stress that *how* they strike us is profoundly influenced by our cultural climate and degree of musical education): they have their own 'logic', and have no subject-matter of a non-musical kind. They *arouse* affective states in us, sometimes states we value very deeply, but this neither presupposes nor entails that music represents or expresses emotion, including that of the composer. We want to listen to music because the sounds interest us aesthetically and because we value the states they sometimes occasion in us; to describe this situation by saying that music is in some sense the 'language of the emotions' confuses the issue, and causes us to listen to music in the wrong way, as if it were conceptual. Such listeners try to work out the 'meaning' of each theme, key change, cadence and so on. Hanslick contends that in a linguistic sense of 'mean', nothing is 'meant' by music at all: it is just that our interpretative habits acquired from literature and mimetic visual art are being carried over, inappropriately, to an art form to which they simply do not apply. The nearest analogue in visual terms for the way in which music delights us is the pleasure caused by certain non-mimetic forms: music 'pleases for its own sake, like an arabesque, a column, or some spontaneous product of nature – a leaf or a flower' (*ibid*. p.53). The appropriate way to respond aesthetically to music is neither to look in it for non-existent 'meanings', nor to use it as a sort of narcotic with which to stimulate emotional daydreams unrelated to the music itself: the appropriate way to respond to music is to contemplate what is there in the musical work of art: 'the artistic and original combination of sound' (*ibid*. p.92).

One of the points of particular philosophical interest with which Hanslick supplements this view concerns the account he gives of the role in talk about music of predicates whose primary use is to refer to the emotions. Hanslick has stressed, not only that music is non-mimetic and non-conceptual, but that its aesthetic value resides in purely musical properties of sound. Add to this the notion that music is not really like anything else ('has no prototype in nature', *ibid.* p.50) and it follows that music is very difficult to talk about. Musical sounds do indeed exhibit a logic of their own (i.e. appear to have to develop in certain ways) but this logic is incommensurable with that of language. Thus,

> we are compelled to speak of it either in dry, technical terms, or in the language of poetic fiction. All the fantastic descriptions, characterizations and periphrases are either metaphorical or false. What in any other art is still descriptive is in music already figurative... In music there is both meaning and logical sequence, but in a musical sense; it is a language we speak and understand, but which we are unable to translate.
>
> *(Ibid.* p.50)

His first assertion, then, is that, where the use of emotion-predicates is justified at all (i.e. does not result in false statements), such usage is metaphorical. The terms are used to refer to purely musical properties. We are justified in using terms like: grand, graceful, proud, ardent, etc. 'but all these terms are exclusively suggestive of the musical character of the particular passage' *(ibid.* p.53).

Interestingly, he then goes on to make a second assertion which is logically independent of the first one and that is that the emotion-predicates can be replaced by others with no loss of descriptive power whatsoever. Provided we are aware of the figurative nature of the usage, emotion-predicates can be used of music,

> But we may with equal justice select them from a different order of phenomena, and call a piece of music 'sweet, fresh, cloudy, cold'. To be descriptive of the character of a musical composition, our feelings must be regarded in the light of mere phenomena, just like any other phenomenon which happens to present certain analogies.
>
> *(Ibid.* p.53)

The justification for the use of any term used figuratively of music, Hanslick argues, lies in suitable analogies which obtain between the character of the music in question, and the phenomenon which the term describes in non-figurative discourse. His second thesis concerning talk about music is that emotion-predicates have no irreplaceable role in such talk. There are other metaphors which do not use emotion-predicates which are, in his view, just as apt and informative. Emotion-predicates, he contends, have no special status in describing music.

Many of the points Hanslick makes in his book seem to me correct. He is right, for instance, in his view that, in his sense of the term, many people never *listen* to music at all: their aesthetic response is not directed by the musical work, but approximates instead to a pleasant, drowsy reverie with music in the background. And no doubt this casual inattention has a good deal to do with much of the nonsense that is talked about music, often characterized by unexamined assumptions about what the composer is supposed to have felt while writing the work. Yet while all this is so, there are a number of important difficulties of a philosophical kind in his theory, and qualifications which must be added to it, of which I will mention a few, beginning with some points arising from the negative argument designed to prove that music cannot represent emotion.

In the first place, the concept of representation with which Hanslick is working is questionable. He assumes (so far as one can tell) that for x to represent y, x must copy or imitate y: the argument that music cannot represent emotion turns on this assertion as does the supplementary argument that, even if music could represent emotion, its aesthetic value would be independent of that fact. Now there is reason to believe that the concept of representation is not by any means as straightforward as that (see Essay Six).

It can be argued in reply, however, that even if this premise is defective, the substance of Hanslick's negative argument can be recast so as to avoid it. Let us drop the term 'represent': yet there remains the powerful assertion that a definite emotion is a complex, one constituent of which is what I have called a propositional content, i.e. a belief or beliefs about the object of the emotion. If this analysis is correct, then, since music is a non-conceptual medium, it still follows that musical sound cannot imitate a definite emotion. Hanslick will have shown that, if music resembles anything, it certainly does not resemble definite emotions, being incapable of conveying the propositional contents which individuate them.

Presupposed in Hanslick's analysis of definite emotions is the assumption that they form a homogeneous class, i.e. that all definite emotions can be analysed in the way he suggests. In his discussion of this argument, Malcolm Budd challenges this assumption. He argues that there are some feelings which do not involve a definite thought, and gives the example of cheerfulness, which he calls 'either a quality of character or a mood' (Budd, 1985, pp. 24–5). If this assertion is correct, and if other examples can be found, then Hanslick's analysis will be true of only a sub-class of emotions, leaving open the possibility that music might express some other types of emotional state.

The suggestion, implicit in Budd's argument, that one should focus on moods is an astute one, since many of the predicates used to describe music are drawn from the class of those we use primarily to refer to moods rather than emotions: music can be light-hearted, melancholy, despairing, and so on. The difficulty, however, is to analyse the concept of a mood without an undeletable reference to reactions which are characteristic of persons in the given mood. These reactions will involve judgements, not indeed about specific objects (since moods, unlike emotions, are not directed at specific objects) but which will be of a recognizable type whatever the situation or object may be which impinges on the person in the mood. Part of what it is to be melancholy is to judge events under descriptions which buttress the mood; in a cheerful mood, the same events would reinforce *that* mood, and be judged differently.

Whether or not this particular argument is successful, a general point about expression emerges from this phase of Hanslick's argument with great clarity, and that is that no useful study of musical expression can proceed without addressing the issue of the analysis of the concept of emotion. Hanslick's argument sharply brings to our attention the important point that emotions have a propositional content; and consideration of it rapidly shows that to speak of 'the emotions' as if they were a neatly homogeneous class, with an entirely uniform analysis, is simplistic. Even if the analysis of moods involves a propositional content, it does not do so in the same way as that of definite emotions: a mood is reflected in a type of judgement about objects, rather than having a specific object. It should be clear by now that we are not likely to get very far in working out whether music does or does not express or represent or embody emotion without a reasonably clear grip on what we take an emotion to be; and the same is true of expression in the other arts.

Turning to Hanslick's positive claims, the first point to note is a purely logical one. In the negative stage of his argument, Hanslick argues for the view that music can represent no definite emotion; in his positive argument, he claims that the aesthetic value of music is purely musical, residing in properties of the music itself, and not resultant from any relation the music has to anything outside itself. The logical point to note is that even if the negative claim is true it does not entail the positive one. This does not of itself show that Hanslick's argument breaks down irremediably at this point: he could reply that the only serious contender there has ever been to be the extra-musical feature from which music draws its aesthetic value is the emotions; and that is a reasonable assertion. If he can show that music does not represent emotion, his positive thesis is to that extent more plausible; but plausibility is *all* that the negative argument can give it. The negative and positive theses are logically independent, i.e. the truth or falsity of either does not entail the truth or falsity of the other. Hanslick's method in the sections of the book which develop his positive, (almost) autonomist thesis is to try to give this positive view ever greater plausibility, by exhibiting its conse-quences and attempting to show that they fit the musical facts better than any others; and by showing that certain other popular views (e.g. that music is like language; that musical effects are somehow grounded in mathematics) cannot be sustained. Whether or not his positive thesis is plausible depends to a large degree on the acceptability of these corol-laries.

A second point concerning Hanslick's positive argument is as follows. He lays great stress on the thesis that musical sound exhibits or exemplifies movement: it is in virtue of its movement that he claims it can represent the dynamic aspects of emotion, and he makes movement part of the 'essence' of music: 'The essence of music is sound and motion' (*ibid*. p.48). Now there is no doubt at all that movement (or its contrary, stasis) is a centrally important property of music; but it is necessary to add a complication to Hanslick's theory by pointing out that this movement is of an odd kind: as many philosophers have pointed out, in musical movement nothing moves (i.e. because in its ordinary sense, movement involves change of spatial location, and in music nothing moves from one place to another). The commonest way philosophers have of describing this phenomenon is to classify this type of movement as a special type of property of the music called an *intentional* property.

This use of the term 'intentional' is a technical one in philosophy. The term itself was used by medieval philosophers, but its modern currency and sense is due to the German philosopher and psychologist Franz Brentano (1838–1917) who argued that intentionality (in his sense) is a property unique to mental phenomena by means of which they can be distinguished from physical phenomena (Brentano, 1973 edn). Brentano claims that mental phenomena have the property of being always directed upon an object, and that these objects have what he calls 'intentional inexistence'. What he means is this: I cannot want or hope or imagine (etc.) without wanting or hoping that or imagining (etc.) *something* (mental phenomena always have *objects*); but it does not follow from the fact that I want something that what I want exists (and so the objects of mental events have a special type of being he calls 'inexistence'). Interpretations of Brentano vary, but need not detain us here. His view applies to the point in hand as follows: musical move-ment (like the objects of mental phenomena) exists only in the presence of a mind. It is mind-dependent in a way which some other properties of musical sound are not. There are meters, for instance, which can measure changes in loudness; but there is no instrument of any kind which measures musical movement: it exists only when the musical sound is heard by a person. Much the same point is made by other philosophers who call movement a *virtual* property of music, i.e. a property which exists only when music is perceived (e.g. Langer, 1953, p.107).

That Hanslick misses this point out is not fatal to his view, since what he says can be recast to take account of it. I stress it, first because it is inherently important, secondly because a full defence of Hanslick would have to include it, and thirdly because, as a part of other theories of music, it can have important consequences. For example, the aesthetician Roger Scruton accepts the thesis that musical movement is intentional, but combines it with two further premises: (i) that there is a defensible sense in which music can be said to be expressive and (ii) that the expression is grounded in, or only possible because of, the movement. Now if the movement is intentional, so is the expression.[15]

In what he asserts to be the consequences of his positive thesis, Hanslick, as we have seen, is emphatic on the issue of the use of emotion-predicates in describing music. As I indicated earlier, he makes two, logically independent, claims on this issue: (i) that all uses of these predicates to describe music are figurative; and (ii) that in all cases, the emotion-predicates can be deleted and replaced by other predicates (again used figuratively) drawn from another area of phenomena with no loss of meaning. He also asserts that, whatever terms drawn from non-musical areas are used to describe music, they refer to purely musical phenomena: no doubt the non-musical phenomena do bear analogies of some sort to the music, and this he clearly takes to be the justification for the figurative use; but these analogies, he holds, do not involve any relation between the music and the non-musical phenomena such that the former draws on the latter for its aesthetic value or significance.

The first of these assertions is acceptable: since music cannot literally have emotions, then the usage of emotion-predicates to describe it must be non-literal or figurative. However, it is important to stress that this assertion is logically independent both of Hanslick's positive thesis and of its denial: the thesis that emotion predicates are used figuratively of music does not of itself entail either that the aesthetic value of music resides in purely musical features, or that this value resides in a special relation with something extra-musical, like emotion. It is compatible with both these theories.

The second assertion – that emotion-predicates are always deletable from descriptions of music – is less easy to sustain. The easiest way to show this is by means of examples. Take the following assertion: 'The last movement in Tchaikovsky's Sixth Symphony (an *adagio lamentoso*) exhibits despair.' If Hanslick is correct, then it should be possible to find other ways of describing the character of the music by means of other non-emotional, figurative predicates. Perhaps, it might be argued, this movement could be likened to a landscape and described as 'bleak'; but the movement does not have the character of a bleak landscape, but, if it is bleak, of a bleak mood. I very much doubt if any term not drawn from the vocabulary of emotions or moods could describe the character of this music as well as does 'despair'.

Once again, however, it is necessary to be clear that, even if Hanslick's second assertion is untenable, and that emotion-predicates do have some special aptness in the description of music, it does not follow from this alone that Hanslick's positive thesis is false, i.e. it does not follow from the fact that emotion-predicates are sometimes especially apt and irreplaceable that the aesthetic value of music is derived from a link with the emotions. Nor, clearly, does the unacceptability of Hanslick's second assertion entail that his positive claim about musical value is true: the thesis that emotion-predicates are irreplaceable in the description of music is of itself logically neutral between autonomist and heteronomist views of musical value. (For a more complex and detailed discussion of related issues, *cf.* Budd., 1985, pp. 31–6.)

What conclusions can be drawn from this very brief survey of Hanslick's views? Concerning his negative argument, we have seen that he is working with a rather simple concept of 'representation', but that nevertheless what he says does involve us in a profitable, close scrutiny of the concept of emotion. I have argued that his argument needs to be extended a little to cover moods. If we accept the central premise in this argument – that the analysis of definite emotions and moods must involve propositional contents – it follows that music cannot imitate any definite emotion or mood. This has the effect of making one very cautious about much that is said about music. This argument alone, irrespective of the psychological data to be considered briefly in the next section, should make one very hesitant about making any claims about the state of mind of the composer based on the musical work.

Further, I have argued, against Hanslick, that emotion-predicates are sometimes ineliminable without loss of meaning from descriptions of music; but it should be clear that, whatever it is about the music that makes us want to use these predicates of it, it cannot be some form of close resemblance to definite emotions or moods, because a non-conceptual medium cannot closely resemble a state the analysis of which includes a propositional content.

Concerning his positive thesis (that the aesthetic value of music resides in purely musical features) we have seen that this is logically independent both of his negative argument, and of his arguments concerning the figurative use and eliminability of emotion-predicates in connection with the description of music. I have also argued that it requires some refinement in respect of the concept of movement in music. An important point to note in connection with autonomist assertions of this kind ('musical value is purely musical'; 'music means itself'; 'music is not like anything else', and the like) is that there is no set of non-figurative terms in which to indicate what these purely musical aesthetic features are which are the alleged locus of aesthetic value, and so such views are very difficult to prove. Ultimately, autonomists have to say: just listen, and you will hear the purely musical features. (It should be clear that the aesthetic features Hanslick has in mind are not the same as the class of features referred to by the technical vocabulary of music: notes, intervals, chords, and so on. The aesthetic properties in some way result from these, but are logically discrete from them.) On the other hand, some features of the autonomist case are very attractive: it is the most plausible way of explaining why we value those pieces of music (of which there are many) which we take to be aesthetically delightful and yet which do not invite description in terms of emotion-predicates. Again, the autonomist insistence that the unique and central aesthetic experience furnished by music arises from following the perceptible changes in the musical sound itself (and neither fantasticating about its supposed 'meaning' nor daydreaming with the music not attended to) many listeners find to be an exact account of what they do.

Perhaps Hanslick's greatest strength is the clarity with which he discriminates between questions in musical aesthetics which have too often been elided. Many of these we have already noted. In conclusion we can note one more. He is quite clear on the point that, even if his positive thesis is true (that the aesthetic value of music resides in purely musical features intrinsic to the music), this still leaves untouched an issue which is just as important but quite independent of it, and that is the question of how it is that music can cause in us the sometimes quite profound reactions it does. By what means sound can move us, he says, is a mystery (*ibid.* pp. 78–9) and it still is. The point I wish to stress here is this: even if it could be shown, for example, that music shares some properties of emotions, or, on the other hand, that it is quite unlike emotion, neither conclusion of itself would explain how it comes about that musical sound causes us to be moved and delighted in the many ways it does.

Before we leave musical aesthetics, I would like to draw one or two general conclusions from the arguments of the three preceding sections. These arguments suggest that, if there is a link between music and emotion of an aesthetically important kind, it must be far more subtle and unobvious than that envisaged in the heteronomist views of Cooke or Langer; and from Hanslick one can learn that autonomist views, attractive though they are in many ways, are extremely difficult to prove. Principally, however, the general point emerges that the musical transaction is extremely complex, far more so than casual thought would suggest: the view (which has been very widely held) that this transaction is illuminated by regarding it as a process whereby a composer expresses emotion in a work which stimulates the same emotion in the listener, simply will not stand scrutiny. We have learned to discriminate sharply between (a) the question of what the composer might feel; (b) the question of what it is about some pieces of music which makes us want to describe them by means of emotion or mood predicates and what these descriptions mean; and (c) the question of what we feel while listening to the music and how the music causes us to feel it.

With these findings in mind, I will now consider what I have called the aesthetic transaction more generally (i.e. not just in relation to music) to see what light, if any, each of its stages sheds on the concept of expression, and vice versa.

3 Expression and the Aesthetic Transaction

So far in this essay, we have looked at two areas in which the notion of expression or of a special relation between art and emotion has been thought to be especially illuminating: the definition of art, and the aesthetics of music. I would now like to look at the concept of expression in a slightly different way. Let us accept that art cannot be *defined* in terms of expression. It might still be the case that the expression of emotion is an important (though not a defining) factor in understanding what I have called the aesthetic transaction: what artists do when they create works of art, what these works are like, and what we experience in their presence.

The section which follows accordingly has three sub-divisions: the artist; the work of art, and the spectator, a term which I shall use as a shorthand way of referring to any person aesthetically experiencing, as opposed to creating, a work of art, whether by means of sight or hearing or any combination of the senses. A useful way of approaching any theory of expression is to see what it states, presupposes or implies about each of these aspects of the subject. All the theories we have considered so far can be set out in this way, and I will refer to them briefly as we go along, in conjunction with some new material. I will argue that, for a number of reasons, expressive properties are most satisfactorily construed as properties of the work of art itself, and not, as has been advanced by various writers, transfused into the work (in ways to be explained) by either the artist or the spectator.

The artist

As we have seen, a number of the classic theories of expression regard this concept as illuminating the nature of what artists do when they are working creatively. Tolstoy and Collingwood occupy the opposing ends of a spectrum in the detail of their accounts of what actually occurs in creative thought. For Tolstoy, the process is fairly straightforward: the artist feels an emotion, for example, a sentiment of 'human brotherhood', wishes to convey this to others, and sets about fabricating a suitable vehicle calculated to arouse the same emotion in those who come into contact with it. For Collingwood, the essence of artistic activity lies in the articulation of the nature of an inchoate feeling in the artist, and the work of art (a mental state) is the articulated product of this process. (Langer sometimes speaks as if she is committed to a very similar view.) For Tolstoy, artists know exactly what experiences they wish to transmit; for Collingwood, the artist's feelings are not fully known or comprehended before the work of art is made; the gift lies in working out clearly precisely what they are.

Moreover, one of the most frequently quoted of Wordsworth's remarks on the nature of poetry appears to bear out the view that the creation of this art form at least is a species of emotional expression. In the 'Observations Prefixed to the Second Edition of *Lyrical Ballads*' (1800) he remarks that 'poetry is the spontaneous overflow of powerful feelings' (in Rhys, 1970, p.187). Yet his comments in the rest of this passage, which amplify this remark, are such as to give one pause. Wordsworth stresses that what a poet does is to *recollect* a previously felt emotion whilst in a state of 'tranquillity' (*ibid.* p.188); and even when this tranquillity is replaced by a mental state in which an emotion is present comparable to that which is recollected, there is always a difference from the primary experience of the emotion in that 'the mind will, upon the whole, be in a state of enjoyment' (*ibid.*), i.e. even when the feelings recollected are of a painful kind. It emerges from the full text of Wordsworth's description, in effect, that the process of the creation of poetry is not really like a 'spontaneous overflow of powerful feelings' at all, but is a psychological state of a much more unusual kind.

Other remarks by artists and facts brought to light by scholars of the creative process make it doubtful whether this process can properly be described as one of expression. Thus, for example, Hector Berlioz, whom one could not accuse either of being a passionless man or of writing passionless music, notes that only *once* in his life did he write a piece of music under the direct influence of an emotion he sought to embody in the music itself. Devastated by his first encounter with the actress Harriet Smithson (whom he married five years later), he spent some time unable to sleep or think, and wandered the streets of Paris in a state near distraction. On his return from one of these wanderings he wrote a setting to Moore's poem 'When he who adores thee', a 'heart-rending farewell' – 'It is the song called "Elégie" which comes at the end of my collection "Irlande". This is the sole occasion on which I was able to express a feeling of the sort directly in music while still under its active influence' (Berlioz, 1977 edn, p.96). Normally, as Berlioz makes clear, inspiration came to him unbidden. Asked by the Grand Duke of Weimar whether he had written the duet for two girls from *Beatrice and Benedict* by moonlight in a romantic spot, Berlioz had to disillusion him:

> Your Grace, it sprang from one of those impressions of nature that an artist stores deep inside himself, to be released at some later time when it is needed, no matter where one happens to be. I sketched the music of that duet one day at the Institute, during a speech by one of my colleagues.
>
> (*Ibid.* p.495)

The Grand Duke, missing the point completely, replied: 'That speaks well for his eloquence. He is clearly quite an orator!'.

Again, scholars of Mozart have established that his last three symphonies, which have very different expressive characters, were composed concurrently; and the same is true of the equally dissimilar last three piano sonatas of Schubert. To suppose that, in cases such as these, the artists oscillated between different emotional conditions which they then proceeded to express is, to put it mildly, implausible. What then does go on in periods of creative thought?

Whilst next to nothing is yet known about the physical basis of creative thought (i.e. about the way the brain functions at such times), there are two major psychological points about this type of thinking which are very well attested. The first concerns the extent to which creative thought is voluntary or subject to the conscious will, and to what extent it is involuntary and beyond the conscious control of the artist.

From ancient times, it has been noted that creative thought at any rate begins with an involuntary impulse. The term 'inspiration' is derived from Latin words which mean 'to breathe into', and the ancient way of describing the process of creative thought was to regard the artist as 'breathed into' by the Muses. The earliest significant version of this view occurs in Plato's dialogue *Ion*, where Plato argues that the poet is not responsible for what he creates, but is merely a vehicle for the afflatus of the Muses. The poet can create only when inspired to a condition of ecstasy. In some modern thought, the role of the Muses has been taken over by the unconscious mind, and the issue has become that of determining the role of the unconscious in the creative process. Artists and other creative thinkers have made introspective reports on this matter, and the picture which emerges is roughly as follows.[16] Prior to the start of the process which leads to the creation of a work of art, the artist leads a mental existence much like that of non-creative thinkers, and receives impressions, lives through the varied experiences of life, etc., much as the rest of us do. But whereas with most of us these experiences are simply absorbed, with the artist they appear to trigger, in ways not yet understood, the impulse to create and a new organization of material evolves in the unconscious. This impulse to creation appears to be involuntary: it can neither be forced by the conscious will, nor eluded by it once begun. The degree to which this initial impulse emerges into consciousness in an inchoate or a nearly finished form varies considerably from artist to artist; but that artists feel that *it* comes upon *them* (and not vice versa) is a point reported over and over again. The following remarks are by Jorge Luis Borges:

> Walking down the street or along the galleries of the National Library, I feel that something is about to take over in me. That something may be a tale or poem. I do not tamper with it; I let it have its way. From afar, I sense it taking shape. I dimly see its end and beginning but not the dark gap in between. This middle, in my case, is given me gradually. If its discovery happens to be withheld by the gods, my conscious self has to intrude, and these unavoidable makeshifts are, I suspect, my weakest pages.

> (Borges, 1972, p.101)

Borges here appears to state that nearly all of his works are delivered by the unconscious, and that relatively little intervention by the conscious mind is needed. If so, he is in that respect somewhat untypical. The majority of artists would agree with his report of something indefinite taking shape 'from afar' to begin with, but few are fortunate enough to have all the rest supplied in the same way. For most, what follows is a period of very intense work, which may last from days to years, in which all the resources of technique and all the conscious apparatus of judgement are deployed to elaborate the initial, involuntary impulse. There may be further, as it were subsidiary gifts from the unconscious on the way, but these are all subjected to conscious scrutiny. The standard or paradigm against which the work of elaboration is judged is the initial impulse, which whilst not fully present to the conscious mind, appears to inform all subsequent judgements made in the work of elaboration, and which finally determines when the work is finished.[17]

In summary, then, the first major psychological point is this: the creative thought process which culminates in the production of a work of art begins with a deliverance from the unconscious, and this initial, inchoate idea is then worked on, consciously and deliberately (though often with subsidiary inspirations) until the work is deemed to be finished.

The second major psychological point is as follows: the creative process outlined above takes place within a tradition or in reaction to it. No artist functions in a psychological vacuum, but rather in the context of a framework of past and current practice, no matter how original or inventive or imaginative or creative the artist might be. Ernst Gombrich has provided the classic statement of this view in *Art and Illusion* (Gombrich, 1960). Gombrich addresses the question as to why it is that the history of art is a history of discernible styles (rather than a history of unclassifiable, random quirks) and bases his thesis on psychological set theory. Roughly speaking, a style is the manifestation of a mental set which governs the perception of an artist. Such sets are extremely difficult to invent, and are generally perfected only over a period of time by a number of artists each changing the set a little. Moreover, the psychological grip exerted by an articulated set is immense (this is one factor which accounts for conservatism in taste), and to change a set significantly requires creative powers of a very high order. Major changes of set are generally found at first to be unintelligible (e.g. the abandoning of tonality in Western music or of perspectival depiction in painting) until the public can master the new set and begin to gauge its aesthetic potential. Thus, ascriptions of originality, creativity, etc. are all made against a background of estimates of past and present achievement. Artists, and indeed other creative workers, articulate their works with reference to the achievements of others, and that they do so is a matter of psychological necessity. There are psychological limits to how much can be invented or changed in one go. *(Cf.* also Collingwood, 1938, p.318, for much the same point.)

What emerges from this briefest of surveys of artistic creativity in this: it is not the case that in their work artists always or even primarily express their own emotions in any sense akin to that in which we express our emotions in non-aesthetic contexts. Of course, it is often the case that they do seek to construct works of art which provide a satisfying emotional experience for their spectators by means of the mechanisms of aesthetic expression, but the way in which this is done is not greatly clarified by assimilating it to the expression of emotion: the process of aesthetic expression is a great deal more complicated than this turn of phrase suggests. Philip Larkin summed the matter up with unpretentious clarity:

> – you write because you have to. If you rationalize it, it seems as if you've seen this sight, felt this feeling, had this vision, and you've got to find a combination of words that will preserve it by setting it off in other people. The duty is to the original experience. It doesn't feel like self-expression, though it may look like it.

(Larkin, 1982, p.58)

The work of art

Works of art are often, though by no means invariably, such that, in describing them or in justifying aesthetic verdicts passed on them, it is necessary to refer to their expressive properties. We readily use of works of art predicates whose primary usage is in non-aesthetic contexts and whose function it is to ascribe emotions or moods to persons (or, in some cases, to other types of animal). Thus Mozart's Fortieth Symphony is a deeply sad piece of music; the mood of Shakespeare's *The Tempest* is one of serene acceptance; the mood of Picasso's *Guernica* (Plate 4) is outrage, and so on. It is important to grasp that these properties are aesthetic properties of the work itself and inhere in it: Mozart's Fortieth Symphony is sad, whether or not it makes us feel sad.[18] If a critic were to maintain that *Guernica* is jolly or Mozart's Fortieth Symphony is cheerful, we would conclude that they were making a mistake.

A number of philosophical and psychological problems are generated by the view that expressive properties are properties of the work of art. We have come across these issues individually in earlier sections: we can now review them together.

The first is that expressive properties are *aesthetic* properties of the work of art, and share the unusual features of other properties in this class. The most significant of these is that aesthetic properties 'emerge' from non-aesthetic ones in a way it is impossible to reduce to a set of rules or laws. This applies to music, for example, in the following way: there is no set of rules for the manipulation of the elements of music such that following them will guarantee the production of music of a given expressive character: there is no combination of melody, rhythm, harmony, pitch, timbre, rhythm and tempo which will guarantee sad or cheerful or melancholy (etc.) music; and the same is true for all the other forms of art. The creation of works with given aesthetic properties requires both creativity and judgement. Moreover, the philosophical analysis of aesthetic properties is itself a problem of some complexity, as we have seen in the view, referred to in the discussion of Hanslick, that these properties are intentional. This matter has already been dealt with in Essay Two: the point to note here is that the analysis of aesthetic properties in general applies to expressive properties in particular.

Secondly, the view that expressive properties are properties of the work of art generates a problem in the philosophy of language. Since works of art are not persons, some account is needed of the sense in which emotion-predicates are used of them. A work of art cannot literally have an emotion, and some considerable effort has gone into trying to work out in precisely what senses these predicates are used in aesthetic discourse: we have already seen how, for instance, Hanslick addresses this issue, claiming that emotion-predicates are used figuratively of music, and are eliminable from descriptions of it. Like the preceding issue concerning aesthetic properties, the logical analysis of emotion-predicates as applied to works of art is a subject in itself, and has already been discussed in Essay Three. I raise it again here first because it is an important consequence of the view of expressive properties I am advocating (a complete defence of this position would include a view on this problem); and, secondly, because it illuminates very clearly how ramified a phenomenon aesthetic expression is. Some of the difficulties involved in the various sorts of analysis available are set out very clearly in the essays by Hepburn and Hospers, referred to in note 18, above.

Thirdly, a different but no less important point concerning the expressive work of art came to light in the discussion of Tolstoy's views: it will be recalled that what Tolstoy values is the quality of the emotion communicated by a work of art, rather than the work itself. He neglects a central feature of aesthetic expression, namely that the aesthetic object (the work of art) is not regarded merely as a tool or vehicle or means with

Colour Plate 1   Vincent van Gogh (1853–90) The chair and the pipe, *1888, oil on canvas. Reproduced by courtesy of the Trustees, the National Gallery, London.*

Colour Plate 2   Pablo Picasso (1881–1973) Weeping Woman, *1937, oil on canvas. Tate Gallery, London. © DACS 1991.*

Colour Plate 3   Rembrandt van Rijn (1616–69) Self-portrait, *c.1663, oil on canvas. Wallraf-Richartz-Museum, Cologne 388. Photo: Rheinisches Bildarchiv, Köln.*

Colour Plate 4 Pieter Bruegel the Elder (c.1525–69) The Fall of Icarus, c.1554–8, oil on canvas. Musées Royaux des Beaux-Arts de Belgique, Bruxelles. Photo: G. Cussac.

Plate 1   Deer, painting from ceiling of main chamber, Altamira cave system.
Photo: Mansell Collection.

Plate 2   Mei Ping blossom vase for
holding branches of prunus blossom
c.1450, ceramic with blue-painted
decoration. Victoria and Albert
Museum, London c.114.1928.
Reproduced by courtesy of the Board
of Trustees of the Victoria and Albert
Museum.

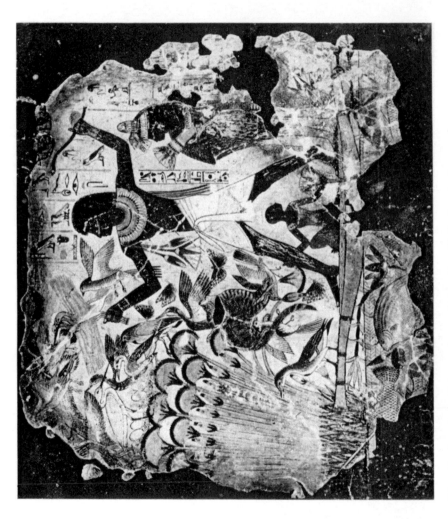

Plate 3   *Egyptian of high rank attended by his wife fowling in the marshes c.1500–1400 BC, mural in tempera. From a tomb in Thebes. XIX Dynasty. Photo: Mansell Collection.*

Plate 4   Pablo Picasso (1881–1973) Guernica, 1937, oil on canvas. Prado, Madrid. © DACS 1992.

Plate 5   Paul Klee (1879–1940) The Tightrope-walker *[Der Seiltänzer]*, *1923, water-colour and oil-coloured drawing on paper. Paul Klee Foundation, Museum of Fine Arts Berne 1923.21.F36. © 1992 DACS, London, COSMOPRESS, Genf.*

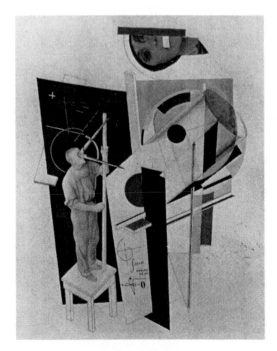

Plate 6   El Lissitzky (1890–1941) Tatlin working on the monument, *illustration for Ilya Ehrenburg's* Six tales with easy endings, *1924, photomontage. Collection of Eric Estorick family.*

which to stimulate an emotion, since if it were, any other means of conveying the emotion (e.g. a suitable brain implant or drug) would do just as well, and this is not how aesthetic expression is regarded. Different embodiments of expressive properties in works of art are not inter-substitutable: the particular work is ineliminable from the aesthetic experience. There are, for example, very many works of art which embody poignancy evoked by a sense of the ephemeral nature of life, from the poems of Wang Wei to the paintings of Watteau; but none of these is in any sense a substitute for or equivalent to another. Clearly, this aspect of expression is closely linked to the notion that works of art are in some non-trivial sense unique.[19]

Fourthly, the issue of how aesthetic expression works – which features of works of art can be the basis from which expressive properties emerge (the mechanism of expression, so to speak) – is an enormous question with little agreement over the answer. Cook, Langer and Hanslick each give a different view on the issue in its most mysterious form, i.e as it applies to music. Cooke, it will be recalled, argues that certain notes have an inherent emotional character and Langer regards music as isomorphic with the patterns of emotional life. Again, Ozenfant wishes to ground the effect of painting ultimately in tropisms, built-in reactions of the human organism to form and colour. Hanslick says something like this, but admits that the matter, as regards music, is in effect a mystery.

A great deal of the answer (or rather, answers) to this question, when it emerges, will be psychological rather than philosophical and so lies outside the scope of this essay; but it is possible to see at least some of the main divisions in the explanation. In the first place, the mechanism of aesthetic expression is likely to be rather different according to whether the work of art in question is mimetic or non-mimetic. Where a work of art depicts human beings, or needs to be performed by human beings as representational elements in the work (i.e. in drama, ballet and, to some extent, opera, where the persons are not functioning in the same way as, for example, musicians playing a piece of instrumental music), one can see how part of the explanation of the mechanism of expression will go – our ordinary non-aesthetic responses to persons will be in play, but crucially modified by the aesthetic character of the situation (*cf.* Essay Four, on aesthetic experience). A more complex version of this explanation, needing a good deal of input from the psychology of learned responses to style, might well work for mimetic sculpture and painting, and for described persons or feelings in literature. This sort of account will also work for depictions of aspects of nature other than persons.

The greatest difficulties occur in accounting for the expressive power of non-mimetic works, aural (music) or visual (abstract painting, architecture and some works of sculpture). There are no persons here, depicted or described, to provide a ready locus for expressive properties in the work; but that these works are expressive is precisely the source of the puzzle. Perhaps some sort of tropist account will turn out to be part of the answer, but it will be only a part. As has been hinted above in the discussion of Cooke, the varieties of style in the music of different continents is very marked, reaching down to technically very basic musical elements and the tropist accounts put forward to date will not go far in explaining this fact. Once again, a great deal appears to require explanation in terms of learned responses to styles. Again, no account of the mechanism of musical expression can ignore the role of the performer, which is manifestly critical: minute differences of timing, timbre, volume and so on can enhance or effectively neutralize or destroy the expressive properties of the work. In any performing art, what is expressed depends to a considerable degree on the performers.

The spectator

The key assertion of the preceding section is that expressive properties are properties of the work of art itself. This allows the inclusion within expression theory of a datum reported by many spectators, namely that it is possible, within the context of an aesthetic experience, to recognize that a work of art has a certain expressive character and yet be unable to share the emotion or mood in question. I can recognize that a given work is a 'farewell to life', for example, and yet be quite unable to share the emotion embodied in it; or that a given work is profoundly joyous and optimistic, but find this emotion outside my range of possibilities at a given time.

This not uncommon occurrence within aesthetic experience is particularly difficult to accommodate in expression theories which seek to explain the presence of expressive properties in works of art not in terms of properties of aesthetic objects but rather by means of the projection of feelings or emotions onto these works by spectators during the aesthetic experience. Such accounts of expression had a considerable vogue in the period (roughly) from 1850 until the First World War, and it is appropriate to say something about them.

The idea that what we take to be expressive properties of aesthetic objects are in fact features we project onto those objects because of our own emotional condition is the central idea behind John Ruskin's doctrine of the 'pathetic fallacy'.[20] Ruskin tries to explain why it is that certain statements in poetry which, if regarded literally are false, nevertheless please us aesthetically. He introduces his explanation with a quotation from Chapter 26 of Charles Kingsley's novel, *Alton Locke* (1850):

> 'They rowed her in across the rolling foam–
>   The cruel, crawling foam.'
> The foam is not cruel, neither does it crawl. The state of mind which attributes to it these characters of a living creature is one in which the reason is unhinged by grief. All violent feelings have the same effect. They produce in us a falseness in all our impressions of external things, which I would generally characterize as the 'pathetic fallacy'.
>
> (Ruskin, 1987 edn, pp. 363–4)

That is, in certain emotional states, our reason is unseated to some degree by the force of the emotion, and in this state we falsely attribute to nature emotional states which are properly only attributable to us: hence, 'pathetic fallacy', i.e. error caused by the feelings. This theory allows Ruskin to give an answer to the problem he began with, i.e. how we can take aesthetic pleasure in statements which, literally interpreted, would be false. We estimate their truth, in Ruskin's view, by construing them not as descriptive of nature but as descriptive of our emotions:

> Now so long as we see that the *feeling* is true, we pardon, or are even pleased by, the confessed fallacy of sight which it induces: we are pleased, for instance, with those lines of Kingsley's above quoted, not because they fallaciously describe foam, but because they faithfully describe sorrow.
>
> (*Ibid.* p.366)

A more philosophically sophisticated account of aesthetic expression which makes use of the idea of projection was put forward in 1896 by George Santayana (1863–1952), in his short, classic work of aesthetics *The Sense of Beauty*. The psychological concept of projection plays a large part in the argument of this book, the major thesis of which is that beauty is pleasure regarded as a property, not of ourselves, but of an object. In his account of aesthetic expression, Santayana employs in addition another psychological notion, that of association. He begins with a reference to his theory of perception, according to which the organization of perceptual data into the discrete objects of the world as we experience it is an activity carried out by the mind:

> We not only construct visible unities and recognisable types, but remain aware of their affinities to what is not at the time perceived; that

is, we find in them a certain tendency and quality, not original to them, which upon investigation we shall see to have been the proper characteristics of other objects and feelings, associated with them once in our experience. The hushed reverberations of those associated feelings continue in the brain, and by modifying our present reaction, colour the image upon which our attention is fixed. The quality thus acquired by objects through association is what we call their expression.

(Santayana, (b), pp. 147–8)

Thus, according to Santayana, expression always involves two terms: the aesthetic object itself, and the associations it has for us and which we project onto it and perceive as qualities of that object. It is to be emphasized that the set of associations is never *fully* present to consciousness during the experience of expression: were it to be so, then the value of the aesthetic object would lie solely in its associations, and it would not itself be perceived as expressive. The experiences whose residue makes up the set of associations must fade and blur, and 'remain simply as a halo and suggestion of happiness hanging about a scene' (*ibid.* p.149).

Again, the associative process and projection of which Santayana speaks are not to be thought of as unfolding gradually over time – there is no train of association which could be observed by introspection. Rather, the association and projection occur instantaneously in the presence of the aesthetic object. As Santayana puts it,

the process of association enters consciousness as directly, and produces as simple a sensation, as any process in any organ. The pleasures and pains of cerebration, the delight and fatigue of it, are felt exactly like bodily impressions; they have the same directness, although not the same localisation.

(*Ibid.* p.152)

The associative and projective process, then, results in a perception of qualities as direct and immediate as that of bodily sensations: the key difference is that these qualities are experienced as properties of the aesthetic object:

The value of the second term must be incorporated in the first; for the beauty of expression is as inherent in the object as that of material or form, only it accrues to that object not from the bare act of perception, but from the association with it of further processes, due to the existence of former impressions.

(Ibid. p.151)

The concept of projection is employed in a slightly different way in the account of expression referred to as the 'empathy' or *Einfühlung* (literally 'feeling into') theory put forward early in this century in Germany by Theodor Lipps and in England by the essayist and novelist Vernon Lee.[21] (The following remarks are restricted to Lee's version of the theory. Lipps's version is more detailed, but Lee has taken over its key assertions.) Lee starts by asking why it is that human beings very frequently wish to use of inanimate objects terms which can be applied literally only to beings which are alive, usually persons. (The use of mood and emotion-predicates of works of art is one example of this.) Her answer is that it is an instance of a tendency, deeply embedded in human thought processes, for the mind to merge its activities as a perceiving subject with those of the perceived object. It is this tendency which causes us, for example, readily to make an inanimate object the subject of a verb of action, as when we say 'The mountain rises'.

The activity of ours which the theory asserts we attribute to the mountain is, in part, the muscular effort of raising our eyes or head in order to follow the line of the mountain (Lee, 1913, p.62), but Lee hastens to add two important qualifications to this rather simple assertion. The first is that this attribution of properties of the self to objects (in this case that of 'rising' to the mountain) occurs only when the mind is in a disinterested or contemplative state. The thought behind this assertion is as follows: were we to be aware of the activity of rising as *ours*, we would not be inclined to attribute it to an object outside ourselves; but, in a contemplative state, we cease to be aware of ourselves. Our attention is fixed entirely and completely on the object, and so we tend to attribute our activities to it (*ibid*. p.63).

The second qualification is that what we attribute to the object is not just our present activity, but the condensed residue in our memory, so to speak, of all activities of the same kind: in the present case, what we project onto the mountain is what Lee calls 'the general idea of rising' (*ibid*. p.65). It is this complex activity of projection, according to empathy theorists, which is not only typical of aesthetic experience in general, but which explains our attribution of expressive properties, in particular, to works of art.

These theories turning on the idea of projection are serious attempts to give an account of the origin of expressive properties. Were they acceptable, they would go some way to explaining what I have called the mechanism of expression, and would explain why it is that we want to use mood and emotion-predicates of works of art. However, they involve some grave difficulties, of which I will mention two.

The first is that the empathist account of expression will not work even for the sorts of expressive properties it might most readily be thought to fit, i.e. dynamic passions, since even where a work of art has expressive properties of the most intense kind (many works by El Greco or Goya would serve as examples) it is, as has been said, perfectly possible to recognize what is expressed and yet not share the feeling. There are two replies which a determined empathist might make to this objection. The first is that anyone who is unmoved by such works and does not share the feelings expressed is aesthetically insensitive and not appreciating the work fully. Such a reply runs the risk of making the theory irrefutable, since nothing is allowed to disconfirm it. Alternatively, the empathist can argue that the projection of feeling occurs at an unconscious level, thereby permitting the conscious mind to remain detached. The problem with this move, however, is that it results in a theory in which *explicans* (that which explains) and *explicandum* (that which is to be explained) cannot be independently identified: the only evidence for the postulated unconscious projection is the fact it is alleged to explain, and this is no explanation at all.

The second difficulty applies not just to empathy theories but to all accounts of expression which locate the source of expressive properties in the spectator, and it is this: in some cases, what is expressed in a work of art is *new* to the spectator. I do not *recognize* in the work of art something I have felt; I *am informed* about a possibility of feeling hitherto beyond my experience.[22] To take an example from art of the highest quality, the mood which informs the last two piano sonatas of Beethoven or the last self-portrait of Rembrandt (Colour Plate 3) is a species of inner quietude attainable only after a lifetime of experience has been absorbed and mastered. This wise serenity is a state to which few artists attain, and there is no evidence to suggest that it is particularly widespread elsewhere; yet it is expressed in these works and by their means becomes available for contemplation to the rest of us. To account for this is impossible on theories of expression which postulate a mechanism of psychological projection of feeling: how can I project a feeling of which I have had no experience?[23] This is a particularly grave problem for Santayana, who in many of his books stresses that works of art are often sources of *ideals*, i.e. unrealized states of affairs which we have not experienced.

There is a further important point concerning art, emotion and expression as related to the spectator, as follows. I have tried to make clear in the course of this section that the process whereby an artist communicates with the audience is a complex one. What the artist does is not like expressing emotion; not all works of art have expressive properties, and when they do have such properties, it is not always the case that the state aroused in the spectator is analogous to the state described by the predicates used to specify the expressive properties. However, even though all that is the case, it still remains true that the central reason why works of art are valued at all is that they enhance our lives in certain irreplaceable ways, and *one* of the ways in which they do this is via the impact they can have on our emotional condition. Many works of art are valued precisely because of the way they make us feel.

The question arises, however, as to what philosophical account is to be given of what it is to feel an emotion in the context of an *aesthetic* experience. In the discussion of Hanslick, some points emerged about the analysis of the concept of emotion, but the features which emerged (e.g. having a propositional content) are not linked to the notion of aesthetic experience. Now, the qualification 'aesthetic' is likely to make an important difference to the account of emotion which is appropriate in such circumstances (for an extended discussion of aesthetic experience, see Essay Four).

An astute suggestion which must be included in such an analysis is put forward by R.K. Elliott in his paper, 'Aesthetic Theory and the Experience of Art' (Elliott, 1966). Elliott draws attention to a distinction made by Plato (*Lysis*, 217C–218B) between ignorance which is both present in and predicable of a person and that which is present but not predicable of him or her. A similar distinction can be drawn in respect of emotion, which can be present in me but not predicable of me in aesthetic experience:

> the emotion that I feel in experiencing a work of art from within… may be present in me without being predicable of me. It is present in me because I do not merely recognize that the poet is expressing, for example, sadness, but actually feel the sadness; yet the emotion I feel is not predicable of me, i.e. it would be false to say that I *am* sad or even, unqualifiedly, that I feel sad.
>
> (Elliott, 1966, p.147)

Elliott has indicated a very profitable way in which to conceptualize the distinction between the analysis of emotions felt in non-aesthetic contexts and those felt in aesthetic experience. The general point I wish to stress here is that theories which ignore such a distinction or entail that it is untenable are highly suspect as accounts of emotion in aesthetic experience.

4 Conclusion

In conclusion, I would like to set out the main general points which have emerged from this survey of aesthetic expression, and to add one or two concluding reflections.

The most important point is this: that although works of art undoubtedly play an important role in the emotional lives both of artists and of spectators, the nature of that role is not illuminated by thinking of it as some form of expression of emotion, nor is art itself definable in such terms. It is true that artists do seek, sometimes, to create works the experience of which will move us; but they do so by means of a highly complex process which is as intellectually demanding as any one might care to name, and which is very remote indeed from spontaneous emotional outpouring.

Some of the works thus created have aesthetic properties to which we refer by means of a vocabulary drawn primarily from human moods and emotions. That this is so generates a number of philosophical questions, e.g. as to the sense in which these terms are used of works of art. Again, where the works concerned are non-mimetic, as in music, it is extremely difficult to frame a convincing account of why it is that we wish to use this vocabulary.

Discrete from both these sets of issues is the question of what emotional states works of art arouse in us, and how it is that they can do so: once again, this question is extremely hard to answer for non-mimetic works. Again, the emotions aroused in us by works of art, and which we value very deeply, are significantly unlike those felt in non-aesthetic contexts. Indeed, they must be – non-aesthetic emotions are the prime motives for action, their aesthetic counterparts are not.

I will add two points to this summary by way of conclusion. The first is that it is anything but surprising that so much time and effort has been expended by so many in trying to understand precisely how art is related to the emotions. It is the reflection in aesthetic theory of the centrality of the emotional life to human well-being or flourishing or happiness. The state of a person's emotions is at any time a major constituent of that person's overall happiness or misery. In consequence, it is entirely understandable that we should value highly those works of art which enrich the emotional life in the many ways in which they undoubtedly do, e.g. by calming the emotions, by stimulating them, by rendering them more comprehensible and to that extent easier to cope with, or by suggesting new possibilities of feeling. (That works of art do thus enrich the emotional life is part of the answer to Tolstoy's initial inquiry as to what justification there can be for the effort and money put into the entire institution of art.) It is equally understandable that so much time is spent trying to analyse the highly complicated manner in which this enrichment takes place.

Finally, in the discussion of both Tolstoy and Collingwood, I have argued that it is not a necessary condition for being a work of art that the work should have expressive properties, since there are many works of art which it would be difficult to contend are in any non-trivial sense expressive; but it is to be stressed that the examples of works of art which validate this objection (e.g. a good deal of mid-eighteenth-century European music; well-executed topographical paintings; antique maps and so on) are all of a minor kind. I would like to suggest by way of conclusion that there are no works of art one might wish to call great which lack expressive properties, and our estimate of whose greatness is not in some measure grounded precisely in their possession of these properties. Take any major work by Shakespeare or Mozart or Goya or Bernini and examine the reasons for its greatness: in every case, together with reflections on formal properties, skill in handling materials and so on will be reasons which specify expressive properties. But this does not at all add up to saying that 'art is expression'.

Bibliography

Barrett, D.C. (ed.) (1965) *Collected Papers in Aesthetics*, Blackwell.
Beardsley, M.C. (1958) *Aesthetics*, Harcourt.
Berlioz, H. (1977 edn) *Memoirs*, Cairns, D. (trans.) Victor Gollancz.
Borges, J.L. (1972) *Dr Brodie's Report*, Penguin Books.
Bouwsma, O.K. (1954) 'The Expression Theory of Art' in Elton, W. (ed.) *Aesthetics and Language*, Blackwell.
Brentano, F. (1973) *Psychology from an Empirical Standpoint*, Routledge and Kegan Paul.
Budd, M. (1985) *Music and the Emotions*, Routledge and Kegan Paul.
Budd, M. 'Belief and Sincerity in Poetry' in Schaper, E. (ed.) (1983) *Pleasure, Preference and Value*, Cambridge University Press.
Collingwood, R.G.(1938) *The Principles of Art*, Oxford University Press.
Cooke, D. (1959) *The Language of Music*, Oxford University Press.
Elliott, R.K. (1966) 'Aesthetic Theory and the Experience of Art' in Osbourne, H. (ed.) (1972) *Aesthetics*, Oxford University Press.
Ghiselin, B. (1952) *The Creative Process*, Mentor.
Gombrich, E. (1960) *Art and Illusion* Phaidon.
Hanslick, E. (1957 edn) *The Beautiful in Music*, Cohen, G. (trans.) Bobbs-Merrill.

Hepburn, R.W. (1965) 'Emotions and Emotional Qualities' in Barrett, *op. cit.*
Hepburn, R.W. (1984) *'Wonder' and Other Essays*, Edinburgh University Press.
Hospers, J. (1969) *Introductory Readings in Aesthetics*, The Free Press.
Langer, S. (1953) *Feeling and Form*, Routledge and Kegan Paul.
Langer, S. (a) (1957), *Philosophy in a New Key*, Harvard University Press.
Langer, S. (b) (1957), *Problems of Art*, Routledge and Kegan Paul.
Langer, S. (1964 edn) *Philosophical Sketches*, Mentor Books.
Larkin, P. (1982) 'An Interview With *Paris Review*' in *Required Writing*, Faber and Faber (1983 edn).
Lee, V. (1913) *The Beautiful*, Cambridge University Press.
Meager, R. 'The uniqueness of a work of art' in Barrett, *op. cit.*
Mothersill, M. (1961) '"Unique" as an aesthetic predicate', *J. Phil.*, vol. 58.
Ozenfant, A. (1952) *Foundations of Modern Art*, Dover Books.
Rhys, E. (ed.) (1970) *The Prelude to Poetry*, Dent.
Ruskin, J. (1987 edn) Modern Painters, Barrie, D. (ed.), André Deutsch.
Santayana, G. (a) (1936) *Obiter Scripta*, Constable.
Santayana, G. (b) (1936) *The Sense of Beauty*, Scribners, The Triton edn, vol. I.
Tolstoy, L. (1930) *What is Art?* Oxford University Press.
Troyat, H. (1970) *Tolstoy*, Penguin Books.
Wittgenstein, L. (1953) *Philosophical Investigations*, Blackwell.

Notes

[1]   Later on in the work, Tolstoy introduces a very stringent variant of condition (a), when he insists that 'only that is a true work of art which transmits fresh feelings *not previously experienced by man*' (*ibid.* p.147, my italics). But this is so strict a test that it can hardly be taken seriously, especially in view of the very spartan range of feelings Tolstoy regards as valuable.

[2]   Tolstoy is assuming that the feelings transmitted by art will be mimicked or copied in non-aesthetic situations. On this assumption, *cf.* Essay Seven.

[3]   For a summary of reactions, *cf.* Henri Troyat's *Tolstoy*, pp. 735–7.

[4]   Bradley, A.C. (1909; 1965 edn) 'Poetry for Poetry's Sake' in his *Oxford Lectures on Poetry*, Macmillan, pp. 11–12. The painter Ozenfant was equally clear on this point: 'The subject is nothing in itself! it is of value if the fashion in which it is exploited moves us. But the manner of expression has no value if what is said is of no particular significance' (Ozenfant, 1952 edn, p.278). More is said about Ozenfant in the section concerning Deryck Cooke's theory of music, pp. 200–2.

[5]   This objection is based on some remarks by Malcolm Budd in his excellent book *Music and the Emotions*, pp. 123ff. *Cf.* also his essay, 'Belief and Sincerity in Poetry' in Schaper, E. (ed.) (1983) *Pleasure, Preference and Value*, Cambridge University Press, pp. 137ff. Budd is avowedly following Wittgenstein, (1958) *The Blue and Brown Book*s, Blackwell, p.178.

[6]   It is well known that a very similar philosophy of art had been developed somewhat earlier within the traditions of Continental European philosophy by the Italian philosopher Benedetto Croce, 1866–1952, whose philosophical *magnum opus* the *Estetica* appeared in 1902. I have omitted Croce's views from consideration for reasons of space.

[7]   Collingwood makes the same point again later discussing the idea of expression: 'the kind of answer we expect to this question is an answer derived from what we all know and all habitually say; nothing original or recondite, but something entirely commonplace' (Collingwood, 1938, p.109).

[8]   The effects of the medium can be felt also in films, e.g. a part of the aesthetic effect of

the films of the *nouvelle vague* derives from the grainy quality of the fast film stock which was used. The stock also allowed novel lighting effects in scenes with low light levels.

[9] On the dangers of music, *cf.* Plato, *Republic*, 401; *Laws*, 814–6; and Confucius, *Analects*, III, 25; VII, 14; XV, 113; XVII, 18.

[10] In order to keep this section to a reasonable length, I have had to use, unexplained, some of the technical vocabulary of music, e.g. note, interval, scale. If you find this difficult, it might be helpful to bear the following in mind. The music Cooke is concerned with is based on a scale of eight notes, such that the top note of any scale (the octave) is always exactly half the frequency of the bottom note (the tonic). The scale is sub-divided into intervals (called first, second, third, etc., up to seventh) such that each note in the scale bears a constant ratio to all the other notes in the scale, whatever the scale may be: thus the third note of any scale will always be the same proportion of an octave away from its tonic note, and will stand in similarly fixed relations to the other notes of its scale. Cooke's central assertion can be expressed as the thesis that notes which thus stand to one another in invariant ratios have invariant emotional significances.

[11] Hanslick gives more examples, from Handel and Gluck, *op. cit.*, p.35-6.

[12] The debt to Wittgenstein is acknowledged, for example, in Langer, (a), p.79.

[13] This exposition is based chiefly on the version of Langer's views set out in Langer, (a), first published in 1942. In a later work (Langer, 1953), attempting to make her theory internally consistent, she added an extra claim to her theory of music to the effect that it (music) is our most perfect symbol of subjective time-consciousness or 'passage', as she calls it. (She was influenced by Bergson in this later book.) I have deliberately omitted this later variant of her view since it adds nothing of philosophical substance to her earlier account and in any case involves her in some quite serious difficulties over the concept of aural illusions (*cf.* Langer, 1953, chap.7).

[14] This is, of course, a version of the difficulty which besets Collingwood who in his fashion identifies the creative act with the organization of experience at a high level of epistemological generality.

[15] Scruton's views are set out in 'Understanding Music', in his *The Aesthetic Understanding*, Carcanet Press, 1983; and in his 'Analytic Philosophy: the Meaning of Music' in Shusterman, R. (ed.) (1989) *Analytic Aesthetics*, Blackwell.

[16] See the excellent anthology of such reports edited by Ghiselin (1952). Ghiselin has drawn together writings by creative thinkers from all spheres of activity, not just the arts. The consistency of their reports is striking.

[17] Of the major artists I am aware of, the only one to disagree fundamentally with this account of the creative process is Edgar Allan Poe. Poe ostentatiously dissociated himself from any suggestion that the composition of his works was dependent on chance, involuntary inspiration. In his essay, *The Philosophy of Composition* (1846) he claims to have composed his poem 'The Raven' by deductive reasoning. There is every reason to doubt, however, that Poe has here given a complete account of how he worked, and there are large gaps in what he says. He appears to have been in the grip of a character he elsewhere christened 'The imp of the perverse'.

[18] As O.K. Bouwsma once put it, 'the sadness is to the music rather like the redness to the apple, than it is like the burp to the cider.' ('The Expression Theory of Art' in Elton, 1954, p.98); *cf.* John Hospers 'The Concept of Artistic Expression', in Hospers (1969), pp. 142ff.; R.W. Hepburn 'Emotions and Emotional Qualities' in Barrett, 1965, pp. 185ff. and in Hepburn, 1984, pp. 75ff.; and Beardsley, 1958, chapter 7. These pieces all contain references to other discussions of this point.

[19] On this, *cf.* Ruby Meager, 'The Uniqueness of a work of art' in Barrett, 1965, pp. 23ff. and Mothersill (1961).

[20] It occurs in volume III (1854) of Ruskin's massive five-volume work, *Modern Painters*, 1843–60.

[21] Lipps published two important papers in the *Archiv für die gesamte Psychologie*: (1903) 'Empathy Inward Imitation and Sense Feelings' and (1905) 'A Further Consideration of Empathy'. Vernon Lee ('nom de plume' of Violet Paget) published her views in her book *The Beautiful*, 1913.

[22] On this aspect of expression *cf.* R.W. Hepburn: 'The Arts and the Education of Feeling and Emotion' reprinted in his *'Wonder' and Other Essays* pp. 88ff.

[23] There is an interesting discussion from a psychological point of view of late works of this kind in Anthony Storr's *Solitude*, chap. 11.

PART THREE ART, WORLD AND SOCIETY

Truth and representation

Rosalind Hursthouse

Introduction

A frequently recurring theme in the essays in this volume is the relation-ship between a work of art and something outside, or external to, the work of art – for example, nature, or some aspect of reality. Art has been defined by some as 'the imitation of beautiful nature' (Batteux); or it has been said that at least many works of art 're-present' or 're-produce' some aspect of nature or reality. Music has been claimed to represent emotions – an aspect of psychological reality. Tragedy, through what it represents, may, it has been said, help us to an understanding of 'realities that are of great importance in human life' (Essay Four, p.172). Paint-ings have been criticized for failing to represent reality – 'trees aren't really purple and the sky isn't really the colour of butter... the things he paints don't really exist anywhere...' (quoted in Essay One, p.32).

These ideas are all concerned with *representation* as a relation between a work of art and something real (taking 'real' in its widest possible sense) which is external to it. Less obviously they are also all thereby concerned with *truth*, for wherever there is a (purported) representation of something real, there is room for the question: 'Is it a *true* representation or a false one – a misrepresentation of reality?'

However, the preceding essays have made it obvious that the concept of *representation* can be used in a variety of ways. This is in part, though not wholly, the result of its being used as one translation of the ancient Greek word *mimesis* (also translated as 'imitation') which figures essentially in Plato and Aristotle. It is with some of their writings that I shall start.

Enormous significance has been, and still is, attached to the writings of Plato and Aristotle in the theory of art, a significance that may at first sight strike one as disproportionate. For one thing, the ancient Greek concept of art was rather different from ours[1] – how then could Plato and Aristotle have said anything significant about art as *we* think of it? For another, such writings of theirs as we have on what could be described as the theory of art are both small (in comparison with later writers) and limited in scope. Plato does not have a single work on the topic; only a number of scattered remarks and a few sustained passages. From Aristotle we do indeed have the *Poetics*, but it is primarily concerned with tragic drama, and his complementary work on comedy is lost. Both philosophers make only the most passing references to painting, sculpture and architecture, and none to Greek vases (subsequently greatly revered as works of art). Though both have something to say about music, the little we know about ancient Greek music is still enough to make it fairly certain that the music they are talking about is very unlike the sort of music that subsequently developed in the western world.

So why is such significance attached to their writings in the theory of art? A large part of the answer to that question is simply that the writings *are* those of Plato and Aristotle, and as such were studied, in the original Greek or in Latin translation, by nearly all scholars and by most well-educated people in Europe, from at least the thirteenth century until almost the beginning of this one, and thereby provided a set of common reference points. They were appealed to, or castigated, as authorities, ransacked for insights, used as springboards, reinterpreted to fit contemporary views, endlessly quoted – and misquoted. And not, of course, just on art, but on all the other concepts that, as previous essays show, bear on theories of art – concepts such as those of nature, human nature, reality, knowledge, the role of reason and emotion in our lives, the capacities of the human mind, and so on. Their thoughts reappear in thinker after thinker, sometimes as a brightly clear reflection, sometimes as no more than a flickering shadow. To this day, their thoughts inform ours, whether we know it or not. So we return to them on the theory of art, despite their limitations, in part to see what we, thinkers in the late twentieth century, want to make of them, and in part to understand better the background against which so many other thinkers about the theory of art have written.

They serve as an introduction to at least two major themes in the theory of art: art as morally educative or formative, and art as 'representing' (or 'imitating' or 'copying') nature or reality.

The first thing we must note is that, for Plato and Aristotle, the two themes are inseparably linked by the concept of truth, because they hold an objectivist view of morals. The current idea that there are no such things as objective moral truths, that each moral opinion is 'equally valid' is one that they both rejected. So for them, the first theme mentioned above takes the form of the question:

(i) Can art be morally educative or formative by conveying moral truths, or by aiding our grasp and understanding of moral truths, and hence give us moral knowledge?

This links the first theme with the second, for the interest Plato and Aristotle have in the second is:

(ii) Can art truly represent reality, and, in particular, can it represent moral reality (and hence convey moral truths and yield moral knowledge)?

The second thing we must note is that they both discuss art (particularly poetry and painting) in terms of the concept of *mimesis*. The difficulty with this concept is that it does not correspond exactly to any concept of ours. In some contexts it is obviously correct to translate it as 'imitation' or 'copy', in others as 'representation', in others as 'mimicry', and in others as 'impersonation' or 'enactment'. This means that when we read Plato and Aristotle in translation, some things they say about 'representation' (i.e. *mimesis*) appear to us very odd. They lump together things that we think of as very different; or they say that something follows from something else when it seems obvious to us that it does not. Of course, this apparent oddity sometimes arises from other sources – it is hardly likely that we will find the thought of two ancient Greeks entirely familiar to us, nor need we be afraid to say that occasionally they make mistakes. But it is worth bearing in mind that any apparent disagreement we have with them about the truth of a sentence in which any of the words 'copy', 'imitation', 'representation', etc. (and their related adjectives and verbs) occurs, *may* be the result of a mismatch of translation.

1 Plato

The Republic *Book 3*

Plato's views on art are to be found in several of his dialogues, but most famously in *The Republic*, his work on the ideal state. Plato thought that a just society was only possible if the rulers were 'philosopher kings' and he attached great importance to the upbringing and education of the people who were to become these rulers (the 'Guardians'). Boys' education, in the Athens of Plato's time, consisted of learning to read and write (and presumably to do very simple arithmetic), physical education, music, and – the most extensive part – the learning of poetry.

Acclaimed poets – especially Homer, but also the dramatists – were learned off by heart and recited. Moreover, the recitation was not gabbled parrot-fashion; the boys were expected to deliver the poetry as actors would, with feeling and appropriate gestures. (This latter fact, that the recitation of poetry involved imaginative identification with the characters, plays an important role in one of Plato's arguments, as we shall see.) So in *The Republic* we find a discussion of the role of poetry (and, to a very minor extent, prose) in the ideal society, and the first sustained defence of censorship.

The discussion is further extended to cover other arts. Although the words we translate from the ancient Greek as 'arts' and 'artists' are more literally to be translated as 'crafts/skills' and 'craftsmen/technicians', Plato fortunately gives examples of the sort of 'crafts' or craftsmen he is discussing, and these tend to be of what we would call 'art', rather than such things as carpentry, or tailoring, arithmetic or logic. Before the discussion of education begins he has mentioned painting, embroidery[2] and work in materials such as gold and ivory; also sculptors, painters, musicians, poets and playwrights.

The discussion begins at the end of Book 2, where, having raised the question 'What kind of education shall we give the Guardians?', Plato immediately lays down restrictions on what the content or subject-matter of poetry can be (Plato, 376). The very beginning of education or upbringing consists in telling children stories; these, he says, are all derived from the poets, and many of them are unsuitable. They are unsuitable insofar as they encourage the children who hear them 'to form opinions the opposite of those we think they should have when they grow up' (*ibid.* 377), i.e. *false* opinions about such important matters as the nature of the gods and the heroes (who are sons of gods), or whether death is preferable to slavery. So the first restriction that is laid down is that the content matter of poetry must encourage *true* opinions about such matters. Note that this still permits the representations of weak or wicked people – 'less reputable women characters or... the bad men whom those we are bringing up as Guardians of our state will be ashamed to imitate' (*ibid.* 388).

In the next section Plato goes on to place further restrictions on such representation. He does this by restricting the form that poetry in the ideal state may take. (We are, remember, assuming that poetry will not only be read, but read aloud and performed by the young.) If the poetry in question is dramatic, then in one's performance or recitation one will always be speaking in the person of a particular character – *representing* him or her – a character who may be not only male or female, but also good or bad, noble or base. If the poetry is epic, then sometimes one will be speaking in the person of a character and sometimes one will be speaking just as the narrator. It is only in lyric or elegiac poetry that one will speak only as a narrator.

Plato argues that the only sort of character whose 'representation' can play a proper part in the education of the Guardians is that of a *good* man; hence, he concludes, all dramatic poetry (whose recitation would necessarily involve impersonating or representing all sorts of undesirable characters) must be banned; and epic poetry must be written in such a way that 'the proportion of representation will be small' (*ibid.* 396) – limited to the direct speeches of good men, especially when the good man 'is behaving with steadiness and determination, and only failing in a few respects and to a limited degree, owing to illness or love or drink or some other misfortune' (*ibid.*).

Plato then goes on to discuss music. Greek music mostly functioned as an accompaniment to songs; and certain 'modes', known to us by names such as 'the Mixed Lydian', 'the Ionian', etc., were, apparently, very strongly associated with the content of the songs. Hence Plato can say with confidence, for example, that 'the Mixed Lydian and the Extreme Lydian are suitable for dirges' (*ibid.* 398), that the Ionian is used for drinking songs and so on. Given this association, he is able to ban a number of modes precisely because they go with unsuitable content – such as dirges and lamentations. The other 'arts' are then dealt with by a somewhat remarkable extension, leading to the conclusion that 'the object of education is to teach us to love beauty' (*ibid.* 403). (It is important to realize that the abstract noun translated here as 'beauty' (*to kalon*) can equally accurately, albeit more clumsily, be translated as 'the fine' or 'the honourable', which is, in Plato and Aristotle, the major *moral* concept.)

The restriction of content   It is easier to pick up a general idea of what Plato is arguing in these passages than pay due attention to the details. But the general idea may, unfortunately, be misleading. Many people have skimmed through the first argument here (on the restriction of content) and picked up the general idea that Plato is prepared to censor poetry in order to ensure that it should 'aim at producing the right moral effect' in the young (*ibid.* 378). Certain sorts of stories must be prohibited 'before they breed vicious habits in our young men' (*ibid.* 392).

Now this argument for censorship – of literature, paintings, music, films, television (remember what people said in the 50s about Rock and Roll?) – is one that has been common, and is used to this day. But in this general utilitarian form ('Such and such will have a bad moral effect on people, therefore it ought to be banned/censored'), the argument omits a crucial detail of Plato's argument. This is his constantly reiterated claim that the passages he is intending to cut from the poets are all *false* and, moreover, false about very important matters, namely the nature of the Good and Wise. *The* fault to be found with 'the greater part of the stories current today' is that of 'misrepresenting gods and heroes' (*ibid.* 377). The stories are 'quite untrue' (*ibid.* 387); the poets make 'stupid mistakes' (*ibid.* 379); their account of the after-life is 'untrue' (*ibid.* 386); much of what they say is 'a wicked lie' (*ibid.* 391). The lies are wicked not simply as lies, but because they are about such important matters.

So the objects of Plato's attack are claimed to have three features: (i) falsehood, (ii) this is wicked or sinful because it is about serious matters, and (iii) it corrupts the young. Only the last one is picked out by the common argument, which is less specific than Plato's. Something suitable for censorship, according to this bit of Plato's argument, has to be made out to be false, as well as wicked, and deleterious (*cf.* 'sinful, inexpedient, and inconsistent...' (*ibid.* 380)) not merely wicked or deleterious.

Hence if someone were to argue (as has been done) that paintings of nudes should be banned, or fig leaves discreetly added, because they breed 'vicious habits in our young', they could not appeal to Plato – or at least, not to this passage in him – as an authority. Human beings really do have genitalia, and do not always have fig leaves attached to them, so the representation of them nude, without fig leaves is no misrepresentation, no untruth, no lie; and thereby, no wicked lie.

However, someone might argue (as has also been done) that pornographic paintings or photographs of women should be banned, on the grounds that they represent women as mere sexual objects or playthings for men. Here the argument may become the same as Plato's, developed as follows. Since women are not mere sexual objects or playthings, the representation is a misrepresentation, an untruth, a lie. Moreover it is a wicked lie, since it is about an intensely important aspect of human values. Moreover 'such lies are positively harmful' (*ibid.* 391), leading men to treat women badly, and women to undervalue themselves and to pander to men's exploitation of them. (The truth of the premises here is not an issue; this is an illustration of how Plato's complete argument might appear in modern dress.)

There is just one point at which Plato suggests that some things might have to be censored even if true (*ibid.* 378); but nothing else in this part of *The Republic* supports the view that anything but wicked lies is to be banned.

The restriction on form   Plato argues not only for restrictions on the content of poetry, but also for restrictions on its form. His arguments for restricting the form poetry may take depend heavily on the fact, mentioned above, that a large part of the education of Greek youths involved their reciting poetry with feeling. Our education is so different that the discussion may no longer seem entirely relevant; nevertheless, it contains several aspects of significance.

His basic objection to the 'representation' or 'impersonation' of anything but good men is that it is dangerous to the characters of the young people involved. 'They must no more act a mean part than do a mean action or any other kind of wrong' (*ibid*. 395), the strong implication being that just as actually doing what is wrong gets one accustomed to it, instead of regarding it with loathing or horror or contempt, so does merely acting wrongdoing.

Now this is a very strong premise about human psychology and how it works, but, although doubtless exaggerated, it is one that many people have held, and do hold, in certain forms. Mothers who allow their very young sons to dress up, and impersonate ('represent') girls, are not infrequently castigated by the sons' fathers as 'bringing him up to be a sissy'. (*Cf.* Plato's claim that the young Guardians will not be allowed to take the parts of *any* women (*ibid*. 395).) Parents nowadays may try to prevent their children, particularly their sons, from playing games involving the enactment (representation) of killing and fighting. (I heard of a playgroup where the children, having managed to turn every allowed game in which human beings, and subsequently animals, were represented, into one which involved killing and fighting, were eventually told that they could pretend to be trees and flowers and mountains and the rain and so on, but nothing else. The next day there they were fighting and pushing and shouting 'You're dead!' 'No I'm not!': they were playing 'Trees and Floods'.) Someone who rejects the Platonic premise may thereby reject this sort of attempt as nonsense. 'It doesn't matter what sort of games you let children play', it may be said, 'as long as you teach them that there is all the difference in the world between acting and real life, and that *real* killing and violence are abhorrent.' But the still current Platonic thought is that the sophisticated distinction between reality and play (or acting, or representation) cannot be grasped clearly by children, and that, in their permitted play, they start to form attitudes to killing, violence, male and female roles, and so on, which will subsequently become extremely difficult to dislodge, perhaps because they will be largely unconscious. (*Cf.* 'Children cannot distinguish between what is allegory and what isn't, and opinions formed at that age are usually difficult to eradicate or change' (*ibid.* 378).)

Suppose we granted Plato his premise about the effects of 'impersonation' or 'representation' on the young. It seems that he still has not completed his argument for banning all dramatic poetry from his ideal state. Why does he not allow that the boys may learn to recite only epic poetry, with its small proportion of (unsuitable) representation, but that the famous Greek festivals, at which comedies and tragedies were performed by professional actors, could continue? He may have an argument for keeping drama out of education (given how it was taught), but where is the argument for keeping it out of the ideal state entirely?

The only candidate in Book 3 of *The Republic* is an argument which appeals to a premise about the ideal state for which he has argued elsewhere. It is supposedly agreed that in the ideal state 'one man does one job (only) and does not play a multiplicity of roles'. The cobbler must stick to his last because one man cannot do more than one job or profession well (*ibid.* 374). So there is no place in it for actors (who play such a multiplicity); an actor 'and his kind have no place in our city' and we shall 'send him elsewhere.'[3]

This argument is distinctly weak, but more devastating ones emerge in Book 10.

The Republic *Book 10*

Book 3 ends with a summary of Plato's views on the importance of the 'arts' in education. A rather different discussion appears in Book 10, claimed by many commentators to have the air of an unsatisfactory appendix to *The Republic* as a whole. Much of it certainly seems inconsistent with what has gone before.

Poetry had been severely criticized in Book 3 for much misrepresentation, the implication being that there could be good and bad (true and false) representation. Plato's arguments for banning some of the true representations entirely (suitably censored dramatic performances by actors) seemed rather weak, as we noted, and in any case, left open the possibility that the ideal state might still contain a fair amount of poetry. But in Book 10 it appears that the sort of representation there is in poetry is no good anyhow.

> The artist's representation is... a long way removed from truth... [The artist is] merely manufacturing shadows at third remove from reality...
> We may assume, then, that all the poets from Homer downwards have

no grasp [knowledge] of reality, but merely give us a superficial representation of any subject they treat *including human goodness.*

(*Ibid.* 598–600; my italics)

How does Plato reach this conclusion? It depends on his metaphysics, his views on the nature of reality. According to Plato in his early and middle period (during which he wrote *The Republic*), the world as we ordinarily experience it is an illusion, a collection of mere appearances, like reflections in a mirror, or shadows on a wall. The real world is the world of the Forms (a word which can also be translated as 'Ideas') – the Forms (or Ideas) of the Good, of Beauty, Justice, the ideal Triangle, Man, and indeed, of the Bed, the Table and so on. The 'knowledge' we derive from our senses of the ordinary world is not knowledge at all, being of mere appearance: true knowledge is of the Forms and is acquired by reason and understanding.

The Forms, according to Plato, exist separately from this world in an eternal unchanging supersensible world, and it is this world which is the proper object of knowledge, that for which the philosopher – the 'lover of wisdom' – yearns and searches. In a particularly famous passage in *The Republic* Plato describes our condition as being like that of prisoners in a cave who are only able to look in one direction because they are chained, and who have a fire behind them and a wall in front. Between them and the wall there is nothing; all that they can see are shadows of themselves and of objects behind them, cast on the wall by the light of the fire. Pathetically, they take these shadows to be real, and have no inkling of the reality that, literally, lies behind them, nor indeed of their own true nature.

This, according to Plato, is our condition while we allow ourselves to be chained by our bodies, our reliance on our senses and emotions. It is only when we reject these and start to use our reason that we are able to turn around, escape from the cave and see, in the light of the sun and the fire the real objects, the Forms, face-to-face and gain true knowledge for the first time.

This view has long been influential in Eastern thinking, and has been no less influential in the West, for it became an important aspect of Christianity. When St Paul says, 'When I was a child, I spake as a child, I understood as a child; but when I became a man, I put away childish things. For now we see through a glass, darkly [ie. in a mirror, obscurely]; but then face to face; now I know in part; but then shall I know even as also I am known,' he is writing in terms of the neo-Platonism which was widely read in his day. In the world of the Forms, the ultimate

Form is that of the Good (or, as it is sometimes translated, the Beautiful, which is the Form Plato is referring to when he says 'the object of education is to teach us to love beauty' as I noted on page 243 above); and much that Plato says about the Form of the Good adapts very readily to claims about the God of Christianity.

So, bearing the above in mind, what are Plato's arguments against tragic poetry? He begins by considering 'the art of representation' as exemplified in painting *and*, notably, by belittling painting. It is compared to holding up a mirror, and the significance of this comparison is that any fool could do it. Later, it is acknowledged that a painter will need skill (*ibid.* 598) and hence not be *any* kind of fool, but, insofar as his skill involves 'knowledge', it would only be 'knowledge' of mere appearances – 'reflections' like those in the mirror – for it is only appearances that he tries to represent (*ibid.*).

Now an obvious objection is that painters may not always try to represent superficial appearances but may indeed try to penetrate beneath them. What goes for depicting beds may not go for depicting people, or goodness or beauty. There was already in Plato's day a distinction drawn between painters who tried to depict character in their portraits and those who did not, but aimed only for likenesses. There were also stories about painters who, failing to find a perfectly beautiful model, would take the eyes from one, the nose from another and so on. Tragic poets are concerned with people, human goodness, and beauty rather than with beds; why should it not be characteristic of them that they seek to penetrate superficial appearances and actually guide their readers and hearers towards an understanding of the Forms? Plato just assumes that this is not so; moreover, having claimed that painters aim only to represent appearances, he maintains that the same is true of poets.

Even if it were true, one might still think that *some* knowledge of reality could be gained even from something which stood a third remove from it. If I am trying to gain true knowledge of the Form of Bird, for example, might not my search for this knowledge be aided by pictures of birds the like of which I have never seen, brought from other countries? Few of us have seen kiwis; it is the pictures of them that aid us towards the knowledge that (as Plato might say) the Form of the Bird is not that of a winged creature.

Plato does not consider the potentially informative aspect of pictures (i.e the way in which they might convey truths and hence give us knowledge), but he has firm arguments against our deriving any knowledge from the poets. First of all, he argues that we should not expect to gain any knowledge from the poets about 'medicine or any similar skilled activity' (*ibid.* 599) on the grounds that if they really did know about these things they would prefer to practise them rather than describe others doing so. (The idea that we might turn to poetry to learn about, for example, medicine, seems quaint to us; but a contemporary of Plato's (Isocrates) was in fact arguing at the time that Homer and Hesiod should be looked to for answers to questions in natural science; one may see in Plato's argument a version of the cynical tag, 'Those that can, do; those that can't, teach'.)

More importantly, Plato argues that we have no grounds for supposing that Homer (or any other tragic poet) knows anything about the sort of thing a poet might be expected to know about – the important things in life, such as how human beings should live, or what human goodness consists in. (It might be noted that, on the tests he demands Homer should pass, we have no grounds for supposing that Plato knew anything about these matters either.) Indeed, if we strip poetry of its poetic colouring, 'reduce it to plain prose', we will find that it amounts to very little (*ibid.* 601).

But we still have no reason to banish tragic poetry entirely; the conclusion is no stronger than the claim that it is rather useless, silly stuff, which 'has no serious value' (*ibid.* 379). But must everything in the ideal state be of serious value? Should nothing be just fun, or entertaining, or thrilling, or move us to our depths?

Plato's stern answer to this is 'No'; anything of this nature makes it even harder to escape from the chains that hold us prisoners in the cave, by appealing to our emotions, feeding them when they ought to be starved (*ibid.* 606). Even if we were to restrict the content in such a way that the poetry did convey truths (in the way that hymns to the gods and paeans in praise of good men might (*ibid.* 607)), we must not admit 'sweet lyric or epic muse' (*ibid.*), for their seductive magic makes 'pleasure and pain become [your] rulers instead of law and the principles commonly accepted as best' (*ibid.*). And, for all that he has said to trivialize poetry, in his final passages on it Plato acknowledges its compelling – its dangerously compelling – power. We know the fascination of drama and poetry 'only too well' (*ibid.*) he says, and we must, 'whenever we listen to it, recite this argument of ours to ourselves as a charm to prevent us falling under the spell of a passion most men have never outgrown. Our theme shall be that such poetry has no serious value or claim to truth' (*ibid.* 608).

It is thought that Plato himself began as an aspiring tragic poet and renounced it to pursue philosophic wisdom under Socrates. But he did not renounce it entirely; it is thought that he wrote at least two poetic epitaphs, and people who read him in the original Greek say that the prose in which his philosophy is written is both of exceptional beauty and highly poetic. Perhaps in part because of these facts (but not because of them alone), a number of commentators have detected in the vilification of poetry in Book 10, the distinct note of someone protesting too much, someone who has not outgrown his passion for poetry and is repeating to himself, 'no serious value, no claim to truth, no serious value, no claim to truth' with some desperation. It is as though he is more acutely aware of the dangers of poetry precisely because he feels its power. One commentator goes so far as to describe the arguments as 'passionate, (and) hopelessly bad', and the attempt to deny the poet's creativity by comparing him to someone holding up a mirror – a mere copyist – as 'extraordinary [and] hysterical' (Annas, 1981, p.344). Be that as it may, it is certainly true that Plato's writings contain, and have thereby inspired, not only the most extreme attacks on poetry and whatever is powerful and moving in great art, but also the most eulogistic descriptions of the uplifting influence of its beauty in our lives. He lends himself (given a merely cursory reading) as we have seen, to repressive censorship, to an extreme asceticism in which everything that engages the emotions or gives pleasure is shunned. Yet he also writes about the love of beauty, of the poet's inspired madness, of the power of beauty and poetry, with a passion that has done much to fuel the criticisms of censorship, the repudiation of the view that art must serve political ends, and the idealization of the emotions and the pleasure that art may generate or express. We have, therefore, not been concerned here to summarize 'Plato's theory of art' but, on the contrary, to appreciate the many diverse strains of thought in his writings.

2 Aristotle

Plato and Aristotle

At the end of his discussion of poetry in Book 10 of *The Republic*, Plato issued a challenge – or perhaps one might call it an invitation. We should give those who love poetry a chance to defend it, he says; and if they can prove to us that drama and poetry 'have a place in well-run society, we will gladly (re)admit them' (Plato, 607). What this defence of poetry requires is showing that it 'doesn't only give pleasure but brings lasting benefit to human life and human society'. It must be shown that poetry has 'serious value [and] claim to truth' (*ibid.* 608).

It is plausible to read the *Poetics* as Aristotle's response to this invitation; however, it is both more and less than that. It is more in that the *Poetics* is Aristotle's own theory of tragic poetry (and to a lesser extent, epic poetry); a theory that forms part of his whole system of philosophy, which embraces his views on moral education, metaphysics, the role of reason and emotion in our lives, knowledge, and so on, just as Plato's views on poetry form part of his system which embraces his views on such things. On the other hand, it is less than a response to Plato's invitation in that it is incomplete (the complementary work on comedy is lost; so is an early dialogue called *On Poets*), and in that it makes little or no attempt to address Plato's arguments directly. Aristotle's whole system is a response to Plato's, and one of the reasons why he does not address Plato's arguments directly in the *Poetics* is that he has put forward his opposing views elsewhere.

The most significant background disagreements between them concern the Theory of Forms and the role of emotion in moral education. Though sharing with Plato the premise that particular different things are given the same name in virtue of something that they have in common, Aristotle rejects Plato's view that this is resemblance to a Form which exists in another transcendent world. Aristotle's Forms, or 'universals', exist in this world; they are the essences of the objects we perceive. He also shares with Plato the premise that the Forms are the proper objects of knowledge – what the philosopher seeks to understand – but, since they are located in this perceivable world it is this world which the philosopher studies by means of perception as well as reason. Plato's asceticism, his scorn for the 'lower parts' of the soul (perception and emotion) which we share with the other animals, is notably lacking in Aristotle, and this disagreement between them becomes particularly acute over the issue of moral education.

According to the writings of Plato's early and middle period, we become good human beings through our theoretical, purely rational, knowledge of the eternal, unchanging, Form of the Good, and this involves suppressing or eliminating, as far as possible, our animal appetites or emotions such as the appetite for food, or love and fear, which are attached to the illusory particulars of this world and thereby keep us in our chains in the cave. (It is not hard to see how influential this view has been on Christianity.) But in Aristotle's view there is no such thing as *the* Form of the Good, and we come to be good human beings, and to understand what human goodness is, not by suppressing our appetites and emotions, but through the correct training of them. Each has its own right form of satisfaction; the pleasure (or pain) proper to it, directed to its proper object.[4] So, for example, where Plato wants the good man to be impervious to fear – to be able, ideally, to suppress it entirely – Aristotle thinks there are things it is *right* to fear. Someone who fears nothing, not even death would be 'a maniac or insensate' (Aristotle (a), 1115b), and someone who does not fear disgrace or dishonour is not admirable, but 'shameless' (*ibid.* 1115a). Where Plato says that the good man's life is so independent of others that the loss of a son or brother will hold the least terrors for him (Plato, 387), Aristotle says there is nothing wrong with a man's dreading 'brutality towards his wife and children' (Aristotle (a), *ibid.*).

Despite these disagreements, there is much that Plato and Aristotle have in common. In particular, they share the view that poetry is like the pictorial arts in being 'mimetic' or 'representational' and it is from Aristotle that the famous phrase 'art imitates nature' is derived. However, the phrase translated as 'art imitates nature' does not, significantly, occur in the *Poetics*. Indeed, the fact that the phrase was, and still is, subsequently so often used to sum up 'Aristotle's view on the relation between art and the external world' is a paradigm example of the way in which he and Plato have been continuously ransacked and misquoted.[5] So it is a mistake to approach the *Poetics* expecting it to discuss the way(s) in which tragic poetry *imitates nature*. What we find instead is that Aristotle unquestioningly takes over from Plato the view that poetry and the other arts (painting, sculpture, music and dance) are imitative or representative and goes on to discuss what poetry imitates without mentioning nature.

The *Poetics*

Aristotle begins by outlining the scope of his work and breaking it down into various subheadings. Our topic is the 'craft' of poetry (epic and tragic), comedy and dithyrambic poetry. (Under this general heading music and even dance appears, the former because, as song, it is a constituent of much poetry (e.g. tragic drama); whether dance is given just as another example of an imitative craft, like painting, or forms part of poetry, like music, is not clear.) He notes that all forms of poetry and music can be described as forms of imitation (following Plato) but immediately introduces an important qualification. All cases of imitation are not the same: (i) they can use different media or (ii) they can imitate or represent different things or (iii) they can imitate or represent things in 'entirely different ways'.

(i) The first is useful for purposes of classification. Painters and sculptors use colours and shapes to represent or imitate things, and this immediately distinguishes them from flautists, dancers and 'the form of craft that uses language alone'.

(ii) What different things can the imitative arts represent? According to Plato, a carpenter would count as an 'imitative craftsman', for he, in making a particular bed, was imitating the Form of Bed. But Aristotle, having discarded the Theory of Forms, has thereby greatly limited the scope of 'imitative crafts'; it now applies mostly to what we would call 'the Arts' – poetry, painting, sculpture and music – and the crafts of carpenters, etc. no longer get included.

Hence it turns out, rather surprisingly, that far from the 'imitative' or 'representative' crafts representing a huge variety of different things, they all deal with people in action, and (by and large) with people who are of either good or bad character (with nothing in between). The 'different things' that can be represented are better-than-us people, or worse-than-us people, or same-kind-as-us people. This yields Aristotle the distinction between comedy and tragedy: the latter represents people better than us; the former, worse. (Later on he also distinguishes between them by saying that tragedy and epic poetry represent serious actions, whereas comedy represents what is ridiculous.)

(iii) Finally, the 'entirely different ways' in which these things (good or bad people) may be represented, within the medium of language, turn out to be the threefold distinction Plato had mentioned – (i) a mixture of narration and 'representation' (Homer), (ii) pure (poet's) narration, or (iii) 'the imitators may represent the whole story dramatically, as though they were actually doing the things described' (*ibid.* 1448a) (drama).

Tragedy

When Aristotle settles down to discussing tragedy, what rapidly emerges from the discussion is the great importance he attaches to plot, or as we might say, '*the* action of the play', a concept which some commentators claim we owe to him. The plot is 'the first and the most important thing in tragedy' (Aristotle (b), 1450b); the tragic poet 'must be more the poet of his stories or plots than of his verses' (*ibid.* 1451b). Why is this so?

It emerges from Aristotle's (stipulative) definition of tragedy. He had said earlier that poetry represents people doing things and people of a certain character. But it subsequently turns out that this is to be taken only as a fairly rough characterization of poetry in general, and tragedy in particular. Tragedy is not really a representation of people, 'but of action and life, of happiness and misery' (*ibid*.1450a). It is not, apparently, really a representation of actions either, but an imitation of *an* action (*ibid*. 1449b, 1450a, 1450b, 1459a and 1461b). And it is the plot of a play which is 'an imitation [representation] of *an* action' (*ibid*. 1451a).

What is *an* action in this sense? Well, it is something which, while having parts which are themselves actions, nevertheless has a certain unity. The parts form a unified whole. But its unity is not simply the result of all the actions in question being those of one agent – 'there are many actions of one man which cannot be made to form one action' (*ibid*. 1451a). Its being a unified whole involves its having a 'beginning, middle, and end' (*ibid*, 1450b) and its parts being related in such a way that if any one of them 'makes no perceptible difference by its presence or absence [it] is no real part of the whole' (*ibid*. 1451a).

The point that a whole action has a 'beginning, middle, and end' (*ibid*. 1450b) is not merely the platitude it might at first sight appear, for all three of these terms are given a technical use by Aristotle. A beginning is 'that which is not itself necessarily after anything else, and which has naturally something else after it'. An end is 'that which is naturally after something itself, either as its necessary or usual consequent, and with nothing else after it'. Hence 'a well-constructed plot, therefore, cannot either begin or end at any point one likes' (*ibid*. 1450b). A middle, prosaically enough is 'that which is by nature after one thing and has also another after it' but the description of an end, and the requirement placed on what it is to be a *real* part of a whole (it has to be present, and where it is), entails that the middle must not occur 'as one likes', haphazardly, either.

The claim that tragedy is an imitation of a single action in this way, turns out to be one of great significance, for it provides Aristotle's ground for claiming that 'poetry is something more philosophic and of graver import than history' (*ibid*. 1451b). This is because poetry's 'statements are of the nature rather of universals, whereas those of history are singulars' (*ibid*.). Why does he say this? To understand it, we must first understand what he means by 'universals'. 'By a universal statement' he says, 'I mean one as to what such or such a kind of man will *probably* or *necessarily* say or do' (*ibid*.). So, let us consider two different kinds of person, a brave one and a coward, in a given situation, one in which they must face danger in order to defend their honour. Aristotle would say that the brave one would necessarily face the danger and that the coward probably would not. If the coward knew he could get away with not facing the danger, that no one but him would ever know he had run away, then necessarily he would run away; if his commanding officer threatened him with execution if he ran away, and was watching, he would probably face the danger. And so on.

This pair – 'probably' and 'necessarily' – occurs in various forms again and again throughout the *Poetics*: in the definition of an end as 'a necessary or usual consequent' of something else (*ibid.* 1450b), in the mention of 'the probable and possible order of things' (*ibid.* 1451b); in the specification of a merely episodic plot ('when there is neither probability nor necessity in the sequence of its episodes') and of how 'peripety or discovery' should arise as 'the consequence, necessary or probable, of the antecedents' (*ibid.* 1452a). The terms are not being used by Aristotle in any technical or 'scientific' sense, but in the ordinary everyday sense in which we would use them (and their opposites, 'improbable' or 'unlikely' and 'impossible') in criticism of a plot.

Now it is noteworthy that, in their everyday use, these terms allow for considerable disagreement between people, and that such disagreement may reflect *different attitudes to life and human nature*. For example, if someone is a cynic, or very pessimistic about human nature, they would probably disagree with Aristotle that a brave man would *necessarily* face danger to defend his honour. If someone were very optimistic about human nature they might say that the coward would *probably* run away if he thought he could get away with doing so, but would not *necessarily* do so. It is Aristotle's view that although, obviously, people do disagree about such matters, this disagreement does not show that the judgements are just a matter of personal opinion, and that none of them is objectively true or false. There is, he thinks, a correct way to think about life, human nature and action; there are objectively correct, i.e. true, judgements to be made about what, in this area, is probable and necessary (and their opposites), and it is such universal truths that are conveyed by the good plot of a good tragic drama and indeed of good epic poetry.

How then does history differ from (tragic) poetry? History is committed to describing what has actually happened, and the trouble with actual events in life (as many novelists have subsequently complained) is that they (usually) lack unity and may be haphazard. Several unrelated things happen and then other things happen and then other things; some happen as a result of what has gone before but many do not. The sequence of actual events is usually just like that in an episodic plot, neither probable nor necessary. So the historian, constrained by the actual sequence of events, cannot convey universal truths as defined, but only particular or 'singular' ones.

Suppose a historian selects a sequence of events which *was* probable and necessary? After all, as Aristotle says 'some historic occurrences may very well be in the probable and possible order of things' (*ibid.* 1451b). May he or she not then convey universal truths as defined? It is unfortunate that Aristotle makes no mention of Plato's near contemporary Thucydides, who expected that his history of the Peloponnesian Wars would be useful in showing a 'clear truth' not only about the events that actually had taken place but also 'about those which are likely to take place in the future – in order of human things, they will resemble what has occurred'. The earlier historian Herodotus, whom he does mention, tends to ascribe great movements of history to individual whim, or the workings of Destiny, but Thucydides, like Aristotle, believed in an unchanging human nature and hence, plausibly, that history could reveal the sorts of things that human beings would probably or necessarily do in certain situations.

Thucydides' view of history as revealing human nature has, so historians tell me, fallen quite out of fashion. Though still popular in the eighteenth and nineteenth centuries, it is now thought to be rather jejune. This is not, of course, to say that modern historians would agree with Aristotle that 'poetry is... of graver import than history'; however, it implies that this is not nowadays to be disputed by maintaining that history, like poetry, conveys universal truths of the sort Aristotle specifies. But since, as I said, Thucydides and Aristotle shared the view of human nature as something unchanging, the question remains of why Aristotle does not admit the possibility that history might reveal universal truths.

It may be that, unacquainted with Thucydides' writings, it simply did not occur to him. Another possibility is that he would say that *if* history did this, it would be a happy accident, because it would just be an accident that some period of the past, or the life of some particular man, happened to form a *plot*; the representation (imitation) of *an* action. But when (poetic) tragedy does it, this is no accident. The poet is a maker of plots; that is his 'function' (or, a better translation of the Greek, 'characteristic activity' or 'business'), whereas the 'function' or business of the historian is to describe what has actually happened, whether it forms a plot or not.

Aristotle's claim that good plots are in accordance with 'the probable and possible order of things' is (characteristically) not an entirely general claim that he makes without qualification. One might think that he was committed to the view that plots must be predictable, but, on the contrary, he points out that 'tragedy... is an imitation not only of a complete action, but also of incidents arousing pity and fear. Such incidents have the very greatest effect on the mind when they occur *unexpectedly*' (*ibid.* 1452a; my italics). And he adds further qualifications to the claim about good plots in his discussion of the five critical objections to poetry and how such objections may be answered.

The five objections are that the piece of poetry in question is 'impossible [the opposite of necessary], improbable, corrupting, contradictory or against technical correctness' (*ibid.* 1461b). With respect to the first, Aristotle says of 'the poet's art itself' that 'any impossibilities there may be in his descriptions of things are faults. But... they are justifiable, if they serve the end of poetry itself – if... they make the effect... more astounding' (*ibid.* 1460b). Indeed, he says later that 'for the purposes of poetry a convincing impossibility is preferable to an unconvincing possibility' (*ibid.* 1461b). And with respect to the 'improbable' he says not only that this may be justified by an appeal to an 'accordance with opinion' but also, rather neatly, that it may be justified 'by urging that at times it is not improbable; for there is a probability of things happening also against probability' (*ibid.*). (This remark echoes an earlier one he had made about the constraints on good characterization. Characters, he says, should (amongst other things) be consistent, and continues 'even if inconsistency be part of the man before one for imitation as presenting that form of character, he should still be consistently inconsistent' (*ibid.* 1454a)).

Truth and representation

The praise of tragedy at the expense of history is indicative of the way in which Aristotle's view of tragedy (at least, and quite possibly of art in general) as mimetic or 'representational' is different from Plato's. A flaw that I pointed out in Plato's argument was his assumption that both painters and poets aim only to represent appearances and hence (given the Theory of the Forms) even the most accurate (and hence best) picture (or poem) was at best a manufactured shadow at third remove from reality. Plato did not allow for the possibility that a painter, in his efforts to represent beauty, might do something other than 'hold up a mirror' to his subject. Aristotle explicitly does allow for this, remarking that:

> As Tragedy is an imitation of personages better than the ordinary man [1448a], we in our way should follow the example of good portrait-painters, who reproduce the distinctive features of a man, and at the same time, without losing the likeness, make him handsomer than he is. The poet in like manner, in portraying men quick or slow to anger, or with similar infirmities of character, must know how to represent them

as such, and at the same time as good men, as Agathon and Homer have represented Achilles.

(Ibid. 1454b)

Now although Plato does not discuss history, one would naturally expect him to argue that history, since it describes what has actually happened in the world of appearances, was at a second remove from reality, and thereby superior to poetry which merely gives fictive representations of history. Aristotle, having abandoned the Theory of Forms, has no reason to denigrate history as being at a second remove from reality. But he does denigrate it for being concerned with singular truths and, in contrast, poetry becomes superior in being concerned with universal truths.

So here, in part, is Aristotle's response to Plato's challenge, 'Show that poetry has serious value and claim to truth'. It has a claim to truth because the poet is a maker of plots, and in the representation of *an* action can convey universal truths. Moreover these are serious truths whereby poetry has serious value, for they concern happiness and its opposite, and the ways in which these are bound up with action *(ibid.* 1450a).

Plato and Aristotle share the view that true happiness (or 'flourishing' or 'blessedness' as the Greek word may illuminatingly be translated) consists in (moral) virtue. Nothing is more important in life than understanding this, but nothing is more difficult than understanding it in its detailed practical application *to* life. Just what is the virtuous action on some particular occasion is what the morally wise or knowledgeable person knows, but such wisdom is very hard to acquire. Plato had demanded that the defender of poetry must show that it 'doesn't only give pleasure but brings lasting benefit to human life and human society' (Plato, 607). Aristotle may be read as responding to this demand by claiming, on behalf of tragic poetry, that the serious truths she represents do indeed bring this.

Early in the chapter on the five critical objections to poetry, Aristotle says, 'It is to be remembered, too, that there is not the same kind of correctness in poetry as in politics or indeed any other art' *(ibid.* 1460b), and many commentators have seen in this remark, amongst others in this chapter, the introduction of the concept of 'poetic' or 'dramatic' or 'artistic' truth. (In particular we might note 'If the poet's description be criticized as not true to fact, one may urge perhaps that the object ought to be as described' *(ibid.)*). Without entering into this debate, we may note, more cautiously, that he is certainly relying on a concept of truth (or reality) which borders dangerously on the ineffable. It may strike us as noteworthy that no example is given of a 'universal truth' which Aristotle thought was represented in any tragedy he mentions.

In this respect, Aristotle stands at the beginning of a practice which is still current. It is a practice in which we unhesitatingly connect talk about truth and the understanding of life and human nature with works of art, not only without specifying *what* truth or *what* understanding is meant, *but without expecting to be able to*. I remember when a whole cycle of the ancient Greek tragedies was performed in London in the 1970s, that one of the commonest reactions of people who had never seen or read them before was amazement that 'they were *so true*' (even today), that the ancient Greeks 'really understood what we are like' (even now) or 'really understood life'. But if one asked (as I did ask some friends who reacted this way), 'What was true about them? What are we like, that they got right? What is it about life that they understood?' not only were people rather surprised and put out at the question, but quite unable to come up with any specific answers. 'Oh well,' people said, 'you know. Truths about love, and family relationships and power – that kind of thing.'

Now I am not decrying the relative incoherence of this sort of response. On the contrary, I shall at the end of this essay try to defend it. At the moment, I am simply drawing attention to the fact that, in responding to Plato's challenge, Aristotle has not said, 'Here is a list of serious truths that I have learnt from poetry'. Instead, he has produced the abstract claim that (good) poetry (truly) represents action and (human) life, i.e. (human) happiness and misery, as these are bound up with (human) action. It conveys universal truths about the kinds of things that a certain type of person will probably or necessarily do, and (extrapolating very slightly from the text of the *Poetics*) about the kinds of things that will probably or necessarily happen in life. He thereby becomes the authority and reference point for hundreds of years of describing and assessing works of art in similar terms – as, for instance, expressing, or conveying, or capturing, or representing, 'human' truth(s). We shall be looking at some recent discussion of this view shortly.

3   Representation in pictures

Introduction

As we have seen, it is Plato and Aristotle who introduce the theme that art 'represents' or 'imitates' reality – is 'mimetic' as we might say, to remind ourselves of the difficulty of translation. As we have also seen, they were primarily concerned with poetry, and the notion of pictorial representation is introduced only as an example. However, in subsequent centuries, the emphasis has gone very much the other way. Though literature continued to be discussed in terms of truth, it was not so often discussed in terms of 'the representation of reality', while, conversely, this (or 'imitation') became *the* term with which to discuss painting.

Plato's Theory of Forms, and Aristotle's related (albeit different) distinction between particulars and universals allowed such discussions a great deal of licence. As we noted when questioning Plato's assumption that the painter will not try to penetrate beneath superficial appearances, the Theory of Forms lends itself well to the claim that the painter should not aim to represent things in this world, but rather Real Beauty – the Form of Beauty abstracted from the imperfect copies of it in this world. In postulating a supra-sensible world, containing things that do not exist in this one, it also lent itself to the idea that a painter was in a particularly good position to teach us a proper reverence for the gods or God. They are rarely, if ever, seen in this world, but can, by the painter's art, be represented in all their majesty and power. At a more mundane level, either Plato or Aristotle could be appealed to in defence of the claim that in representing, say, humans or horses the painter should not aim to copy faithfully some particular model before him, but rather, through his study and understanding of many examples, represent the true nature of Man, or of Horse.

Many other themes ran through and informed such discussions. One was, inevitably, the issue of artistic creativity. If painting is only a matter of copying faithfully what is before one's eyes, then it may seem, as it did to Plato, that although this calls for more technical skill than just holding up a mirror, it does not call for anything profound. But if what is represented is something ideal, or an intelligent abstraction from many particulars, then such representation may seem to call for something profound.

Another theme was the authoritative claim (misquoted, as I have noted, from Aristotle) that art imitates *nature*. In some contexts this figured as an insignificant variant of the view that it represents *reality*, but this was not always so. It is more natural (though not 'more real'!) to talk of 'the laws of nature' than of 'the laws of reality'; and the beginning of this very sentence illustrates another way in which the concept of *nature* (and *the natural*) is not the same as that of *reality* (and *the real*). Given the claim that 'art imitates nature', paintings (and sculpture) could be assessed as more, or less, 'natural', though not, thereby, more or less 'real'.

Although, as I have said, 'representation' (or 'imitation') became *the* term with which to discuss painting and sculpture, it was not limited to that area. Not only did it persist in discussions of literature, but it proved amenable to the discussion of music too. Once again, Plato and Aristotle present fruitful sources of ideas. If art can represent the abstract or pure Form of Beauty, and beauty, so Aristotle tells us, is something whose parts are properly ordered and which is, in some sense, an organic unity, what better example of this can there be than music, the most superbly abstract of the arts, the one that depends essentially on the ordering of its parts into an organic whole? (Prior, that is, to 'abstract' painting.) Or, to take it another way, if art imitates nature, and our emotions are our most 'natural' expressions (being common to all human *nature*), what better example of this can there be than music, which (allegedly) represents, or imitates, or expresses our emotions as no other art can? Or again, on a third reading, if art imitates nature, then music is the only art that *naturally* expresses our emotions; it is the (natural) language of the emotions, rising above the local conventions of, say, English or Hindi. (*Convention* is traditionally opposed to *nature* – an opposition that, once again, derives from Plato and Aristotle).[6]

I am not, of course, endorsing any of the above. I am merely illustrating the ways in which people can think and talk in terms of representation and the related ideas of imitation and nature. The fact that thought and talk about them can range so widely and, many people would say, become so nonsensical, brings me to the topic of this section. In considering the view that art 'imitates' or 'represents' nature or reality, we have not yet said anything about the nature of representation, and it is clearly time that we did.

Since the advent of (what is usually called) non-representational pictorial art in the nineteenth century, there has been an ever growing interest in the concept of representation. The problem can be raised quite generally: what is it for one thing, A, to represent another, B? – where, as substitutions for A we could have, for example, a picture, a diagram, a model, a sculpture, a novel, a poem, a symphony. We could also raise the question about some parts of these things. 'What is it for a line, a patch of blue, a tiny bit of wood or marble, a sentence (a word, a letter), a musical phrase or note to represent whatever it does represent here?' And these examples by no means exhaust the forms 'the' question about representation may take.

We cannot attempt to consider all forms of the questions; instead I shall focus on the one which is of central interest in the theory of art, namely the nature of pictorial representation. Even this, as we shall see, is a subject of great complexity.

Representing reality: the deception view

The idea that pictorial art 'imitates' nature or reality by copying it, or mirroring it – literally re-presenting it – is to be found, as we have seen, as early as the ancient Greeks, and has persisted to this day. But what is meant by 'representing nature or reality'? If we were to sit down with some artist's materials and say, 'Now I shall try to represent reality', just what is it we would be trying to do? What would count as succeeding?

One quite natural answer is that we would be trying to produce something so 'realistic', so life-like, that anyone who saw it would be, at least momentarily, deluded or deceived into thinking that they were really seeing what we had painted a picture of. Let us call this 'the deception model of representing reality'.

As a paradigm example, or standard, of what would count as 'representing reality', this too dates back to the ancient Greeks and has persisted to this day. Stories have always been told about artists producing paintings which would deceive the eye not only of human beings, but even of animals. Pliny recounts the tale of one painter, Zeuxis (whom Aristotle mentions), whose painting of grapes was so 'truly representative' that the birds flew down to settle on them; of another (Apelles) that horses neighed at his picture of horses; and of another that crows tried to land on the painted tiles of his scenery. Vasari tells the same stories: Leonardo da Vinci maintained he had seen dogs attack painted dogs. And in art galleries nowadays one still hears people saying approvingly that, for a moment, they had mistaken the picture for the reality it was a picture of.

However, pictures of *x* that are intended to deceive the viewers into thinking that they are really seeing *x* form their own sub-class; they are *trompe l'oeil* (from the French for 'deceive the eye') paintings, and, far from being typical of realistic paintings, they are rather rare and have special features.

(i) They are limited as to subject matter. A representational picture may be a picture *of* Adam and Eve, or Aphrodite, or the Holy Virgin and the infant Jesus, but it cannot be a *trompe l'oeil* picture of any of them, for no one knows what they look like. And it would be absurd to expect that anyone could mistake a picture of Knowledge triumphing over Ignorance, or of Calumny followed by Repentance and Truth for knowledge actually triumphing over ignorance, or calumny really going somewhere, followed by repentance and truth. And yet for centuries artists who described their aim to be that of representing or imitating nature deliberately produced pictures with this sort of subject matter.

An obvious reply to this point is to try to draw a distinction between literal and non-literal, or more or less basic, descriptions, of what a picture is a picture *of*. A picture *of* the Holy Virgin and the infant Jesus is, say, literally or basically, a picture of a youngish woman and a baby; it is in virtue of further iconographical or symbolic features of the picture that it is a picture of the Virgin and Child, for example that the woman is depicted wearing blue, or that both woman and baby have haloes. Or perhaps it is a picture of the Virgin and Child because it was intended to be, and was painted to occupy a certain position in an altarpiece; similarly, perhaps a picture of three women is a picture of Calumny followed by Repentance and Truth because the artist put a label underneath each woman – 'Calumny', 'Repentance' and so on.

This distinction, between the literal and the non-literal, will be questioned later. But even granting it, it cannot be said that every representational picture of, for example, the Virgin and Child aims to deceive the viewers into thinking that they are seeing a real woman and baby, because of the following two points.

(ii) *Trompe l'oeil* pictures need a special setting. The walls and ceilings of churches, for example, may be painted *trompe l'oeil*, to make it look as though, above the viewers, there was real open sky thronged with beings, and that to their right and left were real open colonnades similarly thronged. But altar pieces can rarely be painted this way, for no one could be expected to think, even momentarily, that, at the far end of the church, there really was a woman holding a baby, a woman who just happened to be invisible from the knees or shins down, and who just happened to be flanked by two much smaller people wearing nothing but figleaves, and that one was glimpsing these people through some oddly ornate golden frame. And yet many artists who painted altar pieces were striving for correct representation.

(iii) *Trompe l'oeil* pictures (and sculptures) are limited as to medium. All etchings and line drawings are out, and all black and white photographs. So too are all unpainted metal or stone statues. But etchings, drawings and bronzes may be described as realistic, as correct representations of reality, and artists' attempts to 'conquer reality', as Gombrich puts it, have not been limited to coloured paintings and statues. The producers of red and black Greek vases, of ceramics, of mosaics, of miniatures, of paintings on fans, of gold salt cellars and bronze doors, have all aimed at, and often succeeded in 'representing reality'. But they did not thereby aim at, nor succeed in, producing *trompe l'oeil* works of art.

So the view that a 'correct pictorial representation' of reality is ideally a picture that deceives the viewers into thinking that they were actually seeing what the picture was of does not apply to the majority of representational pictures. Many such pictures are described as 'truly representative' or 'realistic' or 'correct', without any suggestion that they could deceive anyone. So the question remains unanswered concerning them – if the artists have succeeded in 'representing reality' just what have they succeeded in doing?

The myth of the innocent eye

It might be thought that the basic fault of the deception model is that it insisted on an unnecessary test of what it is for a picture to be lifelike or realistic, namely that it could deceive someone. Why should we not say that, in aiming to produce a picture of *A*, to re-present *A*, artists aimed to produce a copy of *what they saw* when they looked at *A*, in whatever medium they had chosen? Of course a copy, however perfect, has no chance of deceiving if it is in an unsuitable setting or medium, but it may nevertheless be a perfect copy of *what is seen,* may it not?

The difficulty with this attractively sensible view is that it so often involves what Ernst Gombrich has famously called 'the myth of the innocent eye'. It supposes that *what is seen* is simply given, that human observers passively receive visual input, and amongst those observers are representational artists who set themselves the task of re-presenting this. To understand what is wrong with this view, we must first discover what is wrong with the idea of 'the innocent eye' when we are *not* looking at representational objects such as pictures and sculptures.

In first considering the question of how we see the world, many people are tempted towards the view that 'obviously' what happens is that we first passively receive visual information through our eyes, simply seeing what is before us, and then, having been told as it were, how the world appears, subsequently interpret this visual information to arrive at the judgement that we are seeing whatever it is, thereby coming to see it *as* such and such.

The significant features of this view, construed as the myth of the innocent eye, are the following:

1 We can consciously distinguish between the *reception* of visual information (or plain *seeing*) and the *interpretation* of it (seeing *as*).

2 Reception comes first; interpretation depends on it, but not vice versa.

3 Reception is common to all human beings with normal vision; interpretation may or may not vary according to one's expectations, memory, cultural background and so on.

Correspondingly, to reject this view and to claim that the idea of the innocent eye which merely sees or receives is a myth, is to deny each of these three claims, as follows:

1 We can never (or very rarely) consciously distinguish between our reception of visual information and our interpretation of it. As far as our conscious experience goes, there is no such thing as just seeing; we always (or almost always) see *as*. (It should be noted that this is a claim about our conscious experience. Physiological psychologists may well draw a distinction between the 'reception' of visual information (what happens to us physiologically in some parts of the nervous system when light strikes the retina) and 'interpretation' (what happens at the same time or just after in other parts of the nervous system). And they may well call the first 'seeing', and the second 'seeing as'. But they do not – or should not – claim that any one of us is ever conscious of 'seeing'.)

2 Not only does interpretation depend on reception; reception depends on interpretation. The two are interdependent. Hence,

3 There is no reason to suppose or expect that reception is common to all human beings with normal vision. When interpretation varies according to one's expectations, memory, cultural background and so on, so too may reception since (according to (2)) reception *depends* on interpretation.

The demolition of the myth of the innocent eye, though prefigured in earlier philosophers (particularly Kant, as Goodman notes (Goodman, 1976, p.8)) has largely taken place in this century. It has been rejected not only by philosophers, but also by psychologists, anthropologists, and art historians, most notably Gombrich in *Art and Illusion*. The last contains a fascinating discussion of a range of examples illustrating the ways in which 'reception' and 'interpretation' coalesce, most particularly in relation to our perception of shape, size, distance, and colour. As Goodman remarks, in general when we see, we see *as* – 'as things, as food, as people, as enemies, as stars, as weapons' (*ibid.*). We see things *as* close or far away, big or small, receding or approaching, in shadow or highlighted. Even to see an aspect of the world as no more than a something-shaped patch of a particular colour, say, red, is still to see it *as* that – a something-shaped patch of red.

It is tempting to think that, in the seeing of coloured patches of certain shapes, we have hit rock bottom; that although this may indeed be 'seeing as', it certainly does not itself involve any interpretation. Is it not the case, as the myth of the innocent eye holds, that we do just *see* coloured patches of certain shapes, and then interpret them? For example, that I just see a red, or a pale blue patch, and *then* interpret it, coming to see it *as* such and such?

But many people can recount the experience of *seeing the colour of something change* when their interpretation changed. Gombrich quotes the following example.

> I was looking out of the window, watching for the street car, and I saw through the shrubs by the fence the brilliant red slats of the familiar truck; just patches of red, brilliant scarlet. As I looked, it occurred to me that what I was really seeing were dead leaves on a tree; instantly, the scarlet changed to a dull chocolate brown. I could actually 'see' the change, as one sees changes in a theatre with a shift of lighting. The scarlet seemed positively to fall off the leaves, and to leave behind it the dead brown.
>
> (Gombrich, 1977, p.189)

I myself once woke up one morning and saw, draped over a chair at the bottom of the bed, a piece of clothing of a clear Cambridge blue – just like the pale (not the dark) lobelias. Since this is a colour I never wear, I lay there in some perplexity, wondering what it could be (without my contact lenses I was too short-sighted to identify it). Then I realized that it was my dark navy blue trousers in a shaft of light from the window, and, just as the person in the above example found, the pale blue simply vanished. (Unlike him, I could not then say what colour I was seeing there; all I could see was navy-in-a-shaft-of-bright-light.)

One of the most fascinating discoveries we can make about our own visual perception is how very hard it can be to say what colour shadows are (Gombrich, 1982, p.30). Looking across a sunbathed lawn, it may be perfectly obvious that the trees are casting shadows on it. The sun-lit grass is green all right – but what colour are the shadows? Our conscious experience is so much a matter of seeing them *as* shadows-on-grass that we may find it difficult if not impossible to see them *as* a patch of such and such a colour.

Suppose then that 'the innocent eye' is a myth, that the way we see the world excluding representational objects 'depends upon and varies with experience, practice, interests and attitudes' (Goodman, 1976, p.10). Now consider representational objects: they are part of the visible world, so why have I kept them to one side for special treatment? I did so because there is a special problem about them, and room for two quite different views about what is involved in our seeing them *as* representational objects.

Accepting then that the innocent eye is a myth, as far as seeing ordinary unpictured reality goes, we accept that the way we see the world around us is shaped by our own education and training, our language, our expectations, our culture, and so on – there is no such thing as the genuinely innocent eye. And pictures are part of unpictured reality, so the way we see them *as* pictures is also shaped by our education and training, etc.

It is said that some tribes have been found who were unable to recognize pictures *as* pictures, i.e. as re-presentations *of* anything (*ibid.* p.15 n.15). I have no idea whether this is true, but it certainly seems imaginable that if people had grown up in a society in which there were no pictures, and were subsequently introduced to them, they might well be unable to see the most 'lifelike' (as we would say) picture of a dog or a flower or a human being as looking anything like a real dog, or flower or human being. They would just see it *as* a flat, two-dimensional, piece of canvas or paper with some coloured shapes on it.

Now one thing such people would not be able to do is see any distinction between a representational and non-representational picture. But we certainly can. And this is the point at which, as I said, there is room for two quite different views. The question is, 'What enables us to see, or recognize, a representational picture of *x as* a picture or representation of *x*?' And the two different answers are (i) 'Such resemblance as there is between *x* and the picture of *x*' and (ii) 'Convention'.

Answer (i) has to appeal to the distinction drawn earlier between more, or less, basic descriptions of what a picture is a picture *of*. It is agreed that when I see a representational picture *of* the Virgin and Child *as* a picture of the Virgin and Child, my past education and cultural background come into play. I must have learnt not only to recognize pictures, but also have learnt the iconographical conventions according to which this picture of a woman and a child is a picture of the Virgin and Child. But, according to (i), as long as I have been brought up to recognize pictures (and women and children), I do not need to have mastered any conventions in order to see this picture as a picture of a woman and child. I can just see that it is, because I can just see, 'innocently', that it *resembles* a woman holding a child. The resemblance between the picture and what it is a picture of (at a basic level) is really there, waiting for me to be struck by it; and the more realistic the picture, the better it is as a re-presentation, the greater the resemblance.

According to (ii), there is no real resemblance between any picture, no matter how realistic, and what it is a picture of; hence, when we recognize or see a picture *as* a picture of *x*, this cannot be because we are struck by some resemblance between it and *x*. To recognize a picture *as* a picture of *x*, say a cat on a mat, is like recognizing the words of a sentence *as* saying that, for example, the cat is on the mat. Thus the recognition of pictures as *of* this or that, like the recognition of words and sentences as meaning this or that, requires the mastery (albeit unconscious) of sophisticated codes or conventions, in terms of which we must interpret what is before us. Having mastered the conventions, we come to see the picture of *x* as representing *x* and thereby as 'looking like' or 'resembling' *x*. But this resemblance is entirely relative to the code. Given a different set of conventions, the very same arrangement of paint on canvas would be a representation of something else *and* thereby resemble that something else.

According to one proponent of (ii),

> Realistic representation... depends not upon imitation or illusion or information but upon inculcation. Almost any picture may represent almost anything; that is, given picture and object there is usually a system of representation, a plan of correlation, under which the picture represents the object. How correct the picture is under that system depends upon how accurate is the information about the object that is obtained by reading the picture according to that system. But how literal or realistic the picture is depends upon how standard the system is... realism is a matter of habit.
>
> (Goodman, 1976, p.38)

This view, the extreme idea that representation in pictures is entirely a matter of convention and that, as Goodman says, 'Almost any picture may represent almost anything', is one that most people find very hard to accept. For example, it is not accepted by Gombrich; but there was much he said in *Art and Illusion* which lends support to it, and which undermines the simple view outlined in (i). So I will now consider what can be said for the extreme conventionalist view.

Representing reality: the conventionalist view

The initial arguments for the conventionalist view involve attacking the idea that a picture of *x* resembles *x*. And the first argument consists of pointing out and stressing that all pictures resemble each other at least as much as, and it may plausibly be said more than, any one of them resembles what it is a picture of. They are all flat, i.e. two-dimensional, objects, consisting of paint (or something similar) on canvas (or something similar). Anyone sighted who can recognize pictures as such can instantly identify which things in a room are pictures, and which are, say, chairs, vases of flowers, cats, windows with landscapes beyond, and people. Though the pictures may be *of* any of these different things, they do not thereby all look entirely different. On the contrary, pictures all resemble or look like each other.

A second argument, developing out of this one, stresses how little a picture of *x* may resemble *x*. Something can recognizably be a picture of something real while hardly resembling it at all. When children first start to try drawing, what their pictures are pictures of (if anything) is entirely determined (if at all) by their intention. They draw some lines on a page with coloured crayons and they say 'This is Teddy' or 'This is a car'. If they did not tell us, we would not be able to guess. But quite quickly, they get to the stage where we can do more than guess; we know. We can recognize what their picture is a picture of, at least at some level. It's a picture of a house (and they say it's of our house) or of a human being (and they say it's Mum or Dad) or of the sun shining above the sea.

Imagine a child's recognizable drawing of a woman; suppose it is a stick figure. How do we know it is a picture of a woman? Because, say, the figure has a little triangle at about its middle. Does it thereby *resemble* a woman? We can all say, of course, that the triangle 'represents' a skirt and that (some) women often wear skirts, and even that some skirts (flared ones on women with small waists) look triangular. But so what? Why do we not say that it is a picture of a Scotsman in a kilt, or a picture of a woman *wearing a skirt* but not a picture of *a* woman *simpliciter*? (Contrast a stick figure of a man with something on its head; we say, 'Oh, it's a picture of a man *wearing a hat*', not just that it is 'of a man'.)

The answer to 'How do we know it is a picture of a woman?' cannot be, it would seem, 'Because it has a little triangle at about its middle and thereby *resembles* a woman'. On the contrary, the right answer seems to be (something like) 'Because it has that little triangle and *according to our conventions*, this makes it a picture of a woman'. This introduces the third argument, according to which resemblances between xs and pictures of xs, far from being independently 'out there' waiting for us to be struck by them, are actually produced by the pictures.

The child's stick drawings serve to remind us of a great range of pictures which are, in one sense, very simple – some caricatures, lightning sketches, pre-historic cave drawings, many cartoons. Simple in the sense that, like the child's stick figure, they contain very few lines, they are nevertheless recognizable as pictures of x – men, women, dogs, mice, bison, cars, houses, landscapes. But here too, it seems implausible to say that we see them as pictures of x because they resemble x. On the contrary; we see the few lines as resembling the xs because we see them *as* pictures *of* xs – having, according to (ii), mastered the relevant conventions.

It is at this point that many of Gombrich's points from *Art and Illusion* come in to support Goodman's extreme conventionalist view. Gombrich introduced the term 'the language of art' as 'more than a loose metaphor' to capture his insight that artists use 'systems of schemata', 'codes', 'cryptograms' to represent the world, which we, the viewers of their pictures, must learn to decode or decipher if we are to see the pictures *as* pictures of xs. 'When we step in front of a bust,' he says, 'we understand what we are expected to look for. We do not as a rule take it to be a representation of a cut off head' (Gombrich, 1977, p.53). We do not do this, because we have learnt the standard Western conventions for representing busts. We 'read' portraits of heads in accordance with similar conventions, and others concerning the representation of colour. Familiar as we are with the 'code' of black and white photography, we do not 'read' photographs of people as pictures of people with literally grey faces and nothing but grey, black, or white hair.

That pictures *of* xs must be 'read', and can be misread if one has not understood the convention or code the artist is using, is nicely illustrated by a famous story about Picasso.

One day the husband of a woman who was being painted by Picasso called at the artist's studio. 'What do you think?' asked the painter, indicating the nearly-finished picture. 'Well' said the husband, trying to be polite, 'it isn't how she really looks.' 'Oh,' said the artist, 'and how does she really look?' The husband decided not to be intimidated. 'Like this!' he said, producing a photograph from his wallet. Picasso studied the photograph. 'Mmmm,' he said, 'small isn't she?'

Now these three arguments certainly undercut the simple view outlined in (i) above – that we see pictures of x *as* pictures of x simply because they resemble x. We have to master what might be called 'conventions', or 'codes', or 'schemata', in order to see the resemblances. But the point of calling something a 'convention' is usually to convey the claim that it is *arbitrary*, that it might well have been different. But is it the case that the codes and schemata that representational artists in the Western tradition have used might well have been different? This is the point at which Goodman and Gombrich part company, particularly on the issue of representing perspective. Gombrich rejects 'the idea that perspective is merely a convention and does not represent the world as it looks' (quoted in Goodman, 1976, p.10). But Goodman wants to insist that even '[p]ictures in perspective, like any others, have to be read; and the ability to read has to be acquired' (*ibid.* p.14).

Perspective   There are a number of different sources of the idea that, rather than *inventing* perspectival picturing, i.e. producing a new convention, Western artists had *discovered* a convention-independent way of representing the world as it really looks (to, it is agreed, the non-innocent eye).

One is that, looking back over the development of Western art through the Renaissance, we seem to see the artists initially struggling with perspective, then getting better and better, until they *get it right*. We can, it may be thought, just *see* that in some fourteenth-century paintings of receding colonnades, or rooms with staircases and corridors at the back of them, something is wrong, and, in later ones, that they have got it right.

But obviously the conventionalist has a number of responses to this (undisputable) phenomenon. This is what we who have grown up with the conventions of Renaissance art *see*; there is no reason to suppose that someone who has grown up with, for example, the conventions of Japanese art will see the same. Gombrich recounts the story of a twentieth-century Japanese painter whose father, looking at his school drawing of a square box 'in the correct [Western] perspective', said, 'What? This box is surely not square, it seems to me very much crooked' (Gombrich, 1977, p.227).

It is true that the Renaissance artists themselves talked about improvement, and development, and getting things right – but they were, after all, working within the framework of, as once again Gombrich himself says, 'a specific tradition and... a structured area of problems'. Geometrical perspective was the problem they were concentrating on, and why should we not suppose, with Goodman, that they saw their most highly-developed examples of geometrical perspective as 'looking like nature' precisely because it was within the conventions of geometrical perspective that they were trying to represent nature? So this appeal to 'how it seems to us' will not carry the day.

A second source of the idea that perspectival painting embodies the discovery of a convention-independent way of representing reality as it really looks is the impressive authority conferred by 'the laws of geometrical optics'. The Renaissance artists discovered these by painful and painstaking trial and error, but once discovered, they may then be easily taught so that, as Gombrich remarks, nowadays 'many a modest amateur has mastered tricks that would have looked like sheer magic to Giotto' (*ibid.* p.7). No one could plausibly claim that these laws are just a matter of convention (unless they claim that all science is conventional too, in which case the special claim about art loses its point).

But how do the convention-independent laws of geometrical perspective confer convention-independence on the representational nature of a picture painted in accordance with them? As Goodman points out, only in a most artificial way. A picture drawn in accordance with the laws will deliver to the eye a bundle of light rays measurably matching that bundle delivered by the object itself – *if*, that is we discount colour, and *if* the picture is viewed through a peephole, face on, and *if* this is done from a certain distance, and *if* it is done with a single unmoving eye, and *if* several other conditions are met too. But, one might ask, what if any of these odd conditions do not hold? Then of course the bundles of light rays do not match.

So the 'authority' conferred by the convention-independent laws of geometrical perspective amounts to this. *If* certain bizarre conditions – which hardly, if ever, obtain when we look at pictures and what they are pictures of – are met, *then* the picture and the object it is a picture of deliver matching bundles of light rays to the eye if the picture is drawn in accordance with the laws of geometrical optics. Stated in that unsympathetic form, this cannot be taken to confer any authority on perspectival pictures as really looking like reality. For if this were all that was needed we could just specify some other set of bizarre conditions under which a picture and what it was a picture of delivered a matching bundle of light rays and declare triumphantly that this showed that the picture really looked like reality. (Suppose, to adapt a point of Goodman's, that the picture is in perspective distorted in some systematic way, and the bizarre conditions include the fact that it, and/or the object, are to be viewed though a correspondingly distorted lens. 'But we don't look at the world through distorting lenses' someone will say. True, but Goodman's point is that we do not look at it with one eye through a peephole either.)

Finally, there is some temptation to think that photography has conferred convention-independent representational status on the paintings of the past (and present). A truly realistic painting of x, it is thought, looks just like a photograph of x. Until the advent of photography, one might have wondered whether the representation of perspective was not convention-dependent. But photographs prove it is not. The camera, unlike the artist, does not operate within a framework of tradition; it just represents three-dimensional space in a two-dimensional medium in a convention-independent way.

But, as we all know, the camera can 'lie'; that is, can produce pictures that do not 'look like' reality. I am not here referring merely to the well-known fact that photographs of people's faces, or of people or animals in motion can look 'unnatural' (the happily smiling face comes out looking as if the subject is grimacing with pain; the Queen Mother, in her dignified progress towards the Town Hall, looks as if she is lifting her leg at a lamp-post), but to the equally well-known facts about the photographic misrepresentation of size, shape and distance. Amateur photographers soon discover how easy it is to take a photograph in which the feet of the people lying down loom too large, the shape of those standing comes out dumpy, and the mountain which dominated the horizon comes out as a molehill.

So, the argument for (ii) concludes, we have to master the conventions of perspectival representation in order to see perspectival pictures (including photographs) as realistic in that respect. It is because we have mastered the conventions that we see the pictures as resembling reality, not the other way round. 'That a picture looks like nature often means only that it looks the way nature is usually painted' (*ibid.* p.39).

Colour   Initially, similar points can be made about the representation of colour. As we noted before, familiar as we are with the convention of black and white photography, it is impossible for most of us to see a black and white photograph of someone *as* a picture of someone with a literally grey face; and not all black and white photographs of people with hair lighter than dark brown look like pictures of people with grey hair. We are not always inclined to say that colour photographs are more realistic than black and white; indeed there is a tendency to think that black and white photographs give us more realistic portraits than coloured ones do. And no doubt if things had been different, we could have come to see red and white photographs as realistic in the same way as we have with red and black Greek vases.

However, there is, in relation to colour, a formidable objection to the extreme conventionalist view, known as the 'colour-reversal problem'.

Recall that, according to Goodman, the conventions or codes that artists employ are *merely* conventions, and might well have been different. Now consider what this claim means when it is applied to colour. It means that, given one picture, of a red apple on a blue table-cloth, and another picture which is just like the first except that each colour is replaced by a different one, it is *only* our present conventions which make it the case that the first, colour-normal picture, is a realistic picture of a red apple on a blue table-cloth whereas the second, which has, say, a blue apple on a red table-cloth, is not. And against this startling claim, many people have insisted that there must be more to the distinction between them than that.

Goodman, going well beyond Gombrich, stresses 'the analogy between pictorial representation and verbal description' (Goodman, p.40) between the so-called 'language(s) of art' and real language. But the colour-reversal problem shows that the analogy between a patch of red in a picture, and the letters 'r-e-d' can be over-stressed.

That the word for red in English is the letters 'r-e-d' and not 'b-l-u-e' is a convention, and could just as well have been different, and even reversed. But that a painted red apple resembles a real red apple in point of colour and that a blue painted apple does not is something it is hard to imagine being different.

Having noted the colour-reversal problem, we can reflect it back on Goodman's discussion of perspective. To say that we have to acquire the ability to read pictures in perspective is one thing; to say that we can effortlessly acquire the ability to read pictures *as* pictures in perspective *however* the perspective is coded, is a much stronger, and ultimately implausible claim.

In conclusion, what then are we to say is the correct answer to our original question? Do we see pictures of *x*s *as* pictures of *x*s because they resemble *x*s or because we have mastered certain conventions? The answer seems to be: well, a bit (or rather, a lot) of both.

On the one hand, some pictures of *x*s really do resemble *x*s, to the point where (bringing *trompe l'oeil* momentarily back into consideration) they actually deceive not only us, sophisticated masters of convention that we are, but other animals, who cannot be supposed to have learnt to see pictures as resembling what they are pictures of. I don't know whether I believe the stories about the birds pecking Zeuxis' grapes, but certainly my cat was momentarily startled by my printed-cat tea cosy. And Gombrich notes that 'the deterrent and camouflaging forms in plants and animals' depend upon resemblances which predators cannot have been taught to recognize by learning a code of conventions. Resemblance or 'looking like' is not entirely relative to systems, codes, or conventions of representations.

On the other hand, it is partially relative to them. There is 'a degree of plasticity in the way we "see" the world' as Gombrich puts it (Gombrich, 1982, p.28); a plasticity, or degree of 'flex', which enables us to be taught to see resemblances between pictures and the world by mastering conventions. As Gombrich notes (*ibid.* p.27), when Impressionist paintings were first produced, many people did not see them *as* resembling the world at all. But many of us have now become so familiar with the Impressionist 'code' that we find they do. We often see the world about us *as* full of light and movement, and we find that many Impressionist paintings accurately represent these aspects of it.

This 'degree of plasticity' also allows for the fact that the way we see the world may be changed – shaped and moulded – by artists' representations of it, a point which introduces the topic of the next section.

Creating reality

In 'Visual discovery through art', Gombrich takes up one of the many topics discussed in *Art and Illusion*, the theme of artist as creator, which he had introduced there at the beginning of the chapter 'Pygmalion's Power'.

> Ever since the Greek philosophers called art an 'imitation of nature'[7] their successors have been busy affirming, denying, or qualifying this definition. The first two chapters [of *Art and Illusion*] have the same purpose. They try to show some of the limits of this aim toward a perfect 'imitation' set by the nature of the medium on the one hand and by the psychology of artistic procedure on the other. Everybody knows that this imitation had ceased to be the concern of artists today. But is this a new departure? Were the Greeks right even in their description of the aims of the artists in the past?
>
> Their own mythology would have told them a different story. For it tells of an earlier and more awe-inspiring function of art when the artist did not aim at making a 'likeness' but at rivalling creation itself. The most famous of these myths that crystallize belief in the power of art to create rather than to portray is the story of Pygmalion. Ovid turned it into an erotic novelette, but even in his perfumed version we can feel something of the thrill which the artist's mysterious powers once gave to man.
>
> In Ovid, Pygmalion is a sculptor who wants to fashion a woman after his own heart and falls in love with the statue he makes. He prays to Venus for a bride modelled after that image, and the goddess turns

the cold ivory into a living body. It is a myth that has naturally captivated the imagination of artists... Without the underlying promise of this myth, the secret hopes and fears that accompany the act of creation, there might be no art as we know it.

(*Ibid.* p.80)

Taking up this theme of the artist as creator, Gombrich quotes, near the beginning of 'Visual discovery through art' a point from Aristotle's *Poetics.* Considering the question of why people enjoy looking at accurate representations, Aristotle takes this to be a particular instance of our general enjoyment of learning. 'They enjoy seeing likenesses because in doing so they acquire information (they reason out what each represents, and discover, for instance, that "this is a picture of so and so")' (*ibid.* p.12). Gombrich brilliantly reverses the situation, and suggests that the thrill of learning is frequently to be found, not in recognizing the world in pictures, but in recognizing pictorial effects in the world. Artists, he suggests, create their own visions of the world in their pictures, and we discover, with a thrill of recognition, previously unrecognized aspects of our familiar unpictured world.

The details of the ways in which artists' representations of reality may 'transfigure' it for us, not simply re-present it, but present it under new aspects, and create new ways of seeing it, have been well-described by art historians such as Gombrich, and by philosophers of aesthetics (see, for example, Elliott, 1966–7). But my philosophical task here is to relate Gombrich's point, that artists (even the most 'realistic') do not just copy reality but create it, to the preceding discussion of 'Representation in pictures', and to this essay as a whole.

As we saw, Plato denigrated pictorial art by comparing it to holding up a mirror to the world, and maintained that the pictorial artists merely copied appearances or visual images. This view, as we have seen, involves the 'myth of the innocent eye', overlooking the fact that all seeing is *seeing as* and that 'To see at all, we must isolate and select' (*ibid.* p.15). It also overlooks the corresponding fact that to represent at all, the artist must 'isolate and select' and that in doing so he can 'impose his vision on our world' (*ibid.* p.35) thereby creating our world anew for us.

In the brief discussion of 'seeing as', I concentrated mostly on seeing the world *as* categorized into things, and on seeing pictures *as* pictures *of* those things – people, cats, buildings, shadows. But we do not see things only *as* things. We see landscapes – but further, we may see them *as* serene or threatening, domesticated or untamed, static or full of movement. We see some shapes *as* faces, but we may also see those faces *as* familiar or unfamiliar, happy or sad, full of health, or with the shadow of death upon them. And in what they 'isolate and select' to represent, and in the ways in which they do it, artists can enable us to see such things differently.

They can also reveal how they think, consciously or unconsciously, about things by what they represent and the ways in which they do it. This can make us think differently, and, again because of the way in which 'interpretation' and 'reception' are interdependent, this may lead us to see differently.

It is worth reminding ourselves at this point that a great number of the 'representational' pictures of Western art do not, and did not, purport to *copy* reality, simply because what they represented were people and events that the artists did not see and could not have seen. What they represented was either (assumed to be real but) long past (all the scenes from the Bible, Socrates taking the hemlock and so on), or expected in the future (all the scenes of the Last Day of Judgement) or symbolic (the four horsemen of the Apocalypse) or, to a greater or lesser extent, imaginary or invented (such as the Rake's Progress, or scenes depicting battles or other events that happened during a war; of course, artists might have seen such scenes, but in fact they often could not have done so because they were not there). In representing such scenes and people, the artists must choose a particular way in which to represent them, a way partially shaped by their own creative imagination.

Even in portraits or other pictures of people that might be supposed to be 'copied from reality' (in the neutral sense that does not presuppose the myth of the innocent eye, but only that the artists had the people to be portrayed in front of them) the people are still posed in a particular way, with particular surroundings, and particular 'props' (or a particular lack of them). Here, a particular vision of reality is created before it is even copied.

It would, as any art historian would be quick to remind us, be a crass mistake to infer from these points that artists make entirely free choices about how to represent such people and scenes. Their choice is not only limited by the schemata available to them at their time and within their tradition, but by the influences of patronage. If the prevailing tradition dictates, as it did, that Christ be represented as a blond European rather than as a Jew, then artists may, like their contemporaries, have been unable to imagine Christ as looking like a Jew, and, even if, in an imaginative leap, they had conceived of this, it is extremely unlikely that they would have painted it, or, if they had, that the painting would have survived. If the person who commissioned the portrait wants to be represented as a Roman senator in full classical drag, and wants his daughters to be represented as mistresses of the desirable accomplishments of music and embroidery, then the successful artist must find ways to comply.

But even given these constraints, many artists have found themselves with enough scope to represent in significantly different ways. An Annunciation may be represented *as*, say a joyous occasion, calling for celebration, or *as* a solemn one, calling for meditation. The Virgin and Child may be represented *as* a tender mother with a playful baby, or *as* the Queen of Heaven with the King. A scene from the life of Christ can be represented *as* viewed by one of the participants or *as* a scene viewed by a distant spectator (*cf.* Elliott, 1966–7). Recent feminist art historians have detected significance in the way many female nudes are posed – that they are represented *as* passive for example. And war may be represented as glorious or terrible.

I mention the last example particularly, because it serves me as a personal introduction to the topic in the next section. One aspect of the impact of visual art which Gombrich does not emphasize in 'Visual Discovery through Art', nor even, I think, in *Art and Illusion*, is the way in which visual art can create an image of reality which dominates because it is so vivid. I have thought, ever since I started thinking about such things, that war really is terrible, that this is a fact. And the words 'war is terrible' have some power; they evoke connections with suffering, blood, pain and loss. But the words 'military glory', 'honour', 'courage', have a similar power; they evoke connections with suffering, blood, pain and loss nobly borne, and reiterating 'but war is terrible', against those words ('Honour!' 'Courage!'), may start to seem feeble and stale. The familiar words invite, 'Well, war is terrible in some ways, but glorious in others; there are two sides to every question; you can see war in this way or in that way'. And that is what I used to think – reluctantly, but perforce – that there were at least these two ways of thinking about or 'seeing' war. But then I was lucky enough to get to Madrid and see both Goya's paintings on war and Picasso's *Guernica* (see Plate 4). Because I saw them all in the same week I do not know what effect they would have had if I had seen only *Guernica* or only the Goyas, or indeed, only one or a couple of the Goyas, but I certainly know what the effect was of seeing all the paintings I did see. It created in me an image of 'war as terrible' which is *dominatingly* vivid. Now, when I look at pictures which represent war as glorious, or read poems, novels or plays about military glory, or honour and courage displayed in war, or see films about them, or hear music supposed to invoke a passionate willingness to fight for one's country or one's cause, Goya's and Picasso's paintings always come into my thoughts. 'No, no,' they always say, 'don't be fooled. *This* is the way it is – terrible, terrible.'

I do not want this small piece of psychological autobiography to be misinterpreted. I am not asserting (though I would in other contexts, if I were writing moral philosophy), 'It is a *fact* that war is terrible and military glory a chimera' (and pictorial art can teach us this fact about reality). I am not asserting '*The* way to read Goya's war paintings, and *Guernica,* is as saying that war is terrible; that military glory, honour, and courage are a chimera'. There is no context in which I would assert that, because I am not qualified to do so. I am not asserting that these pictures must, or should have, the same effect on you, if and when you see them, as they had on me. All I am asserting, on the basis of an autobiographical example, is that visual art may create in us dominant images of reality, of how things are, where by 'of how things are' I do not mean merely 'of how things *visually* appear' but 'of how "things" – reality or life – may be thought of'.

Such images affect our reaction to the whole world, including our reaction to pictures themselves. As I said above, my reaction to *pictures* representing war as glorious has changed. Representational pictures, though pictures *of* reality, are also part of it, and it is appropriate that I should close this section by considering another story about Picasso which encapsulates this Janus-faced role that pictures play.

Goodman recounts the story according to which Picasso, in response to the complaint that his portrait of Gertrude Stein did not look like her, is supposed to have said, 'No matter, it will' (Goodman, p.33).

This is a story faceted with the ambiguities to which Gombrich lovingly calls attention. Does Picasso's response mean, 'When your vision has been shaped by my vision, you will see *the unpictured world* differently, my art will impose a fresh vision on her face, and then you will see Stein and my portrait of her as similar'? Or does it mean, 'When you have mastered our new code, our new schemata, you will see *the portrait* differently, as falling within a tradition, and then you will see Stein and my portrait of her as similar'? Or does it mean both?[8] The lesson to be learnt from this exploration of representation in pictures is that it can informatively be read as meaning both. Pictures change our way of seeing the world; pictures are part of the world, so pictures also change our way of seeing pictures.

4 Truth in literature

Introduction

In the concluding paragraphs of the preceding section, I wrote about Goya's paintings on war and Picasso's *Guernica* as illuminating and making vivid to me something that I took to be a truth, namely that war is terrible and military glory a chimera. I said that this would serve as an introduction to the topic of this section. It does so in the following way.

If war is terrible and military glory a chimera, *if* this is a truth, it is an important one. *If* true, it would be an example of the sort of truth which, Aristotle would say, must be grasped if one is to have moral wisdom and avoid folly, a truth about life and human nature. (Similarly, *if* war is necessary to preserve justice, and dying for a just cause the most glorious way for a human being to die, that is an important truth, and would be another example: nothing hangs on my being right about war and military glory.) Aristotle claimed that the distinctive mark of tragic poetry was that it gave us this sort of important truth, and this claim of his, generalized to cover other forms of literature, has had its adherents ever since.

The topic of this section is limited to truth in *literature* (and indeed, as the discussion proceeds, it becomes further limited to truth in the novel). But while we consider this topic, we should try to bear in mind the fact that many people find it natural to talk about not only literature but also paintings (and sculpture) and even music as conveying, expressing, illuminating, teaching us truths about 'life and human nature' or 'the human condition' – profound or important truths.

The extent to which people find this way of talking natural varies greatly amongst individuals, though education and training can reduce some of the variation. For example, I used to find such talk about paintings quite unintelligible, but, having been guided around art galleries by people who are much more sensitive to, and intelligent about, pictures than I am, I now find it natural – hence the 'war is terrible' example. It still means nothing to me when applied to music, or to abstract art – but what should I conclude from this fact? I might conclude that I do not (yet) understand abstract art or music properly (and perhaps may never learn to do so). Or (given the fact that abstract art 'leaves me cold', whereas I care about classical music more than I care about any other form of art and am sensitive and intelligent about it) I might conclude that indeed, I do not (yet) understand abstract art, but that classical music simply does not strike me the way it strikes some other people. But, given my past experience of non-abstract art, it would obviously be foolish and arrogant of me to conclude that when other people talk about music or abstract art as conveying, or expressing truths and so on, they are simply talking nonsense.

So, whatever our individual reactions may be, we should, as I said, try to bear in mind the fact that some people talk of paintings and music as conveying profound truths while we are considering the claim that literature does. In what follows, I shall defend the view, derived from Aristotle, that it is a distinctive mark of great literature that it gives us such truths. But, rather than jumping straight to this conclusion, I begin by discussing the contrary view, that literature *as such* does not yield any truths at all – the 'no-truth' theory.

The 'no-truth' theory

What is the point of the italicized phrase in 'literature *as such* does not yield any truths'? It is to make it clear that upholders of the 'no-truth' theory are not denying an obvious and quite undisputable fact about literature, namely that literature uses words, and words combined into suitable sentences are standardly the bearers of truth (and falsehood). A list of words 'red, green, happy' is not a grammatically well-formed sentence and hence not the sort of thing that can be true or false; the words 'Is there honey still for tea?' make a sentence, but not the sort of sentence which makes a statement; but the words 'A thing of beauty is a joy forever' and the words 'In the Spring a young man's fancy lightly turns to thoughts of love' both make sentences which can be assessed as true or false.

Literature abounds with such sentences, a fact that we exploit when we go in for apt quotation. I want to state, as a truth, that there is an essential connection between truth and beauty? I quote Keats – 'Beauty is truth, truth beauty'. I want to state that human beings are incurably optimistic? I quote Pope – 'Hope springs eternal in the human breast'. I want to state that gardens are delightful things? I quote Thomas Brown – 'A garden is a lovesome thing, God wot'. I want to state a cynicism about people's attitudes to marriage? I quote Jane Austen – 'It is a truth universally acknowledged, that a single man in possession of a good fortune, must be in want of a wife'.

It is of course true that poetry tends to be particularly rich in metaphors, and metaphors, when they do occur in statements, are often literally false. 'Life's but a walking shadow' or 'The hounds of spring are on winter's traces', if used as quotations to make a statement, would have to be understood as making the statement metaphorically. But the use of metaphor is by no means peculiar to poetry or even literature more generally; it is a standard feature of ordinary language where metaphorical statements ('I simply *flew* here' ('Then why are you late?') 'He's got a monkey on his back' ('No he hasn't, he's kicked the habit')) are assessed as true or false.

So, it is an undisputable fact that literature gives us truths. But what may be, and is, disputed by upholders of the 'no-truth' theory is the idea that literature *as such* yields truths. Upholders of the 'no-truth' theory do not deny any of the above facts; rather, they claim that in assessing, appreciating, interpreting or evaluating a work of literature as such, the unquestionable fact that the work contains sentences that *can* be assessed as true or false is irrelevant. Faced with such a sentence in isolation, I might ask myself 'Is it true?', i.e. do I or should I believe it? But to ask myself this question when I am reading a poem or a novel, or hearing a poem or a play, is to make a mistake. What arguments can be given in support of this view?

One initial move is uncontroversial. It is undeniable that novels, plays, poems, contain fictional characters and indeed fictional places, and that sentences in the works about such characters and/or places are not to be taken as straightforwardly true statements about the real world. Faced with a sentence in a novel such as 'Paulina Sebesco was quite a newcomer to the village, having lived there for not more than a year and a half by the time Makhaya arrived' (Bessie Head, *When Rain Clouds Gather),* or hearing 'My brother he is in Elysium' (Viola of Sebastian in Shakespeare's *Twelfth Night*), or 'The Wedding Guest sat on a stone' (Coleridge's *The Rime of the Ancient Mariner*), we are not supposed to ask ourselves, 'Is that true? Do I or should I believe it?'

It is said, I do not know with what truth, that one mark of a form of mental handicap is that the people who have it cannot grasp the concept of fiction, but are entirely literal-minded. It is said that when you tell such people a story they take it 'for real' and if you tell them that it is not real, but 'only a story', that the people and places in it do not really exist, they just lose interest. Whether or not there are such people, one can imagine there being people like that, and we would indeed say of them that they did not have the concept of fiction. Closely related to this possibly imaginary case is the real case of people who are said to be philistines about literature. These are the people who say 'I never read fiction; what's the point of reading about a whole lot of people who don't exist?'

Another form of philistine literal-mindedness involves taking a 'nit-picking' approach to literature. It is, so it may be said, a mistake to cavil at a poet's lyric description of a garden in England as full of blooming daffodils and roses, or a novelist's saying that the sinking sun made glorious the façade of the Oxford Divinity School Building. The appropriately well-informed know that daffodils and roses bloom in different months and that the evening sun cannot fall on that particular façade in Oxford, but anyone who picks on this sort of falsehood, and thinks that its presence constitutes some sort of flaw in the novel or poem has made a mistake; they are not approaching the work in the right way, as a *work of literature*.

To grasp the concept of fiction, and thereby of fictional literature, it is said, is to understand that a work of art creates its own imaginary fictive world, which is to be appreciated and assessed in its own right. To compare this world with the real world, by asking oneself 'Do I, should I, believe this?' or by responding 'But that's just not true; I don't believe that', is to cease to engage with the work aesthetically, or as a *work of art*. When one reads a poem or a novel, and thinks about it *as* a poem or novel, all one's beliefs about the real world should be held in abeyance.

It should be noted that this is a very strong claim. Starting from the uncontroversial claims about the status of fictional characters, the upholders of the 'no-truth' theory have reached the conclusion that *none* of one's beliefs should play a part in one's engagement with a work of art. As Arnold Isenberg, one proponent of the 'no-truth' theory has put it, the claim is 'the extreme view that belief and aesthetic experience are mutually irrelevant' (Isenberg, 1954).

It seems, on the face of it, unlikely that such an extreme view can plausibly be upheld, and unsurprisingly it has been subjected to damning criticism.

Isenberg begins with the thought that understanding a sentence is prior to believing it. 'When something is said to us', he says, 'we understand *before* we can assent, and to accept or reject must take further steps in search of evidence' (*ibid*. p.91). If I say to you, 'Tout est pour le mieux dans le meilleur des mondes possibles' you cannot begin to ask yourself, 'Do I believe that?' if you do not understand French and hence know that that sentence means 'Everything is for the best in the best of all possible worlds'. And if I say to you, 'My dog is remarkably intelligent' you will understand me perfectly well but quite possibly, pending my producing some evidence, neither believe nor disbelieve what I say. So far so good. But Isenberg moves from this specific claim (understanding a sentence is prior to, and independent of, believing it) to the general claim 'then it should be possible to understand without being concerned with truth and falsity', and hence that 'the understanding of a poem [is] something independent of [any] belief' (*ibid*.).

Against the 'no-truth' theory

This general claim is elegantly refuted by R.K. Elliott, who shows 'that considerations of truth and falsity are *sometimes* involved both in the interpretation and the evaluation of poetry...' (Elliott, 1966–7, p.68). Consider the opening of one of Shakespeare's sonnets

> So are you to my thoughts as food to life,
> Or as sweet-season'd showers are to the ground.

Is your understanding of these lines independent of your belief that food is necessary for life, or your belief that the ground will not support plant life without water and that it dries out if there is no rain?

Or consider

> He was fresh as is the month of May

and

> Their meetings made December June,
> Their every parting was to die.

I grew up in New Zealand, where (though we do not walk upside down) the seasons are back to front: December is high summer, June winter, May autumn. Had I not been taught, and thereby come to believe, that in Europe spring is in May, summer in June and so on, I could not have understood those lines. I would have had to interpret the pair of lines as describing a rather horrid love-hate relationship, and the first line as irony of some sort, for, as Elliott points out, 'poetic irony depends very often upon our recognition that some poetic proposition is false' (*ibid.* p.79).

(It is sometimes said that *all* interpretations of poems are 'equally valid'. This is not the place to enter into tricky questions about interpretation; and for the purposes of the argument here I shall assume, with Elliott, that there *are* cases of misinterpretation, and take reading 'Their meetings made December June' as 'Their meetings made June December', in the circumstances described, as a clear example of one.)

The general claim that understanding a sentence is independent, not merely of believing it but of believing anything, embodies an ultimately incoherent view of language. Our mastery of language, our understanding of the meanings of words and sentences, is inseparable from our beliefs about the world. If we attempt to imagine a being whose beliefs are totally different from ours but whose language is nevertheless one that we could come to understand, we would soon find ourselves in a hopeless tangle of contradictions and absurdities. (Try to imagine, for instance, that they believe that cats grow on trees, or that snow is warm and green. If, in our attempts to find a translation of their language into ours, we find ourselves translating them as believing such things, we will conclude, not that they have very different beliefs, but that we have the translation wrong.)

But might it not be the case that, although *understanding* a poem cannot be independent of belief, nevertheless evaluation of it can and should be? But here too, Elliott has a telling counter-example. He points out that sometimes – not always, but sometimes – what we admire in lines of poetry is the neat, economical and elegant way in which they state a *truth*. That they state a truth is not all that we admire about them – the neatness, elegance and economy matter too; but that they state a truth is not irrelevant. An equally neat, elegant, and economical statement of a falsehood would not necessarily command the same admiration.

The 'no-knowledge' theory

It seems that the 'no-truth' theory must be rejected. But the initial moves that lead to it looked plausible. The 'no-truth' theorist was surely right to emphasize the importance of grasping the idea that a writer creates her own imaginary world which must not be dismissed as uninteresting because it is not real, nor approached and assessed as though it were supposed to be real. So let us see if the theory can be amended into something less extreme and more plausible. Suppose it were said that literature is not (and hence should not be regarded as) a source of *knowledge*.

We should note at the outset how neatly this formulation avoids being subject to Elliott's criticisms of the 'no-truth' theory. The basis of Elliott's argument was the fact that to understand lines of poetry we have to bring into play many beliefs that we *already* have about the world. These beliefs are part of our common stock of knowledge, many so obvious and mundane that we may easily overlook the fact that we do know them. The order and nature of the seasons, the fact that snow is white and cold, that roses have thorns and die without water, that cats are agile, gold is a precious and shiny metal... If we did not know (and hence believe) that such things were true, poetry, and literature more generally, would be incomprehensible to us. Hence, belief is not irrelevant to aesthetic experience.

But such beliefs are part of our common stock of knowledge; they are things we know already. We do not acquire this knowledge from literature, but, on the contrary, come to literature already equipped with it. Hence, Elliott's points may be admitted, and it may still consistently be said that literature is not a source of knowledge.

As with the 'no-truth' theory, this 'no-knowledge' theory has to be understood as a claim about literature as such. The 'no-truth' theorist did not deny that a work of literature, in virtue of containing sentences which made statements, might happen to contain a truth such as 'Hope springs eternal in the human breast'. His claim was that whether or not it did was incidental to it as a work of literature, and that to approach a poem looking for, or expecting, truths was not to approach it as *a poem.*

Similarly, the 'no-knowledge' theorist need not deny that one might happen to acquire some knowledge from a poem or novel. She may well argue that one could learn something about India from Anita Desai's novels, something about the conditions in Victorian England from Dickens. Of course this itself may be disputed – historians for instance frequently deny the latter; my point is that the 'no-knowledge' theorist is not committed to denying it as part of her claim. Her claim is that whether or not you acquire any knowledge from a work of literature is irrelevant to your understanding and appreciation of it as a *work of literature.* To ask yourself, 'What will I learn (or 'am I learning' or 'have I learnt') from this *work of literature?*' is a mistake. To think of a piece of writing in these terms is not to think of it as a work of literature but as something else – as the mere product of an Indian or nineteenth-century person, for instance.

So, for example, a proponent of the 'no-knowledge' theory might argue that Dickens's *Hard Times* should not be studied as part of a university humanities course centred on industrialization in Britain because its very 'relevance' would interfere with the students' appreciating it *as a novel,* encouraging them to engage with it non-aesthetically, as a social document. If a Dickens novel is to be studied as part of such a course, the students must engage with his greatness as a novelist, not his talents as a social critic and reformer.

This point illustrates the purpose of the 'no-knowledge' theory. Like the 'no-truth' theory, it aims to protect the intrinsic value of works of literature from philistine demands that they should be *useful* in some way. *Hard Times* is not a better novel than, say, *Our Mutual Friend* because it is a better social document, and to think that it is, or even to think that its 'realism' compensates for its other faults sufficiently to make it as good as *Our Mutual Friend,* is to judge both novels by criteria external to them. And this, it is said, is philistinism.

The claim that readers should approach works of literature as having intrinsic value, that is, that they should think of them as things worth reading for their own sake, not for the sake of some knowledge that might be derived from them, is clearly but one side of a coin. The other side is a corresponding claim about what writers are, or should be, up to. They are, or should be, trying to produce something that has intrinsic value, that is worth writing for its own sake. If they start saying to themselves, 'What I am writing will not be worthwhile unless it convinces my readers of the truth of socialism, or the wickedness of industrialization, or the truth of Christianity', their art will be corrupted. (It is indeed often said that the reason why *Hard Times* is one of Dickens's weaker novels is that in it he made his creative imagination subservient to his crusading zeal, instead of giving the former full rein. In the same vein, it is said in defence of Brecht (by non-Marxists who admire Brecht's work) that, whatever he may have intended to do by way of conveying Marxism in *Mother Courage*, his creative genius burst beyond the confines of these intentions to produce a real work of art.)

The claim naturally extends into one about what writers must be allowed to do, and an attack on censorship as inevitably destructive of literature. Writers must not be forced, either directly by law, or indirectly by the pressures of patronage or publication, to think, 'What I am writing will not be worthwhile if it inclines my readers to believe in the hypocrisy of Christianity or the desirability of free enterprise or free love'.

So the arguments for the 'no-knowledge' theory are basically arguments against philistinism. But does our choice lie between these two? Is there a way of rejecting the 'no-knowledge' theory without being a philistine? A promising line of thought is suggested in a paper by Ilham Dilman (Dilman, 1984).

Against the 'no-knowledge' theory: Dilman

Taking it as a premise that Freud has given us psychological knowledge, that he has given us insight into individual characters (in his case histories) and advanced our knowledge of mankind, Dilman argues that the same is true of Dostoevsky. 'Because of what we learn from [his] novels we speak of the truth contained in them, the kind of truth about human beings which makes Dostoevsky a great psychologist' (*ibid.* p.106). He quotes someone as saying 'it is commonplace that Dostoevsky anticipated Freud... all the insights that have become commonplace since Freud were clearly his own' (*ibid.* p.96) and then explores 'what this comes to in the particular case of Dostoevsky's portrayal of Raskolnikov in *Crime and Punishment*' (*ibid.*).

Before going on to discuss Dilman, I must try to make clear what is relevant to the discussion. The question at issue is: Can someone claim that there is knowledge to be derived from a particular novel without thereby revealing themselves to be a philistine, i.e. as someone who has not approached the novel in question as a *work of literature*, but in the wrong spirit? I shall argue that the answer to this question is yes, because Dilman *claims* that there is knowledge to be derived from a particular novel, namely *Crime and Punishment*, without thereby revealing himself to be a philistine; his discussion reveals that he is far from being a philistine.

Why do I emphasize 'claims' in my answer to the question? I do so in order to bring out that this is the key word. What is at issue is *not* whether what Dilman says about Freud or *Crime and Punishment* (broadly, that they both advance our knowledge of mankind) is true. What is at issue is whether he *claims* that such knowledge is to be derived from the novel without thereby revealing himself to be a philistine. So it does not matter (for the purposes of this discussion) if you disagree with him about whether Freud and/or *Crime and Punishment* advances our knowledge of mankind. Nor does it matter if you neither agree or disagree because you know nothing about either Freud or *Crime and Punishment*. In what follows, I make it clear what Dilman *claims* about the knowledge to be derived and that is all we need in order to discuss the question at issue.

To allay any lingering doubts, I will make two confessions. First, personally, I have a very limited respect for Freud and indeed regard much of what he says as pernicious nonsense, and secondly, I have never read *Crime and Punishment*. If the points already made do not serve to convince my reader that knowledgeable agreement with Dilman on Freud and *Crime and Punishment* is irrelevant to the following discussion, then these confessions should serve. Despite these two handicaps, I was able to find in Dilman, viewed abstractly, a striking example of someone who (a) makes a significantly detailed knowledge claim about a novel and (b) is clearly no philistine.

No one who believes, as Dilman does, that Freud was a great psychologist and has advanced our knowledge of mankind would think that his insights can be given by brief paraphrase, or that the advanced state to which he brought our knowledge of mankind can be summarized into idiocies such as 'Everything is motivated by the sexual impulse' or 'All men are in love with their mothers'. So I cast no aspersions on Dilman by saying that his article contains no brisk statement of what we may learn about 'the human soul' or 'the human condition' or 'the psychology of human beings' from *Crime and Punishment*. Here are some examples of the sort of thing he says we may learn.

We may learn about 'the way pride, humiliation, anger and resentment can turn into a force for evil and feed on each other, [about] the way they lend their energy to ideas that inspire the desire for grandeur in the self and contempt for other people' (*ibid*. p.97). We may learn about the way certain ideas – 'the utilitarian, socialist and Nietzschean ideas which were prominent among the young radical intellectuals in Dostoevsky's Russia' can 'reinforce... pride and anger, and organize destructive tendencies' by providing someone with an aim which they would not have had without them (*ibid.*).

We may learn how someone 'under the guise of innocent motherly concern' can try to manipulate her son's thoughts, to play upon his feelings, in her attempt to arrange his life, and how the effect of this in the son will be both to provoke anger and prevent the direct expression of it, making him feel impotent. We may learn how the son of such a mother 'doesn't know how to care for [her] without becoming vulnerable to manipulation and exploitation; he is unable to give without feeling emasculated' (*ibid*. p.100).

We may learn how passivity may be 'a defensive response to [one's] mother's attempt to control [one] through self-sacrifice and indirect accusation' and how someone might use 'the violence that has accumulated in him to break away from this passivity' (*ibid*. p.103). Hence, 'Dostoevsky shows us in one single unusual case... what motivation is like, and gives us a lively awareness of its complexity. More particularly he shows us how a bad conscience and passivity can drive a man to a violent act' (*ibid*. pp. 104–5).

Now someone might say 'We cannot *learn* all those things – about being unable to give without feeling emasculated, or being driven to violence by passivity which is a defensive response to maternal manipulation and so on – from *Crime and Punishment*, nor from Freudian psychologists come to that, because it's all wrong. No one and nothing can *teach* me, or anyone else – i.e. convey the knowledge – that people commit murders because they resent their mothers, because that's just nonsense. A novelist or a psychoanalyst might convince someone of it, but the person who was convinced would not have *learnt* anything thereby. They just would have acquired a set of false beliefs.'

I raise this view in order to dismiss it – not because I think it is false, but because it is irrelevant. For our question, and Dilman's question, is not: Was Freud a great psychologist; did he give us knowledge about mankind, and particularly about motivation? Dilman's question is: *If*

Freud was a great psychologist and did give us knowledge about mankind, was Dostoevsky and did he (despite the fact that he was a novelist and not a clinician; that he created his own fictive world rather than describing real people as Freud did)? Dilman's answer is 'Yes' and an appropriate criticism of this answer must take some other form than saying 'But all the Freudian theory is false'.

One appropriate criticism would be of the form, 'Those things are not what we learn from *Crime and Punishment*. Over-eager to read Freudian insights into Dostoevsky, Dilman has given the wrong (or 'an implausible') interpretation of the novel.' Now Dilman does go on in his article to discuss the problems of interpretation or 'a "correct reading"' of a work, pointing out that 'the question of what is in a play or novel or character, or what the author has put into it, is not a straightforward one' (*ibid.* p.112). But, as I said above, the tricky issue of interpretation is not our concern here, and although an objection to Dilman's interpretation would count as an appropriate criticism of his claims about *what* knowledge we may get from *Crime and Punishment*, it is not an objection which touches on the issue we are concerned with, namely whether works of literature can, as such, yield knowledge at all.

A second appropriate criticism, which does relate specifically to that issue, would have to be something like the following: 'In discussing *Crime and Punishment* as though it yielded us knowledge of human beings, Dilman is not reading the novel *as* a novel, *as* a work of literature, but, in a philistine way, as though it were a piece of clinical psychology. Let us grant, for the sake of the argument, that, as a matter of fact, we can derive an "advance in our knowledge of mankind" from *Crime and Punishment*. But to say this is not to say anything in praise of it *as a novel* or of Dostoevsky *as a novelist*. On the contrary, such facts are quite irrelevant to aesthetic appreciation.'

Such a criticism, though appropriate, is, I would claim, implausible when applied to Dilman, for the following reasons.

(i) Far from treating *Crime and Punishment* as a piece of clinical psychology, Dilman devotes a section of his article to arguing that, precisely because it is a work of fictional literature it makes 'a more vivid impression on the reader than the real thing. This is partly because of the writer's livelier sensibility and his talent as a writer'. The writer, as creative artist

> selects and arranges material... [what] he depicts comes to life because through the artifice of art, he makes available to the reader what he can

imagine… By thus shaping what is shapeless in real life he makes us see things in a new light and more vividly. He makes us not only see them thus, but also feel them. What he depicts moves or disturbs us in a way that its counterpart, in reality may not. *Freud's case histories do not have this power, nor are they meant to have it. Thus the power of art.*

(*Ibid.* p.107; my italics)

Now one need not agree with what Dilman says here, nor even find it particularly intelligible. But whatever one thought of it, one cannot, especially given the two sentences I have italicized at the end, read it and regard Dilman as someone who is not thinking of Dostoevsky as a novelist and *Crime and Punishment* as a work of art.

(ii) The word 'philistine' is a word of abuse, and it might be thought that, as such, there was no restriction on its use – that a speaker could apply it to anyone they despised, for whatever reason. But this it not so; in the Oxford English Dictionary it is defined as 'A person deficient in liberal culture; one whose interests are material and commonplace'. Now I do not deny that 'liberal culture', 'material' and 'commonplace' are, in their turn, terms with a great deal of 'flex' in them, but I would deny that they can be stretched to apply to the attitude(s) Dilman reveals in this article. He is interested in the things he claims Dostoevsky is interested in – 'the conditions that make the soul vulnerable to… evil', in knowledge of the human condition and of 'what life is like'. Far from being material and commonplace these are usually the interests which we describe as profound.

(iii) This thought brings me to my third objection to the criticism, which is just a bald assertion; *viz.* that it is absurd to claim that, in speaking of a novelist as having, and revealing in his work, a profound knowledge of human nature or human beings, we voice no praise of him *as a novelist*. Novelists and novels may be praised, as such, for many features they have, but the view that *this* feature should never figure amongst them has only to be stated baldly to be revealed as nonsense.

An amended knowledge theory

Dilman's article suggests that our choice does not lie between the 'no-knowledge' theory and philistinism. For he provides us, so I have argued, with an example of someone who (a) cannot with any plausibility be described as taking a philistine approach to *Crime and Punishment* or be charged with not reading it 'as a novel', but (b) does claim that there is knowledge to be derived from it. So, bearing him in mind as an example of what we might want to defend, let us consider what a plausible 'knowledge' theory might claim – and not claim.

(i) There is no reason to think that a plausible 'knowledge' theory would make sweeping claims about *all* forms of art yielding knowledge. I cannot myself imagine that an article similar to Dilman's – with its emphasis on motivation – could be written about a piano sonata or a landscape painting. I cannot myself imagine a similar one being written about even a portrait. But perhaps someone else can. As I said at the outset, it would be arrogant of me to jump to the conclusion that what I happen to find unintelligible in talk about works of art yielding truths is always nonsense. It *might* be, but it might not. Either way, a modest knowledge theory can remain uncommitted on this point, adopting a 'Let's see what people come up with' attitude as far as the other arts are concerned.

(ii) Such a theory need not even claim that it embraces all sorts of literature. Once again, an article filled with Dilman's sorts of details could hardly be written about a poem which invoked the delights of spring. So the theory might limit itself explicitly to novels and plays and once again adopt a 'Wait and see' policy about other forms of literature.

(iii) A modest theory need not insist that novels and plays must yield knowledge; that this is a necessary condition that they must fulfil to get into the running as being worth reading.

(iv) Nor, of course, need a modest theory insist that the fact that a novel or play yields knowledge makes it worth reading; that this is a sufficient condition for their being worth reading.

Points (iii) and (iv) call for further comment. Let us compare them with some of Elliott's remarks about truth, for they are closely related. Elliott is careful to point out that 'The view that truth is invariably an aesthetic criterion – that any poem is better insofar as its sentences are true [truth as a sufficient condition of value], worse insofar as they are false [truth as a necessary condition of value] – is indeed a vulgar and philistine error and I am not seeking to defend it. My point is simply that considerations of truth and falsity are *sometimes* involved in... the evaluation of poetry' (Elliott, 1966–7, p.68).

Obviously, if someone claimed that truth was a sufficient condition of value, one could point to turgid or banal verses which were embarrassingly loaded with truths (about say, the dangers of alcoholism); and, contrariwise, if someone claimed truth was a necessary condition of value, one could point to magnificent poems which contained no truths at all (or nothing one thought oneself was a truth – it is possible to imagine an atheist extolling one of Gerard Manley Hopkins's religious poems).

The same points, with the same sorts of counter-examples, can equally obviously be made about knowledge as a sufficient or necessary condition of value in a novel. One could point to turgid novels which yielded one far more knowledge than one wanted about, say, the conditions of Chicago meat workers in the 1920s (to show yielding knowledge is not sufficient); or conversely, to wonderfully rich fantasies which yielded no knowledge of the real world at all (to show that yielding knowledge is not necessary). But such counter-examples would not touch a modest knowledge theory which followed Elliott in saying that the point is that considerations of whether or not a novel yields knowledge are *sometimes* involved in aesthetic appreciation and evaluation of it.

How does this modest knowledge theory compare with Elliott's modest truth theory? Well, it goes beyond it – it is a stronger claim than Elliott's. Elliott was claiming that truths *we knew already* could be aesthetically relevant. Taking that as established, the modest knowledge theory is claiming that some *further* truths may be aesthetically relevant – not ones we know already, but ones we learn from the novel.

However, stated in that form the theory still does not claim much, and so far I have been emphasizing claims that it need not make. But Dilman's article, and the discussion that arose out of considering it, suggests some further claims it might make, which are not so modest and which involve some qualification on (iii) and (iv).

Let us suppose that the modest knowledge theorist has, in accordance with (iii), not said that novels must yield knowledge, and agrees that there can be, for example, fantasies. But suppose we are considering a novel which is not a fantasy but which, like *Crime and Punishment* is about human beings in a world recognizably similar to the real world doing recognizably similar things. And suppose further that we want to say of this novel that it does not yield any knowledge about real human beings, the emotions and ideas that really motivate their actions, because it falsifies life. Its main characters, say, are described as either heroically saintly or satanically wicked, even the children. But no minor character is ever moved to either humbled admiration or understandable irritation with the supposedly saintly; the supposedly wicked, despite their appalling actions and repulsive personalities are presented as having the normal background of loving family and friends. Despite a professed interest in nothing but money and physical pleasure, the wicked must be supposed to devote much time to reading since they are impressively learned; the supposedly saintly are utterly unconcerned with the plight of the poor and apparently unaware of the danger men present to female virginity. And so on and so forth. And, we say, 'Life's not like that; people aren't like that'.

Dilman says he would argue 'that escapist literature, sentimental stories, lie about life', and this is clearly intended to be a criticism of such works as *works of literature*. Yielding knowledge is not a necessary condition of value in a novel – there is nothing *per se* wrong with fantasies which do not purport to be about life – but, Dilman suggests, it is a necessary condition of value in a *novel which is, in some sense, about life*.

So it is not any old sort of knowledge, and thereby truth, which is claimed to be (sometimes) relevant to aesthetic appreciation of a novel. It is said that the publishers Mills and Boon offer guidance to people anxious to write a successful novel for them, and recommend setting the novel somewhere exotic and providing a wealth of factual detail. If that is true, I might acquire a lot of knowledge about, for example, Hong Kong, from a Mills and Boon novel, but I would not acquire any knowledge about life. Quite the contrary; if I took the novel seriously, I would be misled about what life is like.

And now let us look back to the claim of Aristotle with which I started this section. Aristotle claimed that tragic poetry yielded us knowledge of truth. Moreover he claimed that it yielded us knowledge of a special sort of universal truth; not the sort that the natural sciences give us, but the sort that is necessary for moral wisdom – truth about human nature and about life. Having gone through the 'no-truth' theory, Elliott's modest 'some-truth' theory and the 'no-knowledge' theory, we have arrived at a 'some-knowledge' theory which corresponds very closely with Aristotle's. Of course, his is about tragic poetry whereas we have been concentrating on the novel; and he emphasizes truth where we have emphasized knowledge. But had Dilman discussed a play of Shakespeare instead of a novel by Dostoevsky, we would have emphasized poetic dramatic tragedy, and, since knowledge must be of what is true, the 'some-knowledge' theory encompasses a corresponding truth theory. As I said above (p.293), the modest knowledge theory goes beyond Elliott's modest truth theory.

At the end of the section on Aristotle, I said that I would try to defend the relative incoherence of people I asked to tell me *what* important truths they thought were embodied in the ancient Greek plays (see p.259). The *necessary* detail of Dilman's article shows, I think, why such incoherence is understandable. When we are profoundly struck by 'the human truth' in a work of literature, when we think it has increased our knowledge and understanding of life and human beings, the articulation of *what* truth(s), *what* understanding, is not a matter for brisk paraphrase or casual conversation.

As Dilman points out, to judge that a work of literature is true to life, is

> to make a double judgement. First it is to make a judgement about what it is that the work depicts... Secondly, it is to make a judgement about what life is like, and this brings both our values and our experience to bear on the matter.

> (Dilman, p.109)

Our view of 'what life is like', our serious values, and the influence of the complexities of our personal and private experiences, is expressed and revealed in our actions and reactions. To express them in speech is another matter, and not many people can do it easily at all, let alone in response to an unexpected question. The discussion of such matters has its own contexts – in serious discussions with our friends and family, in close encounters with strangers met at strange times, on the psychiatrist's couch. One mark of such contexts is that the speaker is, as it were, allowed a lot of space or leeway. We tell long involved stories about ourselves or people we have known, describing what has made us suffer or feel ashamed, what has made us happy or proud, what we have had mixed feelings about; we struggle to articulate our worries, confusions and doubts. And we do all this in the expectation that our audience is not going to criticize us if we contradict ourselves, or cut our stories or reflections short by saying 'Yes well, what's the point' or 'Make it snappy'. Such discussion requires both a lot of detail, and a sympathetic audience.

So I conclude that the practice of connecting talk about truth and the understanding or knowledge of life and human nature, despite our inability to articulate succinctly *what* truths and *what* knowledge, is not necessarily a practice which embodies an appeal to an ineffable sort of truth, or a queer sort of knowledge as is sometimes claimed. Truths about what life is like, and knowledge of them, are not ineffable or queer; but they are immensely complicated and subtle, expressed more readily in action and reaction than summed up in mere statements, embodied in particulars rather than in abstractions. And they are often to be found in great works of literature.

Bibliography

Annas, J. (1981) *The Republic of Plato*. Oxford University Press.
Aristotle (many edns) *The Poetics*. Quotations from the Ingram Bywater translation; references are to the Bekker numbering.
Cooke, D. (1959) *The Language of Music,* Oxford University Press.
Dilman, I. (1984) 'Dostoyevsky: Psychology and the Novelist', in Phillips Griffiths, 1984.
Elliott, R.K. (a) (1966–7) 'Aesthetic Theory and the Experience of Art', *Proceedings of the Aristotelian Society,* 57, pp. 111–26.
Elliott, R.K. (b) (1966–7) 'Poetry and Truth', *Analysis,* vol. xxvii.
Gombrich, E.H. (1977, 5th edn) *Art and Illusion,* Phaidon.
Gombrich, E.H. (1982) *The Image and the Eye: Further Studies in the Psychology of Pictorial Representation,* Phaidon.
Goodman, N. (1976, 2nd edn) *Languages of Art: An Approach to a Theory of Symbols,* Oxford University Press.
Isenberg, A. (1954) 'The Problem of Belief', *Journal of Aesthetics and Art Criticism,* vol. xiii.
Phillips Griffiths, A. (ed.) (1984) *Philosophy and Literature*, Royal Institute of Philosophy Lecture Series: 16, Cambridge University Press.
Plato (many edns) *The Republic*. Quotations from the Penguin edition, translated by H.D.P. Lee; references are to the Stephanus numbering.

Notes

[1] See Essay One, pp. 4–8.

[2] Embroideries were used as wallhangings.

[3] The social role of the actor and poet is discussed in Essay Seven.

[4] This is the old sense of 'proper', deriving from the same Latin root as 'appropriate'. It does not simply mean, as in modern usage, 'decent' or 'respectable', but 'intrinsic', 'inherent'.

[5] The phrase occurs several times in the *Physics* (his work on nature or the natural world), in contexts where (a) 'craft' or 'skill', not 'art', is certainly the correct translation (the examples are medicine and house-building) and (b) the point that is being made is that the workings of nature, like the activities of craftsmen, are purposive and end-directed. So it has nothing to do with his 'theory of art'.

[6] Although Cooke claims that music is an 'international language' we should note that he does not claim it is 'natural' in the wider sense of being 'inter-continental', or free from the influence of convention and tradition (Cooke, 1959).

[7] Note that Gombrich is probably making the standard mistake here of ascribing this view to Aristotle.

[8] Of course it may simply mean 'I have painted her looking older than she does now, but I know her very well, so I know that she will look like this when she is older'. But it is the other two interpretations which are significant in the context of our present discussion.

Art, Society and Morality

Tom Sorell

Introduction

Of the many philosophical problems concerning art and society, perhaps the most central arise from the fact that novels, films, plays and, less often, paintings and sculptures, can affect people's emotions and influence their actions, sometimes in ways that appear to do harm. Works of art can offend people or make them angry, inspire them to demonstrate and even take violent action. Which of these effects are morally and politically tolerable and which are not? If it is all right for art to disturb people by criticizing their ways of life and institutions, but wrong for art to disturb people by insulting them or by blaspheming things that they hold sacred, then what are the limits of criticism and blasphemy? How is the line to be drawn between art whose whole purpose is sexual arousal, and art which contains, but is not dominated by, erotic material? Is there something morally wrong with art that makes it easier to identify with or have sympathy for criminals? Should art that puts violent disobedience in a favourable light be freely available? These are questions about art that belong to political philosophy. More specifically, they are questions about the consumption or reception of art. There are also questions raised by political philosophy about the creation of art, and about artists. For example, do painters or performing artists such as actors fulfil a socially useful purpose? Or again, is aesthetic production so much influenced by the taste of the politically powerful and wealthy that artists can be said to prostitute themselves?

Not all questions about art and society, however, belong to political philosophy. Some arise from aesthetics itself. In aesthetics a central question is, 'What is good art?', and it is sometimes answered by saying that in order to be valuable, art must have social or political relevance. This is the answer given not only by Marxists, but also by some promoters of the idea of Christian art, such as Tolstoy. Other artists and aestheticians claim, to the contrary, that art should be produced for its own sake and should be judged by autonomous aesthetic standards. In this essay questions about art and society from political philosophy will be given more attention than aesthetic questions about art and society, but both will be discussed.

1 Plato: the social effects of art and the social role of artists

Plato's *Republic* is one work of political philosophy which is sensitive to the ways in which art can exercise a bad influence on people. Plato gives his views in the course of describing how a society would be organized if it lived up to a certain ideal of justice. Though what he describes is an ideal social order, not all of its elements are pure invention. He had his eye on actual Athenian society in the fifth or fourth century BC, and he incorporated into his account of the ideal state many actual practices and institutions, altering others only where they seemed to depart from the standard of justice that he proposed. According to Plato, justice in a state consists, roughly, of everyone fulfilling those socially useful roles that their attainments fit them for (Plato, 433a, p.181). Those who are best at selecting overall goals and making laws, and who identify their own interests with those of the state even at times of peril and hardship, ought to rule (*ibid.* 503B). Those who have a highly-developed sense of honour, a taste for getting things done, a measure of daring and a high degree of conscientiousness are also suited to rule (*ibid.* 535A), but under the guidance of those with a gift for choosing ends and making laws. Finally, those whose talents lie in production, trade and service should involve themselves in the life of the state outside government (*ibid.* 370A–2C), notably its economy.

This, in outline, is Plato's description of the sort of people who should rule and be ruled as citizens if a state is just. There is a class of rulers skilled at choosing ends and another, subordinate class of rulers good at executing these ends. Beneath them is an economic or entrepreneurial class of citizens. Now if the citizens of a just state each fulfil the function they are best suited for, and if the range of possible occupations or functions in the state is determined by the needs of the people who make it up, what need does an artist meet? To adapt the question to Plato's Athens, what need does a performing artist such as a poetry reciter meet, and if there *is* such a need, what makes someone a good poetry reciter or tragedian? What need, for that matter, does a poet meet?

Plato takes up these questions in Book 2 of *The Republic*, after he has described the organization of a society that can cater to people's basic needs (*ibid.* 373A–D), a society that provides a simple, moderate sort of life. This sort of society Plato calls the 'true' state or the 'healthy' state (*ibid.* 372E), and when he entertains the proposal that it might lack something, because people in it would not feed on delicacies or be able to perfume themselves, he agrees to consider additions that would turn it into what he calls a 'luxurious' or 'fevered', i.e. unhealthy, state. The luxurious state calls for a host of occupations unheard of in the simple state: There will be 'hunters and fishermen, and there will be artists, sculptors, painters, and musicians; there will be poets and playwrights with their following of reciters, actors, chorus-trainers and producers...' (*ibid.* 373b). Plato thought that a just state could accommodate some of the trappings of luxury, including an expurgated poetry, but he did not really recognize a social need for artists, sculptors, etc., nor hence a place for them in the just state. Athenians saw a use for artists, in particular poets, but, according to Plato, this was because they had certain misconceptions about what poets and artists could do.

2   Poetry, poets and knowledge

In Athens poets and poems were not uncommonly treated as sources of information. The poets were taken to have direct access to the muses, the daughters of memory, who were supposed to have historical and other knowledge.[1] With such good sources as the muses, poets had claims to knowledge themselves. Even the reciters of poems, who were no more than mouthpieces for the poets, took themselves to have knowledge. In *Ion*, an early dialogue by Plato, a poetry reciter or 'rhapsodist' is interrogated by Socrates who discredits the poetry reciters' claims to knowledge concerning the matters treated in their poems. Plato conceded that the poets themselves sometimes conveyed truth, but this was not because they had knowledge and were communicating it; it was because the gods had knowledge and were inspiring poets, through whom they spoke. The idea that poets were merely inspired or possessed by someone or something else was borne out by their inability to give a reasoned account of the truths that their poems contained.

Plato's way of discrediting the knowledge claims of poets is at the same time a way of denying them a socially useful role – that of historian or reporter or keeper of the public record – to which they might otherwise have had a claim. The only role that seems to remain, once Plato has made his criticisms, is that of providing pleasure through skilled entertainment. This is a coherent role, but Plato has arguments in *The Republic* to show that people who play this role do harm, and hence that they had better not be allowed to play it. Plato's arguments indeed lead to a conclusion stronger than that no one should be allowed to be a professional poet or poetry reciter: they are meant to deprive artists in general of a social role.

3   Imitation in art

The arguments come in Book 10 of *The Republic*. There Plato seems to claim that poetry, as practised by professionals for listeners without the right sort of education, has no place in the state. The reason is that it is imitative or involves *mimesis*, and that 'such representations definitely harm the minds of their audiences, unless they're inoculated against them by knowing their real nature' (*ibid.* 595B). Plato goes on to explain what is wrong with mimesis. What is wrong with it is that it is frivolous and pretentious, and that its products distract us from reality. Its products distract us from reality because in a certain sense they are unreal. The metaphysical assumptions behind the idea that the products of mimesis are in some sense removed from or outside reality have been discussed in Essay Six; I shall concentrate on what Plato thinks is wrong with the activity of mimesis itself.

To see why mimesis is supposed to be frivolous or unserious it helps to begin with Plato's conception of the subject-matter of mimetic poetry:

> [It] represents human beings in action, either voluntary or compulsory; in that action they fare, as they think, well or ill, and experience joy or sorrow.
>
> (*Ibid.* 603C)

Mimetic poetry has a serious subject matter – in fact the very same subject-matter that ethics has. Yet when the poet represents people acting voluntarily or under compulsion and thinking about the result, the poet's purpose is usually not, as in ethics, the serious one of making either the poet or the audience into better people. There may be no serious purpose at all on the poet's part. He may be satisfied if he manages only to get his audience to enter emotionally into the situations he depicts. It may not be his job to do more. As for the audience, they are likely to be satisfied if, with no effort and at no risk to themselves, they can be drawn imaginatively into a dramatic situation. They do not come to be instructed but to be charmed or distracted. In this way it can often happen that, for the sake of a good night out, performer and audience connive in squandering the opportunity for edification or instruction – the opportunity for responding seriously – afforded by poetic subject-matter.

Apart from this, however, Plato claims that there is something wrong when poetry reciters or rhapsodists act out a role of which they have no knowledge: a general's role, say, or a doctor's. This criticism makes sense if poetry-reciters claim to have, or are taken to have, the knowledge associated with their roles, as may have happened in Athens. Plato also seems to have criticized poets themselves for writing about medical or military matters, and even about less specialized crafts or skills, when they were ignorant of them. Once again the criticism would make sense if, as in Athens, poems were regarded as reliable sources of information.

4   Literature and knowledge

Does Plato's criticism of writers who lack specialized knowledge have any force when directed against *modern* novelists or scriptwriters? It certainly does where the novel is 'faction' – a hybrid of fact and fiction – or where a film is a 'drama-documentary', for both of these art forms claim to have a factual basis, and if they are shoddily researched, so that the audience – or even the writer – loses track of what is fact and what is fiction, they are both bad specimens of their kind and potentially very harmful to their audience.

Lack of knowledge can also worsen normal fiction. Someone who sets a story in a hospital or a courtroom risks having it spoiled or marred by an inadvertent mistake concerning hospital routine or courtroom procedure. In some kinds of novel the author's ignorance or idiosyncratic beliefs can also interfere with characterization, since knowledgeability is sometimes an important facet of a central character. In such a case, knowing too little can detract importantly from a work of art even if the reader is not treating it as authoritative about its subject matter. And there is a sense in which knowing too little and being found out is always more of an occupational hazard for a novelist depicting a doctor or a soldier, than for a doctor or a soldier getting on with some medical or military activity. The reason is that the novelist's subject matter is particularly inclusive – the actions and feelings of an indefinitely wide variety of people in an indefinitely wide variety of situations. Perhaps, in a self-consciously postmodernist age, the novelist's subject-matter even extends to the theory of writing itself, and its relation to other branches of theoretical thought. With such a broad subject-matter there is both very great scope for error and no codifiable training to protect a writer against it.

Alongside the risks of knowing too little and letting it show are the dangers of knowing too much and letting it get in the way. This is what happens when authentic detail accumulates to the point of being distracting. In Ian Fleming's James Bond novels, for example, the technique used to establish the hero as a connoisseur of wines or cars is to load the text with exclusive brandnames. Authenticity is overdone in other books when a street dialect is made too conspicuous or the jargon of insiders is used to excess. The only insurance against this, as well as against a lack of research or inaccuracy, is to have a story or character so strong that the misnaming of a Berlin street or one paragraph too many spent describing espionage codes passes the reader by unnoticed. Whether the production of a good story or character results from specialized knowledge, or from knowledge that is concentrated in those who set themselves up as novelists, however, is another question. Plato believed that there was a special ethical knowledge that enabled people to size up correctly the moral worth of characters and people's decisions, hence that would enable people to judge whether such and such an action would be appropriate to a hero or a god – a figure of exemplary virtue – in an epic poem. But he doubted that poets had or could acquire this knowledge, and indeed believed that very few could acquire it. Without necessarily taking Plato's view of ethical knowledge, and without concentrating on epic poetry to the exclusion of films, plays and novels of our own time, we, too, may wonder whether film-makers, novelists or playwrights are more likely to have moral insight or insight into life or virtue than anyone else.

5 The artist as a kind of impostor

We have been considering Plato's claim that poets should not be allowed to speak or be given a hearing because they do not know what they are talking about. Let us now pass on to the point that in mimesis artists have pretensions to being something they aren't. It will be recalled that, according to Plato, everyone in a just state should have an occupation (a) determined by the needs of the people who form the state, and (b) subject to the talents or capacities of the particular individual. Now when it comes to imitation Plato's point is not only that no society *needs* to have on hand impersonators or imitators, but also that there is no real function constituted by imitation. There are real activities – such as those of a doctor or general – which someone can imitate, but no role of being an imitator in the abstract. In this respect the would-be role of an imitator is something like the role of an employee. No one is an employee full stop. They are employed *as* something or to do something, even if the employment consists of doing a variety of odd jobs. Similarly, no one is an imitator full stop. Imitators do what they do by assuming or taking on some definite role. But now the peculiarity of the role of imitator is not just that it is schematic and needs to be further specified, like that of the employee. It is that to be an imitation X is not to be a real X, to be an impersonator of an X is not really to be an X. In other words, not only does the role of imitator require further specification by a practice or activity imitated, but also the imitation of the practice never quite amounts to the practice itself, or at least need not. It is like a shadow or appearance of an activity.

Another aspect of imitation emerges against the background of the connection in Plato's thinking between justice and specialization. To meet the requirements of Plato's idea of justice it is necessary to find the social niche one fits best and stay there. Those with a talent for the pseudo-activity of imitation, or the pseudo-role of imitator, can appear to fill any role without really being suited to it. They are only super-ficially fitted for a niche and really not fitted for any. Such people have no natural place in a just society; moreover, they have the potentially subversive effect of showing, by their apparent adaptability, that people may be suited to some role other than their actual one, or to more than one role – obliterating the framework for a conception of social justice that depends on specialization. It may be on account of the dangers posed for justice, as he conceives it, that Plato is concerned to exclude completely from the state the really chameleon-like figure – someone who can impersonate any type or appear to fill any role.

6   Imitation and appearances

Turning now from imitation to the products of imitation, we come up against the most difficult line of thought in Book 10 of *The Republic*. Plato changes his example of imitative art: poetry rather than painting concerns him, though what he says about painting is supposed to apply to poetry as well. He says that painting imitates appearances (*ibid.* 598B) and that poets are imitators of images. The commentator Alexander Nehamas explains:

> To think of an artist as an imitator of appearance is to think of the
> appearance as the object of imitation, as something existing in the

world before the artist begins to work, as what the artist copies or represents. The appearance in this case is part of the physical object that is the artist's model. To think of an artist as a maker of appearance, by contrast, is to think of the appearance as the product of imitation, as something that comes into being as a result of the artist's work, that is the result of the artist's representation. That Plato does not seem to mark this distinction has some important implications, since it implies that he is thinking of the object of imitation and the product of the imitation as being the same object... It almost seems as if he believes that the painter lifts the surface off the object and transplants it on to the painting... The image is both the surface of the subject and the product of the painter; the difference between the painted (i.e. pictured) bed and the real bed is that, though they have identical appearances, the latter is in three dimensions while the former is only an image with no depth.

(Nehamas, p.62)

Nehamas cites Plato's use of certain Greek expressions as evidence for thinking that Plato identifies appearance with surface, and he thinks that this interpretation illuminates other things that Plato says. If the painter only produces the insubstantial image, no wonder Plato claims that no one who could make both the object and the image would prefer the image (Plato, 599A). Another strength of this interpretation is that it makes the transition from painting to poetry relatively straightforward. There is a sense in which the poet-impersonator takes the surface off Homer's hero and wears it himself. But it is only a surface, not a character, that is transplanted, for the poet-impersonator does not set out to be heroic, and privately he does not know how to be heroic even if he wanted to be. At any rate, he does not get the audience to enter imaginatively into the heroism by *being* heroic. All he does is to go through motions that, *if* the circumstances were dangerous and were believed to be so, would make an agent heroic. A way of summing all this up is by saying that the poet-imitator creates something that has borrowed content and a borrowed attraction for the audience (an attraction derived from that of real heroism), but that has no substance or moral attraction in its own right. In view of this insubstantial and borrowed character, talk of a transplanted surface seems apt. This surface is not worth having if one can have the whole object or a full-scale duplicate, that is, if one can actually witness heroism or see real heroism being reproduced.

This much – about the inferiority of products of mimesis – fits painting and poetry equally. Plato goes on to add considerations that show that poetry is potentially more harmful than painting, and therefore more urgently in need of being outlawed. What makes poetry particularly dangerous, Plato thinks, is that it portrays characters who are in psychological conflict (*ibid.* 603C), characters who are either grieving or rejoicing at how things have turned out as the result of their actions, characters whose emotions have (but perhaps only temporarily) got the better of their reason. Such conflict is an unwholesome spectacle because, according to Plato's psychological theory, it appeals to the lower parts of the soul – appetite and emotion – rather than to the higher part, reason.

7 Questionable elements in Plato

Plato's arguments against poetry and painting are disputable, as is the theory of justice that gives them their background. Nehamas, who is careful in his exposition of Plato and not unsympathetic to his views, wonders whether Plato is right to say that poetry seduces us by making us take pleasure in characters who are distressed or suffering. Nehamas suggests that if Plato had thought harder about claiming that representation is a kind of second-rate reality, if he had considered 'giving representation a status of its own... he might also have noticed that the pleasure of the best people is not at the sorrow represented but at the representation of the sorrow' (Nehamas, p.69). It is not incompatible with taking pleasure at the representation of sorrow, however, that one *also* takes pleasure at the sorrow represented. Nevertheless, Nehamas is right to point out that Plato does not make enough of representation as the object of pleasure. Another, perhaps more central, problem is to do with Plato's claim that unless one has the knowledge necessary for counteracting its effects, mimetic art is harmful. The problem is with Plato's understanding of the kinds of knowledge that serve as antidote to mimesis. One kind consists of knowing what is involved in mimesis, another kind consists of knowing, independently of art, what the good is. For moral knowledge keeps one from being corrupted when evil is made to seem attractive.

Plato's account of the nature of moral knowledge is both difficult and controversial. He thinks of the Good as a Form, that is, as an unchanging and abstract fixed standard that particular actions and characters must measure up to in order to be good. The standard is abstract in that it is supposed to be eternal and unrevisable. It is also a standard somehow set by reality rather than public opinion. Plato rejects the idea that popular approval for a character or action is what makes it good. He also rejects the view that popular approval is evidence for something being good. He holds similar views about beauty. In that case, too, it is conformity with an eternal, fixed standard that makes it true to say, when it is true, that something is beautiful, not the fact that crowds are clamouring to see it in the theatre or art gallery. In these respects, for Plato, goodness and beauty are like straightness and triangularity. They are not a matter of individual opinion or taste, not a matter to be settled by consensus.

Goodness and beauty are also supposed to have a reality apart from the things that are truly said to be good or beautiful, again in much the same way as triangularity is supposed to have an existence apart from wobbly representations of three-sided figures in exercise books or on printed pages. In this respect all 'Forms' or patterns are on a level. They are things that make true judgements true. They are things that one has to be acquainted with if one's judgements are really to express knowledge as opposed to opinion. In other respects, however, the Form of the Good is the pre-eminent Form for Plato, that is, the standard in the light of which all other standards are to be applied. Plato compares the role of goodness in relation to the things that the mind can have knowledge of, to the role of the sun in relation to things that are visible. The comparison, however, is not always convincing. For example, whereas it is the sun that makes other things visible and brings them into existence (Plato, 508A–E), it is unclear how the Good makes other things knowable or generates a knowable subject-matter. How, for example, is the Good involved in knowledge of mathematical axioms? Another problem is to do with what exactly knowledge of the Good involves. Plato compares the initial effect of the Good on the mind to the dazzling effect of the sun on the eyes (*ibid.* 515C–E). If the analogy is taken seriously one is left asking whether we are able to know the good after all, given the difficulties of keeping one's gaze on the sun.

Even if we do not press these points and accept that the Good *is* knowable, Plato's account implies that it is knowable only with difficulty and even then only to a few. Most people, his theory suggests, have the merest inkling of the Good, and are as far from a direct knowledge of it as someone who is imprisoned in a cave with his back to the opening is from seeing the sun. The main impression left by his theory is that knowledge of the Good is extremely esoteric. Even if one allows for the fact that, as Plato conceives it, the Good is not just a standard of moral goodness but of goodness in natural organization and mathematical harmony as well, the account seems to exaggerate the rarity of the Good, to banish it entirely from everyday experience, and to deny it the status of an ordinary object of knowledge. If goodness, and with it the basis of moral valuation, is that difficult to know, no wonder artists are supposed to be bad at moral instruction: on Plato's assumptions the same is true of all but a tiny minority of the human race.

Up to a point Plato's overstatement of the problem of knowing the Good is understandable. He was responding to the ease with which the Athenian public could be swayed into supporting the wrong kind of government and into accepting doubtful claims about what was for the public good. A parable that he introduces in *The Republic* concerning a ship sailed by a deaf, short-sighted master, and crew, none of whom has acquired the art of seamanship (*ibid.* 488A–E), suggests that, where the general public did not deny altogether that there was an art of government or rulership, they tended to take the wrong people to possess that art, namely the demagogues they applauded in the assembly and the actors and poets they applauded in the theatre. Demagogues, poets and actors could not really have knowledge, Plato argued. The successful demagogues only had persuasive power because they told the crowd what they wanted to hear – however much that changed from one day to another. They acquired their skills from sophists who, while good students of public opinion, were not acquainted with any objective distinction between right and wrong. As for the poets and the actors, they were in no better position than the demagogues, being, like them, mere mouthpieces.

8   Anti-Platonic positions

Suppose that Plato was right in claiming that most ordinary people in Athens lacked moral knowledge and therefore were subject to manipulation by the bad moral reasoning of demagogues; it does not follow that he was right about the nature of moral knowledge or about the unsuitability of art as a medium for moral knowledge. On the contrary, it is possible to argue that moral knowledge can be acquired by most people through their own experience of life and the experiences others share with them, as well as through their own and others, especially artists', efforts at imagination. It is even possible to hold that the reception of art is one of the things that makes moral imagination possible for most non-artists. That is, it is possible to hold that through works such as novels we enlarge the range of people we can empathize with, the range of situations we can imaginatively project ourselves into, and therefore the perspectives from which we can assess the rightness of actions or ways of life that we otherwise would never have though twice about.

The position just outlined implies, contrary to Plato, that experience and imagination can be means of acquiring moral knowledge, just what Plato denies when he insists that the Forms are outside experience and that moral education is very exacting and related to or dependent on mathematical education. Before this position is enlarged upon, however, something should be seen of another view which is in many ways closer to Plato's. The view that I have in mind agrees that moral knowledge is knowledge of Forms beyond experience, but it insists, contrary to Plato, that art *is* a medium of this knowledge, that the arts *do* give direct access to the Forms, including the objective Good. Plotinus, a philosopher whose ideas owed much to Plato and who lived and taught in Rome from AD 244, was one of the first to take this approach, but many others have adopted it subsequently. In the next section I shall consider a version of it from the eighteenth century.

9 An eighteenth-century argument against Plato on painting

In *The Political Theory of Painting from Reynolds to Hazlitt*, John Barrell summarizes an anti-Platonic view that had British, French and German adherents in the seventeenth and early eighteenth centuries.

> The first step was to assert that Plato's objections apply only to the abuse of painting, and not to its proper and moral use; though painting was indeed an imitative art, committed still more evidently than poetry to material representations of an apparently material reality, its true function was to represent, not the accidental and irrational appearances of objects, but the ideal, the substantial forms of things. Painting was thus a liberal art insofar as it was an intellectual activity, disinterested, concerned wtih objects which, because ideal, could not be possessed; it was an abuse of painting to practise it in pursuit of objects which, because actual, particular, material, could be made the objects of possession and consumption, and thus appealed to our baser, sensual nature.
>
> (Barrell, 1986, p.14)

When concerned with the ideal, painting was supposed to be a liberal art also in the sense that it was the proper occupation of liberal or free (the Latin '*liber*' means 'free') men of means and in that its products were proper objects of attention of liberal or free men. As for the lesser sort of painting, it did not just have a low-grade, particular and material subject matter; its form of production was also supposed to be low-grade. It was a form of manual labour and could be produced mechanically; its products were only for an audience drawn from the servile classes. When concerned with the ideal, painting had the power of implanting in free men a conception of the public good that an increasingly elaborate division of labour kept people from forming. Those with 'mechanical' occupations or menial status were taken to be less susceptible to the idea of public good, if indeed they had access to it at all.

The anti-Platonic elements in eighteenth-century views of painting were not only to do with the allegedly ideal or purely intellectual content of the better sort of painting; critics of Plato also cited the considerable learning or knowledge necessary for one genre of painting – namely 'history-painting', and also the customary association of painting with people who were well-born (*ibid*. p. 16). But it is hard to see how these responses, and especially the last, meet Plato's reservations about painting. The fact that painting was favoured by the well-born would not have impressed Plato, any more than the fact that in Athenian society the sophists had a following among the wealthy and aristocratic. As for artists with a good training in history, these figures would probably have offended against Plato's belief in specialization as a condition of excellence: the artist-historian runs the risk of being regarded as something less than the best sort of artist and as something less than the best sort of historian.

Coming finally to the power of art to depict the ideal rather than the material, and in particular the morally ideal, Plato would not have denied it. As I have already said, he recognizes a role for art (poetry rather than painting), albeit a highly sanitized art, in moral education. He might, however, have denied that when art was effective in moral education, and therefore socially useful, it derived its worth from the depiction of things or characters belonging to the world of Forms. He could have said, perfectly consistently, that some kinds of art depict good people and good actions, but that to gain access to goodness itself the mind had to operate completely independently of images, even images or personifications of abstract things such as temperance or courage. And apart from disagreeing about whether socially useful art was or could be art concerned with Forms, he might have disagreed with eighteenth-century examples of edifying images.

The specifications for one such image were actually worked out in the abstract by the third Earl of Shaftesbury, who then commissioned someone to paint it. Shaftesbury was interested in the right sort of image to use in the moral education of young aristocrats. In an essay attached in 1713 to his *Characteristicks of Men, Manners, Opinions, Times* first published two years earlier, Shaftesbury described an image, derived from a story by the Greek historian Xenophon, and entitled it *The Judgement of Hercules*. In it, the young Hercules,

> being... retir'd to a solitary place in order to deliberate on the choice he was to make of different ways of Life, was accosted [as the Historian relates] by the two Goddesses, VIRTUE and PLEASURE. 'Tis on the issue of the controversy between these *Two*, that the character of HERCULES depends.
>
> (Quoted in Barrell, *ibid.*)

In the painting which was executed according to this specification Hercules is depicted as he often was in Greek poetry and sculpture, leaning on his club, apparently pensive. To his right, and apparently gaining Hercules' attention, is the standing figure of Virtue, pointing the way to the difficult mountain path of honour and glory for heroic actions. At his feet, on the left, is the half-naked, beckoning Pleasure, apparently equipped to satisfy both hunger and lust. Barrell points out that the choice facing Hercules is not that between virtue and pleasure in general, but between civic, public virtue and private vice (*ibid.* p.29).

There seem to be some serious difficulties with the choice of central character for this painting, difficulties which are anticipated in Plato's worries about the morally equivocal contents of some heroic poetry. Although Hercules was undoubtedly heroic, his exploits in myth were not always those of someone who was morally pure. For example, while tracking down the lion who was ravaging the herds of his supposed father, Amphitryon, Hercules is supposed to have stayed for a night at the house of King Thespius, where he had sex with all fifty of the king's daughters. When Hercules' exploits were virtuous, on the other hand, they did not always exhibit civic virtue. His rescue of Alcestis from the hands of Death, for example, seems only to have benefitted Alcestis and her husband.

Leaving aside the details of *The Judgement of Hercules*, two questions arise. First, does even the better sort of painting have a moral influence of its own, or only one that is borrowed from history or mythology? And second, even if painting does have some effect of its own, is the effect greater than that of written history, poetry or mythology? If the answer is 'No', we do not have a vindication of painting, as Shaftesbury intended. Finally, Shaftesbury's idea that there is a public good that art can educate people to recognize depends on some unduly simple assumptions about the relevant public and its composition. If there is a relatively homogeneous class of aristocrats in charge of a relatively homogeneous, compliant class of 'mechanics', and if there is a homogeneity of nationality or predominant sex that enables patriotism and manly virtue to be promoted as aspects of the public good, perhaps Shaftesbury's idea makes sense. In another sort of society in which there is a much more diverse range of enfranchized groups each with a strong sense of its own identity, the 'public good' one ought to promote may be hard to identify without controversy. A work of art that questions some religious views may be in keeping with a liberal, secular conception of the public good, and yet may offend a religiously-minded minority; a view of the public good attuned to the values associated with machismo may be hard for feminists to identify with; and so on.

10   Moral and non-moral purposes of art

Is it possible to argue against Plato with more success than Shaftesbury? Yes: for one thing, a respectable version of the argument that some fine arts are morally instructive can be constructed, but outside Plato's framework. It is also possible to argue that it is good to have art available even when its benefits are not moral ones.

To begin with the argument for the moral instructiveness of art, the first step is to query Plato's idea that objective standards for judgements of goodness and rightness must have an abstract existence, on analogy with the abstractions that make mathematical statements true. Plato thinks that mathematical statements can be true and yet apply to shifting observational experience, because the things that make them true, geometrical figures, numbers, and their relations to one another, exist and are what they are eternally and immutably – in a realm apart from shifting experience. In the same way, he supposes that moral statements can be true of actions and characters independently of shifting and conflicting moral opinion, because of relations between the actions and characters and eternal, immutable moral standards or Forms. Plato presses the analogy between morals and mathematics too hard, however, when he holds that we do not acquire moral knowledge from experience. The claim that some of our mathematical knowledge is innate and therefore not gained from experience is made plausible in Plato's dialogue called *Meno*, where a slave-boy with no formal education is shown to be able to follow a proof in geometry by native intelligence and the help of a few hints. This is supposed to show that the slave-boy had a latent grasp of mathematical truths quite independently of anything he might have learnt, hence quite independently of experience. The moral of the *Meno* is not quite that experience has no role to play in mathematical education – diagrams available only through experience can *aid* understanding – but they are not supposed to supply any mathematical material for the intellect to work on. After all, a proof in geometry is not a proof concerning a diagram of a geometrical figure, but a proof concerning the figure itself.

When it comes to moral judgement, on the other hand, it is not plausible to say that experience merely acts as a visual aid, making vivid an action or character whose moral worth one is able to figure out on the basis of innate material. In the case of morals it seems straightforwardly true that experience supplies the subject-matter of moral judgement – the situations and actions and individuals we respond to morally – and also that experience refines the standards that we bring to bear on actions, situations and individuals. The fact that experience is variable and yet supplies the subject-matter for moral judgements – the fact that even the moral standards we bring to bear are not innate but implanted in us by, among other influences, our moral teachers, notably our parents, does not mean that the moral judgement cannot be objective in some sense. Roughly speaking, moral judgements are objective when they are not unduly affected by the judger's own interests or idiosyncratic beliefs – that is, when they stand a good chance of being acceptable from an informed and impartial point of view other than the judger's. For a judgement to be objective in this sense is not for it to be made true, when it is true, by things in a realm outside experience: it is for the judgement not to be formed by interests too peculiar to one judger or one kind of judger.

If moral judgements can be affected by experience, even formed by experience, without necessarily lacking objectivity, and if literature can be a means of adding to experience, a means to bring to people's attention situations, actions and characters not encountered in their own lives, then literature can contribute to one's moral education through the situations it adds to one's experience. If a reader is male, middle-class and British, literature can acquaint him with something of the lives of people who are none of those things. Of course, the situations we encounter in literature *need* not be out of the ordinary to be instructive: they may be of a piece with situations we have encountered or lived through and yet be presented in a light we have not considered. In other words, there is a way in which literature can instruct us without adding to the situations one has experienced.

The line of thought just sketched does not base the moral instructiveness of some kinds of art on a supposedly exalted moral subject matter to which art gives us access. Instead, it drops the Platonic assumption that the subject-matter of everyday experience and the subject-matter of objective moral judgement must be different, and it assumes that everyday experience and the subject of literature can be continuous with one another. Now this last assumption can be questioned on two grounds. First, there is the point that experiences which belong to our life histories are experiences of real situations, while the situations described in novels are made up, though sometimes inspired by real life. How can made-up situations be continuous with real situations? Well, in the straightforward way that descriptions in books can be of the same type of episode as we experience in real life. When we recognize situations in novels it is not because we have encountered exactly those situations but because we are acquainted with the same sort of situation. A second objection to supposing that everyday experience and literature can be continuous with one another is an aesthetic one – to the effect that if a work of art deserves the name of literature, for example, it should transform experience and not be subservient to it. According to this point of view, it is aesthetically justifiable, and sometimes necessary, for literature to exaggerate, to distort in the interest of vividness and so on. Art typically demands that characters and situations be larger than life rather than true to life; it usually injects style and colour where in reality it is absent. What art cannot do, according to this point of view, is hold up a mirror to life. The answer to this objection is that art does not have to copy life or mirror it exactly to be able to draw on experience of life. This answer does not imply, as Plato does, that the subject-matter of literature cannot be a truly moral subject-matter, or that ordinary experience fails to put us in touch with the good.

For all of the objections show, then, literature *can* engage and add to the experience that we learn from morally, and it can contribute to our moral education. The same goes for other art forms that tell stories, such as film and opera and, up to a point, representational painting. These art forms can indeed do more than instruct us as individuals. They can help people to understand and live with national traumas – Stalinism in the USSR, Vietnam and the McCarthy trials in the USA, for example. They can also help to identify changes in a national way of life, such as the growth in acquisitiveness in some countries in the West in the 1990s.

Though some kinds of art can do these things, there is no reason to ask all works of art to do so. Often works of art leave things as they are, taking for granted the truth of things we already believe, sticking to situations that do not disturb us, at times aiding a kind of lazy fantasy life that people can retreat into in order to get relief from reality. Instead of saying that this last form of art is bad and the other form good, we can say that one is serious and one is light and that both can harm us and both can benefit us. Serious art can harm us, for example, when it makes us feel less disturbed about evil and less impelled to do good. When, for example, we read a story about a criminal whose terrible crimes are overshadowed by an irresistible charm, or when we are got to be cynical about the motives of someone whose good works really are done sincerely out of good will, then our capacity to tell good from evil and right from wrong may be damaged. Perhaps the difference between great serious art that deals with evil and less successful art that deals with evil, is that the former brings us face to face with evil, makes us feel its attraction and then brings us to our senses, while unsuccessful serious art stops somewhere short of this.[2]

As for light art, it can do us harm by distracting us from what ought to hold our attention: it can provide a means of escape from some situation we should face up to or some task we should see through. Light art can also benefit us, and by the very mechanism of distraction that sometimes counts against it. The reason is the obvious one that in the right circumstances distraction can be refreshing and continued seriousness counterproductive. There are other ways in which art can be improving or beneficial without being morally improving. Certain kinds of visual art, for example, can literally get us to see things in new ways, and can make us understand what is arbitrary and parochial in a certain method of representation. Then again, there is the power of art to activate little-used capacities (like imagination) or rarely-felt emotions (like sheer horror). There is an upshot for the question of the usefulness of art. Instead of saying, as the residual moralizing influence of Plato may incline us to say, that art must be morally improving in order to be beneficial or socially useful, we may say that there is more than one way for art to be socially useful, that being morally improving is one way, while being entertaining or distracting in the right circumstances is another.

11   Art for morality's sake alone

The idea that art is *only* good or beneficial if it is morally improving can nevertheless be given a strong defence in a framework other than Plato's, and I will consider an example of such an approach provided by Tolstoy in *What is Art?*, a work which brings together a short history of aesthetic theory, a lot of provocative art criticism, an account of the decline of Christian belief among the European upper classes from the Middle Ages to the nineteenth century, and a version of Christian ethics which he thinks good art can be useful in spreading.

Tolstoy thinks that the best art expresses and infects people with feelings that reflect different, fairly refined, conceptions of the meaning of life. In general, Tolstoy maintains, human beings live according to conceptions of the meaning of life that over time become more and more clear in the form of religions: religions sum up 'the highest comprehension of life accessible to the best and foremost men at a given time in a given society – a comprehension towards which all the rest of the society must inevitably and irresistibly advance' (Tolstoy, 1930, p.127). He thinks that the religious perception of his own time,

> in its widest and most practical application, is the consciousness that our well-being, both material and spiritual, individual and collective, temporal and eternal, lies in the growth of brotherhood among men – in their loving harmony with one another.
>
> (*Ibid.* pp. 234–5)

This 'religious perception' is supposed to be a version of Christianity, but by this is meant not 'Church-Christianity' or the doctrine codified by some organized religious hierarchy, such as the one in the Vatican, but a way of life modelled as far as possible on Christ's and transmitted by works of art recognized as good by the first Christians, namely 'legends, lives of saints, sermons, prayers, and hymn-singing, evoking love of Christ, emotion at his life, desire to follow his example, renunciation of the worldly life, humility, and love of others...' (*ibid.* p.129).

Good art for Tolstoy was 'Christian' art in the broad sense, and he believed that Christian art

> should be catholic in the original meaning of the word, that is, universal, and therefore it should unite all men. And only two kinds of feeling unite all men: first, feelings flowing from our sonship to God and of the brotherhood of man; and next, the simple feelings of common life accessible to every one without exception – such as feelings of merriment, of pity, of cheerfulness, of tranquillity, and so forth. Only these two kinds of feelings can now supply material for art good in its subject-matter.
>
> (*Ibid.* pp. 239–40)

The art expressing the first kind of feeling – religious art – not only promotes unity among people; it also raises 'indignation and horror at the violation of love' (*ibid.* p.242). Tolstoy says that the primary manifestations of this art are verbal rather than visual, and primarily literary. But he thinks there are very few examples of good religious art: Victor Hugo's *Les Misérables* and Dickens's *A Tale of Two Cities* are included in a short list that also extends to works by Dostoevsky, Schiller and George Eliot (*ibid.*). A story by Tolstoy himself, *God sees the Truth but Waits*, also belongs to this group (*ibid.* p.246n.), but the rest of his artistic production is dismissed as 'bad art', as is most of European artistic production in general. Although a few pictures come into Tolstoy's category of good religious art (*ibid.* pp. 242–3), painting and sculpture are claimed to be less well adapted than literature to the spreading of religious feeling.

In the case of art based on the universal feelings of humanity, Tolstoy thinks that modern examples are hard to find in literature and music. The comedies of Molière and Cervantes's *Don Quixote* have the right 'inner contents' (*ibid.* p.243), but they are marred by the emphasis they give to exceptional feelings and to particular times and places. Tolstoy also mentions his story, *A Prisoner of the Caucasus* (*ibid.* p.246n.). But he thinks one has to look to ancient art for the best specimens of what he has in mind, such as the biblical story of Joseph. In music there are marches and dances which convey human feelings to everyone, but apart from these he mentions only two works by Bach and Chopin (*ibid.* p.245). Universal art comes into its own in painting and sculpture, especially when the subject matter is animals and landscapes. Even ornamental china dolls count for Tolstoy as good universal art (*ibid.* p.247).

Besides having a subject matter that sympathetically promotes unity among people and that conveys universally accessible human feelings, good art in Tolstoy's sense must proceed from a need in the artist, and not be made to order, or be a way of striking a pose. Unless it proceeds from such a need, unless it is also sincere, clear and produced so as to bring the artist closer to his audience, the painting, sculpture, piece of music or literature is not even art (*ibid.* pp. 228ff.). Someone who sets out merely to intrigue his audience, or to allude to things the audience can congratulate themselves for recognizing; someone who makes a virtue of being extremely indirect – such a person is not a producer of art even if the things the person makes require enormous skill to create. Other would-be works of art fail to be art, according to Tolstoy, because they imitate or counterfeit art. Either they are mass-produced according to a recipe, repeating something that has succeeded in the past or that really was art (*ibid.* p.192), or else they assemble willy-nilly the various devices associated with a particular genre. Tolstoy tells the story of having been asked to listen to a reading of a novel of this latter kind:

> It began with a heroine who, in a poetic white dress and with poetically flowing hair, was reading poetry near some water in a poetic wood. The

scene was in Russia, but suddenly from behind the bushes the hero appears, wearing a hat with a feather [in the style of William Tell] (the book specially mentioned this) and accompanied by two poetical white dogs.

(Ibid. p.182)

Finally, if an imitation work of art is not of the kinds already mentioned, it can be 'striking', calling up strong but not, as in true art, elevated, feelings. Instead, it is likely to evoke sexual desire or feelings of horror (*ibid.* p.184).

Tolstoy relegates to the category of imitation art not only the thousands of paintings, musical pieces and novels by run-of-the-mill professional painters, composers and writers but also a number of works generally reckoned great, such as Shakespeare's *Hamlet* (*ibid.* p.225), Beethoven's sonata Opus 101 (*ibid.* p.222), and Wagner's *Ring* (*ibid.* pp. 206ff.). His criticism of 'difficult' and inaccessible art is very bold, and he is often persuasive in his attack on the highbrow and on the critics and art-dealers. When he comes to summarize the effects of a taste for bad art or non-art (*ibid.* pp. 252ff.), he speaks of people who are incapable of being affected by true art. In practice, this means that

people grow up, are educated, and live, lacking the fertilizing, improving, influence of art, and therefore not only do not advance towards perfection, do not become kinder, but on the contrary, possessing highly-developed external means of civilization, they yet tend to become continually more savage, more coarse, and more cruel.

(Ibid.)

Worse than these effects of the absence of art, which are mainly experienced by the upper classes, there are the consequences for all sections of society of the perversion of art, and of the dedication of talented people to the production of empty, or degrading, or unfeeling art.

Tolstoy mentions five such consequences. The first is the wasted effort of producing bad or counterfeit art, wasted effort not only on the part of the performers, writers, composers, painters and the like, but also on the part of the typesetters, set-builders, picture-hangers and so on (*ibid.*). The second consequence is the encouragement of idleness among those who need trivial art to fill out their leisure time. Third, the generally high status enjoyed by producers of impenetrable or counterfeit art breeds perplexity and ultimately disillusionment in those who see how such artists are paid and how they are honoured after their deaths (*ibid.* pp. 255–7). The fourth consequence adds to the disillusion-ment and perplexity: aesthetic concepts start to cloud, sometimes even to supplant, moral ones. Acts that would generally be regarded as vicious are excused if they are done for the sake of art, and ways of life are permitted to artists that would not be tolerated in other people (*ibid.* p.256). Finally, Tolstoy says, the perversion of art encourages feelings that are divisive (patriotism), degrading (sensuality) and irrational (superstition).

12   Objections to Tolstoy

Although many different sorts of question are raised by Tolstoy's account of art, I shall concentrate, to begin with, on two. First, in stressing the value of universality, doesn't Tolstoy neglect the fact that, to some extent at least, a work of art is essentially part of a local tradition which cannot mean the same, or convey the same feelings, to people outside, or unacquainted with, the tradition? Second, might not there be something wrong with making the mark of good art depend on the fulfilment of a *non-aesthetic* purpose, i.e. that of bringing people together?

Overvaluing universality

According to Tolstoy it is essential to art that it set out to unite people – all people – and so it counts against a work if it depends for its effect on a content or technique that will mean something to only some of the people who are exposed to it.

> Art, all art, has this characteristic, that it unites people. Every art causes those to whom the artist's feeling is transmitted to unite in soul with the artist and also with all who receive the same impression. But non-Christian art, while uniting some people, makes that very union a cause of separation between these united people and others; so that union of this kind is often a source, not merely of division but even of enmity towards others. Such is all patriotic art, with its anthems, poems, and monuments; such is all Church art, that is, the art of certain cults, with their images, statues, processions, and other local ceremonies. Such art is belated and non-Christian, uniting the people of one cult only to separate them yet more sharply from the members of other cults, and even to place them in relations of hostility to one other.
>
> (*Ibid.* pp. 238–9)

Tolstoy goes on to contrast non-Christian art with Christian art, even unsuccessful Christian art.

Good Christian art of our time may be unintelligible to people because of imperfections in its form or because men are inattentive to it, but it must be such that all men can experience the feelings it transmits. It must be the art not of some one group of people, or of one class, or of one nationality, or of one religious cult; that is, it must not transmit feelings accessible only to a man educated in a certain way, or to an aristocrat, or a merchant, or only to a Russian, or a native of Japan, or a Roman Catholic, or a Buddhist, and so on, but it must transmit feelings accessible to every one.

(Ibid. p.239)

It is unclear whether in these passages Tolstoy is perfectly consistent; for he supposes that there can be such a thing as good Christian art which is nevertheless imperfect enough in form to be unintelligible, and yet he also insists that good Christian art must be accessible. Leaving aside this problem, however, isn't it true, contrary to Tolstoy, that a certain amount of inaccessibility may be inevitable, and that not all causes of separation among receivers of art are to be deplored?

Taking the point about inevitable inaccessibility first, there is the obvious fact that even works that Tolstoy praises for universality are composed, painted or written in different languages and styles, at different places and times, with references to things that may be difficult, for example, for foreign contemporaries of the artists or future receivers of these works to understand. Then, in the case of literature, changes in a single language and style can bring it about that even later readers of the same language cannot engage with a work as the original readers did. Tolstoy's model of the literary work capable of reaching the widest audience – namely the biblical story – is a good example of something that is now known almost universally in translation rather than the original language, and, what is more, through translations that some think have required revision because modern readers cannot understand them. No doubt there is a certain sense in which the stories in the bible shine through the pedestrian words that the new translations use to express them; equally clearly there is a sense in which, in the interest of accessibility, the aesthetic quality of the work can be said to have declined, along with the modernization and simplification of the language. So not only are there limits to the extent that a work of art can be universally accessible; greater accessibility is sometimes achieved at the expense of art.

Besides the obstacles to universal accessibility posed by time, place and language, which would perhaps affect the understanding of a soup label as much as a novel, there are the conventions of a tradition of art and the influence of exemplary works within that tradition. Having a place in a tradition and the audience's knowledge of it, are important in determining the range of possible responses to a work of art. The knowledge of the tradition or more generally of the style may be an important condition of knowing what to expect and so a condition of being surprised or delighted or disappointed. Facts about the tradition often help to explain why, for example, a literary effect was achieved in one way rather than another, and will expose an otherwise incidental detail of a film as an allusion to some earlier, and exemplary, work of cinema. That the significance of these details is lost on the average reader or cinema-goer does not mean that they are unimportant to reading or viewing; on the contrary, to the extent that there is a difference in the quality of reception for a work of art among different members of an audience or an improvement in the quality of reception in one viewer over time, it may be marked by an acquired sensitivity to details like these. In any case, whether clearly recognizable or not, the tradition or style of a work of art is likely to affect its content and may restrict its intelligibility.[3]

It might be thought that while Tolstoy does not pay sufficient attention to unavoidable limitations on accessibility, still he is right to say that artists should not *add* to the limitations by consciously addressing their works only to fellow members of a particular church or to fellow citizens of a particular country; for won't art that has so exclusive an audience be less accessible and even positively divisive? Not necessarily. A literature or music that is intended only for a given group and not the whole of humanity may be parochial or narrow without being divisive: the people to whom it means nothing may simply be indifferent rather than feel excluded. Second, a literature that encourages patriotic feeling in a particular population may be inspiring to another population that feels, as until recently Eastern Europeans felt, that their countries had lost their old identities. The cultivation of a national literature can, in the right circumstances, be a model for others seeking a common purpose: it need not be a medium for those who want their country to be pre-eminent. Third, it is possible for people in one country to have strong positive feelings for people in another country *through* a national art of that second country. No doubt there are many anglophiles abroad whose affection for England has been heightened or even inspired in the first place by English poetry or the plays of Shakespeare. Similarly, there are those who love Rome because of its ancient imperial art, or who are fond of America and Americans because they adore Hollywood movies.

Art for non-aesthetic purposes

I come now to the second of my two questions about Tolstoy: is he right to insist that the mark of good art is the ability to bring people together and promote feelings of Christian love? The question is not only to do with his particular vision of Christian unity, but with the idea that art should promote and encourage a certain way of life among those to whom it is directed. At this level of generality the question raised about Tolstoy can also be raised about a Marxian conception of art, according to which art is the instrument of different class interests in different social formations, and an instrument of a working-class interest – or more simply an instrument of the people – in a social formation that remedies the injustices of capitalism.

One way of challenging this way of thinking is by asking whether there is such a thing as a working-class interest, and if there is, whether it is the task of art to articulate this interest. But another, and more general, challenge applies to Tolstoy's view as well as to the Marxist one. It can be put by asking whether the purpose of art should be defined in terms of society or a way of life or, even more generally still, by reference to *anything* external to art itself. A danger of supposing that art should be instrumental in the achievement of a non-aesthetic purpose, such as a political one, is that the political purpose can so overwhelm the content of the art that nothing is achieved either politically or aesthetically. We are familiar with institutional sculpture from Eastern Europe, with its predictable clusters of muscular, determined peasants, soldiers and industrial workers. The stilted heroic poses of these figures completely subvert the political purpose of achieving respect for real peasants, industrial workers and soldiers, and the qualities of the sculptures are neutered by the fact that they are – before anything else – institutional, officially commissioned and approved in an official style, with hardly any sign of a personal intervention by the sculptor. The drawbacks of sculptures, novels, and musical compositions with too heavyhanded a political message were clear to Marx and Engels, who complained of 'tendency' literature – novels, plays and reviews which used political allusions to make up for failings of plotting and observation. Much more to Marx's taste were literary productions which did not set out to advertize themselves as socialist, and which let social analysis and criticism speak through dramatic situations or characters. He praised Dickens, Thackeray, Brontë and Gaskell 'whose graphic and eloquent pages have issued to the world more political and social truths than have been uttered by all of the professional politicians, publicists and moralists put together.'[4]

Granted that there is something wrong with a work of art when its political purposes overwhelm its aesthetic ones; is there still something wrong with a work of art when it does not come over as propaganda but is consciously constrained by political purposes? If a right-wing novelist cannot bring himself to make any sympathetic character a Communist or any Communist a sympathetic character, is what he produces a bad work of art? Much depends on the strength of the literary justification for doing what he fails to do. But plainly it is possible for a politically-motivated literary decision to make a book worse, even where the political message is not too obtrusive. So the coexistence of aesthetic and political purposes is sometimes a tense one. On the other hand, there is no reason why there *must* be a tension and in certain works of art – Orwell's *1984*, perhaps – art and politics may coalesce effectively.

Though aesthetic and political purposes need not pull in opposite directions, the fact that they can and sometimes do, throws doubt on the usual Marxist criterion for valuing art by reference to class commitment, and probably also throws doubt on the Tolstoyan criterion of promoting Christian brotherhood. Up to a point, the same complaint about the interference of a non-aesthetic purpose with the aesthetic quality of a work of art can be made where the non-aesthetic purpose is not political at all. Thus Oscar Wilde complains through the character of Vivian in 'The Decay of Lying' (Wilde, 1891) that the aim of being true to nature or true to life can detract from the aesthetic quality of a novel or a play, to such an extent, in fact, that it ceases to be art. Wilde describes a kind of competition between art and life – between invention and subservience to fact – that he thinks results in decadence if life is allowed to prevail over art. He illustrates by taking the case of English drama, and its development into what he claims is the degraded form of the modern English melodrama:

> [T]he magnificent work of the Elizabethan and Jacobean artists contained within itself the seeds of its own dissolution, and... if it drew some of its strength from using life as rough material, it drew all its weakness from using life as an artistic method. As the inevitable result of the substitution of an imitative for a creative medium, the surrender of an imaginative form, we have the modern English melodrama. The characters in these plays talk on stage exactly as they would talk off it; they have neither aspirations nor aspirates; they are taken directly from life and reproduce its vulgarity down to the smallest detail; they present the gait, manner, costume and accent of real people; they would pass unnoticed in a third-class railway carriage. And yet how wearisome the plays are! They do not succeed even in producing that

impression of reality which is their aim, and which is their only reason for existing. As a method, realism is a complete failure.

(*Ibid.* pp. 22–3)

It is unclear from this and other passages whether what offends Wilde is realism, or the vulgarity of the people that are realistically depicted. In either case it is hard to see an *argument* against realism here. There is some plausibility in saying, as Wilde goes on to say, that if fidelity to life and nature were the overriding goal of literature, then many literary works which are careless of factual detail but nevertheless show great imagination would be seriously undervalued. But is this really the consequence of adopting realism as the goal of fiction? Realistic writers do not aim to show things as they are merely by mechanical description or rigid reproduction. Their aim is to give a sense to the facts, to make something of what otherwise would be miscellaneous and dull detail. A difference between police evidence read out at a trial from an incident book and a passage in a good realistic or naturalistic novel is that the details or facts are not just listed or recited in the order in which they took place, but are selectively organized and weighted and paced, so that they come to carry a weight in a narrative that is disclosed in its own time. There is a faithfulness to life or the facts – one is sometimes drawn in and made to live the story – but faith is also kept with what is natural to the character and the plot.

The twentieth-century American writer Flannery O'Connor illustrates this point very well in an essay called 'The Nature and Aim of Fiction'. She comments on a couple of sentences from Flaubert's *Madame Bovary* which describe Emma, at the piano, being watched by Charles. O'Connor translates these sentences as

> She struck the notes with aplomb and ran from top to bottom of the keyboard without a break. Thus shaken up, the old instrument, whose strings buzzed, could be heard at the other end of the village when the window was open, and often the bailiff's clerk, passing along the high road, bareheaded and in list slippers, stopped to listen, his sheet paper in his hand.

O'Connor comments,

> With regard to what happens to Emma in the rest of the novel, we may think that it makes no difference that the instrument has buzzing strings or that the clerk wears list slippers and has a piece of paper in his hand, but Flaubert had to create a believable village to put Emma in. It's always necessary to remember that the fiction writer is much less

immediately concerned with grand ideas and bristling emotions than with putting list slippers on clerks.

Now of course this is something that some people learn only to abuse. This is one reason why strict naturalism is a dead end in fiction. In a strictly naturalistic work the detail is there because it is natural to life, not because it is natural to the work. In a work of art we can be extremely literal, without being in the least naturalistic. Art is selective, and its truthfulness is the truthfulness of the essential that creates movement.

(O'Connor, 1972, p.70)

By this last phrase O'Connor seems to mean the truthfulness of a detail that encapsulates a lot and yet that does not detain the story in the way that a full description of what is encapsulated would detain it. The well-chosen detail gets at what's essential and allows the narrative to proceed, and, as O'Connor goes on to point out, it can also carry the weight of symbolic meaning.

In good fiction, certain of the details will tend to accumulate meaning from the story itself, and when this happens, they become symbolic in their action... [F]or the fiction writer himself, symbols are something he uses as a matter of course. You might say that these are details that, while having their essential place in the literal level of the story, operate in depth as well as on the surface, increasing the story in every direction.

(*Ibid*. pp. 70–1)

In O'Connor's account there is no tension except in 'strict naturalism' between meeting the demands of realism and the demands of art, and it is unclear that she leaves herself open to the sort of objection that Wilde makes. On the other hand, her position is not equivalent to Wilde's, for she stresses the importance to writing of disciplined attention to the world around one, of training oneself to see, rather than of giving oneself up to imagination.

13   Art and social class

Our discussion of the non-aesthetic purposes of certain works of art was prompted by Tolstoy's claim that to be good art, a painting or a novel had to bring people together. In this section I will address other suggestions Tolstoy makes; for example, that art tends to be identified with what wealthy people are willing to pay for as art, and that the artworld and its views about art tend to have an existence independent of people in the wider community and *their* views about art.

The relations between art, or at least fine art, on the one hand, and the wealthy and the artworld on the other, have been taken up by sociologists of art, literary and art critics and philosophers, as well as by novelists interested in art, such as Tolstoy. Sometimes these social relations are considered from the standpoint of an interest in aesthetic theory and its method. People ask whether the concepts of beauty or of the artist can be understood apart from facts about the ideology and social class of those who apply the concepts, or independent of the history of the relevant culture. This sort of question can be pursued alongside the moral one of whether people whose share of economic and social goods is already small, have less access to art and aesthetic enjoyment than those who are better off. Then there is a question, touched upon by Tolstoy himself, that straddles the boundary between morals and methodology, namely whether the 'tastes' and 'interests' of one class exercise too much influence in the determination of what is beautiful or what is real art. Though it is put in terms of social class, the last question could also be pursued in relation to gender or race or nationality. One can ask whether art and artists conventionally regarded as 'great' only seem that way from a male, middle-class, white, European, point of view. Perhaps a different canon – a different set of 'approved' paintings, plays, operas, pieces of orchestral music, poems – could be argued for from a feminist, oriental, working-class, or Third World perspective, for example. Religion may be another background influence on the appraisal of art, as the affair of Salman Rushdie's *Satanic Verses* has shown. A book that some devout Muslims could only see as blasphemous was seen by others, including the chairman of the panel awarding the 1988 Booker Prize, as a work of high literary merit.

14 Sociology of art

The claim that the wider social context affects the classification of things as works of art seems not only true but truistic. But if it is true, then it is natural to expect a kind of overlap between the study of art and the study of society. In other words, if the claim is true, it is reasonable to expect to learn something from the sociology of art. But what exactly? In a paper entitled 'Aesthetic Judgement and Sociological Analysis' (Wolff, 1982), Janet Wolff suggests a question that the sociologist could concentrate on.

> The sociology of art, which explores and identifies the essentially
> ideological nature of all cultural products, raises the pertinent question
> of whether aesthetic value is a chimera – a conception of timeless and

> universal beauty and worth which is itself entirely reducible to politi-
> cal/ideological/class values.   (*Ibid.*)

Or, in other words, is there really such a thing as distinctively aesthetic value?

In the brief investigation of the question in her article, Wolff rejects the idea that works of art have the aesthetic value they have independent of facts about society. For her, social facts do influence aesthetic judgements, and so a knowledge of these facts, or hypotheses about what might explain them derived from sociology, can throw light on aesthetic values. The sociology that Wolff thinks might be useful, however, cannot be a simplistic social theory: she wants nothing to do with a theory that imples that people's aesthetic judgements are a rigid reflection of their class or income group. Such a sociology, she thinks, is ill-equipped to bring out what is special or specific to art. For Wolff, the distinctive nature of art can only be brought out by 'specificity theories', some of which tie the special nature of art to the 'specific codes and conventions of representation' recognized in the art world, as well as particular techniques and skills imparted through art education. Other specificity theories refer to certain aspects of human nature or human experience which great art expresses. Finally, there is what Wolff calls 'discourse theory', which represents art, art history, and art criticism as distinct discourses operating by their own rules, rules which serve as the necessary background for the ascription of aesthetic values. Wolff is attracted to discourse theory because, unlike some of the simpler sociological theories, it does not rule out as irrelevant the question of the social origin of discourse, and it does not assume either that every aspect of a work of art is to be understood by reference to social origins. In particular, the rules of discourse may explain things independently of social origins. But Wolff doubts that discourse theory, which she associates with the work of Michel Foucault, can by itself give an adequate account of aesthetic pleasure.

Wolff wishes both to recognize the peculiar nature of art and to use sociology of art to 'problematize' the value judgements of critics and other members of the artworld; that is, to call in question the authority and apparent objectivity of these judgements. But it is not clear whether it is necessary to problematize value-judgements or whether one can both problematize them and keep art as a distinctive enterprise. To take these matters in order, why is it necessary to problematize judgements that critics or members of the artworld make? Wolff gestures at an answer in remarking that at 'the very moment that criticism presents itself as pure or timeless, its hidden ideological assumptions are asserted': the implication is that the value judgements of critics have a merely apparent objectivity, one that is owed not to the absence of bias but to the concealment of bias in the form of an unspoken ideological perspective and social position. 'Those who accord "value" to works of art and cultural products', she says,

> are empowered to do so by particular social and power relations in society, which situates them as critics and accreditors of art. They are to be found in establishments of higher education, departments of English literature, at universities, as reviewers and critics on certain prestigious journals, and as the mediators or 'gate-keepers' in publishing and the art-market. The criticism of art or literature is thus executed by a specific sector of the population, with its own particular social origins, mediators and ideologies. In England, at any rate, the class composition of this powerful minority is clearly unrepresentative of the population at large.
>
> (*Ibid.*)

Suppose Wolff is right about the unrepresentativeness of critics and reviewers. This does nothing to throw in doubt the aesthetic judgements of the critics and reviewers unless the aesthetic judgements are a rigid reflection of the class position of the people who make them. Wolff does not show that having certain social origins blinds one to certain aesthetic properties of works of art, and the fact that critics from the same social class often disagree sharply among themselves – not uncommonly in ways that reflect a variety of different political positions – tends to discredit the idea that there is a simple relation between class position and aesthetic judgement. Finally, it is not clear that critics regularly display the pretensions to objectivity that Wolff thinks sociology could usefully problematize. On the contrary, it is just as plausible that many practising critics would accept straight off that they make judgements from a point of view. As for readers of criticism, they in their turn are unlikely to accept the aesthetic judgements of the experts as unassailable. The belief in the subjectivity of taste is after all much more widespread than the belief that only one kind of taste is acceptable.

If 'problematizing' aesthetic value is a matter of showing that particular judgements of critics are influenced by social background, then it may only show what people accept anyway. Sociology may be able to do more than this, however; it may be able to induce second thoughts not just about the judgements the critics deliver, but about the concepts used to make those judgements. Just as, in Wolff's opinion, the sociology of knowledge has succeeded in generating scepticism about objective truth, so, she seems to think, the sociology of art may generate (presumably healthy) doubts about whether artifacts are objectively beautiful of whether works of art are objectively great:

> [T]he demonstration that knowledge (including science) is interest-related, that the practices of scientists are, in one sense, arbitrary, and that knowledge has a 'provisional' nature, has been widely accepted among sociologists of knowledge. Relativism has become respectable as one position within the sociology of knowledge... But more recently... the problem of truth *has* emerged in a particular form in the sociology of art – namely, in terms of the question about true or valid art.

(Ibid.)

Though it is not completely clear, the implication seems to be that, in time, relativism will be a respectable position in the sociology of art, and that, when this happens, it will be a welcome development. But why relativism in either area – the sociology of knowledge *or* the sociology of art – should be accepted, is never made clear.

15 High culture vs low culture

One of the uses of a sociology of art, according to Wolff, is to make clear the class background of accreditors of art, and to invite second thoughts about what the accreditors say, given that class background. Another question that can be pursued, perhaps by philosophy, is whether it is good or right for the tastes or interests of one social class to exert particular influence. The arbiters of taste or accreditors of art seem to be drawn predominately from a single, and a privileged, class. Why should the taste of this class be authoritative? If there is such a thing as the art recognized by the élite expert minority and the art recognized by the majority, the latter still being art, but an art different from that recognized by the experts, why should it be thought of as somehow less valuable – lower or more popular – than expert-approved 'high art'?

One philosopher who has tried to deal with questions like these is Roger Taylor in *Art, an Enemy of the People*. Rejecting the valuations implicit in the distinction between 'high art' and 'low art', he draws a distinction between bourgeois and popular culture, claims that popular culture is in danger of being appropriated by bourgeois culture, and holds that popular culture deteriorates when it is appropriated. Taylor gives a very detailed and arresting account of how jazz has been taken over in this way, but he notes in passing another and more recent musical example:

> [D]uring the '60s those aspects of popular music rooted in the tradi-
> tions of rock music became of real interest to a young, intellectual
> middle-class public. As this happened so *art*, as an accolade, became
> tenuously attached to certain forms of this music, but at the same time a
> transformation occurred whereby the category 'progressive art' came
> into being. As this happened so progressive rock established itself as a
> minority interest, and it was within this category that the status of rock
> as an artform was entertained. This, then, was a raid into popular
> culture by the art world.
>
> (Taylor, 1978, p.56)

Taylor acknowledges that what he calls 'a raid' may be welcomed by popular artists as long overdue recognition by the artworld, but he thinks that this recognition is likely to be over-valued by those on whom it is bestowed:

> Art is a badge of success within society, and to have it conferred on
> one's activities, when this is not normal, is to be inclined to bask in the
> value of the award, despite the fact that the total, social significance of
> awarding, in the society, is socially discriminatory against the mass of
> the people. To accept the award as high commendation is to accept, at
> the same time, that one's own life style is inferior. It is also possible that
> if the award is taken too seriously, it can suck the life out of what were
> previously vital activities.
>
> (*Ibid.* p.57)

There is a defensible idea here, but it seems to me to be smothered by a bad argument. The defensible idea is the complex one that 'art' is an honorific term, that accepting an award from the artworld is sometimes a repudiation of one's previous style of life, and that when it is the award may not be worth accepting.

The claim that Taylor actually argues for, however, is that for popular art to accept awards from the artworld is for its practitioner to repudiate a style of life, or at least to make a sign that he or she thinks it is inferior, so that awards to popular art are never worth accepting. Not only does this claim sound too sweeping; it is backed up by the bad argument that the practice of giving awards always discriminates against the mass of the people. To discriminate against people is to single them out for bad treatment that they do not deserve. The practice of giving awards does not necessarily involve discrimination in this sense. It need not involve singling out certain people for special treatment in advance of the competition for the award, and it need not involve bad treatment to those who do not get the award. After all, to fail to get a prize in a competition is not thereby to suffer bad treatment. Bad treatment is suffered only if one's being left out of the prizes results from the judges taking into account things not being tested in the competition. Thus, if someone fails to get an art award because they are black rather than white or because they are in competition with the grandchildren of the man putting up the prize money, who wants them to win, that is one thing; but if they are judged to perform worse by people who do their best to concentrate only on ability, then failing to get the award is not the result of discrimination. It is true that many qualities that help people to get awards in competitions, such as confidence or persistence, are arbitrarily distributed, just as beauty, physical strength and intelligence are. But this source of unfairness, if that is what it is, is not the sort that is at issue in Taylor's diagnosis of the 'social significance of awarding'. He seems to think that there is something that discriminates against the mass in the very idea of having awards – and this, I am claiming, is wrong. Awards do single people out, but this need not involve mistreating people who do not get the awards.

The claim of mistreatment would perhaps make sense if, by labelling someone as an artist or someone's work as art, one were saying, 'You and your work can be admitted to high culture, but your friends and colleagues and their work are not good enough to be included.' But to suppose that this is the message behind recognition by the artworld is in one way too generous to the artworld and in another way not generous enough. It is too generous, because a work of popular art is unlikely to achieve the status of high art just by being recognized by the artworld. It is more likely to be given some rather humbler status, reflected in guarded phrases like 'interesting' or partly-condescending phrases like 'earthy' or 'exuberant'. In this way the artworld keeps its options open and popular art and artists at its fringes. But, by the same token, the artworld does not elevate the noticed work of art or artist to a position above other popular artists. The phrases 'interesting' or 'exuberant' do not necessarily work to exclude other popular art or popular artists.

Is there perhaps an argument other than Taylor's for the position he puts forward? There is a strong argument against accepting awards from the artworld for works that are supposed to protest against the standards of the artworld, or against the standards of the bourgoisie at large, but this does not amount to a general argument against popular art ever accepting the awards of the artworld, for popular art is not always, and may not even typically be, protest art, or art that is supposed to stick in the throats of the bourgeoisie. It seems to me that leading examples of popular art in the UK, such as the television serials 'Coronation Street' or 'Eastenders', are directed at and intended to appeal to as wide an audience as possible. They are directed at a mass audience not in the sense of 'mass' that contrasts with 'élite' or 'bourgeois' but in the sense of 'mass audience' that means 'big audience'. For makers of this sort of popular art to accept the awards or praise of the bourgeoisie is not necessarily for them to acknowledge inferiority or for them to sell out. On the other hand, the acceptance of such awards by jazz musicians can be interpreted in Taylor's way, since, as he shows, jazz *is* a form of protest art. But how typical of popular art protest art is, and how typical of protest art jazz is, are questions that Taylor does not properly answer. He is also unclear about what constitutes the award of artistic status to popular art. Is artistic status bestowed only when popular culture is praised or given an award, or is it enough to be noticed by the artworld, even if the notice is not all that friendly?

Having raised these questions, let us move on and look into Taylor's account of the harm that was supposed to be done to jazz when it was given the status of art – when art critics started to write favourably about it and when musicologists started to pay attention to it. On the one hand, according to Taylor's account, 'the history of jazz has been anti-European, anti-white, anti-bourgeois, anti-art' (*ibid.* p.155). On the other, under the influence of European critics, white American musicians, and black jazzmen who were attracted to the acceptably elevated but also fringe status of art for jazz, it has been absorbed into the 'art process'. With that absorption has come the decreasing significance of jazz as a catalyst for popular, mass experience (*ibid.*).

The extent to which jazz became a mass or popular art form is not always clear from Taylor's account. Partly this is because at times he seems to classify jazz as a music of black Americans that was diluted or hijacked when white musicians and audiences became involved, and at other times he seems to describe it as having had from the start a mixed-race following and authentic white as well as black practitioners. If it was primarily a black art form that was taken over, in the first place by poor whites, later by middle-class Americans and eventually by Europeans, then jazz is not so much an instance of popular culture as of minority culture, and the threats to its authenticity and vitality may have more to do with racial than with class divisions. Ostensibly, however, Taylor's thesis is that the transformation of popular culture into 'art' is a means of *class* domination. The concepts of race and of class overlap in their application, but they are not equivalent, and there is a difference between saying that jazz is proletarian or working people's art and saying that it derives its significance from the experience of blacks in New Orleans about a century ago.

Another unclarity in Taylor's account can be identified by asking whether examples of high art remain examples of high art when they start to have a wide following, or whether things that started out as an art-form with a wide audience continue to be popular art when they lose their following. If a piece in the classical orchestral repertoire starts to have a popular following when it is used in the programme music of the UK ice-dance champions, then does the wide audience start to link up with the high-brow classical orchestral repertoire, or does the piece used by the ice-dancers, despite its place in the repertoire, fall out of high culture, having been taken over by a mass audience? What if the classical orchestral repertoire has a wide popular following in some countries, as perhaps it does in the USSR, or as perhaps grand opera has in some parts of Italy? Do concerts of serious orchestral music and grand opera locally lose their status of high culture? These questions seem to me to be urgent for an account like Taylor's, for he assumes that popular art can be sufficiently independent of high art to be threatened with take over by high art, and perhaps the boundary between the two is in fact not so clearly drawn, at any rate in every case, as Taylor seems to think.

Even if Taylor is right, however, and the boundary between art and popular culture is quite firm, what is supposed to be the practical lesson of the cautionary example that he thinks jazz provides? Is it that critics and other members of the artworld should ignore a popular art-form, lest they spoil it by their attentions? Is the idea that the right way of appreciating these art-forms is only as an ordinary member of an audience and not as a representative of the establishment – be it the 'art' establishment or any other? Is it that a policy of separate development ought to be pursued by popular and high art? When Taylor concludes by saying that 'art is a value that the masses should resist' (*ibid.*), what form should the resistance take? Why isn't it possible – and desirable – for people's taste to span the divide between high and low culture?

A recent controversy involving the film critic of a newspaper in Dallas, Texas, puts the possibility and desirability of straddling the divide between high and popular culture in an unusual perspective. In an article on the controversy in the *New Yorker*, the American writer, Calvin Trillin, raised the sort of question we have been discussing.

What, exactly, does a main-line American daily newspaper do about movies like 'The Night Evelyn Came Out of the Grave' and 'Malibu Hot Summer' and 'Bloodsucking Freaks'? Does he pick one out, on a slow week, and subject it to the sort of withering sarcasm that sometimes, in his braver moments, he sees himself using on his executive editor? Does he simply ignore such movies, preferring to pretend that a person of his sensibility could not share an artistic universe with such efforts as 'Mother Reilly Meet the Vampire' and 'Driller Killer' and 'Gas Pump Girls'?

(Trillin, 1986, p.73)

According to Trillin, this was the problem that the Dallas *Times-Herald* solved toward the end of 1981 when its film reviewer, John Bloom, invented the alter ego of Joe Bob Briggs and started a column that catered for 'exploitation pictures' – films given over to soft pornography, monsters, martial arts and blood-and-guts – as John Bloom catered for art-films and mainstream movies. Around Dallas, exploitation pictures were shown in a thriving network of drive-in cinemas: Joe Bobb wrote from the point of view of an enthusiast for both drive-ins and the films they showed, and adopted the slang and the supposed outlook on the world of a rural Texan.

Trillin describes the double life of John Bloom, the serious film critic, and John Bloom alias Joe Bob Briggs, connoisseur of exploitation pictures:

An admirer of foreign films, Bloom wrote essays on [French new-wave film makers like Truffaut and Godard] while Joe Bob was rating movies according to the amounts of innards displayed ('We're talking Glopola City') and the number of severed body parts that could be seen rolling away, and the number of breasts exposed ('the garbanza factor'). Bloom wanted Joe Bob to 'talk about movies the way most people talk about movies: they give the plot, with emphasis on their favourite scenes, then they sum up what they think of it.' Joe Bob tended to tell the plot ('So this flick starts off with this bimbo [woman] getting chained up and killed by a bunch of Meskins [Mexicans] dressed up like Roman soldiers in bathrobes'), and his summaries eventually developed into his best-known trade-mark: 'Sixty-four dead bodies. Bimbos in cages. Bimbos in chains. Arms roll. Thirty-nine breasts. Two beasts (giant lizard, octopus). Leprosy. Kung fu. Bimbo fu. Sword fu. Lizard fu. Knife fu. Seven battles. Three quarts blood... Joe Bob says check it out.'

(*Ibid.* p.74)

Material of this studied tastelessness attracted a large readership. Some apparently took Joe Bob's column to be a satirical treatment of a male chauvinist, racist, anti-Communist Texas backwoodsman, while others, including experienced reporters employed by the Dallas *Times-Herald*, took the material at face-value (at any rate to begin with). The column had a wide audience outside Dallas. It was syndicated and reprinted weekly in newspapers throughout the USA.

In 1985 Joe Bob's column went too far. It satirized in racially offensive terms a rock song recorded in aid of African famine relief. The local outcry led to the cancellation of 'Joe Bob goes to the Drive-In' in the Dallas *Times-Herald*. It was not quite the end of Joe Bob, however. John Bloom started a cabaret act in the persona of his alter ego, and a number of weekly instalments from the column were collected and published as a book in America in 1987. A UK edition appeared in 1989 (Bloom, 1989).

Does 'Joe Bob goes to the Drive-In' offer a model for reviews of parts of popular culture that even the popular press does not reach? To the extent that it was taken seriously by a section of the Dallas *Times-Herald* readership who liked exploitation pictures, and who took the column to speak to them in their language, it seems that it may: it invented a voice apparently appropriate for the audience of exploitation pictures, and it seems to have identified and counted all the things that, for this audience, matter to making one exploitation picture better than another. That the column was apparently intended to send up or satirize exploitation pictures and their audiences seems to be neither here nor there. Whatever the intention of John Bloom, he seems to have hit upon a means of presenting reviews of the previously unreviewable. That these reviews showed little interest in the films does not mean that their form was on the whole an inappropriate one, though it probably often went over the top because its main object was satirical.

The phenomenon of Joe Bob seems to me to show that even the most dubious parts of popular culture can be connected with their own outposts of the artworld – their own critics and reviewers – without the art world necessarily falsifying or taking over that part of popular culture, as Taylor claims. Whether it is desirable to find new forms of criticism or review for outlying parts of popular culture may be an open question in the case of exploitation pictures, which can be offensive at times. The desirability may be easier to make out in the case of more harmless 'pulp' fiction or pop videos. An artworld that extends to Mills and Boon publications and the latest Bananarama single need not threaten popular culture or condescend to its consciousness in the way that Taylor seems to fear. Similarly for an artworld that recognizes fringe art. The descendents of the underground press routinely review what are supposed to be fringe art and artistic events in terms that are recognizably different from mainstream criticism, but which do not condescend either. These reviews do not seem to me to show the imagination or daring of Joe Bob, and they are not nearly as funny, but they do seem to me to be creditable attempts to make accessible art that might otherwise go unnoticed.

16   Social involvement, criticism and detachment

Different art forms are sometimes sustained by different sections of society. They have distinctive followings or audiences and sometimes depend on the shared experience of these for their significance. That is one way in which art can depend on society. Perhaps jazz started out relying for its significance on the experience of people with dealings in a certain quarter of New Orleans. Other, broadly comparable art forms – rimbetika in the big Greek port of Piraeus near Athens, flamenco in Seville, fado in Lisbon – may also exhibit a comparable dependence on the experience of those locals who are its main consumers. Art can also depend on society, however, when it seems to stand outside society, to struggle against it, or to challenge its laws and conventions. Solzhenitsyn's novels draw their subject-matter from Stalinist Russia and indeed have a strong claim to document their time and place. Nadine Gordimer's novels are critical of the South Africa they portray. Victorian society provided not only the conditions exposed by Dickens as shameful: it also formed Dickens himself. How can the detachment necessary for criticism of Victorian England or Stalinist Russia or apartheid South Africa be achieved given the involvement of these writers in the conditions they are writing about?

Involvement does not always inject bias, but it can limit the writer's perspective in ways that are identifiable by the reader, while at the same time being the kind of involvement that allows for authentic description. If involved in the right way the author is caught up but not carried away by his or her society or one of the classes within it. Dickens may have managed only a partial detachment of the sort needed for the conditions he described. Or so Terry Eagleton has claimed, with some plausibility. He has pointed out how Dickens's way of *resolving* the problems of his characters often shows a certain class bias, despite the fact that this bias is partly overcome in the *description* of the problems. According to Eagleton, Dickens belonged to the petty bourgeoisie, and this class, positioned between the proletariat and bourgeoisie, had a freedom of intellectual manoeuvre not available to the bourgeoisie proper or to the proletariat. 'Ambiguously placed within the social formation, the petty bourgeoisie was able on the whole to encompass a richer, more significant range of experience than those writers securely lodged within a single class' (Eagleton, 1976, p.125). Rather like the *émigré* writers of a later period, Dickens, Hardy and other petty bourgeois writers were 'open to the contradictions from which major literary art was produced'. According to Eagleton, the same petty bourgeois class position which enabled Dickens to get a vantage point on, and provide criticism of, the chancery courts, the education system and the working conditions in the industrial north of England, also circumscribed the criticism and explained Dickens's eventual endorsement of bourgeois values. Eagleton considers the case of *Oliver Twist*. 'The novel argues at once that Oliver is and is not the product of bourgeois oppression, just as the 'real' world of bourgeois social relations into which he is magically rescued is endorsed against the 'unreal' world of poverty and crime, while simultaneously being shown up by that underworld as illusory' (*ibid*. p.128).

A petty bourgeois class position is supposed to help Dickens get the right perspective on the 'contradictions' between bourgeoisie and proletariat in Victorian society, according to Eagleton. According to Robert Boyers, the device of viewing political involvement and its costs from the perspective of the private lives of those involved helps Nadine Gordimer to get the right sort of critical purchase on apartheid, and on people on both sides of its divide (Boyers, 1985, pp. 121–46).

Gordimer herself has a theory of what novels should do, and it confirms Boyers's reading. In an interview in 1983, she spoke about what a novel must be like to serve the, in her opinion, desirable function of giving social history.

> Again this slippery element of truth comes into it. We come back to Balzac. What he wrote was history, a remarkable social history of part of nineteenth-century France. The requirements there are not just truth to events, you could check dates in any history, but an attempt to discover what people think and feel and most important, the most important requirement to my mind, would be to make a connection between their personal attitudes and actions and the pressures of the historical period that shapes such actions. So if you are living at a time when one portion of the population is extremely affluent and the other is very poor, the historical importance of that work of fiction would be in how it would show that that extremely affluent group managed to justify their existence to themselves, never mind the world... I think that is where the novelist goes much further than the historian. The

historian can tell you the events and can trace how the events came through the power shifts in the world. But the novelist is concerned with the power shifts within the history of individuals who make up history.

(in Cooper-Clark, 1986, pp. 82–3)

Gordimer does not say in so many words that writing through a personal or individual perspective affords its own sort of critical distance from a political situation, while straight history provides another, but I think that this is strongly implied. And whether or not she thinks of the individual perspective in exactly this way, it may be that her work makes use of it for the purpose of detachment. Boyers certainly reads Gordimer in this way, basing his view on quite a wide range of her output.

Boyers's principal claim is that Gordimer has 'reconceived the very idea of private experience and has created a form that can accommodate microscopic details of individual behaviour and sentiment without suggesting for a moment that individuals are cut off from the collective consciousness and political situations characteristic of their societies' (Boyers, p.122). Boyers considers the example of *The Conservationist* (1974) in which Mehring, the central character, is a sort of prototype of a not very self-conscious, affluent, white South African in his relations with blacks. As Boyers reads it, *The Conservationist* gradually elaborates a distorted self-understanding that Mehring has of himself and of the wider political situation, and this is subjected to implicit criticism. The criticism, however, like the politics it is directed at, comes filtered through Mehring's consciousness.

Gordimer's *Burger's Daughter* (1979), is another novel in which the problems of South Africa are viewed through individual lives. The Burger of the title is a white activist opposed to apartheid whose death has taken place before the action in the book. His story is told largely through the recollections of his daughter, who constantly measures her own life by his example. The activist father has relations to all sections of South African society, not only the blacks but also the Afrikaaner *volk* into which he was born. Through the memory of his daughter, Burger's history crosses the generation gap: his daughter is asked to do things by other second-generation activists who assume automatically that she will carry on her father's sort of life. Up to a point she is repudiated or criticized by black activists of her generation for belonging to a white activist community they feel is living vicariously on their suffering. In this way, again indirectly, a picture is built up of a certain sector of political division in South Africa. For a time the daughter escapes to

Europe, which provides Gordimer with a device for accentuating detachment. Boyers comments:

> A considerable portion of *Burger's Daughter* is set outside South Africa, in a comfortable European setting among persons for whom politics is an occasional topic of conversation rather than a matter of life and death. Nothing can better point up the meaning of politics than the absence of politics Rosa [the daughter] confronts in France.
>
> (*Ibid.* pp. 140–1)

Not that life in France is compared unfavourably to that of committed activists in South Africa. Through the character of the ex-wife of the dead activist the predictability and narrow vision of the white, anti-apartheid activists is brought out.

Boyers's reading of Gordimer suggests that she has devised a number of literary solutions to the problem of achieving the distance required for criticism of her society. Class position may create conditions of detachment in Dickens. And other ways of achieving detachment may be worked out by other writers. There is no need to hold that the social involvement of writers must compromise their ability to criticize society.

17　Social involvement and the obligation of restraint

Even if the artist's involvement in a society does not rule out the sort of detachment required for criticizing the society, does it not impose obligations to the rest of society that conflict with artists' aims, such as the obligation not to give great offence and the obligation to obey the law even if the law restricts freedom of expression? Whether an artist or anyone else is obliged to avoid giving offence is not a clear-cut matter. Some people are easily offended. Others try to deflect fair criticism by seizing on the form in which it is delivered and side-stepping its substance. In short, there are cases where to take offence is unreasonable or where creating offence is not an overriding consideration against doing something. If the thinly-disguised original of a character in a work of fiction feels subjected to a libel because the novel or story places his character in questionable circumstances after having given a virtual biography of the real person, then this may be a case where taking offence is reasonable. But if, without launching an attack on anyone in particular, a TV play puts in a bad light a certain type of person – some representative of the 'enterprise culture', say, or some militant left-wing local councillor, to take two clichéd figures from the Britain of the 1980s

– then, while many viewers may be offended at what they take to be extreme political bias in the images being conjured up, it is not therefore clear that the play should not have presented either figure in that light. Of course, much depends on the details, but I hope it will be clear that the cases are different.

Besides politics and religion, race and sex are difficult subjects for the artist to take up without being, at one extreme, inoffensive to the point of being boring, and, at the other, insulting or defamatory. The case of Joe Bob's film reviews, seen now not as the prototype of straight-faced reviews of exploitation pictures, but as a piece of satire concocted by John Bloom, is in point, since prejudice against women and racial minorities was part of the persona expressed through Joe Bob. Other cases, to do with sex and religion, have cropped up in Britain in the last twenty years. During that period at least two films, the satirical 'Life of Brian' and Martin Scorsese's 'Life of Christ' have caused offence great enough for legal proceedings to have been threatened. About ten years ago the newspaper *Gay News* was privately prosecuted for blasphemy when a poem it published suggested that while on the cross Christ had had a homosexual fantasy about a Roman centurion. More recently, blasphemy has been alleged against Salman Rushdie's *Satanic Verses*. In an earlier day, writing about sex rather than religion was more likely to generate controversy, as in the prosecution of D.H. Lawrence's *Lady Chatterley's Lover*.

The question of whether a given work of art is better classified as mere pornography or as erotic art is just as good a vehicle for the discussion of the social responsibility of the artist as a question about religion or politics, and I shall take it up in preference to the cloudier issues of minority religions, death threats from foreign powers and the status of prophets raised by *Satanic Verses*.

A recent, and philosophically sophisticated discussion of pornography, which also takes into account research about its psychological effects, and the implications of regulating it in the UK, is contained in the *Report of the Committee on Obscenity and Film Censorship (1979)*, written under the chairmanship of Bernard Williams.[5] The 'Williams Report' does not quite broach the question of whether an artist breaks a moral or social obligation by producing something that causes offence, but it does go into the related matters of whether offence caused by sexually explicit material amounts to a harm, and whether, if it does, it is the sort of harm that justifies a legal prohibition of pornography. It also considers the question of whether pornographic material can have artistic merit, and whether there is a difference between the pornographic and the erotic. The question I shall consider is related to that about offence and harm. When sexually explicit material goes beyond the point where it causes nuisance and becomes either deeply offensive or harmful, does it justify the judgement that the artist should not have produced it, or that it should be taken out of public view?

In pursuing this question it is reasonable to start by accepting the explication of the term 'pornography' given in the 'Williams Report', as well as an observation from the Report about the aesthetic merit of most of the pornography actually sold or in circulation. The term 'pornography', according to Williams,

> always refers to a book, verse, painting, photograph, film... We take it that, as almost everyone understands the term, a pornographic representation is one that combined two features: it has a certain function or intention, to arouse its audience sexually, and also a certain content, explicit representations of sexual material (organs, postures, activity, etc.) A work has to have both this function and this content to be a piece of pornography.

> (Williams, 1981, p.103)

On this understanding of what is meant by 'pornography', and taking seriously the Committee's knowledge of what the typical piece of pornography is like, it seems uncontroversial to accept the claim that 'almost all the pornography sold across (or under) the counter, or seen in the cinema, is from any artistic point of view totally worthless' (*ibid.* p.105). This claim – about the lack of artistic merit of the typical piece of pornography – has to do with what constitutes the

> definite *genre* of pornographic work, which consists almost exclusively of pornographic representation of sexual activity, often complex. There is no plot, no characters, no motivation except relating to sexual activity, and only a shadowy background, which may involve a standard apparatus of a remote and luxurious *château*, numerous silent servants, and so forth.

> (*Ibid.* p.104)

It is because the film or book is, as a rule, entirely empty of plot, character, etc. that its claim to be art or to have artistic merit, if indeed it puts forward any such claim, is negligible.

Typical pornography must, of course, be distinguished from books and films which, while predominately pornographic, are not exclusively so, as well as books and films which, though they have pornographic content, are not predominately works of pornography. Finally, and at the most respectable end of the spectrum, room must be made for works where sexually explicit and titillating material is part and parcel of a work that is accomplished in all those areas of plotting, character development and so on that most pornography does not bother with. It is to this category that *Lady Chatterley's Lover* might belong, for example. Only the non-typical pornographic work, the kind to be found at the *Lady Chatterley* end of the spectrum, allows one a basis for asking seriously whether pornography can be art, or whether, when a work of pornography or a work with pornographic parts causes offence, that takes away from the moral standing of an artist.[6]

Confining ourselves, then, to the cases where there are reasons for classifying the film, novel, or painting as a work of art, would the fact that it offended on account of its sexual content show by itself that something morally wrong had been done in producing the film, novel, etc.? As already said, there is such a thing as unreasonable offence, and so the fact that some activity causes feelings of distaste or indignation is not always morally significant. In the case of the representation of sex for the purposes of sexual arousal, however, there are several reasons why it might be thought that taking offence was always reasonable.

Some of the reasons are given in the 'Williams Report'. To begin with, pornography

> crosses the line between private and public since it makes available in the form, for instance, of a photograph, some sexual act of a private kind and makes it available for voyeuristic interest: since it is itself a public thing, a picture book or a film show, it represents already the projection into the public of the private world – private, that is to say, to its participants – of sexual activity.
>
> (*Ibid.* p.97)

A further reason for considering even the pornographic content of a genuine work of art offensive, is that it can be, and is perhaps legitimately experienced as, foisted or forced on a viewer or reader who neither wants nor expects it (*ibid.*). Again, pornographic material often 'encourages a view of women as subservient, and as properly the object of, or even desirous of, sexual subjugation or attack' (*ibid.* p.58). If these are ways in which pornographic material can reasonably offend people, even offend them deeply, is there any sense in which the artistic quality of the material can redeem it or compensate for the offence? Or, alternatively, if the producer of the work is a bona fide artist, someone, let us say, the rest of whose work unquestionably qualifies him for the title, is there something in his role of artist that exempts him from blame? If by describing sex explicitly he trespasses onto what is private and should not be made public, is he immune from the blame that would attach to a mere voyeur because it is his business as an artist to 'explore' sexuality and question or break down divides like that between private and public?

To take the question of redemption by artistic quality first, it seems to me that the answer can be 'Yes'. The BBC production of Dennis Potter's play *The Singing Detective* is perhaps a case in point. An explicit sex scene in the play, which represents the protaganist's childhood memory of discovering his mother with her lover, is repeatedly shown in flashback. There are other sex scenes, but none as explicit as this one. *The Singing Detective* as a whole cannot reasonably be regarded as pornographic, but there is some reason to think that this scene counts as pornographic content within a non-pornographic work. I say that there is only 'some reason' to think this, because we are using the term 'pornography' to cover not only explicit sexual material, but material intended to arouse people sexually, and it is not clear that this is the purpose of the scene in Potter's play. Even if the scene *is* pornographic in this sense, however, it does seem to be redeemed by the insight it gives into the protagonist's unsuccessful marriage, his feelings for his father, who suffered the effects of the mother's infidelity, and his own fears (justified as it turns out) of a betrayal that is partly sexual.

There are other cases in which artistic quality does not so much 'redeem' content that is arguably pornographic as give a purchase on the work other than by way of the sex it depicts, that is, by way of the technique of the artist. The 'Williams Report' gives the example of Indian erotic sculpture and 'many pornographic Japanese prints of the eighteenth century, works of the admired artist Utamaro and others, which are regarded by artists as brilliant achievements' (*ibid.* p.106). These works may come into the interesting category in the 'Williams Report' of 'pornographic works of merit that cannot reasonably be regarded as offensive' or they may come into the category of those pornographic works whose initially offensive effects give way to aesthetic appreciation (*ibid.* p.107).

18   Pornography and harm to women

Pornography is sometimes described in such a way that it includes everything from the titillating, glossy, widely-distributed magazine to films and videos catering to those with a taste for rape and other extremes of violence. Can so broad a definition, which probably covers *The Singing Detective* just as much as material with no aesthetic value whatever, be used justifiably in legislation that restricts the sale and importation of pornography? Or must distinctions be made between an arguably tolerable 'soft' pornography and a less tolerable or straight-forwardly *intolerable* 'hard' pornography? There are campaigners who argue that these distinctions are not relevant, on the ground that the whole spectrum of pornography encourages violence against women, including rape. Recently this view received some official support in the UK when the chairman of the Broadcasting Standards Council, set up under 1990 legislation, commented on the need to ban television broad-casts of pornographic movies. 'Pornography', he said, 'is basically rapists' television.'

The question of whether pornography, soft *or* hard, encourages violence, was examined in detail in chapter 6 of the 'Williams Report', which took seriously the possibility that soft pornography might be more sexually arousing, and therefore more dangerous, than anatomi-cally more detailed hard pornography. After a careful review of many different kinds of evidence, however, the report concluded that there was at best a weak case for believing that pornography had been a stimulus to acts of sexual violence in England and Wales in the 1960s and 70s (*ibid.* p.80). An important shortcoming of even the most systematic investigations that the committee considered was that there was no reliable measure of the amount of pornography available in the period studied. On the other hand, periods during which the investiga-tions assumed that pornography was increasing in availability did not coincide very well with periods in which the rate of recorded rape and sexual assault was increasing. The rate of increase in rape and sexual assault seemed to have increased rapidly *before* pornography was supposed to have become widely available. What is more, the rate of increase in rape and sexual assault was apparently slower than the rate of increase in crime generally. The Report admitted, however, that reported rape and assault may only be a fraction of the rape and assault that actually takes place.

Is there an argument for restricting or banning pornography if its effects on women fall short of bodily violence? For example, would a ban or severe restriction be justified on the ground that pornography debases women by treating them as sex objects? As before, much depends on how broadly pornography is defined – whether it is to include 'pin-ups' and *Playboy*, and, differently, *The Singing Detective* – in addition to hard pornography. The issue is complicated if, as even some campaigners against pornography are prepared to concede, there is a distinction between pornography and sexually explicit material that is intended to arouse, but in which men and women are depicted as equals and there is no hint of violence. According to some views, material of this latter kind comes into the category of acceptable 'erotica' rather than pornography. A related distinction sometimes made in this area is between pornography that caters for problems of male sexuality and pornography that acknowledges the pleasure it is possible for women to take in pornography. There can be no doubt that a great deal, perhaps the vast bulk, of pornographic material, does depict the domination of women and does confine the role of women to that of gratifying male lust, sometimes with an improbable enthusiasm. All of this is so, and it provides a compelling reason for restricting most of what is actually produced. But it leaves entirely open the question of whether pornography must mistreat women, as well as the question of how feminists should regard erotic literature produced by female writers (see Chester, 1987).

19   Offence and aesthetic purpose

Let us turn from objections to pornography based on its effect on women and consider another issue. When explicit sex is used both to arouse the reader and fulfil an independently intelligible artistic purpose, such as to convey the intensity of a romantic relationship between two characters, or to convey how a class or racial division could be bridged or some taboo could be broken, does this purpose mitigate any offence caused or even give a kind of immunity to moral criticism if it was sincerely attempted to solve an aesthetic problem?

It seems doubtful that immunity to moral criticism *is* conferred by having the role of artist, even if the artist has only aesthetic motives for producing something that causes offence. In a recent British case, a London art gallery owner was prosecuted for exhibiting a sculpture in which freeze-dried human foetuses were incorporated into earrings. The gallery owner had a reputation for promoting *avant garde* but serious work, and the artist appeared to be sincere in holding that the use he made of the foetuses had a purely aesthetic motivation. Neither the gallery owner nor the artist appear to have intended the offence they caused to the few who saw the sculpture and the many more who heard or read its description. Nevertheless, the offence was real, and not felt only by those who were squeamish or particularly vociferous as anti-abortion campaigners. This seems to be a case in which the offence was reasonable, and even predictable, though it was not intended, and though it was brought about by people who may not have foreseen it.

It might be thought that though the offence in the case just described was real, the importance of upholding the freedom of expression is overriding. So while the offence sometimes caused in the exercise of the freedom of expression is not wiped out by the value of freedom of expression, it might be thought to be overwhelmingly counterbalanced by it. But if the value of free expression is that weighty, it is worth asking what makes it so. Four factors are sometimes mentioned as a general justification, not all of them equally relevant to pornography. I follow the formulation given by the American Norman Dorsen, who begins with the point that 'free speech permits the fulfilment of individuals by presenting their views (and therefore themselves) without legal restraint' (Dorsen, in Gostin, 1986, p.124). Dorsen comments that 'this is a goal of the highest order' and even quotes approvingly a US Supreme Court Judge who claims that the ultimate purpose of the state is to make citizens free to develop their faculties. The second and third grounds for the exercise of free expression are drawn from the nature of democracy. If the many are to rule instead of the few, then public debate may be necessary for wise legislation, and freedom of expression necessary for useful public debate (*ibid.*). Free expression may also afford a means of hindering those in government in the excessive use of power (*ibid.*). Finally, and fourthly, 'free expression helps to advance knowledge and reveal truth'. In explaining this ground for free expression Dorsen speaks of the tendency of adversarial public debate to weed out false opinion.

Even if these grounds for a right of free expression are seen as sound, only the first comfortably fits freedom of artistic expression. The second and third do not. For while it is true that a political novel or poem or film, perhaps even a political painting, may contribute to public debate in a democracy or even introduce a point of view that is not given weight by an autocratic government, not all works of art can be expected to do these things, and those that do may even be untypical. So the political grounds for free expression do not seem to be grounds for artistic expression in general. The same can be said of the fourth ground. Debate and criticism can, perhaps, weed out falsehood in some areas, but it is unclear that art typically contributes to debate and criticism with this effect. On the other hand, art can plausibly be said to be an activity that contributes to personal fulfilment, and personal fulfilment is valuable. It is not, however, necessarily valuable enough to uphold even where it involves giving deep offence to others. It only seems to be if freedom of expression is allowed to range over everything from freedom of speech in political debate to freedom to put scientific hypotheses to the test.

Bibliography

Barrell, J. (1986) *The Political Theory of Painting from Reynolds to Hazlitt*, Yale University Press.
Bataille, G. (1985 edn) *Literature and Evil*, Marion Boyers.
Bloom, J. (1986) 'American Chronicles: The Life and Times of Joe Bob Briggs, so far', *New Yorker*, 22 December.
Bloom, J. (1989) *Joe Bob goes to the Drive-In*, Penguin Books.
Boyers, R. (1985) *Atrocity and Amnesia: the Political Novel since 1945*, Oxford University Press.
Chester, L. (ed.) (1987) *Deep Down: New Sensual Writing by Women*, Faber.
Cooper-Clark, D. (1986) *Interviews with Contemporary Novelists*, Macmillan.
Dorsen, N., 'Is there a Right to Stop Offensive Speech...', in Gostin, 1986, pp. 122–350.
Eagleton, T. (1976) *Criticism and Ideology*, Verso.
Feinberg, J. (1985) *Offense to Others*, Oxford University Press.
Gordimer, N. (1983) Interview in the *London Magazine*, February, pp. 74–88; reprinted in Cooper-Clark, 1986.
Gostin, L. (ed.) (1986) *Civil Liberties in Conflict*, Routledge.
Moravcsik, J. and Temko, P. (eds) (1982) *Plato and Beauty, Wisdom and the Arts*, Rowman and Allanheld.
Nehamas, A., 'Plato on Poetry and Imitation in *Republic* 10', in Moravcsik and Temko, 1982, pp. 47–88.
O'Connor, F., 'The Nature and Aim of Fiction', in Fitzgerald, S. and Fitzgerald, R. (eds) (1972) *Mystery and Manners*, Faber.
Plato (1968 edn) *The Republic*, H.D.P. Lee (trans.), Penguin Books; references are to the Stephanus numbering.
Sharpe, R.A. (1988) 'Culture and its Discontents', *The British Journal of Aesthetics*.
Taylor, R. (1978) *Art, an Enemy of The People*, Harvester.
Tolstoy, L. (1930 edn) *What is Art? and Essays on Art*, A. Maude (trans.), Oxford University Press.
Urmson, J.O. 'Plato and the Poets', in Moravcsik and Temko, 1982.
Wilde, O. (1891) *Intentions*, Methuen.
Williams, B. (1981) *Obscenity and Film Censorship*, Cambridge University Press.
Williams, R. (1977) *Marxism and Literature*, Oxford University Press.
Wolff, J. (1982) 'Aesthetic Judgement and Sociological Analysis', *Aspects*, no. 21.

Notes

[1] J.O. Urmson, in 'Plato and the Poets', writes: 'In the *Iliad* Homer's first request to the Muse was that she would tell him what caused Achilles and Agamemnon to quarrel, and throughout the *Iliad* he continues to ask the Muses... for factual information: "For you are goddesses, and are present, and know all things, but we have only hearsay and know nothing" ' (*Iliad*, Book II, ll. 484–5) (Urmson, p.126).

[2] In one of the essays in *Literature and Evil*, George Bataille (1985 edn) suggests that through the character of Heathcliffe, who exercises such an attraction on a sympathetic heroine, and who may himself represent a kind of emancipation from 'all prejudice of an ethical or social order', Emily Brontë's *Wuthering Heights* is an example of successful serious art concerning evil.

[3] R.A. Sharpe has called my attention to the related but distinct case where an artistic production, such as a work of cinema, has to be coded to get by the censor, and decoded by the audience.

[4] Marx and Engels, 'The English Middle Class' quoted in Williams, 1977.

[5] I use the abridgement prepared by Williams (Williams, 1981). Page references are to this volume unless otherwise indicated.

[6] Though there are those, such as George Steiner, who think that even 'high-porn' is a perversion of literature. For a summary of his and the other main views on the relation of pornography to literature, as well as useful discussion, see Feinberg, 1985, pp. 129ff.

PART FOUR ART AND VALUE

The Evaluation of Art

Colin Lyas

Musée des Beaux Arts
About suffering they were never wrong,
The Old Masters: how well they understood
Its human position; how it takes place
While someone else is eating or opening a window or just walking
                                        dully along;
How, when the aged are reverently, passionately waiting
For the miraculous birth, there always must be
Children who did not specially want it to happen, skating
On a pond at the edge of the wood:
They never forgot
That even the dreadful martyrdom must run its course
Anyhow in a corner, some untidy spot
Where the dogs go on with their doggy life and the torturer's horse
Scratches its innocent behind on a tree.

In Brueghel's *Icarus*, for instance: how everything turns away
Quite leisurely from the disaster; the ploughman may
Have heard the splash, the forsaken cry,
But for him it was not an important failure; the sun shone
As it had to on the white legs disappearing into the green
Water; and the expensive delicate ship that must have seen
Something amazing, a boy falling out of the sky,
Had somewhere to get to and sailed calmly on.

                                    (Auden, 1968, p.28)

Introduction

In *On Art and the Mind* Richard Wollheim writes:

> The third painting that I want to consider is one of Rothko's canvases
> from the Four Seasons series, now hanging in the Tate; to my mind one
> of the sublimest creations of our time... The greatness of Rothko's
> painting lies ultimately, I am quite sure in its expressive quality, and if
> we wanted to characterise this quality – it would be a crude charac-
> terisation – we would talk of a form of suffering and sorrow, and
> somehow barely or fragilely contained. We would talk perhaps of

some sentiment akin to that expressed in Shakespeare's *Tempest* – I don't mean, expressed in any one character, but in the play itself.

(Wollheim, 1973, p.128)

To read such a declaration is to be immediately reminded that works of art are objects of value to us, in the sense, at least, that we queue to see them, spend money on them, invest our time in seeing, reading or listening to them. All of this indicates that we place a value on them. This raises two immediate questions, which constitute, in part, the subject of this section. The first is, 'what are the features for which we value art?' The second is this: Wollheim expresses a belief about Rothko's painting, and the question arises, 'can such beliefs be supported by reasons for believing them true?' For if they can, then criticism would be a rational enterprise, in the sense that one could demonstrate the truth of one's claims. If they cannot, then we seem to be left with the possibility that such expressions of belief are no more than the expression of our personal likes and dislikes, or, as some put it, a 'subjective' matter.

The first of these questions, it has to be noted, raises a cluster of other questions, many of which are dealt with in other essays in this book. Thus, to begin with, not all of the reasons for which we might put a value on a work of art are obviously relevant to its value *as* art. I may buy a picture in order to cover a damp patch on the wall or play a Beethoven symphony in the car to conceal the rattle from the engine, but these reasons for choosing the painting or the symphony do not seem to be reasons for valuing them as art. More interestingly, perhaps, and this is a matter addressed by Sorell in Essay Seven, in his discussions of Plato and Sim in his discussions of Marx in Essay Eleven, we may like or dislike a work because we do or do not assent to its moral or political stance: but then the question arises whether to attend to the moral or political content of a work is to attend to it as art, a question which Oscar Wilde and Clive Bell answered firmly in the negative (see, for example, Bell, 1915).

I do not wish prematurely to close off the results of discussions of these questions in the other essays. To avoid questions about the relevance of this or that way of evaluating art I shall, therefore, try to take as examples of the value features that we apply to art, only features that are, if anything are, features for which we unquestionably do value art. If others – for example, the political and moral features of works of art – turn out also to be relevant to art, then the account that I give of our evaluation of art will apply to a wider set of features than those upon which I concentrate in this section. I shall, in addition, ask questions about the relevance of one hotly debated way of talking about art, a way that involves reference to the creator of a work of art.

But there is a deeper problem than this. For to ask what the features are in terms of which we value art is to assume that the whole activity of taking an interest in the value of art makes sense. That activity, however, is in two ways a problem. For, first, it can be argued, as discussed in Essay Seven, that the activity of ascribing value to a work may be a front under which the prejudices of a middle-class, white bourgeoisie are imposed upon a wider population in a form of cultural imperialism. That argument is not, however, the most sceptical one about evaluation. For even if it is true that the canons of a certain class are no good guide to important value features of art, it is still possible that there should exist other, better candidates and that evaluation should survive as an activity in a less prejudiced state. The more radical problem about evaluation, as is well demonstrated by Sim in Essay Ten, is raised in continental aesthetics, where the question is posed as to whether evaluation has any place in criticism at all. I shall make some comments about that matter at the end of this section, when we have some clearer view of what the evaluation of art involves. For we will then be in a position to understand better what the attempt to undermine this activity involves.

1 How problems about evaluation arise

In the Introduction to this essay I raised the question whether value claims made by commentators on works of art could be justified. This, I have pointed out, is secondary to the question whether or not the demand for justifications and proofs in criticism is ultimately intelligible. Putting that aside for the moment let us begin by noting that the demand for justifications and proofs in criticism – among those who believe in the intelligibility of that activity – is likely to arise in two situations. First, having read what Wollheim has to say about Rothko, one might then look at the painting and fail to see anything of the sort. All one sees, perhaps, is two patches of colour on a background of another colour. In that situation one is likely to be sceptical as to whether the picture has the qualities that Wollheim attributes to it, and then one is likely to ask for a proof or demonstration that it does indeed have those qualities. But the demand for proof procedures may arise in a second way, which may be illustrated by two responses to a concert which included a performance of Webern's *Six Orchestral Pieces*. Writing in *The Times* (17 December 1983), Bernard Levin castigated this music, referring to it with derision as 'plinks and plonks' and 'horrible sounds'. Writing in the *Sunday Times* (18 December 1983), the music critic Nicholas Kenyon referred to the music as one of the 'miracles of modernity'. Here there is a disagreement between informed critics, and the temptation is to suppose that unless one critic can be proved to be right and the other wrong all the two critics can be doing is expressing their own personal likes and dislikes. Without a procedure that will settle such disagreements, criticism seems to be an entirely subjective matter.

Such a conclusion is likely to have far-reaching consequences. Governments are often asked to give money to the arts. Now if the arts are merely a matter of personal preferences, it might seem that a government ought, given that resources are not endless, to give money to what pleases most people: and this is unlikely to be grand opera, symphony concerts or demanding fiction, these being, it is said, minority interests. Unless we can show that there is a way of supporting the claim that this work is better, more important, than that work, we seem to have no way of supporting claims that certain kinds of human activities are more deserving of support than others. When, however, we turn to theorists for some answers to questions about the nature and rationality of critical evaluation we find surprisingly few. Some, indeed, seem almost to denigrate the question. Thus one of the most important recent aestheticians concludes a highly-praised work by writing:

> It will be observed that in this essay next to nothing has been said about... the evaluation of art, and its logical character. This omission is deliberate.[1]

(Wollheim, 1980, p.153)

We can, however, find important approaches to the question of the rationality of criticism, one in the work of the influential aesthetician, Monroe Beardsley and one in the work of an equally influential writer, Frank Sibley (see also Savile, 1982 and Mothersill, 1984). Before I turn to them I shall make some prefatory remarks about criticism and reasoning.

It is often thought that if criticism is to be a rational enterprise, then critics have to be able to give reasons (that is, statements that their readers believe or can be brought to believe) which make it reasonable to believe in the truth of their assertions about a picture, sculpture, poem, novel, play, concerto, and so forth. Those who want criticism to be a reasonable enterprise may want it to be possible to support judgements of the kind that Wollheim gives by deductive arguments or by inductive arguments.[3] In the first case they want it to be possible to give the reader or hearer statements which, if accepted, entail deductively the truth of a judgement about a work of art. And if that were possible, a commentator could prove the truth of her or his judgement. Failing that, they want it to be the case that the reader or hearer can be given statements which, if true, make it probable (and thus reasonable to believe) that a particular judgement about a work of art is true. I shall consider how this is applied by theorists, beginning with Monroe Beardsley, who in his book *Aesthetics* appears to be looking for deductive reasons for judgements about the merits of art, that is to say, for statements which, if true, logically entail the truth of such judgements about art. If that were the case, then we could reason so that people accept our judgements by getting them to accept statements that entailed those judgements and from which those judgements deductively or logically followed.

2 Beardsley's account of evaluation

That Beardsley is looking for a deductive account is suggested by the way he looks for statements that can be offered as reasons for judgements that can be called 'safe' (Beardsley, 1962 and 1963). To accept such statements is to be forced to accept that a work has something good about it. That conclusion then follows logically from the statements. Beardsley, however, encounters an immediate difficulty which can be explained by saying that a genuinely deductive reason ought to be *general*. If sharpness is a reason for thinking a knife good, it must be a reason for thinking that any knife that has sharpness is good for that reason. Similarly, if honesty is a reason for praise, that is because honesty always makes the person who has it a better person. It would be absurd if the sharpness which made this knife good as a knife were the very thing that made that knife bad as a knife, or if the honesty which contributed to the goodness of this person as a human being contributed to the badness of that person as a human being. Similarly, if answering the mathematics paper correctly is to be a reason for giving one student high marks, it has to be a reason for giving any student who has given the right answers high marks.

Beardsley's problem, now, is that if reasons have to be general, then there appear to be no such things as genuine reasons that can be offered in support of judgements made of works of art. For the kinds of reasons we give for saying that a particular work is good seem not to have the required kind of generality. Take, for example, humour. It is tempting to think that one might say, 'The humour contributed to the goodness of this work', and thus to make the presence of humour a reason for thinking there is something good about the work that contains it. Unfortunately the very humour that makes one work better may make another worse. The kind of humour that occurs in the porter scene in *Macbeth*, immediately after the death of Duncan, is held, controversially perhaps, to mar that play. Again the humour of the sub-plot of the film *The Accidental Tourist* (director: Lawrence Kasdan, 1988) might be thought too farcical to be appropriate to its delicately wry main plot. In addition, balance seems to count both ways: one who made Klee's *Tightrope-walker* (Plate 5) more balanced by straightening up the skewed white band that runs from top to bottom, would ruin the picture by making it more balanced. But if the possession of a quality is to be a reason for thinking one thing good, then, so it is alleged, it must be a reason for thinking anything that possesses that quality is also good; and this, we have seen, is said not to be the case with respect to the qualities in terms of which we praise works of art. Hence, there seems to be no such thing as reason-giving in aesthetics. Hampshire, indeed, links this conclusion to the fact that each work of art is original and unique (Hampshire, 1954). If each is unique, could we bring them all under general rules for determining merit and demerit?

Beardsley attempts to deal with this matter by distinguishing levels of judgement. On the first level he claims that there are three general or basic criteria of merit in art: unity, complexity and intensity. These are indeed, he thinks, general reasons that deductively support the claim that the work has merit. Thus, to accept the claim that a work is unified or complex or intense is to accept that there is something good about it, and we can therefore prove the claim that the work has something good about it by getting our hearer or reader to agree that it is unified, etc. Other statements like 'it is humorous' or 'it is graceful' are 'risky' (Beardsley, 1963, p.297): one might concede that the work has the property in question without conceding that it is good. However, if we can link these 'risky' judgements to the basic criteria, if we can show, for example, that the humour contributes to unity, then it can be cited in support of the judgement that the work is good.

Beardsley's analysis is in two parts. There is the part that argues that certain judgements – for example, the claim that the work has humour or grace – are not general because they can equally support the claim that there is something right or the claim that there is something wrong about the work. I return to this claim later in my discussion of Sibley's views. Then there is the part that argues that certain statements, for example, the statement that the work is unified, always support judgements of merit. These are therefore genuinely general reasons which deductively support judgements about works of art; and that looks mistaken.

Consider, first, that almost anything, whether or not art, can have unity. So until we know what 'aesthetic' unity is, we are no further on with our understanding of art. Second, works intended to be art can have a unity that is not aesthetic unity. To use Sibley's example, a bad novel may be unified in that it consistently, though woodenly, preaches a coherent political doctrine. But it may have no aesthetic worth. Unity is not, then, unqualifiedly an aesthetic criterion. Thus an assertion that unity is present cannot provide the kind of statement that would deductively entail that the work is good. Indeed some kinds of unity, the unity of a pale pastel colour for example, might lead as well to the judgement that the work is insipid and banal as to the judgement that it is unified in some sense that makes the work good. Thus, even the judgement that the work is unified seems to be able to go both ways, and thus seems not to be a general reason. Further, although we can think of cases in which a work might have unity, complexity and intensity and be good, we can also think of cases in which there is intensity, complexity and unity and also badness. An object might be complex in the variety of ugly features that it has: furthermore, these ugly features might all reinforce an overall impression (a unity) of ugliness; and the result might be something intensely ugly. I conclude, therefore, that Beardsley has not found statements that we can make about a work of art that logically entail judgements of merit. His unity, complexity and intensity are not general (irreversible) reasons of the kind for which he is looking.

3   Sibley's account of aesthetic evaluation

The account of aesthetic evaluation that follows is derived from the writings of Frank Sibley (see Bibliography). In what follows I set out the elements of his views. I shall make a start on them by looking at some of the things that are said about works of art. These fall into various groups, and I begin by looking at three groups of remarks. Understanding the relations between these groups helps one to understand the questions about rationality, objectivity and subjectivity that I have been raising.

Consider, first, remarks such as the following: 'there is an alliteration in line three', 'the first movement is in C major', 'there is a patch of red colour in the bottom left hand corner'. Following Sibley, we may call such remarks 'non-aesthetic'. No special power of discrimination is required to make such comments, indeed, if we sought to say things about a work on which we are all likely to agree, these are the sorts of things we would be likely to say.

Second, there are remarks such as, 'the lines are graceful', 'the colours are delicate', 'the composition is balanced', 'the face expresses sorrow', 'the poem is witty', 'the music is jolly'. We will call these, following Sibley, 'aesthetic judgements'. In making these judgements we do appear to exercise powers of taste and discrimination. To make such judgements we have to do more than note the mere colours, sounds and words of a work.

Third, there are remarks such as, 'the novel is a brilliant *tour de force*', 'the play is worthless', 'the music is magnificent', 'this is a superb painting'. Here we pass what we may call an 'overall verdict' on the work before us.

These groups of remarks appear to be related. A critic might say, 'what gives the picture its balance is the patch of red in the lower left hand corner'. In Klee's *Tightrope-walker* (Plate 5), what gives the pictures its vertiginous quality is the fact that the white band running from top to bottom is (like the tightrope-walker's pole), not at right angles to the frame of the picture. Again, in Wordsworth's poem 'Lines composed above Tintern Abbey', what gives the lines, 'In which the heavy and the weary weight, /Of all this unintelligible world', their heavy quality is the way in which, for example, the stresses fall in immediate succession on the words 'weary' and 'weight', thus re-doubling their force. In these cases a non-aesthetic remark, 'has a line that is not at right angles to the picture frame', 'has successive stresses on the words "weary" and "weight"', 'has a red patch in the lower left corner' is linked to an aesthetic judgement that a work is balanced or vertiginous, or that a line has a weary, heavy quality.

Similarly, an aesthetic judgement may be linked to an overall verdict. One might say, 'what makes it such a good painting is the balance of the composition, the delicacy of the colours, the expressive-ness of the face'. The overall verdict 'it is a very good painting' is supported by remarks about the aesthetic qualities to be found in it.[2] The support, it is worth remarking, however, tends to be *ex post facto*. We first arrive at a judgement and tend only to support it if called on to do so, or if curiosity intervenes.

We seem then to have aesthetic judgements supported by reference to non-aesthetic judgements, and verdicts supported, in their turn, by aesthetic judgements. When the kind of support that is involved here is understood we will be in a position to deal with the problems that have been raised about rationality and subjectivity.

The second element in Sibley's account is the claim that discrimination and judgement in the arts is a matter of perception. In order to appreciate the grace of a painting we have to see that grace. In order to appreciate the expressiveness of a piece of music we have to perceive that expressiveness. If we are to appreciate the emotional quality of the death of Cordelia in *King Lear*, we have to perceive that it has that quality. Not only do we have to see, feel, hear the qualities of a work of art in order to appreciate it, but these are precisely the capacities that we want to acquire when we set out to become more discriminating about the arts. It is not enough for us to read Wollheim and so come to believe on good authority that Rothko's picture has a sublime expressiveness. We want to see and feel that expressiveness for ourselves. The aesthetic judgements that I referred to above are, then, a species of perceptual judgement.

Scepticism about aesthetic reasoning

I said earlier (pp. 351–3) that those who are interested in aesthetic judgements (and that includes all of us who pay attention to what is said about art whether it be said about heavy-metal rock music or the sonatas of Beethoven) are often interested in whether those judgements can be supported by reasons. Given the truth of the things I have outlined from Sibley's work we can say now say the following.

If, in seeking an ability to discriminate aesthetically, we are seeking to see, hear and feel, then it is difficult to see how proof or demonstration by inductive or deductive reasoning can be any part of what we want from criticism. What we want is to *see* for ourselves, and reasons have no place in helping us to reach our perceptual goal. The explanation is a simple one. We can have reasons for opening our eyes to look at something, for going to see it, for looking in its direction. But, given that our eyes are open and looking in the right direction, we can have no reasons for *seeing* something. The question 'Why are you looking at the rain?' makes sense. I can justify doing that. But I cannot in the same way justify my seeing the rain, if I am looking at it. That being so it would seem that all the critic can do is help us to see something that she or he has seen by directing our attention in certain directions by procedures to which we shall come shortly (pp. 365–6 below). These procedures can indeed direct my attention to what I may, in consequence of that direction, see. But I doubt that these procedures should be called 'reasoning' in the senses in which we normally use that term. For the critic cannot *reason* me into *seeing* that something has a certain property by giving me propositions from which it follows that I will see that it has.

LYAS

The critic can, as we shall see, reason me into *believing that* a thing has a certain property by giving me reasons: but I do not want merely to believe *that* a painting, say, has a certain property. I want to *see* that property for myself. Wordsworth was right in the Preface to *The Lyrical Ballads* to express scepticism about the possibility of *reasoning* his readers into approbation of those poems.

Sibley makes an important claim about the relation between what I called 'aesthetic' and what I called 'non-aesthetic' judgements that supports this scepticism about the relevance of reasons to criticism. From the non-aesthetic descriptions of a work, its colours, shapes, alliterations, and the like, we can never *deduce* an aesthetic description (Sibley, 1959). I might see that the vertical white band in Klee's painting is not parallel to the sides of the painting without being able to deduce that the painting therefore has a vertiginous quality. And if I can see a red patch in a certain position in a painting, I cannot deduce merely from that fact that the painting is balanced, even if it is the position of that red patch that makes the picture balanced. Both the discriminating and the non-discriminating can see that the Wordsworth line that I quoted has a certain pattern of stresses. But if the undiscriminating cannot perceive that this pattern is responsible for the heavy feel of the lines, they are hardly likely to be able to deduce this from the stress pattern. Now, if I cannot deduce the aesthetic from the non-aesthetic, citing the presence of the latter can scarcely count as a reason for believing the former to be present.

I have, then, expressed some scepticism about whether, granted that our aesthetic judgements are perceptual, critics can support them with reasons. Why, then, do critics say such things as 'what makes this picture balanced is the position of this patch of colour'? For in such cases they do appear to be supporting their judgements by reasons. To explain what may be happening here, we may now introduce another component of Sibley's account: the distinction between two uses of the term 'reason'.

Sometimes, to give a reason is to give a justification for a belief or an action. We can, for example, say 'My reason for believing that I am mortal (Z) is that I am a human being (X) and all human beings are mortal (Y)'. Here X and Y are reasons that justify my belief that Z because X and Y entail Z. We have seen that such reasons are not readily available to the critic, granted that we want the critic to help us to *see* the qualities of a work.

The term 'reason' is, however, used in another sense. Here to give a reason is not to give a justification but to give an explanation. We may say 'The reason it is cold today (X) is the presence of an area of low

358

pressure over Scotland (*Y*)'. This explains the coldness, but in no intelligible sense constitutes a justification for it.

Sibley suggests that when a critic says 'the reason why it is balanced is the presence of the red patch in the bottom left hand corner', he or she is *explaining* the source of the balance by saying what is responsible for the presence of that quality. That explanation can be tested by imagining the patch in a different place and seeing whether the picture remains balanced. But although the critic is giving an explanation of why the picture is balanced, she or he is not giving a justification for the belief that it is balanced. To be a justification, the citation of the presence of the red patch in a certain position would have to give the hearer a reason for concluding that the picture is balanced. But merely to be told that there is a certain colour patch in a certain position in a picture allows us to conclude nothing about whether it is balanced or not. To know that we have to look and see. When we have seen that the picture is balanced we may well be able to explain that a certain patch of colour in a certain position is responsible for the presence of that quality. But the presence of a patch of colour in a certain position can never justify the claim that a work has a certain aesthetic quality.

4 What criticism can be

We are now in a position to come to a preliminary understanding of the possibilities for criticism. We may consider two directions, so to speak, in which the critic might attempt to go. First, the critic might start with a neutral, descriptive account of the non-aesthetic features of a work of art. One might count stresses, alliterations, metaphors, harmonies, changes in tempo, transitions of key. One might describe the position of colour areas and so forth. There is sure to be fairly general agreement about the truth and falsity of such descriptions. I do not deny the utility of this: we have to see what is there. Since the effect of the work depends on its words, colours, sounds and their combinations, anything we miss here may lead us to miss what depends on these combinations. But then the critic, having given this 'objective' description might seek to *deduce* from them conclusions about the value features of the work. *If* what I have taken from Sibley is correct, then there is no way in which this can be done. No non-aesthetic description can ever entail conclusions about the presence of aesthetic qualities in the work. Those qualities have to be seen for themselves.

There is an historical point to be made here. In the early years of this century advances in the physical sciences led to the belief that criticism should be reformed along scientific lines. This meant that stress was to be laid on the publicly observable and measurable. Only so could criticism be objective. Under the influence of this idea the Russian Formalists (see Ehrlich, 1981) attempted to carry out such a programme. They would count the distinctive patterns of words, sounds and combinations of sounds and words of a text. But having done so, it was quite unclear what light this threw on our understanding of the literary work as an object of *value*. For, in the light of what I have said, there is no way of deducing conclusions about value from neutral descriptions of the components of a work. Trotsky was, to my mind, rightly scathing about the whole procedure.

> Having counted the adjectives, and weighed the lines, and measured the rhythms, a Formalist either stops silent with the expression of a man who does not know what to do with himself, or throws out an unexpected generalization which contains five per cent of Formalism and ninety-five per cent of the most uncritical intuition.
>
> (Trotsky, 1960, p.172)

There seems little future in beginning with a description of what is supposedly public and objective about a work and them attempting to *deduce* conclusions about its value qualities from that description. That direction for criticism is ruled out. The alternative is to move in the other direction. One first attempts to grasp the value qualities of a work by careful reading, looking and listening. I shall say more about how we can be helped in this task at a later stage. Having grasped these value features one may then explain how they depend on details of the written, visual or audible work. The task of the critic on this account is to help us to see, hear, feel, the value features of the work. Having done so there remains the task of showing how these value features depend on the fine details of the texture of the work of art; how, for example, *this* word, or *that* colour patch, or *that* chord is essential to the overall effect. Consider the following lines:

But now secure the painted vessel glides,
The sunbeams trembling on the floating tides;
While melting music steals upon the sky,
And softened sounds along the waters die:
Smooth flow the waves, the zephyrs gently play,
Belinda smiled, and all the world was gay.

(Alexander Pope, 'Rape of the Lock')

Something of the effect of the lines is easily grasped: a summer's day on the river, full of light, a scene one could have imagined an impressionist wishing to depict. The critic's task is to help us to grasp this effect. But having grasped that effect it is possible to explain how it is produced by the sounds, the meanings of the words and the rhythms of the work (in this work the vowel sounds will be especially important to that effect). My point is that one starts with the attempt to grasp those effects of the poem which make it seem valuable to us and only then does one try to trace these back to textures of the work upon which they depend. But that grasping is a matter of coming to see for oneself, perhaps with the help of others, something that is there to be perceived. It is not something that we can be reasoned into. That, as I have argued, follows from the fact that it is a *perceptual* experience that we are after.

We can now explain a certain kind of problem experienced by many who are novices in criticism, for example, students of English who are asked to write a criticism of a poem. It is common in their answers to find remarks to the effect that the rhyme scheme is so and so, that there are alliterations in certain places, that onomatopoeia is to be found, that there is an ambiguity in such and such a line. But the student then has the greatest of difficulty in linking this to any coherent characterization of the quality of the poem. The reason is that the student has started from the wrong end. The place to start is with the attempt to grasp such things as the expressive quality of the poem: Is it mawkish, glib, ironic, witty, sad? If sad, is the quality of the expression of the sadness, for example, too excessive or too commonplace? Having done that it is possible then to ask how the rhyme scheme, the stress pattern, the vowel sounds, the alliterations contribute to the achievement of that effect. I fear that novitiate criticism is inadequate because, under the influence of a model of science as the only avenue to truth, with the consequent flight from judgement into calculation and quantification, people shrink from encouraging students to talk about value and quality of expression. This is all written off as a subjective matter. 'How do you mark this stuff?' a professor of Chemistry asked of a creative writing course with which I was involved – as if *he* had an algorithm which allowed him mechanically to establish who were the imaginative and creative experimenters among his students. And so bad philosophy impoverishes the capacity of human beings to perceive the value-qualities of works and so deprives them of sources of joy. In consequence they are reduced to mumbling about the publicly observable aspects of a work with no idea how these relate to the value of that with which they are confronted, and no idea, even, wherein that value may reside.

5   Overall judgements

So far I have tried to establish that when critics say such things as 'this picture is balanced because of the position of the red patch in the lower left-hand corner' they are not giving a proof or justification but rather an explanation. What should we say, though, when a critic offers the presence of aesthetic features in support of an overall verdict – as when the critic says, 'The reasons it is such a good novel are the grace of the writing, the wit of the dialogue, the unity of the plot and the exactness of the characterization'?

One problem here is the wish that reasoning be *general*. What counts for merit in one work must count for it in another. But since an aesthetic feature, such as humour, may be cited as the reason for the merit of one work and a reason for the demerit of another, there is no such generality in aesthetic reasoning.

Merit and neutral terms

It may be conceded that what Sibley calls 'non-aesthetic features' can never be the kinds of general reasons for ascribing merit and demerit for which some are looking. The same red patch in the same position that makes for balance in one picture may be the very thing that makes another picture unbalanced. Hence the absurdity of searching for infallible rules for producing balanced compositions. Where we are making a non-aesthetic judgement there is no oddity in saying that the same feature that contributes to the excellence of one work contributes to the poverty of another. Non-aesthetic judgements can, without oddity, be held to count either way. They are, so to speak 'neutral' as to merit and demerit judgements (see Sibley, in Fisher, 1983). But not all judgements made about works of art function in this neutral way. Having said, 'It's the red patch in that corner that makes it so good', I can, without oddity, say of another picture, 'It's the red patch in the corner that makes it so bad'. But I cannot with the same lack of oddity say 'What makes it bad is its wit, or its grace, or its intelligence'. If I say the wit makes it bad I cannot just leave it at that, as I might if I were to say 'it's the red patch that spoils it'. A *special explanation* is needed. This is because wit, for example, *is* generally thought to make that which has it better. It is a *good-making* feature. (Beardsley, so Sibley argues, errs because he runs together the true claim that judgements like 'it has red patch in the left hand corner' which can go either way without oddity, with the false claim that judgements like 'has a humorous scene in act 2' can go either way, and so cannot be used to give general reasons for overall verdicts (*ibid.*).)

Why is it, then, if humour is generally a good-making feature, that some could think that it is the humour of the 'porter scene' that spoils *Macbeth*? Here we need to introduce the notion of a *prima facie* merit or demerit. There are some properties that can count for (or against) the merit of the thing that possesses them. But in certain circumstances that positive or negative charge, so to speak, can be nullified. (Think of courage, which we think of as a good thing, but which may make the damage done by a bad person even worse.) Hence wit, humour, grace and so forth will always be assumed to count for the merit of a thing unless some special reason is given why in a particular case they do not. Hence, to say something is witty and to leave it at that will be assumed to have said something favourable about it. Wit is a merit term. In this it contrasts with a judgement like 'has an alliteration in line three'. We just don't know from this, taken in itself, whether it is meant to count for or against a judgement of merit.

Wit, then, and many other qualities, *are* generally taken to be merit qualities. Does it then follow that criticism can be a rational (reason giving, proving) activity? It might seem so. I earlier characterized reasoning as giving a statement from which the truth of another statement logically followed. And can't we suppose that I might say that from the fact that a work is witty, graceful, or intelligent, it follows logically that it is good, or has something good about it? For such things as wit, grace and intelligence are good-making qualities. This is not so.

Consider, first, that wit is only *prima facie* a merit. It is not enough for us to know that wit, say, is generally a merit in order to be able to conclude that a work which actually has it is therefore good. We have to see that wit actually is a merit in that work. This requires a judgement which cannot be replaced by any mechanical sort of proof procedure. We have to ask such questions as, 'Is the wit out of place? Does it clash with other features of the work, as the "porter scene" in *Macbeth* is sometimes alleged to do?'

Some, including Sibley, have pointed out that merits fall into two classes. Some are 'additive'. The merits that make for a good knife (strong handle, rustproof, sharp, etc.) are additive. If a knife has those qualities it is a better knife than if it didn't, and the more such qualities it has the better the knife it is. So, too, I suspect with the qualities which make for intelligence.

But some merits, notably those we cite in art and morality, are not additive but 'interactive'. It isn't just a matter of adding them up, where more means better. Intensity, grace, wit, deep expressiveness, are all merits of art but these merits can pull in opposite ways in the same work.

Wit may clash with intensity in a play just as beautifully delicate colours may not go well with dynamic lines in a picture. We have to *see* how the merits go together. This again requires judgement, taste, discrimination. It cannot be reduced to any sort of guaranteed proof procedure. So even though wit can be *prima facie* a reason for thinking that the work which has it is good, there is still no possibility of giving cast-iron proofs or demonstrations of our judgements of works of art. In the sense sought by Beardsley and which he attempts to capture in his 'general canons', no overall judgement can be absolutely safe in the sense that it is entailed by the statement that a work is, say, unified, complex or intense. In the end perception and judgement are ineliminable.

6   Conclusion

I began by saying that there is sometimes divergence in our judgements of art. We fail to see in a picture, say, what a writer claims is there. Again, two apparently well-qualified critics may offer incompatible judgements. In such situations it is tempting to ask the critic to prove to us that what she or he says is true; and this amounts to asking the critic to give us statements (reasons) which would entail in some way the truth of his or her claims. It now seems that this cannot be done. If the critic makes an aesthetic judgement ('the picture is balanced', say), there is no way this can be deduced from any set of non-aesthetic statements that we all might agree to be true of the work. Nor is it obvious that any reason that would convince us that we ought to believe what the critic says would satisfy us (e.g. 'All competent critics say it is witty, so probably it is'). This gives us some reason for believing that the work is witty, but will leave us dissatisfied. We want to see the things which the critic claims to have seen, and, so I have argued, it is in the nature of perception that we cannot be reasoned into that (see pp. 357–8). What we want from art we cannot be reasoned into.

Nor are matters any different when we come to critical verdicts, that is, to overall judgements of the work. To be sure, the claims that a work is witty, graceful, elegant, sensitive, unified in composition and the like, establish a presumption that it is good. But again we need an exercise of judgement, which we cannot be reasoned into deductively, in order to test whether that presumption holds. In short, if it is asked whether criticism is a rational enterprise, where that means 'Can we deduce the aesthetic from the non-aesthetic?', the answer is 'No'. And if it is asked, 'Can we deduce overall verdicts from claims that a work has properties such as wit, grace and the like?' the answer is a limited 'Yes'. For such properties are *prima facie* merits. The 'yes' is limited, however, by two considerations. First, if we know that a work has certain *prima facie* merits, we have a basis on which to make a judgement of overall goodness and badness. But there is no way of reasoning us into seeing that a work has wit, grace and the like. The primary source of the knowledge that a work has such properties comes from experience of it, not from reasoning about it (though I can have second-hand evidence for this based on the reports of others; reports that may motivate me to study the work myself). Second, even when we know that the work has the *prima facie* merits, there is no way of deducing that it is therefore good. We still have to make the judgement that the merits hang together in the right way. That, again, is a matter of experiencing the work and involves the exercise of judgement rather than the exercise of deductive reasoning. Indeed, there are cases where the wit may be so out of place that it makes a work bad, and then wit ceases altogether to be a good-making feature, so that even though the work has wit, there may be nothing good about it.

It has always been claimed that art cannot be mechanically created, that there are no hard and fast rules for producing good art. (If there were, we might all become good artists.) Nor, it has often been said, are there hard and fast rules that we can learn what will infallibly guide us to right discriminations. My remarks in the foregoing justify those claims by establishing some truths about what might be called the 'logic' of art appreciation.

7 Critics and criticism

I began this essay by raising the question whether critics could give proofs for their assertions about the value features of works of art. Those who think that critics must be able to do this if criticism is to be a well-founded enterprise think that what critics do must be analogous to what mathematicians or scientists do. The critic offers an assertion, a conclusion, and then secures our belief in that conclusion by offering arguments, that is by offering other statements, which if accepted give us reasons for accepting, reasons for *believing that* conclusion. In contrast to that model of what criticism must be I have offered the idea of art appreciation and evaluation as involving *perception* of certain features of works of art, rather than *belief that* those works have those features. And since we cannot reason people into perceiving things, it followed that it is not reasons that we want from writing about art.

What we do want is help in seeing, hearing, feeling for ourselves what others claim to see, feel and hear in works. The helpful writer is one who helps us to do that by awakening and directing our perception. This is not done by arguments that lead from premises to conclusion. Those arguments may be in order when it is a matter of securing belief, but they are inappropriate when the task is to bring about a kind of perception. This is not to say that writers about art have no ways of helping us: it is only to say that they do not help us by demonstrative proof of beliefs. The ways are those appropriate to helping people to see. They include the following (see Sibley, 1959 and Hermeren, 1988): first, some non-aesthetic feature hitherto unnoticed, may be pointed out. Since the value features of, say, a painting, depend on its colours, tones, forms, etc., if some aspects of these are missed, then some value features arising from their presence may also be missed. Thus we may fail to see why Pieter Bruegel's picture *The Fall of Icarus* is humorous and thought-provoking (Colour Plate 4). Indeed a viewer might wonder why it is called *The Fall of Icarus* at all, since no dramatic plunge by a man with melting waxen wings is to be seen. Then, someone points out the small splash in the sea, and this may help bring home the force of the painting. Second, we may just point out the features that we want others to see. 'Notice the irony', we may say, 'in the fact that Hamlet spares his murderous uncle, on the grounds that, since he is praying, he may undeservedly go to heaven, at the very moment when his uncle is finding it impossible sincerely to seek repentance'. Third, we may link non-aesthetic and aesthetic remarks: 'Look how the corners of the mouth are not defined in the *Mona Lisa*. Don't they give the face an enigmatic and mysterious expression?' Fourth, we may use similes and metaphors: of Mondrian's *Broadway Boogie-Woogie* we might say 'It is like the frenetic movement of jazz music'. Fifth, we use contrasts and comparisons: 'Suppose the whip were pointing the other way in Stubbs's *The Duke of Richmond's Horses at Exercise*, wouldn't the unity of the composition be lost?' Or we may say, 'Doesn't it remind you a bit of Dickens?' Sixth, we use bodily movements. I was singing in a *Messiah* once and the conductor showed me the quality he saw in a passage of the music by a swooping movement of the hand. And I might do this before a picture in order to help someone to see some quality I have noticed in the work to which that gesture seems appropriate. All these are ways of helping someone to perceive what we see, hear or feel about a work of art. They are not guaranteed to succeed, but then neither is argument. But since what we are after is perception, these are the methods we have to use. In the end they amount to ways of drawing people's attention to something that is to be perceived.

8   The shortcomings of induction

In the foregoing I have argued that critical comments of the kind I quoted from Wollheim are not provable by deduction. If that is what people want when they ask that criticism be rational, then what is sought is not to be had. However, there are two sorts of procedures that go by the name of reasoning: deduction and induction.[3] So, it might be asked, even if criticism cannot be deductive, can it at least be inductive?

Though I believe that we cannot deduce statements about the presence of aesthetic qualities from statements about the presence of non-aesthetic qualities, I do not wish to deny that we can use induction. That this is a picture by Rembrandt might constitute a good reason for believing that it is a masterpiece and for looking at it more carefully than at some other paintings. Again, I might argue that most of the balanced pictures I have seen have had a patch of colour in a certain position (hardly a likely possibility). And then I might claim that since this new picture has such a patch in such a position, it, too, is probably balanced.

This, however, will not do. For, first, although an inductive argument might gives me a reason for *believing that* a work of art has a certain property, it does not give me what I want, namely the rewards attendant on *perceiving that* it has. Second, the kinds of induction that I have cited rest on the claim that, to take my example, most pictures that we have seen that have been balanced have had a colour patch in a certain position. But how was that claim established? It can only have been established by, first, *directly* seeing the balance in the picture and then later correlating the presence of balance with the existence of a colour patch in a certain position. But if it is possible to see balance directly, why then does not the critic help us to see that rather than engaging in a dubious form of inductive reasoning designed only to give us second-hand beliefs about qualities of works of art, qualities we would dearly love directly to see?

There is an important corollary of what I have said. There have been efforts in the history of aesthetics to find some non-aesthetic feature of a work (usually a measurable one) which is an infallible index that the work has value. And if there were such a feature critics could indeed prove their claims that a work has value merely by engaging in measurement. Indeed, any one with a good ruler could be a competent critic. One such feature was the Golden Section. If we draw a line and then strike a line at right angles to it, it will be found that we nearly all divide the line at the same place. The ratio of *AB* to *BC* in the diagram below (Figure 1) is the same as the ratio of *BC* to the length *ABC* of the whole line. This ratio is indeed pervasive in nature, for example in the distribution of

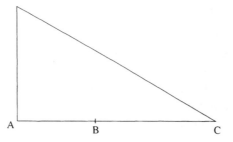

Fig.1   The Golden Section

seeds in a sunflower head, and some have argued that this ratio underlies all pictures which we find valuable, so that to find this ratio in a picture entitles us to conclude that the picture which contains it will be a good one. This, as Croce, for example, pointed out, is useless (Croce, 1953, chap.14). For, first, even if every good picture somehow exhibits this ratio, this would at most allow us to conclude, once we have detected that ratio, that the picture has value. But it will not do anything to help us see that value, and that, I have argued is what we most want to be able to do. We want to see the value features, and not merely believe that a work has them. Second, the claim that all pictures in which we can find the Golden Section exhibited are good seems dubious. We just cannot rule out by *fiat* the possibility that a work might exhibit the Golden Section and be bad or not conform to it and be good. And that leads to a third comment. How is the claim to be tested that there is an unfailing correlation between the fact that a work exhibits the Golden Section and the fact that a work has merit? Presumably we take a work and see if it has merit: then we look and see if it exhibits the Golden Section: or alternatively we find the Golden Section in the work and then look to see if that work has merit. But then two things have to be said. First, that test procedure concedes the possibility that we might find the Golden Section in a work and then discover that the work is not good; or, alternatively, that we might find that a work is good and then not find any evidence of the Golden Section in it. But if either is possible, then there is no *necessary* connection between the possession of the Golden Section and merit. For the test procedure concedes that the correlation might break down. How else could it be a test procedure? Second, the test procedure envisages us seeing that a work is good directly and *then* looking to see if the Golden Section is exhibited in it. But if we can see directly that works have merits, we do not need to have recourse to potentially unreliable claims about the connection between the presence of the Golden Section and the presence of merit features in order to arrive at second-hand *beliefs* about the presence of those merits.

9 Objectivity and subjectivity

We are now in a position to say something about an earlier question (see pp. 351–2), the question of the objectivity and subjectivity of aesthetic appreciation. That question arose because of a feeling that critics make variant judgements of a work of art, so that unless there were some way of deciding between those judgements, everything would be a matter of mere personal preference.

I want, first, to make a point entailed by what I have said earlier. Some have thought that unless critics could prove their judgements by giving reasons, then criticism would be a subjective matter. I have said that such proofs are not central to criticism. Some will conclude from this that criticism is not a rational, objective matter. This does not follow. All that follows is that if criticism is an objective matter, its objectivity cannot depend on the kinds of proofs that I have ruled out as not central to criticism. To establish that because proofs are not central to criticism, criticism is therefore a subjective matter, one would have to establish that proof by argument is the only way of establishing the truth of one's claims. This, as we shall see, is by no means obvious. For example, the truth of the claim that the traffic light is green seems rather to be established by observation than by argument. The fact that I cannot argue people into seeing that it is green does not establish that it is not green, nor that I have no rationally defensible way of getting people to see that it is (for example, by directing their gaze in a certain direction). Now, I am inclined to say a statement about something is an objective statement about that thing if there is some way of establishing that it is true or false of that thing that it is as the statement says it is. But it is a mistake to think that the only available way of establishing such things is by argumentative proof. Observation might do as well. Hence the unavailability of such proofs in criticism shows nothing as yet about the impossibility of objectivity in criticism. Nor does it establish that criticism is irrational. The statement that a traffic light is green is not one that can be conclusively demonstrated by deductive proof to someone who cannot see that it is that colour. It does not follow from this that we speak irrationally every time we say that a traffic light is green.

The second point I wish to make, before I come to the main body of my comments on the matter of the objectivity of criticism, is this. Even if in our comments on art we are giving voice to our own responses, it does not follow that any comment is as good as any other. It is compatible with the view that critics are articulating their own responses to the work that we can distinguish between good and bad criticism. This conclusion was argued by Hume in his essay 'Of the Standard of Taste'. There Hume claims that certain factors may disqualify a judgement as inadequate. There are, that is, and as Hume puts it, 'certain general principles of approbation or blame'. Thus we discount judgements when we suspect a defect in a physical organ: the judgements of the colour-blind about pictures or the tone deaf about music have a lesser claim on us than those made by people with normal vision and hearing. Again, there are such things as experience and practice. Those with them establish a claim on our attention. The judgements of those who are widely experienced in reading poetry can have a weight lacking in the judgements of those who have read only a few verses. Yet again, works of art are complex things which deserve long and detailed scrutiny. Hence we tend to discount judgements which are based on a hasty perusal. Similarly, we suspect judgements where we suspect prejudice. These cases ought to be sufficient to convince us that even if we are reporting our personal responses when talking about works of art, not anything goes. There can be good and bad criticism, even if critics are reporting on their own experiences of art.

But the main comments I wish to make on the matter of subjectivity and objectivity are a consequence of the argument that I have given earlier, and which I derived from certain observations of Frank Sibley, that aesthetic discrimination is to be thought of as perceptual (see pp. 357–8 above). From this it follows that one way to show that aesthetic judgement is subjective would be to show that perceptual judgements are subjective.

10   Perceptual judgements and aesthetic judgements

This raises the larger philosophical issue as to whether all perceptual judgements are subjective. Discussion of this issue would take me well beyond the scope of this essay, although, to the extent that it is not here resolved, my present argument is not wholly complete and securely founded.

I adopt, instead, a different strategy. I begin by noting that in our everyday discourse we accept that our perceptual judgements sometimes report on how the world is, rather than on how we feel or react to the world. Thus, the courts believe that statements about the colours of traffic lights can be objective. For they believe that a claim by a motorist that a light was red or green can be true or false of that light: it was either red or it was green, and that is a matter that is not determined on the mere say-so of any passing motorist. Our everyday presumption is that perceptual judgements do report, subject to the testable possibilities of error, how things are, and, to that extent, are to be thought of as objective. Given that there is this presumption, we can at least ask whether our aesthetic perceptual judgements have the objectivity that, in our non-philosophical moments, we attribute to our other perceptual judgements.

Suppose that Sibley is right to claim that aesthetic judgement is a perceptual matter. In the light of what I have just said one cannot deduce from the mere fact that such discrimination, and the critical judgements that follow its exercise, is perceptual and that it is therefore subjective; i.e. where this means that such judgements tell us only about the feelings of the judger rather than about how the world is. We need an argument for that conclusion. What are the possibilities of argument here?

The only alternative, short of a radical attack on the possibility of there being objectivity in perceptual judgements, is to argue that although our ordinary non-aesthetic perceptual judgements about such things as colour are objective, our aesthetic judgements are not. But one who argues this has to show that there are differences between our ordinary perceptual judgements and our aesthetic judgements and that these differences are sufficient to show that the latter are, whereas the former are not, subjective.

One line of approach is to argue that we are in large part agreed in our colour judgements. On the other hand there is massive disagreement about our aesthetic judgements. This degree of disagreement is taken as an index of the greater subjectivity of our aesthetic judgements.

This line of approach is seriously flawed. For, first, it is not clear that there is massive disagreement in aesthetic judgements. When haste, ignorance, prejudice, inexperience and the like are discounted what is striking is the amount of agreement there is about what is good and great in art. Where there is disagreement it is sometimes patchy. Two people may agree on the greatness of Mozart, Beethoven and Shakespeare but disagree over Mahler. Even here the way this is put is significant: one is likely to say 'I cannot see what you see in Mahler'. The language used here suggests that there may be something to be seen, but that one is *blind* towards it. And this blindness may be overcome by further experience and discussion, just as one may come to see that one saw too much in a work of art for reasons which have to do with one's own personal circumstances or lack of taste. Again, where there is disagreement it is often about contemporary or near contemporary art. The history of appreciation is full of cases of raging debates about what was once *avant-garde*: Beethoven, T.S. Eliot, Ibsen, Matisse, Beckett,

Stravinsky have all been the subject of fierce controversy. But again it is easy to overstate the disagreement. After a period of time, the status of the disputed art is gradually settled and its position and merit more clearly seen. It as if these new works temporarily dazzled us and therefore upset our powers to make accurate discriminations. But once the eye and ear became accustomed to the new art, its status ceased to be a subject of such fierce controversy.

It is, then, possible to overstate the amount of disagreement when seeking to show that aesthetic judgement is less objective than our ordinary perceptual judgements. Even if it were not, however, the mere fact of disagreement shows nothing. This is for two reasons. First, when there is disagreement in aesthetic matters we should be as much interested in the quality of the disagreement as in its quantity. As Hume pointed out, we have to ask whether all the parties involved are equally competent. The fact that an ignoramus about literature, or insensitive reader after a casual reading, comes to a different opinion about James Joyce's *Ulysses* from a careful and experienced reader, shows nothing that supports a case for subjectivity: no more than the fact that a colour-blind man makes a different claim about the traffic lights from a fully-sighted man shows anything about the subjectivity of colour perception.

A more important point is this: questions about majorities and minorities have no bearing, in themselves, on the question whether or not a matter is subjective or objective. It is possible to imagine that only a few of us have a full range of perceptual abilities with respect to colour, but we might nonetheless be right when we said that a light was green rather than red. It is possible for the majority to be colour blind without this making an objective colour language impossible. This, after all, is the situation at present with respect to wine-tasting. Those who, by blind testing, can make discriminations accurately between various wines are in minority. But we do not deny that they have the capacity to discern real differences. Similarly it is possible that those capable of discriminating accurately between the various works of Rembrandt, not all of which need be equally good, are in a minority. This does not of itself count against the belief that they are capable of noticing real distinctions.

11   Colour language and conditions for objectivity

In the light of the foregoing comments some, notably Sibley, have adopted the following procedure. They claim that we should ask, first, on what is the presumed objectivity of our colour language based? What conditions does such a use of language by human beings have to meet if it is to lay claim to objectivity? Then we should ask whether those conditions are also met by the language that we use of works of art (see Sibley, 1968).

One thing is clear. The objective colour language that we ordinarily believe that we have, did not come to us because we proved to ourselves that things were coloured and then devised a language for talking about their properties. How, if we could not see that things were coloured, would we ever have had the idea that they might be?

Our colour language rests upon a set of physical abilities and upon there being some point in our marking an aspect of our world that we notice when our eyes are turned to it. That language developed over time. During its development we developed our present understanding that changes in colour due to changes in light, illness, eye defects and so forth were only apparent changes of colour. And so we gradually developed our present understanding of the conditions under which it made sense to say that things were coloured. Since what we are dealing with is a language, and since a language is an intersubjective means of communication, the colour language rests in the end on a kind of agreement in judgement. Moreover it is linked to the group who in their performances make the maximum range of discriminations (Hume, *Essays*). (This is why the colour blind, even if a majority, are not the reference group against which the truth of colour judgements is tested.) The colour language that we possess, and which, we take it, is used to describe features of things, rests in the end on an agreement in judgements among those who are able visually to make certain sorts of distinctions and upon nothing more – and in particular not upon argumentative proofs that things are coloured.

If we put the matter this way we might be tempted to argue thus and by analogy. (This is, indeed, the central thrust of the kind of argument offered by Sibley, 1968.) At a certain stage of their development human beings started to respond in certain ways to certain of the objects, both natural and manmade, about them. They said of these things that they were graceful, witty, elegant, garish, expressive and so forth. And with that awareness developed the language of talking about these things. As that language developed, so it would be noticed that different people made different judgements. But it was also thought that those differences could often be put down to things like haste, impairment of organs, prejudice and the like. And as the language developed, so judgements made by those who were hasty, impaired and prejudiced were discounted as irrelevant to questions whether things really had certain features. At a certain point it was possible to say that an objective aesthetic language had emerged. Grace, elegance, wit, no less than redness, were thought to refer to properties of things. People agreed in their attribution and believed that right and wrong were possible with respect to those attributions. (We correct a child who, having had a deer pointed out to it as graceful applies the same term to one that is halt and lame.) Where there were disagreements we had explanations – haste, impairment of organ and so forth. So, it is arguable that there is an analogy between the development of our colour language and the development of our aesthetic language, and that the conditions which make it possible for the one to function as a way of making true and false statements about things make it possible for the other so to function.

There are, to be sure, differences between the colour language and the aesthetic language. First, though judgements made in both these uses of language share sources of impairment (haste, carelessness and impairment of organs), aesthetic judgements have an additional source of impairment; for aesthetic judgements, unlike colour judgements, often require considerable experience, intelligence and maturity if they are to be accurate. Children can see redness as well as adults, but small children are less likely to see the meritorious or demeritorious qualities of *Ulysses* than adults. The requisite experience is simply not there. Second, colours are not dependent qualities. When I see that something is red, there is nothing else I have to see in order to see that it is red. But in order to be able to see that a line is graceful, I have first to see a curved line. Often, then, with aesthetic qualities, we need to have seen something on which the aesthetic quality depends. This opens up a further explanation of divergent judgements beyond those that we have for colour judgements. For if someone does not see that upon which the aesthetic property depends, then she or he will not see the aesthetic judgement that depends on it. One who has not seen the small splash in *The Fall of Icarus* cannot see the wit emergent from it.

I have, then, suggested that we do ordinarily treat the use of colour terms as objective, in the sense that they report on how things are. I have suggested that their objectivity is founded upon an agreement in judgement among those who use these terms. I then suggested that our use of aesthetic terms was analogous to that, and that in consequence not only do they function as a language in which we can report on what our eyes and ears tell us, but that there is as much a case for saying that they are objective as there is for saying that our colour language will be objective even though people cannot be reasoned into seeing and hearing things. The objectivity of aesthetics is the objectivity of an observational, perceptual language. Those who deny this seem to me to have an unduly limited model of what objectivity must be. They think that objectivity is to do with provability by argument. I claim that it has to do with telling people to look and see, and the critic's job is to help them see. And I would claim that I have as much right to say that Oscar Wilde's plays are in themselves witty as I have to say that a traffic light is red.

I should stress that all I have offered is a line of approach which is in the last resort based on the claim that an analogy exists between our use of colour terms, and our right to claim that the judgements that we make using them are objective, and our use of aesthetic terms. That line of approach has this in its favour: in aesthetics we use our eyes and our ears to make judgements. It is, then, not stupid to suppose that the aesthetic judgements that we make by the use of our senses should be compared for their objectivity with the colour judgements that we make by the use of our eyes. But the line of approach that I have suggested needs a great deal more work. I offer it in order to provoke the reader to thought, and to invite alertness to a possible prejudice in those who use the term 'objective' in such a way as to link that word too closely to the procedures of science and mathematics – disciplines that for perhaps too long have been the only permissible models of objective discourse.

12 Disanalogies between colour language and aesthetic language

Here I must mention some possible difficulties, which seem to me to be central to the question whether there are disanalogies between our colour language and our aesthetic language.

First let me remark that we seem to have ways, with respect to such things as colour perception and wine-tasting, of publicly testing whether those, who claim to be discriminating differences which we cannot perceive, are in fact doing so. Thus, if someone claims that the wine in this bottle tastes differently from the wine in that bottle, we can put the wines in two identically-appearing bottles, which we have secretly marked, and then swap them about in such a way as to test that it is really a difference in taste that the person making the perceptual claim is basing his or her judgement upon. But if a person claims that one picture differs from another with respect to its grace, say, we do not seem to have this alternative open to us. For since we are dealing with different pictures there will always be some difference between them in respect of their non-aesthetic properties, for example, the shape of their lines, or the positioning of their patches of colour, and this difference will be additional to any difference they may have with respect to their grace. So we can never be entirely sure that a person who claims that two objects differ with respect to grace, or any other aesthetic property, is really discriminating between them on the basis of a difference in their grace as opposed to some other discriminative difference which, as two separate aesthetic objects, they must have.

More important, perhaps, is the following fact. We feel that colour perception and our ability to discriminate between wines rests on our physical constitution. Those who can make such judgements derive their authority from the possession of what are recognized as the proper physical organs of perception and from the fact that we have the means of testing whether those organs are working properly. But the judgements we make on art require us not merely to possess certain physical organs. They are affected by our culture, race, gender, traditions, education, and individual psychologies.[4] Indeed, I think this is one of the things that led Hume to think that in the end there was an irreducible element of the subjective in them.

But now, it could be argued that since the judgements that we make are in the end a function of the culture to which we belong mediated by our individual psychologies, and since there is no external objective point from which we can judge the comparative worth of different cultures and psychologies, so our judgements of works of art are in the end relative and culture dependent. Where, then, is the source of the authority with which we proclaim this or that work *really is* moving, beautiful and funny?

And here I concede that if the demand that our judgements be objective is the demand that we find some Archimedian point outside all cultural value systems from which we can decide which value system gets it most right, then objectivity is not to be had. Nor do I wish to deny that as our cultures and individual preferences change, so our judgements change also. But equally it does not seem to me to follow from this that we are left with what amounts to the extreme subjectivist claim that in judgement anything goes. We know that the possibility of speaking at all depends in the last resort upon the fact that groups of human beings share interests, senses of what is important, funny, striking, interesting and stimulating. Within and between those groups of agreements there can be agreements that this is funny, this graceful, this elegant, this moving – agreements that may be shifting and, provisional, since they may change as we learn and live. That no more shows that we can say what we like about anything using aesthetic terms than the fact that there might be people so constituted as to make different sorts of colour discriminations from the ones that we make shows that we can say what we like, within the group of people who are constituted as we are, about the colours of things. And to say that not anything goes within a culture in the use of aesthetic and colour language is to mitigate the claims of extreme subjectivists.

13 Subjectivity and objectivity: a misleading dichotomy

I conclude with this thought: the terms 'objective' and 'subjective' are commonly thought of as exclusive alternatives. Either something is an objective matter or it is not, and if it is not it must be subjective. I am inclined to suggest that any simple dichotomy misleads so that rather than treating subjectivity and objectivity as exclusive alternatives, we should think of them rather as two poles of a spectrum. At one end we might find entirely subjective remarks. A candidate for inclusion here a remark such as 'I like strawberries'. This, it is said, makes no claim about the qualities of strawberries, but merely reports how I, a subject, respond to them.[5] At the other end of the spectrum there will be judgements which will be thought to be entirely objective: the judgement that triangles have three sides, perhaps. But for most of us, a large percentage of our judgements, including our judgements about art will be more or less objective (or subjective). My judgement of *Othello* may be objective to the extent that it avoids haste, prejudice, ignorance and the like, but my response may also be dependent on things which are part of my personal life history. The point I wish to make is that the fact that my judgement is for these latter reasons not entirely objective (since I cannot assume that we all have the same sort of psychology or cultural background) does not make it entirely subjective, whatever that means.

In the foregoing remarks I have talked (in a deliberately provocative way) about the nature of aesthetic appreciation and evaluation. I have tried to show that such appreciation is not the kind that can helpfully be supported by deductive or inductive reasons, but it is not for that reason alone obviously irrational and subjective.

14 The enterprise of critical evaluation

I wish to make good a promise made on page 351 above. There I said that the whole enterprise that I have undertaken assumes that evaluation is an integral part of criticism, an assumption, which, as Stuart Sim in Essay Ten on recent continental aesthetics makes clear, has been vigorously denied.

The question I have raised is the subject of much contemporary debate and will only be settled when some of the questions that Sim raises are answered. Here I will make two comments of my own.

First, I have argued that the attribution of value to works of art is a part of the way that human beings in fact respond to those works – a way that displays itself in such characteristic activities as choosing to spend our time and money in attending to and acquiring works of art, and in attending to and acquiring this rather than that work. Moreover, I argue that these appreciative activities are founded upon and constitute refinements of certain propensities that we have from our earliest childhood – such as the propensity to be pleased by colour, rhythm, verbal play, imitation and the like. The expression of aesthetic preferences is *deeply* rooted in our lives. Now the *fact* that an activity *is* deeply rooted in our lives is not of itself a reason for believing that that activity is beyond criticism. Religion, for example, is deeply rooted in human culture, but that has not prevented some from arguing that it should not be. Granted, though, that a form of response, such as aesthetic evaluation, *is* a deeply entrenched aspect of human existence, then two responses are possible. One response is to accept that it is deeply entrenched and then to attempt to show, as I have attempted to show in my discussion of evaluation, that this or that account of it is better than others. The other response is to argue, *not* that the enterprise of evaluation of art has hitherto been ill-conceived, and could be better reconstructed (which not only commits the theorist to the existence of the activity of evaluation but lays on that theorist the onus of saying how it might best be performed), but rather, and more radically, that the whole enterprise is indefensible. (Modern theorists, including Derrida and some Marxists often seem to me to hover uneasily between these alternatives – see Essays Seven, Ten and Eleven.) But that more radical argument takes on a heavy burden. The onus lies, on anyone who deploys it, of showing that something that we naturally do in our expressions of delight and preferences, namely evaluate art – something deeply rooted in our lives and seemingly unpernicious – is in fact wrong. (Moreover, not wrong in that it expresses a limited and inferior view of what evaluation should be, but wrong in that there is something wrong about evaluation as such.) And how is that radical argument to proceed? How do we show that something that arises naturally with and from the forms of our human life *should* be no part of that life?

One way would be to show that, although those propensities are a part of our human nature, that nature would be better without them (just as it might be argued that selfishness is innate to humankind but that human life would be better if we could eliminate it). And then the theorist becomes embroiled in problems that have haunted philosophy since the time of Aristotle: namely the problem of giving some plausible account of what counts as a good life for a human being, and the problem of showing how the activity of aesthetic evaluation goes against the realization of that good life. But then, the notion of the good state of a human being (a state which has no place for aesthetic preference) and its superiority to a more retarded state in which aesthetic evaluation still functions, reintroduces the very notions of comparative evaluation, hostility to which animated the sceptic about critical evaluation. The more radical way (and I refer here to the way in which Derrida stands within the tradition of Nietzsche) would be to claim that human beings, with their natural human propensity for evaluation, are in some sense or other an inferior step along the way to a state that surpasses the 'human-all-too-human'. For, as Nietzsche put it, in what looks to me a peculiarly old-fashioned sort of species-denigration, the 'beyond-man' that is to come as much surpasses man as man does the ape. (Here we glimpse how interesting contemporary critical theory can be, raising as it does deep and unsettling questions about the whole status of the notion of human beings.) But even if a plausible account can be given of a *progression* from the all-too-human, with its questionable attachment to judgements, that account, involving as it does, the notion of progression, seems itself to rest on those very kinds of judgements between better and worse which those who deploy the argument apparently wish to eliminate.

My second comment is that quite apart from the problem of correctly analysing it, value is a problem for contemporary theorists. This, as we have seen, is partly the result of the misconceived belief that only in a value-free, precise, quantitative science, such as physics, can objectivity and truth be found (pp. 359–61). The rest, including aesthetic judgement is messy, imprecise and subjective, and many would like to be rid of it all together. But since, as I remarked at the outset, our dealings with art are dealings with things that we attend only because we place a value on them, to get rid of value seems to be to get rid of art altogether. The problem for those who are suspicious of values because they are messy, subjective and imprecise is to give an account of art that also gives a coherent account of what it is to value art *as* art. (See Sim's account of the problems Marxists such as Eagleton have encountered in giving an account of art that makes sense of the value that we place on art, which illuminates this difficulty in an instructive way – Essay Eleven, pp. 458–9.)

Bibliography

Auden, W.H. (1968) *Selected Poems,* Faber and Faber.
Beardsley, M. (1962) 'The Generality of Critical Reasons', *Journal of Philosophy.*
Beardsley, M. (1963) 'The Discrimination of Aesthetic Enjoyment', *British Journal of Aesthetics.*
Bell, C. (1915, 2nd edn) *Art,* Chatto and Windus.
Croce, B. (1953) *Aesthetic,* Ainstie, D. (trans.), Peter Owen.
Ehrlich, V. (1981) *Russian Formalism,* Yale University Press.
Elton, W. (ed.) (1954) *Aesthetics and Language,* Blackwell.
Fisher, J. (ed.) (1983) *Essays on Aesthetics,* Temple University Press.
Hampshire, S., 'Logic and Appreciation', in Elton, 1954.
Hermeren, G. (1988) *Aesthetic Concepts,* Lund.
Hume, D. (undated) *Essays,* Ward Lock.
Mothersill, M. (1984) *Beauty Restored,* Oxford University Press.
Savile, A. (1982) *The Test of Time,* Oxford University Press.
Sibley, F. (1959) 'Aesthetic Concepts', *Philosophical Review.*
Sibley, F. (1968) 'Colours', *Proceedings of the Aristotelian Society.*
Sibley, F. (1978) 'Objectivity and Aesthetics', *Proceedings of the Aristotelian Society,* Supp. Vol.
Sibley, F., 'General Criteria in Aesthetics', in Fisher, 1983.
Trotsky, L. (1960) *Literature and Revolution,* University of Michigan Press.
Wollheim, R. (1973) *On Art and the Mind,* Allen Lane.
Wollheim, R. (1980, 2nd edn) *Art and its Objects,* Cambridge University Press.

Notes

[1] This may seem puzzling given the initial quotation (pp. 349–50 above), but see, however, the final supplementary essay to the second edition of *Art and Its Objects* (Wollheim, 1980, pp. 227–40).

[2] A fine example of this sort of writing, and one that deserves close attention, is to be found in Piper, D. (1984) 'A Painting in Words', *The Listener,* 20–27 January.

[3] Inductive reasoning can be exemplified by my acceptance of the truth of the statement that every one of a large group of swans that I have examined in a group of countries is white does not deductively prove that the next swan that I encounter will be white. But it gives me *some* (inductive) reason for believing the statement that it *probably* will be. So we have inductive or probabilistic reasoning.

[4] Some have argued that our perception of colour is culturally determined, a thesis often confused with the claim that what we notice and how we describe it is culturally determined.

[5] Incidentally, if it is thought that a subjective comment is one that lies entirely outside the realm of rational assessment, then it is not clear what is subjective. Some would say humour is a subjective matter. But if I take you to the theatre and, when the curtains open to reveal an unremarkable drawing room, you burst into hysterical laughter, I am disinclined to say, 'To each what she or he finds funny'. I want to know *why* you are laughing, that is to say your reasons for laughing: and that brings it within the scope of rational consideration.

Criticism and Interpretation

Colin Lyas

Introduction

Critics have commonly been thought to engage in at least two major activities. First, they pass judgements on the merits and demerits of works of art and, in the case of music, dance and drama, on performances. Second, they offer interpretations of works of art.

I have argued in Essay Eight that the task of judgement involves the critic in identifying the value features of works of art (and so writing about them as to draw them to the attention of others). But works of art may be valued for many different reasons, and it is not always obvious that all of these reasons are equally relevant when treating an object *as* a work of art. Until we know something about what is relevant to the interpretation and judgement of a work of art we are in no position properly to characterize the critic's activities. In this essay I make a start on this task by discussing one highly contentious issue, namely the relevance to criticism of references to the creator of a work of art, and in particular the relevance of references to the intention of the artist. I do so by constructing, and then commenting upon, one kind of argument for the irrelevance of references to artists and their intentions.

1 The relevance of references to artists and their intentions

An argument

Let us begin with what seems to be an obvious claim, namely, that the job of the critic is to talk about an entity called 'the work itself'. It is the critic's job to talk about such things as *Hamlet,* Elgar's Cello Concerto, Picasso's *Guernica* (Plate 4) and Michelangelo's *David.* It is about the value features of these works that we wish to know. To be sure, there are problems about the nature, or what is called the 'ontological status' of those objects which are called works of art (see Essay Three). For the present we can set these problems aside and begin with what ought to be an axiom of relevant criticism: the job of the critic is to talk about the work of art. If the critic deviates from this to make some other thing the focus of attention, then what is said is irrelevant to criticism, no less than it would be irrelevant for me, when asked to tell you about Morocco, to talk instead about Malta.

The almost trivial-seeming characterization of the critic's task that I have just given in fact functions as the first premise of an important argument designed to rid criticism of the need to refer to, or know anything about creators of works of art.

The second premise of this argument might seem to be equally obvious. For it is the claim that the work of art is one thing and that its creator is another, separate thing. Work and artist, we might say, are discrete entities. This claim has considerable plausibility. For there is a philosophical principle which says that two things are different if what is true of the one is different from what is true of the other. But it would appear self-evident that what can be truly said of a work of art is different from what can be truly said of its creator. It is true of Leonardo's *Mona Lisa* that it hangs on a certain wall in the Louvre, but this is not, happily, true of Leonardo. It is true of Picasso's *Acrobat on a Ball* that its colour is predominantly blue. This was not true of Picasso. It is true of Beethoven's Fifth Symphony that it can still be heard in a concert hall: this is not true of Beethoven. So, it is said, work and artist are distinct entities.

Let us put together these two premises of the argument:

(P1) The relevant critic's task is to talk about the work.

(P2) The artist is distinct from the work she or he produces.

From these two premises we can draw the following conclusion;

(C) Anything the critic says about the artist is irrelevant to the task of a critic.

It is important to see what is not denied by those who use this argument. It is not, for example, denied that an investigation of the lives of artists and the story of the creation of their works is a legitimate activity. It is not, however, *criticism* but, as Beardsley and Wimsatt say in 'The Intentional Fallacy' (in de Molina, 1976, p.6), 'literary biography'. Again we may study the economic and social conditions of the time in which the work was written in order to understand how these reacted with the individual psychology of the artist to produce the work. This, though, is literary history, the study of the genesis of the work. But, the claim is, it is one thing to study how a work that has certain merits and demerits came about, another to ascertain what merits and demerits it actually has.

A further argument

A further argument reinforces this last claim. Because works of art and artists are distinct we could imagine two directions of argument. First, starting with the work itself, we might use that work as a piece of evidence from which we might make inferences about the person who wrote it and about his or her state at the time that it was written. So, some have used Hamlet's disgust with sexuality as a basis for an inference that Shakespeare himself was disgusted with things sexual. But this, the argument goes, has nothing to do with criticism. It is to use one thing, the work, as a springboard to talk about another thing, the artist. The inference takes us away from the thing which should be the object of our attention, the work, towards another entirely separate thing, the artist; and since it is the task of the critic to talk about the work, that inference must be irrelevant to criticism, although it may be entirely legitimate if the task is biographical. Alternatively, starting with information about the artist, we might use that information in order to make inferences about features we might possibly find in the work. But then that sort of inference is in principle unnecessary (though in practice it might give us a short-cut to an understanding of the work). It is unnecessary because if the work does have a certain property, then that property must be detectable in the work itself. If it is thus detectable, then we need only study the work to find it. We don't have to rely on artists to tell us what properties are to be found in works. Indeed, even if they were around to tell us what properties are to be found in the work, we would in the end have to look at the work in order to test the truth of what is claimed. But if in the end we have to go to the work to verify the presence of certain properties in it, would it not be more efficient to go there to start with, and so avoid an unnecessary digression through the artist's biography? The upshot of this line of argument is that inferences from work to artist are irrelevant to criticism because they take us away from the study of the work to the study of some other thing. And inferences from what we know about the artist to what we can know about the work are unnecessary. If we want to know what properties the work has, we need only look at *it*. So references to the artist are either irrelevant or unnecessary.

Criticism and genetic studies

These earlier arguments are buttressed by other considerations. Thus a study of the genesis of a work of art seeks to trace the political, economic, historical and cultural pressures which, working on a particular human being with a particular psychology, produced the individual work of art. Such a study is possible and legitimate as a branch of *history*. But two things ought to be noted about these genetic studies. First, we normally undertake them because we have already, and independently of such studies recognized the merit of the text whose genesis we seek to explain. We study the genesis of, say, Wordsworth's poetry because we already know that it is great poetry. So it looks as if critical judgments of value precede and give a point to genetic studies of works of art.

The primacy of evaluational studies over genetic studies is reinforced by a further point. We can study the genesis of any human product, and doubtless for each such product a complex and interesting story will emerge, be the product the writing on the back of a cornflakes packet, Hitler's *Mein Kampf*, or *Hamlet* . But then the question arises: What makes a genetic enquiry into a work a part of the study of *art*? The answer seems to be: When the object we are studying is a work of art. But that seems to suggest that we have to have a way of identifying something as a work of art independently of any study of its genesis. To be sure, once we know that we have a work of art before us, then we can be assured that a study of its genesis is part of the study of art. How, though, are we to mark off what is art from what is not? One suggestion, made by Beardsley, is that works of art differ from other things in that they possess certain sorts of value features. But if that is so, then the primacy of critical over genetic studies has been established. For what makes the genetic study of a work a part of the study of art is the decision that that work has certain sorts of values; and what is to decide that other than the evaluational activities of the critic? Those activities are, therefore, foundational to the study of works of art. (This is certainly what happens in practice.) For until critics have done their work, we do not know whether the object whose genesis we are studying is a work of art, and, so, will not know whether our investigation into its genesis is part of the study of art.

This has profound consequences. Thus a central activity of Marxist literary studies has been the determination of the social and economic origins of works of art. Important and interesting as the results of those studies have been, they only count as literary studies because a different kind of study has established that the objects of their investigations *are* works of literature. Trotsky glimpsed this when he wrote:

> It is very true that one cannot always go by the principles of Marxism in deciding whether to reject or to accept a work of art. A work of art should, in the first place, be judged by its own law, that is, by the law of art. But Marxism alone can explain why and how a given tendency in art has originated in a given period of history; in other words, who it

was who made a demand for such an artistic form and not for another, and why.

(Trotsky, 1960, p.178)

It is compatible with what I have said that what this or that culture calls 'art' may vary. The conditions governing the use of the term 'art' are themselves social and cultural in that they reflect a common understanding that the speakers of a culture possess for the use of the term 'art'. But it is, nonetheless, one thing to ask whether an object is, according to that understanding, properly to be called 'art' and another to ask for an account of the genesis of any particular work of art.

I have cited various arguments for the exclusion from the activity of criticism of references to and knowledge of artists. Those arguments are sometimes supplemented by practical considerations. Sometimes little or nothing is known about the artist, as seems to be the case with Shakespeare. Even then, however, criticism manages to continue, from which it is concluded that knowledge of and reference to the artist cannot be essential to criticism.[1] Again, it is said, knowing something about the artist often leads us to read things into a work that are not there or otherwise to respond inadequately to it. Many are charmed, on first reading, by Auden's poem *Lullaby*, which begins 'Lay your sleeping head my love/Human on my faithless arm'. The discovery that Auden was homosexual often causes an adverse reaction. Hence the claim that it is better to exclude such biographical knowledge. Yet again it is said that artists are not the best judges of their works: they can lie, misread or misjudge the importance of what they have done. Better therefore to leave them out when their works are being evaluated.

The argument evaluated

I want now to look at the argument I constructed earlier. The argument ran:

(P1)   The relevant critic's task is to talk about the work.

(P2)   The artist is distinct from the work she or he produces. Therefore,

(C)   Anything the critic says about the artist is irrelevant to the task of a critic.

When we evaluate an argument of this sort we may ask two questions. First, is the argument valid? That is, does the conclusion follow from the premises. Second, we may ask whether the premises *are* true. For if I do not (on good grounds) accept the premises of an argument, I am not obliged to accept anything that follows from them.

It seems to me that the argument meets the first condition: its conclusion follows from its premises: it is valid. The question, therefore, becomes: are the premises true? I am not inclined to contest the first of these premises and so it follows, if I am to reject this argument, that I must find something wrong with the second.

I have said that the appeal of this second premise (P2) comes from the fact that many of the things we say about a work of art are true of it but not true of its creator. I may call Ravel's *Pavane for a Dead Infanta* sad, but it does not follow that Ravel was sad when he wrote it. Even where a work and its artist share a feature, say both are heavy, what we are referring to when we say that the work is heavy differs from what we are referring to when we say that its creator is heavy.

So, it seems, we can talk about the sadness of a work without talking about the sadness of its artist, about its colours without talking about the colours of its artist, and so forth. That, then, supports the second premise of the argument I have constructed.

The artist and the work

But, now let us take a different range of cases.

In *The Rhetoric of Fiction* Wayne Booth writes thus about *Lady Chatterley's Lover*:

> In short whatever unfairness there is in this book lies at the core of the novel... If we finish this book with a sense of embarrassment at its special pleading... it is ultimately because no literary technique can conceal from us the confused and pretentious little author who is implied in too many parts of the book.
>
> (Booth, 1961, p.81)

And F.R. Leavis writing on George Eliot's *The Mill on the Floss* says:

> But when the novelist touches on these given intensities of Maggie's inner life the vibration comes directly and simply from the novelist, precluding the presence of a maturer intelligence than Maggie's own. It is in these places that we are most likely to make with conscious critical intent the comment that in George Eliot's presentment of Maggie there is an element of self-idealisation. The criticism sharpens itself when we say that with the self-idealisation there goes an element of self-pity. George Eliot's attitude to her own immaturity as represented by Maggie is the reverse of a mature one.
>
> (Leavis, 1962, pp.54–5)

These passages draw our attention to a cluster of terms commonly used by critics. They include terms like 'pretentious', 'glib', 'facile', 'mawkish', 'immature', 'intelligent', 'sensitive', 'witty', 'perceptive' and 'discriminating'.

The propensity of critics to use these kinds of terms creates a difficulty for the second premise of the argument that I have offered for the eliminability from criticism of knowledge of and references to artists. That premise would have us believe that for any term that a critic uses we can ask the question, 'Is that term used to refer to the artist or to the work?', where it is thought that to refer to the one is not to refer to the other.

Let us then take a term like 'perceptive' and ask whether, as used by a critic, it refers to the work or to the artist. In favour of the former is the fact that the claim that the work is perceptive is justified by reference to the details of the work. But against the belief that it is the work and not the artist that is being referred to is the fact that terms like 'perceptive' are used by critics of creators of works (Leavis refers to Eliot and Booth to Lawrence). Now the fact that critics *do* talk in this way does not show that they are right to do so. But, then, those opposed to authorial reference might say how they propose to handle the kinds of comments that I have quoted.

I wish to suggest that if we were asked, 'Which are you referring to when you use the term "perceptive" – the artist (but not the work) or the work (but not the artist)?' – we have no clear reply. For, in the kinds of cases I have quoted we seem to be talking about both at once. Indeed, the best answer is that we are referring to a quality displayed by the artist in the work. The referent of the term 'perceptive' as it is used by a critic is the-artist-as-she-displays-herself-in-the-work; for though in such cases we justify our claim that the work is, say, perceptive by reference to details of that work, what we are talking about is the *artist* as she or he has immanently shown her or himself *there*. That is to say, in some cases at least, the question, 'Are you talking about the artist or the work?', admits of no clear answer. And then the claim of premise (P2) that the work is one thing and the artist another, distinct separate thing, appears to be undermined.

It is not without interest here that Wimsatt, who earlier joined with Beardsley in the attempt to eliminate reference to artists, in fact comes to a position close to the one that I have advocated. For he writes:

> What we meant... and what in effect I think we managed to say, was that the closest one could ever get to the artist's intending or meaning mind, outside his work, would still be short of his *effective* intention or

operative mind as it appears in the work itself and can be read off from the work.

(Wimsatt, in de Molina, 1976, p.36)

But is this not just my claim that sometimes we are talking about the artist as displayed in the work? And does this not count against the second premise of the argument that I have constructed, which asks us to believe that work and artist are entirely separate things? Even Wimsatt, one of the foremost proponents of the view that we should talk about the work and not the artist, is forced to concede that sometimes to talk about the properties of a work just *is* to talk about the features of the artist's mind that are displayed in it.

To summarize, then, for the second premise of the argument (P2) that we are considering to be true it *must* be true that for any and every term that the critic uses we can sensibly ask the question: 'Is that term being used to refer to the artist (in which case it is not being used to refer to the work) or to the work (in which case it is not being used to refer to the artist)?' But the terms that we are now considering seem to refer to an artist detectably present in the work. So, in using these terms the critic, though referring to the work, must also be referring to the creator of the work. In that case, given that the use of these terms is legitimate in criticism, a matter to which I return later, it follows that some kinds of critical comments about a work of art necessarily involve reference to the creator of the work and the argument I constructed against that possibility rests on a false premise and so fails. But before I examine the possible replies to what I have said I wish to clarify more precisely what I have claimed.

I do not wish to claim that when we say that a work is perceptive or witty, say, we commit ourselves to the unqualified claim that the person who wrote, painted or composed it was generally a witty or perceptive person. This goes beyond the evidence. For we can well imagine that the writer of a witty novel turns out to be a dull bore when invited to enliven a post-prandial discussion. All I wish to claim is that when we say that a work is perceptive we are committed to saying that its creator, whatever his or her general character, *there*, on *that* occasion, displayed perceptivity. And that can be said without taking any interest in the lives and loves of the artist, and without engaging in any absurdly romantic idolatry of artistic geniuses.

Further, I do not wish to say that an interest in the immanent artist must be the only kind of interest we should take in a work of art. But I do wish to claim that aspects of the artist's character and intelligence may be visible in a work, and that, consequently, we cannot have given a full account of that work if we do not include reference to those of its aspects.

Possible replies: the dramatic speaker

Various replies have been made to my suggestion that sometimes reference to a work may necessarily involve reference to its creator. I begin with an influential line of thought, first found in Beardsley and Wimsatt's article (*op. cit.*). They write:

> Even a short lyric poem is dramatic, the response of a speaker... to a situation. We ought to impute the thoughts and attitudes of the poem immediately to the dramatic *speaker*, and if to the author at all, only by an act of biographical inference.[2]

> (Beardsley and Wimsatt, in de Molina, 1976)

Here we are invited to believe that when a creator produces a work, say of literature, a fictional person is created who speaks the work. When we attribute personal qualities to the work, it is to this fictionally created speaker that they should be attributed, and not to the author. Thus Beardsley writes in *The Possibility of Criticism*:

> A poem can, of course, be used in performing an... act – it may, for example, be enclosed in a box of candy or accompanied by a letter endorsing its sentiments. But the writing of a poem, as such, is... the creation of a fictional character performing a fictional... act.

> (Beardsley, 1970, pp. 58–9)

Again, in his *Aesthetics* he writes:

> In every literary work, therefore, there is first of all an implicit *speaker* or voice: he whose words the work purports to be... The speaker is not to be identified with the author of the work... Clearly Conan Doyle's use of the word 'I' in the Sherlock Holmes stories does not give this pronoun a reference to any actual person (certainly not to himself)... Why then must we assume that when Keats or Shelley uses the pronoun he is always referring to himself.

> (Beardsley, 1958, pp. 238ff.)

The claim, then, is that when we are talking about a work of art, the personal-quality terms that we use of it refer not to the artist in the work but to a fictional person created by that artist to speak the work.

This argument is a dubious one. For if Beardsley and others who have invoked the notion of a dramatic speaker are right, then when we say that a *work* is perceptive, for example, we are saying that some *fictional* dramatic speaker of that work, be it explicit, as in first-person narratives, or implicit as in the novels of Jane Austen, is perceptive. But often this is manifestly not so. Thus the fictional dramatic speaker of the Sherlock Holmes stories, Dr John Watson, is bluff, uncomprehending and obtuse. But the stories themselves are perceptive, sensitive, intelligent and witty. In using these terms of those stories we are not, then, talking about the fictional dramatic speaker of those stories. But who else could we be talking about but the controlling intelligence who through those works presents that obtuse fictional dramatic speaker to us, and who, in so presenting it, displays qualities of intelligence and character? And who is that controlling intelligence if not the author?

We must, then, I suggest, distinguish a speaker *in* the work (Watson, for example) from the speaker *of* the work (Conan Doyle, for example) who presents the work, complete with its dramatic speaker, to us. It is true, as Beardsley says, that we cannot always identify the speaker in the work with the author of the work. But that is not to show that we cannot identify the speaker of the work with the creator of the work.

The essence of Beardley's claim (Beardsley, 1970, *ibid.*) is that to create a literary work of art is to engage in a kind of pretence or play-acting in which one invents a speaker through whom to present the work.[3] There are fascinating issues here, which have to do with questions about the relevance, if any, of sincerity in art.)

The element of truth in Beardsley's claim is that novelists, musicians and painters can pretend, in their works, to beliefs, feelings, attitudes and qualities that they do not actually have. Thus, a sensitive artist might, for financial gain, create a mawkish work. And then, Beardsley says, we can see why we should never attribute the personal qualities of a work to its creator. For the creator might merely be putting on a cunning pretence to have those qualities.

But there is a difficulty here. A creator indeed can, for example, write a work in which she or he pretends to be glib, mawkish and pretentious. But a creator can hardly write a work in which she or he pretends to be intelligent, witty and perceptive when she or he is not. Hence, when we find a work which itself has these qualities it makes no sense to assume that an artist is pretending to have these qualities, when she or he does not in fact have them. If these are qualities of the work they have to be qualities of its *creator* as displayed *there*.

There is a further problem about the attempt to ignore the controlling intelligence of the artist entirely. If we do, then we will find it hard to give an account of such central devices as irony and parody. Thus, in his *A Modest Proposal*, Swift castigates those who have produced a certain kind of destitution in Ireland. He does so by writing what could be the speech of one who proposed to cure the problems of the surplus child population of Ireland by breeding babies as a source of meat. The notion is brilliantly conceived and carried out. But the whole point would be lost if we missed the fact that *Swift*, the creator of the work, is engaging in an act of irony. We need to know that the creation of the pretence is an *actual* act of irony in which the literary creator displays *his* wit, verve and imagination to a high degree. And that knowledge requires not only a knowledge of intention but also of the artist's historical and other circumstances.

Possible replies: the irrelevance of personal quality terms

The introduction of the notion of the dramatic speaker does not, then, allow us to avoid reference to artists by critics. This brings us to a second strategy: that although to refer to the personal qualities is to talk about an artist manifested in the work, this does not make references to artists relevant to criticism. Alan Tormey, at the end of a work in which he seeks to deny that talk about works of art in any way involves reference to their creators, has to concede that 'an art work may be an expression' of its creator's attitudes, emotions and qualities of mind (Tormey, 1971, p.118). He does not, as Beardsley tried to do by introducing the notion of a dramatic speaker, try to show that a work cannot be thought of as embodying the thoughts, emotions and attitudes of its creator. But Tormey then adds, 'the sense in which art is an expression of the mind and character of the artist does not establish a relevant distinction between art and any other form of human activity'(*ibid*. p.123). Tormey is saying, therefore, that the only things to which the critic can relevantly attend in art are things which works of art do not share with things that are not art. He must, therefore, think that, if we mark works of art off from things that are not art, then works of art must have properties that things which are not art do not have. These properties will be the things that make art *art*, and, if we are interested in talking about art *as* art, these are the only properties to which we should attend. But, the argument must continue, things other than art can also, as he concedes that art does, express the actual attitudes, emotions, feelings and qualities of character of human beings. Works of art *share* this capacity with other human activities, such as sermonizing or making political speeches. But since Tormey believes critics should confine themselves to what art does *not* have in common with other human activities and products – that is to say, to things which are special to art – it is no part of the critic's task to refer to the articulation of attitudes, emotions, feelings and qualities of character in works of art, even if those works do in fact display those attitudes, emotions and beliefs of their creators.

Various things need to be said about this argument. First, it runs counter to the fact that many practising critics *do* think it relevant to talk about the articulation of the personal qualities of artists in the works of art they create. In the passage I have quoted from Leavis (p. 386, above) he says that his remarks about the immaturity displayed by George Eliot in her works are made 'with conscious critical intent'. Of course, as I said earlier, practising critics might get it wrong, but before we conclude that they do we need a good argument to that effect.

Second, Tormey's argument seems to be that the critic should attend to no features of a work of art that are also to be found in things which are not art. This would be extraordinarily sweeping. Thus works of art share certain properties, for which they are regularly praised, with natural things, for example, colour, shape, grace, elegance and dynamism. But it looks absurd to say that it would be irrelevant for a critic to talk about these features just because things which are not art also possess them. So the mere fact that things other than works of art display personal qualities is in itself no reason for believing that a critic cannot relevantly refer to those qualities.

Possible replies: doubts about persons

The third reply to my claim that sometimes we can detect in a work of art a controlling intelligence to which qualities such as, for example, pretentiousness and perceptivity can be attributed, goes much deeper than the two I have so far mentioned.

The view I have sketched talks about a mind or controlling intelligence that can be detected *in* the work and characterized by the use of a certain vocabulary. And now, by way of an introduction to the third reply to this claim, we may consider an important difference between the replies of those who work within what may loosely be called the 'anglo-american' tradition in philosophy (for example, Beardsley and Tormey) and those working in a continental European tradition (for example, Barthes, Foucault, Lévi-Strauss and Derrida). What I have to say introduces, in a preliminary way, matters that are to be more fully dealt with in Essay Ten.

Beardsley and Tormey do not query the existence of individual persons with minds and personalities. What they seek to show is that no reference need be made to a certain group of those minds and personalities, namely the minds and personalities of artists. One reason for this, upon which I have tried to cast some doubt, is the belief that we can distinguish between the mind of the artist and the work produced by that mind, it being the critic's task to talk only of the latter. In the what may be called the 'European continental tradition' we find a more radical approach, namely one which raises fundamental questions about the coherence of our traditional beliefs about persons. Lévi-Strauss writes, for example, that 'the goal of human sciences is not to constitute man but to dissolve him' (Lévi-Strauss, 1962, p.326). Foucault writes that 'man is only a recent invention, a figure not yet two centuries old, a simple fold in our knowledge, and that he will disappear as soon as that knowledge has found a new form' (Foucault, 1966, p.15) and that may be read as the suggestion that we need to think about our concept of a person.

The relevance of this line of argument to our present discussion is patent. I have argued that in talking about works of art we can talk about the persons, the men, women, human beings, who produced them. But if our traditional beliefs about persons are called into doubt, then it becomes much less clear what we are doing when, as critics, we refer to those persons we call 'artists'.

Although this matter is more fully discussed in Essay Ten I will say some preliminary things about its bearing on my earlier discussion. First, the history of much recent theory of criticism begins as a reaction to the French philosopher Descartes. Central to Descartes's philosophy was a distinction between two kinds of substances: the mental and the physical. This is a *dualistic* philosophy. The body, for example, is physical, but linked to it, in some way, is another entity, a mind, the seat of thought, feeling and personality, which is a different sort of thing from the physical body.

It is said to be a part of this view that physical things get their meaning from the activity of minds. Thus a word is a physical entity, a sound or an ink mark that can be physically described. As such it is dead and devoid of meaning. A word gets a meaning when a individual mind, a person speaking, attaches a meaning to it, or imposes a meaning on it by an act of intending that meaning for it.

That this is an incoherent view can be seen if we consider the case of Lewis Carroll's Humpty Dumpty who tried to operate in the way envisaged on the view attributed to Descartes. At one point Humpty Dumpty says to Alice 'there's glory for you'. Alice, puzzled asks what he means by 'glory'. He replies, 'by "glory" I mean "a fine knock down argument"'. Alice objects that 'glory' does not mean 'fine knock down argument'. Humpty Dumpty loftily replies, 'When I use a word it means just what I want it to mean, nothing more nor less.'

The problem is how Humpty Dumpty is ever to make his meaning clear. For he explains the word 'glory' by using the phrase 'a fine knock down argument'. But on his account *this* phrase also gets its meaning by his willing a meaning onto it. So, suppose he says, 'by "fine knock down argument" I mean "custard tart"'. But now the question repeats itself for this phrase: what is the meaning of 'custard tart'? The upshot is that if meaning is only to be given by individual acts of will, then we get into an infinite regress. Everytime a new phrase is offered as the meaning of an earlier phrase, we can ask what that new phrase means, and so on for ever. If this is Descartes's view, it follows that meaning can never be made clear.

If meaning *is* to be made clear, it will be because in explaining meaning we appeal not to private acts by means of which individuals assign meaning to their words, but to a public, interpersonal structure of understanding which, independently of the whims of individual speakers, gives meaning to *our* language. It is that public structure that gives words their meaning, not an individual speaker's intentions.

But now this argument turns into an attack on the very notion of a person as a discrete consciousness of the kind envisaged by Descartes, a consciousness which gives meaning to our world. For how will that consciousness express itself? One way will be by saying 'I...' But now how does the word 'I' get its meaning? As we have seen it cannot get its meaning by the imposition of a meaning upon it by an individual act of will. The individual cannot say 'by "I" I mean...', for how did the words, whatever they are, by which he explains *his* meaning of the term 'I', get *their* meaning? Once again a regress looms. Hence, we seem forced to conclude that even the word 'I' has the meaning that it has, not because an individual imposes a meaning on it by an act of will, but because the public rules of a language themselves give sense to the notion of a person. And from that the conclusion is sometimes drawn that the concept of a person, and so our sense of what we are as persons, is given us by the public, meaning-giving structures of the language. But those structures are open to alteration, criticism, change. (They may, for example, embody ideas that we come to find unsatisfactory, as when it is alleged that our concept of a person is too male-centred.) And from this it is said to follow that the notion of a person is not the concept of some entity, lying *behind* and giving meaning to our words, our actions and our world. It is a notion constituted by the mutable structure of public rules that give a meaning to the notion of a person. And, it is then concluded, this undermines the notion of a person as an individual consciousness responsible for the meaning of its utterances; and that, in turn, undermines the claim that we should refer to artists if we wish to understand works of art.

This striking line of thought has three implications. One, which I do not investigate here, is that deep questions are raised about the concept of a person. Some, indeed have said that persons are no more than the points at which the meaning-giving structures of our language intersect and become concretized. We do not give meaning to language, it gives meaning to us (see Culler, 1975, chapter 1).

A second implication of the argument is that we need to be suspicious of the notion of a person that is said to be found in Descartes – the notion of a person as an immaterial, private, meaning-giving entity lying somehow '*behind*' the physical body. Here I remark only that from the fact that we can do away with that unsatisfactory notion of persons, it does not as yet, follow that we can do away with the notion of a person altogether. All that follows is that what we can say about persons is determined by what our language allows us to say about them. And this is compatible with the line of approach that I have adopted in the talking of 'the-artist-in-the-work'. What we learn when we learn to use terms like 'perceptive', 'pretentious', 'witty' and the like allows us to read from texts evidence of a mind at work *in* them. This does not commit us to the view that we are inferring from the text the presence of a shadowy entity, a mind as envisaged by Descartes, lurking behind the work with the right to impose whatever meaning it likes upon it. To say that the author is present in the work is not to give the author a dictatorial control over what we may find, including what we might find out about her or him, *in* that work, by using the public, meaning-interpretative structures of our common language.

A third thing which is thought to follow from the arguments that I have been discussing is the irrelevance of knowledge of, and reference to, the author in settling questions about the meaning of a work of art, including its verbal meaning. I now turn to the more detailed discussion of this.

2   Interpretation and intention

I said at the beginning of this essay that critics often offer interpretations of works of art. I shall discuss one aspect of that activity, namely the question whether interpretation, in the sense of determining what a work means, requires any reference to the artist. This has been vigorously denied in twentieth-century critical theory.

Meaning and interpretation

Turning to the first of these issues, it does not seem unnatural to think that questions about what a person meant by saying *p* might be resolved by asking that person what was *intended* by saying *p*. The question 'What did you mean by that remark?' is an invitation to the speaker to clear up ambiguities by telling us what he or she intended to say. Indeed, E.D. Hirsch has asserted that a determinate meaning requires a determining act of will, so that the meaning of an utterance is determined by finding out what the speaker intended to say. Without such an intention every utterance is, he says, indeterminate in meaning, or ambiguous.

First, there is the 'Humpty Dumpty' argument that I have already mentioned (pp. 393–4 above). The result was that on this account meaning is never made clear. Hence the view that meaning is given to words by individual acts of intention entails that the meaning of no word can be explained. One could not even explain one's meaning to oneself. For to do that one would have to say 'By this word I mean...', and produce a phrase or word of explanation. But then one would have to give that word or phrase a meaning by another word or phrase, and so on for ever.

The conclusion seems to be that if we are to explain our meaning to others we have to do so by using words which have a meaning in a public language, which are used according to an understanding which we all accept. And this looks right. When I speak I do not, typically, *give* the words I use a meaning. I use them as *already* having a meaning. They had that meaning before I was born and will continue to have that meaning when I am gone. A word gets its meaning from a public structure which is not the possession of any individual speaker.[4] But if all this is so, why do we need reference to individual artists and their intentions in order to discover the meaning of a literary or any other work of art? All we need to do is bring to a text our knowledge of the structure of rules that give words their meaning and then read that meaning off from the text. If we are in doubt, we need to consult dictionaries and not authors. Beardsley can therefore write:

> It is in its language that the poem happens. That is why the language is the object of our attention and our study when its meaning is difficult to understand. It is not the interpreter's task... to draw our attention off to the psychological states of the author.
>
> (Beardsley, 1970, p.34)

And Sartre writes:

> words... became things themselves. And when a poet joins several of

these microcosms together the case is like that of painters when they assemble their colours on the canvas.

(Sartre, 1950, p.229)

Here we have the clear view that the meaning of a word is what it is regardless of what the author might say about what he or she would have liked to have said, just as the colour of a coloured patch is what it is regardless of what its painter would have liked to have painted.

So the argument is: since the public rules of the public language and not individual and private acts of intention determine the meaning of words, it follows that if we want to know what a text means, we should see what the rules of the language allow it to mean. We should not investigate what the writer would have liked to say. As Beardsley put it in *Aesthetics*, there is a difference between what a speaker meant (wanted to say) by certain words and what those words mean (what he actually did say). It is the latter we are interested in, if we are interested in the meaning that a text actually has, and it is the rules of the public language that tell us that.

But doesn't reference to intention help to resolve ambiguities?[5] Here there is an important argument. First, suppose that someone says something ambiguous, for example, we hear someone say, 'I like my secretary better than my wife.' This is ambiguous between, 'I prefer my secretary to my wife' and 'I like my secretary better than my wife does'. Suppose we ask the speaker which he meant, and he offers the latter interpretation. Beardsley would argue that this does not make the original utterance any less ambiguous. It merely replaces it with a new utterance whose meaning is now unambiguous. But by the rules of our language, the first utterance is ambiguous, and no amount of intending can take away that property from it. The ambiguous meaning of the first utterance is determined by the structure of our public rules for assigning meaning. No publicly stated act of intention can make that utterance unambiguous. All it can do is replace that utterance by one which, by the public structures of rules, is unambiguous.

To summarize, I have tried to state as forcibly as I can some of the arguments that have been offered for the view that we do not need reference to the intentions of the artist when our critical task is the interpretation of literary texts. Meaning is a property conferred on words, actions and institutions by the structure of the public language and not by individual acts of willing meaning onto words, acts, etc. It follows that the task of determining meaning falls to the reader (hence the emergence of what are called 'reader-response' theories). The reader brings an accumulated body of public understanding to the text and, using that understanding, assigns a meaning to it. Where a reader is in doubt, it is in virtue of a lack of competence with part of that public domain; in which case what is needed is not a reference to the artist but reference to a dictionary or a more competent speaker. On this account reference to intention in the determination of meaning is unnecessary.

Structuralism, Sartre and authorial choice

First, a structuralist account, which allows us to assign a determinate meaning to a text by the use of a structure of meaning-giving rules may take an over-optimistic view of the extent to which the rules we have mastered for the use of language can help us when our task is the discovery of the meaning of a text. For the use of language is creative and always extends beyond the rules we have mastered for its under-standing. Thus we learn the rules for the word 'vivid' as rules which tell us that certain colours can be characterized by the use of this word. Then out of the blue someone says of an expression, such as Tom Lehrer's famous warning to graduating students, 'soon you'll be sliding down the razor blade of life', 'What a vivid turn of phrase'. Here 'vivid' is projected, so to speak, into a new context for which nothing in the rules we hitherto learned can prepare us. Yet we manage to make perfectly good sense of this creative extension of our language. So it is when, having learned the meaning of the term 'deep' with respect to oceans, we hear feelings called 'deep', or having learned 'blue' with respect to colours we hear someone say that he feels blue today (see Wittgenstein, 1969, p.137). So, a structuralist account seems to take no account of the way in which we can *creatively project* the structures that we have learned. This is something that *persons* do, and so the structuralist attempt to reduce persons to passive reflections of the structures of language overlooks the fact that language requires individual human beings *creatively to operate the structures* of a language. This is, I think, related to Stuart Sim's comment (Essay Ten, p. 424) that structuralism can say little about the content or psychological effect of a text.

This line of argument, however, does not, as yet, reinstate the artist as a source of meaning. It is still the reader who has to see the possibility of creative extensions of language. A new use of a word by an author which no reader could follow would not be a creative extension in the (public) *language*, and the author would not manage to *say* something, if no reader could grasp the point of the creative projection of language.

The next thing I wish to show, therefore, is that even if we accept the view that meaning is assigned to texts by readers, this entails nothing about the eliminability of authorial reference. For such a view is compatible with the belief that mental qualities of authors may be detected in texts and relevantly referred to by critics. For even if the meaning of the words that a writer uses in a text is determinable by the public rules of the language rather than by reference to a private intention of a speaker, nothing has been done to show that artists cannot show themselves and their personal qualities in their works in ways which it is relevant for critics to note. For the words of a text are put together by an authorial act which can show us the author's character and intelligence at work. This point was clearly (although, I suspect, reluctantly) seen by Sartre. Sartre pointed out that at every stage of the production of a work of art the artist is confronted by choices. A novelist, for example, chooses whether to be an omniscient or first-person narrator, to telescope a long passage of time into a few pages and so on. At *every* stage the artist has to make a choice: to juxtapose these colours rather than those, to use this word rather than that, to use this chord when others were available. A work is the result of a set of choices, and from that set of choices there can emerge a strong sense of the mental, emotional and other qualities of character of the artist who made those choices. If we understand that at a certain point in a piece of music a composer could have gone into a minor key for cheap emotional effect, we may praise her or his intelligence and disicrimination in resisting that obvious temptation.

Sartre, as I have said, saw this clearly. For though suspicious of references to authors (who, he thought, had no right to dictate to readers how their works should be read), he clearly saw that evidence of authorial choice (what we have seen Wimsatt describe as 'the operative mind or effective intention' of the author) *could* be read from the work, for the work is a repository that bears the evidence of successive acts of choice. So Sartre writes:

> If I pack six months into a single page, the reader jumps out of the book [i.e. the illusion of fictional reality is spoiled for the reader]. This... raises difficulties that none of us has resolved and which are perhaps partially insoluble, for it is neither possible nor desirable to limit all novels to the story of a single day. Even if one should resign oneself to that, the fact would remain that devoting a book to twenty-four hours rather than to one, or to an hour rather than to a minute, implies the intervention of the author and a transcendent choice.

(Sartre, 1950, p.229)

Similarly Wayne Booth writes in *The Rhetoric of Fiction*:

> Even if we eliminate all… explicit judgements, the author's presence
> will be obvious on every occasion when he moves into or out of the
> character's mind – when he 'shifts his point of view' as we have come
> to put it… The author's judgement is always present, always evident to
> anyone who knows how to look for it… Though the author can to some
> extent choose his disguises, he can never choose to disappear.
>
> (Booth, 1961, p.20)

So even if the meaning of a text is determined by the reader deploying
the rules of the public language, that meaning, once assigned, may (will)
reveal the presence of the author in the text (whether or not that author
wishes this), and that in turn will reveal (regardless of authors' wishes
and sometimes to the detriment of their achievements) the personal
qualities of the author, qualities to which, as we have seen, critics such as
Leavis wish to attend. That authors cannot make their words mean what
they want, does not stop them revealing critically relevant aspects of
their personalities through the particular use of those words.

Meaning and intention

All that the arguments I have mentioned have shown is this: the meaning
of a text cannot be there as the result of a prior act of willing by the artist
in which a personal meaning is willed onto the words that are used. But
that is compatible with the view that when we assign a determinate
meaning to an utterance (always granted that the notion of determinate
meaning makes sense – see below and Essay Ten) we can do so because
we can detect *in* that text an intention to say this rather than that.
Ambiguity is present when we cannot detect such an intention in an
utterance. But we *can* make our meaning clear because we can make our
intentions clear *in* speaking. Intention can be made manifest in action,
including our speech actions (how else could it be made known). When
it is made manifest as it often is, in our speech actions, then our meaning
is made clear. The rules of a public language do not replace our meaning-
intentions with other ways of assigning meaning to our utterances. They
are, rather, the apparatus which allow us to make our intentions, and so
our meanings, clear.

I find it striking that Beardsley himself is forced, when he comes to a
particular problem of interpretation, to link meaning to intention. He
takes the case of Housman's poem *1887*, written on the occasion of
Queen Victoria's Golden Jubilee. Frank Harris wrote to Housman

congratulating him on the splendid irony of this work, a description which Housman angrily rejected. Beardsley asks, 'was the poem ironic or not?' One alternative he thinks is to say that the poem is ironic, if Housman says so. But he wishes to reject this alternative. The other alternative, he says, is to have the poem read by 'competent' readers, and if they say it is ironic, then it is ironic, whatever Housman says (Beardsley, 1958, p.26). But there is a fudging in Beardsley's treatment, for he writes that if it is decided that the poem *is* ironic, then Housman's *unconscious* intention must have 'guided his pen more that his consciousness can admit'. But this seems to link his interpretation to an assumption about the *real* (as opposed to the professed) intentions of the author, for once Beardsley has found what he thinks to be the correct interpretation, he then immediately relates this to what Housman *really*, albeit unconsciously, intended.

Similarly, Wimsatt, writing on this same poem and about Housman's denial of any intended irony says:

> Here a statement made in retrospect and under provocation, a kind of profession of loyalty to a sovereign, stands in sharp contradiction not only to the cunning details of the poem in question but to the well known sceptical and cynical cast of the poet's canon.

> (Wimsatt, in de Molina, 1976, p.36)

But, again, this concedes that the poem is ironic because all the evidence is that *Housman*, despite his protestations, is showing his customary cunning and scepticism. (And, incidentally, whose can the 'cunning' and 'scepticism' of the poet's canon be, if not *Housman's*?)

Conclusion

I conclude with a final point, which takes us to the frontiers of present discussions and to the following essays. The structuralists and Beardsley clearly both believe that a work must be able to have a determinate meaning if criticism is to be possible. And I have claimed above that determinate meaning is linked to a recognition of intention. Beardsley, indeed, believes that the very *possibility* of criticism is linked to the possibility of assigning determinate meaning to texts, only so can we test the rightness and wrongness of critical interpretations: the right interpretation being one that accords with the determinate meaning of the work. So Beardsley says:

> What is wanted... is a constructive theory of meaning in literature that will show, in fact, it is possible for literary texts to have an independent

existence and to exercise their own controlling authority over the efforts of the literary interpreter.

(Beardsley, 1970, p.31)

Now one of the significant differences between structuralism and post-structuralism comes to this: the former appears to accept and the latter to query the notion of determinate meaning (see Essay Ten, p. 427). And from this follow some of the problems that some have had with the writings of a post-structuralist such as Derrida. For, as Sim points out (p. 429), one question will be how the determinate thesis that meaning is indeterminate can be expressed, granted that that thesis is true. Again, there will be questions, given that texts have no determinate meaning, about what criticism is to be: what, for example, if this is not a misguided question, might make one piece of criticism more significant than another? Post-structuralists are not without resources in attempting to answer these question. In asking them and examining the answers we become involved in matters that are the topic of vigorous and important contemporary debates, debates which, as I have tried to indicate, raise questions not merely about art, but about human beings and the sort of culture in which they live and might live.

Bibliography

Beardsley, M. (1958) *Aesthetics*, Harcourt Brace and World.
Beardsley, M. (1970) *The Possibility of Criticism*, Detroit.
Booth, W. (1961) *The Rhetoric of Fiction*, Chicago University Press.
Carroll, L. (1962 edn) *Alice's Adventures in Wonderland* and *Through the looking Glass*, Penguin Books.
Culler, J. (1975) *Structuralist Poetics*, Routledge and Kegan Paul.
Foucault, M. (1966) *Les Mots et les Choses*, Paris.
Leavis, F.R. (1962) *The Great Tradition*, Penguin Books.
Lévi-Strauss, C. (1962) *La Pensée Sauvage*, Paris.
de Molina, D. (ed.) (1976) *On Literary Intention*, Edinburgh University Press.
Sartre, J.-P. (1967) *What is Literature?*, B. Frechtman (trans.), Methuen.
Tormey, A. (1971) *The Concept of Expression*, Princeton University Press.
Trotsky, L. (1960) *Literature and Revolution*, University of Michigan Press.
Wimsatt, W. and Beardsley, M., 'The Intentional Fallacy', in de Molina, 1976.
Wimsatt, W.K., 'Genesis', in de Molina, 1976.
Wittgenstein, L. (1969) *Blue and Brown Books,* Blackwell.

Notes

[1] I have immediate doubts about the conclusiveness of this argument. From the fact that we can perform an activity without knowledge of a particular set of facts it does not follow that we could not perform that activity *better* if those facts were available to us.
[2] Beardsley and Wimsatt, incidentally, do not mean by a 'dramatic speaker' a character like Hamlet.

[3] This, it must be said, looks far fetched. Was Pasternak, to take an important case, creating a pretended speaker for liberal humanism in his epic novel *Dr Zhivago*? And, to take a different sort of case, was Mahler creating a fictional pretence to soul-searching when he composed his music?

[4] One meaning of the term 'structuralism' is related to this point. Structuralism is the view that meaning is given to words and social actions by the structures of meaning that exist independently of the will or whim of individual speakers (see Essay Ten).

[5] Some have talked as if ambiguity were intrinsically a good thing in poetry. I doubt it.

Structuralism and post-structuralism

Stuart Sim

Introduction

Aesthetics and criticism

Aesthetics on the continent can present a very different face from that of its Anglo-American counterpart. The aesthetic theory that has emerged from France in recent decades, for example, has provoked some very hostile reactions in the English-speaking world. 'Structuralist' and 'deconstructionist' aesthetics, to name the two most influential theories involved, remain matters of considerable controversy, with the latter theory in particular often drawing accusations of intellectual irresponsibility and unintelligibility on this side of the channel. (As one editor of the leading deconstructionist theorist Jacques Derrida has complained, Derrida seems always 'willing to risk equivocation for the sake of a pun' (Newton Garver in the preface to Derrida, 1973, p.xxiv).) It is not just the aesthetic theories of structuralism and deconstruction that have come under fire but also the schools of criticism they have generated. In comparison to our own tradition it is probably fair to say that continental aesthetics assumes a much closer connection between philosophical theory and the practice of critics (Marxism might be cited as another example of this tendency). Anglo-American criticism, with a few significant exceptions, is in general markedly less theory-conscious in its approach to artistic artefacts, and less concerned to make the artefact fit into a preconceived world view.

Criticism has been one of the major growth areas of twentieth-century intellectual life and the nature of its relationship to aesthetic theory has become an increasingly important topic. The questions that would typically arise in such an enquiry would include the following:

On what grounds do critics make their value judgements?

To what extent can these judgements be philosophically grounded?

To what extent *should* these judgements be philosophically grounded?

The answers will vary depending on the philosophical tradition from which one starts. In what follows I will be exploring the nature of structuralist and deconstructionist aesthetics and their theories of meaning and aesthetic value, paying particular attention to the way that philosophical theory has informed the practice of critics in each case, with a view to revealing some of the major differences separating continental from traditional Anglo-American aesthetics.

1 Structuralism

The Saussurean legacy

Structuralism is an aesthetic theory based on certain key philosophical assumptions:

(i) that all artistic artefacts (or 'texts', as they are more usually referred to by structuralists) are exemplifications of an underlying 'deep structure';

(ii) that texts are organized like a language with their own specific 'grammar';

(iii) that the grammar of a language is a series of signs and conventions which draw a predictable response from human beings.

The objective of structuralist analysis is to reveal the deep structures of texts. Structuralism has its basis in 'semiology' (or 'semiotics'), the theory of signs. According to semioticians all systems are made up of signals to which the individual responds in an agreed or conventional way. To take one of the most elementary sign-systems by way of example, an individual registers the proper response to a green traffic light when she puts her car in motion again. 'Green means go': the light has been understood as a sign which sanctions the performance of an action, or dictates an appropriate response. Semiology is the study of how signs operate within systems and of what codes govern their meaning. Sign-systems will vary quite considerably in degree of complexity – traffic lights have a very restricted grammar compared to that of texts and narratives – but the signal-response model will always form the basis of their operations.

Semiology can be traced back mainly to the work of the Swiss linguist Ferdinand de Saussure, one of the founders of structural linguistics.[1] Saussure's *Course in General Linguistics* propounds a theory of language as a self-contained system which exists within the wider field of semiology: 'Linguistics is only a part of a general science of semiology; the laws discovered by semiology will be applicable to linguistics, and the latter will circumscribe a well-defined area within the mass of anthropological facts' (Saussure, 1974, p.16). Structuralist analysis is largely the product of semiology and structural linguistics, but it also draws heavily on Russian formalism (a school of literary theorists that flourished in the 1920s) and on anthropological theory. I will say a few words about these last two theories before going on to consider Saussure's structural linguistics in more detail.

Russian formalism is the source of a key structuralist concept known as 'transformation'. Transformation provides for narratives to be studied in terms of the way the basic elements are varied, or 'transformed', by different authors or cultures. In the work of the influential Soviet theorist V. Propp, which is particularly concerned with folktales, such basic elements as landscape, setting, character's appearance, dress and social station can be, in Propp's terminology, transformed by being reduced, amplified, deformed, inverted, intensified, weakened, or substituted, so that the final narrative form of each individual folktale is subtly varied from other examples of the genre (Propp, in Maranda, 1972, pp. 139–50). While the basic elements will always be present – landscapes, settings, characters, etc. – they will never appear in quite the same arrangement across a range of narratives. They will be transformed in each case, and it is the point of structuralist analysis to chart and compare such transformations.

The anthropology of Claude Lévi-Strauss extends this method of analysis into primitive myth to show how a basic structure (for instance a creation myth) can be made to vary from culture to culture. The idea of an underlying, yet formally variable, structure is central to the structuralist enterprise: 'a structure is a system of transformations', as the structuralist psychologist Jean Piaget has remarked (Piaget, 1971, p.5), and 'all known structures... are, without exception, systems of transformation' (*ibid*. p.11). Literary structures are, therefore, systems containing a series of transformations of basic narrative elements. Piaget claims that 'the notion of structure is comprised of three key ideas: 'the idea of wholeness, the idea of transformation, and the idea of self-regulation' (*ibid*. p.5). Wholeness (the totality of the system), transformation (the variation of the system's constant elements), and self-regulation (the system's internally-operative grammar) are all ideas that are derived from Saussure's *Course in General Linguistics*, and it is there that we start our analysis of structuralist methodology in detail.

Saussure regards language as, above all, a self-contained system. He differentiates between language as a system *(langue)* and language as a set of utterances *(parole)*. *Langue* comprises rules and procedures, *parole* behaviour (which does not always conform to the rules, as in the case of dialect or colloquial speech), and it is with the former that his interest primarily lies. Chess provides him with a useful analogy for *langue's* self-contained, systemic nature:

> In chess, what is external can be separated relatively easily from what is internal. The fact that the game passed from Persia to Europe is external; against that, everything having to do with its system and rules is internal. If I use ivory chessmen instead of wooden ones, the change has no effect on the system; but if I decrease or increase the number of chessmen, this change has a profound effect on the 'grammar' of the game... everything that changes the system in any way is internal.
>
> (Saussure, *op. cit.* pp. 22–3)

The concepts of wholeness, transformation and self-regulation are all used in this passage. Chess is a whole system which can appear in different contexts (Persia, Europe), while still maintaining its identity. It admits transformations: ivory chessmen can be substituted for wooden, but their playing function does not alter. The game has its own specific rules and grammar, so it is internally self-regulating in the sense of setting limits to what can occur during the game. Even if there is tinkering with the rules (increasing or decreasing the number of pieces, for example), it has to take place within the context of the game's grammar; structures can only change internally and in terms of the existing relationship of their constituent elements.

The most thought-provoking part of *Course in General Linguistics* is the discussion on the nature of the linguistic sign. Saussure contends that there are three notions involved in a word: *signified*, *signifier* and *sign*. A signified is the mental concept which, according to him, a word is designed to convey; a signifier is the sequence of sounds or letters (in Saussure's formulation the 'sound-image') by which we refer to that concept; a sign is the union of signified and signifier in an act of understanding ('united in the brain by an associative bond', as Saussure puts it (*ibid.* p.66)). When we see or hear the word 'dog', we know what it means, that it is a sign for a dog, because we have matched our concept of dog with the sound-image 'dog'.

The most important characteristic of the sign is that it is arbitrary, which means that there is no necessary connection between a concept and the sounds which conventionally serve as its signifier. As Jonathan Culler has noted:

> Since I speak English I may use the signifier represented by *dog* to talk about an animal of a particular species, but this sequence of sounds is

no better suited to that purpose than another sequence. *Lod*, *tet*, or *bloop* would serve equally well if they were accepted by members of my speech community. There is no intrinsic reason why one of these signifiers rather than another should be linked with the concept of a 'dog'.

(Culler, 1976, pp. 19–20)

This principle of arbitrariness, Saussure claims, 'dominates all the linguistics of language' (Saussure, *op. cit.* p.68). The idea that the sign is arbitrary implies that meaning is conventional, something agreed upon by a linguistic community using a given language-system. Meaning is a product of the internal relations of a given system, the matching of signifiers to signifieds to construct signs. Though it might appear to be, this is not a recipe for anarchy. We inherit our individual language-system rather than create it from scratch each generation, and signs and meanings do not change arbitrarily or at any individual's whim. Yet signs do change over time. 'The principle of change is based on the principle of continuity' (*ibid.* p.74), which introduces one of the most important distinctions in *Course in General Linguistics*: the distinction between *diachronic* and *synchronic*.

Synchrony deals with the totality of a phenomenon, diachrony with some particular aspects of that totality ('language state' and 'evolutionary phase' respectively in Saussure's words (*ibid.* p.81)). To return to the chess analogy, the game plus its grammar (rules and procedures as to how the various pieces are permitted to move) is a synchrony. An actual move within a game – of a pawn, for example – is a diachronic event. Synchrony is static and outside time, diachrony is dynamic and in time.

To demonstrate how synchronic and diachronic are perceived to interact, I quote from Howard Gardner's introduction to structuralist analysis, *The Quest for Mind*; the subject in this case being French intellectual life from Descartes to the twentieth-century:

A structural analysis of the French intellectual tradition

Synchronic Elements (always present from 1650 to 1900)	interest in mind; detached objectivity; desire to synthesize all knowledge; special status of human beings; unique properties of language; interest in, but disdain for, previous philosophy; respect for mathematic (logical) thinking
Diachronic Elements, Reversible (alternate in importance from 1650 to 1900)	primary interest: in the individual/in society primary interest: in French culture/ in the variety of world cultures; primary interest: in logical-mathematical thought/in the affective life and aesthetic aspects of thought

Diachronic Elements,	interest in findings of modern science
Irreversible (of	rejection of introspection
increasing importance	search for empirical data and confirmation
from 1650 to 1900)	

(Gardner, 1976, p.24)

Gardner's analysis displays a close application of Saussurean theory, with synchrony providing the principle of regularity and diachrony the dynamic force through which effects and changes are produced. Wholeness here equals 'the French Intellectual Tradition' over a certain period of time; transformations of constant (i.e. synchronic) elements are to be noted in the reversible and irreversible diachronic elements, and the system is seen to be self-regulating in that all reversible and irreversible elements stand in some relationship to the continuing synchronic elements. A perpetual belief in the special status of human beings may be expressed in the study of either the individual or society. The rejection of introspection and an interest in the findings of modern science are logical outgrowths of an overall commitment to detached objectivity. The structure varies, but at any given point it is a recognizably whole and self-regulating structure which can accommodate change. There is always such a thing as 'the French Intellectual Tradition', and it will be defined by the presence of certain essential elements, but it can develop in a multitude of ways.

Saussure thinks in terms of system-bound binary oppositions – 'language is characterized as a system based entirely on the opposition of its concrete units' (*ibid*. p.107) – and his theory of value reflects this. Units have no value except within the system in question, and are interdependent; their value, for Saussure, 'results solely from the simultaneous presence' (*ibid*. p.114) of other units. The value of a unit of a system is the product, respectively, of

(i) a *dissimilar* thing that can be exchanged for the thing of which the value is to be determined; and

(ii) *similar* things that can be *compared* with the thing of which the value is to be determined (*ibid*. p.115).

What this means is that any element within a system can *substitute* for any other element of that system, or can be *compared* to any other element in the system (unit A is similar to unit B in ways p, q and r, dissimilar in ways x, y and z, etc.). For Saussure, value is to be equated with *function*. To enquire about the value of an element of a system is to be told about its *rôle* in the system.

Value is therefore considered to be relative to a system and to be dependent upon binary relations in all cases; which is to say that there is no such thing as *intrinsic* value, no specific quality holding over time (although structures, of course, *do* hold over time and independently of all systems). Knights and pawns have a determinable value vis-à-vis each other in chess, but that value could be reversed (substitution), and the pieces in question would then take on a different value with respect to the other pieces on the board, along with a new set of similarities/dissimilarities. The value that any object, including an aesthetic object, has, is dependent on the grammar of the system in which it is viewed. What Saussure encourages is a purely formal, or function-oriented, approach to the question of value. Like the parts of a machine, the elements of a system are defined by how they interact with each other. Thus, 'language is a system of pure values which are determined by nothing except the momentary arrangement of its terms' (*ibid*. p.80), and 'signs function... not through their intrinsic value but through their relative position' (*ibid*. p.118).

This formalism has since become a characteristic of structuralist analysis, and has lately been attacked by many post-structuralist thinkers. Jacques Derrida considers structuralism's obsession with form and system to be sterile, claiming that '*Form* fascinates when one no longer has the force to understand force from within itself. That is, to create' ('force' stands for something like 'creative urgency' in Derrida) (Derrida, 1978, pp. 4–5). Derrida's concern is to undermine what he regards as the tyranny of form – a tyranny which is held to inhibit the creative imagination – and in this sense he is going well beyond Saussure to propound a far more radical concept of aesthetic value (this topic will be treated in more detail in section 2 below).

Saussure's theory of relations, and hence his notion of value, is based on the *syntagmatic/paradigmatic* distinction. The idea here is that words acquire relations by being strung together in sequences called 'syntagms'. A syntagm is a combination of words composed of two or more consecutive units constructed according to the rules of syntax: for example, 'God is good' and 'If the weather is nice we'll go out' (Saussure, *op. cit*. p.123). Each word stands related to the next word in the sequence as it unfolds, and normal discourse – spoken or written – is constructed in this manner. Words also acquire relations of a different kind from outside normal discourse, and these so-called *associative* relations (now usually referred to as *paradigmatic*) are not linear in nature. Since they are held to depend on the experience, and particular mental processes, of the individual ('their seat is in the brain', as

Saussure puts it (*ibid.*) they fall into no predictable pattern. There can be no grammar of the associative. One possible associative/paradigmatic group suggested by Saussure goes as follows: teaching, teach, education, apprenticeship. While the connections between these particular words are fairly obvious, if one were to continue the sequence one would eventually reach a point so far removed from the original starting word as to suggest no rational, or grammatically determinable, connection between that word and the final word of the sequence.

The process involved in making such associative connections from word to word is very similar to that outlined two centuries before by John Locke as 'association of ideas':

> some of our ideas have a *natural* correspondence and connexion one with another; it is the office and excellency of our reason to trace these, and hold them together in that union and correspondence which is founded in their peculiar beings. Besides this, there is another connexion of ideas wholly owing to *chance or custom*. Ideas that in themselves are not at all of kin come to be so united in some men's minds that it is very hard to separate them; they always keep in company, and the one no sooner at any time comes into the understanding but its associate appears with it; and if they are more than two which are thus united, the whole gang always inseparable, show themselves together.

> (Locke, 1964 edn, pp. 250–1)

What Saussure and Locke are suggesting is that words set off a chain of associations in the mind; that certain associations cluster around a given word in the mind (because of the individual's personal experience), and that the sequence is not logical in construction. No 'fixed order of succession' (Saussure, *op. cit.* p.127) is involved in the case of associative relations; the order will depend on the psychology and experience of the individual in question.

Deconstruction relies heavily on this notion of paradigmatic relation. Derrida and his followers make extensive use of punning and word-play, activities which are dependent on the principle of association – association of sound, for example. The procedure is designed to challenge the emphasis traditionally placed on logically-constructed thought-patterns in our culture, and suggests a much more random motion for thought. Saussure himself is unwilling to go this far, arguing that even though the whole system of language is based on the principle of the arbitrariness of the sign – that is, the lack of any necessary connection between signifier and signified – this would lead to 'the worst sort of complication if applied without restriction' (*ibid.* p.133):

by which he means that discourse as we know it would tend to break down, perhaps into a chaos of private languages. The mind, therefore, Saussure claims, 'contrives to introduce a principle of order' *(ibid.)* to guarantee that discourse between individuals can take place. There is what he calls a 'limiting of arbitrariness' *(ibid.)*. (Saussure's arguments are not particularly strong on this issue of 'limiting', and it is a weakness that, as we shall see, Derrida exploits with some success.)

To summarize the main points of Saussure's argument: language is a self-contained system consisting of signs. Signs consist of a signifier and a signified. The sign is arbitrary, signifier and signified having no necessary connection to each other; although once the system is in operation the human disposition towards patterning will have the effect of imposing a sense of order and coherence on signs. Within any system, meaning is conventional, value relational (that is, defined in terms of the internal relations between elements in that system). Relations are either syntagmatic (linear) or paradigmatic (associative). All systems are analysable in terms of their diachronic and synchronic elements. Linguistics is the study of language-systems and it provides a methodological model for the study of all other systems. It is to be subsumed in its turn under the more general science of semiotics, the study of signs and how they operate within systems.

Structuralism has adopted much of the terminology to be found in *Course in General Linguistics*, as well as the substance of its methodology. Signifier/signified, synchronic/diachronic, syntagmatic/paradigmatic are the stock in trade of structuralist analysis. The basic concerns of structuralists are to demarcate the boundaries of the system being studied (its wholeness), identify its syntax and the relations holding between its syntactical elements (its self-regulation), and then view their findings in both diachronic and synchronic perspective where transformations of the relevant elements can be traced. To a structuralist, any system is amenable to semiotic analysis, although obviously some will yield greater insights about the way we live than others (traffic lights only go so far). The arts have proved to be a fruitful area of study, with literature, film and painting all responding well to structuralist analysis.

Literature tends to fall into genres (though not always neatly so), and genres can be treated as systems each with their own particular set of rules and grammar. Murder mysteries, for instance, contain a murder, a mystery surrounding the identity of the murderer, a pattern of detection, and, usually, the ultimate discovery of the murderer. These stock formal elements signal the text's genre to its audience although they can be presented in a variety of ways. The murder may occur at various points in the narrative – there may even be several murders. Then the murderer may be identified gradually or may be unmasked suddenly or confess voluntarily. Different examples of the genre will handle the stock conventions in their own particular manner, which is the principle of transformation in operation. Thus Umberto Eco in *The Name of the Rose*, Raymond Chandler in *The Long Goodbye*, and Agatha Christie in *The Murder of Roger Ackroyd*, can be seen to distribute the elements of the murder mystery genre throughout their narratives in their own very individual fashion. Using the basic murder mystery model (murder, mystery, search for and discovery of murderer) the critic will be able to subject a range of narratives to sophisticated comparative analysis, such as the cataloguing of similarities and dissimilarities. A vast amount of data can be easily and methodically assembled, and the tracing of transformations in a genre over time can be very revealing about literary and cultural development.

Lévi-Strauss: myths and transformations

Structuralism is a powerful technique for purposes of formal analysis, particularly comparative formal analysis of transformation in its many and various guises. It enables us not only to construct classifications of phenomena (as in the case of the historical phenomena in the Gardner table (pp. 409–10 above), for example), but also to reveal the underlying structure, grammar, and capacity for creative transformation of those phenomena: to seek what Culler has called 'the system behind the event' (Culler, 1975, p.30). In terms of method, structuralism remains true to its basic model, Saussurean linguistics.

Lévi-Strauss's work on primitive myth, one of the key areas of his anthropological studies, shows the method to excellent advantage, particularly its overriding concern with the transformation of structural elements. In *The Raw and the Cooked* he works his way painstakingly through a group of apparently disparate South American Indian myths to argue that 'in all these instances we are dealing with the same myth... the apparent divergences between the versions are to be treated as the result of transformations occurring within a set' (Lévi-Strauss, 1969, p.147) (structuralists tend to gravitate towards notions of unity in this way). The process by which a Bororo tribal myth 'The bird-nester's aria' is transformed into the Ge tribal myth 'The Origin of Fire' and its several variants, and subsequently into a Sherente tribal myth on the origin of water, 'The Story of Asare', is charted with quasi-mathematical precision by Lévi-Strauss, as the following summary suggests:

Let us suppose two myths, which we will call M_x and M_y, and which happen to be linked by a transformation relation:

$$M_x \underset{(f)}{\rightarrow} M_y$$

If we agree that $M_y = fM_x$, does there exist a myth $M_z = fM_y$, in connection with which we can prove that it reconstitutes M_x by means of a transformation symmetrical to the one that produced M_y from M_x, but operating in the reverse direction? In other words, after establishing that a Sherente myth about the origin of fire (M_y) is a transformation of a Bororo myth about the origin of water (M_x), can we now find a Sherente myth (M_z) explaining the origin of water which takes us back to the Bororo myth which was our starting point, and at the same time confirms the following isomorphism:

$$\left[\begin{array}{c} M_z \rightarrow M_x \\ (f) \end{array} \right] \approx \left[\begin{array}{c} M_x \rightarrow M_y \\ (f) \end{array} \right] ?$$

Such a myth does in fact exist among the Sherente.

(Lévi-Strauss, *op.cit.* p.199)

Lévi-Strauss presses the case for wholeness, transformation and self-regularity with considerable conviction. The 'only justification' for structural analysis, he claims,

> lies in the unique and most economical coding system to which it can reduce messages of a most disheartening complexity, and which previously appeared to defeat all attempts to decipher them. Either structural analysis succeeds in exhausting all the concrete modalities of its subject, or we lose the right to apply it to one of the modalities.

(*Ibid.* p.147)

It is just such an insistence on the totality of explanation of structural analysis, its capacity to 'exhaust all', that has spurred post-structuralist thinkers like Derrida to criticize structuralism as authoritarian. Reducing the complexity of messages equals curbing imagination and creativity in Derrida's view. We also have a problem at such points with the structuralist method's *essentialism*. That is, structure is functioning as an ultimately irreducible essence of discourse in Lévi-Strauss's case, as a foundation of discourse that lies beyond any need of proof. Basic structures are simply assumed to exist.

Gardner has likened the quest for underlying structures to what he calls 'the quest for mind' in modern French intellectual history. Like the mind, structure seems to have an independence of operation and non-material quality, and it poses similar problems as a source of explanation for human behaviour. In many ways we face a worse problem with structure than with mind since the former has deterministic overtones. Deep structures appear to work independently of human agency, suggesting that the task of criticism is primarily a scientific exercise in identification and classification of the forces acting on and through individuals, who cannot be said to be in any control of the process. There is thus a hidden metaphysical commitment to determinism to be taken into account in structuralism.

One of the consequences of structuralism's scientifically-minded approach is the tendency to reduce phenomena to tabular display, as in the following examples drawn from *The Raw and the Cooked* (Figures 1 and 2).

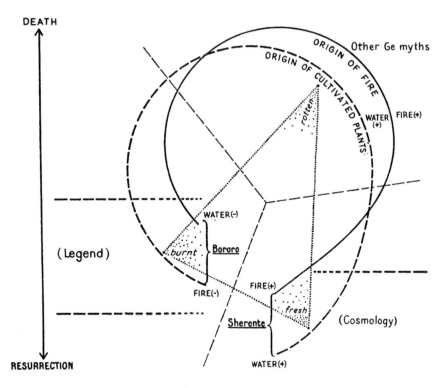

Figure 1 Interrelationship of the Bororo and Ge myths about the origin of fire or cultivated plants. (Lévi-Strauss, op. cit. p.194)

$\begin{cases} \triangle & \text{man} \\ \bigcirc & \text{woman} \end{cases}$

$\triangle = \bigcirc$ marriage (disjunction of marriage : #)

$\triangle$ $\bigcirc$ brother and sister (their disjunction : |——|)

$\triangle$ $\bigcirc$
$\triangle$, $\bigcirc$ father and son, mother and daughter, etc.

T   transformation

$\longrightarrow$ is transformed into

$\begin{cases} : \\ :: \end{cases}$ $\begin{array}{l}\text{is to . . .} \\ \text{as . . .}\end{array}$

/   contrast

$\begin{cases} \equiv \\ \not\equiv \end{cases}$ $\begin{array}{l}\text{congruence, homology, correspondence} \\ \text{noncongruence, nonhomology, noncorrespondence}\end{array}$

$\begin{cases} = \\ \neq \end{cases}$ $\begin{array}{l}\text{identity} \\ \text{difference}\end{array}$

$\approx$ isomorphism

$\begin{cases} \cup \\ // \end{cases}$ $\begin{array}{l}\text{union, reunion, conjunction} \\ \text{disunion, disjunction}\end{array}$

$\begin{cases} \longrightarrow \\ \#\!\!\longrightarrow \end{cases}$ $\begin{array}{l}\text{conjoins with . . .} \\ \text{is in a state of disjunction with . . .}\end{array}$

f function

$x^{(-1)}$ inverted x

+ , −   these signs are used with various connotations depending on the context: plus, minus; presence, absence; first or second term of a pair of opposites

Figure 2 *'Table of Symbols'* in Lévi-Strauss's The Raw and the Cooked, *p.ix.*

What becomes questionable in such cases is the degree to which the analysis is capturing, or even addressing, the aesthetic qualities of the narratives under scrutiny. Visual displays tell us nothing whatsoever about how narratives are received by readers, nor how or why they have the effect, personal or cultural, that they do. These have been traditional aesthetic and critical concerns. Analysis conducted on Lévi-Strauss's lines operates primarily at the level of formal description, with no evaluative interpretation being offered. Aesthetic value is reduced to a by-product of transformation and remains stubbornly system-bound, a matter of formal relations rather than psychological or sociological effect. If we see aesthetic theory as centrally concerned with providing criteria to account for psychological and social effects and value, and in the process establishing a basis for critical interpretation, then it could be argued that structuralism is deficient in precisely those areas where there is most need for aesthetic theory.

This tendency to formalize mythic narrative can be carried to extreme lengths. A case in point is the work of the Russian structuralist Dmitry M. Segal on North American Indian myth, where three variants are noted:

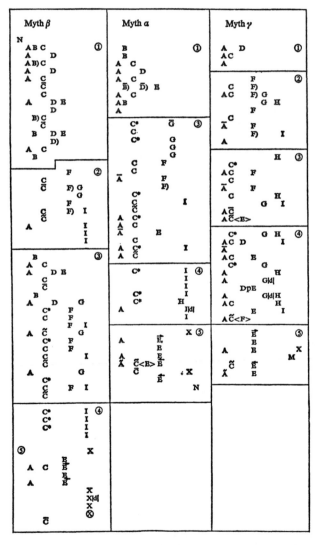

Figure 3   Symbolic transcription of the three variants of the (North American Indian) myth. (Segal, in Maranda, 1972, p.223)

Each symbol in these tables stands for an element of the basic story ('the outcast hero'), such as,

A   The hero is in a state of repudiation (in a condition of rejection),

Ã   Modification of A. Here in the sense of the hero's active reaction to events, and

Ä   Complete negation of all the components of A (*ibid.* pp. 217, 221).

Once again there is a sense of a process in which questions of aesthetic value and meaning are being elided, and when we pass from theory to criticism such questions are not so easily avoided. We normally expect critics to make value judgements, and we normally expect them to do so according to specified, or specifiable, criteria. It could with some justice be argued that myth is not designed for aesthetic effect (although it might well come to inspire it in time), and that I am looking for different things in such narratives than structural anthropologists are, but it is nevertheless necessary to consider carefully the procedures of structural anthropology since it has come to be so influential in the development of structuralist criticism.

Barthes: narrative and its codes

Complexity of coding (and by extension the complexity of meaning that can be read into it) might be put forward as a source of aesthetic value in structural analysis, and Roland Barthes suggests as much in *S/Z*, his *tour de force* reading of Balzac's novella *Sarrasine* in terms of its major narrative codes:

> To interpret a text is not to give it a (more or less justified, more or less free) meaning, but on the contrary to appreciate what *plural* constitutes it. Let us first posit the image of a triumphant plural, unimpoverished by any constraint of representation (of imitation). In this ideal text, the networks are many and interact, without any one of them being able to surpass the rest; this text is a galaxy of signifiers, not a structure of signifieds; it has no beginning; it is reversible; we gain access to it by several entrances, none of which can be authoritatively declared to be the main one; the codes it mobilizes extend *as far as the eye can reach*, they are indeterminable.
>
> (Barthes, 1975, pp. 5–6)

This celebration of plurality of meaning (*polysemy* in Barthes's terminology) argues that density of coding – 'the codes it mobilizes extend *as far as the eye can reach*' – is where the text's value lies. The reader co-operates with the text, in Barthes's view, to produce rather than just consume meanings. There is no central meaning to a text – no 'structure of signifieds' – but rather a multitude of possible readings for the reader to construct: 'we gain access to it by several entrances'.

The text which has greatest complexity of coding is the so-called *writerly* text, which is opposed to the *readerly* text. Writerly texts encourage the reader to produce meaning, readerly texts merely to consume meaning. (The mark of a writerly text, in Richard Howard's opinion in the preface to *S/Z*, is that 'it makes upon us strenuous demands, exactions' (*ibid.* p.xi).) The terms are not specifically historical in their application – the eighteenth-century comic novel *Tristram Shandy* by Laurence Sterne, for example, would qualify as a writerly text just as easily as James Joyce's twentieth-century modernist novel *Finnegan's Wake*. Most genre fiction – detective thriller, science fiction, historical romance, etc. – would be describable as readerly, with its formulaic plots ostensibly promoting passive consumption on the reader's part. Writerly texts tend to draw attention to the act of writing itself (hence the reference above to *Tristram Shandy*, a text which deliberately and elaborately draws attention to its own artifice), whereas readerly texts usually try to efface their literariness, often by the use of techniques of realism which encourage the reader to treat fictional characters as real people, and, in Barthes's opinion, to delimit considerably the reader's range of response. (In art we can similarly talk about 'painterly' paintings, where the spectator's attention is deliberately drawn to the act of painting itself. Abstract art qualifies as painterly, and can be contrasted with, for example, Victorian narrative painting, where content, and specifically *moral* content, can be considered to be of predominant interest.)

Barthes is operating at the boundary line between structuralism and post-structuralism in *S/Z*, in that he is beginning to question such notions as wholeness and closed structure. There has been a switch from an author-centred to a reader-centred analysis, from consumption of meaning to active production of it. Barthes is one of the major proponents of the 'death of the author' notion; that is, removal of consideration of the author as central to criticism (see pp. 422–3 below). Yet, although Barthes is edging towards post-structuralism and a far more anarchic method of dealing with texts than the Lévi-Strauss tradition would allow, elements of that tradition remain. There is still a noticeable tendency to eschew evaluation. The individual 'appreciates' the plurality of a text rather than interprets it in the old-fashioned sense of *explication de texte* – that is, the narrowing down of a narrative to what are taken to be its main themes and concerns – by the professional critic for the benefit of the lay reader. There is also the tendency to stay at a formal level, to catalogue codes and their networks of interaction. And if we have moved from a closed to an open structure (one with codes extending into infinity) as an ideal, we are nevertheless still mainly concerned with structure, those insistent networks of interaction just mentioned, as well as with coding within the text.

Barthes's writerly-readerly distinction may be seen as an attempt to introduce a more conventional theory of value into structuralism, and thereby to counter the frequently-voiced charge that textual content is largely irrelevant to structuralists: all narratives have structure, codes, transformations, signifieds, signifiers and signs, after all – Mills and Boon romances no less than the complex texts of Sterne and Joyce. Although it is an interesting attempt, it can be challenged on several counts. It is neither precise enough – one can readily imagine endless, and probably unresolvable, debates over attribution of specific texts to the categories in question (*either* writerly *or* readerly) – nor as open-minded as criticism ideally should be; readerly texts by implication warrant less attention by critics and readers alike since they are held to encourage passivity. Neither is it self-evident that, accepting the distinction for the moment, writerly and readerly texts actually function in the way Barthes claims they do. Writerly texts such as *Tristram Shandy* are arguably just as manipulative of the reader's responses as any readerly text is assumed to be; Sterne manipulates you to accept his vision of the world, and humankind, as being at the mercy of blind chance. When it comes to coding, it is by no means clear that complexity on the writerly model could not be found in even the most formulaic of readerly texts – such as fiction of the Mills and Boon type. Barthes's atomization of *Sarrasine* into tiny units or syntagms (often of only a few words or so) for analysis, may, given a little ingenuity, be possible with *any* literary text: in which case his value criterion collapses and one text becomes much like any other as far as the critic is concerned. As an evaluative criterion, with moralistic connotations in this instance of 'writerly good, readerly bad', the writerly-readerly distinction is not wholly successful in rescuing structural analysis from the 'content irrelevant' charge.

Elsewhere Barthes can be seen operating in a more orthodox structuralist manner. In the essay 'Structural Analysis of Narratives' he claims that,

> either a narrative is merely a rambling collection of events, in which
> case nothing can be said about it other than by referring back to the
> storyteller's (the author's) art, talent, or genius – all mythical forms of

chance – or else it shares with other narratives a common structure which is open to analysis, no matter how much patience its formulation requires. There is a world of difference between the most complex randomness and the most elementary combinatory scheme, and it is impossible to combine (to produce) a narrative without reference to an implicit system of units and rules.

(Barthes, 1977, p.80)

At such points Barthes displays the familiar structuralist concern with order (note how dismissive he is of chance) and with deep structure ('implicit system'). Barthes proceeds to construct a 'functional syntax' for narrative: 'How, according to what "grammar", are the different units strung together along the narrative syntagm? What are the rules of the functional combinatory system?' (*ibid.* p.97). The reference to function is a revealing one: structuralists are ultimately concerned with the identification and description of functions to the exclusion of meaning and value, at least as those latter phenomena are traditionally construed.

In 'The Death of the Author' Barthes outlines his theory that 'the Author' is an outmoded concept and that texts can operate on their own without reference to authorial objectives and intentions. This is yet another plea for a reader-centred criticism. 'To give a text an Author is to impose a limit on that text, to furnish it with a final signified, to close the writing' (*ibid.* p.147), Barthes insists. The argument depends on a conception of the self that recalls that of David Hume. One of the consequences of Hume's researches into the nature of causality, during which he famously claimed that there was no necessary connection between causes and effects, was that he was led to deny that there was any such thing as an enduring self. Hume saw individuals as bombarded by an endless stream of sense-impressions from the outside world, and the self accordingly was for him merely a 'bundle or collection or different perceptions, which succeed each other with inconceivable rapidity' (Hume, 1962 edn, p.302). Nothing apparently tied those perceptions together such that we could be justified in speaking of a fixed personal identity or a self that endured over time. The picture that emerges from Hume is of an entity caught in the fleeting present and struggling to make sense of it in any wider perspective. A similar picture emerges from Barthes when he states that 'Linguistically, the author is never more than the instance writing... there is no other time than that of the enunciation and every text is eternally written here and now' (Barthes, 1977, p.145). (This enables him, by the way, to dismiss the claims of expression theory because it would require a fixed personal identity to do the expressing, and that is precisely what both he and Hume are denying is possible.) Authors have no more of a fixed identity over time in Barthes than the self does in Hume.

Turning this argument against Barthes, his analysis of the self must call into question the authority of his own utterance: the death of the author is also surely the death of the critic. Criticism, if it is still legitimate to call the practice that in the apparent absence of value judgements, is reduced to an exercise in identifying signs in order to reveal their underlying networks of signification. This is an anti-authoritarian argument in more senses than one, and it ends with a firm commitment to the cause of the reader: 'the birth of the reader must be at the cost of the death of the Author' (*ibid.* p.148). The social status of the artist has been considerably downgraded by Barthes, and we are at the opposite end of the spectrum from Plato's notion of the artist as an individual dangerous to a well-ordered society (see Essay Seven). Plato was centrally concerned with the effects of art in his aesthetics, whereas structuralism typically avoids this issue; so it is perhaps not surprising to see the contribution of the creative artist being marginalized by Barthes.

Barthes pushes structuralism to its limits. If we start with self-regulating grammars and deep structures, it is quite logical to end up with the 'death of the Author'. From this point of view texts take on a life of their own seemingly independent of human agency. Barthes also demonstrates the limits of structuralism in that he begins to question the notion of closed structure, as well as the determinism it implies, and to embrace a concept of plurality of meaning that might look anarchic to older-style structuralist analysts on the look-out for orderly deep structures underlying all discourse. The writerly-readerly distinction also manages to draw attention to one of structuralism's major weaknesses: its formal theory of value, where value becomes equated with function. Barthes threatens more post-structuralism than he delivers, however, and periodically makes strategic retreats behind structuralism's barriers of wholeness, transformation and self-regularity. He is still concerned to reveal 'the system behind the event', where any given narrative 'shares with other narratives a common structure which is open to analysis'.

The evaluation problem

As an aesthetic theory structuralism is vulnerable at several points. Structure remains a questionable concept resting on dubious assumptions. For all Barthes's manoeuvres to build individual creativity into the reading process, structure continues to have a reality independent of readers: human beings discover or appreciate it, not control or direct it.

The formalism of the theory must remain a problem in that it leads to a form of criticism which can say very little about the content of works of art, and, by extension, their psychological effect. The notion of a process by which authorial intention, however loosely conceived, is translated into reader-effect, is missing in the structuralist enterprise. Effect is almost a 'no-go area', and no number of diagrams, tabular displays, and lists of codes can reveal anything very substantial about the impact of a narrative on an individual, why a given narrative might draw critical acclaim or displeasure, or be compared favourably or unfavourably with others. In the Anglo-American tradition such factors have generally remained of primary interest to critics, and that constitutes a significant area of difference between them and the continentals.

What has tended to happen in practice in structuralist criticism is that an author's oeuvre is examined in terms of an assumed ideal structure (spatial and geometrical references abound in such criticism, as Derrida has noted (Derrida, 1978, pp. 20–1)), and then each individual work is compared to this ideal structure. Essentialism is to the fore in such cases: behind each text is supposed to be an essential structure, well or badly realized by the author. Structuralist analysis also blurs the distinction between the aesthetic and the non-aesthetic: phenomena tend to be treated in much the same manner on either side of the divide, advertizing and artistic texts equally, for example. The evaluative aspect of aesthetic theory, which some thinkers would consider to be its most important one, is marginalized. There is often a studied avoidance of psychological and social evaluation in structuralism. Barthes's attempt to rectify this situation by introducing into structuralist analysis the evaluative criterion of writerly-readerly founders on imprecision. Complexity of coding could also be regarded as an evaluative criterion, but again, at best an imprecise one. A criticism or an aesthetic theory which does not provide the means to evaluate artefacts in a social and psychological sense, ultimately can only appear somewhat impoverished. Marxists have argued that there is in fact a disguised theory of value at work in structuralism, and that analytical processes in which the human dimension is suppressed serve some particular class interest (see Essay Eleven).

2 Post-structuralism

Derrida and deconstruction

Barthes's work reveals with particular clarity both the strengths (universality of application, for instance) and weaknesses (the lack of a theory of value) of structuralism, and also, eventually, the method's limits and limitations. Universality of application might be regarded as a weakness as well as a strength, since one largely knows before the event what a structuralist will say. Confronted by practically any social phenomenon – fashion, advertizing, the arts, myths, cultures – the structuralist responds in much the same way. The method becomes highly predictable in its operation, which is one of the starting points for Derrida's critique of structuralism. The 'structural consciousness', he argues, contents itself with being 'a reflection of the accomplished, the constituted, the *constructed*' (*ibid.* p.5); that is to say, it classifies ('reflects') rather than interprets or creates. Derrida's work is part of a broad intellectual movement, ranging over several disciplines, called post-structuralism, which has reacted against institutional structures and received authority in general. The initial thrust of Derrida's attack is against philosophical structures (he has a tendency to talk rather grandly of dismantling 'Western metaphysics' or 'Western thought'), but his researches repeatedly lead him into the field of aesthetics and criticism, and he has in fact spawned a highly influential school of criticism.

Deconstructionist aesthetics involves very different assumptions from those of structuralism: namely:

(i) that texts, like language, are marked by instability and indeterminacy of meaning;

(ii) that given such instability and indeterminacy neither philosophy nor criticism can have any special claim to authority as regards textual interpretation;

(iii) that interpretation is a free-ranging activity more akin to game-playing than analysis.

The point of deconstructionist criticism is to demolish the illusion of stable meaning in texts.

Derrida's starting-point is in Saussurean linguistics and the notion of the arbitrariness of the signifier. On the basis of this arbitrariness, Derrida proceeds to construct a sustained attack on what he considers to be the authoritarianism of Western thought, and in particular its commitment to essentialism. The clearest example of that essentialism in Western thought is the phenomenon known as 'logocentricity': the belief that words are representations of meanings already present in the speaker's mind. Speech is seen to be in direct contact with meaning; that is, at one remove only from the speaker's thought (this is what is known as 'phonocentricity'). A written word, however, is at one further remove from meaning. It is a written representation of a spoken representation, standing in relation to a spoken word as a spoken word does to the original thought where the meaning is considered to lie. Derrida rejects this conception of meaning as a fixed entity awaiting representation by either a spoken or written word: 'meaning is neither before nor after the act... the notion of an idea or "interior design" as simply anterior to a work which would supposedly be the expression of it, is a prejudice' (*ibid.* p.11). Derrida's claim is that meaning is being regarded as an ideal form ('interior design'), located in the mind, which can only be captured imperfectly by words. The critical reference to 'interior design' signals the anti-structuralist drift of the deconstructive enterprise. There are no pre-existing meanings, structures, or essences to be taken into account in Derrida's universe, and there will be no attempt to limit arbitrariness there.

Derrida wishes to replace the search for a pre-existent essence or 'interior design' with what he calls 'the joyous affirmation of the play of the world and of the innocence of becoming, the affirmation of a world of signs without fault, without truth, and without origin which is offered to an active interpretation' (*ibid.* p.292). Signs that are without fault, truth and origin are signs whose meaning has not been fixed in advance and really are arbitrary. Instead, their meaning at any given point will depend on the ingenuity of the reader's unlimited 'active interpretation'. Derrida is calling for a free play of sign and meaning, unrestricted by any limiting notion of structure: what Culler has called 'the pleasure of infinite creation' (Culler, 1975, p.248). Creation of this kind is undertaken by the reader; as Madan Sarup has pointed out, for a post-structuralist, reading 'has become performance' (Sarup, 1988, p.4). Reading-as-performance, with its strong echoes of Barthes's writerly text situation, starts from scratch, with no preconceived ideas about structure, meaning or intention, and thereby mounts a challenge to Western culture's commitment to rationality and logical thought. V. Leitch has neatly summed up the deconstructive project as a celebration of 'playfulness and hysteria over care and rationality' (Leitch, 1983, p.246). To indulge in playfulness and hysteria (irrational and unpredictable behaviour) is to deny that 'principle of order' that Saussure saw as necessary to the 'limiting of arbitrariness' and the maintenance of discourse. The spectre of his 'worst sort of complication', the breakdown of communication, looms.

The deconstructionist view of structuralism is that it 'lends support to the traditional idea of the text as a bearer of stable meanings and the critic as a faithful seeker after truth in the text' (Sarup, 1988, p.43); the truth in this case being the structural essence of a text and its network of codes. To be a 'faithful seeker' is to be committed to logocentrism in one's criticism, in the sense that the concept of 'structure' takes over from 'meaning', and the relationship between structure and artwork becomes analogous to that between meaning and word: the latter in each case being a material representation of the former. The task of the structuralist critic is to reveal the structure that is deemed always to have been there, the 'interior design' hidden behind the surface of the work of art. It is to catalogue pre-existing networks of interaction. Derrida's accusation is that structuralists are *imposing* a form on textual material rather than discovering one, and that such a practice puts limits on human creativity – or 'active interpretation' as he dubs it. Mainstream structural analysis, under such a reading, would register as an exercise in passive classification rather than 'active interpretation'.

Rather than stable meanings and the authority of the critic, Derrida offers us undecidability of meaning and critical play with language. The American deconstructionist critic Geoffrey Hartman has insisted that words are characterized not by stable meanings, but by 'a certain indeterminacy of meaning' (Hartman, in the Introduction to Bloom, *et al.*, 1979, p.viii). Deconstruction sets out to demonstrate that indeterminacy, and employs a variety of strategies to do so. Punning and word-play, for example, play a significant role in deconstructive criticism – leading to that charge mentioned earlier of Derrida's willingness to risk equivocation for the sake of a pun – mainly because they suggest a shifting or diffused field of meaning: a given word or phrase constantly conjuring up similar-sounding, but possibly very dissimilar in meaning, words or phrases. One of Derrida's most important concepts, *différance*, is based on word-play, combining as it does two French words with a similar sound-quality (*différence* and *différance*, 'difference' and 'deferral' respectively). The constant possibility of shifting between the two meanings of *différance* illustrates Derrida's point that meaning is never determinate and stable (all words are marked by *différance* in Derrida's view), and in his reading of the history of structuralism those are precisely the assumptions that are being made.

Deconstruction finds in structuralism a particularly entrenched version of all that it considers to be unacceptable in the tradition of Western rational thought. Derrida's aesthetic theory derives from his critique of metaphysics, and in particular his critique of what he calls the metaphysics of presence. He sees Western metaphysics, from Greek philosophy onwards, as being crucially dependent on the notion of binary opposition (Saussure, as we saw, relied heavily on the notion in his theory of value – see pages 410–11). In binary oppositions such as speech/writing, subject/object, signifier/signified, and word/meaning, one side of the opposition is always considered to be subordinate to the other. Derrida claims that speech, for example, is consistently accorded greater status than writing in Western philosophical discourse because it is felt to be closer to the original thought in the speaker's mind, and thus less contaminated by mediating, and potentially distorting, literary devices and tricks of writing. Speech is felt to have a sense of immediacy and authenticity that writing lacks. This assumed quality of immediacy is what Derrida defines as the 'metaphysics of presence', and he strenuously opposes it. The point of Derrida's project is to dismantle such oppositions and show that no hierarchy in fact exists: to show that writing is not subordinate to speech, and so on. If there is no 'interior design' of meaning for speech to express then it *cannot* claim authority over writing. Neither can meaning claim authority over word if it is indeterminate, unstable, and in a permanent state of 'active interpretation'. Meaning is in fact both *differed* from itself (non-identical to itself) and constantly *deferred* (never fully present, fixed, or complete). The metaphysics of presence is thus exposed as a myth.

If the metaphysics of presence collapses then arbitrary signs become a real possibility. Derrida's argument for the arbitrariness of signs involves an attack on the 'transcendental signified', that is, a concept which is held to be totally independent of other concepts. Without such a transcendental signified there could be no final meaning to any sign. Logocentrist discourse, in Derrida's view, assumes the existence of such transcendental signifieds. God, Platonic Forms, and the Cartesian mind would all stand as examples of the transcendental signified, being what Derrida would call 'originary' in not having to depend on other entities for their existence. This is to say that God, Platonic Forms, and the mind, are *foundations* of philosophical discourse (thus Descartes, for example, on the basis of what he takes to be the self-evidently true proposition *cogito ergo sum*, can construct a theory of knowledge). Derrida rejects this idea, and his metaphysical position in general can be described as anti-foundationalist. He does not believe that self-evidently true propositions or axioms are anywhere to be found. Structure presents itself as just such a foundation of discourse, and structuralism is held by Derrida to be built on an illicit assumption.

Deconstruction is to be regarded as a series of strategies designed to undermine the assumptions, untenable assumptions in Derrida's view, on which Western philosophical discourse, as well as all those discourses which rely on it as a source of foundations (critical discourse, for example) are based. Traditional philosophical discourse, as far as Derrida is concerned, cannot function without a transcendental signified or a metaphysics of presence, and deconstruction seeks to unmask those pretensions. We might define Derrida as anti-metaphysical as well as anti-foundationalist, and, as I hope to demonstrate shortly, by traditional standards the propounder of what amounts to an anti-aesthetics. Derrida may mistrust metaphysics but he also remains aware that he is caught within that same metaphysical tradition that he is attacking. It has been a standard criticism of Derrida that he relies, at least implicitly, on precisely those notions he attacks – stability of meaning, non-arbitrary signifiers, deep structures of thought – in his own writing. If meaning slips to the extent that Derrida claims it does, it is difficult to see how he could communicate this to us without similar slippage occurring – yet clearly he feels that he can, otherwise he would hardly undertake the practice of critique. *Différance* may have two simultaneous meanings, but it has *only* two and those two are quite clear. This is an obvious criticism to make, but a powerful one nevertheless, I would argue. Puns and word-play are only effective if they can be compared to normal, syntagmatically-structured discourse; indeed they are parasitic on it.

Sarup defends Derrida from the charge of being parasitic on the tradition he is calling into question, as follows:

> The usual superficial criticism of Derrida is that he questions the value of 'truth' and 'logic' and yet uses logic to demonstrate the truth of his own arguments. The point is that the overt concern of Derrida's writing is the predicament of having to use the resources of the heritage that he questions.
>
> (Sarup, 1988, p.58)

It might be countered that what Sarup calls a 'heritage' is simply the way the world is – and that it could not be otherwise. Perhaps there *are* identifiable truths in human existence (that a thing is one thing rather than another, that it has a discrete identity, for example). J. Hillis Miller, another Derrida-influenced American literary critic, has referred to the fact that, ironically enough, deconstructive texts 'contain both logocentric metaphysics and its subversion' (Hillis Miller, 1977, p.59), but argues that the process of deconstruction, although apparently self-cancelling and nihilistic, is still worth continuing. Derrida himself speaks of the work of deconstruction as an act of resistance from within:

> I do not believe in decisive ruptures, in an unequivocal 'epistemological break', as it is called today. Breaks are always, and fatally,

> reinscribed in an old cloth that must continually, interminably be undone. This interminability is not an accident or contingency; it is essential, systematic, and theoretical.
>
> (Derrida, 1981, p.24)

It must be assumed, however, that a resistance movement has an ultimate objective. The state in which 'active interpretation' and 'innocence of becoming' occur might well be posited as that ultimate objective, at which point Derrida is moving well beyond traditional conceptions of value.

It is in the area of value, particularly aesthetic value, where Derrida is at his most radical, as well as most questionable, as a theorist. The value of deconstructing texts, of laying bare their indeterminacy of meaning and lack of truth, structure or essence, is presumably that one is making an individual contribution to the breakdown of received authority (there is an implicit, arguably anarchistic, political dimension to Derrida's theories). Punning and word-play overturn normal expectations of critical discourse and might be seen to be demolishing not just the authority of the author, but also the authority of the critic. This is the 'Death of the Author' notion extended well beyond Barthes. We no longer have explications of texts in deconstruction, but freewheeling supplements to them in which the critic plays games with texts in order to score anti-metaphysical points about linguistic indeterminacy. This might be described as the covert use of aesthetics for ideological, in this case apparently anarchistic, ends.

There is a move away from value judgements in deconstruction, but of an even more radical kind than structuralism sanctions. For the deconstructionist, in Geoffrey Hartman's words, 'interpretation no longer aims at the reconciliation or unification of warring truths' (Hartman, 1981, p.51): that is, it no longer seeks to 'reduce messages' to an 'economical coding system' in the Lévi-Straussian manner. It is questionable whether the term 'interpretation' is even justified in this case, since normally it is taken to mean interpretation in terms of a scheme of some kind, having pretensions to truth of some kind. But these pretensions, however loosely defined, are precisely what Derrida sets himself against; the assumptions lying behind deconstruction are predicated on the inadmissibility of such criteria. Texts become mere excuses for an anti-metaphysical, quasi-political programme, and their value comes to reside in the degree to which they help to further that programme. It is no accident that deconstructionist critics have tended to be attracted to texts that self-consciously exploit the indeterminacy of language and ambiguity of meaning, hence the appeal of English Romantic poetry (Wordsworth, Shelley, *et al.*) and James Joyce's fiction to many American deconstructionists.

Aesthetic value and meaning are no longer seen to be products of the operations of a system, and have become fleeting and unstable phenomena which can never be recaptured or even properly communicated. They must always be considered to be in a process of 'becoming', instead of being directed towards a pre-arranged goal as in the case of structuralists such as Lévi-Strauss. In Derrida's scheme of things meaning is endlessly being produced and just as endlessly being erased, so that there are no fixed points of reference for critics to orient themselves by (Hume's dilemma all over again). Value judgements of the traditional kind become impossible under the circumstances, and the value of reading is now seen to be located in the 'active interpretation' of the reader. Value has shifted from the system to the reader, although this carries the implication that each reader will become increasingly isolated from other readers. If structuralism systematically excludes the human dimension from aesthetic theory – a case of the death of the individual subject as well as the death of the author – then deconstruction in some sense reintroduces it, but at the price of individual isolation: 'active interpretations' by their nature remain very private things.

The Yale School: playfulness and hysteria

Deconstruction has had a far greater impact in America than it has in Britain. Surveying the recent American academic scene in literary studies, Paul A. Bove has remarked that, 'deconstruction effectively displaced other intellectual programs in the minds and much of the work of the literary avant-garde' (Bove, in Arac, *et al.*, 1983, p.6). In the forefront of this avant-garde has been the so-called Yale School: the critics Geoffrey Hartman, Harold Bloom, Paul de Man and J. Hillis Miller. The most exuberant of these critics, stylistically speaking, is Hartman, whose *Saving the Text* (a commentary on Derrida's *Glas*), provides ample evidence of the deconstructionist desire to transcend value judgement by means of playfulness and hysteria.

Saving the Text is particularly heavy on pun and word-play, and Hartman makes several provocative claims for the pun, notably that it is 'beyond good and evil', that is, beyond value judgement ('there is no such thing as a bad pun' (Hartman, 1981, p.46)). Because the pun works in an associative, reflex way, Hartman contends that it escapes questions of value. It acts like a resistance movement within logical thought, and since any word is susceptible to punning (even if at times this requires some tiresome ingenuity on Hartman's part, as in 'This then is Derrida's crucifixion of the Word, that is, cruci-fiction' (*ibid*. p.62), meaning must always be considered problematical and liable to slip. The point of deconstructive criticism is to *accelerate* this process of slippage (whereas Saussure would want to *limit* it), and its success in so doing would presumably provide the criterion of its value. Good criticism under such a scheme would undermine texts' pretensions to stability, although the paradox must remain as to how we could recognize such a collapse without relying on a concept of stability of meaning as a source of comparison.

However we judge deconstruction, it is clear that traditional textual interpretation is not what it delivers, as the following example of linguistic game-playing from *Saving the Text* (deliberately chosen for its density of texture) would suggest:

> That the word 'knot' may echo in the mind as 'not' is one of those small changes that an analyst or exegete are trained to hear. 'When thou has done, thou has not done'. There are so many knots: Donnean, Penelopean, Lacanian, Borromean, Derridean. At the beginning of *Glas*, the similarity in sound of *Sa* (acronym for 'savoir absolu') and *Sa* ('signifiant') is such a knot with a positive philosophic yield. Yet because of the equivocal, echo-nature of language, even identities or homophonies sound on; the sound of *Sa* is knotted with that of *ca*, as if the text were signalling its intention to the Freudian Id ('Es'); and it may be that our only 'savoir absolu' is that of a *ca* structured like the *Sa*-signifiant: a bacchic or Lacanian 'primal process' where only signifier-signifying-signifiers exist.
>
> (*Ibid*. pp. 60–1)

Several of the problems posed by deconstructive criticism crop up in this passage: although ingenious, it is somewhat relentless in its pursuit of 'homophonies' as a means of altering the logical, step-by-step, process of the argument, as it is in its avoidance of explanation (by no stretch of the imagination can it be considered a gloss on Derrida). The passage has something of the density of significance and reference of modernist poetry rather than the transparency of discourse traditionally valued by the Anglo-American critical fraternity. That is how it is probably best read, as creative writing; but that takes us a long way from traditional literary criticism and standard preconceptions of it. The Anglo-American critical establishment has rarely aspired to be 'creative' in this manner. It would probably regard playfulness and hysteria on the Hartman model as an abdication of the critic's responsibility towards the audience.

Anti-aesthetics

One of the implications of Derrida's deconstruction of Western metaphysics is that philosophy can claim no special status towards other disciplines. If, as Derrida argues, philosophy itself cannot be grounded – there being no self-evident truths or transcendental signifieds around to perform that service – then it cannot function as a legitimate source of grounding for other activities, such as aesthetic theory or literary criticism. Criticism, far from being an applied form of a theory, however loosely formulated, in its turn derived from a philosophical position, can now claim equality with philosophy. Christopher Norris has interpreted this 'equality' to mean that literary criticism can be turned back on philosophy, and in what he calls 'the revenge of literary theory' (Norris, 1983, p.3) he subjects the work of a range of major philosophers (Austin, Wittgenstein, *et al.*) to rhetorical analysis. The aim is to show that philosophers are just as much caught up in the problems of language as are any other writers; that philosophers too are essentially engaged in the business of writing narratives, of persuading by means of literary figures appealing to the emotions, rather than proving by means of rational argument. Norris's task, as he conceives it, is 'to explore the various ways in which philosophy reveals, negotiates or represses it own inescapable predicament as written language' (*ibid.* p.12). Deconstruction also has to face this 'inescapable predicament' and must presumably be as much undermined by it as mainstream philosophy is, but Norris's application of deconstruction takes us even further down the road to an anti-aesthetics. If all discourses are merely rhetorical narratives of a greater or lesser degree of plausibility directed at the senses rather than the reason, then aesthetic judgement becomes an increasingly problematical activity. No one judgement could be considered to be preferable to another, indeed no grounds would exist by which comparison of judgements could be made.

Deconstruction seems to be calling for a rejection of value judgement, although, as was the case with structuralism, there are implicit values to be noted in its theories. It puts forward a theory of reading in which the value is deemed to lie in 'active interpretation', that is, the rejection of received authority (both critical and authorial) in favour of irreverent game-playing with the text. Behind this call lurk unacknowledged political commitments about the need to destabilize institutional structures. The value of criticism in the deconstructionist scheme of things is that it upsets the authority of texts, and demonstrates both the instability and endless plurality of meaning possible in a text's 'play of differences' (total apprehension of meaning, in the sense assumed by the 'metaphysics of presence', being considered impossible). Exactly what claim to authority deconstruction itself can have, given the 'inescapable predicament' identified by Norris and Sarup, remains unclear, but it does provide a corrective to the predictability associated with structuralist analysis. This is not a theory where we can all but know beforehand what the critic will say – a sequence of puns may lead us anywhere. The theory-of-value problem in deconstruction is that its values have no foundation, nor according to the theory is such a foundation even possible. What deconstruction is notably successful in doing, however, is drawing attention to the hidden commitments (to essentialism and determinism, for example) of other theories such as structuralism.

Post-modernism

Anti-aesthetics might also be the way to define post-modernism. The work of Jean-François Lyotard, in particular his book *The Postmodern Condition*, has just this implication in its rejection of large-scale, all-embracing theories of explanation: 'grand narratives', or 'metanarratives', as Lyotard calls them, with Marxism being a prime example. Lyotard is excluding the possibility of discourses being grounded in any traditional philosophical manner. Once again, as in Derrida, transcendental signifieds (such as the 'dialectic of history' in Marxism) are ruled out. Inasmuch as there is a concept of grounding in *The Postmodern Condition*, it is to be found in 'narrative' (*petit récit* as opposed to *grand récit*). By 'narrative' Lyotard seems to mean any sequence of events. The virtue of narrative to Lyotard is that it is self-justifying and self-validating: 'it certifies itself in the pragmatics of its own transmission' (Lyotard, 1984, p.27), as he puts it. Narrative simply *is*; it requires no further justification or license from any 'grand narrative' for its operation or existence. Lyotard directs our attention to the use made of narrative, rather than speculating on what narrative as such means (perhaps recalling Wittgenstein's claim that 'the meaning of a word is its use in the language' (Wittgenstein, 1976, p.20)). Under such a reading, narrative is perceived to be liberating on a personal level, while grand narrative is totalitarian and authoritarian.

Lyotard's work shows a concern similar to that of Derrida in its desire to transcend, or somehow bypass, value judgements. All discourses again are treated as equal, with no particular claims to precedence (both Lyotard and Derrida are uncompromisingly anti-hierarchical in outlook). Any discourse you care to name is, to Lyotard, simply a narrative: a sequence of ideas which either strikes its audience as plausible or not, congenial or not, but which has no sustainable claims to transcendental authority. The value of a particular narrative to Lyotard might well lie in its modesty as regards claims to authority: grand, all-embracing narratives, such as Marxism or Christianity, are to be avoided at all costs. What is not clear is how, in the absence of workable criteria, we can assess the claims of competing rhetorics.

Lyotard's theories centre on the individual. They might be said to involve a rather romanticized conception of the individual, who is pictured by Lyotard as being dominated by systems and theories (grand narratives), and in the process as having lost any sense of creativity and freedom for manoeuvre. Lyotard wishes to set this embattled individual free from the chains of grand narrative, that is, from pre-existing systems of explanation. There may be covert ideological assumptions at work here of at least a libertarian, and quite possibly an anarchistic, kind: the wish to dispense with value judgement tends to carry such implications.

As an aesthetic theory post-modernism has, as one might expect from the name, involved a reaction against what modernism has stood for. Such terms are not necessarily historically-bound, and one might have modernisms and post-modernisms in previous eras. Precise definitions of post-modernism are hard to come by ('incredulity toward metanarratives' (Lyotard, 1984, p.xxiv) is one of Lyotard's characteristically cryptic efforts), but it does seem to revolve around rejection of most of the assumptions of twentieth-century modernism, such as the obsessive concern with form, the preference for abstract or non-realist forms, and the desire to effect a complete break with the past. Post-modern artists, architects and writers are generally quite happy to rework traditional forms, although they tend to do so in a very knowing, often cynical manner. Irony and pastiche are the staples of post-modern creative practice, which suggests that post-modernists have little real feeling for the past or for its system of values.

The reaction against value judgement is even stronger in the work of Jean Baudrillard, whose outlook is considerably more anarchistic than Lyotard's (he speaks of the theorist's task as being 'speculation to the death', which suggests 'active interpretation' pushed to extremes (Baudrillard, 1984, p.89). In Baudrillard's world there would appear to be no direct contact with objects, events or other beings, but only with their simulations. So complex has modern culture become in terms of communication media that it is all but impossible to differentiate between image and reality. In practice, the image has taken over from reality, with the television image becoming more 'real', and more authoritative, than the actual live event: 'the cinema and TV are America's reality' as Baudrillard notes mysteriously (Baudrillard, 1988, p.104). Baudrillard's work is perhaps best approached as an updated version of Marshall McLuhan: 'the medium is the message' stated in extreme, and even apocalyptic terms (one of Baudrillard's essays is entitled 'The Year 2000 will not take place' (Baudrillard, in Grosz, *et al.*, 1986, pp.18–28)). In his book on American culture, *America*, Baudrillard consistently refuses to judge the artefacts he is confronting (buildings, landscapes, lifestyles), and argues that we should not discuss their value, but merely experience them. There is more than a touch of Eastern-style mysticism to Baudrillard's views (Zen Buddhism comes to mind), and we reach the outer limits of anti-aesthetics at such points. Judgement is no longer even to be attempted by the commentator.

3 Conclusion

Meaning, value and semiotic theory

The rejection, or at least suspicion, of value judgement is a common theme running through structuralism, deconstruction and post-modernism. Nevertheless, despite themselves, each one might be said to imply a theory of value of sorts in that they have, unacknowledged or otherwise, metaphysical and political commitments. On the one side, we have determinism and authoritarianism (structuralism), on the other indeterminism and some form of anarchism (deconstruction and post-modernism). A general trend towards an anti-aesthetics can be noted; that is to say, a trend towards a theoretical position with an oppositional stance to the basic assumptions of traditional aesthetics (that value judgements can be made, that criteria can be established for making those value judgements through the use of philosophical theory). The major theoretical shift that takes place between structuralism and post-structuralism is a move from essentialism to anti-essentialism: from a world featuring stable structures to a world of flux and indeterminacy. Whereas structuralist aesthetic theory assumes an underlying unity to existence and seeks to demonstrate this at work in texts, deconstructionist aesthetics argues for *a lack* of unity and sees texts as exemplifying this. In critical terms of reference this represents a move from description and classification to anarchic game-playing, but in each case we remain within the framework of semiotics, with Saussurean linguistics remaining the major point of reference.

The viability of the anti-foundationalist position in Derrida and Lyotard remains a major question. If meaning is always, and necessarily, in the process of being deferred (never fully present to any individual, never totally complete in itself) then deconstructionist writing must be caught in the same bind. If all discourses are merely narrative then equally so is Lyotard's, and much of the authority of his utterances disappears. Part of the problem lies in the desire for universality of application, with regard to meaning, on the anti-foundationalist side of the divide. Derrida wants to say more than that in some cases meaning is relative or plural; he wants to claim that in *all* cases it is relative and plural, and, indeed, that it can never be reduced to criteria of truth-value. He asks us to choose between all meaning being rigidly fixed, or all meaning being radically unstable. The debate is presented in a polarized form. Most of us would be quite willing to accept that meaning is not always completely stable (the art of poetry largely depends on just such a premise), without thereby feeling this licenses a swift transition to the position of claiming that all meaning at all times can *only* be unstable: how could one possibly *prove*, or even *test*, such a proposition?

Some question marks must also be placed over the total rejection of textual explication. At some level this remains a useful activity (it is hard to envisage teaching in the humanities without some such procedure at some stage, in which case its pragmatic value at least could be established), and it is an overstatement of the case to see the act of explication – criticism's traditional objective – as *necessarily* authoritarian. Authorities can be transcended, and readers are possibly less impressionable, and also possibly less respectful towards critical 'authority' than Derrida or his followers imagine. The state of 'innocence of becoming' is, in fact, a highly sophisticated one that can only be reached after going through the textual-interpretation stage. Reference points can only be jettisoned after they have been learned and absorbed.

Deconstructive criticism is grounded in deconstructive philosophy and its particular reading of the Western metaphysical tradition. The deconstructive critical enterprise is, therefore, very much open to attack on the basis of its grounding theory's validity. If Derrida's arguments on logocentricity, identity and meaning fail, then much of the point of deconstructive criticism is inevitably going to be lost. To a much larger extent than usual, this is a criticism that stands or falls on the validity and reputation of its underlying philosophy (although similar remarks might be directed at Marxist criticism (see Essay Eleven)). Given that it is less tied to an explicit philosophical programme and is correspondingly more pragmatic in its operation, traditional Anglo-American criticism largely avoids this pitfall. Structuralist criticism might well survive better in the long run than deconstruction, in the sense that even if its essentialist assumptions about underlying structures prove spurious, it still generates illuminating data about the internal relations of texts; an aspect of textuality likely to remain of appeal to critics of almost all persuasions.

Even if ultimate philosophical justification were not forthcoming, however, deconstructive critical practices might survive in some form. Neither punning nor word-play *needs* philosophical justification: their value is presumably psychological; but when philosophical claims are made for them as techniques for demolishing metaphysical assumptions, then that is an entirely different matter. When a criticism is so explicitly linked to a philosophical programme then it has to expect to be judged in fairly rigorous terms. On that basis, considerable problems remain as regards deconstruction. In the final analysis, traditional conceptions of value and meaning are not so easily dispensed with.

Bibliography

Arac, J., Godzich, W. and Martin, W. (eds) (1983) *The Yale Critics: Deconstruction in America*, University of Minnesota Press.
Barthes, R. (1975) *S/Z*, Miller R., (trans.), Jonathan Cape.
Barthes, R. (1977) *Image-Music-Text*, Heath, S. (trans.), Hill and Wang.
Baudrillard, J. 'The Structural Law of Value and the Order of Simulacra', in Fekete, 1984.
Baudrillard, J. 'The Year 2000 Will Not Take Place', Foss, P. and Patten, P. (trans), in Grosz, 1986.
Baudrillard, J. (1988) *America*, Turner, C. (trans.), Verso.
Bloom, H., *et al.* (1979) *Deconstruction and Criticism*, Continuum.
Bove, P.A. 'Variations on Authority', in Arac, 1983, pp. 3–19.
Culler, J. (1975) *Structuralist Poetics*, Routledge and Kegan Paul.
Culler, J. (1976) *Saussure*, Fontana Modern Masters.
Derrida, J. (1973) *Speech and Phenomena*, Garver, N. (ed.), Allinson, D. B. (trans.), Evanston Illinois.
Derrida, J. (1978) *Writing and Difference*, Bass, A. (trans.), Routledge and Kegan Paul.
Derrida, J. (1981) *Positions*, Bass A., (trans.), Athlone Press.
Fekete, J. (ed.) (1984) *The Structural Allegory: Reconstructive Encounters with the New French Thought*, Levin, C. (trans.), Manchester University Press.
Gardner, H. (1976) *The Quest for Mind*, Coventure.
Grosz, E.A. *et al.* (eds) (1986) *Futur-Fall: Excursions into Post-Modernity*, Power Institute Publications.
Hartman, G. (1981) *Saving the Text*, John Hopkins University Press.
Hillis Miller, J. (1977) 'Ariachne's Broken Woof', *Georgia Review*, 31, pp. 44–60.
Hume, D. (1962 edn) *A Treatise of Human Nature*, Macnabb, D.G.C. (ed.), Fontana/Collins.
Leitch, V. (1983) *Deconstructive Criticism, An Advanced Introduction*, Hutchinson.

Lévi-Strauss, C. (1969) *The Raw and the Cooked*, Weightman, J. and D. (trans), Jonathan Cape.

Locke, J. (1964 edn) *An Essay Concerning Human Understanding*, Woozley, A.D. (ed.), Fontana/Collins.

Lyotard, J.-F., (1984) *The Postmodern Condition: A Report on Knowledge*, Bennington, G. and Massumi, B. Manchester University Press.

Maranda, P. (ed.) (1972) *Mythology: Selected Readings*, Penguin Books.

Norris, C. (1983) *The Deconstructive Turn*, Methuen.

Piaget, J. (1971) *Structuralism*, Routledge.

Propp, V. (1972) 'Transformations in Fairy Tales', in Maranda, 1972.

Sarup, M. (1988) *An Introductory Guide to Post-Structuralism and Postmodernism*, Harvester Wheatsheaf.

Saussure, F. (1974) *Course in General Linguistics*, Bally, C., Sechehaye, A. and Reidlinger, A. (eds), Baskin, W. (trans.), Peter Owen.

Segal, D.M., 'The Connections between the Semantics and the Formal Structure of a Text', in Maranda, 1972.

Wittgenstein, L. (1976) *Philosophical Investigations*, Anscombe, G.E.M. (trans.), Blackwell.

Notes

[1]   Sign theories have been put forward by many others, notably including the American philosopher C.S. Peirce.

Marxism and Aesthetics

Stuart Sim

Introduction

Art and value

One of the most influential strains in aesthetic theory during the twentieth century, particularly on the continent, has been that of Marxism. Marxism is the prime example of a politically motivated aesthetic theory, and it is a theory which accordingly lays great stress on the didactic role of the arts. Of all aesthetic theories Marxism is the one most explicitly tied to a political programme. Value is probably the area of greatest contention in Marxist aesthetics, but despite the arguments of competing schools on the issue there is general agreement that, at some point, the arts must be considered to be subsidiary to politics. Differences can be sharp – Soviet socialist realism, as we shall see, is a world away from Brechtian 'epic theatre' theory or French structuralist Marxism – but no Marxist theorist is likely to deny that the arts are part of a process of ideological struggle, nor that their ultimate objective is didactic in the sense of either striving to reinforce or to subvert a given society's dominant values. This essay will be concerned with tracing the debate on value in Marxist aesthetics from Marx through to the late twentieth century.

Marxism is less of a monolithic body of theory than sometimes it has been made out to be (Eastern bloc, Third World, and Western Marxism, for example, have followed very different lines of development in the twentieth century), but some common features can be identified amongst its many variants, such as the requirement to judge all activities of a society, its artistic activities included, in political perspective. Under such a reading works of art may further or retard the class struggle, be progressive or regressive in their effect on their audience. Cruder forms of Marxism disparage, or even on occasion censor, works which fail to meet didactically oriented criteria (as in the case of Stalinist Russia's suppression of works by a wide range of creative artists, such as the composer Dmitri Shostakovitch, for alleged ideological 'incorrectness'), whereas Marxism in its more sophisticated forms shows a greater interest in determining exactly why given works have the effect they do. Yet underneath both crude and sophisticated Marxism lies a similar compulsion to situate artworks within a political context. (It is worth pointing out that 'political' is a term with a very wide range of reference to a Marxist, embracing the structure of social relations as well as politics in its institutional sense.) Regardless of the particular theory of value involved, this will remain a constant factor in Marxist aesthetic enquiry.

Art's value to a Marxist, therefore, is to be politically determined. Both artwork and artist are to be analysed according to political criteria, although that leaves considerable room for debate as to the exact value of individual works of art, or artistic styles, within a given society. It is a debate going right back to Marx himself. There is, for example, his famous analysis of the value of Greek art and literature in *Grundrisse*. Marx stresses that Greek art and literature are 'bound up with certain forms of social development' (political structures, mythology, etc.), and speculates as to why it is 'that they still afford us artistic pleasure and that in a certain respect they count as a norm and as an unattainable model' (Marx, 1973 edn, p.111), when the forms of social development in question have long since disappeared. The problem arises because Marx espouses a progressive theory of social development. He sees mankind as evolving through a series of historical stages – from tribalism through feudalism to bourgeois capitalism, and then eventually communism – to become more advanced beings in all senses, including the production of art. Modern art, being the product of mankind's highest stage of social development, ought by rights to exert the greatest effect and to supersede the art of the past – to have the greatest value, as it were.

The answer that Marx puts forward in explanation of the difficulty he experiences is the somewhat notorious 'childhood of humanity' argument.

> A man cannot become a child again, or he becomes childish. But does he not find joy in the child's naïveté, and must he himself not strive to reproduce its truth at a higher stage? Does not the true character of each epoch come alive in the nature of its children? Why should not the historic childhood of humanity, its most beautiful unfolding, as a stage never to return, exercise an eternal charm? There are unruly children and precocious children. Many of the old peoples belong in this category. The Greeks were normal children. The charm of their art for us is not in contradiction to the undeveloped stage of society on which

it grew. [It] is its result, rather, and is inextricably bound up, rather, with the fact that the unripe social conditions under which it arose, and could alone arise, can never return.

(*Ibid.*)

This is, as David McLellan has rather tartly remarked in his biography of Marx, 'no direct answer' (McLellan, 1973, p.292) and by twentieth-century standards it looks to be patronizing about mankind's past. There is nevertheless an important principle being established at this point, and it is one that few Marxist theorists would care to dispute: that works of art do not transmit eternal truths over time. In the literary theorist Pierre Macherey's words, 'the Homeric poems did not make their appearance in the trappings of a false eternity' (Macherey, 1978, p.70); which is to say that, for a Marxist, they make no eternally valid statements about 'the human condition'. Instead, Homeric poems, like any other great works of art, have to be recreated and reappropriated by each generation in terms of the specifics of its own ideological struggle. The main thrust of Marxist aesthetics will be to contextualize artworks within that progressively unfolding ideological conflict, in order to determine how the arts are helping to form ideological attitudes.

Art and the base/superstructure model

Politics, in the broad sense mentioned earlier, will therefore be the ultimate determinant of a given work of art's value, but the precise nature of the relationship between the arts and politics remains a matter for dispute. Whether the arts can claim a 'relative autonomy' from the realm of politics and economics has again been much debated in Marxist circles of late (both Marx and Engels had earlier floated such an idea in their writings). Even the notion of a relative autonomy, with its implication that partial escape only can be made from political and economic constraints, gives away the unequal nature of the relationship and directs us back to consideration of the base/superstructure model on which so much of Marxist cultural theory depends. Marxism assumes that society consists of an economic base (the production of goods by labour) and a 'superstructure' comprising a range of social activities, such as the arts, religion, the law and education. The economic base is held to determine, in some sense, the form that the activities in the superstructure will take: 'the mode of production in material life determines the social, political, and intellectual life processes in general' (Marx, 1968 edn, p. 356) (note that 'political' here refers to institutional politics). Thus a society structured on capitalist principles gives rise to an educational system based on competition, and a conception of the arts heavily imbued with the notion of individualism (the heroic author, painter, composer, etc. communicating a personal vision), since competition and individual effort form the cornerstone of *laissez-faire*, free-market economic theory.

Early Marxist aesthetic theorists saw the relationship between the arts and the economic base as essentially a reflective one, thus the arts reflected the ideology of a society, an ideology determined by economic factors. Reflection theory, for many years one of the major paradigms in Marxist aesthetics, postulated a somewhat passive role for the arts in the ideological process. 'The art of a decadent epoch "*must*" be decadent; this is inevitable; and it would be futile to become indignant about it', as Georgi Plekhanov, one of the leading reflection theorists, insisted (Plekhanov, 1936, p.93). More recent theorists – structuralist Marxists such as Louis Althusser and Pierre Macherey, for example – have argued for a much more complex relationship between the arts and the economic base, to the extent of claiming a relative autonomy for the arts as a social practice. Nevertheless, the base is invariably the dominant partner in the relationship, and, as with all superstructural phenomena, the arts will be viewed against an ideological background that is base-derived. Engels makes this very plain when in a letter to Heinz Starkenburg he states that

> Political, juridical, philosophical, religious, literary, artistic etc., development is based on economic development. But all these react upon one another and also upon the economic base. It is not that the economic position is the *cause and alone active*, while everything else only has a passive effect. There is, rather, interaction on the basis of the economic necessity, which *ultimately* always asserts itself.
>
> (quoted in Siegel, 1970, p.10)

For all that there is interaction, in the final analysis it is the economic base that is considered to hold the key to superstructural development. (Identifying the point at which that 'ultimately' takes effect has proved a considerable headache to several generations of Marxist aesthetic theorists, it should be said.)

The objective of Marxist theory in general is to alter the economic base obtaining in a capitalist society, a base reinforced by a variety of superstructural practices, to one involving less exploitation of the working classes whose labour created that society's wealth. In a capitalist society there is vastly unequal distribution of wealth and profit across the social classes, and Marx's response is to call for a change in ownership of the means of production, leading to the 'dictatorship of the proletariat' in which the working class assumes control of a society's industries and institutions. All his writings from the *The Communist Manifesto* (1848) onwards are directed towards this goal of class struggle against an exploitative socio-economic system. And the arts, if one accepts the idea of their having a relative autonomy, become one more means of contriving to bring this about. Marxist aesthetics 'presupposes a far-reaching and active influence exerted by art on various spheres of material and cultural life, the participation of art in the process of transforming the real world' (Zis, 1977, p.8). This would suggest the need for a reassessment of artistic history in terms of the current struggle being waged, and also for a reassessment of the role of the artist in generations to come. Put crudely, artists henceforth will be treated as being either *for* or *against* the progressive ideology – that of Marxism. The positive side of such an injunction is that it encourages artists to take their socio-political role seriously, and to understand the power, for good or ill, that the arts can have in forming people's ideas and attitudes. The negative side can be seen in the censorship and distortion that resulted in Stalinist Russia from an over-zealous application of class-struggle principles to creativity.

The law of art and the law of politics

The implications of Marxist theory for artistic freedom will be considered in due course, but it would have to be acknowledged that there are strong imperatives within Marxism towards censorship of politically suspect material (a category for which it is difficult to give precise guidelines). Marxist aesthetics does not as such entail censorship, and there have been many dissenting voices against it throughout its history, but Marxist politicians are not averse to adopting Plato's solution (discussed in Essay Seven) when it comes to potentially socially subversive poets and artists, and expelling these figures from the commonwealth. Leon Trotsky's assertion in the 1920s that, 'A work of art should, in the first place, be judged by its own law, that is, by the law of art' (Trotsky, 1960, p.178), has not always been heeded, and is in contradiction with the views stated above. Indeed, it is not clear that a law of art, if we mean by that a law for constructing value judgements that is independent of political considerations, is even possible under a Marxist scheme. Given the belief that economics 'ultimately' are the determining factor of all superstructural activities, then it would seem that the analysis of the work of art will always be reducible to ideological criteria, to what we might call 'the law of politics'. It is a moot point whether there can even be a law of art such as Trotsky suggests, except in the rather simplistic sense of checking that formal procedures, say the rules of counterpoint in musical composition, have been correctly executed.

Marxism is an aesthetic theory which insists on a didactic role for the arts, and in practice this has most often led to a strong commitment to 'realism' as an artistic style because of its assumed greater powers of accessibility to a mass audience. To quote the art historian Francis Klingender, a staunch supporter of realism,

> Realism, the attitude of the artist who strives to reflect some essential aspect of reality and to face the problems set by life, is from its very nature popular. It reflects the outlook of those men and women who produce the means of life. It is the only standard which can bring art back to the people today.
>
> (Klingender, 1975, pp. 48–9)

Realism is a notoriously difficult term to define (and when it comes to an art such as music, it is of dubious relevance anyway), although both A.A. Zhdanov and Georg Lukács (whose work will be looked at more closely below) attempted to do just that in conformity with Marxist political imperatives. What realism, as conceived above, tends to encourage is a highly partisan form of aesthetics, in the sense that works dubbed non or anti-realist are treated as politically undesirable. In Lukács's case this led to the rejection of modernist literature as inappropriate, indeed inimical, to the cause of socialism.

Not all Marxist theorists would agree with this commitment to realism, and an anti-realist countertrend might be identified: a trend which would encompass Bertolt Brecht, Walter Benjamin, the Dada and surrealist movements (many of whose members were overtly Marxist in their political sympathies), and, latterly, structuralist Marxism. What these modernism-inclined figures and movements share is a desire to experiment and to break with the past. Before Stalinism and socialist realism established themselves in the Soviet Union, Constructivism, very much an experimental and anti-traditional form of art (it sought to combine art, science and technology, and had certain stylistic similarities to Cubism), had a considerable vogue, but, in general, artistic experimentation has not been very well received in twentieth-century Marxist political circles. Orthodox Marxist theorists have been prone to dismiss experimental or anti-realist art such as Constructivism as anti-socialist in spirit. 'Consciousness, experiment... function, construction, technology, mathematics – these are the brothers of the art of our age', boldly proclaimed the Constructivist artist and theoretician A.

Rodchenko (quoted in Karginov, 1979, p.90), but within a few years, as the art historian Margaret A. Rose has noted, the movement was 'virtually eliminated from official Soviet art history' (Rose, 1984, p.153). (See Plate 6.)

Both sides, realist and anti-realist, have a different vision of art's role in society, and some of the major positions in Marxist aesthetics will now be examined to see how these differences are manifested. To 'bring art back to the people today' can mean, on one side of the realist divide, to speak to the people at large in a voice which is both readily understandable and employs the 'correct' political register ('It should be comprehensible to the masses and loved by them' as Lenin puts it (quoted in Klingender, 1975, p.49)); or, on the other side, to challenge the people, by means of experiment and novelty, to reject traditions and ways of thinking which are held to be outmoded as well as politically suspect. While the two positions have similar underlying objectives, to make art politically relevant and publicly accountable, their methods are radically different and perhaps ultimately incompatible with each other. It is over the question of experimentation, particularly in the case of modernism, where some of the sharpest exchanges in twentieth-century Marxist aesthetics have taken place.

1 Socialist Realism

Plekhanov and reflection theory

Reflection theory holds that the value of art lies in its being a recorder of social trends. We have only to look at the art of a historical period, according to the Plekhanovite view, to understand what kind of period it is ideologically speaking. Decadent periods produce decadent art and, conversely, politically progressive periods produce progressive art. It is a measure of the complications involved in this area that progressive, under a Stalinist regime, came to mean stylistically conservative and thematically traditional in the manner of nineteenth-century realism, a style which is generally held to reflect the ideals of the socio-economically progressive middle class of the time (and, even more insidiously, that any art produced under such a regime that met with official approval became, by definition, progressive).

Plekhanov's attack on abstract art provided one of the major sources of Soviet socialist realist theory. His critique of Cubism is a case in point. In *Art and Social Life* (1912) he criticized Cubism as belonging to the 'art for art's sake' movement, and in consequence being tainted by association with a bourgeois ideology which sought to keep art separate from politics. Cubist art, as Margaret Rose has pointed out, 'represented to Plekhanov a subversion of his belief in the duty of art to reflect accurately social reality' (Rose, 1984, p.121). Artistic 'decadence' of this kind mirrored a socio-political decadence, almost amounting to a celebration of it. Under such a reading abstract art, by its very nature, could not constitute a critique of social evils and became value-loaded in the wrong way: effectively, it was a part of the mechanism whereby bourgeois society kept its politics hidden.

Socialist realism was very much affected by this reading and brought similar arguments to bear against the Constructivist movement. To move away from realism in painting – eventually a very tightly specified type of figurative realism – was to move away from the masses and thus to deny art's political value. Formal experimentation of any kind was frowned upon, and the upshot was an art heavily committed to figurative representation and idealized forms. Art became relentlessly upbeat and optimistic in mood, and just as relentlessly propagandistic. Hence the vogue that there was for heroic-looking workers engaged in socially progressive labour in Soviet, and subsequently Chinese communist, painting. Whether this was an 'accurately reflected' social reality was highly debatable. It was, however, how social reality *ought* to be if the political theory involved, Marxism, was accurate in its analysis. The value of the art was to be determined by the extent to which it reflected that politically constructed Marxist 'reality'.

Zhdanov: Art as social engineering

Similar constraints were applied to the other arts as well. The keynote address of socialist realism was Zhdanov's speech to the Soviet Writers' Congress in 1934, when, echoing Stalin, he called upon each writer to become 'an engineer of human souls', whose task was 'to depict reality in its revolutionary development'. Zhdanov, Stalin's cultural commissar, then proceeded to spell out what such 'engineering' was to involve

> the truthfulness and historical concreteness of the artistic portrayal should be combined with the ideological remoulding and education of the toiling people in the spirit of socialism. This method in *belles lettres* and literary criticism is what we call the method of socialist realism.'
>
> (Zhdanov, 1977, p.21)

'Engineer of human souls', 'ideological remoulding and education': art's didactic role is made unmistakably clear by Zhdanov. This is art reduced to propaganda and artistic value is defined in exclusively political terms. The creative artist under such a scheme is little more than a state functionary whose capacity for social criticism, which is ironically enough one of art's *most* revolutionary characteristics, has all but been withdrawn. Post-Zhdanov, the artist must reflect what the political rulers decree that reality to be. There are definite echoes of Platonic aesthetics in this circumscription of the artist's role, and, as Rose aptly has remarked, 'What was to be "engineered" were not only the "souls" of the workers but... the souls of the artists themselves' (Rose, 1984, p.148).

Art as a form of social engineering is a concept of which Plato undoubtedly would have approved, and it is striking how close Zhdanov can be to the Platonic line on aesthetics. In Plato, as in socialist realism, political considerations are always primary and the didactic imperative is the only acceptable one for artistic activity to display. The discussion on dramatic art in *The Republic* is uncompromising on this score.

> Suppose, then, that an individual clever enough to assume any charac-
> ter and give imitations of anything and everything should visit our
> country and offer to perform his compositions, we shall bow down
> before a being with such miraculous powers of giving pleasure; but we
> shall tell him that we are not allowed to have any such person in our
> commonwealth; we shall crown him with fillets of wool, anoint his
> head with myrrh, and conduct him to the borders of some other
> country. For our own benefit, we shall employ the poets and story-
> tellers of the more austere and less attractive type, who will reproduce
> only the manner of a person of high character and, in the substance of
> their discourse, conform to those rules we laid down when we began
> the education of our warriors.
>
> (Plato, 398A–B)

It is precisely this 'more austere and less attractive' type of writer that Zhdanov wishes to encourage, and, as in Plato's case, those who choose not to conform will be banished from the commonwealth, although in Stalinist Russia the opportunity for self-censorship will first of all be extended to the dissident before the exclusion principle (exile or imprisonment) is applied. (The question arises as to whether such a literature would have much appeal to the masses; but if the state prohibits the production of any other kind then the problem is rather cynically circumvented.) In Plato too there is a commitment to an idealized reality peopled by larger-than-life heroic figures. 'Both poets and prose-writers', he claims, are

> guilty of the most serious misstatements about human life, making out
> that wrongdoers are often happy and just men miserable; that injustice

pays, if not detected; and that my being just is to another man's advantage, but a loss to myself. We shall have to prohibit such poems and tales and tell them to compose others in the contrary sense.

(*Ibid.* 392B)

Prohibition means that when a poet refuses to conform 'we shall be angry and refuse him the means to produce his play' (*ibid.* 383C). The state is to control the arts and it will fall to the politicians, as it will also in Zhdanov's commonwealth, to set the ground-rules.

You and I, Adeimantus, are not, for the moment, poets, but founders of a commonwealth. As such, it is not our business to invent stories ourselves, but only to be clear as to the main outlines to be followed by the poets in making their stories and the limits beyond which they must not be allowed to go.

(*Ibid.* 379A)

Platonic and socialist realist aesthetics have similar underlying objectives, and the history of the latter provides a graphic illustration of what can happen when politics are allowed to dominate the artistic imagination. Perhaps, as the American political commentator I.F. Stone suggests in his study of Socrates, 'Plato provides Leninist dictatorships with a precedent they cannot find in Marx and Engels' (Stone, 1988, p.129). Each theory fears the affective power of literature, indeed of the arts in general, and it may well be that both of them overrate this power considerably. A direct correlation is assumed between what people see or read and what people believe and then proceed to act upon. Both theories would appear to conceive of reception as a fairly passive process, in which a highly impressionable individual uncritically consumes works of literature and the ideological assumptions encoded within them. The obvious solution is to censor those works deemed to feature socially unacceptable views, and to substitute for them others containing approved sentiments, the assumption being that the mass audience will just as uncritically absorb the one as the other. The judging process is being dictated by political considerations and scant attention is being paid to any law of art. There is no suggestion that art might entertain, or that pleasure might be taken as a primary criterion of value, in either Plato or socialist realism. Where politics sets the agenda such things can only appear escapist, and escapism can have no part in a social system so heavily committed to didacticism.

Many of the concerns of socialist realism are prefigured in neoclassicism, an aesthetic theory heavily based on the writings of such classical figures as Plato, Aristotle and Horace, and which dominated European aesthetics from the Renaissance through to the later eighteenth century. Neoclassicism had a similar commitment to didacticism (although its ideological orientation was very different, being more concerned with the promotion of moral virtue than of class consciousness), but it allowed greater scope for pleasure in the reception process. Poets, as the Elizabethan neoclassical theorist and poet Sir Philip Sidney noted, 'imitate both to delight and teach: and delight to move men to take that goodness in hand, which without delight they would fly as from a stranger' (Sidney, 1970 edn, p.224). What is posited here in Sidney's *Apologie for Poetrie* (1591) is a working relationship between education and entertainment that is often missing in socialist realism, where delight is in short supply and the bias is rather unrelievedly towards education. What Sidney and Zhdanov agree upon is the affective power of literature and that affective power's didactic implications:

> for if it be as I affirm, that no learning is so good, as that which teacheth and moveth to virtue; and that none can both teach and move thereto so much as poetry: then is the conclusion manifest, that ink and paper cannot be to a more profitable purpose employed.
>
> *(Ibid.* p.248)

Substitute 'political virtue' for Sidney's moral 'virtue' and 'literature' for 'poetry', and you have a statement with which Zhdanov could heartily agree.

There are definite echoes of Sidney-style neoclassicism in socialist realism, in that both theories are concerned that the arts should provide appropriate models of behaviour for the audience to imitate or to be inspired by. Ultimately, however, socialist realism is closer to the Platonic tradition. Given socialist realism's bias towards censorship, as well as its narrow view of the artist's social role, the question arises as to whether such a limited aesthetic theory can be defended. A defence of a kind can be mounted on the censorship issue. Few sociologically-based aesthetic theories would be willing to sanction complete artistic freedom of expression – pornography often provides an interesting test case for feminists, for example – and in that respect socialist realism differs only in degree. Neither is self-censorship an unknown side-effect of other aesthetic theories: most creative artists in most generations tend to conform to the 'rules'. It is the extent of restriction of subject-matter and formal experimentation that mark socialist realism out for special attention. Politics may be present in many other aesthetic theories, but with the exception of Plato, none is as explicit about its politically-inspired programme – nor about the censorship that backs it up.

Some defence is possible, too, of the socialist realist's conception of the artist's social role as 'the engineer of human souls'. Creative artists have traditionally set out to communicate some vision of the world, no matter how obscure and eccentric that vision may be, and their work can have a profound effect on its audience. In that sense most artists are to some extent aspiring to be 'engineers of human souls', and a measure of responsibility must surely be attached to the process. To disclaim any responsibility in such cases would be to deny the affective power of one's art. There are too many extant examples of this affective power in action successfully to deny the premise: Dickens's novels drew attention to many of the social evils of the day, and in some cases provoked legislation to correct such evils. To call Dickens an 'engineer of human souls' seems entirely justified under the circumstances. He sought through his novels to arouse the audience's social conscience, and he manifestly succeeded in doing so. What might be objected at this point is that no one questions that some art is like this, and that it can be admirable; but it seems excessive to demand that *all* art be like this, or to claim that engineering *alone* can explain aesthetic success.

More recently Jean-Paul Sartre put forward a variant of the 'engineer' argument, when he called for writers to engage directly with the political issues of the post-war world in his major work of aesthetic theory, *What is Literature?* (1947):

> When the whole of Europe is preoccupied before everything else with reconstruction, when nations deprive themselves of necessities in order to export, literature… reveals its other face. Writing is not living. Neither is it running away from life in order to contemplate Platonic essences and the archetype of beauty in a world at rest. Nor is it letting oneself be slashed, as by swords, by words which, unfamiliar and not understood, come up to us from behind. It is the practising of a profession, a profession which requires an apprenticeship, sustained work, professional consciousness, and the sense of responsibility.

> (Sartre, 1967, p.172)

This 'sense of responsibility' requires that an author must write 'in such a way that nobody can be ignorant of the world and that nobody may say that he is innocent of what it's all about' (*ibid.* p.14). Whether the state is justified in forcing authors to write in this way is another question, and Sartre is by no means calling for official censorship of literature that does not meet his criteria. Sartre was no supporter of Zhdanov or Stalin:

in fact many of his plays of the 1940s, which certainly engage with the era's political problems in a very confrontational manner, were viciously attacked by pro-Zhdanovite elements in the French Communist Party. Yet in hindsight his aesthetic arguments have an ironic similarity to Zhdanov's (Sartre was impeccably 'realist' in approach both as theorist and dramatist, and in his later career was fairly openly Marxist too). Where Sartre differs is in objecting to the element of compulsion involved in Zhdanovism, as well as to the notion of political correctness: 'the opponent is never answered; he is discredited' (*ibid.* p.190). Sartre wants the artist to have a significantly greater degree of personal freedom than Zhdanov could countenance, although he is just as insistent as the latter regarding the artist's responsibility to society and equally unwilling to allow the law of art alone to dictate criteria of aesthetic value. Politics intrudes forcefully in both cases. Zhdanov, and Plato before him, effectively demands state-approved propaganda, whereas Sartre calls for individually initiated intervention by writers in political debates. The difference is a crucial one and should not be under-estimated, but all parties assume that artists have a socio-political role to fulfil which, given the proven affective power of art, they cannot readily ignore. Socialist realism may be to most people an unattractive and often cynical theory, but its starting premises – that art should be didactic, that artists have political responsibilities – are neither unreasonable nor indefensible in social or philosophical terms.

Lukács and 'critical realism'

Zhdanovist socialist realism was largely geared to the demands of judging, and directing, the output of currently practising socialist creative artists. Lukács's critical realism, on the other hand, is a way of judging the work of non-Marxist writers, both past and present, from a Marxist perspective. Lukács is not opposed to socialist realism, but he does maintain an attitude of healthy scepticism towards its claims as an aesthetic theory and the knee-jerk response it can generate from its supporters: 'if every mediocre product of socialist realism is to be hailed as a masterpiece, confusion will be worse confounded' (Lukács, 1963, pp. 10–11). The reference here is to the tendency – widespread amongst Soviet critics – to judge works according to their political correctness rather than their artistic merit.

Lukács's thesis in *The Meaning of Contemporary Realism* (1957) is that twentieth-century bourgeois literature can be broken down into two main styles, 'modernism' and what he calls 'critical realism'. Modernism is marked by an obsession with formal experimentation, a concern with technique at the expense of narrative content, and an intense subjectivity that pictures human beings as essentially isolated and alienated from their fellows. Overall, the modernist presents a very despairing view of 'the human condition', and seems to see little real opportunity for change. Alienation is generally regarded as part of man's nature by modernists, whereas for the Marxist it is a state induced by a certain kind of socio-political system (bourgeois capitalism). It is the work of such authors as Franz Kafka, James Joyce and Samuel Beckett that Lukács takes as being representative of the modernist ethic. Critical realism, on the other hand, is realism much in the nineteenth-century understanding of the term (linear narrative, credible situations and characters based on real-life models, literate and transparent writing style) plus what Lukács refers to as a sense of 'critical detachment'. Properly deployed, as in the fiction of the German author Thomas Mann (*Doktor Faustus, Buddenbrooks*, etc.), this critical detachment 'places what is a significant, specifically modern experience in a wider context, giving it only the emphasis it deserves as part of a greater, objective whole' (*ibid.* p.51).

In the highly polemical style of Lukács's writing the bourgeois author is pictured as being confronted by a clear choice of value systems: 'It is the dilemma of the choice between an aesthetically appealing, but decadent modernism, and a fruitful critical realism. It is a choice between Franz Kafka and Thomas Mann' (*ibid.* p.92). The value of bourgeois literature for Lukács, therefore, is to be determined by its critical realist content; that is, by the extent of critical awareness that it displays of a society's overall mechanisms of operation. Rather like Sartre, Lukács demands that the author write in such a way that nobody can be ignorant or innocent of the world. The fictional individual must be presented within a cultural context where ideology is visibly shaping his or her social being. Since modernism insists that the world is full of isolated, alienated individuals apparently independent of political processes (Kafka's Josef K. in *The Trial*, for example, or Beckett's Vladimir and Estragon in *Waiting for Godot*), then as a style it has to be valued much lower in Lukács's aesthetic scheme. What this adverse value judgement results in is a rejection of some of the most highly-regarded authors of the twentieth century, and an explicit criticism of the anti-realist tradition in literature.

Probably any pre-twentieth century author whose style is anti-realist and who believes that alienation is the natural condition of humanity, would suffer downgrading under Lukács's criteria. If we consider eighteenth-century English narrative fiction as a case in point, a Lukácsian analysis could justify treating Laurence Sterne as politically regressive in *The Life and Times of Tristram Shandy* (a novel featuring most of the modernist 'sins' of Lukácsian aesthetics), as opposed to the socio-politically aware, and therefore aesthetically progressive, realism of Daniel Defoe. In novels such as *Moll Flanders* and *Roxana* Defoe contrives to reveal the economic roots of individual alienation, and would in consequence be far more likely to win the critical realist's approval. The criterion of value is again seen to be explicitly politically motivated. Progressive works from the past can be appropriated in the current class struggle; thus, in the example given above, Defoe is to be valued for his narratives' exposure of the effect of capitalist economics on sexual relations (Moll and Roxana are forced, in the absence of male protectors, to turn to prostitution to survive). Sterne's failure to provide a similarly realistic context for his alienated hero would render *Tristram Shandy* ideologically suspect, a case of the author misleading his readers as to the real character of human nature and social relations. He would be guilty, therefore, of promoting that condition known to Marxists as 'false consciousness': the failure to see through the contradictions of one's ideology, and the acceptance of those contradictions as part of the natural order of things.

Although ultimately not as harsh in his judgement as the Zhdanovist school, Lukács is similarly concerned to exclude politically unacceptable works and authors from consideration by a Marxist readership. There are several problems with such an approach, most notably that the farther back in time one goes the more it involves anachronism. A Lukácsian might argue that as long as texts are still being read, then, no matter how old they may be, they are helping to form attitudes and are therefore politically sensitive. Once that principle of sensitivity is accepted, then texts automatically lay themselves open to politically-oriented analysis. Nevertheless, there are still some highly questionable assumptions involved in sorting texts into progressive and regressive categories irrespective of cultural context. Apart from the anachronistic implications, there is, as with Roland Barthes's readerly-writerly distinction (discussed in Essay Ten), the problem of whether precise discriminations can always be made. And they need to be made if the line being adopted is that Franz Kafka is bad, Thomas Mann is good: little provision is made for a middle ground in such cases. Politically speaking, one can see the rationale for such a division, but it runs the risk of turning criticism into a fairly mechanical exercise, where experimental texts only have to be dubbed modernist to enable the critic to fall back on the appropriate political clichés. The tag of modernism functions much like a government health warning to deter both critic and reader alike.

The realist tradition in Marxist aesthetics, as both Zhdanov and Lukács suggest, is essentially backward-looking in its distrust of experimentation, and authoritarian in operation (this is less true of Lukács perhaps, but still he adheres to the fundamental objectives of socialist realism). It calls for a highly prescriptive aesthetics, almost invariably tending to polarize debates – *either* Kafka *or* Mann – as well as expecting a high standard of political correctness in works of art. Socialist realist aesthetics in particular involves a tight system of social control in which the artist obeys the instructions of the aesthetic theorist, who in turn obeys the instructions of the political theorist. There is small scope for deviation or artistic innovation in such a system, and the economic base very much drives the superstructure, with artists being placed under an obligation to tailor their works to the demands of that economic base as determined by politicians. Lukács is a less dogmatic theorist than Zhdanov, but he is still authoritarian and prescriptive in his method. The modernism/critical realism division acts to close off debate, and is clearly politically motivated in its insistence that authors be condemned for presenting 'false' models of the human condition. Lukács is no less suspicious than Zhdanov is of formal experimentation. Such an activity challenges the stability of the theorist's cultural models, and is thus less easily turned to polemical account. There is an argument to be made for didacticism in the arts (neoclassicism makes it very successfully on behalf of moral virtue), but ultimately it is a very narrow-minded, and perhaps even anti-artistic didacticism that is being called for in socialist realism. Lukács's version of socialist realism is much more self-critical than most, but the theory has in general been an unappealing blend of censorship and authoritarianism.

2   Anti-realist Marxist aesthetics

Brecht and epic theatre

Not all Marxist aesthetic theorists have taken the realist route towards value, and a counter-tradition can be identified whose most important contributors have been Bertolt Brecht, Walter Benjamin, the Frankfurt School and the structuralist Marxist movement in France, all of whom will now be considered in turn. There is an acute sense of scepticism about reflection theory amongst such thinkers, which is neatly summed up in Brecht's remark that 'If art reflects life it does so with special mirrors' (Brecht, 'A Short Organum for the Theatre', 1978, p.204). (Eagleton's gloss on Brecht's method is worth quoting also: 'The play... is less a reflection of, than a reflection *on*, social reality' (Eagleton, 1976(a), p.65): this is to say that the dramatist does not simply reflect, but decides *what* to reflect and also what *form* the reflection will take.) Brecht's theories have been enormously influential on dramatic aesthetics, and they are conspicuously anti-realist in sentiment. The objective of Brechtian, or 'epic', theatre is to break the illusion of reality created on the stage and also to prevent audience identification, in an emotional sense, with dramatic character. In Brecht's view the illusionism propagated by realist theatre, which he refers to disparagingly as 'culinary' (that is, wholly pleasure oriented), diverts attention away from the characters' political condition; and it is that condition which Brecht, as a Marxist, considers to be of paramount importance.

The trick for Brecht is to make plain the social forces that lie behind a dramatic situation; as his close associate, the critic Walter Benjamin, noted, 'Epic theatre... does not reproduce conditions but, rather, reveals them' (Benjamin, 1973, p.4) (that is, it is not to be construed as just another form of naturalism). Included in this act of revealing is the actual staging of the play itself, and Brecht works against the illusion of reality by making the mechanics of theatrical production evident, so that the audience is never left in any doubt that it is watching a staged rather than a real event. What Brecht calls 'the alienation effect', whereby the audience is actively prevented from treating the drama on the stage as reality, or identifying with the dramatic characters, is obtained by a variety of techniques: for example, stylized acting (in the manner of circus or Chinese theatre, for instance); exaggerated gestures; continually interrupted stage action (songs, music); avoidance of 'realistic' scenery. Implicit in such a method, given its continual disruption of both the stage action and traditional audience expectations of what serious theatre should involve, is the idea that theatre should do more than just entertain; indeed Benjamin argues that 'Epic theatre casts doubt upon the notion that theatre is entertainment' (*ibid.* p.9). In fairly standard Marxist fashion Brecht conceives of theatre as didactic, although he insists that didacticism need not exclude pleasure.

> When we call the other theatre, the one that is hostile to us, merely culinary we create the impression that in our theatre we are against all fun, as though we could not imagine learning or being taught other than as an intensely unpleasurable process... Yet the act of recognizing of which we speak is itself a pleasurable act... That man can be changed by his surroundings and can himself change the surrounding world, i.e.

can treat it with consequence, all this produces feelings of pleasure.

(Brecht, quoted in Benjamin, 1973, pp. 12–13)

Didactic intentions are rarely stated this positively in Marxist aesthetics, and there is yet again an echo of neoclassicism's 'delight and teach' principle to be noted when Brecht argues that, 'the act of recognizing is a pleasurable act' to the spectator.

In its experimentation with dramatic form, Brecht's epic theatre brings to a head one of the central problems in Marxist aesthetics: the issue of whether form, and not just content, can be revolutionized. It was on just such an issue that Brecht clashed with Lukács in the 1930s, and that Zhdanov and his disciples clashed with the avant-garde Constructivists. Benjamin argued for a revolutionary art which developed not only new themes, but also new techniques of communicating them: 'We must rethink the notions of literary forms or genres if we are to find the forms appropriate to the literary energy of our time. Novels did not always exist in the past, nor must they necessarily always exist in the future' (*ibid.* p.89). Behind this commitment to formal experimentation lies a very different conception of aesthetic value than is called for in the Leninist tradition. The point is to unsettle the audience rather than to reinforce its prejudices, whether politically of the left or right. Brecht makes this clear when he puts forward the following criterion for determining aesthetic value: 'Anything that was worn out, trivial, or so commonplace that it *no longer made one think*, they did not like at all ("You get nothing out of it"). If one needed an aesthetic, one could find it here'. Terry Eagleton is particularly enthusiastic about this formulation as a basis for a Marxist theory of aesthetic value, arguing that

> When Shakespeare's texts cease to make us think, when we get nothing out of them, they will cease to have value. But why they 'make us think', why we 'get something out of them' (if only for the present) is a question which must be referred at once to the ideological matrix of our reading and the ideological matrix of their production. It is in the *articulation* of these distinct moments that the question of value resides.
>
> (Eagleton, 1976(b), p.169)

There are some problems here which a socialist realist would be quick to point out. Eagleton himself raises the question of 'why', but the socialist realist would be more likely to be concerned with 'what': what people think, and whether they think the correct thing. Brecht seems to allow the possibility of a range of responses to a play, and that would be anathema to the 'engineers of human souls' with their distinctly authoritarian and prescriptive slant. We are back with the issue of social control, and how large a part it should play in an aesthetic theory. It is on that issue that the realist/anti-realist divide in Marxist aesthetics is at its very sharpest.

Adorno and musical modernism

Modernism in general seems to create problems for Marxist theorists and modernism in music is no exception. It was Shostakovitch's brushes with modernism in the 1930s, as in his opera *Lady Macbeth of Mtsensk*, which brought him into direct confrontation with the Communist Party and forced him to adopt a considerably more conservative approach to composition thereafter. When it comes to music, realism is not an issue. The term hardly applies to this art. What is being demanded in this case is consonance and melody of the kind found in eighteenth and nineteenth-century classical music. Modernist composers broke the rules of musical composition, as taught in the academy, to create a sound-world which was in general harsh and discordant, and at variance with the classical tradition. Under Stalinism, conservative tastes dominated in music no less than in art and literature, and dissonance, which modernist composers actively cultivated, came to be treated as a mark of political decadence.

Until quite recently twelve-tone music (the method of composition devised by Arnold Schoenberg in the early twentieth century whereby tonality and its procedures were completely rejected) has been widely considered to be the most extreme form of modernism, and dissonance, in music. Whereas tonality organizes the twelve tones of the Western chromatic scale into seven-note scales, each with its own tonal centre or keynote, and prescribes precise rules whereby modulations can be made from one scale to another, Schoenberg's twelve-tone system dispenses with such groupings and controlled modulations to produce a music which is, to most ears, startlingly dissonant, unmelodic, and lacking in development. Twelve-tone music provides another interesting test case for Marxist critics – given its dissonance it is highly unlikely ever to appeal to the masses in approved Leninist fashion – and there is a provocative, although not uncritical defence of it by one of the leading figures of the Marxist-oriented Frankfurt School of Social Research, Theodor Adorno. In *The Philosophy of Modern Music* (1948), Adorno, prefiguring Lukács's method in *The Meaning of Contemporary Realism*, polarized the debate into a stark choice – in this case a choice between the musical aesthetics of Schoenberg and those of Igor Stravinsky. Some of the latter's work can be described as modernist too (his revolutionary early ballet score *The Rite of Spring* (1913), for example), but when Adorno was writing this particular book Stravinsky had consciously turned his back on experimentation and was instead imitating and reworking older styles and forms of music. This part of his career is referred to as his neoclassical phase (ironically enough, a decade or so after *The Philosophy of Modern Music* was published, Stravinsky made use of twelve-tone technique in several works).

To Adorno the neoclassical style in music amounted to a regression, a refusal to face the modern world and its problems by taking refuge in safe, traditional modes of expression: 'The seemingly positive return to the outmoded reveals itself as a more fundamental conspiracy with the destructive tendencies of the age than that which is branded outrightly as destructive. Any order which is self-proclaimed is nothing but a disguise for chaos' (Adorno, 1973, p.xvi). Stravinsky's neoclassical compositions, 'music about music-making' (*ibid.* p.185) in Adorno's dismissive phrase, fail to express the tensions of twentieth-century life (a residual commitment to reflection theory seems to underpin Adorno's analysis) and, in effect, reinforce the widespread public prejudice against novelty and experiment in music. Adorno's argument is quite close to Benjamin's at this point, in particular to the latter's plea that the modern artist 'rethink the notions' of 'forms or genres'. Thus Stravinsky the neoclassicist is anti-progressive in 'imagining that the responsible essence of music could be restored through stylistic procedures' (*ibid.* p.135). Even Stravinsky's ostensibly progressive early works are ideologically unacceptable in that the ballets *The Rite of Spring* and *Petrushka* deal with what Adorno calls 'the anti-humanistic sacrifice to the collective' and 'the blind affirmation of a situation recognised by the victim' (*ibid.* p.145). The narrative of each ballet pictures a helpless individual trapped by fate and circumstance. It is a profoundly pessimistic vision of the human condition, and to Adorno it is a highly suspect vision politically speaking because it encourages us to believe that there is no way of escaping from our predetermined fate. Stravinsky represents 'false musical consciousness' in his fatalistic outlook no less than in his stylistic conservatism (*ibid.* pp. 7–11).

Schoenberg's music, on the other hand, is identified with progress. He is a 'radical composer inspired by a drive for expression' (*ibid.* p.xvi), who rejects traditional musical forms and the outmoded ways of thinking that they represent. Rejection of tradition is taken to be a fundamental part of the modernist creed: 'The procedural method of modern music questions what many progressives expect of it: structures perfected within themselves which might be exhibited for all time in museums of opera and concert' (*ibid.* p.32). Adorno is arguing that progressiveness requires that artistic forms and structures, no less than political ones, be subjected to revolutionary change. To continue with traditional modes, to fail to 'rethink the notions' of creative activity, is to deny the possibility of historical change and, by extension, to collude with the forces of reaction – which is on Adorno's polemical reading precisely Stravinsky's 'sin'. Tonality for Adorno is part of a politically reactionary, class-ridden past which the revolutionary-minded composer must oppose, rather than simply adapt to propagandistic purposes as socialist realism directs.

> All the tonal combinations employed in the past by no means stand indiscriminately at the disposal of the composer today. Even the more insensitive ear detects the shabbiness and exhaustion of the diminished seventh chord and certain chromatic modulatory tones in the salon music of the nineteenth century... It is not simply that these sounds are antiquated and untimely, but that they are false. They no longer fulfil their function. The most progressive level of technical procedures designs tasks before which traditional sounds reveal themselves as impotent cliches.
>
> (*Ibid.* p.34)

Schoenberg's development of a non-tonal music represents a decisive break with a 'shabby and exhausted' tradition, and it qualifies as the most progressive music of its day. It seems impeccably radical to reject the authority of tonality and its weight of tradition. Stravinsky's return to older compositional models in the post-First World War period, and the restrictions placed on Soviet composers of the 1930s and '40s, whereby tonality became an index of political 'correctness', stand condemned as regressions to an ideologically suspect past which can have no relevance to present-day needs. (Stravinsky's practice is the more suspect for Adorno because, unlike Soviet composers, he made a free choice to turn the clock back.)

Much hinges on Adorno's identification of tonality with false consciousness. If tonality is to be taken as a product of bourgeois society (as realism was for Brecht and Benjamin), then adherence to it by socialists does seem on the face of it reactionary and in bad faith. The thoroughgoing Marxist will reject all aspects of bourgeois culture as being compromised. Adorno, like Brecht, Benjamin, and the Constructivists before him, demands that musicians be revolutionary in their own sphere, avoiding the shabby, the exhausted, the clichéd. The issue at stake is the social role of creative artists, and whether they best serve a revolutionary political creed by being revolutionary in artistic terms (experimental, anti-realist), or, as Lenin insisted, by being 'comprehensible to the masses'. Adorno espouses the former position, claiming that the radically-minded musician has a duty to break what he calls 'the blind domination of tonal material' (*ibid.* p.68). In doing so, however, twelve-tone composers must move well beyond the position of mass comprehensibility, thus exposing themselves to charges of élitism (one of the cardinal sins of Marxist politics) in the act of expressing the sense of crisis of their times. Tonality equals conservatism to Adorno, whereas it equals comprehensibility to a socialist realist (Lukács's attack on literary modernism has a similar underlying commitment to comprehensibility). On the one hand the artist is exhorted to be a nonconformist and on the other a conformist; although a socialist realist would phrase it differently, glossing conformism as a socially responsible political correctness sanctioned by cultural necessities.

The problematical status of the artist under Marxism – rebel or state functionary – has never been satisfactorily resolved, although it does seem that Western Marxists have been more likely than their Eastern counterparts, from socialist realism onwards, to defend the former status. As we saw in Plato's case, the fear of art's affective power, and its potentially unpredictable consequences as far as individuals are concerned, runs deep, and the artist-as-rebel poses precisely that problem to a highly-planned, centralized society on the traditional Marxist model. The value of artists to society, from a realist perspective, is their ability to communicate politically approved material in an accessible and imaginative manner ('delight and teach'). To modernism-inclined Marxists such as Adorno, artists are to be valued for their talent at challenging tradition. This idea that aesthetic value is to be derived from conflict contrasts sharply with the fundamentals of the realist position and promotes a very different attitude towards authority. Each side lays itself open to a charge of false consciousness by the other in its commitment to, respectively, radical individualism or collective conformity.

There is much to take issue with in Adorno's reading of modernism. In the first place he is just as dogmatic in his way as the realist tradition in Marxism that he sets out to supplant. The route may be different, but we are still offered only one true way – the way of experiment and anti-traditionalism – to aesthetic truth and value, and, by extension, to political correctness. Neither is it clear that Schoenberg's radicalism is as anti-authoritarian as Adorno claims. Twelve-tone music may free the composer from 'the blind domination of tonal material' but it substitutes another, possibly even more severe, domination in its place (even Adorno admits the 'terrible discipline' of twelve-tone technique (*ibid.* p.116)). The rules of twelve-tone composition, such as the necessity to avoid tonal centres, to base a piece entirely on a 'tone row' (a particular sequence of all twelve notes in the chromatic scale), and to process such rows through a range of mechanical manoeuvres (retrograde, inversion, etc.), look even more inhibiting to the creative imagination than tonality does to most outside observers – which is not to deny the expressive possibilities within such restrictions. Strict twelve-tone method arguably imposes far greater limitations on the composer than does the tonality of classical counterpoint or sonata form, and the tone row's authority, for Schoenberg and his followers, is taken to be total.

It is also questionable whether artistic radicalism is always to be regarded as simultaneously politically radical. One of Adorno's Frankfurt School colleagues, Herbert Marcuse, continued to argue vigorously for such a connection well into the 1960s, seeing radical and experimental art as one of the leading manifestations of political radicalism in the United States in the sense that, by estranging themselves from the social order and its conventional expectations, experimental works called that order's validity into question. Few Marxist theorists would now wish to push this line of reasoning too far. A recent commentator on Marcuse's aesthetics, Stephen Eric Bronner, has remarked: 'It is time to recognize that formal experimentation will not *necessarily* have a more critical and emancipatory content than a representational emphasis upon content' (Bronner, in Pippin *et al.*, 1988, p.130). The form/content distinction is not the easiest to defend at the best of times, but in Bronner's terms of reference, Adorno is claiming just such an emancipatory effect for Schoenberg's technical (that is, formal) innovations.

The politics of modernism is one of the most complex topics in Marxist aesthetics, and serious music is one of the most difficult areas in which to pursue it (the plea for mass communication is of doubtful relevance as far as serious music goes: Schoenberg may not have achieved the mass popularity of pop music, but then neither has Stravinsky, nor for that matter Beethoven). Adorno makes a brave attempt to open up serious concert music to sophisticated ideological analysis, but it remains the most resistant of the arts to such a procedure. False consciousness is an irritatingly vague notion – more a term of abuse than a precise analytical notion – but it seems even vaguer than usual when applied to non-narrative art (it is noticeable that Adorno concentrates on the narrative of Stravinsky's ballets when he requires examples). Given the range of conclusions amongst Marxist theorists as to what can count as false consciousness in the arts (realism or modernism, depending upon your perspective) it is perhaps not surprising that the notion does not figure quite so prominently in more recent Marxist aesthetics – structuralist Marxism being an excellent example.

3 Structuralist Marxism

Althusser and Macherey: Art and ideology

Structuralist Marxism largely derives from the work of the French philosopher Louis Althusser, who drew on structuralism (see Essay Ten) to some extent in his reformulation of Marxist theory. A major criticism that is often levelled against structuralism is that it lacks a human dimension, playing down the role of 'the subject'– the individual human being – in favour of self-regulating and self-validating structures (thus the 'death of the author' notion to facilitate the autonomy of the text). Althusser is open to a similar objection in that his theory of society, or 'social formation' as he tends to call it, consists of a set of monolithic-looking 'practices' (economic, political, ideological, and theoretical) within which human beings have to operate. 'Historical process without a subject' is how Althusser's critics have dismissively described his outlook. Althusser also refers to his philosophy as anti-humanist, thus further distancing himself from beliefs in the autonomy of the individual subject.

The most inventive part of Althusser's philosophy, as well as the most relevant for the development of Marxist aesthetics, is his theory of ideology, a theory which his disciple Pierre Macherey applies to the problems of literary aesthetics in his highly influential book, *A Theory of Literary Production*. In works such as *For Marx* and *Reading Capital*, Althusser differentiates sharply between 'ideology' and 'science'. This may seem unexceptionable enough, but for the fact that Althusser subsumes Marxism, which its detractors would define as an ideology, under the heading of science. Ideology, he argues, 'is a matter of the *lived* relation between men and their world... not the relation between them and their conditions of existence, but the *way* they live the relation between them and their conditions of existence: this presupposes both a real relation and an "*imaginary*", "*lived*" relation' (Althusser, 1977, p.233). Ideology, therefore, is the domain of beliefs, and beliefs by their nature offer only partial explanations of the way the world and society work (as in the case of religions or metaphysical systems), and are also often self-contradictory. Science on the other hand – most notably that highly-developed science of society, Marxism – is the domain of knowledge and thus supersedes ideology. Whereas ideology, of whatever variety, tries to disguise its internal contradictions (explaining away sexism, racism, and economic exploitation by means of religious doctrine, for example), science works to reveal those contradictions such that we can see exactly where injustices are being perpetrated. Not only is science the domain of knowledge, it is also a way of discovering and creating new sources of knowledge by the use of its analytical techniques: 'it produces... new objects of possible knowledge and new problems about them', as Macherey and a collaborator note (Balibar and Macherey, in Young, 1981, p.98 n.1). Between ideology and science there lies what Althusser refers to as an 'epistemological break': on the one side there is belief, and on the other side knowledge. It is a break which is said to occur in Marx's own work in the mid-1840s, marking the transition from a pre-scientific to a scientific state of mind.

Although he subscribes to the theory that, in the last instance, the economy is the dominant practice in a social formation – that base takes precedence over superstructure, as the more orthodox Marxist would put it – Althusser argues for a relative autonomy for the various practices to be found in a society. Thus he can hold that there is a dynamic relationship between art and both ideology and science:

> *I do not rank real art among the ideologies,* although art does have a quite particular and specific relationship with ideology... Art (I mean authentic art, not works of an average or mediocre level) does not quite give us a *knowledge* in the strict sense, it therefore does not replace knowledge (in the modern sense: scientific knowledge), but what it gives us does nevertheless maintain a certain specific *relationship* with knowledge. This relationship is not one of identity but one of differen-ce... [T]he peculiarity of art is to 'make us see', 'make us perceive', 'make us feel' something which *alludes* to reality... What art makes us *see...* is the ideology from which it is born, in which it bathes, from which it detaches itself as art, and to which it *alludes.*
>
> [Balzac and Solzhenitsyn] give us a 'view' of the ideology to which their work alludes and with which it is constantly fed, a view which presupposes a *retreat...* from the very ideology from which their novels emerge. They make us 'perceive' (but not know) in some sense *from the inside,* the very ideology in which they are held.
>
> (Althusser, 1971, pp. 203–4)

'Real' is having to do a great deal of work here, and it is by no means clear how it is to be recognized; but it is from such a position that Macherey goes into action to show how literature can be turned to account by Marxism to reveal the inner workings of ideology.

Literary aesthetics will be in the front line of class struggle for Macherey. When critically read, fictional texts will disclose the internal contradictions of the ideological system within which they were written; contradictions that an ideology will normally seek to hide from scrutiny. 'Ideology's essential weakness is that it can never recognize for itself its own real limits. At best it can learn of these limits from elsewhere, in the action of a radical criticism, not by a superficial denunciation of its content' (Macherey, 1978, p.131). Macherey's concern is to establish the grounds for such a radical criticism that will go beyond the surface characteristics of a text – theme, formal structure, writing style – to identify the ideological contradictions encoded within it, a technique which has been dubbed 'reading against the grain' (and an example of which follows shortly). Texts are for Macherey as much producers of ideology as reflectors of it. Authors are not 'creators', in the romantic sense of the word, but 'producers', who consciously rework the raw material of an ideology, such as the beliefs and assumptions which are all around them in everyday life, in a determinate way for a determinate audience. 'A book never arrives unaccompanied', Macherey writes. 'It is a figure against a background of other formations, depending on them rather than contrasting with them' (*ibid*. p.53). That is to say that a book is a production, which entails a network of social relations lying behind it. This may seem to be something of a platitude, but some critical schools, New Criticism being an outstanding example, have denied that such factors as production and context have any relevance to the study of texts. To the New Critic a literary text is a self-contained artefact to be studied in terms of the internal relations of its elements (literary figures, etc.).

Macherey's theory of ideology depends heavily upon the notion of contradiction, and in one of his most quoted phrases he describes ideology as being 'the false resolution of a real debate'. The following example should help to explain how this process works. In a capitalist system individual competition is actively encouraged in almost all spheres of life, this being the basis of 'free market' economics. Individual competition is not the only way to run a society – other models exist around the globe at any one time, and can also be found in history – but capitalists want to present it as both the most natural way and the highest state of human development. Competition is therefore seen to be part of 'human nature', an innate characteristic and not an ideological issue, for human nature lies beyond the reach of ideology. The real debate for a Marxist would be the justice or otherwise of the competitive ethic and the social relations that proceed from it, but that is a debate which cannot be properly articulated within a capitalist framework (a prime case of an ideology failing to 'recognize for itself its own real limits'). In Macherey's view, 'ideology exists precisely in order to efface all trace of contradiction' (*ibid.* p.131), and the 'real debate' that contradiction would create, but it can only do so if it can prevent those contradictions from being recognized. Competition must not seem to be a problem, it must just seem to be part of 'human nature'.

The virtue of the text, and this is where aesthetic value primarily lies for Macherey, is that it both contains ideological contradictions and can be made to reveal them. Written texts become ideology made visible for the critic willing to look for it:

> The text constructs a determinate image of the ideological, revealing it as an object rather than living it from within as though it were an inner conscience; the text explores ideology... puts it to the test of the written word, the test of that watchful gaze in which all subjectivity is *captured*, crystallised in objective form. The spontaneous ideology in which men live (it is not produced spontaneously, although men believe that they acquire it spontaneously) is not simply reflected by the mirror of the book; ideology is broken, and turned inside out in so far as it is transformed in the text from being a state of consciousness. Art, or at least literature, because it naturally scorns the credulous view of the world, establishes myth and illusion as *visible objects*.
>
> (*Ibid.* pp. 131–3)

To elaborate on a previous example, Defoe's novels *Moll Flanders* and *Roxana* 'explore ideology' and 'put it to the test of the written word', by revealing the contradictory position of women in early eighteenth-century society. Required to be paragons of virtue but prevented by the pressures of patriarchy from being so, women are trapped in ideological contradiction. What cannot be seen clearly at the time in the 'spontaneous ideology' of everyday life (Roxana is eventually treated by her author not so much as a victim of double-standard morality, but as an unrepentant sinner) can be seen now in the unfolding of the narrative. The author has unwittingly revealed the contradictions buried within his own ideology.

For the critic who goes beyond analysis of the thematic and structural components of the text, who reads against the grain (as with the

Defoe example above), the contradictions and gaps of an ideology begin to disclose themselves. The critic becomes not so much a critic of the text as a critic of ideology, and there is no longer any need for an overtly judgemental aesthetics (Mann over Kafka, Schoenberg over Stravinsky). Any and all narratives – realist and anti-realist – will prove amenable to such a method of analysis, which seeks less to judge a text (Macherey regards the text as a means 'to escape the false consciousness of self, of history, and of time' (*ibid*. p.132)) than to identify how it articulates the inner workings of an ideology. As in structuralism, the text rather than the author will form the real focus of attention. The text is taken to reveal from within the shortcomings of an ideology, although as Eagleton has pointed out this involves some special pleading for the 'scientific' (that is, Marxist) method of reading being employed. 'Science or theory is not, in Macherey or Althusser, itself viewed as an historical product, but rather intervenes into history from some apparently transcendental vantage point' (Eagleton, 1986, p.20). Scientific Marxism is seen to be a self-evidently true theory, and the measure by which other social and philosophical theories can be declared false, and it somehow mysteriously escapes the historical process and the need to prove its starting premises. Since these starting premises – for example, that all human history is the history of class struggle, and that societies evolve in a dialectical manner with the successive exploiting classes eventually being overthrown by the exploited ones – are metaphysical notions that remain to be proved, Marxism appears to be deficient in philosophical foundations. Such a deficiency can only call its claims to truth into question.

Macherey's literary theory of value may be less judgemental of individual texts and authors than socialist or critical realism, but it is no less politically motivated. The value that literature has for Macherey is that it enables the reader-against-the-grain to mount a critique of bourgeois ideology. Literature does not so much reproduce (that is, reflect) ideology as *produce* it for a structuralist Marxist, and it produces it complete with contradictions and gaps. Much of the value of literary narratives is deemed to lie in what they do *not* say, in their significant absences (lack of recognition of ideological contradictions, or tacit acceptance of them as simply part of 'the human condition'). There are things that the text is 'ideologically forbidden to say' (Eagleton, 1976(a), p.35), and it is these things in particular that the critic must search out. From such a perspective literary texts constitute a history of ideology for critics to work on, and it is the scientific critic's duty to 'interrogate' the text as Macherey puts it in a revealing phrase which brings Marxism's adversarial character to the fore (Macherey, 1978, p.132), to make it reveal its ideological secrets. The political dimension that invariably informs Marxist aesthetic theories is plainly recognizable.

Macherey's work raises again the question of whether the arts are being reduced to a sub-division of politics in Marxist theory. While Macherey's theory of literary production translates easily into critical practice, it leaves open the question of how we discriminate between individual texts. In a sense Macherey is not much interested in this; texts are first and foremost ideological artefacts to him, and the question of relative value is incidental. Much in the manner of structuralism, Macherey avoids the issue of value judgement, and although Eagleton has tried to plug this gap with a Brecht-derived criterion of value (the 'makes you think' criterion) in *Criticism and Ideology*, this, as we have seen earlier, creates more problems for the Marxist than it actually solves. We seem no closer to reaching principles for the long-sought law of art than ever. Indeed, the problem of the law of art might be cited as the major one facing Marxist aesthetics. It is easy to see how a law of politics can be devised for judging the arts, and this particular survey of Marxist aesthetics has revealed several variants, but it is much more difficult to see how a law of art that is not simply a disguised law of politics can be constructed from within Marxism.

Eagleton and aesthetic value

The chapter entitled 'Marxism and Aesthetic Value' in Eagleton's *Criticism and Ideology* provides an interesting case study of the conflict between the law of art and the law of politics (it is where the 'makes you think' criterion is introduced). Eagleton is anxious to avoid the crudeness of socialist realism and the 'either/or' approach of critical realism, yet he also wants to be able to make value judgements. Thus the classical humanism of Ben Jonson's poetry is, in Eagleton's opinion, to be preferred to that of the now little-read Walter Savage Landor (1775–1864), Jonson's being in tune with the spirit of his times whereas Landor's later version is dismissed as 'an elaborate shell sucked of substance'. There are echoes of Adorno's anti-neoclassicism in such a judgement, and the comment that Landor is 'in full flight from history' (Eagleton, 1976(b), p.186) reinforces them. Few literary critics are likely to disagree with the value judgement of Jonson over Landor, but being 'in full flight from history' seems a problematical candidate for a law of art criterion. Eagleton goes on to remark that Landor's contemporary Wordsworth was also in full flight from history in *The Prelude*, but that this reaction generated a work of greater 'contradiction and complexity' than any of Landor's, and one 'haunted by certain spiritual and historical possibilities'. Eagleton obviously feels that Wordsworth makes you think more deeply than Landor, but it is by no means clear why, and the law of art involved seems fairly obscure.

In the last paragraph of the chapter, and of the book, Eagleton strikes a despairing note which suggests just how intractable the law of art problem is to the Marxist theorist. 'If Marxism has maintained a certain silence about aesthetic value, it may well be because the material conditions which would make such discourse fully possible do not as yet exist' (*ibid*. p.187). This is to postpone discussions about the law of art for the foreseeable future – effectively until capitalism collapses. Meanwhile, one assumes, the law of politics will continue to hold sway and the arts will of necessity remain a sub-division of politics. The relative autonomy claimed by Althusser begins to look less than plausible at such points, and in many ways Eagleton undermines the theory he has set out to extend by demonstrating just how little independence aesthetics actually has in a Marxist framework.

4 Conclusion

The conclusion Eagleton reaches suggests that at the current stage of development of Marxism the law of art has to yield to the law of politics – and that perhaps a law of art cannot yet be formulated. If that is the case, and the foregoing survey of some of the major positions in Marxist aesthetics seems to provide much corroborating evidence for the view, then aesthetic value can only be politically constructed and didactic, thus raising again the spectre of social control and Platonic aesthetics at its most sinister. No one in the anti-realist camp is advocating such social control, indeed Brecht and Benjamin are vigorously denying the Marxist credentials of such control, but neither is there any significant dissent from the notion that the arts must be part of a programme of socio-political reform. The argument between realists and anti-realists is over the manner in which the artist, and critic, operates within that programme, not over the validity of the programme itself. Realists are more prone to argue for an exclusion policy than anti-realists, and also to be stricter in their application of the law of politics to the arts. Value judgements are easier to make on the realist side too, but that need not mean that either side is any less committed to the objective of revolutionary change: methods, not objectives, are at issue.

Eagleton has spoken of 'the Marxist tradition's embarrassment over the question of aesthetic value' (*ibid*. p.174), but perhaps this is a false problem. Given Marxism's all-embracing tendencies, and the general reluctance of Marxists of all persuasions to relinquish the 'last instance' thesis concerning the economic base's determining power over super-structural activities, it is better to concede that, in Marxism, aesthetic value simply *is* a sub-class of political value and could not be otherwise. What is really at stake in this debate is what goes into that concept of political value: how restrictive it is going to be, and how much scope it is going to allow for individual initiative and interpretation?

Bibliography

Adorno, T.W. (1973) *Philosophy of Modern Music*, Mitchell, A.G. and Bloomster, W.V. (trans), Sheed and Ward.

Althusser, L. (1971) *Lenin and Philosophy*, Brewster, B. (trans.), Verso.

Althusser, L. (1977) *For Marx*, Brewster B. (trans.), Verso.

Balibar, E. and Macherey, P. 'On Literature as an Ideological Form', in Young, 1981.

Benjamin, W. (1973) *Understanding Brecht*, Bostock, A. (trans.), Verso.

Brecht, B. (1978) *On Theatre*, J. Willett (ed. and trans.), Eyre and Spottiswode.

Bronner, S.E. 'Between Art and Utopia: Reconsidering the Aesthetic Theory of Herbert Marcuse', in Pippin, 1988.

Eagleton, T. (a) (1976) *Marxism and Literary Criticism*, Methuen.

Eagleton, T. (b) (1976) *Criticism and Ideology*, Verso.

Eagleton, T. (1986) *Against the Grain*, Verso.

Karginov, G. (1979) *Rodchenko*, Thames and Hudson.

Klingender, F. (1975) *Marxism and Modern Art*, Lawrence and Wishart.

Lukács, G. (1963) *The Meaning of Contemporary Realism*, Mander, J. and N. (trans), Merlin Press.

Macherey, P. (1978) *A Theory of Literary Production*, Wall, G. (trans.) Routledge and Kegan Paul.

Marx, K. and Engels, F. (1968 edn) *Selected Works*, Lawrence and Wishart.

Marx, K. (1973 edn) *Grundrisse*, Nicolaus M., (trans.), Penguin Books.

McLellan, D. (1973) *Karl Marx: His Life and Thought*, Macmillan.

Pippin, R., Feenberg, A. and Webel, C.P. (eds) (1988) *Marcuse: Critical Theory and the Promise of Utopia*, Greenwood.

Plato (many edns) *Republic*; quotations from the H.D.P. Lee translation (Penguin); references to Stephanus numbering.

Plekhanov, G.V. (1936) *Art and Social Life*, Lawrence and Wishart.

Rose, M.A. (1984) *Marx's Lost Aesthetic: Karl Marx and the Visual Arts*, Cambridge University Press.

Sartre, J.-P. (1967) *What is Literature?*, Frechtman B. (trans.), Methuen.

Sidney, Sir Philip (1970 edn) *Selected Poetry and Prose*, Kalstone, D. (ed.), Signet.

Siegel, P.N. (ed.) (1970) *Leon Trotsky on Literature and Art*, Path.

Stone, I.F. (1988) *The Trial of Socrates*, Jonathan Cape.

Trotsky, L. (1960) *Literature and Revolution*, University of Michigan Press.

Young, R. (ed.) (1981) *Untying the Text*, Routledge and Kegan Paul.

Zhdanov, A.A. (1977) 'Soviet literature – the richest in ideas: the most advanced literature', in *Soviet Writers' Congress 1934*, Lawrence and Wishart.

Zis, A. (1977) *Foundations of Marxist Aesthetics*, Judelson K. (trans.), Central Books.

Index

Aagaard-Morgenstern, L. 24, 28
abstract art 17, 19
  and socialist realism 447–8
  and truth 280–1
action
  and beauty 56
active discovery
  in aesthetic experience 166, 167
Adorno, T.W. 459–64, 469
aesthetic, origins of word 112
aesthetic appreciation
  and Institutional Theory 30–2
aesthetic attitude 9, 111
aesthetic concepts ix, 63
aesthetic descriptions 49
aesthetic experience viii, xi–xiii, 9,
111–78
  and contemplation theory 117–25,
  132–3
  and disinterestedness 134–44
  form and 'significant form' 144–50
  history of 112–14
  nature of 115–17
  and psychical distance 156–65
  and will-lessness 125–32
aesthetic expression
  Tolstoy on 185
  see also expression
aesthetic grounds
  authentic performance of a work on
  88–9
aesthetic judgements 356–7, 358, 362–5
  objectivity and subjectivity in 369–70
  and perceptual judgements 370–2
  see also value judgements
aesthetic judgements 356–7, 358
aesthetic perception ix, 64, 65, 67,
112–13, 152
aesthetic qualities ix–x, 41–73, 113
  of imitations 103
  and non-aesthetic qualities 63–7
  in ready-made works 35, 36
  of reproductions 100
aesthetic reasoning xxi–xxii, 357–9
aesthetic significance
  and judgements of beauty 52–3
aesthetic value 326–8
  and deconstruction 431
  Eagleton on 469–70, 471

  see also value
alienation
  effect, in epic theatre 457
  and modernism 454
Althusser, Louis 444, 464–5, 470
Alton Locke (Kingsley) 229
America (Baudrillard) 436
Analysis of Beauty (Hogarth) 42–3
animals
  and the concept of beauty 6, 41–2
Annas, J. 250
anti-aesthetics
  and deconstruction 433–4
  and post-modernism 434–6
appreciation
  and Institutional Theory 30–2
Aquinas, Thomas vii, 120–1, 122, 123,
124, 127, 130, 134, 144, 156
architecture
  and formalism 58
  materials used in 193
Aristotle vii, 10, 112, 121, 127, 134, 144,
156, 280, 281, 294
  and aesthetic experience 125, 133
  on beauty 41–2
  and the concept of art 5–6
  and contemplation theory 118–21
  on representation 239–41, 250–61
Art, an enemy of the people (Taylor)
328–32
Art (Bell) 1, 19, 53, 59, 148
Art and Illusion (Gombrich) 224
Art and the Aesthetic (Dickie) 30–1
Art as Experience (Dewey) 150–6
Art of Poetry, The (Aristotle) 6
artefacts
  beauty in 53
  works of art as 20, 21
artistic creation
  Tolstoy on 185–6
artists
  and expression 221–5
  personal qualities of 391–2
  separation from works of art 383–95
'artkind instance' 166
'attention', concept of
  and psychical distance 161
Auden, W.H. 349, 385
audiences

and aesthetic experience 118, 120
and the authentic performance of a
work 88
mass 331, 332
and musical performances 91, 92
and Shakespeare's plays 93
see also spectators
Augustine, Saint
on beauty 41
Austen, Jane 281, 390
Austin, J.L. 22–3, 433
authenticity
and aesthetic appreciation x–xi,
106–10
in fiction 302
of performances x, 88–93
authors
Macherey on 466
as outmoded concept 422–3
avant-garde art 21–2, 29, 32–3
awards in the artworld, acceptance of
329–31

Bach, J.S. 69, 87, 89, 92
Bacon, Francis 171
Balibar, E. 465
Barrell, John 308, 310
Barthes, Roland 419–23, 426, 430, 455
Batteux, Charles 7–8, 9
Battle of San Remo, The (Uccello) 60
Baudrillard, Jean 435–6
Baumgarten, A.G. 112, 113, 114
Beardsley, Monroe xiii, 9, 30, 31, 171,
172
on aesthetic experience 165–70
on criticism and interpretation 384,
387, 389, 390, 391, 392, 396, 397,
400–1, 401–2
and the evaluation of art 352, 353–5,
362, 364
Beautiful in Music, The (Hanslick) xvi, 58
beauty
and aesthetic experience 114, 120–1,
122–4, 130, 135–6, 137, 138–9,
139–40, 143, 172, 173, 174
and art ix, 10, 44, 53–6
causal theories of 48–50
and the concept of art 12
concepts of 6, 9
decline of 53–6
and feeling 9, 44–8
in music 211
normative accounts of 50–3

Plato on 306
and proportion 41–4
and psychical distance 159
regularity concept of 42–3, 44, 45
and truth 281
Beauty Restored (Mothersill) 56
Beckett, Samuel 454
Beethoven, Ludwig van 60, 61, 70, 71,
84, 88, 97, 98, 106, 232, 463
Bell, Clive ix, xvi, 1, 19, 24, 34, 36, 53,
54, 104, 350
and aesthetic experience 144–50, 156,
157
Dewey on 152–3
and formalism 57, 59–60, 61
Benjamin, Walter 446, 456, 457, 460,
461, 470
Berlioz, Hector 222
Binkley, Timothy 24, 28–9, 30–1, 34, 114
Bloom, Harold 427, 431
Bloom, John (alias Joe Bob Briggs)
333–5, 339
Booth, Wayne 386, 400
Borges, Jorge Luis 223–4
Bove, Paul A. 431
Boyers, Robert 336, 337, 338
Bradley, A.C. 184
Brecht, Berthold 287, 446, 456–9, 461,
470
Brentano, Franz 216
'Briggs, Joe Bob' (John Bloom) 333–5,
339
Brillo Box (Warhol) 22, 29, 31, 32, 34, 35,
63
Bronner, Stephen Eric 463
Brown, Thomas 281
Bruegel, Pieter 366
Budd, Malcolm 206–7, 214, 218
Bullough, Edward xiii, 9, 30, 158–61,
162–5
Burger's Daughter (Gordimer) 337–8
Burke, Edmund 43–4, 48, 49, 54

Cage, John 4, 37
Canterbury Tales (Chaucer) 94
cave-paintings, pre-historic 26, 27, 29
censorship
in literature 287
Plato on 243–4
and socialist realism 452
in Stalinist Russia 441–2, 445
Chandler, Raymond 414
Chaucer, Geoffrey 94

Lightning Source UK Ltd.
Milton Keynes UK
UKOW011352200911

178968UK00002B/75/P